SYRIAN-KURDISH INTERSECTIONS IN THE
OTTOMAN PERIOD

NEW LANDSCAPES IN MIDDLE EAST STUDIES

General Editor: Stefan Winter, Université du Québec à Montréal

Advisory Board

Dyala Hamzah, Université de Montréal
Colin Mitchell, Dalhousie University
Paul Sedra, Simon Fraser University

Syrian-Kurdish Intersections in the Ottoman Period

EDITED BY STEFAN WINTER AND
ZAINAB HAJHASAN

UNIVERSITY OF TORONTO PRESS
Toronto Buffalo London

© University of Toronto Press 2024
Toronto Buffalo London
utorontopress.com

ISBN 978-1-4875-5440-8 (cloth)   ISBN 978-1-4875-5688-4 (EPUB)
                                  ISBN 978-1-4875-5687-7 (PDF)

New Landscapes in Middle East Studies

Library and Archives Canada Cataloguing in Publication

Title: Syrian-Kurdish intersections in the Ottoman period / edited by Stefan Winter and Zainab HajHasan.
Names: Winter, Stefan, 1970–, editor. | HajHasan, Zainab, editor.
Description: Series statement: New landscapes in Middle East studies | Includes bibliographical references and index.
Identifiers: Canadiana (print) 20240359410 | Canadiana (ebook) 20240359429 | ISBN 9781487554408 (hardcover) | ISBN 9781487556884 (EPUB) | ISBN 9781487556877 (PDF)
Subjects: LCSH: Kurds – Syria – History. | LCSH: Turkey – History – Ottoman Empire, 1288–1918.
Classification: LCC DS94.8.K8 S97 2024 | DDC 956.91/00491597 – dc23

Cover design: Louise OFarrell
Cover images: (Top) *Rumkale*, 2022, photograph by Muhsin Soyudoğan; (middle) *Mehmed Salih Bedirxan*, © Archives Bedir Khan; (left) *Hawar Mountain*, 2018, Kurd Dagh, photograph by Fexrî Abdo; (bottom) *Millî Ibrahim Paşa and Son Visiting with Foreign Dignitaries and Officials in Aleppo*, c. 1906, © Albert Poche Collection, Aleppo.

We wish to acknowledge the land on which the University of Toronto Press operates. This land is the traditional territory of the Wendat, the Anishnaabeg, the Haudenosaunee, the Métis, and the Mississaugas of the Credit First Nation.

University of Toronto Press acknowledges the financial support of the Government of Canada, the Canada Council for the Arts, and the Ontario Arts Council, an agency of the Government of Ontario, for its publishing activities.

 Canada Council for the Arts / Conseil des Arts du Canada

 ONTARIO ARTS COUNCIL / CONSEIL DES ARTS DE L'ONTARIO
an Ontario government agency
un organisme du gouvernement de l'Ontario

 Funded by the Government of Canada / Financé par le gouvernement du Canada

Contents

List of Maps and Illustrations   vii

Archival Series Abbreviations   ix

Introduction   3

Part One: Kurdish Origins and Territorialities in Diachronic Perspective

1 Nusaybin under the Ottomans   17
   TOM SINCLAIR

2 The Qizilbash Reconsidered: The Role of the Kurdish Arabgirlu Tribe in the Early Safavid State   56
   MUSTAFA DEHQAN AND VURAL GENÇ

3 The ʿAfrin District under Ottoman Rule, 1516–1921   75
   STEFAN WINTER

Part Two: Kurds in Western and Urban Syria

4 Locating the Kurds in Ottoman Jordan and Palestine in the Sixteenth Century   111
   ZAINAB HAJHASAN

5 The Lebanese Junblats and the Canbolads: A Case of Mistaken Identity   128
   ABDUL-RAHIM ABU-HUSAYN

6 Warlords and Landlords: The Kurdish Presence in Central Syria in the Eighteenth and Nineteenth Centuries   137
   DICK DOUWES

vi Contents

Part Three: Kurdish Tribalism and Tribal Control in the Jazira

7 *Waqf* versus *Miri* Nomads: Taxation, Endowment, and Settlement
Practices in Northern Syria in the Eighteenth Century 161
KEIKO IWAMOTO

8 Bekir Bey and the Making of a Reşwan Nobility at Rumkale 179
MUHSIN SOYUDOĞAN

9 The Berazi Tribe of Suruj and Their Rebellion in the Tanzimat
Period 207
MUHSIN SEYDA

10 The Reşwan in Central Anatolia: Tribal Settlement and Sheep Trade
in the Nineteenth Century 223
YONCA KÖKSAL

11 Warfare and Alliances in Ra's al-'Ayn: Hamidiye Regiments,
Bedouin Tribes, and Ottoman Governors, 1895–1905 243
ERDAL ÇİFTÇİ

Part Four: Syrian Kurdish Elites of the Late Ottoman Period

12 Kurdish Naqshbandi-Khalidi Sheikhs of Damascus in the
Nineteenth Century 273
METIN ATMACA

13 Alliances and Competition in Kurdish Networks in Late Ottoman
Syria: The Example of the Bedirhani and Baban Families 287
BARBARA HENNING

14 Between Ottomanism and Kurdism: Mehmed Salih Bedirhan and
'Abd al-Rahman Yusuf in Damascus 308
MARTIN STROHMEIER

Afterword 337

Contributors 347

Index 351

Illustrations and Maps

Illustrations

3.1 Variant designations of the Liva-ı Ekrad, sixteenth–seventeenth century 80

3.2 Ravendan (Ravanda) castle 83

3.3 Order in the Antioch *shar'iyya* court registers regarding the Qilîçlo Kurds in Cum 90

3.4 Western edge of the Kurd Dagh (*nahiye* of Derbisak), overlooking the 'Amq Plain 94

3.5 Farm near Rajo, Syrian Kurd Dagh (2002) 107

8.1 Kuloğlu family tree 183

8.2 Rumkale castle 189

8.3 Stepped well in Rumkale 202

10.1 The Cihanbeyli *yayla* (pasturage), Ankara 238

11.1 Extract from a map by Mark Sykes showing the tribal composition of northeastern Syria 251

11.2 Mark Sykes's visit to Milli İbrahim Paşa's tent 254

11.3 Zühdü Bey, *mutasarrıf* of Zor 264

11.4 Shaykh Faris Paşa, chief of the Shammar 265

14.1 Mehmed Salih Bedirkhan in Damascus, January 1915 313

14.2 Abd al-Rahman Pasha al-Yusuf 326

Maps

1 Kurdish Syria and adjoining regions 2

2 The Ottoman Kurd Dagh 85

3 The Reşi Dağı–Suruj region 206

4 Reşwan pasturages and settlement areas in central Anatolia 228

Archival Series Abbreviations

BOA – T.C. Cumhurbaşkanlığı Osmanlı Arşivi, Istanbul

A.MKT – Bab-ı Ali Sadâret Evrâkı Mektubi Kalemi
A.MKT.MHM – Sadaret Mektubi Kalemi Mühimme
A.MKT.MVL – Sadaret Mektubî Kalemi Meclis-i Vala
A.MKT.NZD – Sadaret Mektubi Kalemi Nezaret ve Devair
A.MKT.UM – Sadaret Mektubi Kalemi Umum Vilayat
A.RSK – Bab-ı Asafi Ruus Defterleri
AE.SABH.I – Ali Emiri Sultan Abdülhamid I
AE.SMST.III – Ali Emiri Sultan Mustafa III
AE.SSLM.III – Ali Emiri Sultan Selim III
BEO – Bab-ı Ali Evrak Odası
C.AS – Cevdet Askeriye
C.DH – Cevdet Dahiliye
C.DRB – Cevdet Darphane
C.ML – Cevdet Maliye
C.ZB – Cevdet Zabtiye
CRAD – Cezayir ve Rakka Ahkam Defterleri
D.BŞM – Başmuhasebe Kalemi
D.BŞM.MHF – Başmuhasebe Kalemi Muhallefat
DH.MEM – Dahiliye Memurin Kalemi
DH.MKT – Dahiliye Nezareti Mektubi Kalemi
DH.MUİ – Dahiliye Muhaberat-ı Umumiye İdaresi
DH.SAİD – Dahiliye Nezareti Sicill-i Ahval İdare-i Umumiyesi
DH.ŞFR – Dahiliye Nezareti Şifre Kalemi
DH.TMIK.M – Dahiliye Nezareti Tesri-i Muamelat ve Islahat
 Komisyonu ia
DH.TMIK.S – Dahiliye Nezareti Tesri-i Muamelat ve Islahat
 Komisyonu ib

x Archival Series Abbreviations

GŞS – Gaziantep Şeriye Sicilleri
HAD – Haleb Ahkam Defterleri
HAT – Hatt-ı Hümayun
HR.MKT – Hariciye Nezareti Mektubi Kalemi
HR.SYS – Hariciye Nezareti Siyasi
HR.TH – Tahrirat-ı Hariciye Kalemi
İ.DH – İrade Dahiliye
İ.MBH – İrade Mabeyn-i Hümayun
İ.MVL – İrade Meclis-i Vala
İE.DH – İbnülemin Dahiliye
İE.ML – İbnülemin Maliye
KK – Kamil Kepeci
MAD – Maliyeden Müdevver
MB.İ – Mabeyn İrade
MD – Mühimme Defterleri
MKM – Mühimme-i Mektume Defterleri
MŞAD – Maraş Ahkam Defterleri
MV – Meclis-i Vükela
MVL – Meclis-i Vala
MZ – Mühimme Zeyli Defterleri
ŞD – Şura-ı Devlet
ŞKT – Şikayet Defterleri
ŞŞAD – Şam-ı Şerif Ahkam Defterleri
TD – Tahrir Defterleri (Defter-i Hakani)
TKGM – Türkiye Kadastro Genel Müdürlüğü
TSMA – Topkapı Sarayı Müzesi Arşivi
Y.A.RES – Yıldız Sadaret Resmi Maruzat Evrakı
Y.EE – Yıldız Esas Evrakı
Y.MTV – Yıldız Mütenevvi Maruzat Evrakı
Y.PRK.AZJ – Yıldız Perakende Evrakı Arzuhal Jurnal
Y.PRK.UM – Yıldız Perakende Evrakı Umum Vilayetler Tahriratı

Other Collections

AA – Political Archive of the German Foreign Ministry (Auswärtiges
   Amt), Berlin
A/AS – Aleppo/Awamir Sultaniyya (Centre for Historical Docu-
   ments, Damascus)
A/MS – Aleppo/Mahkama Shar'iyya (Centre for Historical Docu-
   ments, Damascus)
AHK.d – Ahkam Defterleri (Vakıflar Genel Müdürlüğü, Ankara)

E-L/SL – Correspondance politique et commerciale, Série E-Levant / Syrie Liban (Archives du Ministère des Affaires étrangères, Paris – La Courneuve)

H/MS – Hama/Mahkama Shar'iyya (Centre for Historical Documents, Damascus)

EVM.d – Evamir Defterleri (Vakıflar Genel Müdürlüğü, Ankara)

FER.d – Ferman Defterleri (Vakıflar Genel Müdürlüğü, Ankara)

FO – Foreign Office (National Archives, London)

FP – Fonds Poche (Poche-Marcopoli Archives, Aleppo)

MKT.d – Mukataa Defterleri (Vakıflar Genel Müdürlüğü, Ankara)

SYRIAN-KURDISH INTERSECTIONS IN THE OTTOMAN PERIOD

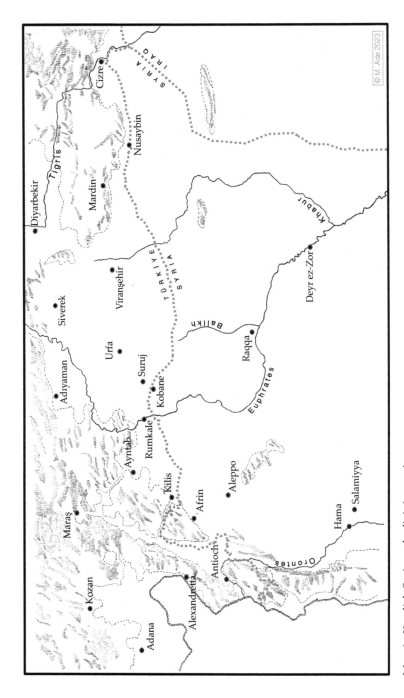

Map 1. Kurdish Syria and adjoining regions

Introduction

This edited volume is a collective exploration of an area that has never been the object of sustained enquiry, the Kurdish presence in Ottoman Syria. It reflects a shared feeling among the authors that while the field of Kurdology as a whole has made great strides this past decade, we still lack the critical mass of documentary knowledge and concrete case studies about the Kurds of and in Syria that would enable us to establish their history as a proper subfield of Ottoman Kurdish studies. The following chapters stem from the longstanding research projects or simply the wider areas of interest of a very disparate group of researchers from Canada, Türkiye, Cyprus, the Netherlands, Germany, Iran, Japan, Jordan, Lebanon, Syria, and the United States. They do not aim to provide a holistic picture of the Kurds of Ottoman Syria, something which would be as yet premature, but rather to contribute to and begin texturing the corpus of primary research available to scholars, in hopes of laying down some basic orientations and lines of enquiry for what might eventually develop into a more monographic treatment of the subject.

Not all of the contributions in this collection deal exclusively or even primarily with the territory of modern Syria, which was not delimited as such in the Ottoman period, and even the *vilayet* of Syria created in the late nineteenth century did not encompass the northern reaches of Aleppo and Mesopotamia where most of the country's Kurds live today. "Syria" as a historical entity is thus a construct, albeit one with key implications for students of Ottoman and Kurdish history especially. The area's removal from lands usually seen as more central to Kurdish concerns or "Kurdistan" properly speaking; the importance of local sources and literature, principally in Arabic; and now the difficulties of travelling and conducting research in the country as well as the geopolitical sensitivities inherent to the topic all help explain why

4 Introduction

Syria has generally been neglected in wider Ottoman Kurdish studies and therefore merits our attention. It has become a standard exercise in work on Ottoman Syria to point to the historical contingency and changing associations of the name, or of similarly unsatisfying pendants such as Anatolia, Lebanon, Bilad al-Sham, etc.[1] In recent and more politically-oriented literature, the modern coinage "Rojava" is sometimes used to characterize the region as "western" Kurdistan, but it occurs in no sources from the period and is thus rarely used in a historical context. Syrian, in this collection, is meant to be inclusive of a complex territorial reality of vital concern to the history of the Kurds rather than an exclusive or formal jurisdiction.

Nor is the focus in every contribution even necessarily on Kurdish actors per se. Several deal instead with specific geographic locales or Ottoman government policies that constitute an essential framework for the topic but not with particular communities as such; others deal with figures such as the Canpolads or the Bedirxans who were only later and retrospectively cast as agents of Kurdish history. What this collection seeks most fundamentally to illuminate are the junctures and crossings of Kurdish lives, Syrian geography in the broadest terms, and Ottoman rule. It touches on Kurdish populations that have existed in the land of Syria for centuries, as much as on nomad groups with only fleeting or periodic contacts in the area under the specific parameters of Ottoman government. Some of the contributions treat the historical origins and development of what is today the most important linguistic minority in republican Syria; others tell of distinct groups that flourished in the region in an imperial context but that ultimately emigrated again or were assimilated into modern Syrian, Lebanese, Palestinian, and Jordanian society.

The history of the Kurds in greater Syria under the Ottomans is in large measure one of mobility, forced or voluntary settlement, state repression, the struggle for autonomy, or the quest for individual advancement. A key challenge in writing the history of an essentially rural and tribal people is of course the nature of the sources. Educated Kurdish speakers always existed in Ottoman Syria, but it is commonly admitted that they did not begin writing as or even identifying as

---

1 Thomas Philipp, "Identities and Loyalties in Bilad al-Sham at the Beginning of the Early Modern Period," in *From the Syrian Land to the States of Syria and Lebanon*, ed. T. Philipp and Christoph Schumann (Beirut: Ergon, 2004), 9–26; James Reilly, *Fragile Nation, Shattered Land: The Modern History of Syria* (London: I.B. Tauris, 2018), 3, 76–86.

Introduction   5

"Kurds" until the very end of the empire. A written prose literature in Kurmancî Kurdish, the dialect or group of dialects spoken by Syrian Kurds, did not exist before the twentieth century and has only begun to develop on a large scale in recent decades, particularly in Turkey/ Türkiye and among the Kurdish expatriate community, while historians have only intermittently explored oral accounts and folk literature as a possible source.[2] Arabic and Turkish narrative chronicles, as well as western travel and consular literature, provide a wealth of anecdotal information about Kurds in Syria, but generally reflect the interests and biases of their urban, non-Kurdish authors. The overwhelming mass of historical information used in the studies in this volume therefore comes from Ottoman-era archives, primarily those of the central administration in Istanbul, and to a lesser extent from the *shar'iyya* court registers of several key provinces. Of course these materials too invite caution, in that they provide an ideal, normative, picture of what Ottoman government meant to achieve vis-à-vis Kurdish and other subject groups in the region, and not what was actually occurring on the ground or what was really achieved in the end. Scholars especially of the well-worn Tahrir Defterleri (tax census registers), which are put to use alongside other records in several of the contributions to the present volume, have warned of their "pitfalls and limitations" as a source for social and economic history. They have recalled the necessity of understanding them in the precise fiscal context in which each was composed, allowing for the fact that certain population groups and sources of revenue are not covered, and cross-checking the registers with other sources.[3] Numerous historians of Syria have relied on the Tahrir registers, albeit not always critically, to provide a picture of what the Ottoman state knew of real or potential fiscal resources in rural areas throughout the region in

---

2   See Alexandre Jaba, *Recueil de notices et récits kourdes servant à la connaissance de la langue, de la littérature et des tribus du Kourdistan* (St. Petersburg: Académie Impériale des Sciences, 1860); Oskar Mann, *"Our Steppe is Vast...": Kurdish Epics and Tribal Stories from Urfa, 1906*, ed. Barbara Sträuli (Wiesbaden: Harrassowitz, 2021), as well as the contributions to the popular literary journal *Bîrnebûn* (Stockholm, 1997–).

3   Heath Lowry, "The Ottoman Tahrîr Defterleri as a Source for Social and Economic History: Pitfalls and Limitations," in *Studies in Defterology: Ottoman Society in the Fifteenth and Sixteenth Centuries* (Istanbul: Isis Press, 1992), 3–18; Metin Coşgel, "Ottoman Tax Registers (Tahrir Defterleri)," *Historical Methods* 37, no. 2 (2004): 87–100, https://doi.org/10.3200/HMTS.37.2.87-102. For northern Syria see especially Margaret Venzke, "The Ottoman Tahrir Defterleri and Agricultural Productivity: The Case for Northern Syria," *Osmanlı Araştırmaları* 17, no. 17 (1997): 1–13.

6 Introduction

the sixteenth and seventeenth centuries. In the following, they are understood, much like the equally well-known Mühimme executive decrees, Şikayet fiscal complaint registers, Vakıf (pious foundation) records, and a full range of ministerial and other governmental papers from the Tanzimat period, not as objective representations of provincial realities by an abstract Ottoman state, but as authoritative claims on resources by individual and sometimes rival agents or agencies of the state.

Most important for our purposes, the identification in Ottoman administrative sources of certain groups by ethnic labels such as "Ekrad" (from Arabic *Akrad*; Kurds) meant that they were indeed perceived as a distinct social-linguistic collective, whether this collective was explicitly recognized as a "tribe" or by one of the many terms for discrete population groups (*aşiret, kabile, boy, cemaat, taife*, etc.) in Ottoman usage. Many other Kurdish-speaking people, whether families or individuals, were simply not identified as such in Ottoman sources. The fact that the term "Ekrad" systematically implied a rural or pastoral social formation has in fact been used by modern-day detractors of Kurdish ethnic identity in Turkey to argue that it referred *only* to lifestyle and not to Kurdishness/Kurdish-speakingness per se ("the word Ekrad does not mean Kurds whatsoever"), thereby intimating that there was no historically significant Kurdish presence in Anatolia or Syria and Iraq after all. (The inverse argument, that "Turkoman" was also just a sociological term and implies no Turkish identity whatsoever, is never encountered.) For Syria, certainly, claims of this sort can easily be disproven with reference to the voluminous Arabic historiography on local or migrant population groups that already figure prominently in the Ayyubid and Mamluk eras and that were unmistakably perceived as ethnic Kurds; readers of the present volume may of course read into the Ottoman terminology regarding the *Akrad/Ekrad* in Syria whatever they see fit.

The interest of many of the contributions to this volume lies precisely in the fact that the Kurds of Ottoman Syria did not live in isolation, but relayed tribal affiliations and politics from Anatolia and Iraq; interacted with indigenous Arab, Turkoman, Armenian and other populations; traded with or settled among urban communities; and grappled and negotiated with local and imperial Ottoman authorities. From the Ayyubid period, which saw the settlement of numerous Kurdish military troops to confront the Crusaders through the development of Kurmancî Kurdish print media under the French Mandate, Syria has been a pivotal yet underappreciated crossroads of Kurdish history. In the contemporary theoretical sense, our perspective on the Ottoman

Introduction 7

period is perhaps also "intersectional" in so far as the socioeconomic marginalization of tribal pastoralists, the widespread indifference to the provincial periphery and to the "Arab" provincial periphery especially in modern scholarship, and the negation of Kurdish identity and rights in virtually every state of the region are in many ways overlapping and mutually determining. It is not intersectional in the sense that the available source material has not yet allowed us to take up questions of coinciding race, gender, or sexual discrimination – arguably the key blind spot of this and many other works on the history of Middle Eastern rural society. By turning a light on the societal and geographical fringes of the Ottoman, the Syrian, as well as the Kurdish past itself, however, it is hoped that this collection will at least aid in establishing some frames for future enquiry.

Contributions

The chapters in this volume are arranged in four thematic sections while adhering to a roughly chronological order. The first section addresses some basic *longue-durée* parameters of Kurdish history in Syria, beginning with Tom Sinclair's multi-secular survey of Nusaybin (city and countryside) under the Ottomans. Building on and extending his encyclopedic investigation of eastern Anatolia in the late medieval and early Ottoman period,[4] his description of this important centre of eastern Christianity, Turkic expansion, and finally Ottoman colonization provides the ideal spatial and temporal segue to the question of the Kurdish presence in Syria. On the basis of a broad review of primary and secondary literature, Sinclair is able to trace the vicissitudes of settlement, economy, and society in and around Nusaybin, in particular the rising power of local tribes and the concomitant decline, and finally the disappearance, of the Christian population at the end of the Ottoman era. In many ways, the city of Nusaybin, and with it Kurdish-populated northeastern Syria in general, never entirely recovered from the Mongols' destruction of trade routes in the region in the medieval period.

The contribution by Mustafa Dehqan and Vural Genç deals with Kurdish populations that were only notionally linked with Syria, but whose actions fundamentally helped orient Ottoman concerns in the region in the sixteenth century: the Shamlu-affiliated Arabgirlu tribe and other Kurdish groups who entered into the Qizilbash (Kızılbaş)

---

4 Thomas Sinclair, *Eastern Turkey: An Architectural and Archaeological Survey*, 4 vols. (London: Pindar Press, 1987–90).

8   Introduction

confederation and became principal elements of the Iranian Safavid state. The authors further show how Arabgirlu figures continued to inhabit high offices in the seventeenth century, demonstrating to what degree not only Turkomans, as is often suggested, but also Ottoman-based Kurds played an essential role in the establishment of the great Shiite rival empire. This in turn, Dehqan and Genç suggest, resonated with local Kurdish leaderships in Syria at the time of the Celali governor rebellions.

Chapter 3 in part 1, by Stefan Winter, provides another long-term historical overview of a key Kurdish area of Syria, the ʿAfrin district in the province of Aleppo, from the Ottoman conquest to 1921. Relying mainly on Tahrir, Mühimme, and Şikayet documents, as well as court registers from Aleppo and Antioch and later narrative literature, he recalls the different phases of Ottoman governance vis-à-vis the local Kurdish population, from the cooptation of indigenous leaders in the sixteenth century to the increasing integration of autonomous tribal structures, and finally the attempts to reassert more central control in the Tanzimat and Young Turk periods. He concludes that the Ottoman state consistently sought to recognize and incorporate the distinctly Kurdish tribal population as such.

Part 2 encompasses studies on three relatively restricted Kurdish communities in the western and central Bilad al-Sham (Syria). The first, perhaps fittingly, examines the Ottoman-era presence of what are likely among the oldest Kurdish groups in the region: the descendants of tribal military units settled in Palestine and Transjordan by the Ayyubid dynasty in its struggle against the Crusades. Following on the seminal work of Boris James that chronicles the slow marginalization of the Kurds under the Mamluks, together with the crystallization of an eastern "Kurdistan" in the late medieval periods,[5] Zainab HajHasan here draws on Ottoman tax census records to reconstitute the town quarters (*mahalle*), villages, agricultural activities, and religious bequests (*waqf*) still associated with the Kurdish community in the early modern era. While only a small population in the Ottoman era and today completely assimilated, HajHasan shows how this distant holdover from the medieval period continued to be identified as Kurdish under Ottoman imperial rule.

Mount Lebanon, meanwhile, despite the importance of numerous Kurdish lordships in the ʿAkkar, Kura, and Jabal ʿAmil districts

---

5   Boris James, *Genèse du Kurdistan : Les Kurdes dans l'Orient mamlouk et mongol, 1250–1340* (Paris: Éditions de la Sorbonne, 2021).

Introduction 9

under Ottoman rule, is unfortunately not the subject of a separate investigation in this volume. Instead, we are honoured and privileged to reprint a lightly edited version of one of the most foundational yet under-recognized studies in the field, which the great historian of Ottoman Lebanon, Abdul-Rahim Abu-Husayn, agreed to contribute before his unhappy passing in early 2022. "The Lebanese Junblats and the Canpolads: A Case of Mistaken Identity," which was originally published in the in-house proceedings of the 1998 CIEPO conference in Vienna, definitively disproves one of the most oft-repeated myths of modern Lebanese history, namely the ostensible link between the Druze "Joumblatt" family and the Kurdish Canpolad dynasty of Kilis, but has been remained largely unknown even to the scholarly world.[6] Drawing essentially on Arabic narrative and biographical literature from the time, the chapter shows that the Junblats were in fact already long established in the Shuf mountains of Lebanon by the time of the Canpolad revolt in Kilis in the early seventeenth century. It is offered here in fond testament to Prof. Abu-Husayn's legacy and in hopes that it will finally receive the attention it commands.

The last chapter in part 2 shifts the focus further south to Hama, where Dick Douwes investigates the establishment of Kurdish military entrepreneurs under the auspices of Ottoman rule, and their subsequent transformation from "warlords" to "landlords" as they begin to substitute investment in livestock farming, agriculture, commerce, and landowning for their previous military-administrative prerogatives. Concentrating ultimately on the Berazî and Millî families, Douwes's contribution extends his previous work in the *shar'iyya* court records of Hama and other provincial sources to provide a vivid illustration of the gradual assimilation of Kurdish tribal elements into mainstream Syrian society.

Part 3 goes to the heart of the question of major Ottoman Kurdish tribes present on or around Syrian territory. In an important revisionist study, Keiko Iwamoto reviews the fiscal-administrative status of the Yeni-İl and Aleppo Turkomans and the Reşwan and Kilis Kurds, mapping out the critical difference that while the former were committed to imperial *waqf* foundations, the latter remained subject to regular state (*miri*) taxation. On the basis of an extensive survey of nomad groups in the archives of the Vakıflar Genel Müdürlüğü in Ankara, she is also able to show that

---

6 Markus Köhbach, Gisela Procházka-Eisl, and Claudia Römer, eds., *Acta Viennensia Ottomanica: Akten des 13. CIEPO-Symposiums (Comité International des Études Pré-Ottomanes et Ottomanes) 21–25 September 1998* (Vienna: Institut für Orientalistik, 1999), 1–6.

10   Introduction

the tribes themselves could play on the confusion between the two parallel systems in an attempt to escape paying their dues, and implicitly raises the question of whether the state's assignment of Turkoman confederations to *waqf* foundations and Kurds to regular tax collectorships bespeaks a conscious policy of ethnic differentiation in Syria.

Another revisionist study touching on the Reşwan is offered by Muhsin Soyudoğan, who chronicles the rise of a notable family of the Reşi tribe in the south Anatolian fortress town of Rumkale on the Euphrates in the late eighteenth and early nineteenth century. Likely of Yezidi origin, related to the larger Reşwan confederation but not included in the same fiscal structure, the Reşi Kuloğlu dynasty represented one of the leading autonomous powers in the area before the Ottoman attack on Rumkale and execution of Bekir Bey in 1814. As such their story sheds light not only on an important Kurdish-dominated tribal territory of northern Syria/Mesopotamia, but also on the beginning of processes of state centralization that would confront all Kurds in the region in the nineteenth century.

Growing state pressure on tribes is precisely the subject of the third chapter in part 3, in which Muhsin Seyda retraces the rebellion of the Berazî tribe around Suruj between 1840 and 1845. Drawing on government documents but also on the local oral tradition, he shows how the Tanzimat regime's new policy of military conscription in the area crystallized resistance among the Kurdish population, leading to armed insurrection but ultimately not serving to mobilize the local nobility politically as in other parts of the empire. Translated from Arabic for this volume, Seyda's study of this particular event is one of the first of its kind to integrate source material in Kurmancî Kurdish and should stand as a model for future research.

Following a similar line of enquiry, Yonca Köksal's chapter returns to the Reşwans and highlights the effects of their forced settlement in central Anatolia in the nineteenth century, and especially their changing role in the Ottoman sheep trade. Despite the violence and coercion of the Tanzimat-era tribal settlement project, leading livestock traders of the Reşwan, Cihanbeyli, and other confederations actually came to new wealth with the end of provisionist policies and price controls in the Empire and rising demand on the Istanbul meat market in the second half of the century. Grounded in her far-ranging work on Ottoman provincial administration in the reform period, Köksal's contribution serves to recall how extensively Kurdish pastoralists with ties in Syria and elsewhere were integrated in the imperial economy.

Finally, Erdal Çiftçi examines Kurdish-Arab tribal relations in northern Syria/Mesopotamia at the very end of the nineteenth century and

Introduction   11

the turn of the twentieth century. Detailing how major rivals such as the Millî Kurds and the Shammar Bedouin entered into frequent alliances with the Ottoman governors of Deyr al-Zor and Diyarbekir in their own regional struggles, or gained the backing of the central government as Hamidiye Regiments, he paints a picture of a complex world of tribal autonomy, "tribal diplomacy," and immersion in Ottoman provincial politics at the end of empire.

In part 4, the focus is back on central Syria, primarily Damascus, and not on Kurdish tribal groups but on Kurdish individuals who came to the great Arab provincial capital to make their careers as Ottoman functionaries, scholars, and gentlemen in the nineteenth century. It opens with a study on the Khalidi family of the Naqshbandi Sufi order, in which Metin Atmaca traces the emigration of the leading family shaykhs from Sulaymaniyya to Baghdad and on to Damascus in the 1820s. Here they founded their own distinctive Naqshbandi branch, which continued to attract above all Shafi'i Kurdish scholars and Sufis, while at the same time constituting one of the principal currents of reformist Islam in all Syria, the last representative of which was in fact the late grand mufti Ahmad Kaftaru (d. 2004). Despite the fact that Hanafism was and remained the dominant juridical school (*madhhab*) in Syria under the Ottomans, the Kurdish newcomers and other followers of the Khalidi-Naqshbandi branch continued to benefit from official patronage, were integrated into the scholarly networks of the city, and in fact became a key conduit of the Shafi'i establishment in Damascus.

The last two chapters both address aspects of the family which, through its publishing activities and community leadership, would ultimately play a role in the Kurdish movement far beyond the confines of Syria, the Bedirxans (Bedirhans). Barbara Henning dissects an 1894 court case against Hüseyin Bedirhan, the local governor of 'Akkar in northern Lebanon, which he tried to have moved elsewhere on account of the ostensible hostility of the governor of Beirut, a member of the rival Kurdish Baban family of notables. His claim of an ancient "feud" existing between the two families, according to Henning, was essentially a self-serving, self-orientalizing myth, with little bearing on the Babans' equally modernist and reformist credentials, designed to move the proceedings to friendlier territory in central Syria, where the Bedirhans had more political support.

In the final chapter, Martin Strohmeier compares the career paths of two leading Kurdish notables of Damascus, Mehmed Salih Bedirhan and 'Abd al-Rahman Paşa al-Yusuf, against the backdrop of the absolutist regime of Abdülhamid II, Young Turk opposition, the rise of Turkish and Arab nationalism, and the growing awareness of Kurdish

12   Introduction

identity in Syria and the wider empire. While the former failed to gain significant office under the Ottomans and instead helped steward a Kurdish cultural awakening, the latter, a high state functionary, belonged to the city's Ottoman Arab elite. Both nevertheless espoused the common cause of Ottoman modernism, exemplifying the range of complementary identities, networks, and activities available to Kurds of late Ottoman Syria.

Note on Kurdish Names and Transliterations

Needless to say, no collection of individual research papers will ever adequately cover the history of the Kurds of Ottoman Syria in all the breadth and depth the topic deserves. Nor will there be a consensus on the pertinence of all the subjects, sources, methodologies and lines of questioning deployed in the present volume – perhaps not even among the different contributors themselves. Rather than enforce a particular thematic or ideological unity, we have preferred in essence to let the differing approaches speak for themselves, and hope that their very diversity will spark further interest and ideas for future research.

We have also not insisted on uniformity in the rendering of personal and place names. Part of the objective of this volume is of course to afford the Kurds more space within the fields of Ottoman and Syrian history, and as such we have encouraged the use of Kurmancî Kurdish spellings of personal, tribe and place names, using the modern Kurmancî translation of Mihemed Emîn Zekî Beg's classical *History of the Kurds and Kurdistan*, published by the pioneering Istanbul-based Kurdish language publisher Avesta, as a general guide.[7] The point of many of the studies, and of the volume as a whole, however, is that most of the characters and issues presented here operated at the crossroads of Ottoman (Turkish), Syrian (Arabic) and Kurdish history and historical representations, so that the authors have in general not found it useful or advantageous to favour the relatively recent (and not fully standardized) Latin-script Kurmancî renderings of traditional names and terms, especially when they occur in the context or source materials of Ottoman or Arab provincial history. As a result, most names of individuals (including Kurds) with standing in the state administration will have been rendered in modified modern

---

7   Mihemed Emîn Zekî Beg (d. 1948), *Dîroka Kurd û Kurdistanê*, translated from Sorani Kurdish by Ziya Avci (Istanbul: Avesta, 2002).

Turkish (e.g., Mehmed, not Mehmet, Muhammad or Mihemed), while geographic names in Syria, or formerly associated with Syria, will usually appear according to the modified transliteration system for Arabic of the *International Journal of Middle East Studies* – with a good deal of tolerance for variations across and even within the individual contributions. The index will encompass variant spellings and may be used as a rough guide for conversion. While much more can and should doubtless be done in the name of correct Kurmancî Kurdish philology, it is hoped that these compromises will be seen as pragmatic and conducive to the exercise of seeing the Kurds of Syria within the greater whole of Ottoman history.

PART ONE

Kurdish Origins and Territorialities in Diachronic Perspective

1 Nusaybin under the Ottomans

TOM SINCLAIR

The city of Nusaybin lay on the plain of Upper Mesopotamia in a stretch overlooked from the north by the escarpment of a limestone plateau. Ninety kilometres to the east, the river Tigris issued on to the plain from a gorge in the plateau and soon came to the city of Jazirat ibn 'Umar (Cizre). Traffic from Baghdad, which had followed the Tigris upstream to the city of Mosul, continued upstream up the river's east bank, crossed at Jazirat ibn 'Umar and then came westwards to Nasibin/Nusaybin. Strictly speaking there was a more direct way between Mosul and Nusaybin, which crossed the angle made at Jazirat ibn 'Umar. In the Ottoman period it was not guarded, was subject to robbery, and lacked facilities for provisioning.[1] To the west, tracks continued over the plain to Ruha/Urfa, ultimately to Aleppo. From Nusaybin, after a day's travel over the plain, a track climbed northwest to the city of Dara and so to Mardin, whose clifftop citadel crowned an isolated sector of the escarpment; Mardin gave access to Amid/Diyarbekir and so to cities in Anatolia, Armenia, and Iran.

Nusaybin serves as a bridge of sorts between the central Kurdish regions (regularly though not systematically referred to as "Kurdistan" in Ottoman sources) and the area known in antiquity and again today as Syria. This chapter concerns essentially the city and its condition under

---

1 Tavernier, taking this route (which required only five days of travel) to Mosul in 1644, bought all his provisions at Nusaybin. He found water, though not especially fresh, in only two places, one of which was a "méchante fontaine." After four days' travel, he and his party saw the ruins of a bridge over a small river, and those of a fortress. *Les Six Voyages de Jean-Baptiste Tavernier qu'il a fait en Turquie et en Perse et aux Indes* (Amsterdam: Joannes Van Someren 1678), 1:191–2. For a six-day journey, *Jacut's Geographisches Wörtherbuch*, ed. Ferdinand Wüstenfeld (Leipzig: Brockhaus, 1866–73), 4:787. See also pp. 33 and 47–8 below.

18   Tom Sinclair

the Ottomans. The damage done to trade, especially by the Mongols in the thirteenth century, and the routing of commercial traffic elsewhere, substantially explain Nusaybin's state in this time. A short throwback to the Middle Ages serves too as a bridge between the successive medieval Kurdish regimes in the region, including the Marwanids of Upper Mesopotamia and the Ayyubids of Hisn Kayfa, and the more fragmented picture of the Ottoman period. A look at the late medieval period also helps us to understand the relationship between the city and the surrounding plain under the Ottomans, including the Kurdish population of the plain and the ties between them, the commercial situation, the Ottoman authorities' policies and capabilities, and the city's Christian population.

Before the Period of Ottoman Rule

In the tenth to thirteenth centuries CE the city, much fought over, nevertheless prospered.[2] The principal source of prosperity was trade, as just described; but the plain round about supported wheat, barley and rice, and the river Hurmas (or Jaghjagh), rising in the limestone hills above, watered orchards and gardens.[3] The factor which brought to an end the period of commercial efflorescence in the city's history was the Mongol invasions, not because of any violent devastation but because warfare in sectors further west with the Mamluks of Egypt and Syria prohibited the passage of substantial quantities of commercial traffic along the avenue of Upper Mesopotamia.[4] By the early fourteenth century the city was in a state of decline and ruination.[5]

---

2 See E. Honigmann and C.E. Bosworth, "Nasibīn," in *Encyclopaedia of Islam*, 2nd ed. [*EI2*], ed. H.A.R. Gibb et al. (Leiden: Brill, 1960–2008), 7:983–4. An updated article on "Nasibīn," with more bibliography, is currently under preparation by the present author, *Encyclopaedia of Islam Three*, ed. Kate Fleet et al. (Leiden: Brill, 2013–). In particular, see Halil Kök, *Musul Atabeyliği: Zengiler (Musul Kolu, 1146–1233)* (Ankara: Türk Tarih Kurumu, 2013).

3 On trade, Thomas Sinclair, *Eastern Trade and the Mediterranean in the Middle Ages: Pegolotti's Ayas-Tabriz Itinerary and its Commercial Context* (Abingdon: Routledge, 2020), 49–50, 51–3. On the introduction of rice cultivation to the district, Marius Canard, "Rice in the Middle East in the first centuries of Islam," in *Production and the Exploitation of Resources*, ed. Michael Morony (Ashgate, UK: Routledge, 2002), 156.

4 Sinclair, *Eastern Trade*, 70–1.

5 Ibn Battuta, *Voyages d'Ibn Battûta*, ed. and tr. C. Défrémery and B.R. Sanguinetti (Paris: Anthropos, 1969), 140; Guy Le Strange, *The Lands of the Eastern Caliphate: Mesopotamia, Persia, and Central Asia from the Moslem Conquest to the Time of Timur* (New York: AMS Press, 1976), 95. Jean Maurice Fiey, *Nisibe : métropole syriaque orientale et ses suffragants des origines à nos jours* (Leuven: Peeters, 1977), 110.

Nusaybin under the Ottomans   19

In the field of Christian life, too, Nusaybin had a glorious past to look back to. Among a population known as Syrian, which spoke a language called Aramaic whose literary form is called Syriac, an early and inchoate school of theology developed here. It was no coincidence that Nisibis was a wealthy city, designated in treaties from the late third century to the sixth century as the premier market city for trade between the Sasanian and Roman, subsequently Late Roman, empires. When a treaty of 363 CE parted Nisibis (as it then was known in Greek and Roman sources) from the East Roman Empire and gave it to the Sasanian Empire of Iran and Iraq, the school was transferred to Edessa/Urfa. Here the school espoused and ramified a dyophysite Christology, in other words the view that Christ had two natures, a divine and a human.[6] In 489 the school at Edessa was closed and the scholars migrated back to Nisibis, where they continued as the leading theological institution of the Church of the East; the latter substantially adopted the school's Christological stance. The school's position of pre-eminence lasted until the late seventh century CE.[7]

By the time of the treaty of 363 CE, after which the influential teacher and writer Ephrem moved to Edessa, the Church of the East was fully formed and independent of the wider imperial Church, whose network of patriarchs (including Rome and Constantinople) and bishops accounted for the territory of the two Roman empires, East and West.[8] In the Church of the East an episcopal structure had taken shape by the end of the third century CE; the Church recognized itself as independent in 410 CE.[9] It was now that the metropolitanate of Nisibis was founded; this was a group of bishoprics under the care of a bishop of

---

6 On the treaty and exodus of population in 363, see Averil Cameron and Peter Garnsey, eds., *The Late Empire, AD 337–425* (Cambridge: Cambridge University Press, 1998), 79, 424, 439, 442. On Nisibis as a market city, see Hubert Cancik and Helmut Schneider, eds., *Brill's New Pauly: Encyclopaedia of the Ancient World* (Leiden: Brill, 2006), 9:778. On the schools, see E. Kirsten, "Edessa," in *Lexicon für Antike und Christentum*, ed. Theodor Klauser (Stuttgart: Anton Hiersemann, 1959), esp. 571–81; Adam Becker, *Fear of God and the Beginning of Wisdom: The School of Nisibis and Christian Scholastic Culture in Late Antique Mesopotamia* (Philadelphia: University of Philadelphia Press, 2006), chap. 3.

7 Becker, *Fear of God*, chaps. 4–9.

8 For the patriarchates and episcopal organization and role of the East Roman Empire's imperial church, see Cameron and Garnsey, 238–40, 240–5, 246–50; Averil Cameron, Bryan Ward-Perkins, and Michael Whitby, eds., *Late Antiquity: Empire or Successors, AD 425–600* (Cambridge: Cambridge University Press, 2000), 731–41.

9 Wilhelm Baum and Dietmar Winkler, *The Church of the East: A Concise History*, tr. Miranda G. Henry (London: Routledge Curzon, 2003), 7–11, 14–21.

20 Tom Sinclair

higher rank, the metropolitan. The metropolitanate covered the plain of Upper Mesopotamia as far east as Jazirat ibn 'Umar (Syr. *Gazarta*) at the Tigris crossing, and districts at the east end of the Upper Tigris basin further north.[10] Overlooking the city of Nisibis from the lip of the escarpment were two monasteries founded in the fourth century CE, and another, that of Mar Ibrahim of Kashkar, founded in the late sixth century.

The formation and autonomy of the Church of the East were possible because the church's whole fabric of adherents, bishoprics, etc., always lay in the territory of the Sasanian Empire, which was generally hostile to and sometimes at war with the Roman, subsequently the East Roman, Empire. Edessa was a frontier city of the East Roman Empire, Nisibis of the Sasanian Empire. In any case such an autonomy made it relatively easy for the church to adopt a Christology which the greater Roman church (comprising both the Western and the Eastern Roman Empires) never fully espoused. The formula of the Council of Chalcedon (451 CE) came near to doing so. The Church of the East believed Christ had two natures, a divine and a human, and that this accounted for all Christ's actions on earth. The Chalcedonian formula accepted the two natures; there were differences nevertheless, but in any case, by this stage the Church of the East was well separated from the wider body of the imperial church.[11]

To understand the state of Nisibis in the Late Antique period, as well as the Ottoman period, it is helpful to introduce here a church and a Christological formula, in some ways the polar antithesis of that espoused by the Church of the East, which was equally present at Nisibis early in the city's existence as a Christian centre. The Monophysite position is that Christ had just one nature, neither solely a divine one nor a solely human one. That single nature existed in Christ the human being who walked on the earth and died to save mankind: as Frend put it, "the Monophysites held that after the incarnation the two natures became one, so that all the thoughts and acts of the Saviour were those

---

10 David Wilmshurst, *The Ecclesiastical Organisation of the Church of the East, 1318–1913* (Leuven: Peeters, 2000), 40–1.

11 The Church of the East claimed that each nature could exist only in its own *hypostasis*, the concrete and individual realization of that nature. According to the Chalcedonian formula, on the other hand, the two natures, united yet different, existed in just one *hypostasis*. For the Church of the East, Baum and Winkler, *Church of the East*, 22–3, 39; W.H.C. Frend, *The Rise of the Monophysite Movement* (Cambridge: Cambridge University Press, 1979), 13–14. For Chalcedon, see Cameron, Ward-Perkins, and Whitby *Late Antiquity: Empire or Successors, AD 425–600*, 810–14; Frend, *Monophysite Movement*, 1–6, 16–20 on Council of Ephesus.

of a single unitary being, God in Christ."[12] Putting the theological positions succinctly, we may say that whereas the Dyophysite theology explains how the Christ who walked on earth, was crucified, and did many actions characteristic of humans, managed to be human, the Monophysite explains how He managed to be divine.

The Monophysite position was attractive to monks and lay populations in Alexandria and the African provinces, as well as in Syria. Chalcedon (451) effectively put an end to any chance of agreement with the imperial church, despite subsequent attempts to weld the Monophysite with the Chalcedonian view.[13] The East Roman emperor Anastasius and a particularly articulate advocate of Syrian Monophysitism, a bishop named Severus, tried between 513 and 521 to make Monophysitism the standard doctrine of the imperial church. However, in 521 there started a general persecution of Monophysite adherents in the provinces.[14] Beginning almost straightaway after the Council of Chalcedon, but gathering strength from about 530, a separate hierarchy was gradually formed; by 566, twenty-seven bishops had been consecrated. The hierarchy covered Syria, Cilicia (north of Antioch), and Upper Mesopotamia, reaching as far as the monasteries of the Tur 'Abdin, the plateau behind the escarpment overlooking Nisibis.[15] This was a single church known as the Syrian Orthodox or Jacobite church. As with the Church of the East, in Upper Mesopotamia the Syrian Orthodox population was Syrian and Aramaic-speaking, and the written language was Syriac. In addition to this Syrian Orthodox branch, Monophysitism also became the creed of the church of Armenia, with one difference.[16] Armenia was geographically contiguous with the Syrian populations of Upper Mesopotamia. Monophysitism also was the creed of the Coptic

---

12 W.H.C. Frend, "Monophysitism," in *Encyclopedia of Religion*, ed. Mircea Eliade (New York: Macmillan, 1995). See also Frend, *Monophysite Movement*, 16–20, 46, 120–30, 205–6, 210–12.

13 Frend, *Monophysite Movement*, 136–40, 166, 167, 175, 184–90.

14 Frend, 221–36, 272–3; V.L. Menze, *Justinian and the Making of the Syrian Orthodox Church* (Oxford: Oxford University Press, 2008), 111–36, 152–3 for more detail.

15 Frend, *Monophysite Movement*, 260–1, 283–9, 293; Menze, *Justinian*, 149–58, 175–86.

16 The creed of the Armenian church relied essentially on the Council of Nicaea (325), where it was agreed that Christ was *consubstantial* with God. See Vrej Nerses Nersessian, "Armenian Christianity," in Ken Parry, ed., *The Blackwell Companion to Eastern Christianity* (Malden, MA: Blackwell, 2007), 23–46. On Armenia's relations with Rome and Constantinople and the development of Monophysitism there, Garth Fowden, *Empire to Commonwealth: Consequences of monotheism in late antiquity* (Princeton: Princeton University Press, 1993), 104–6, 108–9.

22 Tom Sinclair

church of Egypt and of churches in Nubia and Ethiopia.[17] A Syrian Orthodox metropolitan of Nisibis is known in 631; thereafter, however, and up till the twelfth century we know only of Syrian Orthodox bishops rather than of Syrian Orthodox metropolitans of Nisibis.[18]

After the late seventh century the Church of the East entered its days of glory: on the one hand an extraordinary missionary drive to Iran, Afghanistan, and China, and on the other a strong presence in the Abbasid empire, whose capital was Baghdad. Under the Mongols too (mid-thirteenth to mid-fourteenth century) the church prospered.[19] But afterwards there took place a sudden and severe retraction, whose speed seems never to have been fully explained, and at the turn of the fifteenth and sixteenth centuries the church found itself restricted mainly to northeast Iraq (Mosul and district), to Amid/Diyarbekir and places in the Upper Tigris basin east of that city and the mountains south of Lake Van and the adjacent part of Iran (Salmas and nearby). The patriarchs' first known residence was at Gazarta/Cizre (1497, 1502), after which the patriarch made a move to the monastery of Rabban Hormizd, north of Mosul (Shim'un V, 1504–38).[20]

The Syrian Orthodox church, too, grew from its beginnings in the fifth century until reaching a climax of numbers and extent of clerical hierarchy in the twelfth and thirteenth centuries, despite losses in the tenth century. Like the Church of the East it suffered a severe decline. At the beginning of our period (c. 1500) it was limited to the city of Amid/Diyarbekir; northeast Iraq, in particular the city of Mosul; some monasteries near Mosul; the Tur 'Abdin (the rolling plateau behind the scarp overlooking Nusaybin, where monasteries are mixed with villages); and to sundry congregations in Syria.[21]

---

17 On Nubia and Ethiopia, see Fowden, *Empire to Commonwealth*, 109–19, 129–31, 132–3, 135–7.

18 Ernst Honigmann, *Le couvent de Barṣaumā et le patriarcat jacobite d'Antioche et de Syrie* (Leuven: L. Durbecq, 1954), 138–9.

19 Baum and Winkler, *Church of the East*, chaps. 2 and 3.

20 Heleen Murre-van den Berg, *Scribes and Scriptures: The Church of the East in the Eastern Ottoman Provinces (1500–1850)* (Leuven: Peeters, 2015), 21–3, 300–6. Strictly one should count also the remnant in India. For more on Rabban Hormizd, see J.M. Fiey, *Assyrie Chrétienne : contribution à l'étude de l'histoire et de la géographie ecclésiastiques et monastiques du nord de l'Iraq* (Beirut: Imprimerie Catholique, 1977), 2:390, 545. On the nearby Alqosh, see Fiey, *Assyrie Chrétienne*, 390–1, 395; Wilmshurst, *Ecclesiastical Organisation*, 42.

21 François Michaeau, "Eastern Christianities (eleventh to fourteenth century): Copts, Melkites, Nestorians, and Jacobites," in *Eastern Christianity*, ed. Michael Angold (Cambridge: Cambridge University Press 2006), 377–9, 380, 383–4, 386, 389, 391–3. On the twelfth and thirteenth centuries, see brief reference in Paulos Gregorios,

The Ottoman City in the Sixteenth Century

Having sketched the historical background and theological beliefs of the Christian communities represented in Upper Mesopotamia at the beginning of Ottoman rule there, we shall now look at the city as it was, exactly at the beginning of Ottoman rule. To be precise, the critical date seems to be June 1516, when a battle took place on the plain below the city of Mardin. An Ottoman army advancing from Amid/Diyarbekir, which had been finally taken in September 1515, inflicted a defeat on the forces of the Safavid administration in Upper Mesopotamia. The victory was won near the small town of Koçhisar, earlier Dunaysir. It allowed the Ottoman army to bring under control towns and cities on the plain as far east as Mosul and west towards Ruha/Urfa; gained also were towns overlooking the Tigris basin further north such as Ergani and Çermik. The walled city, but not citadel, of Mardin, was easily taken.[22] Probably in April 1517 the grim, cliffed citadel of Mardin was finally taken, and this secured the whole region.[23]

The small city of Nusaybin then occupied a site on the west bank of the river Hurmas/Jaghjagh, which rose in the plateau overlooking the plain from the north. The city wall, of cut stone, described a rough circle. The wall at this stage was in good condition and surrounded by a ditch.[24] In the wall were gates, to east and west, and to north

---

"Syrian Orthodox Church of Antioch," in *The Encyclopedia of Religion*, ed. Mircea Eliade (New York: Macmillan, 1995), 14: 227–30. Situation c. 1500: Murre-van den Berg, *Scribes and Scriptures*, 34. The Syrian Orthodox church had an Indian arm too, but this was founded in the seventeenth century; see Gregorios, "Syrian Orthodox Church of Antioch," 14:229.

22 Nejat Göyünç, *XVI. Yüzyılda Mardin Sancağı* (Ankara: Türk Tarih Kurumu, 1991), 25–8, 30–4. On Amid, see Göyünç, *Mardin Sancağı*, 17–18.

23 Göyünç, *Mardin Sancağı*, 32–4.

24 Evliya Çelebi ibn Derviş Mehemmed Zıllî, *Evliya Çelebi Seyahatnâmesi: Topkapı Sarayı Bağdat 304 Yazmasının Transkripsiyonu, Dizini*, ed. Seyit Ali Karaman and Yücel Dağlı (Istanbul: Yapı Kredi Kültür Sanat Yayıncılık, 2001), 332. Leonhardt Rauwolff suggests the walls were in defensible condition. See John Ray, ed., *A Collection of Curious Travels and Voyages* (London: S. Smith, B. Walford, 1693), 1:211. However Evliya, writing a century later, implies a dilapidated wall. On the shape of the city wall's course, see John Kinneir, *Journey through Asia Minor, Armenia, and Koordistan in the Years 1813 and 1814* (London: Murray, 1818), 443. He talks of the *circuit* of the city walls, and of a *circumference*, suggesting a roughly circular perimeter. Elif Keser-Kayaalp, "The Cathedral Complex at Nisibis," *Anatolian Studies* 63 (December 2013): 137–54, https://doi.org/10.1017/S0066154613000070, assumes the city wall described a rectangular shape. I am grateful to Garth Fowden for recommending this article.

24   Tom Sinclair

and south. Streets ran east-west and north-south between the gates, crossing in the centre of the walled area.[25] The east gate gave on to a twelve-arched bridge over several rivulets of the Hurmas; at the bridge taxes on travellers were collected.[26] The city wall's circumference was around five kilometres, and its diameter about two kilometres.[27] However, much of the walled area was uninhabited, as we argue below. In particular, areas towards the southwestern and western sectors of the walls were probably uninhabited and ruined.[28] The medieval citadel had survived; it was probably in defensible form, though would have required extensive restoration, and probably, too, in use by the authorities at least as a depot for arms and munitions. It probably stood to the northeast, just north of the bridge.[29] Further

---

25 Evliya Çelebi, 4:332 on the gates. In the thirteenth century the easterly gate, justly, was known as the Sinjar Gate (Fiey, *Nisibe*, 105). It is likely that the east-west street was broader than the north-south one. The tenth-century geographer Muqaddasi remarked that the city's market extended from gate to gate. See Muḥammad ibn Ahmad Muqaddasi, *Kitab Ahsan al-Taqasim fi Ma 'rifat al-Aqalim*, ed. Michael J. De Goeje (Leiden: Brill, 1906), 160. This would most likely run between the east gate, in front of which taxes were extracted, and the west gate. An uninhabited strip running across the city site is described in a report later than Evliya. This must have been the footprint, as it were, of the market, but without the booths and tents which probably constituted it in the tenth century. On the streets, see Keser-Kayaalp, "Cathedral Complex," 138, arguing in part from the present layout.

26 Evliya Çelebi, 4:332. For the twelve arches, Gertrude Bell, *The Churches and Monasteries of the Ṭur 'Abdin*, introd. and notes Marlia Mundell Mango (London: Pindar Press, 1982), 142 and pl. 69. [British] Admiralty War Staff, Intelligence Division, *A Handbook of Mesopotamia*, vol. 4, Northern Mesopotamia and Central Kurdistan (London: 1917), 576, talks of a bridge to the south (not east) over three arms of the river, but this must be the same bridge, wrongly placed.

27 Mustawfi, in the fourteenth century, estimated the circumference at 6,500 paces (Le Strange, *Lands of the Eastern Caliphate*, 95); Kinneir in the early nineteenth century, at three miles or more (Kinneir, *Journey*, 443). Discussed by Keser-Kayaalp, "Cathedral Complex," 138.

28 Naval Intelligence Division, *Turkey* (Oxford: Oxford University Press, March 1943), 2:576. These areas were uninhabited but contained ruins in the early twentieth century. In this sector the line of the city wall is perhaps indicated by a road, at present passing through fields, which circles round from a westerly to a northerly direction. Eduard Sachau, *Reise in Syrien und Mesopotamia* (Leipzig: Brockhaus, 1883), 392, talks of squared blocks on the line of the walls "west south-west" of the ruined church next to the fourth-century baptistry, on which pp. 26, 48, and 49 below. Sachau also writes that features of these blocks suggest the position of a gate, which might be the west gate or a gate subsidiary to the axial north and south, east and west gates.

29 The tenth-century geographer Muqaddasi mentioned such a citadel, remarking that it was built of stone and cement. See Muqaddasi, *Kitab Ahsan al-Taqasim*, 140; discussed by Fiey, *Nisibe*, 89. See also Kök, *Musul Atabeyliği*, 342–3, where a siege of the city in 600/1204 by one of the atabegs of Mosul is related. The walled area was easily taken, but

Nusaybin under the Ottomans 25

up the west bank, and watered by the river, were market gardens, growing flowers, and orchards.[30] Within the city walls were mosques, hammams, a caravansaray and *sebils* (multi-mouthed fountains); the water for mosques, hammams, and *sebils* was supplied from the river.[31] Of the mosques, that known as the Zeynelâbidin Zaviyesi stood towards the city's south side. It was said in a sixteenth-century Ottoman *defter* to have been built by Jihangir Ak Koyunlu, who ruled here from 1452; this may mean that the mosque was repaired (not built *de novo*) in the mid-fifteenth century.[32] Of the hammams some may have gone back to the tenth century or earlier.[33] It is doubtful if the two madrasas mentioned by the traveller Ibn Jubayr after his visit in 1184 had survived upright.[34] Equally

---

the citadel resisted and the attempt to take it was eventually abandoned. That the walled area was easily taken on this occasion does not mean its defences were inadequate. In 628/1231 a Mongol force appeared in front of the city, but the city did not open its doors and the Mongol force went to Sinjar instead (Kök, *Musul Atabeyliği*, 422–5). After the rapid expansion of the city's population in the mid-sixteenth century (below, pp. 26–9), a "Kale Mahallesi" was created, presumably on the citadel's site. Since the inhabited area probably expanded towards the north, this new *mahalle* (neighbourhood) probably lay in that direction: for the citadel a site against the city wall and overlooking the river would have made sense. Buckingham in the second decade of the nineteenth century found a square citadel still standing. James Silk Buckingham, *Travels in Mesopotamia: Including a Journey from Aleppo to Baghdad* (London: H. Colburn, 1827), 249–50. It may be that this citadel is the building described in the mid-eighteenth century as a tower on the city's east side, near the bridge: Carsten Niebuhr, *Carsten Niebuhr's Reisebeschreibung nach Arabien und andern umliegenden Ländern* (Copenhagen: Möller, 1778), 2:379.

30 Evliya Çelebi, *Evliya Çelebi Seyahatnâmesi*, 4:332.
31 Evliya Çelebi, 4:331–2. Here we relate those aspects of Evliya's mid-seventeenth century account – circular city wall, gardens and orchards, mosques, hammams, and *sebils* – which must have been valid for the early sixteenth century too. Rauwolff's (in English translation) "full of conduits and springs" must refer to the water supply system and *sebils* (Rauwolff in Ray, *Collection*, 211). Other aspects, below pp. 25–6.
32 Göyünç, *Mardin Sancağı*, 58, 122. The mosque may have been the same, or on the same site, as that mentioned by Muqaddasi in the tenth century (*Kitab Ahsan al-Taqasim*, 140). However the mosque in question, according to Muqaddasi, stood in a central position, so the identity of the two is not certain.
33 Hammams were reported, again, by Muqaddasi (*Kitab Ahsan al-Taqasim*, 140).
34 Muhammad Ibn Jubayr, *The Travels of Ibn Jubayr*, ed. W. Wright (New York: AMS Press, 1973), 240; discussed by Fiey, *Nisibe*, 102. They may be the same as those seen by Ibn Battuta in the early fourteenth century (*Voyages d'Ibn Battûta*, 2:140). Evliya Çelebi has a sentence reserved for the number of *medrese*s, *sıbyan* (primary) schools, *tekke*s, hammams, and caravansarays, but in each category the space for the relevant number is left blank (*Evliya Çelebi Seyahatnâmesi*, 4:322). It is possible that this sentence is a template, as it were, rather than a record of anything Evliya saw or heard of. So it is preferable not to assume, merely on the ground of their presence in the list, that categories such as *medrese*s and *tekke*s were actually represented on the city site.

26   Tom Sinclair

the hospital and *ribat*s (here apparently buildings to shelter social and religious activities) founded by the Mosul *atabeg*s' vizier Jamal al-Din Muhammad in the mid- or late sixth/twelfth century seem not to have survived the general abandonment and ruination of the Mongol and immediately post-Mongol periods.[35] Perhaps one or two of the three synagogues noticed in the 1170s by a Jewish visitor were standing, no doubt in a state of dilapidation or collapse; the Jews who settled here in the mid-sixteenth century might well have repaired or substantially rebuilt one of them.[36] Besides the above buildings there were at least two churches: the ancient baptistery known misleadingly as the church of Mar Yaʿqub (St. James), which again stood towards the city's south wall, and the church of Mar Batala, which had been rebuilt in the 1480s.[37] Above the city one of the monasteries founded during the Late Antique period was probably functioning: this was Mar Awgin, from which monks were chosen in c. 1497 and again in 1502 or 1503 to go to the Church of the East's communities in India; the patriarch who ordained the two monks from the monastery in 1497 was buried at Mar Awgin.[38] The monastery of Mar Awgin continued to function at least until 1629; before that the Church of the East metropolitan of Nisibis, to be discussed below, had resided there from 1587. Two other monasteries may have been inhabited in 1517, continuing their work throughout the sixteenth century, though the evidence dates from later in the sixteenth century or the early seventeenth century. The last evidence for the habitation by monks at the monastery of Mar Melke comes in 1588. Mar Yohannon is known in 1610.[39]

Now let us come to the city's population, which naturally has a direct bearing on the state of the city, its ruination or revivification and so on. In a fiscal census of 924/1518, in other words barely a year after the region was secured for the Ottoman Empire, there were in the city 114 Muslim *hanes* or households plus thirteen *mücerreds* or bachelors, and ninety-eight Christian *hanes* plus twenty-one Christian *mücerreds*. So there were rather over two hundred households in all and, allowing an average of five to the *hane*, a total population of around 1,100 persons. Nusaybin was the centre of a *nahiye*, sub-division of a *sancak*, in this case that of Mardin, which in turn formed part of the vast *eyalet*

---

35 Kök, *Musul Atabeyliği*, 125, 488. Ibn Jubayr (previous note) also saw a hospital. Ibn Battuta may have seen the hospital (*Voyages d'Ibn Battûta*, 2:140).

36 Fiey, *Nisibe*, 101; below pp. 28 and 29.

37 On baptistery, below, pp. 48 and 49; on Mar Batala, Fiey, 111.

38 Murre-van den Berg, *Scribes and Scriptures*, 21–2.

39 Fiey, *Nisibe*, 114, 139, 142–3; Wilmshurst, *Ecclesiastical Organisation*, 43–7; 352–4.

or *beylerbeyilik*, in other words the province, of Amid. Looking at the remainder of the *nahiye* at the same date, we find 115 Muslim households with twenty-one *mücerreds* and 114 Christian households with nil *mücerreds*. Here there is certainly an element of undercounting; some villages were not surveyed. The tax revenue of the *nahiye* as a whole went to the *beylerbeyi*, or governor, of the Amid province; in other words, no *sipahis* or *zaims* – both categories were Ottoman cavalrymen – were settled here.[40]

The low population numbers might be put down, not only to the city's general collapse after the Mongol occupation, but also to a flight from the city as a result of the recent fighting and to a general abandonment of the Mosul-Urfa-Aleppo corridor, perhaps for the same reason. We can test this explanation by looking at the following fiscal census, that of 932/1526. Here we find 183 Muslim *hanes* in the city and 151 Christian *hanes*; so certainly there has been an increase. In the *nahiye*'s villages there are 509 Muslim households, but strangely, no Christian households at all.[41] To an extent the jump in the number of Muslim households is due to a catching-up process whereby previously unsurveyed villages are brought into the tax net; Christian villages are perhaps not surveyed at all, on the ground that there is not sufficient change to justify the resurvey.

Matters become clearer when we look at other aspects of the villages. Of the sixty-nine villages, sixty-seven are now in the *hass*, or tax-producing estate, not of the Amid *beylerbeyi*, but of the sultan himself. The *beylerbeyi* now enjoys no tax revenues from the *nahiye*.[42] Here we see an arrangement that will later turn out to be quite common in the Mardin *sancak*: the inclusion in the sultan's *hass* of villages inhabited by tribes, not merely to channel revenue into the total of the sultan's resources but also to keep the tribes under control.

By 947/1540 Nusaybin had become a *kaza* (the area within the authority of a given Muslim judge) rather than a *nahiye*. Mardin had in a sense been downgraded to the same status, that of a *kaza*. From this we should conclude, not that the town or the *nahiye* of Nusaybin had grown, but that the province of Diyarbekir had been enlarged to embrace expanses of the prairie further south as far as the Euphrates. This required the creation of new administrative entities, all within the same province. By 954/1547 Nusaybin had become a *sancak*; Mardin

---

40 Göyünç, *Mardin Sancağı*, 38–9, 81–2, 149.
41 Göyünç, 83.
42 Göyünç, 56–7, 147, 149.

28 Tom Sinclair

had equally been upgraded.[43] Such an upgrading this time probably did recognize a growth in the town itself as well as the whole province's expansion.

Such a growth in the town becomes apparent from a register of 972/1564, much of whose information was tabulated in *Land an der Grenze* by Göyünç and Hütteroth.[44] The city was now composed of eight *mahalle*s or neighbourhoods; from the document of 947/1540 referred to above, it emerges that the city then had only two *mahalle*s. In 1564 there were 1,651 Muslim households, 738 Christian households, and thirty-seven Jewish ones – this seems to be the first evidence of Jews in Nusaybin during Ottoman rule. Five of the *mahalle*s were composed of both Muslim and Christian households. The Mahalle-i İmam Zeynülabidin contained twenty-five Muslim households and eleven *mücerred*; it must have lain towards the south edge of the walled area, as it is here that the Zeynülâbidin Zaviyesi stands. The Mahalle-i Cemaat-ı Gebrân ("Mahalle of the Community of Infidels," where the Gebrân would normally be understood to be Christians) consisted of 169 Christian households, sixty-two Christian *mücerred*, and nine Jewish households, with one Jewish *mücerred*: this *mahalle* presumably lay around the ancient baptistery named after St. James. These two *mahalle*s can be considered the oldest; in the first years of Ottoman rule they were probably the only thickly populated parts of the city, the remainder of the population being sprinkled over areas further north within the walls. The İmam Zeynülâbidin and the Cemaat-ı Gebrân *mahalle*s apart, we learn of a Mahalle-i Kale ("Citadel Mahalle"), in which dwelt fifty-eight Muslim households and twelve *mücerred*. Above we argued that the medieval citadel had survived, probably against the city wall rather to the north of the easterly gate, to the sixteenth and seventeenth centuries; it seems to have been occupied at least until the mid-eighteenth century.[45] Perhaps the ground within and immediately outside the citadel had previously been free of habitations. The existence of this small *mahalle*, then, seems to indicate an influx of population and an expansion of the city's settled area. The other *mahalle*s can be imagined as spreading north of the two original ones; none of them

---

43 Göyünç, 43–7, 52, 58, 147, 151.

44 Nejat Göyünç and Wolf-Dieter Hütteroth, *Land an der Grenze: Osmanische Verwaltung im heutigen türkisch-syrisch-irakischen Grenzgebiet im 16. Jahrhundert* (Istanbul: Eren, 1977).

45 In the mid-eighteenth century the equipment was moved from the citadel of Nusaybin to that of Mardin (see below, pp. 44–5). It follows that the citadel was occupied at least until then.

Nusaybin under the Ottomans   29

seems to be formed particularly on one group, for example Muslims or Christians.[46] It is a matter for speculation where in the city's walled area the *mescid* and *medrese* endowed c. 1549 by a Hacci Şah-Kulu were built: no doubt their foundation helped in the city's development, and perhaps the *mescid* became the centre of a new or developing *mahalle*.[47]

The population increase over the years since 1526, when there had been 183 Muslim and 151 Christian households, can in part be explained by an improvement in agriculture and animal breeding, in turn brought about by the greater security offered by the Ottoman administration. Nusaybin was a market town; an increase in the production of the city's dependent agricultural district employed more people in the town's market functions, as did the export of agricultural produce to other *sancak*s.[48]

It is also possible that the town's population increase was due in part to an increase, again induced by greater security, in the volume of inter-regional trade, for instance in the use of the tracks coming from Baghdad and Mosul on the one hand and Aleppo and Ruha/Urfa on the other. The 1564 document seems to offer little help on the question; just one clue can be found, the presence for the first time of a Jewish contingent in the town's population and of a substantial Armenian one too.[49]

---

46 On the population totals and *mahalles*, Göyünç and Hütteroth, *Land an der Grenze*, 128–31.

47 Göyünç, *Mardin Sancağı*, 58. Hacci Şah-Kulu was appointed in 1549 as chief officer of the force guarding the "Berriye Ağzı" beneath Mardin; see p. 35 below.

48 The *kanunname* or code of tax regulations mentions taxes on horses, sheep, and goats, and a tax on shops. Ahmed Akgündüz, *Osmanlı Kanunnâmeleri ve Hukuki Tahlilleri*, V. Kitap: *Kanunî Süleyman Devri Kanunnâmeleri*, II. Kısım. *Kanunî Devri Eyâlet Kanunnâmeleri* (Istanbul: Fey Vakfı, 1992), 486 (from *tahrir defter* TD 998 in the Başbakanlık Arşivi). Published also by Göyünç, *Mardin Sancağı*, 169.

49 Jews: pp. 26 and 28 above. Armenians: Rauwolff in Ray, *Collection*, 1:211. The paucity of surviving coinage from the period rather militates against the proposition of increased trade. The surviving Ottoman issues from Nusaybin are the seven types of *mangır*, a heavy copper coin, struck in the name of the Ottoman sultan Süleyman I (1520–66). Rolf Ehlert, *Umlaufgeld im Osmanischen Reich* vol. II: *Suleyman der Prächtige* (Heidelberg: Ehlert, 2021), 129–30. See also Atom Damalı, *Osmanlı Sikkeleri Tarihi / History of Ottoman Coins* (Ankara: Nilüfer Damalı Vakfı Yayınları, 2010–14), 2:683. Copper coins on the whole were for local use rather than trade, and those in Damalı were commemorative issues struck at the beginning of the reign of Süleyman I. Nevertheless a number of different issues were struck at Mosul, all in 926/1520, but in all three metals and to different designs. Damalı, 2:663–7; similarly at Mardin (Damalı, 2:643–9) and Ruha/Urfa (Damalı, 2:684–8). For rare subsequent issues, Ömer Diler, *Islamic Mints / İslam Darp Yerleri*, ed. Emire Nur Diler, J.C. Hinrichs, and Garo Kurkman (Istanbul: 2009), 2:1096, 1233. After Süleyman I, only at Mosul was there further minting over a broad spectrum of metals and types (982/1574–5), at the beginning of Murat III's reign: Damalı, 3:1030–3. See also Diler, *Islamic Mints*, 2:1096.

30　Tom Sinclair

The three *nahiye*s of which the Nusaybin *sancak* was composed have an interesting story to tell. The town of Nusaybin lay at the northern edge of the *sancak*'s territorial expanse. The three *nahiye*s extended southwards, the middle one (Nehr-i Dere) from the town itself and the other two from the *sancak*'s northerly boundary. Of these, the Nehr-i Cali lay around a series of streams to the west of the town, then extended further south over agricultural land and prairie. Of the villages, twenty-eight belong to the sultan's *hass*, as before. Another sixteen are *hass-ı mir-liva* (*hass* of a *sancakbeyi*). However, some of these villages are the *hass* of *sancakbeyi*s outside the *sancak* of Nusaybin, for example Hisn Kayfa/Hasankeyf at the southern border of the Tigris basin further north. This mosaic of *sancakbeyi hass* was a common arrangement, designed apparently to prevent given *sancakbeyi*s from building up a local power base. A further twenty villages are *zeamet*s, taxable estates to support a *zaim* or cavalryman somewhat superior in status and resources to the *sipahi*, beneficiary of a *timar*. So for the first time we come in contact with the cavalry soldiers who at the time supplied an essential component of Ottoman armies on campaign. Of the *timar*s themselves there are twenty-two within this *nahiye*, but of these only seven are villages in the proper sense. Most are *mezraa*, a unit of cultivable land not attached to a village, but available for agricultural exploitation and, normally, under exploitation.[50]

In the Nehr-i Dere, the central *nahiye* which follows the river Hurmas southwards, we find something similar, though with a tribal twist. Twenty-two villages belong to the sultan's *hass*, but only two to the *hass* of the *sancakbeyi*. Nine are *timar*s, this time all fully villages rather than *mezraa*s. But besides these we find a separate category, twenty villages (strictly three of them *mezraa*) lived in by a tribal unit called the Sarılı (Ṣārılū): this unit is called in the document a *cemaat*, a clan, sub-division of an *aşiret* or tribe, according to anthropological terminology. Of these twenty villages, eight are part of the sultan's *hass*. Only one belongs to the *sancakbeyi*'s *hass* and the remainder are *zeamet*s and *timar*s (the *mezraa*s, naturally, falling to the *timar*s).[51] Here again we see an imperial accommodation with a tribe, strictly a tribal section.

The Kertuvan *nahiye*, starting to the east of the town, lay athwart a series of streams parallel with the Hurmas. Here again the *hass-ı hümayun*, the sultan's *hass*, predominates. Forty of the villages are so committed: of these some are inhabited by *cemaat*s. Seventeen are tied to the *sancakbeyi*'s *hass*. Twenty-one, with a sprinkling of *cemaat*s, were allocated as *zeamet*s: twenty-four as *timar*s, though in one village lived a

---

50　Göyünç and Hütteroth, *Land an der Grenze*, 223–6.
51　Göyünç and Hütteroth, 227–9.

Nusaybin under the Ottomans   31

taife, which may mean a whole tribe as opposed to a tribal section, and an Arab tribe as opposed to a Turkish or a Kurdish one.[52] Lastly come four villages, all *hass-ı hümayun*, including two lived in by different *taifes*, one the Şütürāñ and the other the Al-i Arab.[53] In the *sancak* that neighbours that of Nusaybin to the east, Akçakale, eleven villages were tied to the sultan's *hass* and a further twenty-four to that of the *sancakbeyi*. There follow ten *zeamet*s and fifteen *timar*s, of which seven are *mezraa*s. But then comes a separate section devoted to the villages of the *cemaat* of Şah Nasibi. Here seven villages belong to the sultan's *hass*, five to a *sancakbeyi*'s *hass*, this time that of the *sancakbeyi* of Nusaybin, and ten are *timar*s.[54] As for the products grown in the villages of the *nahiye*, these were mainly wheat and barley; in each of the *nahiye*s there was also rice cultivation.[55]

The next view we have of the city and its dependent district comes in the mid-seventeenth century narrative of Evliya Çelebi, the relentless investigator of the Ottoman Empire's provinces on behalf of the central government. In Evliya's account Nusaybin was still a *sancak* in the province of Diyarbekir. The government still maintained a garrison in the city; in addition there was a force of janissaries. The defensive walls were now in ruined condition, no doubt because a rising population meant an increased demand for building material. In addition, for such a small community the upkeep of a wall of such wide circumference could not be justified. Within the walls there were 700 two-storeyed houses, therefore a drop in the number of households of about half since the census of 1564. We are told there was a *bezestan* or lockable building for the storage and sale of valuable products such as silk and spices; it is not clear if this was the same as the caravansaray known in the mid-sixteenth century.[56] On Mt Izla there was a mosque of Noah

---

52 *Ta'ifa/taife* means simply a group or category of people.
53 Göyünç and Hütteroth, 229–34.
54 Göyünç and Hütteroth, 234–8.
55 Göyünç and Hütteroth, 113–15, 281, 295. See also Akgündüz, *Kanunnâmeleri*, vol. V–ii, 488–90.
56 *Evliya Çelebi Seyahatnâmesi*, 4:332. Concerning the drop in population, it is possible that a configuration of the built area noticed by Jean de Thévenot, *Suite de voyage du Levant* (1674; quoted in Fiey, *Nisibe*, 115) in 1656, therefore at a date close to that of Evliya's visit, is relevant. Thévenot reports that the city's built area consisted of two quarters divided by a narrow strip worked for agricultural purposes. Could this strip have been in origin the city's east-west shopping street described by Muqaddasi in the tenth century (discussed in Fiey, *Nisibe*, 89)? In the city population's sixteenth-century expansion, the strip might have been built over with makeshift houses, but in the subsequent contraction the houses could have been levelled and the strip returned to agricultural use.

32   Tom Sinclair

at the source of the river Hurmas; this was the spot where Noah's ark came to rest after the flood. The Aşdi Kurds worshipped there during the summer months. This tribe's well-kept villages were to the west of the town of Nusaybin; however the tribe's chief resided in the city of Mardin. Of course the story that Noah's ark came to rest at the source of the Hurmas is a local version designed to attract worshippers from Nusaybin and its villages: the standard version had the ark come to rest on Cudi Dağı, a long mountain beyond the Tigris to the east, and overlooking Jazirat ibn ʿUmar and Zakho. However the picture of a *ziyaretgâh* visited by Kurds on the mountain above Nusaybin is both fascinating and convincing.[57]

Unencouraging, however, is Evliya's account of the town and its hinterland. First, the *sancak* now included 105 *timar*s and twelve *zeamet*s; altogether the *sancak* supported 900 soldiers, made up of *zaim*s, *sipahi*s, and *cebelü*s, the mounted followers of *sipahi*s.[58] In the survey of 1564 the totals were forty-four *zeamet*s and fifty-nine *timar*s. While the total loss of minor taxable estates (*zeamet*s and *timar*s) is not great (117 falling to 103), a switch from *zeamet*s to *timar*s has taken place. This perhaps suggests that some of the estates initially allocated as *zeamet*s were too poor to support a *zaim*. Perhaps, too, the type of military operation for which the cavalrymen were needed in this region had changed: no longer was there a need to assemble large armies for invasions and pitched battles. But *zaim*s and *sipahi*s were still needed in border peacekeeping against Safavid forces and for law enforcement in the vicinity.

Evliya's few remarks about the villages suggest decline in an environment of insecurity. The villages are without produce, he states; they are not maintained. This is because of depredations and damage by three tribes: the Keys Urbânı, the Mevali Urbânı, and the Aşdi. Of these the Keys (Arab. "Qays"), according to Evliya, lived on the plain well south of Mardin and Nusaybin. This Arab tribe was known in northern Syria in the ninth and tenth centuries. The Mevali (Mawali) are not mentioned elsewhere in Evliya, though he talks of the Urbanlar as based, again, south of Mardin and Nusaybin. By Urbanlar (Bedouin) he presumably means both the Keys and the Mevali. The Tayy, too, lived south of Mardin: we shall meet them later in the region east of Nusaybin. The Aşdi we have already located in villages west of the city, and Evliya mentions them in yet another geographical position, this time at the Kend-beli, a pass on the way between Mardin and the city of

---

57 Evliya Çelebi, 4:333.
58 Evliya Çelebi, 4:332.

Nusaybin under the Ottomans 33

Sinjar: here they and another Kurdish tribe, the Şekaki, ambushed and robbed travellers.[59] The result of all the depredations by tribes and the consequent failure of the villages as food suppliers was a weak soldiery. Perhaps Evliya means one that did not always come up to complement and was inadequately equipped.[60]

Given the drop in the town's population from around 1,400 households in 1564 to 700 at Evliya's visit and the poor state of the villages after depredations by local tribes, we must ask how this deterioration came about. First, the whole corridor along which Indian and other spices were carried from Baghdad up the Tigris to Mosul, then across the plain of Upper Mesopotamia through Nusaybin, Urfa, and Ayntab to Aleppo was now substantially out of use. In the tenth to thirteenth centuries Nusaybin had been sustained by this traffic. Under Ottoman rule in the sixteenth century the spice trade between the head of the Persian Gulf at Basra on the one hand and Aleppo in Syria on the other enjoyed a certain revival. However the caravans preferred to follow the Euphrates upstream, certainly through the desert, past 'Ana and Hit, to Bir/Birecik (west of Urfa) and from there to Ayntab and Aleppo. From Bir goods could be floated downstream on rafts.[61] The Tigris route to Mosul was occasionally followed for reasons of safety and local trade. Silk produced at Baalbek in Lebanon, and traded in Mardin, was in high demand at Mosul, particularly in the first half of the sixteenth century; cotton cloth woven at Yazd in Iran came through, presumably crossing the Persian Gulf and then traded in Baghdad; Mosul exchanged different types of cloth with Mardin, from which Nusaybin must have benefited, and cities in the upper Tigris basin further north.[62] Essentially, however, Nusaybin lost out on the revival of the grand export lines by which Asian spices reached Europe and Constantinople.

The other main item of trade exported to or transported through the Ottoman Empire was Iranian silk, grown principally in the mountains overlooking the south shore of the Caspian Sea. During the sixteenth

---

59 Evliya Çelebi, 4:44, 447. On the Qays in the ninth century, Hugh Kennedy, *The Prophet and the Age of the Caliphates* (London: Longman, 1986), 150, 155, 169; C. Bosworth, "Uḳaylids," in *EI2* 10:786–7; S.H. Winter, "The Province of Raqqa under Ottoman Rule, 1535–1800," *Journal of Near Eastern Studies* 68, no. 4 (October 2009): 256, https://doi.org/10.1086/649610.

60 Evliya Çelebi, *Evliya Çelebi Seyahatnâmesi*, 4:332.

61 Halil İnalcık and Donald Quataert, eds., *A Social and Economic History of the Ottoman Empire, 1300–1914* (Cambridge: Cambridge University Press, 1994), 249, 338–40.

62 Dina Khoury, *State and Provincial Society in the Ottoman Empire: Mosul, 1540–1834* (Cambridge: Cambridge University Press, 1997), 34–5.

34   Tom Sinclair

century, naturally with certain interruptions or disruptions in periods of war, the most stable route followed a northerly line through Asia Minor starting at Tabriz, then passing through Erzurum, Sivas, and Ankara and ending at Bursa.[63] The alternative line of export from Tabriz came past the cities of the north shore of Lake Van, then down into the upper Tigris basin and to the great walled city of Amid, now Diyarbakır. From Amid to Ayntab and Aleppo the most practical route was to rise over an easy pass on the north side of Karaca Dağ and circle round the mountain to arrive at Urfa. It can be seen that Nusaybin again was left out of the business generated by this traffic. Some traffic, it seems, came through Mardin and so on to the plain, turning westwards towards Ruha, but even this would have no reason to pass through Nusaybin.[64] Traffic on the Amid route was limited during the first half of the sixteenth century, and with good reason: Ottoman attacks on the Lake Van cities took place in 1534 and again in 1548, and in a counter-invasion of 1552 the Safavid shah took Archesh/Erciş and Khlat/Ahlat.[65] However in the second half of the sixteenth century the silk trade through Aleppo took off, reaching even higher volumes in the century's last quarter.[66] Here, then, was a hard economic reason (that the haulage of Iranian silk took routes which avoided Nusaybin) why Nusaybin could not recover its former trading function, and therefore size and wealth, in the sixteenth century.

There was a second reason, evidently related to the first, even if exact relations of cause and effect cannot be traced. We have already referred to Evliya's mid-seventeenth century remarks about the depredations inflicted on villages of the Nusaybin *sancak* by three tribes. Evliya mentions, too, that the Yezidis of Sinjar, the elevated region southeast of Nusaybin, raided and plundered the villages of the Mardin *sancak*, whose

---

63   İnalcık and Quataert, *Social and Economic History*, 227–30, 245.
64   İnalcık and Quataert, 224.
65   1533: Ebru Boyar, "Ottoman Expansion in the East," in Suraiyya Faroqhi and Kate Fleet, eds., *The Cambridge History of Turkey* (Cambridge: Cambridge University Press, 2013), 2:119–20; Orhan Kılıç, *XVI. ve XVII. Yüzyıllarda Van (1548–1648)* (Van: Van Belediye Başkanlığı Kültür ve Sosyal İşler Müdürlüğü, 1997), 15. For 1548: M. Fahrettin Kırzıoğlu, *Osmanlılar'ın Kafkas-Elleri'ni Fethi (1451–1590)* (Ankara: Sevinç, 1976), 179–80, 182–205. For 1552: Kırzıoğlu, *Kafkas-Elleri*, 212–15; Kılıç, *Van*, 21.
66   Niels Steensgard, *The Asian Trade Revolution of the Seventeenth Century: The East India Companies and the Decline of the Caravan Trade* (Chicago: University of Chicago Press, 1974), 176–81, 384–5, 437; Edmund Herzig, "The Rise of the Julfa Merchants in the Late Sixteenth Century," in Charles Melville, ed., *Safavid Persia: The History and Politics of an Islamic Society* (London: I.B. Tauris, 1996), 316–18; Inalcık and Quataert, *Economic and Social History*, 244.

Nusaybin under the Ottomans   35

borders in fact extended well to the southeast: such raids may have taken place at points in time earlier than the mid-seventeenth century, the time of Evliya's visit.[67] We have already referred to the presence of tribally-inhabited villages in the *sancak* of Nusaybin itself. In 1549, as we have seen, the central government appointed a *zaim* (beneficiary of a *zeamet*), Hacci Şah-Kulu, as the captain of a guard placed over the Berriye Ağzı, the "Berriye passage," which meant a part of the plain beneath Mardin leading to the district of Berriyecik further west. Such an appointment implies a threat to traffic in the locality, a threat which it was the captain's duty to counter.[68] It also implies that there was traffic passing along the north edge of the plain, most likely commercial traffic coming through Mardin, descending to the plain and turning westwards towards Aleppo.

Further west lay other sources of danger to commercial traffic. The district of Berriyecik (normally a *sancak*) lay athwart the possible lines of movement towards Aleppo. The eastern boundary of Berriyecik fell around thirty-five kilometres west of Mardin, or more exactly of a point on the plain immediately below Mardin. The easterly portion of Berriyecik, the *nahiye* of Tel Bism, stretched westwards from a corner of the escarpment here; some of the larger villages lay near the road. Further west was the *nahiye* of Viranşehir: the small town of Viranşehir stood among the ruins of a late Roman city, that of Tella. The volcanic soil here was less suitable for permanent settlement, and in various parts of the *nahiye* tribes or tribal sections had made their winter quarters.[69] Their summer habitat was to the northeast, mostly on Bingöl Dağı and in the Erzurum district, but also in the Tigris basin near Hasankeyf.[70] Now it can be seen that a tribe relying on distant summer pastures, and deriving relatively little income from its winter habitat, would pose a danger to caravans and other parties passing through that winter habitat.

---

67 Evliya Çelebi, *Evliya Çelebi Seyahatnâmesi*, 4:48–51 for a punitive expedition by Melek Ahmet Paşa. In the mid-sixteenth century Rauwolff travelled from Mosul directly to Sinjar and so through the Jabal Sinjar to the classic east-west route Jazirat ibn 'Umar-Nusaybin and so to Nusaybin itself. Before Sinjar his party was attacked by Kurds, and again on the following day. Rauwolff in Ray, *Collection*, 206–11. Further back along the track, Arab and Kurdish tribes had been disrupting traffic between Baghdad and Mosul and from Mosul onwards, for example in 1581 and the 1590s: Khoury, *State and Provincial Society*, 39–40.

68 Göyünç, *Mardin Sancağı*, 51–2; Göyünç and Hütteroth, *Land an der Grenze*, 24.

69 Göyünç and Hütteroth, 24, 54–5, 188–207.

70 Gündüz, *Türkmen Aşiretleri*, 138–41; Nejat Göyünç, "XVI. Yüzyılda Güney-Doğu Anadolu'nun Ekonomik Durumu (Kanunî Süleyman ve II. Selim devirleri)," *Türkiye Tarihi Semineri. Metinler/Tartışmalar 8–10 Haziran 1973*, ed. Osman Okyar (Ankara: Hacettepe Üniversitesi, 1975), 85–6, 94.

36 Tom Sinclair

Not on the great east-west road, but near it, in the great hollow behind the citadel of Mardin, were the winter quarters of various sections (*cemaat*) of the Millili (later Milli) tribe as well as the residence of the whole tribe's chief. The villages lived in by one of the *cemaat*s were all *hass-ı hümayun*: we have discussed the reason. Beside the Millili *cemaat*s there were others, though the parent tribes are mostly unnamed in the documents. One *cemaat* is identified as Kurdish, though here the parent tribe is named.[71] Here too the potential for disruption of passing traffic was obvious.

The transference to a completely different line on the ground (Ana and Hit as opposed to Mosul, Nusaybin, and Urfa) of traffic carrying particular sorts of goods and the danger from robbers and tribespeople are intertwined and it would be hard to name one phenomenon as cause and the other as effect. It is more instructive to look at the way the two factors, the low volume of traffic and the presence of tribes whose members sometimes got out of hand, played out on the ground.

At the height of the city's medieval prosperity, one would travel westwards in one day from Nusaybin to a settlement now called Sercihan. Here the way to Mardin via Dara would part from the road along the plain to Ruha, Ayntab, and Aleppo. There had been a substantial fortress here, no doubt built in the early sixth century CE at the same time as Dara, which it was designed to protect. Originally this fortress, rectangular in shape, had twelve towers.[72] In the sixteenth century parts at least of the fortress still survived;[73] even in 1814, the date of Kinneir's visit, five towers could be made out.[74] There is no way of knowing whether in the sixteenth century, as in the nineteenth, part or all of the civilian settlement, a village, lay on the fortress site, but at any rate the fortress gave the village a certain security.[75] A document of 957/1550 tells us that the settlement was in a derelict state and the Muslim inhabitants were being beset by robbers. Four men, a man and his three sons, had requested permission

---

71 Göyünç and Hütteroth, *Land an der Grenze*, 151–62. The *nahiye* was named Kuh-ı Mardin ("Mountain of Mardin"), though it was in reality a deep bowl. On Millili *cemaat*s, Göyünç and Hütteroth, *Land an der Grenze*, 154–7. On the Kurdish *cemaat*, 161–2.

72 Sachau, *Reise*, 393–4; he notes the similarity of its walls' large, rectangular blocks to those of Dara and argues for a similar date.

73 Thévenot in the mid-seventh century found several stretches of wall. See Thévenot, *Suite de voyage du Levant*, 2:91.

74 Kinneir, *Journey*, 441; compare William Ainsworth, *Travels and Researches in Asia Minor, Mesopotamia, Chaldea, and Armenia* (London: John W. Parker, 1842), 2:117. The settlement's name suggests a caravansaray, but no physical evidence of a caravansaray has been found.

75 On the nineteenth century, Sachau, *Reise*, 393.

Nusaybin under the Ottomans   37

to bring twenty families (*hane*) to settle here. Permission was given, and as a reward or inducement the newcomers were exempted from a tax, the *avarız*. However, conditions were such that they were unable to settle, and returned to their tribe, (significantly) the Milli. New applicants were given permission in 972/1564.[76] Going forwards on the road towards Ruha, the *kasaba* (so-called) or small town of Koçhisar had 176 households in the mid-sixteenth century.[77] But in the late twelfth and early thirteenth century a city, Dunaysir, had sprung up here, precisely in response to a surge in long-distance trade; an impressive Great Mosque, was finished in 601/1204.[78] Finally, on the track from Sercihan through hills towards Mardin, Dara, a significant, well-defended city until the thirteenth century CE, but in the early fourteenth century already deserted by the greater part of its population, was a village of 175 households. To be sure it contained a dye-house, probably connected to the weaving industry in Mardin, a watermill, and a *zaviye*.[79]

Within such a scenario it is surprising to find a corner of this district of Upper Mesopotamia with solid evidence of long-distance trade. However, we mentioned that the appointment of an officer to guard the *Berriye ağzı* beneath Mardin suggested that traffic did pass that way, and the list of goods on which taxes are defined in the *kanunname* of 932/1526 shows clearly that some long-distance traffic did pass at least through the city of Mardin. Among the taxable goods are cloth from Yazd in Iran; other cloth from Aleppo, Damascus, Baalbek, and Egypt; satin, silk brocade, and gold brocade from Rum (Anatolia, probably from Sivas and Tokat); and finally European cloth.[80] The Yazd cloth

---

76 Göyünç, *Mardin Sancağı*, 70–1.

77 Göyünç, 66.

78 Yaqut ibn ʿAbdullah al-Rumi al-Hamawi, *Muʿjam al-Buldan*, ed. Ferdinand Wüstenfeld (Leipzig: N.p., 1866–73), 2:612; Thomas Sinclair, "The Amid-Mardin Triangle as a Node of Routes in the 12th and First Half of the 13th Century, with a brief look at two subsequent periods," in *Central Periphery: Art, Culture and History of the Medieval Jazira (Northern Mesopotamia, 8th–15th centuries)*, ed. Lorenz Korn and Martina Müller-Wiener, (Wiesbaden: Reichert, 2017), 184; Le Strange, *Lands of the Eastern Caliphate*, 96. For Dunaysir as a slave market, Kök, *Musul Atabeyliği*, 360–1.

79 On the city's decline, *Voyages d'Ibn Battûta*, 2:142. According to him the area within the city wall was now empty, though a village had formed outside the enceinte. See Le Strange, *Lands of the Eastern Caliphate*, 96–7. On the sixteenth-century village, Göyünç, *Mardin Sancağı*, 64, 148. Strangely a memory of Dara's Late Antique past survived at least until the mid-seventeenth century: Evliya Çelebi, *Evliya Çelebi Seyahatnâmesi*, 4:44. The memory, with all its contradictions, is valuable.

80 Akgündüz, *Kanunnâmeleri*, V–ii, 479 (from *tahrir defter* TD 998; the *kanunname* is repeated in TD 117 of 972/1564; Akgündüz, V–ii, 173–5.) This *kanunname* is published also in Göyünç, *Mardin Sancağı*, 164–8. Trade discussed in Göyünç, "Güney-Doğu Anadolu'nun Ekonomik Durumu," 95–7; Göyünç, *Mardin Sancağı*, 128–9.

38   Tom Sinclair

must have reached Mardin by the Lake Van route described above; it is significant that no Caspian silk is mentioned. Aleppo and Damascus cloth would naturally reach Mardin by the Ruha road. Likewise the European cloth, having been disembarked at the port of Payas in the Gulf of Iskenderun, would reach Mardin via Aleppo. Goods from central Anatolia (Sivas, Tokat) could come down through Malatya. Apart from the imported cloth, silk cloth was woven in the city of Mardin itself, and other cloth in two villages near the city.[81] These industries are not irrelevant to long-distance trade, given that from Mardin one could travel to distant cities in a number of directions. In any case we do not know the scale of the traffic in any of the imported cloths or that of the local production of cloth.

Local Christians, Kurds, and Arabs

We have now to return to Nusaybin and determine as far as possible who the Christians of Nusaybin and its surrounding countryside were in the mid-sixteenth century. As presented above, the number of Christians (without distinction of creed) in the town of Nusaybin had grown fast until in 1564 it reached 738 households.

In 1528 and 1536 a Syrian Orthodox metropolitan of Nisibis is known who was responsible for bishoprics at Urfa and Gerger (the latter a mountain town in the southern Taurus overlooking the Euphrates from a great height).[82] A list of 1581 includes a Timothy, "epimetropolitanus" of the Antioch district and "metropolitan" of the cities of Raqqa, Nisibis, and the Khabur district. The list suggests that Timothy was both metropolitan of the Antioch district, together with the three cities named, and bishop of a diocese, in the proper sense, consisting of those three cities. In practice he may have had no function in the Antioch district at all.[83] At any rate with Nisibis present in both references, the presence of a Syrian Orthodox congregation in the city of Nusaybin and its villages in the sixteenth century is very likely.

As for the Church of the East, the metropolitanate of Nisibis continued to exist, though its purview was somewhat different from the original: the dependent region was described as Mardin, Amid, and

---

81   Akgündüz, *Kanunnâmeleri*, V–ii, 482; discussed in Göyünç, "Güney-Doğu Anado-
     lu'nun Ekonomik Durumu," 87; Göyünç, *Mardin Sancağı*, 66–7, 137–8.
82   Fiey, *Nisibe*, 112.
83   Honigmann, *Couvent de Barṣaumā*, 176–7. A similar list recording the presence of
     bishops at a council of 1579–80 calls Timothy simply the bishop of the region of
     Antioch, Mardin, Nisibis, and Khabur.

"all Armenia." Amid may be taken to cover perhaps the whole of the upper Tigris basin, which stretches east of Amid. In this case the principal difference with the original formula of geographical coverage was that the whole upper Tigris basin rather than the districts at its east end was meant; and the city of Amid, now the seat of a large Ottoman province, was taken as the geographical marker for that region. The city of Mardin is a new element in the formula, and here again its inclusion reflects the economic and administrative importance of the city. In 1562 the metropolitan of Nisibis renovated the ancient baptistery attributed to St. James and endowed it with vineyards and farming estates; this accords with the picture of an expanding city population. The same metropolitan is known again in 1573 and 1575, then in 1610.[84]

In the meantime, however, a group of the church's faithful, opposed to the practice of hereditary succession in the katholikosate, chose Sulaqa, the abbot of Rabban Hormizd in northern Iraq, to be the new patriarch. But in order to make the appointment secure and in order to tie the church more closely to the institutions of a stronger and more stable church and to western powers such as Portugal, they decided to bring the church under the wing of the Church of Rome. Sulaqa was sent to Rome; on his return he was eventually ordained katholikos (April 1553).[85] The union with Rome brought a foreign allegiance, where there had been no allegiance before, and the acknowledgment of a different Christological position, but not a difference of rite in the church service.

In the Church of the East as a whole, the ordination of Sulaqa caused a split, between Uniate congregations and their patriarchs, on the one hand, and non-Uniate congregations, still with patriarchal residence at Rabban Hormizd, and with a different line of patriarchs, on the other. Support for Sulaqa had been strongest in the city of Amid and its vicinity and in the region of Siirt, at the eastern and therefore opposite end of the upper Tigris basin. Sulaqa, before he died in 1555, consecrated metropolitans at Amid and Gazarta/Cizre and bishops at Mardin, Siirt and Hisn Kayfa/Hasankeyf (the latter against the southern hills overlooking the upper Tigris basin). Some of these appointments, for example Gazarta, Amid, and Hasankeyf, were perhaps made in order to counter opposition to Sulaqa and his faction, from monks and lay congregations

---

84 Fiey, *Nisibe*, 112–14; Wilmshurst, *Ecclesiastical Organisation*, 42, 44, 73. The two authors' accounts and dates conflict.

85 Murre-van den Berg, *Scribes and Scriptures*, 44–51. M. Moosa, "Nestorian church," in *Encyclopedia of Religion*, ed. Eliade, 6:369–72; Charles Frazee, *Catholics and Sultans: The Church and the Ottoman Empire 1453–1923* (London: Cambridge University Press, 1983), 56–8; Wilmshurst, *Ecclesiastical Organisation*, 348.

40   Tom Sinclair

in those places. Nusaybin, too, had its share of opponents to Sulaqa. The monastery of Mar Awgin above Nusaybin, too, seems to have been opposed to Sulaqa and his policies.[86] The appointments by Sulaqa at Amid (a metropolitanate) and Mardin had a tendency to diminish the authority and following of the ancient metropolitanate at Nisibis.[87]

Meanwhile strange events were taking place within the Church of the East, which must have affected the congregation in Nusaybin. The two rival hierarchies within the Church changed allegiances and, in the end, swapped doctrinal positions. A non-Uniate (Rabban Hormizd) patriarch made contact with papal emissaries as early as 1584, and in 1586 he made a profession of Catholic faith, although it was not accepted in Rome. The successor patriarch sent messages, then envoys, to Rome. A synod in Amid agreed to union with the Catholic church and accepted the Catholic creed, but Rome did not accept the text of the profession of faith. Afterwards it was the turn of the Catholic church to make approaches; but these, for a variety of reasons, including the opposition of local Kurdish lords and Ottoman administrators, failed.[88]

On the other hand, the Uniate church seems to have thought again, partly perhaps because it no longer enjoyed strong support in the region of Amid, which originally had been the principal cockpit of the Sulaqa movement's politics and theology. The patriarchs in the Sulaqa line continually moved their residence, ending in the Salmas district, well away from Upper Mesopotamia. Its final move into the Hakkari mountains is well-known. But by 1660, as Murre-van den Berg puts it, "both patriarchates were completely independent of Rome." The Sulaqa line in the last decade of the seventeenth century lost its Catholic creed, falling back into the traditional dyophysite Christology; moreover in 1692 it cut its lines of communication with the Papacy.[89]

A third, breakaway, Uniate hierarchy was recognized by the Pope in 1696; this perhaps reflected a disappointment on the part of Rome with the negligent tendencies of the Uniate hierarchy with which the Pope had negotiated terms of dependence and acknowledgment in 1553.[90]

---

86   Murre-van den Berg, 48–9, 51, 52.

87   Wilmshurst, *Ecclesiastical Organisation*, 42, 52. Wilmshurst suggests that he was appointed as a counterweight to the appointment of Catholic bishops in Amid and Mardin; by implication this means to shield the non-Uniate members of the congregation in Nusaybin.

88   Murre-van den Berg, *Scribes and Scriptures* 52–3, 55–61. See also Baum and Winkler, *Church of the East*, 117, 118–19.

89   Murre-van den Berg, 59; see also Frazee, *Catholics and Sultans*, 209.

90   Frazee, 209, 211; Baum and Winkler, *Church of the East*, 119. The two do not agree in every detail.

Nusaybin under the Ottomans   41

This third hierarchy was the patriarchate of the Chaldaeans of Diyarbekir ("Chaldaean" being the misconceived term for the Uniates of the Church of the East). Its first patriarch was recognized by Rome in 1670. Between 1693 and 1731 Diyarbekir and Rabban Hormizd battled for the allegiance of congregations in Upper Mesopotamia. The result was a division in which Amid and Mardin fell to the patriarchate of the Chaldaeans of Diyarbekir; and Mosul, well to the east, fell to Rabban Hormizd. The division was made up only in 1830. The ancient Rabban Hormizd line acquired the diocese of Amid in 1791, but its last two patriarchs came from the Diyarbekir Chaldaean line. On the other hand, northeast Iraq had been much Catholicized owing to the efforts of Dominican missionaries.[91]

The question now arises how these radical changes in church politics and theological alignments affected the congregations in Nisibis and its surrounding villages. In the first place the historic metropolitanate of Nisibis was brought to an end a few years after the appointment of the last metropolitan. In 1616 the metropolitanate's whole territorial remit was split between three dioceses: Amid, Beth Zabdaï (with seat at Jazirat ibn ʿUmar/Cizre), and Hisn Kayfa.[92] This seems to mean that Nisibis and its district stayed on the whole loyal to the non-Uniate church. However, after Sulaqa's creation of Uniate bishoprics at Amid and Mardin and the resulting contraction of non-Uniate congregations, the case even for a bishopric, let alone a metropolitan, at Nusaybin, could not be made out. The Church of the East congregation at Nusaybin was now attached to the diocese of Amid. By 1644 Nusaybin's Church of the East congregation seems to have been there on equal terms with the city's Armenians, mentioned in the sixteenth century; the latter had a bishop and several priests.[93] Probably the Armenians had come for reasons of commerce; however, the times seem not to have been propitious.

It is the ancient baptistery, wrongly attributed to St. James even if he is buried in a crypt beneath, about which visitors to Nusaybin in the sixteenth to eighteenth centuries inform us best. The French commercial explorer Tavernier, after his visit of 1644, wrote, as we said above, that the church was in the possession of the Armenians. Thévenot visited the town in 1656. His comment on the church is that a small space,

---

91 Murre-van den Berg, *Scribes and Scriptures*, 61–2, 65, 69–72.
92 Fiey, *Nisibe*, 113, 114; Wilmshurst, *Ecclesiastical Organisation*, 43. Note that a subsequent patriarch, consecrating bishops for Mosul, Mardin, and Salmas, consecrated none for Nisibis: Wilmshurst, *Ecclesiastical Organisation*, 355.
93 Tavernier, *Les six voyages*, 1:190; Fiey, *Nisibe*, 115.

42   Tom Sinclair

the church's kernel, has been closed off; and this is where the Syrians *and* Armenians celebrate their services.[94] Let us interpret this as follows.

The church was a richly decorated baptistery finished in 359/60 (the Seleucid year 571). At the initiative of Mar Ya'qub (St. James) a cathedral of substantial size had already been built (over the years 313–20) in a position to the west of the baptistery's site; the distance between the two was a matter of twenty metres or so. The baptistery consisted of a square chamber of limited ground dimensions but with high walls, and a narthex or forechurch, originally perhaps with two open arches to north and south. Some of the congregation would have waited in the narthex, sheltered from sun or rain, before entering the baptistery by a wide, decorated doorway. The burial crypt of Mar Ya'qub (d. 338) is underneath the floor of the baptistery, but is entered by a stairway from the narthex.[95] Against the north wall of both was added in the eighth century CE a new church, longitudinal rather than square.[96] What Thévenot means by the kernel of the church is presumably the somewhat cramped but vertically tall baptistery rather than the narthex to the west. It is the baptistery which was shared by the Armenians and Syrians; in the space of a dozen years (1644 to 1656) the Church of the East had made some arrangement with the Armenian church to hold services at different times.

Thévenot's short account reveals a further circumstance, whose significance can be appreciated, on the one hand in the light of the split between the ancient line of patriarchs residing at Rabban Hormizd and the Catholic line which followed Sulaqa's consecration in 1553, and on the other hand, in the light of this story's continuation in the seventeenth century. According to Thévenot the Armenians of Nusaybin (with own bishop and priests) were Catholics. Of course the conversion of Armenians in the region or nearby to Catholicism is a parallel case to that of the Church of the East; papal motives for a missionary drive among the

---

94 Thévenot, *Suite du voyage de Levan*, 92; Fiey, 115.

95 Keser-Kayaalp, "Cathedral Complex," 140–9, 151.

96 Fiey, *Nisibe*, 74–6; Sinclair 1987–90, 3:344–5. Keser-Kayaalp argues that the northerly chamber is not an eighth-century church but a structure contemporary with the baptistery and narthex. The arguments are not entirely convincing, in particular the assertion that the masonry of the northerly chamber's east wall shows no discontinuity with that of the baptistery's east wall. For more photographs and the building sequence, Bell, *Churches and Monasteries*, ed. Mundell Mango, 143–5, pls. 70–83. Excavations to the south of the baptistery complex have revealed a platform originally executed in mosaic. The latter was then covered with a flooring of stone slabs, perhaps for an open-air church, as there was an apse in the east wall (Keser-Kayaalp, 144–5.) But indications of date are lacking, and it is unclear if this southern building, or space, was joined on to the baptistery complex's south wall, and if so how.

Armenians are the same as in the story of Catholic efforts towards the Church of the East. As early as 1584 a College for the Armenians had been founded in Rome with the purpose of training missionaries sent to the Armenians and of teaching Catholicism to the Armenians themselves. Capuchins (a branch of the Franciscan monastic order) started work in Aleppo in 1623 and in Mosul in 1638. In addition, Franciscans were active in the city of Amid/Diyarbekir from 1643 to 1658.[97] The Capuchin and Franciscan missions were not sent primarily to communicate with the Armenians of Mosul and Amid, but it seems likely that the Armenians of Nusaybin had been prosyletized from Amid, and perhaps more Armenians had come from that city. As a source of the Nusaybin Armenians' Catholicism, Mosul too is a possibility.[98]

Returning now to the plain of Mesopotamia and to Nusaybin and its environs, we have to observe that, in tandem with conditions elsewhere in the Ottoman empire, the basic parameters required for a living from the soil or from commerce had been further infracted. The government had limited control of the tribes. Central government to some extent had lost control even of its own organs and agencies in this district of Upper Mesopotamia.

As early as 1007/1599 we find the Mardin *sancak* in the hands not of a *sancakbeyi* but of a *voyvoda*. The *voyvoda* was meant to carry out the duties of a *sancakbeyi*, but was appointed for specific periods such as one year or three years. He levied taxes on his own account, and sometimes at least was given a precise list of the taxes he was entitled to extract. Instead of forwarding the taxes to the central government, he had to send a pre-agreed sum to the central treasury. The basis of his appointment and remuneration resembled the later *iltizam* system, where the *mültezim* or beneficiary of the taxes paid a given sum to the government in return for the tax revenue from a given estate.[99] The

---

97 Murre-van den Berg, *Scribes and Scripture*, 39, 42. See also S. Peter Cowe, "Church and Diaspora: The Case of the Armenians," in *The Cambridge History of Christianity*, vol. 5, *Eastern Christianity*, ed. Michael Angold (Cambridge: Cambridge University Press, 2006), 432–3.

98 The missions sent specifically to contact Armenian communities seem to have targeted Constantinople and other cities further north such as Erzurum and Tokat. Moreover, the effort started later (1685) than Thévenot's visit to Nusaybin (1654). See Cesare Santus, *Communication in sacris, coesistenza e conflitti tra le comunitàcristiane orientali (Levante e Impero Ottomano, XVII–XVIII secolo)* (Rome: École française, 2019), esp. 309–16, 320–4, 359–65.

99 F. Adanır, "Woywoda," in *EI2* 11:215. For the activities of the *voyvoda* of Amid, and the possibilities for exploitation of the position, Ariel Salzmann, *Tocqueville in the Ottoman Empire: Rival Paths to the Modern State* (Leiden: Brill, 2004), 91, 128–9, 134, 138, 141–3, 166–8.

44   Tom Sinclair

advantage to the central government was that it received a certain sum in cash at the start of the appointment. The drawback was that the *voyvoda* had complete freedom within the *sancak* or other administrative unit: he was prone to overexploitation, including over-extraction of taxes. At least in Mardin the appointment of *voyvoda*s continued after Mardin and Nusaybin passed from the *beylerbeyilik* of Amid to that of Baghdad, apparently in the early seventeenth century.[100]

As regards Nusaybin, the most ominous outcome was not the appointment of *voyvoda*s in the seventeenth century, but the non-appointment in the eighteenth century of any officer at all to run the *sancak*'s affairs. This for a date around 1131/1719 we learn from a document noting appointments within the empire. The document is a *sancak tevcih defteri* or *sancak* appointments register, though in practical terms it is a register of the holders of posts in provincial administration at various levels throughout the empire. The first date noted is Rebiülahır 1131/March 1719.[101] The document notes that the post of *sancakbeyi* of Nusaybin is empty.[102] This might not be especially disturbing; as personnel is shifted from post to post or retires, vacancies can be expected. All the same the document's purview is not confined just to the one date: it is filled in as the appointments are made. Perhaps this situation can be explained by a comment of the German traveller Niebuhr in the mid-eighteenth century: the *sancak* of Nusaybin was administered by an official appointed by the *voyvoda* of Mardin.[103] The *voyvoda* of Mardin, himself an appointee, was hardly likely to choose for Nusaybin a man of the best calibre, or one that would put the interests of the *sancak* above those of the *voyvoda* on whom he was dependent. Equally it is not surprising that the *voyvoda* of Mardin delayed in making a choice of officer for Nusaybin. In the 1719 document a related post, the *alaybeyilik*, is also registered as vacant: the *alaybey* was an officer responsible for gathering the *sancak*'s available troops as war or other emergency approached.[104]

A further aspect of the loosening of government control is the abandonment of Nusaybin as a serious military centre in 1154/1741. In that year the military material (*mühimmat*) of the citadel was taken

---

100 Göyünç, *Mardin Sancağı*, 45–6, 53–4; Yusuf Halaçoğlu, *XVIII. Yüzyılda Osmanlı İmparatorluğu'nun İskan Siyaseti ve Aşiretlerinin Yerleştirilmesi* (Ankara: Türk Tarih Kurumu, 1988), 52–3.

101 Fahreddin Başar, *Osmanlı Eyâlet Tevcihatı (1717–1730)* (Ankara: Türk Tarih Kurumu, 1997), 14–16.

102 Başar, *Osmanlı Eyâlet Tevcihatı*, 21, 112.

103 Niebuhr, *Carsten Niebuhr's Reisebeschreibung*, 2:381; Göyünç, *Mardin Sancağı*, 59.

104 Göyünç, *Mardin Sancağı*, 28, 245.

Nusaybin under the Ottomans   45

to the citadel of Mardin.[105] *Mühimmat* would include cannon, stores of muskets, bullets, swords, etc. The removal did not mean that no military presence was maintained thereafter, but without *mühimmat* the presence was weak and the military contingent would have been quite unable to impose order on the surrounding Arab and Kurdish tribes or to intervene in any kind of violent incident.

Regardless of exact causes, let us look at the situation on the *sancak*'s territory and nearby. In 1715 and 1716, for example, peasants were abandoning their homes because of raids by Bedouin tribes, mentioned earlier in this chapter in the context of sixteenth- and seventeenth-century Upper Mesopotamia.[106] The government through its provincial organization made attempts to settle the tribes, or sections of them. The Milli tribe, resident in the "Kuh-i Mardin" behind the city of Mardin in the mid-sixteenth century, had in 1707 been moved elsewhere in the Mardin *sancak*, presumably to one of the *nahiye*s on the plain. But from their new habitat they merely continued the plunder they had carried out from their former habitat. For this reason they were moved to the district of Raqqa in Syria. The city of Raqqa lies around eighty kilometres south of the present Turkish border at a point where another river, the Balikh, flows into the Euphrates. (The town of Bir/Birecik, at the highest navigable point on the Euphrates, stood some twenty-five kilometres north of the present Turkish border and somewhat further west than Raqqa.) Now the district of Raqqa offered (paradoxically, perhaps) poorly irrigated land which was at the same time sufficiently isolated to prevent winter and summer migrations. Before the Milli, other tribes had been forcibly transferred to this district. But the policy encountered a series of factors that collectively dragged at its viability. Among the worst of these was a lack of water.[107] Realistically the resettled tribes could not quickly abandon a transhumant way of life for a sedentary one; moreover their presence caused friction with established villages, which themselves were sometimes abandoned.[108] A rebellion took place in 1697.[109] The Milli tribe, having been moved to

---

105 Göyünç, 58–9, quoting Mardin Şeriye Sicili no. 203. By "Nusaybin Kalesi" must be meant the citadel on the riverbank, since the broken-down city walls offered no protection.

106 Halaçoğlu, *İskan Siyaseti*, 135, see also 54, 85.

107 Cengiz Orhonlu, *Osmanlı İmparatorluğunda Aşiretlerin İskanı* (Istanbul: Eren, 1987), 91–2, 110.

108 Orhonlu, *Osmanlı İmparatorluğunda Aşiretlerin İskanı*, 42–4, 89–91.

109 Caroline Finkel, *Osman's Dream: The Story of the Ottoman Empire, 1300–1923* (London: John Murray, 2005), 310, quoting Silahdar Fındıklı Ağa, *Nusretnâme*; Defterdar Sarı Mehmed Paşa, *Zübde-i Vekayiât*.

46   Tom Sinclair

the Raqqa district in 1711, escaped from it in 1713.[110] Another example of the tribes' violent and lawless tendencies is furnished by the Mukri tribe, which in 1734 was settled in empty villages in the *sancak*s of Mardin and Nusaybin.[111] We do not know the continuation of the episode, but empty villages tell a certain story, and it seems unlikely that the purpose of settling the tribe in those villages was merely to provide the villages with a population.

Populations, Conditions, and the City, Mid-Eighteenth to Early Twentieth Century

From the mid-eighteenth century at least, the open plain both east and west of Nusaybin was occupied largely by Arab and Kurdish tribes, all free of any form of government control. We pointed out earlier that no government control was possible once the military equipment was withdrawn from Nusaybin in 1741. The tribes do not seem to have been transhumant, but the tribal families lived mainly in tents, implying a reliance principally on animal rearing. The territory between Nusaybin and Mosul, well to the east, was dominated by the Tayy, an Arab tribe. In the mid-eighteenth century this tribe was aggressively seizing territory from others.[112] But its influence and power had somewhat diminished by the end of the nineteenth century. We hear also of the Shammar tribe.[113] In the other direction, towards and nearly as far as Mardin, the plain was ruled by a tribal entity which seems to have differed slightly from the Tayy in internal organization. In the early nineteenth century, during a visit by the British traveller Buckingham, the man at the heart of this tribal entity was known to the visitor as "Sheikh Farsee."[114] The information is unspecific, but we can imagine a perhaps small tribe to which other tribes, and village communities, were subject. Buckingham mentions a shaykh at Amuda, rather to the south of the territory of "Sheikh Farsee," who "commanded many of the villages in the neighbourhood." This perhaps is an indication of the nature of "Sheikh Farsee's" rule. Buckingham himself had to pay a tribute (not a customs

---

110 Halaçoğlu, *İskan Siyaseti*, 136; Orhonlu, *İskan*, 110.
111 Halaçoğlu, 69.
112 Orhonlu, *İskan*, 113.
113 Sachau, *Reise*, 389–90. Towards Mosul, local domination was shared with a Kurdish tribe, the Jarjariyya. On the latter, Jean Otter, *Voyage en Turquie et en Perse, avec une relation des expéditions de Tahmas Kouli-Khan* (Paris: Frères Guerin, 1748), 263.
114 Buckingham, *Travels*, 241.

Nusaybin under the Ottomans 47

toll or road tax) to "Sheikh Farsee."[115] In both areas (east and west of Nusaybin) lived Kurds, whether in tents like the Arabs or in villages; in these districts, surprisingly, apart from the distant Jarjariyya, no Kurdish tribe existed in which the village or tented communities could be subsumed.[116] Beyond Mardin, on the plain and in the great hollow vale behind the city, were other Kurdish tribes, apparently different from those of the early sixteenth century, but presenting just the same threat to commercial traffic as in that century.[117]

In general, the conditions seem to have been highly inimical both to agriculture and to trade, even if to a degree both were carried on. Traffic still came up from the port of Basra via Baghdad and Mosul.[118] But robbery along the length of the road was rife. It occurred certainly between Baghdad and Mosul.[119] From Mosul to Nusaybin the shorter and more direct way through desert could be taken, but it ran near Jabal Sinjar, home of the Yezidis much feared for their uninhibited raiding activity. Moreover, the longer road up the Tigris to Jazira and then westwards offered convenient halting places and better provisioning.[120] Even so robberies took place on the "safer" route too. Olivier, travelling just after the turn of the eighteenth century, was told of a holdup by Arabs where goods and cash were handed over.[121] Finally tolls, in lawful or in unlawful quantities, had to be paid. Nusaybin was among the most expensive toll points. At the bridge here one paid both a customs charge and a travel fee (Turk. *bac*). Strangely these were paid to different officials, the travel fee or road tax to a nominee of the *voyvoda* or governor of the Mardin *sancak*, in which Nusaybin lay, and the customs tax to a nominee of the *beylerbeyi* or governor of the Diyarbekir province – and yet the Mardin *sancak* belonged to that province.[122] To sum all these

---

115 Buckingham, 235, 241–2.

116 Tents: Thévenot, 91. Villages: Buckingham, *Travels*, 235; Horatio Southgate, *Narrative of a Tour through Armenia, Kurdistan, Persia, and Mesopotamia* (New York: D. Appleton, 1840), 116.

117 *Diary of Major E. Noel on Special Duty in Kurdistan* (Basra: N.p., 1919), 60, admittedly information collected in the early twentieth century.

118 For some examples in the mid-eighteenth century, Otter, *Voyage*, 196, 214, 222, 253.

119 Otter, 195, 196, 222.

120 Kinneir, *Journey*, 432–3; Southgate, *Narrative*, 120; Ainsworth, *Travels and Researches*, 2:119–23 (note that sometime in the early nineteenth century a governor of Mosul built two forts in order to provide some security along the route); James Fletcher, *Notes from Nineveh: And travels in Mesopotamia, Assyria and Syria* (London: Colburn, 1850), 165 (halting places, provisions).

121 Guillaume Olivier, *Voyage dans l'empire othoman, l'Égypte et la Perse : fait par l'ordre du Gouvernement* (Paris: H. Agasse [1801]–1807), 260.

122 Olivier, 254–65.

48   Tom Sinclair

matters up, an interesting example, and the most detailed, can be given. The German explorer Niebuhr travelled in 1766 along the road from Mosul past Nusaybin to Mardin, where he paid both the customs toll and the *bac* (road money). The caravan was made up of 1,400 camels and 500 or 600 horses. One hundred fifty armed guards protected the caravan and its 2,000 bales of saleable goods. The number of travellers, whether associated with particular goods under carriage or not, was 400.[123] The numbers are eloquent: in dangerous conditions one could make the journey, but it was safer as well as more economical to organize such huge caravans, with 150 armed guards. However, these would have to be assembled at much longer intervals.

The same traveller, Niebuhr, visited the town too. He reported 150 houses, in the sense of physical structures rather than families; and badly built. From our evidence concerning the deficits and dysfunctions of local government and the danger from tribesmen and robbers, the drop in population from Evliya's figure of 700 houses a century earlier does not surprise us. Coming to the question of the religious groups, it appears the Armenians now had exclusive use of the baptistery. The "Jacobites" [that is, Syrian Orthodox] conducted services in the eighth-century chapel against the baptistery's and narthex's north side; but there was not always a priest available. For burials and baptisms a priest had to be brought from Mardin.[124] However the monastery of Mar Melke on Mt. Izla was certainly inhabited at the same date, 1766.[125] A depressing picture in any case: mention of the Jacobites/Syrian Orthodox alone implies that the Church of the East's congregation had left the town, going either to nearby villages or to other towns or districts. Nineteenth-century evidence suggests that the Syrian congregation worshipping at the church here may well have belonged to the Syrian Orthodox church. Can we be sure? Even if Niebuhr had a precise picture of each church's history and Christology, there was plenty of room for confusion.

On the assumption that the Syrian congregation here belonged at the time to the Syrian Orthodox church rather than the Church of the East, what accounts for the abandonment of the town by the Church of the East congregation? Had that congregation migrated to a city such as Mardin, or else eastwards to the region of Gazarta/Cizre or perhaps Rabban Hormizd north of Mosul? If so, the migration could be

---

123 Niebuhr, *Reisebeschreibung*, 2:374; Göyünç, *Mardin Sancağı*, 55; Göyünç, "Ekonomik Durumu," 97. Göyünç draws from Niebuhr the conclusion that trade in the sixteenth century was lively!

124 Niebuhr, 2:380; Fiey, *Nisibe*, 116.

125 Fiey, 143.

Nusaybin under the Ottomans   49

explained either by a wish to join other non-Uniate Church of the East congregations in a city or district with a stiffer and larger population than in Nusaybin, or by the very unsafe conditions in the countryside and on the roads near the town.

The next news we have of the town comes from the Frenchman Olivier after a visit in 1791. According to Olivier, Nusaybin had to be countedas a village, not a town. It had scarcely 1,000 inhabitants, implying around 200 households. However, these were nearly all Kurdish and Arab, although there were some "arméniens jacobites."[126] This is the first explicit reference since the census of 1564 to Muslims residing in the town, though it seems likely that there had always been a Muslim element, small or large, in the meantime. An Armenian [sic] priest celebrated services in the eighth-century church built against the north face of the baptistery and narthex.[127] But then who were the "arméniens jacobites"? In Olivier's phrase, one can see an original account given to him in which Jacobites and Armenians would have been mentioned as members of the two different churches. One may deduce that the Syrian Orthodox held their services in the baptistery proper since the Armenians held theirs in the eighth-century church. After his visit, the two groups would be conflated in Olivier's understanding. The Armenians would be the Catholic Armenians of Niebuhr's reference. The Armenians and Jacobites remained heavily outnumbered, nor was the town's permanent population increasing. Two accounts based on visits in the 1810s state that much of the city site was occupied by tents; one said Kurdish tents only, the other said a mixture of Kurds and Arabs.[128] At the American missionary Southgate's visit in 1837 there were still only 150 houses.[129] The church added to the north face of the baptistery and narthex had now been taken over as a fodder store for the garrison's horses.

Times were soon to change. The central government succeeded in mounting campaigns against the Kurdish tribes, which had gained control over the city of Mardin. In 1836 an Ottoman army moved against Cizre, then occupied by Bedirhan Bey, the prince of Bohtan (the mountains north-east of Cizre); on the way back it attacked the Yezidis of Jabal Sinjar, the complex of hills rising out of the Mesopotamian plain south-east of Nusaybin.[130] In 1838 another Ottoman army surrounded

---

126 Olivier, *Voyage*; Fiey, *Nisibe*, 117.
127 Olivier, 247; Fiey, 116–17.
128 Kinneir, *Journey*, 443–4; Buckingham, *Travels*, 249.
129 Southgate, *Narrative*, 119.
130 John Guest, *The Yezidis: A Study in Survival* (London: KPI, 1987), 69.

50   Tom Sinclair

Jabal Sinjar and the Yezidis surrendered; they were allowed to stay on the mountain. But barracks were constructed at Nusaybin and a garrison installed.[131] This, it seemed, was part of an attempt to re-establish Nusaybin as a military centre and generally upgrade the site.[132] The barracks were to the north of the inhabited area, and it is highly likely that they were built with the masonry of the medieval citadel noticed by Buckingham as late as 1816. At some point, perhaps after the creation of the new province of Mosul in 1845, the barracks were emptied and the garrison moved to Mosul.[133]

In the mid-nineteenth century, during the so-called Tanzimat or reforms beginning in 1840, local government was reorganized several times. Up to 1840 it seems that Nusaybin continued as a *sancak* in the province of Diyarbekir. But sometime between the beginning of the reforms in 1840 and the year 1845, Nusaybin became a part of the *kaza* of Mardin, which was included in a newly-created province (*vilayet*) of Mosul. In 1845, Mardin was upgraded to the status of *sancak*, and Nusaybin correspondingly to that of *kaza*. In 1869 Mardin, with Nusaybin, was moved back to the province of Diyarbekir and remained there until the end of the Ottoman period.[134] The Tanzimat, of which the administrative reorganizations mentioned earlier were part, combined with the effects of European economic upswing, brought about a certain security and a linkage to other regions of the Ottoman Empire. But these changes were slow in coming about.

The British missionary Badger visited Nusaybin several times between 1844 and 1850. At the earlier of these two dates Nusaybin was inhabited by 300 families, most of them living in tents; they were Arabs of the Tayy tribe. The Jacobite and Armenian communities accounted for only twelve families between them, and had neither church nor priest. There were now four Jewish families; previously the town's Jews had numbered forty families.[135]

---

131 Guest, *The Yezidis*, 7. The official responsible for their construction seems to have been a Mirza Paşa, *mütesellim* or governor of the *sancak* of Mardin. Oswald Parry, *Six Months in a Syrian Monastery* (London: H. Cox, 1895), 224; Fiey, *Nisibe*, 118.

132 Ainsworth, *Travels and Researches*, 2:118.

133 Parry, *Syrian Monastery*, 224, 225. By 1894, however, the barracks had become the residence of the *kaymakam* (governor) of the *kaza* of Nusaybin. See also Sachau, *Reise*, 391.

134 Mehmet Taştemir and Banu Bilgicioğlu, "Mardin," in *Türkiye Diyanet Vakfı İslam Ansiklopedisi* (44 vols., Istanbul: Türkiye Diyanet Vakfı, 1988–2013), 28:43–51, here 47; Kemal Karpat, *Ottoman Population, 1830–1914: Demographic and Social Characteristics* (Madison: University of Wisconsin Press, 1985), 132–5, 176–7.

135 Fiey, *Nisibe*, 119.

Nusaybin under the Ottomans   51

In the mid-nineteenth century the Syrian Orthodox began to play a more decisive part in the town's history. In 1865 they gained possession of the baptistery, having secured from the Grand Vizier a decision to that effect. The Syrian Orthodox congregation within the town had grown (Fiey surmises that families had come in from the surrounding villages). The Syrian Orthodox restored the church in 1872, rebuilding the baptistery's roof and building new chambers for the priest or bishop.[136] The monastery of Mar Awgin on Mt. Izla was now inhabited. The first evidence of habitation this century comes in 1838 (Church of the East monks), then in 1842–3 (Syrian Orthodox monks).[137] Later it was the residence of two Syrian Orthodox bishops. The monastery was inhabited by monks up to the First World War; in 1912 a bishop again resided here.[138] In 1881 a Syrian Orthodox diocese of Nusaybin was created, split off from the diocese of Mardin; however, this diocese was to be reincorporated in 1912 into that of Mardin. The Syrian Orthodox had exclusive rights over the church. In the *kaza* of Nusaybin (therefore including the villages) they outnumbered the Armenian Catholics, though strangely the Armenians of the Gregorian church were the largest Christian community in the *kaza* as a whole. In the town, however, the Muslim element predominated. Some Jewish families had been expelled from Mardin and made a strange addition to the whole corpus of religious denominations represented in Nusaybin. They are mentioned in a letter by the British consul for Kurdistan dated March 1879.[139] In general the town was growing; cultivation in the countryside was on the increase. In the 1890s, nevertheless, there were still only around thirty Syrian families in the town (as opposed to the villages) as against 300 Muslim and 150 Jewish ones.[140]

The disturbances, intercommunal fighting, and massacres that in 1895 affected the mountain district of Sasun and the city of Amid so violently and with such destructive consequences, affected also the Christians of Nusaybin. Kurds attacked the Christian quarter of the town. The Tayy Arabs, remarkably, then chased them out of the town. The Kurds then turned their attention to the villages, burning and pillaging fourteen of them.[141]

---

136 Fiey, 119–21, 131.
137 Wilmshurst, *Ecclesiastical Organisation*, 47.
138 Fiey, *Nisibe*, 126, 139, 140, quoting several visitors.
139 Fiey, 121, 122, 123, 127, 128.
140 Parry, *Syrian Monastery*, 224–5; but Sachau, contemporary of Parry's, suggests 200 houses (*Reise*, 391).
141 Fiey, *Nisibe*, 123; David Gaunt, *Massacres, Resistance Protectors: Muslim-Christian Relations in Eastern Anatolia during World War I* (Piscataway, New Jersey: 2006), 43.

52   Tom Sinclair

By the time of the First World War massacres of June 1915 the Christian side of Nusaybin's population consisted of 400 families, divided as follows: there were ninety Armenians, probably belonging to the Catholic hierarchy, and apparently with their own church, presumably built recently. Besides the Armenians there were Syrian Orthodox and Chaldaeans (the name initially coined to denote Uniates), though at this stage the original Uniates were established in their villages high up in the Hakkari mountains, and in effect we probably have to do with the successor of the hierarchy in the Church of the East, which initially refused union with the Church of Rome. It seems that the Chaldaeans had no priest.[142]

The whole story of small Christian communities and Kurdish and Arab neighbours in an Ottoman provincial town ends on a grim and soulless note. Arrests of the Christians were made in summer 1914 and the arrested persons were put in jail. The non-Armenian prisoners were let out, only to be arrested later.[143] The town's Armenians were killed on 15 and 28 June 1915, the Syrian Orthodox on 16 August. A further massacre on the town's outskirts followed in September.[144] The massacres in Nusaybin belie the theory that the authorities' only target was Armenians. It does not seem that any exception was made for women, as Muslim custom normally suggested; but the children were shared out among Muslim families and the shaykh of the Tayy tribe saved some of those adults who evidently were about to be targeted.[145]

It was therefore to a tiny town, without Christian inhabitants, that the Baghdad railway came in 1917.[146]

---

142 Fiey, 128; Gaunt, 25. On the Armenians, Raymond Kévorkian and Paul Paboudjian, *Les Arméniens dans l'Empire ottoman à la veille du genocide* (Paris: Arhis, 1992), 59, 415. The figure comes from a census by the Armenian patriarchate in Istanbul carried out in 1913–14 (Kévorkian and Paboudjian, *Les Arméniens*, 57), but it seems likely the Patriarchate's aim was to record all Armenians, not just Gregorian ones.

143 Gaunt, 76.

144 Gaunt, 77, 159, 176, 440. On the shifts of policy towards non-Armenian Christians, Uğur Üngör, *The Making of Modern Turkey: Nation and State in Eastern Anatolia, 1913–1950* (Oxford: Oxford University Press, 2011), 92, 95–6, 97–8.

145 Fiey, *Nisibe*, 129. In general various Armenians, some of them perhaps from Nusaybin, fled to settlements in northern Iraq. They were sheltered in particular by the Yezidis of Sinjar. See the *Review of the Civil Administration of Mesopotamia* from Sir A.T. Wilson (London: HMSO, 1920) (Cmd. 1061; Parliamentary Papers, House of Commons, Session 1920, vol. 51), 50; Wallace Lyon, *Kurds, Arabs and Britons: The Memoir of Wallace Lyon in Iraq, 1918–44*, ed. D.K. Fieldhouse (London: I.B. Tauris, 2002), 63, 182.

146 Ulrich Trumpener, *Germany and the Ottoman Empire, 1914–1918* (Princeton: Princeton University Press, 1968), 305, see also 285, 300, 306–7. Before the First World War

Conclusions

In this survey of Nusaybin's history in the Ottoman period we dwelt on the relations between the city, the relevant commercial networks and conditions on the roads, and the Kurdish-inhabited surrounds: the plain and the foothills of the massif to the north. We looked first at Nusaybin's medieval history as a means of explaining, at least in part, the city's condition under the Ottomans and why outstanding aspects of its past – its trade and culture, the theological school – could not have been recreated in the Ottoman period. Our throwback to the late Middle Ages also served to link previous regimes, where Kurdish political structures either were in absolute control or else existed within the tissue of wider states, with the more fragmented Kurdish tribal patterns, and almost exclusively rural life, of the Ottoman period.

We have been limited in our ability to consult primary sources in the original language. For Syriac sources we are dependent on Fiey and Wilmshurst and others; for Ottoman ones, mostly on Göyünç, for his extensive study of sixteenth-century *defters* and other documents. In the one case language has been the barrier; in the other, access to documents and the time required to check them. On the other hand the publications of these scholars have tended to purvey the information in the primary sources just as we find it in the text; in other words the publications contain raw information, of course carefully extracted and presented. The scholars in question proceed only to a limited extent to the drawing of conclusions on the basis of the data which they have made available with such accuracy. We on the contrary have taken the data and precisely built conclusions from it. We have also combined the information furnished by one current of scholarship, the Syriac, with that furnished by the other, the Ottoman; and interesting historical conclusions have resulted.

At the beginning of this chapter we implicitly posed the question, Could Nusaybin have returned to its prosperous medieval days, when the extensive walled area on the west bank of the Jaghjagh was filled with houses, not to mention churches, mosques, madrasas, a functioning citadel, and other public buildings? We described the conditions in

---

construction had started from Baghdad towards Mosul, but it was only in 1940 that the line from the Amanus mountains in northwest Syria all the way to Baghdad was completed. (Trumpener, 7–8, 316.) On the construction of the sections preceding the final link with Nusaybin, Trumpener, *Germany and the Ottoman Empire*, 283; Manfred Pohl, *Von Stamboul nach Baghdad: Die Geschichte einer berühmten Eisenbahn* (Munich and Zurich: Piper, 1999), 171–3.

the open countryside and concluded that the danger to trade from robbers and undisciplined tribe members was present from the very start of Ottoman rule over the district. Instead of the authorities' achieving an appropriate measure of control over the tribes, the latter got more out of hand in the seventeenth and eighteenth centuries. Moreover, from the beginning of Ottoman rule the relevant traffic from Baghdad took as a standard route the alternative via the Euphrates through Ana, Hit, and Raqqa. Regular, substantial trade, which might have sustained an impressive city, was to all intents and purposes precluded, and in the circumstances the city could not have recovered even to the size of a comfortably prosperous market town, let alone a cultured medieval city.

We also emphasized at the beginning of the essay the role of Nisibis as the site of an influential theological school in the Church of the East from the late fifth to the late seventh century. The city became, too, the seat of a metropolitan responsible for the sector of the plain as far as Beth Zabdaï, with its city of Gazarta/Jazirat ibn 'Umar, and for districts in the upper Tigris basin further north. Implicitly, again, we were looking for clues as to whether the city of Nusaybin could have regained something of these roles.

A prosperous, sizeable city would have been easy ground for a theological school to emerge and develop in; but under Ottoman rule Nusaybin was never prosperous. The church itself was much reduced, confined now to the northeast corner of the Mesopotamian plain and to settlements in the upper Tigris basin; there was no case for a school. Moreover, the Church of the East was no longer in its earlier position, whereby it was territorially within the Sasanian empire, subsequently the Umayyad and Abbasid empires. As far as belief was concerned, it had much more in common with the Christian population of the Late Roman, subsequently the Byzantine, empire. Now there was just one empire, which worked according to standard Muslim precepts, and no position within the border of a rival empire. The Church of the East had lost the position by which it could be at the same time independent of one empire, with which it shared at least a religion, though not Christological precepts, and dependent on another, with which it had no religious ties whatever. The mid-sixteenth-century recourse to the Church of Rome was no surprise: in the circumstances one would naturally resort to a power outside the Ottoman empire in order to win one's battles within the Ottoman-enclosed church. That the metropolitanate of Nisibis was abolished nearly a century after the Ottoman Empire won the territory of Mardin and Nusaybin is hardly surprising either.

The fluidity of Nusaybin's population in the Ottoman period is striking. In 1644, for example, most of the town's population was either Armenian or else belonged to the Church of the East. In the mid-eighteenth century the Christian population consisted of Armenians and Syrian Orthodox. In the mid-nineteenth century there were only twelve Christian families and most of the others were Arabs of the Tayy tribe living in tents. But if there was one factor or element that constantly kept the town's Christian populations alive, it was the physical structures of the baptistery complex, attributed to St. James. Even though the different denominations competed for control of the church, and even given the circumstance that only one or perhaps two of the denominations could actually worship in it at any one time, the church was a robust symbol, which provided a measure of stability to all the Christian communities.

2 The Qizilbash Reconsidered: The Role of the Kurdish Arabgirlu Tribe in the Early Safavid State

MUSTAFA DEHQAN AND VURAL GENÇ

Introduction

In the study of Safavid history, the term "Qizilbash" (Kızılbaş) is generally taken to denote a group of tribes, Turks or Turkomans, who helped Shah Ismail found the Safavid dynasty in 1501. This emphasis on the Turkish element in Safavid history has been reflected in the last decades not only in regard to the early period of the Safavid venture but also in studies on the later Safavid shahs. However, we need to reconsider the assumption that the Qizilbash tribes were a uniquely Turkish community. In focusing on the role played by Kurdish Qizilbash in early Safavid-era politics, this chapter seeks to revisit the phenomenon per se.

The Qizilbash represented one of the most important challenges to central state authority in Iran, Anatolia, and Syria in the sixteenth century and continued to effect political upheaval and change well beyond. The movement and its dynamics have been a key research topic in Iran and Turkey for many years. Our aim in this contribution is to set forth the role played by Kurds in the early Qizilbash movement and to underscore the fact that contrary to the dominant paradigm, it was not only Turkoman but also Kurdish tribes that played a significant role in its emergence. The majority of these tribes were not directly tied to Syria. It is known, however, that the Canpolads, the Kurdish rulers of Kilis in the later sixteenth century, regarded the Qizilbash question as an important political issue on which to ground themselves. This does not mean that they espoused Qizilbash tenets: As can be observed in their correspondence with the Ottoman sultans, the Canpolads in fact distanced themselves from Qizilbash doctrines and declared that they were proud of being Sunni. The Canpolads' case suggests that the issue of Kurdish involvement in the Qizilbash movement also resonated in

The emphasis on the Qizilbash as Turkish tribes may be said to have come about when the Safavid period first began drawing the attention of western scholarship.[2] This happened as early as the late sixteenth century, when several important travelogues were published, in quick succession, through which the mysterious and enigmatic character of the Qizilbash was unveiled before an eager European audience.[3] It is thought that the Qizilbash included several Turkic tribes that played a unique role in the emergence of the Safavid dynasty. The fundamentally nationalist interpretation in this regard culminated in the work of Faruk Sümer,[4] and since 1976, numerous academic publications referencing Sümer's work have defined the Qizilbash as an exclusively Turkish confederacy.[5] In recent decades, scholarly views on the Turkishness of all Qizilbash tribes have become quite dominant in Turkey, with the work of Tufan Gündüz and his students even stressing the Qizilbash as a historical vehicle of Turkish nationalism.[6]

---

1 See Mustafa Dehqan and Vural Genç, "Kürdlükten Çıkmayub: Janfulad Husayn's Complaint against Sultan Mehmed III," *Journal Asiatique* 306 (2018): 167–71.

2 Working independently, Kasrawi (1927) and Toğan (1957) concluded the Safavids themselves were Kurdish in origin. See Ahmad Kasrawī, "Nizhad wa Tabar-i Safawiyya," *Ayanda* 17 (1927): 358–64; Zeki V. Toğan, "Sur l'origine des Safavides," in *Mélanges Louis Massignon* (Damascus: Institut Français de Damas, 1957), 3:347–57. On the origins of the Safavids, see also Michel M. Mazzaoui, *The Origins of the Safawids: Šīism, Sūfism, and the Ġulāt* (Wiesbaden: F. Steiner, 1972).

3 See for example, Mohsen Saba, *Bibliographie française de l'Iran. Bibliographie méthodique et raisonnée des ouvrages français parus depuis 1560 jusqu'à nos jours* (Paris: Bibliothèque Nationale, 1951), esp. 161–3; Sibylla Schuster-Walser, *Das safawidische Persien im Spiegel europäischer Reiseberichte (1502–1722): Untersuchungen zur Wirtschafts-und Handelspolitik* (Baden-Baden: Grimm, 1970); Ayfer Karakaya-Stump, "The Emergence of the Kızılbaş in Western Thought: Missionary Accounts and their Aftermath," in *Archaeology, Anthropology, and Heritage in the Balkans and Anatolia: The Life and Times of F.W. Hasluck, 1878–1920*, ed. David Shankland (Istanbul: ISIS Press, 2004), 329–53.

4 Faruk Sümer, *Safevi Devletinin Kuruluşu ve Gelişmesinde Anadolu Türklerinin Rolü* (Ankara: Türk Tarih Kurumu, 1976).

5 See for example, Irène Mélikoff, "Le problème Kızılbaş," *Turcica* 6 (1975): 49–67; Masashi Haneda, *Le Chah et les Qizilbaš* (Berlin: Klaus Schwarz, 1987); Kathryn Babayan, "The Safavid Synthesis: From Qizilbash Islam to Imamite Shi'ism," *Iranian Studies* 27 (1994): 135–61; Fariba Zarinebaf-Shahr, "Qizilbash 'Heresy' and Rebellion in Ottoman Anatolia during the Sixteenth Century," *Anatolia Moderna* 7 (1997): 1–15.

6 Tufan Gündüz, *Anadolu'da Türkmen Aşiretleri/Bozulus Türkmenleri 1540–1640* (Ankara: Bilge, 1997); Tufan Gündüz, *Son Kızılbaş Şah İsmail* (Istanbul: Yeditepe, 2010); Tufan Gündüz, *Kızılbaşlar, Osmanlılar, Safeviler* (Istanbul: Yeditepe, 2015). See also Ali Rıza Özdemir, *Türk Hakanı Şah İsmail* (Ankara: Kripto, 2018).

58   Mustafa Dehqan and Vural Genç

Other scholars, however, in identifying the Qizilbash as mostly Turkic do not associate them with Ottoman "Turkishness" or modern Turkish identity. Therefore calling the Qizilbash "Turks" in the Iranian context has little to do with modern nationalism; it is more a question of language use and ethnic identity. It is of course important to avoid anachronisms in assigning such identities: in the pre-modern period, we understand that identifiers such as "Kurd," "Turk," and "Persian" were not stable markers, but part of the way in which very mixed populations strove to create distinctions among themselves.

In Iran, a country which has maintained a high level of literary production throughout its history and continues to exert its influence on the political and the religious spheres of the former Safavid world today, there have been surprisingly few studies on the history of Qizilbash tribes per se. The work that has stood out most is diplomat and scholar Nasr Allah Falsafi's *Tawayif-i Qizilbash.*[7] Strictly speaking, however, Iranian authors including Falsafi have used this term to designate the Turkish or Turkoman tribes that helped Shah Ismail and later Safavid shahs run the empire.[8] Modern Iranian studies on the Qizilbash tribes appear largely unrelated to questions of nationalism, as in Turkey.

The above-mentioned studies do offer some nuanced appreciations ethnic constitution of the Qizilbashes. Sümer's account ends before the conclusion of the origins of the tribes, but sometimes, where the Kurdishness of some of them is beyond doubt, he does indicate that there were tribes of Kurdish origin, presumably in the modern ethnic sense.[9] Overall, however, he has little information to impart beyond the Kurdish origin of a given tribe and fills in the rest with Turkification rhetoric. Some important scholarship on the question that is often overshadowed by Sümer's work is that of Abdülbaki Gölpınarlı, which served to establish the Shiite religious nature of the Qizilbash in particular. Gölpınarlı in effect describes two separate and independent groups: a) the Turkoman Qizilbash tribes, and b) the Kurdish Ahl-i Haqq community of western Iran. It is important that, according to Gölpınarlı, there is no functional difference between these two groups.[10]

---

7 Nasr Allah Falsafi, *Zindigani-yi Shah Abbas-i Awwal* (Tehran: Ilmi, 1996), esp. 205–32, 265–8.

8 See for example Firuz Mansuri, "Pazhuhishi darbara-yi Qizilbash," *Barrasiha-yi Tarikhi* 10, no. 4 (1975): 145–62; Muhsin Bahramnizhad, "Tahlili bar Yik Farman az Dawran-i Hukumat-i Shah Safi (1038–1052), Takapuha-yi Bithamar dar Hall-i Ikhtilaf-i Turkan-i Qizilbash wa Gurjiyan wa Payamadha-yi Tarikhi-yi An," *Ganjina-yi Asnad* 22 (2012): 22–42.

9 See, for example, Sümer, *Safevi Devletinin Kuruluşu,* 53.

10 Abdülbaki Gölpınarlı, "Kızılbaş," *İslam Ansiklopedisi* 6 (1965): 789–95.

The most important in-depth study in this regard is Roger Savory's portrayal of the Qizilbash in his *Encyclopaedia of Islam* article. He locates the origins of the Qizilbash in the Turkoman tribes, but at the same time suggests that the term was also applied to certain non-Turkish-speaking Iranian tribes that supported the Safavids, for example the Talish and the Qarajadagh (Siyahkuh), as well as Kurds.[11] Savory unfortunately does not mention the source for this statement, but he apparently had access to the text of the *Alamara-yi Amini*, at least in regard to the Qizilbash tribes of Talish and Siyahkuh.[12] On the other hand, there are other primary sources such as the *Tarikh-i Qizilbashan*[13] and the *Tarikh-i Alamara-yi Abbasi* which refer to Kurds among the Qizilbash and provide evidence to the effect that they were not exclusively made up of Turkish groups.[14] Ottoman documents (and chronicles) that occasionally apply the term "Qizilbash" to Arabic-speaking Twelver Shiites in Lebanon have been used to suggest that some of these populations may have had an origin in the Safavid Qizilbash movement; in fact the term was only used in a legal sense, without any ethnic or tribal connotations.[15]

Walter Posch's extensive research on Alqas Mirza sheds light on the diversity of the Qizilbash tribes, suggesting they were comprised of individuals from various ethnic and social backgrounds, including nomads and settled people as well as Kurds and Turks. The *Beyan-ı Menazil-i Sefer-i Irakeyn* of Matrakçı Nasuh, for instance, indicates that the Qizilbash were recognized by their contemporaries as a heterogeneous group and often referred to as "heretics of mixed origin." Posch divides the Qizilbash tribes into six distinct groups: (a) those considered Qizilbash in the strict sense; (b) Turkish (Oghuz) tribes; (c) royal tribes; (d) Kurds and Lurs; (e) Şeyh Avand; and (f) other groups. His examination of Safavid sources also shows that certain Qizilbash tribes, including the Ustajlu as a whole and the sub-tribes Khinislu and Çemişkezeki, as well as the Bayburtlu of the Rumlu, were considered to have mixed origins. According to Posch, the homeland of the Ustajlu,

---

11 Roger M. Savory, "Kizil-Bash," *The Encyclopaedia of Islam*, 2nd ed. EI2 (1986), 5:243–5.
12 Fadl Allah Ruzbihan Khunji Isfahani (d. 1521), *Tarikh-i Alamara-yi Amini*, ed. M.A. Ashiq (Tehran: Mirath Maktub, 2003), 267.
13 Anon., Tarikh-i Qizilbashan, Malek National Library (Tehran), Ms. 6284, fols. 99r–113r.
14 Willem Floor, *Safavid Government Institutions* (California: Mazda Publishers, 2001), 129–31.
15 Stefan Winter, "The Kızılbaş of Syria and Ottoman Shiism," in *The Ottoman World*, ed. Christine Woodhead (London: Routledge, 2012), 171–83.

who are well known in the literature as a Turkoman tribe, was in fact Bingöl, suggesting they may have been of Kurdish descent. These he distinguishes from Kurdish tribes such as the Ruzegi, Ardalan, Siyah Mansur, Zanganeh, Chegeni, Pazuki, and Dunbuli, which were explicitly identified as Kurdish or Iranian Kurdish by Iskandar Beg Munshi and Sharaf Khan. These Kurds attained significant positions within the Safavid Empire's military establishment mainly during the time of Shah Tahmasb. This distinction serves to highlight the recognition of the diverse origins of the Qizilbash and the categorization of different tribes based on their ethnic identity, as observed in Safavid primary sources.[16]

In recent times, some scholars have also referred to the "Kurdish Qizilbash" when dealing with the modern Bektashi-Alevi communities of eastern Anatolia.[17] The latter is of course a new name for Alevi Kurds inhabiting Anatolia, with no evident link to the Qizilbash tribes at the time of Shah Ismail. Local Kurdish historians, whose works have largely escaped the notice of other researchers due to their limited circulation, have sometimes claimed, though without providing proof, that Alevi Kurds are related to Shah Ismail and his Kurdish Qizilbash followers.[18] The Qizilbash genealogies of certain individuals and clans in Kurdish-populated parts of Turkey are folkloric at best,[19] but it is important that they relate their own Alevi identity to that of the Safavids by claiming the two groups are offshoots of the same religious movement.

The above-mentioned secondary works have been of vital importance for those who are interested in Safavid history. These materials, however, are by no means sufficient to explain the existing problems in the academic literature. Large gaps still exist not only on Turkish Qizilbash tribes but also on the part played by the non-Turkish Qizilbash in the Safavid state. The principal goal of this paper is to present primary

---

16 Walter Posch, *Osmanisch-safavidische Beziehungen 1545–1550: Der Fall Alḳâs Mîrzâ* (Vienna: Österreichische Akademie der Wissenschaften, 2013), 183–6, 195–7.

17 Ayfer Karakaya-Stump, "Documents and Buyruk Manuscripts in the Private Archives of Alevi Dede Families: An Overview," *British Journal of Middle Eastern Studies* 37 (2010), 273–86, esp. 278; Rıza Yıldırım, "The Way of Muhammad/ Ali: Qizilbash Religion in Early Modern Iran and Anatolia" (PhD diss., Emory University, 2024).

18 Many of these studies based on oral tradition are unfortunately of poor quality; see for example Mehmed Bayrak, *Êzidî-Kızılbaş-Yaresan Kürtler (Belgelerle Kürdistan'da Gizili Dinler)* (Ankara: Özge, 2014).

19 See for example Melville Chater, "The Kizilbash Clans of Kurdistan," *The National Geographic Magazine* 54 (1928): 485–501.

source materials which contain new information about the Kurdish Qizilbash that has been neglected so far.

Qizilbash: Definition and Demarcation

The term *Qizilbash* did not have a firm meaning throughout Safavid history, but should be seen as an object of political, religious, and social discussion. Our purpose here is not to present an extensive history of the term, which underwent important changes in signification over the course of two centuries. A comprehensive study would have to include a review of all Persian and Ottoman primary sources, as well as European-language materials on Safavid history, which are not relevant to the present study.[20] What we would like to do here instead is to substantiate the suggestion that the primary sources do not demonstrate a unique Turkish or Turkmen origin of the Qizilbash tribes as claimed in some secondary sources.

The word *qizilbash* (*sorkhsar*) or "redhead" seems to have a satisfactory etymology, being derived from *qizil*, "red," and the noun *bash*, "head." Such a compound is also seen in *yishil bash*, "green-head," which is a well-known exchange of *qizil* for the older term *yishil*, denoting a Sufi order of Bukhara in the sixteenth century.[21]

In its general sense, the term "Qizilbash" is used loosely to designate a wide variety of "extremist" Shiite sects whose common characteristic was the wearing of red headgear.[22] It was also used by the Ottomans as a derogatory term applied to the supporters of the Safavids, often in rhyming combinations such as *Qizilbash-i bad-maash*, *Qizilbash-i awbash*, *Qizilbash-i qallash*, *Qizilbash-i kufr-fash*, *Qizilbash-i na-tarash*, etc.[23] Apart from this pejorative sense, the Ottomans also used the term

---

20 For a detailed discussion of the term, see Shahzad Bashir, "The Origins and Rhetorical Evolution of the Term Qizilbash in Persianate Literature," *Journal of the Economic and Social History of the Orient* 57, no. 3 (June 2014): 364–91, https://doi.org/10.1163/15685209-12341352; Sajjad Husayni, "Siyr-i Tatawwur-i Manai-yi Wazha-yi Qizilbash," *Mutaliat-i Tarikh-i Islam* 32 (2017): 73–101; Ayşe Baltacıoğlu-Brammer, "One Word, Many Implications: The Term 'Kızılbaş' in the Early Modern Ottoman Context," in *Ottoman Sunnism: New Perspectives*, ed. Vefa Erginbaş (Edinburgh: Edinburgh University Press, 2019), 47–71; Posch, *Osmanisch-safavidische Beziehungen*, 164–6.

21 Hayrullah Efendi, *Devlet-i Aliye-i Osmaniye Tarihi* (Istanbul: Süleyman Efendi Matbaası, n.d.), 7:14.

22 For example, see Khunji Isfahani, *Tarikh-i Alamara-yi Amini*, 45.

23 See for example Selânikî Mustafa Efendî, *Tarih-i Selânikî (971–1003/1563–1595)*, ed. M. İpşirli (Ankara: Türk Tarih Kurumu, 1999), 2:478, 729.

"Qizilbash" when defining the Safavid realm. It should be added that "Qizilbash" could also cover anyone who supported the Safavids in the Ottoman world. 'Izz al-Din Shir Bey, the Kurdish emir of Hakkari, is a good example for delineating the meaning of "Qizilbash." In one of his Persian reports, Idris-i Bidlisi labels this emir "a deviant Qizilbash" because of his support for Shah Ismail,[24] even though he was otherwise known as a faithful Sunni Muslim.[25]

The Safavid usage of the term traditionally corresponds to a well-known story regarding Sheikh Haydar and Imam Ali. According to this story, Sheikh Haydar, having been instructed in a dream by Imam Ali, devised a distinctive scarlet or crimson head covering (*taj*) with twelve pleats (*tark*) in commemoration of the twelve *imam*s of the *ithna-'ashari* Shiites.[26] In many Safavid chronicles the term is applied in its general sense to the state (*dawlat-i Qizilbash*) and its army (*lashkar-i Qizilbash*).

With these definitions in mind, let us now turn to other primary sources. From existing original accounts, we get the impression that the tribes to whom the term Qizilbash is applied simply possessed a Shiite ideology, and there is no mention that these tribes were exclusively of Turkish origin. Rather, the mutual admiration and friendship between non-Turkish Qizilbash tribes and the Safavid shah has served as the source for some historical accounts, among which the famous historian Khunji Isfahani's monumental *Alamara-yi Amini* stands out. Here, it is clearly mentioned that the followers of Junayd and Haydar were based in Anatolia (Rum), Talish, and Siyahkuh, where Iranian (including Kurdish) communities were living.[27]

For a succinct history of Qizilbash Kurdish tribes, one may also benefit from the account in Sharaf Khan Bidlisi's *Sharaf-nama*. Within Kurdish tribal society there were marginal religious factions politicized by the Safavid shah. According to Sharaf Khan, the non-Sunni Kurdish Pazuki tribe originally came from Adilcevaz, the region west of Lake Van, and had become Qizilbash because of their military and political preferences, and especially because of their "non-orthodox" religious doctrines.[28] In actuality, Sharaf Khan regarded anyone who fought with

---

24 Topkapı Sarayı Müzesi Arşivi, Istanbul [TSMA]: E. 1019.
25 Başbakanlık Devlet Arşivleri Genel Müdürlüğü Osmanlı Arşivi, Istanbul [BOA]: Bâb-ı Asafî Ruûs Kalemi [A.RSK] 1/9, no. 950.
26 Anon., *Alamara-yi Shah Ismail*, ed. A. Muntazir Sahib (Tehran: Bungah-i Tarjuma wa Nashr-i Kitab, 1963), 26; Muhammad Yusuf Wala Isfahani, *Khald-i Barin*, ed. M.H. Muhaddith (Tehran: Mawqufat-i Afshar, 1993), 53.
27 Khunji Isfahani, *Tarikh-i Alamara-yi Amini*, 267.
28 Scheref, Prince de Bidlis, *Scheref-nameh ou Histoire des Kourdes*, ed. V. Véliaminof-Zernof (St-Petersburg: Académie Impériale des Sciences, 1860–2), 1:328. For details

The Qizilbash Reconsidered   63

the Safavids during the Ottoman military expedition as Qizilbash, even though this was not the case with the Pazuki tribe. As mentioned in the *Sharaf-nama*, they were a non-Sunni Kurdish tribe with a great interest in "heresy," and this fact allows us to refine our understanding of the Pazuki tribe as a Kurdish Qizilbash group with a religious (not political) affinity to the Safavid state. In the reports he sent to Sultan Selim, Idris-i Bidlisi makes several references to them and corroborates that the Pazuki tribe, ruling around Bidlis, was deeply loyal to the Safavid shah.[29]

Ottoman registers also mention Kurdish Qizilbash tribes in the Safavid period. It is very interesting to note that, according to some Ottoman reports, it was sometimes Kurdish rather than Turkoman tribesmen who adopted the Qizilbash creed. The term Qizilbash appears as the epithet of a well-known Kurdish emir of the Kalhur area, where Shiite tendencies were very common, in some sources.[30] According to the investigations of Baghdad's governor in 985/1577, there were a large number of "heretic Shiites" in Kalhur province. The report suggests that they found a leader in the Kurdish *bey* of the frontier *sancak* of Derne, Qubad Beg of Kalhur.[31] The point here is that the governor of Baghdad once tried to imprison the Qizilbash Qubad Beg, and interestingly encouraged the court to appoint a "Sunni" in his stead.[32] On the other hand, the sixteenth-century Ottoman tax registers known as the

---

on the Pazuki tribe, see TSMA: E. 1019; Abu'l-Mahasin Yusuf Taghribirdi, *Hawadith al-Duhur fi Nada al-Ayyam wa'l-Shuhur*, ed. W. Popper (Berkeley: University of California Press, 1930–1), 466–7, 473–4; Iskandar Beg Munshi Turkman (d. 1634), *Tarikh-i Alamara-yi Abbasi*, ed. I. Afshar (Tehran: Amir Kabir, 2008), 2:644; Posch, *Osmanisch-safavidische Beziehungen*, 196–7.

29 See Vural Genç, "İdris-i Bidlîsî'nin II. Bayezid ve I. Selim'e Mektupları," *Osmanlı Araştırmaları* 47 (2016): 147–208, esp. 179, https://doi.org/10.18589/oa.582976.

30 For details on both the Kalhur area and the tribe, see Katib Çelebi (Mustafa ibn 'Abd Allah Hacci Halife, d. 1657), *Cihannümâ* (Istanbul: Matbaa-yı Amire, 1824), 449; Qadi Ahmad ibn Sharaf al-Din al-Husayn al-Husayni Qummi (d. 1606), *Khulasat al-Tawarikh*, ed. I. Ishraqi (Tehran: Tehran University Press, 1980–4), 1:175–6, 190; Anon., "Risala-yi Asami-yi Ashayir-i Kurd az Asr Nasiri," in *Pazhuhish-ha-yi Iran-shinasi 12*, ed. Muhammad Samadi (Tehran: Mawqufat-i Afshar, 2000), 554–5.

31 On Derne and Qubad Bey, also known as Kubadgün, see BOA: Mühimme Defteri [MD] 6, no. 206; MD 12, no. 806; MD 55, no.190; Turkman, *Tarikh-i Alamara-yi Abbasi*, 2:650, 660.

32 MD 31, no. 141; MD 32, nos. 416, 418. Several other documents refer to Qubud Beg's imprisonment but do not mention his Qizilbash identity. However, it is quite likely that the Safavid *halife*s mentioned in these accounts were in contact with Alevi Kurdish groups of eastern Anatolia. See, for example, MD 23, nos. 173, 186, 451, 452, and 696, all dated from 985/1577–8.

tahrir defterleri show that the Qizilbash constituted the majority of the population in the area.

The examples mentioned above constitute important evidence with regard to how the term Qizilbash was defined. But it is important to note that the majority of these references to Kurdish Qizilbash tribes do not cover the period of Shah Ismail. They refer only to the reign of Tahmasp I and to the Kurdish Qizilbash affiliated with him, regardless of differences in ethnicity, political creed, or other contextual circumstances. Apparent references to Kurdish tribes as supporters of Shah Ismail will be discussed below, but before we proceed, one clarification seems necessary: as Bashir argues in "The Origin and Rhetorical Evolution of the Term Qizilbash," the early Safavid sources affirm that Qizilbash were bound to the dynasty through religious as well as political ties. But only a few sources refer to these tribes as the Qizilbash, while others use more generic terms such as *sufi* and *ghazi*.[33] In other words, it is interesting that some of the earliest Safavid court historians such as Hirawi and Gunabadi do not use the term Qizilbash.[34] It is only in the seventeenth century, with the decline in their power, that references to the term Qizilbash and its symbolic weight increase.[35] There is an important lack of information on the early years of the Safavids.

The Qizilbash Confederation Including Kurdish Tribes

The Qizilbash tribes of the Safavid dynasty belonged to what has been called by several writers the "nations" of Anatolia, northern Syria, and the Armenian highlands, and they were for the most part ethnically Turkish. The greater tribes were subdivided into as many as eight or nine clans. The most important of these include the Ustajlu, Rumlu, Shamlu, Takkalu, Dhulqadr, Afshar, and Qajar; others such as the Warsaq and Baharlu are occasionally listed among the great tribes.[36]

---

33 Bashir, *The Origins and Rhetorical Evolution*, 368.
34 See for example Sadr al-Din Ibrahim Amini Hirawi (d. 1535), *Futuhat-i Shahi*, ed. M.R. Nasiri (Tehran: Anjuman-i Athar wa Mafakhir-i Farhangi, 2004); Qasimi Husayni Gunabadi, *Shah Ismail-nama*, ed. J. Shuja Kayhani (Tehran: Farhangistan-i Zaban wa Adab-i Farsi, 2009).
35 Bashir, *The Origins and Rhetorical Evolution*, 369.
36 For a list of Qizilbash tribes, see Anon., *Tadhkirat al-Muluk: A Manual of Safavid Administration*, trans. V. Minorsky (Cambridge: Cambridge University Press, 1980), 16–17; Anon., *Tarikh-i Qizilbashan*, ed. M.H. Muhaddith (Tehran: Bihnam, 1982); and esp. Rıza Yıldırım, "Turkomans Between Two Empires: The Origins of the Qizilbash Identity in Anatolia (1447–1514)" (PhD diss., Bilkent University, Ankara, 2008), 284–5, where the Ekrad-ı Seyyid Mansur [*sic*] are mentioned among the Qizilbash tribes.

The Kurdish groups of the Qizilbash confederacy are generally said to have belonged to three tribes, the Arabgirlu, the Chamishgazaklu, and the Yigirmi-dört. Kurdish representatives of the Ispir tribe were, however, also frequently encountered on Kurdish soil.[37] The issue of identifying the Khinislu as a Kurdish tribe of the Qizilbash, which arises in a number of different contexts, can be discussed only within the realm of historical conjecture. It is important to note that the Khinislu were a tribe from northern Kurdistan that is repeatedly mentioned among the Qizilbash tribes.[38] The primary area of control of the Kurdish emir of Khinis was the Khinis plain (Dohuk region), inhabited interestingly by a certain "Khinislu" community. But the emir's territory always extended south of the Murat Su as well.[39] Posch provides substantial evidence that the Khinislu belonged to the Ustajlu. Nevertheless, their affiliation remains unclear and their Kurdish ancestry is occasionally questioned.[40]

In order to find more information on the Qizilbash Kurdish tribes, we may ask questions such as: What is their origin? What is their history there? Were they the original inhabitants of the country, or did they succeed other, no longer extant, ethnic groups? However interesting such questions may be, they are unlikely to find a definitive answer. The history of Kurdish tribes during the early Safavid period is, at best, very uncertain, and very little is known of the Kurdish tribes of the Qizilbash.

The Arabgirlu

As the adjective Arabgirlu indicates, the tribe's name refers to the Arabkir/Arabgir region which, according to Idris-i Bidlisi and his son Ebu'l-Fazl Efendi, was the western-most district of Kurdistan.[41] The district lies on the slopes of a valley running north-eastwards towards a tributary of the Upper Euphrates, the Angu Çay/Arabkir Çay, where the inhabitants' attitude towards Safavids' official doctrines was very

---

37 For Ispir as a Kurdish *liva* of Erzurum, see BOA: Kamil Kepeci [KK] 248:3 and KK 240:56 (dated Cemazi I 994/May 1586). For Ispirlu as a Qizilbash tribe, see Sümer, *Safevi Devletinin Kuruluşu*, 107–9.

38 See Anon., *Tadhkirat al-Muluk: A Manual of Safavid Administration*, 14, n. 3; Qummi, *Khulasat al-Tawarikh*, 1:63; Anon., *Tarikh-i Qizilbashan*, 25.

39 BOA: Tahrir (Defter-i Hâkânî) Defteri [TD] 189:36; TD 294:6–8; and Katib Çelebi, *Cihannümâ*, 416:425.

40 Posch, *Osmanisch-safavidische Beziehungen*, 189.

41 Ebu'l-Fazl ibn Idris (d. 1574), *Zeyl-i Heşt Behişt (Salim-nâma)*, Ms. AEfrs 810, Millet Kütüphanesi, Istanbul, fol. 30v., fol. 32r.

friendly.[42] According to the *Tarikh-i Qizilbashan*, the Arabgirlu tribe was from the Arabgir district, which belonged to Chamishgazak.[43] The Arabgirlu are recorded by Sharaf Khan as an "Iranian" Kurdish tribe, by which he means those tribes which were in the service of the Safavids and subscribed to Qizilbash doctrines.[44]

Without reference to the ethnic origin of the tribe, John E. Woods points out that "rising to prominence under the Safavids as a part of the major Shamlu Qizilbash confederate clan, the Arabgirlu of central Anatolia saw limited service with the Aqquyunlu in the second half of the fifteenth century."[45] This integration took place when Shah Abbas sent them to Khorasan to defend the Safavid borders against the Uzbeks. Settled in the Safavid-Uzbek frontier, the Arabgirlu tribe incorporated itself into the most prestigious tribe of the region, the Shamlu-Qizilbash confederation, which had migrated from Damascus, Aleppo, and northern Syria in the first years of Shah Ismail.[46] In addition to Sharaf Khan's statements, another clear reference to the Kurdishness of the tribe can be traced in *Tarikh-i Alamara-yi Abbasi*. In his chronicle, Iskandar Bey Turkoman underscores that Haqverdi Sultan Arabgirlu was one of the most prominent Kurdish Qizilbash amirs of Azerbaijan.[47]

The Arabgirlu tribe almost always occupied a prominent place in the population of the Qizilbash confederacy. Living in the east of Anatolia, the Qizilbash Kurds of Arabgir had to execute their power vis-à-vis the Sunni Kurds in the area.[48]

The Chamishgazak(lu)

The Chamishgazak(lu) are named for a thinly populated district of Dersim southwest of Erzincan, situated in a valley sloping down to the Dagar Su.[49] According to Sharaf Khan, this was a well-fortified

---

42 On the historical background of Arabgir, see Vural Genç, *Kim Bu Mülke Kondu Bundan Ezeli: Arabgir Yerleşim, Nüfus, Toplumsal Hayat ve Ekonomi 1518–1847*, III (Istanbul: Kerem Aydınlar Vakfı, 2020).

43 Anon., *Tarikh-i Qizilbashan*, 49.

44 Scheref, *Scheref-nameh ou Histoire des Kourdes*, I:323; Anon., *Tarikh-i Qizilbashan*, 25.

45 John E. Woods, *The Aqquyunlu: Clan, Confederation, Empire* (Salt Lake City: The University of Utah Press, 1999), 185.

46 Anon., *Tarikh-i Qizilbashan*, 5.

47 Turkman, *Tarikh-i Alamara-yi Abbasi*, 2:1084.

48 Budaq Munshi Qazwini, *Jawahir al-Akhbar*, ed. M. Bahramnizhad (Tehran: Mirath Maktub, 2000), 237; Turkman, *Tarikh-i Alamara-yi Abbasi*, 2:1084.

49 Mehmet Ali Ünal, *XVI. Yüzyılda Çemişgezek Sancağı* (Ankara: Türk Tarih Kurumu, 1999), 4, 26, 54, 57–8.

Kurdish principality surrounded by thirty-two castles and consisting of sixteen *nahiyes*. Its vast territory was the reason Sharaf Khan states that the name Chamishgazak was a synonym for Kurdistan.[50] The same can also be said of Ebu-l-Fazl Efendi, who uses the term "Kurdistan-i Chamishgazak."[51]

Chamishgazak has received much scholarly attention on account of its Qizilbash tendencies. Due to their interest in Shiism, Sharaf Khan categorized the Chamishgazak as Qizilbash tribes by establishing their affiliation to Iran.[52] A modern study even claims the Chamishgazak as an *ithna-'ashari* (Twelver) Shiite community, and thus relates them to the ongoing controversy concerning the western Chamishgazaks of northern Kurdistan, for whom Shiism was simply a demonstration of "heresy," and the eastern Chamishgazaks of northern Khorasan who understood and accepted it in its religious meaning. The question remains unresolved as to how much religious continuity there was between the Chamishgazak tribe in Kurdistan and that of Khorasan (before their well-known immigration to Khorasan during the reign of Abbas I).[53]

There are no details on the Qizilbash tribes of Chamishgazak in the Safavid sources. In the Pertek chapter of the *Sharaf-nama*, the tribes of Chamishgazak are identified simply as "Chamishgazakiyan."[54] This is corroborated by Ottoman registers, according to which the principal tribes of Chamishgazak (some of which had Shiite leanings) were: Behramlu Ekrad, Disimlu Ekrad, Hasirlu Ekrad, Kızıl Mağaralu Ekrad, Zervereklu Ekrad, and Şeyh 'Ömerlu Ekrad.[55]

The Yigirmi-Dört

The Yigirmi-dört ("Twenty-Four") Kurdish tribe is a heterogeneous constellation of Kurdish groups brought together in a confederation sometime between the early sixteenth and the seventeenth century. The question of how and when this confederation was formed is something of a riddle, which arises mainly from the poor evidence we have.

---

50 Scheref, *Scheref-nameh ou Histoire des Kourdes*, 1:163.
51 Ebu'l-Fazl, *Zeyl-i Heşt Behişt*, fol. 25v.
52 Scheref, *Scheref-nameh ou Histoire des Kourdes*, 1:323.
53 For an authoritative discussion on this issue, see Kalim Allah Tawahudi, *Harikat-i Tarikhi-yi Kurd bi Khurasan dar Difa az Istiqlal-i Iran* (Mashhad: Wasi, 1980), 3:173.
54 Scheref, *Scheref-nameh ou Histoire des Kourdes*, 1:171.
55 TD 998, 169–71.

68 Mustafa Dehqan and Vural Genç

As Sümer indicates, what is certain is that the Yigirmi-dört were a Qizilbash tribe who helped Shah Ismail establish the Safavid state.[56] Surprisingly, Sümer does accept the Kurdish identity of the tribe. To be sure, this was a group of twenty-four clans in Qarabagh in the Caucasus.[57] Sharaf Khan categorized these clans as "Iranian Kurds," that is, the Shiite Kurdish tribes known both religiously and politically as Qizilbash.[58]

It is also possible to compare this tribe with the Otuz-iki ("Thirty-Two") Qizilbash tribe of the same area, first recorded in 1604 as followers of Abbas I, when they submitted to the latter's forces upon the Safavid recovery of the neighbouring region of Qarabagh from Ottoman occupation. The Yigirmi-dört were associated with, or were part of, the Qajar Qizilbash tribe of Qarabagh, while the Otuz-iki persisted in its association with the Jawanshir and Muqaddam tribes.[59] The Yigirmi-dört are also sometimes considered a Kurdish tribe.[60]

Most of the sources describe the Yigirmi-dört as a confederation starting in the period of Abbas I, rather than from the early Safavid period. There is no evidence of the involvement of their representatives in the establishment of the Safavid state, but according to the *Ahsan al-Tawarikh*, we may assume that the Sufis and Kurds of Qarabagh who helped Shah Ismail included the Yigirmi-dört as well.[61]

The Rise of Shah Ismail and Pro-Safavid Kurdish Emirs

Shah Ismail, the leader of the Safavid order whose newly-founded empire stretched from eastern Anatolia to Khorasan in the early sixteenth century, is a much studied and much romanticized figure in the history of

---

56 Sümer, *Safevi Devletinin Kuruluşu*, 188.
57 Abbas Quli Aqa Bakikhanuf, *Gulistan-i Iram*, ed. A. Alizada, Muhammad Aqa Sultanof, Muhammad Azarli, Ezhder Ali Asgharzada, and Fazel Babayef (Baku: Farhangistan-i Ulum-i Jumhuri-yi Shurawi-yi Susiyalisti-yi Azarbayjan, 1970), 106, 114; Turkman, *Tarikh-i Alamara-yi Abbasi*, 2:1025; Vladimir Minorsky, *Studies in Caucasian History* (London: Taylor's Foreign Press, 1953), 34n1.
58 Scheref, *Scheref-nameh ou Histoire des Kourdes*, 1:323.
59 Richard Tapper, *Frontier Nomads of Iran: A Political and Social History of the Shahsevan* (Cambridge: Cambridge University Press, 1997), 68.
60 Prince Sharaf al-Din Bitlisi, *The Sharafnama or the History of the Kurdish Nation-1597-Book One*, trans. Mehrdad Izady (California: Mazda Publishers, 2005), xx–xxi.
61 Falsafi, *Zindigani-yi Shah Abbas-i Awwal*, I:209. The name is preserved in the political geography of present Azerbaijan. There was a village called Iyirmidördler in the Agdam region, now occupied by Armenia. Another village called Otuzikiler is located in Imishli district of Azerbaijan. People of both villages spoke Kurdish until around 1930 but gradually assimilated into the Azeri Turkish community after Sovietization.

The Qizilbash Reconsidered   69

Iran. His brutal intimidation of enemies is almost as legendary as his military power. Shah Ismail's actual relationship with Kurdistan in the early sixteenth century was, contrary to modern mythology, limited. Indeed, Shah Ismail's Kurdish policy had two main aspects. The first was his well-known macabre policy against Sunni Kurds, whose scope has been wrongly understood as representing a Safavid plan of action against all Kurds.[62] The second was his policy towards Qizilbash Kurds.

Kurdistan did not fall into the hands of Shah Ismail as easily as other regions. This is perhaps the main reason why he chose to follow a harsh policy against Sunni Kurds. His imprisonment of Kurdish emirs (from Sunni principalities) was seen in the Kurdish chronicles of the time as a calamity.[63] When eleven Kurdish emirs presented themselves at Khoy to pay homage to the shah (c. 1510), he imprisoned most of them and appointed in their stead rulers chosen from among the Turkoman Qizilbash tribes. It is true that it was Khan Muhammad Ustajlu (and not the shah) who was behind this incident. Besides this personal affair, there was also a Kurdish-Turkoman rivalry for control over eastern Anatolia and the trade routes leading from Iran to Syria that passed through the region.[64]

Between the Kurdish Qizilbash chieftains and Shah Ismail, however, there was a religious affinity which in some cases was formed without political ties. Kurdish scholars have been conspicuously silent in chronicling this relationship, though a significant number of sources exist that give us reasonably clear insight into the nature of such Kurdo-Safavid contacts. For example, Chamishgazak was Shiitized to a greater extent than ever before in the country's history. The career of Hajji Rustam Beg of Chamishgazak bears witness to this fact. When Shah Ismail sent his general Nur Ali Khalifa against Chamishgazak, Hajji Rustam Beg gave up all his castles without any resistance. He went in person to the Safavid court where the shah received him in audience and made him the governor of a district in Iraq, in the region of Chamishgazak. According to Sharaf Khan, it is clear that Hajji Rustam Beg had a long-lasting desire to form an alliance with the Safavids. This is evidenced by the many warriors he used to fight on the Safavid side at Chaldiran.[65]

---

62 See Jafar Nuri and Firiydun Nuri, "Wakawi-yi Ruykard-i Shah Ismail I bi Shurish-i Umara wa Saran-i Kurd (907–30)," *Payam-i Baharistan* 13 (2011): 272–81.

63 Scheref, *Scheref-nameh ou Histoire des Kourdes*, 1:156.

64 Akihiko Yamaguchi, "Shah Tahmasp's Kurdish Policy," *Studia Iranica* 41 (2012): 101–32, esp. 106–7.

65 Scheref, *Scheref-nameh*, 1:164; Feridun Beg (d. 1583), *Münşe'âtü'l-Salâtīn* (Istanbul: Takvimhane, 1858), 1:353–4; Celâl-zâde Mustafa (ö. 1567), *Selim-nâme*, ed. A. Uğur and M. Çuhadar (Istanbul: Millî Eğitim Bakanlığı Yayınları, 1997), 613; Ünal, *XVI. Yüzyılda Çemişgezek Sancağı*, 15–16.

70 Mustafa Dehqan and Vural Genç

Hajji Rustam Beg was certainly not a supporter of peaceful coexistence with the Ottomans, though he was unable to reject the Ottoman victory over the Safavids. What was, however, Selim I's objective in murdering him (on 2 Rajab 920/1 September 1514)? It appears that Hajji Rustam Beg was realistic enough to understand the Ottomans' great superiority at the time, but Selim hated him because of his Kurdish Qizilbash activities and the role he played in Chaldiran and beyond. According to contemporary Ottoman documents, it is also clear that he spied on the Ottomans for Shah Ismail.[66]

Kurdish Officials at the Safavid Court: The Case of the Arabgirlu

In the first decade of the sixteenth century, it is reported that there were approximately 7,000 Qizilbash *murid*s (followers) of the Safavids in Anatolia, making up a very important part of the total military population of the Safavid state.[67] A significant presence of Kurdish Qizilbash *murid*s in Anatolia dates from the same decade, with the Arabgirlu Kurds regularly resident in the Arabgir district (in the Chamishgazak area) since 1501. The Arabgirlu tribe, which immigrated to Iran following the Shah's invitation, probably originated in both the city of Arabgir and its villages. Although we do not have any hard data in this regard, the first cadastral survey of Arabgir from 1518 mentions that thirty-one of fifty-seven villages, that is, more than half, were abandoned and desolate, indicating a great mass migration and dispersal. This suggests that the migration from Arabgir to Iran in the spring of 1500 may have been from these settlements.[68] If that is the case, we must accept that there might have been some Turkoman-Qizilbash groups among the Arabgirlu tribe. The fact that the Safavid chroniclers emphasize the Kurdish identity of the tribe may also indicate that the Turkomans among them were in the minority. It is reasonable to accept that the Qizilbash Kurdish tribe of Arabgirlu played a role in the establishment of the Safavid state and Shah Ismail's battle against the Aqquyunlu. But to what extent can it be legitimately argued that they were loyal supporters of Shah Ismail in the early history of his political movement? At this point, other sources must be introduced into the debate.

Some neglected primary sources mention the Arabgirlu Kurdish tribe supporting Shah Ismail in the battle of Chaldiran. They had 1,000

---

66 TSMA E.6672; E.11839.
67 See Sümer, *Safevi Devletinin Kuruluşu*, 18–20.
68 Genç, *Kim Bu Mülke Kondu*, 1:36–7.

The Qizilbash Reconsidered   71

soldiers in the Safavid army at Chaldiran.[69] It is important to mention that Arabgirlu officials were not only secondary Qizilbash officials, but important chieftains on their own part, who participated fully in the military elite of the Safavids at the time of Shah Ismail. 'Abd al-Karim Agha-yi Arabgirlu is a case in point; not only was he the main chieftain of the Arabgirlu tribe, he was also one of the two Safavid commanders during the campaign of Shah Ismail in Mazandaran in 1504.[70] Another Arabgirlu official at the court of Shah Ismail, known as Mihtar Shah Quli-yi Arabgirlu, is found in the Safavid sources, but no detail is given and the historical context places him at a later date than Abd al-Karim Agha. The only historical detail of his role in the Safavid court that can be ascertained is that he was the senior royal horse keeper of Shah Ismail.[71]

Stronger evidence regarding the role played by the Arabgirlu Kurdish tribe in the Safavid court may be derived from the assignment of Arabgirlu chieftains to important bureaucratic and military positions at the court of Tahmasp I. A particularly notable example is Khalil Sultan Arabgirlu, who was Tahmasp I's representative in the struggles between Sharaf Khan I, the Kurdish emir of Bidlis, and Ulama Sultan Takkalu, in 1532–4.[72] Besides the bureaucratic position held by Khalil Sultan during the reign of Tahmasp, it should also be mentioned that Qara Wali Arabgirlu, a Qizilbash military commander, worked to crush the revolt of Hajji Shaykh Kurd in 1541.[73]

We also know the names of at least some of the Arabgirlu chieftains from the period of Tahmasp I. In 1553, we hear of Kamal al-Din Ulugh Beg Arabgirlu serving as an envoy from Tahmasp I to Humayun Shah,

---

69 Talikîzâde Mehmed (d. 1606?), Şâhnâme-i Âl-i Osman, Topkapı Sarayı Müzesi Kütüphanesi, Istanbul [TSMK], III. Ahmed Kitaplığı, Ms. 3592, fols. 87r.–87v.; Haydar Çelebi, *Haydar Çelebi Ruznâmesi*, ed. Y. Senemoğlu (Istanbul: Tercüman, 1976), 30–1.

70 Hirawi, *Futuhat-i Shahi*, 227.

71 Abd al-Hussayn Nawai, *Rijal-i Kitab-i Habib al-Siyar* (Tehran: Anjuman-i Athar wa Mafakhir-i Farhangi, 2000), 258–9; Vural Genç, "From Tabriz to Istanbul: Goods and Treasures of Shah Ismail Looted after the Battle of Chaldiran," *Studia Iranica* 44 (2015): 227–76, esp. 253.

72 Şem'î, *Terceme-i Tevârîh-i Şeref Han*, ed. Adnan Oktay (Istanbul: Nubihar, 2016), 255. For details on the political struggles between Sharaf Khan I and Ulama Sultan, see TSMA E.4080; BOA: Bâb-ı Âlî Sadâret Evrâkı, Mektûbî Kalemi [A.MKT] 1/10; KK 1764:126; J.L. Bacqué-Grammont, "Quinze letteres d'Uzun Süleymân Paşa, beylerbey du Diyar Bekir (1533–1534)," *Anatolia Moderna* 1 (1991): 137–86, esp. 143–8.

73 Hasan Rumlu (d. 1577), *Ahsanu't-Tawarikh: A Chronicle of the Early Safavids*, ed. C.N. Seddon (Baroda: The Gaekwad Series, 1931–4), 1:296.

the Mughal sultan of India.[74] Hilhil Bahadur Arabgirlu, whose activities during the Iran campaign of Süleyman I procured some victories to the Safavid armies, was of the Arabgirlu Kurds.[75] He was also in the personal service of Sam Mirza.[76] Mention should also be made of Mahmud Agha-yi Arabgirlu, the chief of Tahmasp I's hunters, who had previously been the *ishik aghasi bashi* (master of ceremony) of the Shah, in 1533.[77] And it appears that the office was taken over from Mahmud Agha-yi Arabgirlu by Avjishan Arabgirlu.[78]

Although the presence of Arabgirlu officials at the Safavid court continued in later years, the situation under Ismail II's rule was relatively quiet. It is certain that there were contacts between the Arabgirlu Kurdish tribe and the Shah at this time, but we only see Hasan Beg Halwachi Ughlu-yi Arabgirlu as an official at the court of Ismail II in 1577.[79]

The Arabgirlu connection to the Safavid court, however, was not about to disappear. Abbas I masterfully used more Arabgirlu chieftains to balance the power of the Turkic Qizilbash officials. One of these may have been Husayn Khan Beg Shindaki Arabgirlu, who was a senior military commander and the *qurchi bashi* (head of royal guards) of Abbas I. He played a role in the revolt of Malik Jihangir as the Safavid military commander and in the incursions against the Georgians in 1615.[80]

Another Arabgirlu chieftain who has been widely cited is Muhammad Quli Beg Arabgirlu. In 1596 we hear of Muhammad Quli Beg as Abbas I's envoy to the Uzbek ʿAbd Allah Khan;[81] two years later, he was chosen as the Safavid envoy to the Ottoman court.[82] It is certain that Muhammad Quli Beg returned to Iran, probably around 1600, as Abbas I appointed him commander of the Safavid frontier garrison in

---

74 Colin Mitchell, "The Sword and the Pen: Diplomacy in Early Safavid Iran, 1501–1555" (PhD diss., University of Toronto, 2002), 312, 335.

75 Shah Tahmasb (d. 1576), *Tadhkira-yi Shah Tahmasb: Sharh-i Waqayi wa Ahwalat-i Zindagani-yi Shah Tahmasb-i Safawi bi Qalam-i Khudash*, ed. And al-Shukur (Berlin: Kaviani, 1922), 40.

76 Martin Dickson, "Shah Tahmasb and the Uzbeks" (PhD diss., Princeton University, 1958), 76.

77 Sümer, *Safevi Devletinin Kuruluşu ve Gelişmesinde Anadolu Türklerinin Rolü*, 104.

78 Qummi, *Khulasat al-Tawarikh*, 223.

79 Turkman, *Tarikh-i Alamara-yi Abbasi*, 218.

80 Turkman, 688.

81 Turkman, 444, 457; Fazli Beg Khuzani Isfahani, *A Chronicle of the Reign of Shah ʿAbbas (Afzal al-Tawarikh)*, ed. Kioumars Ghereghlou (Cambridge: Gibb Memorial Trust, 2015), 228.

82 Khuzani Isfahani, *Afzal al-Tawarikh*, 279; Selânikî, *Tarih-i Selânikî* (971–1003/1563–95), 814–15.

The Qizilbash Reconsidered 73

the castle of Andkhud, in Transoxiana, in 1602.[83] Among the Arabgirlu officials with similar responsibilities was Khan Ahmad Beg Arabgirlu, who was the commander of the castle of Lar, in southern Iran (1601).[84] Some of the Arabgirlu chieftains employed by Abbas I remained inside the scope of interest of his successors. One example is Isfandiyar Beg Arabgirlu, who was the chief hunter of Abbas I. He was a very close (*muqarrab*) official to the Shah, and besides his several meetings with Abbas I, he was also the Safavid envoy to Shirwan and Georgia in 1614–15.[85]

Isfandiyar Beg died in 1623. The important role he played at the court of Abbas I, as a very close person to him, was to have a major influence on what happened to other Arabgirlu officials at the time. Kamal Beg Arabgirlu and Murtada Quli Beg Arabgirlu, the sons of Isfandiyar Beg, enjoyed the strong support of Abbas; the former was appointed as the successor of Isfandiyar Beg.[86] It was possibly under the influence of Isfandiyar Beg that his brother, Ismail Beg Arabgirlu, was appointed by Abbas I as *binbashi* military commander.[87]

In addition to those already mentioned, a number of other, secondary Arabgirlu chirftains with more limited roles at the Safavid court are known from history: Husayn Ali Beg Arabgirlu, Ali Quli Beg Arabgirlu, Haqqvirdi Sultan Arabgirlu, and Yahya Beg Arabgirlu.[88] Members of the Arabgirlu Qizilbash tribe continued to serve the Safavid shahs in both the army and palace bureaucracy for more than two centuries, from 1504 until the collapse of the Safavids. Safavid chronicles are in agreement that the members of the Arabgirlu tribe occupied some preeminent offices in the palace (*ilchi, rikabdar, wazir-i qurchiyan-i khassa, ishik aghasi bashi*, and *avji bashi*) which were (often) handed down from father to son. Thanks to these offices, they also had the privilege of being close to the Safavid shahs.

Conclusion

The Qizilbash were the most influential group who shaped the policy of the Safavid era. There were many who criticized them in their

---

83 Isfahani, 319.
84 Isfahani, 310.
85 Isfahani, 644, 677–9.
86 Isfahani, 876.
87 Isfahani, 685.
88 Turkman, *Tarikh-i Alamara-yi Abbasi*, 164, 1084; Mulla Jalal al-Din Munajjim, *Tarikh-i Abbasi ya Ruznama-i Mulla Jalal*, ed. Sayf Allah Vahidnia (Tehran: Intisharat-i Vahid, 1987), 401–5.

capacity as one of the most powerful groups in the Safavid movement. They played a decisive role in the practice of both religion and politics. Whatever they thought and whatever they did, they drew the attention of both early chroniclers and modern historians. Starting in the 1580s, information about the Qizilbash spread throughout Europe, through travelogues and the development of scholarship on the Safavid state to wider debates in the representation of the Safavid shahs and their concepts. A major concern in these fields, especially in modern studies, was the national view that posited a solely Turkish identity of the Qizilbash tribes. Close study of the evidence considered in this paper, however, proves that this sentiment is not well founded. While Turkish tribes were probably dominant in the Qizilbash community in terms of percentages, the significance of the Kurdish part of the Qizilbash should not be overlooked.

The aim of this paper has been to provide an overview of the roles and positions of Kurdish Qizilbashes at the beginning of the Safavid venture. A central argument was that Safavid studies have tended to marginalize the role played by Kurdish tribes in the establishment of the Safavid state by relegating it to the domain of "Turkish studies." The evidence of Kurdish Qizilbash individuals' fame and influence in the early Safavid state as presented in this paper draws attention to the many overlooked Kurdish elements in this context.[89]

---

89 The authors express their most sincere gratitude to Nikolay Antov, Ufuk Erol, and Amelia Gallagher for their comments and advice. They also wish to thank Rıza Yıldırım, Rudi Matthee, and Georgio Rota, without whose support and help this study could not have been produced. We remain responsible for the faults and deficiencies of this chapter.

3 The ʿAfrin District under Ottoman Rule, 1516–1921

STEFAN WINTER

The modern-day ʿAfrin District (Mintaqat ʿAfrin) in the northwestern corner of Aleppo province is among the oldest areas of Kurdish settlement in Syria. Named for the ʿAfrin River (the Aprê or Oinoparas of antiquity), and for the town of ʿAfrin established as an administrative centre under the French Mandate in the 1920s, the district encompasses the southern portion of the medium-altitude inland massif colloquially known as the "Kurd Dagh" (from Turkish Kürd Dağı; "Mountain of the Kurds") or Çiyayê Kurmenc, and formally associated with a Kurdish tribal population since at least the region's incorporation into the Ottoman Empire in the early sixteenth century. The object of this chapter is to trace the political-administrative history of the ʿAfrin district from this period through the early twentieth century on the basis of Ottoman archival records, and show that the Ottoman government consistently recognized and sought to extend the local Kurdish population a degree of autonomy as such.

The study draws on central government sources (principally Tahrir tax cadastres, Mühimme executive decrees, and Şikayet complaints registers), as well as on provincial *shar ʿiyya* court records from Aleppo, Antioch, and Hama that provide clues on the fiscal organization, local leaderships, brigandage, and police measures in the district throughout the period of Ottoman rule. The first part reviews its official incorporation, in the sixteenth century, as the "province of the Kurds" (liva-ı Ekrad), and attribution, along with the governorship of Aʿzaz or Kilis, to the Kurdish Canpolad family. Following the end of the rebellion of ʿAli Canpolad in 1607, however, these sources suggest that local authority was left largely in the hands of the Oqçî-Izzeddînlo and Qilîçlî confederations, the former likely derived from an originally Yezidi rival to the Canpolads, and the latter for a while constituting a key private fiscal reserve of the Ottoman court in Istanbul. The study concludes

76   Stefan Winter

with an examination of attempts to reassert more centralized control over the region in the Tanzimat and Hamidian periods, suggesting that the Ottoman government nevertheless continued actively to cultivate local Kurdish notables as state intermediaries in the district.

The Province of the Kurds

Following the annihilation of the Mamluk army in Syria on 24 August 1516 (on the plain of Dabiq just 45 km due east of modern-day 'Afrin), the city of Aleppo and its hinterland were initially maintained as a regional governorate (Mamluk *niyaba*; Ottoman *eyalet*) and placed under the authority of Karaca Ahmed Paşa, one of sultan Selim's leading generals on the campaign. According to the Ottoman court official and historian Feridun Ahmed Bey, "the Turkoman and Kurdish *beys* in the environs of Aleppo were granted [their] localities in charity" by Selim in late August.[1] With the conclusion of the overall war against the Mamluks in the summer of 1517, however, all the new conquests in the area, including Aleppo, 'Ayntab, Malatya, and Birecik, were reorganized as standard military provinces (*sancak*) and incorporated into a single "governorship of Arabia" (*vilayet-i Arabistan*) or *eyalet* of Damascus, under the ex-Mamluk viceroy Canberdi al-Ghazali, until his revolt against Ottoman rule in 1520 and defeat at the hands of a new military campaign to Syria in 1522.[2]

The earliest trace of Aleppo's actual integration into the provincial administrative system dates from 1518, when the Ottomans carried out the first of several tax censuses (*tahrir*) in the area. In this census, a large part of the local Kurdish population is reckoned as belonging to four distinct tribal confederations or tax divisions, the most important one of which appears under the heading of "Kurdish groups attached to 'Izzeddin Bey, emir of the Kurds" (*Tavaif-i Ekrad tabi-i İzzeddin Bey mir-i Ekrad*). The other divisions are identified as the "Alikanlu [Kurdish: Xelîkanlo] group, also known as the Halil-Beylu," likewise under the overall authority (*tabi-i*) of 'Izzeddin Bey; the "Çobi group, also known as the Eşkal"; and the Süleymaniye. Together, these divisions encompassed a total of seventy-three "tribes" (sing. *cemaat*), the vast majority of which are simply identified by the name of an individual leader (shaykh or *kethüda*), and many of which are noted as being based in a

---

1 Feridun Ahmed Bey (d. 1583), *Mecmua-ı Münşeatü's-Selatin* (Istanbul: N.p., 1848), 1:428.
2 Enver Çakar, "XVI. Yüzyılda Şam Beylerbeyiliğinin İdarî Taksimatı," *Fırat Üniversitesi Sosyal Bilimler Dergisi* 13 (2003): 354–8.

The 'Afrin District under Ottoman Rule, 1516–1921   77

particular village or in the Kurdish Quarter (Mahalle-i Ekrad) of Aleppo. Larger tribal divisions, that is, ones that carry an abstract collective name (ending in *–iyya* in Arabic or *–lu* in Turkish) and that are wholly or partially represented in the region, include the Mûsa-Beylo Kurds, the Kılıçlı (Qilîçlo; see below), and sections of the Millî confederation.[3]

'Izzeddîn Bey, according to the sixteenth-century Aleppine historian Muhammad Ibn al-Hanbali, was a scion of a local Yezidi dynasty, the Mend, who had already served the Mamluks as "emir of the Kurds" in the region before basically being reinvested in the same position by Karaca Ahmed Paşa upon the Ottoman conquest in 1516. Cunning and deceitful, 'Izzeddin managed to arrange for the execution of his rival from the other great Kurdish lineage in the area, the Ibn 'Arabo (Canpolad) family, and continued to serve the Ottomans as a government intermediary with the local Kurds until his death in 1541–2.[4] After that, the Ibn 'Arabos were able to reimpose themselves as the dominant Kurdish leadership. Again according to Ibn al-Hanbali, Canpolad Bey ibn Qasim, the head of the Ibn 'Arabo clan, in fact married the widow of 'Izzeddin Bey, "the enemy of his father," and took over (*tamakanna*) not only his houses in Kilis and Aleppo, but also his faction of supporters among the Yezidi community.[5] Canpolad and his heirs would of course go on to occupy the *sancak* governorship of Kilis (and of other districts such as Balis and Jabala) for many years and finally even the provincial governorship of Aleppo, before 'Ali Paşa Canpolad's ill-fated participation in the Celali revolts and execution in 1611.[6] Interestingly, it is

---

3 T.C. Cumhurbaşkanlığı Devlet Arşivi (ex-Başbakanlık [BOA]), Istanbul: Tahrir Defteri [TD] 93:695–732. See also Coll., *397 Numaralı Haleb Livâsı Mufassal Tahrîr Defteri (943/1536)*, vol. 1 (Ankara: T.C. Başbakanlık Devlet Arşivleri Genel Müdürlüğü, 2010), 40–2; Mustafa Öztürk, *16. Yüzyılda Kilis Urfa Adıyaman ve Çevresinde Cemaatlar/Oymaklar* (Ankara: Berivan Yayınevi, 2018), 29–46. On the reckoning of the Turkman population in the same region see Enver Çakar, "Les Turkmènes d'Alep à l'époque ottomane (1516–1700)," in *Aleppo and its Hinterland in the Ottoman Period / Alep et sa province à l'époque ottomane*, ed. Stefan Winter and Mafalda Ade (Leiden: Brill, 2019), 1–27.

4 Muhammad ibn Ibrahim Ibn al-Hanbali (d. 1563), *Durr al-Habab fi Tarikh A 'yan Halab*, ed. Mahmud al-Fakhuri and Yahya 'Abbara (Damascus: Wizarat al-Thaqafa, 1972), 1:ii, 890–3.

5 Ibn al-Hanbali, 1:ii, 437–41. See also Charles Wilkins, "Ottoman Elite Recruitment and the Case of Janbulad Bek b. Qasim," in *The Mamluk Ottoman Transition: Continuity and Change in Egypt and Bilad al-Sham in the Sixteenth Century*, ed. Stephan Conermann and Gül Şen (Göttingen: V&R Unipress/Bonn University Press, 2022), 2:155–80.

6 See Şenol Çelik, "XVI. Yüzyılda Hanedan Kurucu Bir Osmanlı Sancakbeyi: Canbulad Bey," *Türk Kültürü İncelemeleri Dergisi* 7 (Fall 2002): 1–34; Wilkins, "Ottoman Elite Recruitment."

78   Stefan Winter

the Canpolads, not the 'Izzeddins, whom the famous Kurdish historian Şerefxan Bidlisi (d. 1603) connects with the legendary Mend dynasty.[7] Despite the fact that the Canpolads were never subsequently identified with Yezidism, it appears that some sort of filiation through 'Izzeddîn Bey remained critical to legitimizing their rule over the Kurdish populations in the region.

What is perhaps most significant about 'Izzeddîn Bey is not only that he was of the Yezidi religion, which was severely proscribed by the Ottoman state, but that the "İzzeddin Bey Kurds" continued to constitute a fundamental administrative and fiscal unit in the area even years after his death. In 1536, a portion of the İzzeddin Bey Kurds was attached to the newly-created *liva* of A'zaz (later Kilis), as suggested in the detailed (*mufassal*) provincial census TD 181; in 1552, a series of summary (*icmal*) registers covering crown domains (*hasha-ı padişah*) in both the provinces of Kilis and Aleppo still list a number of the area's Kurds under the rubric "Tavaif-i Ekrad-ı İzzeddin Bey."[8] The term continues to be used in TD 493, a *mufassal* tax census for the *liva* of Aleppo in 1570, though no longer as an independent tax category but as the affiliation (*tabi-i*) of a number of groups in the area. The same information was carried over without change into the sixth and final Aleppo *tahrir* TD 610 in 1584.[9] 'Izzeddin Bey himself last appears to be mentioned in the prologue to a prebend (*timar*) register for the "Liva-ı Ekrad-ı İzzeddin" in 1587–8, where the new incumbent is under strict instructions to collect the requisite taxes, defend the province's poor against oppression, and "keep the Kurdish tribes [*aşayir*] under control." Interestingly, 'Izzeddin's name in this instance is followed not by his normal title of Bey, but with the somewhat ominous invocation "may God on High preserve him from ruin [*fesad*] on Judgement Day," likely an insinuation regarding his Yezidi identity.[10]

---

7   See Chèref-ou'ddine, *Chèref-Nâmeh, ou Fastes de la Nation Kourde*, trans. and ed. François Bernard Charmoy (St. Petersburg: Académie impériale des sciences, 1873), 66–77.

8   BOA: TD 181:90; TD 280:365–8, TD 378, TD 391. A number of İzzeddin Bey groups, according to a 1540 tax code (*kanunname*) for the Boz Ulus Turkmen confederation, had also migrated to the *vilayet* of Diyarbekir, where they subsequently owed their taxes. See Ömer Lutfi Barkan, *XV ve XVIıncı Asırlarda Osmanlı İmparatorluğunda Ziraî Eknominin Hukukî ve Malî Esasları* (Istanbul: İstanbul Üniversitesi İktisat Fakültesi Yayınları, 2001), 144. On other branches of the İzzeddin Bey Kurds settled elsewhere (especially in Birecik), see Yusuf Halaçoğlu, *Anadolu'da Aşiretler, Cemaatler, Oymaklar (1453–1650)* (Istanbul: Togan Yayıncılık, 2011), 3:1154–5.

9   TD 493; TD 610; see also *397 Numaralı Haleb Livâsı Mufassal Tahrîr Defteri*, 1:8–9.

10 Ömer Lutfi Barkan (d. 1979), "Türkiye'de imparatorluk devirlerinin nüfus ve arazi tahrirleri ve Hâkana mahsus istatistik defterleri (II)," *İstanbul Üniversitesi İktisat Fakültesi Mecmuası* 2 (1940): 229.

The 'Afrin District under Ottoman Rule, 1516–1921   79

Whatever the case may be, the regional importance of the İzzeddin Bey Kurds, whether counted as tribes or groups (*cemaat; taife*) or attributed to specific localities, continued to be reflected in the naming of the province of Kilis. Whereas the towns of A'zaz and Kilis originally composed a single sub-district (*nahiye*) of the province of Aleppo, the new *liva* they formed in 1536 is alternately, apparently haphazardly, referred to in contemporary sources as the Liva-ı Azaz (with Kilis, or "Kiliz" in an older spelling, constituting one of its main centres), the Liva-ı Ekrad ve Azaz (province of the Kurds and A'zaz), Liva-ı Ekrad ve Kilis (province of the Kurds and Kilis), Liva-ı Ekrad-ı Kilis (province of the Kurds of Kilis), Liva-ı Kilis "*nam-ı diğer*" (also known as) Liva-ı Ekrad, or just Liva-ı Ekrad, viz. Ekrad Sancağı, with A'zaz generally constituting a simple *nahiye* within the *liva* (figure 3.1).[11] A revised tax register composed in 1590 at the behest of Husayn ibn Canpolad identifies the province as the Liva-ı Ekrad-ı İzzeddin (province of the Kurds of İzzeddin), but this formulation does not appear elsewhere.[12] The province was later reincorporated into the *eyalet* (regional governorate) of Aleppo, and was still known as the Sancağ-ı Ekrad-ı Kilis by the time of Evliya Çelebi's travels through the region around 1648.[13] The name seems largely to have disappeared by the eighteenth century, when the province of A'zaz/Kilis, as will be seen further on, was more commonly administered as a large tax farm (*mukataa*) rather than as a unit of the classical provincial military hierarchy.

In addition to a number of Kurdish groups already mentioned in the previous Aleppo registers,[14] the Liva-ı Ekrad ve Azaz as formed in 1536 also encompassed a vast Kurdish tribal population that was not necessarily tied to the province territorially. Thus TD 181, a detailed (*mufassal*) tax register containing the original tax code (*kanunname*) for the province, lists only two actual *nahiyes*, A'zaz and Cum (see below), but also thirty-five major populations (*taife*), including sections of the Saçlo, Mûsâ-Beylo, Millî, Reşî, and Reşwan confederations, all of which are either explicitly identified as Kurdish or are known as such from other sources. These thirty-five *taife*s comprise a sum total of 316 individual

---

11 Not to be confused with the *sancak* of Klis (Hersek Kilisi; Kliški) in Dalmatia (Croatia).

12 İbrahim Hakkı Konyalı (d. 1984), *Abideleri ve Kitabeleriyle Kilis Tarihi* (Istanbul: Fatih Matbaası,1968), 145–6.

13 Evliyâ Çelebi ibn Derviş Mehemmed Zıllî (d. 1682), *Evliyâ Çelebi Seyahatnâmesi*, ed. Yücel Dağlı, Seyit Ali Kahraman, and Robert Dankoff (Istanbul: Yapı Kredi Yayınları, 2005), 9:180; see also Öztürk, *16. Yüzyılda*, 21–3.

14 *397 Numaralı Haleb Livâsı Mufassal Tahrîr Defteri*, 1:40–6.

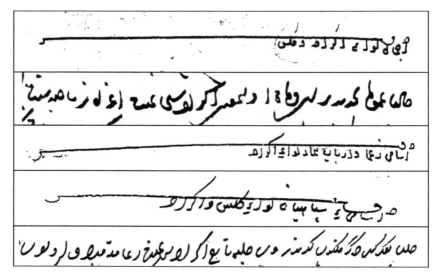

Figure 3.1. Variant designations of the Liva-ı Ekrad, sixteenth–seventeenth century

tribes (*cemaat*; *oymak*), generally named for their *kethüda*, of which the majority are noted to be resident not in the *liva* but attached to other provinces throughout the region, principally Hama, Urfa, Adana, Malatya, Birecik, Hısn-ı Mansur, Gerger, and Kahta.[15] While a full demographic tabulation of these tribes (along the lines of the very numerous studies on the Turkomans of Aleppo we dispose of) is not within the purview of the present article, the material from TD 181 makes clear that the Liva-ı Ekrad ve Azaz was in fact among the key institutions, if not the key institution, of the Ottoman Empire's government of the Kurds in the early modern period.

The autonomous character of the province of the Kurds in the first century of Ottoman rule is also underlined by the fact that it was considered to constitute its own judicial district or *kaza* (Arabic *qaḍā'*). As Mustafa Öztürk has rightly stated, it was not unusual for the Ottomans to confer on larger tribal confederations the status of a *kaza*,[16]

---

15 TD 181:73–223.
16 Mustafa Öztürk, "İzziye Kazasının Kuruluşu ve Milli Mücadeledeki Yeri," *Tarih Araştırmaları Dergisi* 24 (2005): 30–3, https://doi.org/10.1501/Tarar_0000000208.

The 'Afrin District under Ottoman Rule, 1516–1921   81

and to designate a judge to live and even travel with them if they were itinerant. Later examples from the region include *kadıs* appointed to the Lek (Lekwan) Kurds, the Boz Ulus Turkmen, and the Reşwan Kurds.[17] A judge assigned specifically to the İzzeddin Kurds is mentioned at least as early as March 1572, after he and other local *kadıs* wrote to the Sublime Porte to report that members of the Oqçî-Izzeddînlo division in Maraş were refusing to provide campaign contributions, and had instead attacked and robbed villages and merchants in the area.[18] Similarly, an order from January 1577 instructs the *"kadı* of the Kurds" (*Ekrad kadısı*) as well as the governor of Kilis-A'zaz to follow up complaints about some Yezidis waylaying and robbing travellers on the road between Aleppo and 'Ayntab.[19] In the spring of the following year, the İzzeddin *kadı* was ordered to join his counterparts from Kilis city and from Sivas to repress acts of brigandage that had been committed by the Reşî and other groups "resident in the *kaza* of the Kurds"; a few weeks later, the same official was instructed to find and recapture several convicts whom a gang of Kurds had managed to liberate from the grasp of a local village captain (*subaşı*).[20]

Numerous additional documents point to the challenges of integrating and ruling the tribal hinterland of Kilis in the sixteenth century. In 1566, for example, Canpolad Bey, the governor of Kilis at the time, was warned that "some of the Kurds attached to your province" were engaging in "vice and corruption" and had fled to Diyarbekir, where he was to send soldiers to help capture them; a couple of local Kurdish shaykhs characterized as "thieves and criminals," meanwhile, were to be deported to Rhodes.[21] The Canpolads were of course frequently also called upon to organize Kurdish auxiliary forces in the province to contribute to imperial military ventures. Another time, in the fall of 1577, a different *sancak* governor of Kilis was told to "get his hands on" two Kurdish individuals who were leading something of a tax revolt in the province. A year later, however, in the fall of 1578, the Sublime Porte sent orders to the governor of Sayda and Beirut, asking for the release of some Kurds from the galleys who had previously been accused by Canpolad's son Ja'far Bey and the *Ekrad kadısı* of hindering the collection of war material for a campaign to Basra.[22]

---

17 BOA: Şikayet Defterleri [ŞKT] 4:122:508, 509; ŞKT 14:4:15; ŞKT 23:157:725; ŞKT 24:23:71; ŞKT 41:257:1136; ŞKT 55:265, no. 2; ŞKT 60:334, no. 1; ŞKT 104:136a, nos. 3, 4.
18 BOA: Mühimme Defteri [MD] 16:280–1:535.
19 MD 29:85:205; MD 31:257:568.
20 MD 33:374:770; MD 34:85:192; Öztürk, *16. Yüzyılda*, 23–4.
21 MD 5:403:1067; MD 5:521:1426.
22 BOA: Mühimme Defterleri Zeyleri [MZ] 3:289:728; MD 31:384:853; MD 35:249:626.

82   Stefan Winter

In modern Turkish historiography it has become commonplace to note that the term "Ekrad" as used in Ottoman documents only signified a pastoral or tribal population and not a "Kurdish" ethnic identity per se – so as to imply (and sometimes to claim outright) that such groups were essentially really of Turkish origin. Beyond the fact that Arabic sources had already been using the words *Kurd* or *Akrad* in the plural to designate the Kurdish-speaking populations in these same regions for centuries, however, and that imperial bureaucrats did, in a handful of instances, label certain groups as "Kurdish Turkomans" (Türkman-ı Ekrad) or "Turkish Kurds" (Ekrad-ı Türkman), when they were unsure as to their affiliations, our sources suggest that the Ottomans were perfectly willing and able to differentiate precisely between the Kurdish and the equally numerous Turkic-speaking tribal elements in the *eyalet* of Aleppo. The very care with which the state authorities sought to incorporate a distinct military-administrative unit for the Kurds around Kilis, on the basis of well-established Mamluk precedents and initially indeed with Mamluk-era personnel, indicates the Ottomans had every benefit in correctly sizing up, categorizing, and governing one of the region's key rural populations as such.

The *Nahiye* of Cum

If the *"liva* of the Kurds" originally appears to have been constituted around tribal groups associated with ʿIzzeddin Bey, the region's village population was also, and increasingly, governed on a territorial basis within the framework of the Empire's classical provincial administration. In the sixteenth-century Ottoman *tahrir* records, the Kurdish population in the area regarded as the "Kurd Dagh" was concentrated in four *nahiye*s or provincial sub-districts extending along or near the course of the ʿAfrin River: Ravendan, Cum, Amık, and Derbisak. Of these, Cum was by far the most important, forming the heart of the province of Aʿzaz-Kilis after 1536, and lending its name to the "Cum Kurds" as a corporate fiscal entity in the seventeenth century.

The *nahiye* of Ravendan, which was named for the medieval Kurdish castle of Ravendan (figure 3.2),[23] near the source of the ʿAfrin River and approximately eighteen kilometres north-northwest of Kilis,

---

23 Likely derived from "Rawand," that is, the Rawwadid tribe from which Salah al-Din and the Ayyubid dynasty originated. See also Ahmad Mahmud Khalil, *Siyaha fi Dhakirat Jabal al-Akrad (Kurd Dagh)* (Damascus: Dar al-Zaman, 2010), 16.

Figure 3.2. Ravendan (Ravanda) castle
Photo by Stefan Winter.

encompassed between sixty and eighty-five villages in the sixteenth century. Of these, up to twelve villages, in addition to numerous uninhabited farm plots (*mezraa*), are noted in the Tahrir registers at any one time as being "in the hands of" (*der yed-i*) or "belonging to" (*tabi-i*) Kurdish groups – for the most part the Mûsa-Beylo tribe.[24] The smaller *nahiye* of Amık, for its part, was centred on the plain or "depression" of Amık (Arabic/Ottoman ʿ*Amq* or ʿ*Amīq*) on the lower course of the ʿAfrin River, where it empties into the marshes and lake of Amık just north of Antioch.[25] Only two or three of its forty to fifty villages were associated with Kurdish groups in this period, although the Kurdish Amiki tribe, well attested in Ottoman documents from the second half of the seventeenth century onwards, appears to have been named for the district, despite its spelling with a *kaf* rather than with a *qaf*. Tax farm arrears registers from the early eighteenth century also refer to the

---

24 TD 93:283–321; *397 Numaralı Haleb Livâsı Mufassal Tahrîr Defteri*, 1:216–30.
25 The lake was only formed through tectonic activity stemming the Orontes River in late antiquity, and drained again in modern times to permit agricultural development and the construction of Hatay airport.

84   Stefan Winter

"Ekrad-ı Amık" (Kurds of Amık).[26] The northern extension of the Amık plain east of the Amanos range formed the *nahiye* of Derbisak, and was largely dominated by the Turkoman Zulkadir confederation. But it also encompassed the westernmost edges of the Kurd Dagh around Shaykh al-Hadid, one of the main centres of the Kurdish Qilîçlo tribe (see below).

The *nahiye* of Cum, meanwhile, was named for the plain of Juma (Kurdish Cûmê) stretching along the middle course of the ʿAfrin River at the foot of the Kurd Dagh, to the west of modern-day ʿAfrin. The appellation al-Juma was already current in the medieval period.[27] The Ottoman district was predominantly centred on the west bank of the ʿAfrin, with most of the east bank forming part of the *nahiye* of Jabal Samʿan. In 1518 and 1526, when Cum was still part of the *sancak* of Aleppo, the district encompassed some three dozen villages and as many uninhabited *mezraa*s. Approximately half of all these are explicitly attributed to *Ekrad*, including several groups which remained under the fiscal control of ʿIzzeddin Bey. By way of comparison, five villages in the district are noted as belonging to Turkoman groups, and one *mezraa* as belonging to an Arab tribe.[28] In 1536, when Cum was one of two districts (the other being Aʿzaz itself) forming, together with the area's Kurdish tribes, the new *liva* of "Azaz ve Ekrad," it continued to encompass thirty-five villages plus associated *mezraa*s. While many of these were again linked with Kurdish populations, the great majority of their revenues were now specifically assigned to the imperial crown reserve (*hass-ı şahi*), the provincial governor's reserve (*hass-ı mir-liva*), a private beneficiary (*mülk*), a *waqf* foundation, or a *timar* prebend. Only in three minor instances are some "remaining charges" (*sair rüsum*) still noted as being in the hands of ʿIzzeddin Bey.[29] In later registers as well, the district of Cum appears, alongside Aʿzaz and the separate tribal groups under ʿIzzeddin Bey, as the heartland of the Kurdish sedentary population in the province.[30]

---

26 BOA: Maliyeden Müdevver [MAD] 4455:41.
27 ʿImad al-Din Ismaʿil Abu'l-Fidaʾ (d. 1331), *Taqwim al-Buldan*, ed. Joseph Toussaint Reinaud (Paris: Imprimerie Royale, 1840), 50; ʿAli Ibn Khatib al-Nasiriyya (d. 1439–40), *Al-Durr al-Muntakhab fi Takmilat Tarikh Halab*, ed. Ahmad Fawzi al-Hayb (Kuwait: Muʾassasat ʿAbd al-ʿAziz Saʿud al-Babtayn, 2018), 2:789, 4:1922.
28 TD 93:323–43; TD 146:748–99. This latter register has the particularity of listing all the villages and *mezraa*s of Cum together in alphabetical order.
29 TD 181:73–87.
30 TD 280:365–8; TD 378:21–3; TD 391:333–6.

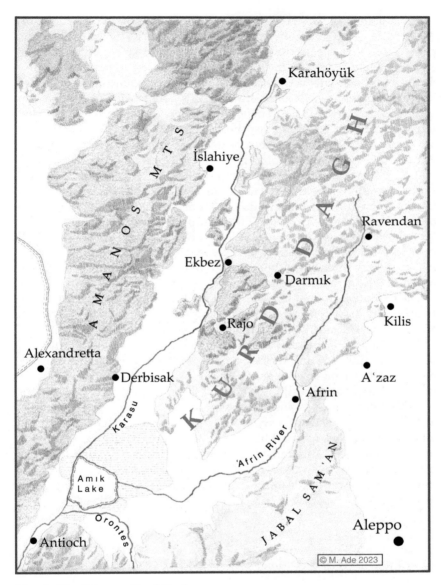

Map 2. The Ottoman Kurd Dagh

86 Stefan Winter

Beyond its inclusion in the tax cadastres first of the province of Aleppo, then of A'zaz (Kilis) in the sixteenth century, the *nahiye* of Cum per se does not appear often in Ottoman records. In November 1672, to cite only a few examples, the *kadı* of Kilis was asked to ensure that produce from the district be distributed in town on the basis of fixed market prices (*narh-ı cari*).[31] From around 1716 to at least 1725, the holder of a major *zeamet* (military benefice) on Kanj and other villages of Cum fought a running battle against the *voyvoda* (*sancak*-level tax collector; see below) of Kilis, whom he repeatedly accused before the Sublime Porte of overstepping his prerogatives and oppressing the local population.[32] In several villages whose revenues were assigned to minor *waqf* foundations, the imperial authorities occasionally had to intervene to coordinate the collection of dues.[33] Cum was maintained as a *nahiye* of the new *kaza* of Kilis in the Tanzimat period and figures as such in the *salname*s (administrative yearbooks) of the time.[34] As late as 1912, members of the Poche family of merchants in Aleppo could write the *mudir* (district director) of "al-Juma" to request his support in bringing to market the area's commercial crop that season.[35]

The vast majority of references to Cum, however, concern its Kurdish tribal population, who are increasingly identified simply as the "Cum Kurds" (Cum Ekradı) or the "Cum tribe" (Cum aşireti). Already in May 1595, an imperial janissary officer was attacked and robbed in the village of Cindîres in Cum, where he had gone to investigate the murder of three other janissaries a few weeks before; according to the janissary's subsequent deposition in court, the local Kurds were known to be stockpiling weapons and were responsible for various crimes in the area.[36] The "Cum Kurds" perhaps first appear under that name in 1688, when they, along with the Mûsa-Beylo tribe and other *reaya* (subjects) of the *kaza* of Kilis, complained of the depredations of another Kurdish tribe, which had caused many of the residents to flee and settle instead down around Antioch, leading to an important revenue shortfall back in Kilis.[37] A few years later, after the Ottoman Empire had embarked

---

31 ŞKT 7:100:338.
32 ŞKT 82:251, no. 3; ŞKT 99:109, no. 3; ŞKT 104:253a, no. 2; ŞKT 105:393, no. 1; ŞKT 105:413, no. 1.
33 ŞKT 119:178, no. 2; BOA: Şam-ı Şerif Ahkam Defterleri [ŞŞAD] 2:67, no. 5.
34 Cengiz Eroğlu, Murat Babuçoğlu, and Mehmet Köçer, *Osmanlı Vilayet Salnamelerinde Halep* (Ankara: Global Strateji Enstitüsü, 2007), 153.
35 Poche-Marcopoli Archives, Aleppo: FP 383:527.
36 MD 73:236:550, 551; MD 73:442:976.
37 ŞKT 12:85:397.

The 'Afrin District under Ottoman Rule, 1516–1921   87

on an ambitious program of tribal settlement (*iskan*) in the region, the Sublime Porte gave orders to protect the Cum Kurds against excessive demands for contributions, beyond what they were already paying in regular taxes, on the part of some local bedouin chiefs.[38] Similarly, in 1698 and again in 1703, "Cum *reaya*" belonging to the Qiliçlo tribe complained of being illegally shaken down for *khuwwa* ("brotherhood" dues) by the Arab *çöl beyi* (desert emir) whenever they tried to bring camel caravans in to Aleppo for the purpose of trade.[39] Of course the violence could go the other way too: In 1709, a taxlord of the Cum and Ravendan districts was accused of having gathered together forty or fifty Kurdish "thugs" (*eşkıya*) to steal provisions and oppress the rest of the local population.[40]

What would appear to account for the state's growing interest in the "Cum Kurds" as a collective is their establishment as a private fiscal reserve (*hass*) of the Ottoman queen dowager or Valide Sultan in the second half of the seventeenth century. Similar to the Yeni İl Turkoman confederation, which was actually "given" (*temlik*) to the mother of Murad III in 1579 and subsequently included as a revenue source in the *waqf* foundation of the "Atik Valide Sultan" mosque complex in Üsküdar,[41] the Cum or "Kilis Kurds" as well as the Reşwan Kurd confederation of south-central Anatolia appear to have been assigned to Turhan Sultan, the vastly influential mother of Mehmed IV, after her formal regency had ended and she began to invest herself in building projects such as that of the Yeni Cami in Eminönü, Istanbul. The earliest evidence we have in this regard dates from 1668, when her official steward (*kethüda*) petitioned the Sublime Porte to obtain various sums that were due to her from sources throughout the region, and to ascertain that Kurds from her Kilis *hass* who had been convicted of violent crime remain imprisoned in the citadel of Aleppo.[42] Following Turhan's death in 1683, the *hass* was given to the new Valide Sultan, the mother

---

38 ŞKT 29:264:1171; ŞKT 29:271:1202.

39 ŞKT 30:36:164; ŞKT 37:235:958.

40 ŞKT 55:91, no. 4.

41 MD 39:75–8, nos. 183–91. On the financing of her *waqf* see Ramazan Pantık, "Atik Valide Sultan Külliyesi (1686–1727)" (master's thesis, Hacettepe University, Ankara, 2014), 54–102. Other examples of Valide Sultans being awarded tribal revenues in 1620–1 and 1645 are included in the 1848 edition of Feridun Ahmed Bey, *Mecmua-ı Münşeatü's-Selatin*, 2:292–4.

42 ŞKT 6:133:599; ŞKT 6:165:773, 774; ŞKT 7:100:338. This *kethüda* appears at the same time to have been the acting *mütevelli* or administrator of the Atik Valide Sultan complex; see ŞKT 6:148:670.

88   Stefan Winter

of Mustafa II, around 1697, as indicated by the complaint of her *kethüda* that year that some villagers from Kilis, Cum, the local Turkomans and the Mûsa-Beylo tribe attached to the *hass* had been driven out by other Kurdish groups, which had recently been settled there from Anatolia, and who should thus be sent still further off to settle in Hama and Homs.[43] In 1731, we see the *hass* for incomes from Kilis and Azaz again attributed to the new Valide Sultan, the mother of Mahmud I, who had ascended the throne just the year before.[44]

Although not all of these queen mothers were equally invested in patronage works in Istanbul, securing their revenues was at all times a top priority of the relevant imperial palace bureau. A major concern in the middle decades of the eighteenth century seems in fact to have been that the Cum/Kilis tribal collective might be breaking apart. According to the register books of "sultanic orders" (Awamir Sultaniyya) received in Aleppo in this period, the Cum-Matih tribe had already notified the court in 1690 that, while they had always paid their taxes in full, recently some of their members had left to take up service with powerful figures ("zi kudret kimesneler yanında") in Aleppo, as a result of which the remaining members could no longer fulfil their fiscal obligations. The imperial court (in residence at Edirne at the time) sent instructions that the complete amounts were to be collected from those who had settled in Aleppo, and to not let anyone (presumably meaning the Kurds' patrons) prevent this.[45] Exactly the same issue was raised again in 1735, perhaps not coincidentally soon after the Kilis *hass* had been transferred to the latest Valide Sultan. This time, the governor received orders not only to levy taxes on the three hundred or more individuals of the Cum tribe who had gone to live in Aleppo, but to remove and return them to their "original homelands" (*evtan-ı asliye*) in Kilis.[46]

These appeals do not seem to have addressed the underlying issue, however. In the fall of 1739, the *voyvoda* of Kilis sought and received a *buyuruldı* (governor's order) to permit him to collect taxes from specific sections of the Cum that were once more living in Aleppo; the order is dated, again not coincidentally, only two weeks after the death of Mahmud I's mother and the transfer of the *hass* to a new fiscal agent.[47]

---

43 MD 110:23:97; ŞKT 25:137:543; ŞKT 26:98:531.
44 ŞKT 133:59a, no. 1; ŞKT 133:64a, no. 1.
45 Markaz al-Watha'iq al-Tarikhiyya, Damascus: Aleppo / Awamir Sultaniyya [A/AS] 1:59:109.
46 A/AS 3:170:290.
47 A/AS 4:44:93; A/AS 5:368:739.

The 'Afrin District under Ottoman Rule, 1516–1921   89

In 1747, the Cum Kurds are mentioned as a *hass* of the grand vezir (*sadrazam*), but again, many had moved to Aleppo, while five hundred more members are said to have gone and joined the [S]açlo Kurds at Hama and Homs. These were once again to be returned to their original homes, if they could not give proof of residence for ten years or more in the places they had settled.[48] "The Cum tribe of the Kilis *mukataa* used to be a sizeable tribe," a similar but more detailed order notes the following year, "but because of the weight of their dues, most of the subjects dispersed little by little and moved to Aleppo, Hama, Homs, [Jisr al-] Shughur, Tripoli, and other places. Formerly composed of 1,500 families, only 500 of the said tribe remain today."[49] An entry in the Antioch court registers around the same time (shown in figure 3.3), for its part, states that members of the Qilîçlo of Cum had settled in the Qusayr district above Antioch, and should also be sent back.[50] In 1755, two distinct *hass*es given to Osman III's mother were defined as "Kilis with the Şêxlo," in reference to another of the district's Kurdish tribes, and "Azaz with the al-Wahb," a local Arab tribe.[51] Following her death only a few months later, however, the *hass*es were transferred to a governor of Raqqa, marking the last time either the Cum or the Reşwan Kurds were held by a Valide Sultan until nearly the end of the century.

The Cum Kurds as a collective, and in fact the entire Cum district as such, are hardly mentioned at all any more in the second half of the eighteenth century, if not in very occasional orders to seek tax moneys from those who had dispersed to other areas.[52] The lapsing of the practice of giving the Cum as a private fiscal reserve to the reigning queen mother after 1739 seems to have marked a significant drop in interest for the district on the part of the palace and central administrative authorities in Istanbul, or at least an end to their direct intervention in matters of tax collection in the area. One of the last times the Cum district is mentioned at all in Ottoman documents is a bizarre case from 1793, when a former collector of the Kilis *hass* who was supposedly responsible for "ruining" the *mukataa* was ordered banished by a *fatwa* from the Şeyhü'l-İslam; instead he fled to Cum, where he obviously still had contacts, to take up a life of banditry with the locals.[53] At that time

---

48 A/AS 5:390:774.
49 A/AS 1:138:258.
50 İslam Araştırmaları Merkezi, Üsküdar/Istanbul: Antakya Şeriye Sicilleri Defteri 4:98:179.
51 MD 157:15–16:55; MD 162:402:1144; MD 163:294–5:793; A/AS 6:59:118, 119.
52 BOA: Halep Ahkam Defterleri [HAD] 1:176, no. 1; HAD 2:77, no. 1; A/AS 7:62–3:88.
53 BOA: Mühimme-i Mektume Defterleri [MKM] 1:137:430.

Figure 3.3. Order in the Antioch *shar'iyya* court registers regarding the Qilîçlo Kurds in Cum

the *hass* was back under the authority of the incumbent Valide Sultan, the mother of Selim III, and following his deposition in 1807 it was briefly held by the mother of Mustafa IV.[54] We have no more evidence of the practice after his own deposition and execution in 1808 or in the modern reform era.

Kurdish Tribalism in ʿAfrin

The Ottoman administration of the ʿAfrin district thus closely matched the evolution of Ottoman provincial government in Syria as a whole: 1) the initial retention of Mamluk-era personnel, tax units, and fiscal practices, viz. ʿIzzeddin Bey and the Kurdish groups under his authority, in the

---

54 HAD 6:149, no. 3; HAD 6:191, no. 2. The *hass* is defined here as comprising the "six Kurdish tribes of Kilis," including the Cum.

The 'Afrin District under Ottoman Rule, 1516–1921   91

decades following the conquest; 2) the consolidation and territorialization of the classical provincial military hierarchy in Syria through the definition of new *sancak*s and *nahiye*s, as reflected in the tax cadastres of the sixteenth century; 3) the cumulation and *de facto* privatization of key provincial revenue sources for the benefit of specific palace interests, in this case the newly-defined "Cum Kurds" and their assignment to the Valide Sultan beginning in the mid-seventeenth century. With the decline in influence of palace factions around the queen mother in the eighteenth century, however, and the increasing tendency to grant revenue collection concessions to provincial notables and financiers as cash tax farms (*iltizam*) or even life-time tax farms (*malikane*) after 1695, the Ottoman central authorities began to take more of a laissez-faire approach to the distant provinces and to tolerate and indeed actively promote local autonomy under different kinds of domestic leaderships. In hinterland areas such as the Kurd Dagh and other parts of rural Anatolia and Syria, this often meant recognizing and extending precise fiscal responsibilities to tribal populations not previously associated with the state.

We have just previously referred to the Şêxlo (or Şêxler) Kurds, who were not counted as a separate tax unit in the classical Tahrir registers but who ultimately formed the main constituent of the Kilis *mukataa*. Once again, it is in the period when the Kilis Kurds were first given to the Valide Sultan that they come to the attention of the central authorities, most notably in 1673 for their illegal stockpiling of firearms (*tüfek*) with which they (and others including the Oqcî-Izzeddînlos and the Amîkîs) had apparently begun to terrorize local villages.[55] But they especially gained notoriety with a massive assault on the Amîkîs in 1690, leading to a wide, inter-regional punitive campaign against them and an unsuccessful attempt to deport them to the Harran area.[56] In 1698 they were formally removed from the Kilis reserve and ordered to settle in Raqqa, but this again does not seem to have had any lasting consequences; and by 1741 the Sublime Porte was decrying the fact that the Şêxlos, like other tribes, had partially dispersed to other provinces, causing revenue shortfalls in Kilis.[57]

---

55 ŞKT 5:148:841; ŞKT 8:402:1958; Stefan Winter, "Les Kurdes du Nord-Ouest syrien et l'État ottoman, 1690–1750," in *Sociétés rurales ottomanes / Ottoman Rural Societies*, ed. Mohammad Afifi, Afifi Mohammad, Rachida Chih, Brigitte Marino, Nicolas Michel, and Işık Tamdoğan (Cairo: Institut français d'archéologie orientale, 2005), 252.

56 A/AS 1:22–3:37–9; MD 100:32:97; MD 106:241–2:905.

57 ŞKT 39:47:199; A/AS 4:133, no. 2. According to HAD 1:176, no. 5, different Şêxlo families in fact joined Mahfuz ibn Shillif and Muhammad Rustum Agha, the two most powerful feudal lords (and bitter enemies) in the mountains of Latakia in this period.

92   Stefan Winter

Another group that was frequently assimilated into the Kilis *hass* were the Amîkîs themselves, even though they appear to have resided only in the Amık and Karamort area and should more properly be dealt with in a study of the Kurds of Antioch province. The Mûsâ-Beylos, for their part, were concentrated in the *nahiye* of Ravendan – which for all purposes ceased to exist as an administrative unit with the constitution of the Kilis Kurd collective in the seventeenth century. Like other local tribes, they were originally assigned to İzzeddin Bey, although one tax register from 1536 also suggests that several of their branches were affiliated with the Saçlo Kurd confederation in central Syria.[58] In Ravendan, they were consistently based in the villages, as far as these can be identified today, around Dumancık, Gemrik, Haydariyye (Haydarlar), Mağaracık, and Üçpınar (in what is today in fact the district (*ilçe*) of Musabeyli in the Turkish province of Kilis), as well as Ikidam, Shaltah, Arab Viran, and Tallaq, just across what is now the border with Syria, all on the northeastern edge of the Kurd Dagh, giving the impression of a high degree of settledness and stability.[59] The Mûsa-Beylos do not appear frequently in later Ottoman records, and most of the documents in their regard concern tax arrears and debt collection rather than banditry.[60] A single group or family known as the Çavuşoğulları, belonging to the Mûsa-Beylo Kurds of Kilis, were identified as brigands in 1712, and ordered to resettle in Raqqa.[61] More generally, however, the Mûsa-Beylos, as we have already seen, were repeatedly cited by Valide Sultan officials as a Cum population that had to be protected against the ravages of other tribes; as late as 1782, individual Mûsa-Beylo families were known to have sought refuge in Rumkale from "upheaval" (*ihtilal*) back in Kilis.[62]

Another sedentary population that had a long-established presence in the 'Afrin area was the Yezidis. Members of the religious community first moved from the Lalesh Valley in northern Iraq, under threat of the Mongols, to Syria in the thirteenth century, and appear to have been relatively well integrated under the Mamluk sultanate. They were led by a shaykh 'Izzeddîn, a descendant of the sect's founder, who was however imprisoned for his growing popularity among the Syrian Kurds in 1330–1. A manuscript from the Jabal Sam'an (adjacent to

---

58 TD 93:285–6, 721–3; TD 146:690; TD 181:144–8; TD 378:19.
59 *397 Numaralı Haleb Livâsı Mufassal Tahrîr Defteri*, vol. 1; TD 280:98–9; TD 391:98–9; TD 493:312–29.
60 ŞKT 20:183:785; ŞKT 20:386:1714; ŞKT 43:96:386; HAD 3:247, no. 2.
61 MD 119:917.
62 ŞKT 43:96:386.

The 'Afrin District under Ottoman Rule, 1516–1921   93

'Afrin) indicates that his family nonetheless continued to live in the area for at least five more generations,[63] before Ibn al-Hanbali's account of Izzeddîn Bey of the same lineage serving as "emir of the Kurds" under the last Mamluks and the Ottomans. We have already seen that Yezidis were cited for banditry on the road from 'Ayntab in 1577. But the few Ottoman documents we have in regard to the local Yezidi population also invoke the need to protect it from overzealous taxation.[64] In the Aleppo *shar 'iyya* court registers, a singular entry also records how a "Hamo the Kurd" came before the judge in 1679 to renounce his "false" Yezidi faith and embrace Islam,[65] but the occurrence of names such as "Tawus [Peacock] bint Rashid al-Kurdi" or "Tawus al-Kurdiyya" as property owners in the Kurdish Quarter of Aleppo might also suggest the existence of a certain Yezidi elite with ties to the city.[66] European missionaries and travellers also started to take notice of the Yezidis in northwestern Aleppo (often describing them as nomadic) beginning in the seventeenth century.[67]

The Qilîçlo (Turkish Kılıçlı) tribe, in contrast, was one of the best-documented, but arguably also the most ephemeral, of Kurdish populations of the 'Afrin region. They are well accounted for in the earliest Tahrir registers discussed in the opening section: In the first census for Aleppo from 1518, they can be seen to form an important population element in Shaykh al-Hadid and adjoining villages Sinara, Anqele, Merwan, and İkizce (Hekiçe), on the westernmost edge of the Kurd Dagh overlooking the Amık plain, part of the *nahiye* of Derbisak but assigned for fiscal purposes to 'Izzeddin Bey.[68] In 1526, they are listed as being affiliated with the Çobi Kurds, but seem to have disappeared from Shaykh al-Hadid by this point.[69] The Qilîçlos of Merwan and others are included in the register for the newly independent province of Azaz and the Kurds in 1536, even if they are noted to be residents of Derbisak. Interestingly, this register also presents the tribe as attached to the famous

---

63 John Guest, *Survival Among the Kurds: A History of the Yezidis* (London: Routledge, 2010), 24–6.

64 A/AS 2:140:233; Winter, "Les Kurdes du Nord-Ouest syrien," 251.

65 Markaz al-Watha'iq al-Tarikhiyya, Damascus: Aleppo/Mahkama Shar'iyya court records [A/MS] 34:130:4. I am grateful to Charles Wilkins for this reference.

66 A/MS 1:25:237; A/MS 4:308:1677. I am grateful to Mihran Minassian for these references.

67 Sebastian Maisel, *Yezidis in Syria: Identity Building among a Double Minority* (Lanham: Lexington, 2017), 80–1.

68 TD 93:725–6.

69 TD 146:861, 863, 898, 901, 922.

Figure 3.4. Western edge of the Kurd Dagh (*nahiye* of Derbisak), overlooking the ʿAmq Plain

Millî (Millo) confederation, enumerating multiple sections based in the "eastern province" (Vilayet-i Şark), that is, in the Urfa-Cizre region. At the same time, the *nahiye* of Derbisak with its Qilîçlo-inhabited villages also continues to be included in the register for the *sancak* of Aleppo from the same year.[70] The link with the Millî confederation is not corroborated in later censuses, however, and in fact by 1552 they appear to be confined to the sole village of Merwan (figure 3.4).[71]

---

70 TD 181:156–8; *397 Numaralı Haleb Livâsı Mufassal Tahrîr Defteri*, 1:18, 42, 45, 241, 247, 250; Öztürk, *16. Yüzyılda*, 49, 65.
71 TD 280:103; TD 391:104.

The 'Afrin District under Ottoman Rule, 1516–1921   95

Beyond the Tahrir registers there is relatively little mention of the Qilîçlos in the sixteenth century. A Mühimme order addressed to the governors of Maraş and Aleppo in 1577 includes the Qilîçlos, along with the Oqçî-Izzeddînlos, Şêxlos and others, in a long list of tribes who were under the authority of the *bey* of Kilis-Azaz (presumably one of the sons of Canpolad), but who had migrated to other provinces over time and should be sent back to Cum.[72] It is in the final decade of the seventeenth century that we come across an important cluster of references to the Qilîclos, precisely at a time when the Ottoman state had just initiated a vast program of tribal resettlement (*iskan*) centred on the *eyalet* of Raqqa and was paying increased notice to problem tribes throughout Anatolia and Syria. A significant branch of Qilîçlo Kurds was in fact located in the Hama region in this period, where they were considered part of the fiscal reserve (*hass*) of the "Üsküdar Turkomans" (that is, the Yeni İl confederation, belonging to the Atik Valide Sultan foundation), but where they had come to the negative attention of the imperial authorities not only for sheep rustling but also for quitting the area illegally to settle in Amık and causing harm to villages there.[73] Similarly, in 1695 the governor and *kadı* of Tripoli were told to get their hands on and prosecute some Qilîçlo nomads (*konar-göçer*) who had stolen livestock in the area and murdered some locals, and to inform the authorities in Hama if that was indeed where the perpetrators had come from.[74] Numerous other orders concern the finances, or the depredations, of branches of the Qilîçlo Kurds around Maraş and Elbistan, and plans to settle them in Raqqa or in İç İl (İçel; Silifke).[75]

Given the central government's increasing focus on tribal organization in the late seventeenth century and the tendency to define all the Kurds of the Kurd Dagh as a single collective (assigned to the Valide Sultan), it comes as no surprise that the Qilîçlos of the Shaykh al-Hadid area were subsumed into the "Kilis Kurds" too, even though they were technically residents of Derbisak. We have already seen that

---

72 MD 33:140:280; see also Hüseyin Arslan, *16. Yy. Osmanlı Toplumunda Yönetim, Nüfus, İskan, Göç ve Sürgün* (Istanbul: Kaknüs Yayınları, 2001), 267.

73 BOA: Maliyeden Müdevver [MAD] 9484:47, no. 1; MD 104:46:192; ŞKT 20:293:1282.

74 ŞKT 21:72:331; ŞKT 21:83:384.

75 In Elbistan the Qilîçlo Kurds constituted a *hass* of Ahmed III's sister Hadice Sultan. In addition to the numerous references which can be found in the Mühimme Defterleri through simple keyword searches (Kılıçlı; Kılıçlu), see ŞKT 34:88:397; ŞKT 35:116:481; ŞKT 39:998, no. 3; ŞKT 41:700:3057, 3059; ŞKT 42:191:821; MD 121:44:179; MD 126:77:286. See also Cevdet Türkay, *Başbakanlık Arşivi Belgelerine Göre Osmanlı İmparatorluğu'nda Oymak, Aşiret ve Cemaatlar* (Istanbul: İşaret Yayınları, 2001), 441–3; Mehmet Bayrak, "Binboğalarda Kürt Aşiretleri," *Bîrnebûn* 5 (1998): 56–62.

96   Stefan Winter

the Qilîçlos were described as "Cum *reaya*" (subjects), and had to be protected as such against the excessive demands of the Arab desert emirs, in 1698 and 1703. Widely reputed as caravan drovers, they were also responsible for supplying camels as part of Kilis' contribution to imperial military campaigns.[76] But they were equally castigated for their banditry and frequently subject to *iskan* measures. In 1723, for example, several members of the Qilîçlos and other local tribes, including the Amikis and Oqçî-Izzeddînlos, were accused of plundering villages in the Maraş region; they were to be rounded up by the governor of Aleppo and brought to the eastern border of the province, where they would be taken in charge by the governor of Raqqa for resettlement.[77] A band of over three hundred Qilîçlo, Oqçî-Izzeddînlo, and other Kilis Kurds was accused of having joined together to terrorize the Ayntab region in 1731.[78] In 1750, an imperial official travelling from Damascus to Istanbul was attacked and robbed near the Karamort *khan* north of Antioch by fifteen bandits from the Qilîçlo and the Bektaşlo Kurds, an Amık-area tribe with whom they frequently joined forces. A special commander (*bölükbaşı*) was sent to retrieve the stolen goods and surrender them to the court in Aleppo.[79] A few years later, in 1753, the two groups were again accused of having attacked villages and killed and robbed travellers near Karamort, but also around Antioch and as far as the Altın Özü district in the hill country south of Antioch.[80]

In many cases, government orders were directed against the wider Qilîçlo tribe, and it is not always clear if those members resident in the ʿAfrin region were implicated. Throughout the summer and fall of 1754, for example, Qilîçlos were accused of banding together with Lekvanık, Bektaşlo, Reyhânlo, and "other Kurdish brigands" to raid villages in Elbistan in the course of their seasonal migrations, but these orders only concerned the governors of Adana and Maraş (who were incidentally both of the Reşvan-zade dynasty of Kurdish *beylerbeyi*s) and not the authorities in Aleppo or Kilis.[81] On the other hand, Reşvan-zade Süleyman was transferred from Adana to the governorship of Kilis later that same winter with an express mandate to govern the local Kurds there but also to interdict any more such raids in the Elbistan area.[82] One reason the Qilîçlos may have come under special

---

76 A/AS 3:32:50; Winter, "Les Kurdes du Nord-Ouest," 248.
77 A/AS 2:72:127.
78 MD 138:49:171–6; MD 138:86:325; MD 138:88:332; MD 138:105:365; MD 138:106:366.
79 A/AS 1:335–6:616–18.
80 MD 156:8–9:21; MD 156:46:142.
81 MD 156:179:533; MD 156:191:573; MD 156:239:783.
82 MD 156:281:919.

The Afrin District under Ottoman Rule, 1516–1921   97

scrutiny, to judge by a petition submitted by the religious notables of Maraş in 1770, was not only that they were highwaymen and inveterate criminals, but that they were "a sinister folk of evil-living Kızılbaş [Shiʻis], outside the four Sunni schools of law."[83] Already in 1733, a group of Qilîçlos described as "Rafızıs" (Shiʻi heretics) who had ostensibly been banished to Cyprus had now returned to their old ways in Anatolia, and were either to be executed or resettled anew in Raqqa.[84] A Turkish government report on Anatolian tribes in the 1980s does in fact continue to identify remnants of the Qilîçlo confederation in the region as Imami Shiʻis,[85] but this never actually appears to have been an issue in their treatment by the Ottoman authorities. According to multiple documentary sources, Qilîçlos raiding activities extended throughout the Anatolian hinterland from Maraş to Sivas in the second half of the eighteenth century. As a result of one particularly violent punitive campaign in 1784, the *voyvoda* of Kilis and Aʻzaz was specifically warned that members of the tribe were fleeing to areas under his jurisdiction, where they could expect support (*istishab*) from kinsmen.[86]

We have few documentary references to the Qilîçlos in ʻAfrin in the nineteenth century, suggesting that the state's attempts at tribal control, particularly in the Tanzimat era, were effective in that area at least. Around Maraş too, where the Qilîçlos continued to attract negative attention, for example for robbing foreign teachers from a Protestant missionary school in 1855, they were increasingly subjected to *iskan* measures.[87] During the Turkish War of Independence in 1920, some Qilîçlo Kurds were still based in Maraş, but do not appear to have been present in Kilis or played any role in resistance efforts against the French at Maraş or in the Kurd Dagh.[88] For a tribe that was once among the most mobile and unsettled in the whole region, both the social engineering policies of the reform period and finally the demarcation of the new border between Syria and Turkey after World War I effectively marked the end of their historical being in the ʻAfrin district.

---

83 BOA: Cevdet Dahiliye [C.DH] 246/12280.
84 MD 139:347–8:1342–51.
85 Anon., *Aşiret Raporu* (Istanbul: Kaynak, 1998), 209.
86 MD 182:113:354; MD 182:129:411.
87 BOA: Hariciye [HR.SYS] 81/9; İrade Meclis-i Vala [İ.MVL] 84/1696; Meclis-i Vala [MVL] 1059/61.
88 Tayfur Sökmen (d. 1980), *Hatay'ın Kurtuluşu için Harcanan Çabalar* (Ankara: Türk Tarih Kurumu, 1978), 36; Şinasi Çolakoğlu, *Kilis: Dereniş-Kurtuluş ve Sonrası, 1918-1921-1930* (Ankara: Onur Yayıncılık, 1991), 97–102, 121–3, 126, 133, 135, 137.

98   Stefan Winter

The Oqçî-Izzeddînlo Tribe

Like many of the other Kurdish tribes of 'Afrin, the Oqçî-Izzeddînlos have a historical presence in the area going back at least to the Ottoman conquest and are well attested in the earliest Ottoman sources. Unlike many of the other tribes, however, the Oqçî-Izzeddinlos expanded and consolidated their presence throughout the Ottoman period and into modern times, to the point that a separate *nahiye* was named for them in the nineteenth century. The object of this final section is to trace their history in 'Afrin as a means of illustrating the incorporation and recognition of the Kurdish population element in northern Syria under the Ottoman Empire.

In 1518, the Oqçî-Izzeddînlos are predictably included among the İzzeddin Bey tribes, although the *defter* in question also gives them the alternative name (*nam-ı diğer*) "Millî," suggesting again that they, like the Qilîçlos (and others such as the Amikis), may originally have been affiliated with the much greater Urfa-area Kurdish confederation of that name.[89] In later *defter*s they appear either as a relatively small *cemaat* in villages of Cum and Ravendan, or as a subdivision of the Saçlo Kurds of central Syria.[90] They do not appear to have been named for İzzeddin Bey *per se*, who had his own *ordu* or personal retinue recorded in the tax registers,[91] and who would not have been identified by the simple title of *okçı* or bowman. The name was and remained extremely popular among Kurds in the region, and apparently among Yezidis in particular, raising the question to what degree the eponymous Oqçî Izzeddîn and other figures were not all named in some fashion after the famous 'Adawi shaykh or the Mamluk-era emir.

In any event, the Oqçî-Izzeddînlos quickly acquired a reputation for rebellion against the Ottoman order in Kilis. In the spring of 1572, as we have already mentioned, the *kadı* of the İzzeddin Bey Kurds complained that the Oqçî-Izzeddînlos were refusing to provide campaign contributions and ransacking the Maraş area; a few months later, the governor of Dulkadir (Maraş) had to be mobilized because they were refusing to submit to Canpolad Bey in Kilis and instead attacking travellers and pilgrims, as well as driving "Muslims" from their homes.[92] In 1584, the

---

89 TD 93:703, 731; Enver Çakar, *XVI. Yüzyılda Halep Sancağı (1516–1566)* (Elazığ: Fırat Üniversitesi Basımevi, 2003), 210–11.
90 *397 Numaralı Haleb Livâsı Mufassal Tahrîr Defteri*, 43; TD 181:149; TD 378:19.
91 Öztürk, *16. Yüzyılda*, 43.
92 MD 16:280–1:535; MD 19:106–7:228.

The 'Afrin District under Ottoman Rule, 1516–1921   99

Oqçî-Izzeddînlos, this time identified as forming part of the "Canpolad Kurds," were again accused of fomenting trouble in Maraş and then of killing the *subaşı* (sergeant) of Gerger sent to contain them.[93] In the early decades of the seventeenth century, as the authorities struggled to reassert control in the region after the Celali rebellions, Oqçî-Izzeddînlos continued to make a name for themselves with banditry. It is also from this time, however, that we have references to a specific *mukataa* (tax collectorship) for the İzzeddin (presumably meaning the Oqçî-Izzeddîn) and Reşî tribes of Aleppo attached to the Saçlo Kurds in Hama and the Sahyun, with whom we have already seen they were originally associated in the sixteenth century.[94]

It is with the *iskan* initiative beginning in the late seventeenth century that the Oqçî-Izzeddînlos came to the repeated and close attention of the state. As early as 1697, members of the tribe who had recently been settled in Shaykh al-Hadid apparently tried to claim taxation rights over other residents of the area; a few months later, we see them ordered for the first time to resettle in Raqqa.[95] In 1703, however, a band of Oqçî-Izzeddîn Kurds identified as nomads stood accused again of raiding farms (*çiftlik*) in Kilis and making off with dozens of oxen and other livestock and goods.[96] From then on, their mutiny only became more pronounced: while the governor of Adana was transferred to Aleppo specifically to bring them to court and return the stolen effects, they continued to resist all efforts at control and finally went so far as to kill the *voyvoda* (tax agent) assigned to them by the government, giving rise to orders (no doubt futile) to remove them to Raqqa by force and imprison their ringleaders in the citadel of Aleppo in early 1705.[97]

Official reports of excesses by the Oqçî-Izzeddînlos in the 'Afrin district in this period are too numerous to go over in detail here. As with any such group in the Empire, their appearance in the documentary record as a "tribe" (rather than as individual, tax-paying subjects) is almost automatically and tautologically negative. In 1723, as we have seen, they were part of the Kilis Kurd population that was to be brought to the Aleppo-Raqqa border for resettlement in the desert province, something which does not seem to have actually been carried

---

93 MD 53:97:265.
94 MD 84:49:98; Centre for Historical Documents, Damascus: Hama/Mahkama Shar'i-yya [H/MS] 37:280:786; MAD 6415:147, no. 2.
95 ŞKT 25:137:543; MD 109:21:94.
96 ŞKT 36:325:1299; ŞKT 39:244:1030; ŞKT 39:900, no. 2.
97 ŞKT 41:51:224; ŞKT 41:428:1889; ŞKT 41:671:2943.

100   Stefan Winter

out; over the next years they were repeatedly cited, often in association with other local Kurdish groups, for acts of brigandage and highway robbery throughout the area.[98] They appear to have had regular summer pastures in the Gavur Dağı (Amanos Mountains),[99] which likely brought them into recurring friction with the settled population in both Antioch and Adana whenever they set out from the Kurd Dagh. One particular set of references concerns the Ottoman campaign against Nadir Shah in 1733, to which a unit of Oqçî-Izzeddînlos was assigned, but who attracted notice mainly for stealing from the tents of other soldiers camped at Baghdad, before deserting the campaign to return home to Aleppo.[100]

The imperial authorities once again spent the winter of 1735–6 coordinating provincial forces from Adana, Aleppo, Tripoli, Maraş, and Kars, as well as janissaries from Kilis, to force the Oqçî-Izzeddînlos to a renewed settlement attempt in Raqqa, apparently once more without success.[101] In their continuing resistance against the Ottoman governor of Raqqa, who had been entrusted with the *mukataa* of Kilis in an effort to better control them, they at one point also joined forces with the Mawali bedouin emirs ruling over the northern Syrian desert from Salamiyya (east of Hama).[102] Another uptick in violence was registered in 1756, when the Oqçî-Izzeddînlos and other Kilis Kurds were accused of descending on the plain of Antioch to assault villages and travelling merchants, but also of illegally appropriating farmlands in Maraş.[103] Reports increasingly singled out the Serikanlo or Serektanlo *oymak* (tribal sub-division) as the most seditious; by late 1764 the authorities were noting that the Oqçî-Izzeddînlos were raiding villages as far away as Hisn al-Akrad in central Syria with up to 130 horsemen (*süvari*), and were already responsible at this point, together with their allies from the Mûsa-Beylo and Cum tribes, for robbing one top-level provincial governor (Reşvan-zade Süleyman) and killing another.[104]

---

98 ŞKT 116:210, no. 1; ŞKT 140:522:1843; MD 140:400:1412; A/AS 3:169:288.
99 Tahir Öğüt and Nihat Küçük, "18. Yüzyılda Kilis'te Okçu İzzeddinli Aşiretinin Vergi Direnci," *Akademik Araştırmalar ve Çalışmalar Dergisi* 7 (2015): 56.
100 ŞKT 142:496:1649; A/AS 3:151:258.
101 MD 141:78:288; MD 141:89:342; MD 141:91:346, 365; A/AS 3:205:347, 347a; A/AS 3:206:347b.
102 Öğüt and Küçük, "18. Yüzyılda Kilis'te Okçu İzzeddinli," 59–66.
103 HAD 2:78, no. 2; MD 158:10:20; MD 158:42:100; MD 158:171–2:519; MD 158:303:822; HAD 2:182, no. 2; Cevdet Dahiliye 14242.
104 MD 161:390:1204; MD 163:327–8:882; HAD 3:70, no. 2; HAD 3:82, no. 5; BOA: Ahkam-ı Cezayir ve Rakka [RAD] 24:196, no. 1.

The entire provincial administrative apparatus, including the detailed Mühimme and Şikayet registers we depend on for the rural history of Ottoman Anatolia and Syria, was in large part geared towards tribal control and sedentarization during the first half of the eighteenth century. As such it should come as no surprise, nor be seen as specific to the Kilis Kurds or any other such population, that the state authorities overwhelmingly perceived, categorized, and treated them in terms of *"eşkıyalık"* (brigandage), tribalism, rebellion, and tax liability. What is more striking is that despite the notoriety the Oqçî-Izzeddînlos had achieved by this time, the Ottoman state appeared to be cautiously willing, in the second half of the century, to recognize and co-opt individual Oqçî-Izzeddînlo leaders within a framework of local home rule.

We have already referred several times to the *"voyvoda"* of Kilis. Originally used to designate native Christian warlords and tributaries in the Balkans, the term also came to be applied to the tax collectors and *de facto* governors of imperial crown reserve lands such as the Kilis *hass*, especially with the progressive conversion of classical military *sancak*s into *mukataa* tax collectorships and the growing concentration on tribal control in the seventeenth century.[105] In the district of Kilis, where we see the post replacing that of *sancak-beyi* as early as 1629, or shortly after the end of the Celali rebellions in which the local governor 'Ali Canpolad had of course participated, the *voyvoda* naturally came to play a decisive role in the supervision of the Kurds.[106] For the most part, as we have seen, these relations were conflictual, being based on the collection or extortion of taxes and not seldom ending in violence. On the other hand, the Ottomans well knew that they had to rely on local intermediaries to govern the subject population more effectively, and increasingly began to concede fiscal responsibilities and outright political office to local notable figures (*ayan; vücuh*) throughout the Empire in the eighteenth century.

Already in 1725, for example, the court in Kilis accepted a sworn deposition from the recognized *boy-beyi*s (clan leaders) of the Oqçî-Izzeddînlo, Amîkî, and Mûsa-Beylo Kurds along with other local shaykhs and *ulema*, to confirm that a group of sixteen men farming and fishing near Karamort on the plain of Antioch were indeed longstanding residents of Shaykh al-Hadid, and not tax subjects of Mudiq (province

---

105 Fikret Adanır, "Woyvoda," *Encyclopaedia of Islam* II (Leiden: Brill, 2002), 11:215; Erol Özvar, "Voyvoda," *Türkiye Diyanet Vakfı İslam Ansiklopedisi* (Istanbul: TDV, 2013), 43: 129–31.

106 MD 84:49:98.

102   Stefan Winter

of Hama), as a *waqf* administrator of the latter was trying to claim.[107] Several years later, in 1757, the *boy-beyi*s of "the Oqçî-Izzeddînlos and other tribes and confederations living in the Kilis Plateau" (Cebel-i Kilis; the Kurd Dagh) were called upon directly by the Sublime Porte to interdict all brigandage and ensure the timely collection of taxes and tax arrears that year,[108] committing them nearly on par with the *voyvoda* himself to the good governance of the district and perhaps opening the way to a more formal implication on their part. It is in fact possible that an earlier *voyvoda* had already been chosen from among the local tribes, for an order telling the governors of Aleppo, Tripoli, Maraş, Adana, and Raqqa in 1735 to capture some Oqçî-Izzeddînlo brigands who might have fled to their territories notes that they were making common cause with the ex-*voyvoda* Velî and his sons, who were acting as the "Kurds' gang leaders" (*Ekrad'ın ser-cemiyetleri olub*).[109]

In any event, in 1761 the governor of Aleppo appointed an "elder" (*ihtiyar*) of the Oqçî-Izzeddînlos, Köse Bekir-oğlı Ahmed, as his *kethüda* (steward) for the Kilis *mukataa* with a mandate to collect taxes in a timely fashion and keep the local population under discipline. The appointment was, however, rescinded by the Sublime Porte only a short while later as being "detrimental to the order in the land" (*muhill-i nizam-ı memleket*), with the governor being instructed to find someone more appropriate, and Köse Bekir-oğlı not to interfere in the tax farm's affairs.[110] The Sublime Porte was perhaps more prescient than the governor in its dismissal of the Oqçî-Izzeddinlo *kethüda*. In 1780, another *ihtiyar* of the tribe, Ömer-oğlı el-hacc Velî, came to the authorities' notice for joining with a local army commander and a *sekban* (militia) leader to form a band of Kurdish brigands and loot homes in Kilis and A'zaz, later widening their operations to attack caravans even in the vicinity of Aleppo.[111]

Oqçî-Izzeddînlo leaders also appear to have played a role in the resistance against the Egyptian occupation in the 1830s. We have relatively fewer documentary sources from this and the previous decades, but already in 1834 Egyptian administrators were reporting trouble in the "Kurd Dagh" as the new regime attempted to collect weapons in

---

107   A/AS 2:225:367; MAD 9915:37, no. 2.
108   MD 159:67:184.
109   MD 141:41:140. Velî was incidentally also the name of the principal Oqçî-Izzeddinlo *boy beyi* in 1725.
110   A/AS 6:55:112; MD 162:229:667.
111   A/AS 15:159, no. 2; MD 176:188:578; A/AS 15:350, no. 1.

The Afrin District under Ottoman Rule, 1516–1921   103

the Kilis-Antioch area.[112] Then in May 1839, when Egyptian rule over Syria had already begun to crumble under the effect of various, in part British-armed, tribal uprisings in the coastal highlands, the Oqçî-Izzeddînlo chief "al-Hajj Ömer-oğlı" was reported to have led a cavalry unit against the Egyptian position at Darmık, a strategic promontory on the northern edge of the Syrian Kurd Dagh, and incited the tribes staying in the area to revolt. Al-Hajj Ömer-oğlı had purportedly also assembled one to two hundred cavalrymen, purchasing muskets probably from other rebels in the Gavur Dağı (Amanos Mountains); a force of not less than five hundred government troops would be necessary to quell him.[113]

Three of al-Hajj Ömer-oğlı's deputies had meanwhile rallied the population of nearby Bulamaçlı against the Egyptians, who began to worry that he might raise the entire Kurd Dagh in revolt or join forces with the legendary rebel bandit of the Gavur Dağı, Mıstık Bey (Küçükalioğlu).[114] Interestingly, one of the Egyptian missives also raises the question of whether al-Hajj Ömer-oğlı would be supported by "Köse Bekir-oğlı," very likely the successor to the eighteenth-century Oqçî-Izzeddînlo elder of that same name mentioned earlier.[115] In the end, however, the great revolt anticipated by the Egyptians in the Kurd Dagh does not seem to have materialized. The local Egyptian commander failed to make good on his promise to find and annihilate al-Hajj Ömer-oğlı, while leaders of the Şêxlo Kurds wrote to the Egyptians to assure them that no one else had joined al-Hajj Ömer-oğlı anyway (the few who did were only like "a she-donkey whose foal (*jahsh*) has died"), and that the people of the Kurd Dagh would sooner or later just kick him out.[116]

Regularizing the Kurd Dagh

If the Egyptian forces did not remain in Syria long enough to finish the work of pacifying the coastal mountains, the Ottomans picked up the effort with new vigour in the Tanzimat period. The Fırka-ı İslahiye ("Reform Division"), a special army unit tasked with settling the more refractory tribes and levying recruits in the Gavur Dağ (officially renamed the "Cebel-i Bereket") and the Çukurova, was set up

---

112 Asad Rustum (d. 1965), ed., *Al-Mahfuzat al-Malikiyya al-Misriyya: Bayan bi-Watha'iq al-Sham*, 4 vols. (Beirut: Al-Maktaba al-Bulusiyya, 1986–1987), [Mahfuzat] #3764.
113 Mahfuzat #5813.
114 Mahfuzat #5827, #5836, #5836–17, #5836–35, #5836–50, #5836–59.
115 Mahfuzat #5836–46.
116 Mahfuzat #5836–55, #5836–60, #5844, #5861, #5861–2, #5861–4, #5865–2.

104   Stefan Winter

and dispatched from Alexandretta in the spring of 1865. Part punitive campaign and part press gang, the Division first advanced into the likewise newly consecrated "Kürd Dağı," securing the road to Aleppo and submitting the tribal population to forced conscription (*kur'a*).[117] The great reformist statesman Ahmed Cevdet Paşa (d. 1895), who directed the Fırka-ı İslahiye and left a detailed account of its progress, relates that the Kürd Dağı ("the people of which are all Kurds, and express themselves in Kurdish") was at the time completely under the dominion of Hacci Ömer-oğlu Deli Halil – no doubt still the same, or of the same lineage, as the Oqçî-Izzeddînlo leader cited above. This Deli Halil held numerous other *ağa*s (rural or tribal lords) of the region under his sway, and possessed a mansion (*konak*) in Kilis itself, from whence he routinely interfered in local district affairs: it was "as if the town of Kilis were shared between the government of Aleppo and the Kürd Dağı government."[118]

The previous year, the governor of Aleppo had actually arrested Deli Halil and banished him to Edirne. Deli Halil had managed to return to the Kürd Dağı and resume his old ways, however, so that a military operation was deemed necessary to bring him to heel.[119] In fact Deli Halil fled before the advancing Fırka-ı İslahiye already in late June, following a show of force near Hassa on the eastern slope of the Cebel-i Bereket, leaving the Ottomans free to take the Kürd Dağı virtually unopposed. With the aid of various in-laws and other associates, Deli Halil was able to hold out in the Gavur Dağı for another few months, until, realizing the hopelessness of his situation, he came to offer his submission and join the Fırka in October. This proved to be his undoing: with the entire unit beset by cholera that fall, and quarantine measures only haphazardly applied, Deli Halil soon fell ill and died. Somewhat surprisingly, Cevdet Paşa himself would eulogize him as "a tall, extremely handsome, well-built, robust, well-proportioned, unique exemplar of a soldier and champion warrior."[120]

---

117   Yusuf Halaçoğlu, "Fırka-ı İslahiye ve Yapmış Olduğu İskan," *İstanbul Üniversitesi Tarih Dergisi* 27 (1973): 6–9; Bekir Sami Bayazıt, *1865–1866 Kürt-Dağı, Cebel'i Bereket, Kozanoğlu'ları İsyanı ve Güneydeki Aşiretleri İskânları* (Antioch: Kültür Eğitim Tesisleri, 1989).

118   Cevdet Paşa, *Tezâkir (21–39)* (Ankara: Türk Tarih Kurumu, 1991), 124–5.

119   Cevdet Paşa, 133. On Süreyya Mustafa Paşa of Aleppo, see Mehmed Süreyya (d. 1909), *Sicill-i Osmanî*, ed. Nuri Akbayar and Seyit Ali Kahraman (Istanbul: Türkiye Ekonomik ve Toplumsal Tarih Vakfı, 1996), 1554–5.

120   Cevdet Paşa, 142–4, 152, 168, 174, 179–81; Bayazıt, *1865–1866 Kürt-Dağı*, 221–5.

The actual chief of the Oqçî-Izzeddinlo tribe, Hacci İsmail-oğlu Osman Ağa, and the head of the Şêxlos, Reş Ağa-zade Mehmed Ağa, had submitted soon after Deli Halil's flight, and despite some minor resistance in the north, the Fırka-ı İslahiye was able to bring the entire Kürd Dağı under control by the summer and begin levying army recruits in the local villages. Another reform that was instituted almost immediately was to incorporate the whole plateau as the new *kaza* of İzziye, officially named in honour of Sultan Abdülaziz's son İzzeddin Efendi,[121] but evidently also as a gesture towards the area's historically leading tribe. Abiding by the framework of the empire-wide provincial reform (Vilayet Nizamnamesi) adopted just the year before, the new district encompassed three new sub-districts (*nahiye*) named for the Oqçî-Izzeddînlo, Şêxlo, and Amîkî tribes, in which these were expected to settle. The intent of Cevdet Paşa was finally to separate the *kaza* from Aleppo and attach it instead to a new *liva* to be constituted around the town of İslahiye, so as to break its long-standing association with Kilis.[122]

These administrative-territorial realignments were, however, not set in stone. The *kaza* of İzziye continued to form part of the *liva* of Aleppo, and already in 1876, its three sub-districts, along with a new *nahiye* named for the Mûsa-Beylo Kurds, were reassigned to the *kaza* of Kilis.[123] In the spring of 1896, unnamed tribes from the Kürd Dağı carried out a series of major raids in the Kilis area but also around Hassa in the *vilayet* of Adana, carrying off much livestock.[124] By 1908, we see a *kaza* of İzziye once again joined, like the *kaza* of Cum, to the *liva* of Kilis, with the governorate-general (*vilayet*) of Aleppo repeatedly receiving instructions over the following years to investigate various crimes and abuses of power ostensibly being committed there by the local *ağas*.[125] In 1912, the administrative centre of the *kaza* of Cum was established in Çolak village (Julaqan; Çolaqa, in the lower Syrian Kurd Dagh approx.

---

121 Öztürk, "İzziye Kazasının Kuruluşu," 31, 34–5; see also Saim Yörük, *Fırka-i İslahiye: Cevdet Paşa, Kozan ve Gâvur Dağı Ahvaline Dâir Lâyiha* (Istanbul: İdeal Kültür Yayıncılık, 2017), 37–8.

122 Cevdet Paşa, *Tezâkir (21–39)*, 144–5.

123 Öztürk, "İzziye Kazasının Kuruluşu," 35–40.

124 BOA: Yıldız Sadaret Resmi Maruzat Evrakı [Y.A.RES] 78:64; Sadaret Mektubi Kalemi Mühimme [A.MKT.MHM] 616:48; Tahrirat-ı Hariciye Kalemi [HR.TH] 175:91.

125 BOA: Dahiliye Nezareti Mektubi Kalemi [DH.MKT] 2628:64; Dahiliye Muhaberat-ı Umumiye İdaresi [DH.MUİ] 50–1:46; DH.MUİ 91–1:34; Dahiliye Nezareti Şifre Kalemi [DH.ŞFR] 423:57.

106   Stefan Winter

twelve kilometres southwest of 'Afrin), and that of İzziye in Karahöyük (at the northern-most edge of the Turkish Kürd Dağı, approximately sixty kilometres due west of Ayntab), so that the villagers would have an easier time reaching them for any official business.[126] In a list of district directors of Aleppo province from 1915, both "Okçı-İzzeddin" and Cum are once again identified as *nahiye*s.[127] The division of the Kurd Dagh into two sections therefore in a sense already foreshadowed its permanent partition between Turkey and Syria after World War I. The last Ottoman archival document dealing with the region concerns the appointment of a new director (*müdir*) to İzziye in March 1919 – a week after French forces had occupied Kozan in the northern Çukurova and began their push into the interior to occupy Maraş and all of Syria at the close of the war.[128]

Throughout the Turkish-Kemalist War of Independence (Kurtuluş), the Oqçî-İzzeddînlos under the leadership of Haccî Hannan Ağa would play a key role in the resistance against the French in the region, mainly through guerrilla attacks on the road between Ekbez and Kilis bisecting the Kurd Dagh, but also around Rajo in the southern (Syrian) part.[129] French army reports of the time indicate that in addition to their ravages in the Kurd Dagh, rebel bands from the area were also providing reinforcements to the Kurdish resistance leader Ibrahim Hanano at Aleppo.[130] According to one such report from early 1920, the "Kurdish committees" of Kilis-A'zaz were claiming allegeance to the exiled CUP leader Enver Paşa, although there is no actual proof for this.[131] With the signature of the Ankara Agreement and the end of the French-Turkish confrontation in the fall of 1921, in any event, the Kurdish population of the district became permanently divided between the new states of Turkey and Syria.

---

126 BOA: Şura-yı Devlet [ŞD] 34:40.
127 BOA: Dahiliye Memurin Kalemi [DH.MEM] 222:88. A government report from the same year makes note of the development potential of "beledi" (local) and "cebeli" (mountain) varieties of olives grown in the İzziye and Cum districts; see ŞD 2248:47.
128 DH.MEM 382:42.
129 Öztürk, "İzziye Kazasının Kuruluşu," 40–4; Halil İbrahim İnce, *Millî Mücadele'de Kilis* (Ankara: Atatürk Araştırma Merkezi, 2015), 65–6, 99, 128, 166–8.
130 Archives Ministère des Affaires étrangères, La Courneuve (Paris): Correspondance politique et commerciale, Série E – Levant / Syrie Liban [E-L/SL] 115:60, 79; E-L/SL 116:118; E-L/SL 117:26, 97, 115; E-L/SL 121:21–2.
131 E-L/SL 121:33.

Figure 3.5. Farm near Rajo, Syrian Kurd Dagh (2002)
Photo by Stefan Winter.

The Ottoman state obviously did not follow a single consistent "policy" towards the ʿAfrin area or any other rural district in Syria throughout the early modern period. In line with a general predisposition towards preserving the structures and sometimes even the personnel from the previous Mamluk administration, the Ottomans initially recognized the authority of the Kurdish leader ʿIzzeddin Bey over the tribal population of the Kilis (Kurd Dagh) area and beyond, his objectionable religious identity notwithstanding, before co-opting the rival Canpolad family as governors of the newly-constituted "*liva* of the Kurds" and even of the whole province of Aleppo in the late sixteenth century. Following the Celali rebellions, in which the Canpolads were directly implicated, the tribes of Kilis and of the *nahiye* of Cum in particular were recast as a private fiscal reserve (*hass*) of the Ottoman queen mother, attracting the close scrutiny of the central authorities each time their taxes were deemed to be in arrears or they in a state of rebellion. The first half of the eighteenth century especially has left us with a rich ethnography of the Kurd Dagh tribes, when they and the rest of the pastoralist population in the region became subject to a sustained government sedentarization (*iskan*) program.

It is also from the mid-eighteenth century onwards that we have the first references to an indigenous community leadership, particularly among the Oqçî-Izzeddîn tribe. Both the Egyptian occupation authorities and the Ottoman Tanzimat regime would attempt to subjugate and co-opt these lineages in their efforts to police the unruly Kurd Dagh, using military force and conscription where necessary but also creating new jurisdictions such as the *kaza*s of İzziye, Şeyhli (Şexlo), and Musabeyli, in an endeavour to integrate and serve the local Kurdish population. This "policy" of recognizing linguistic and communal difference, co-opting or creating local intermediaries, and institutionalizing distinct administrative structures can be said to have been in effect in one form or another throughout the Ottoman era. The official negation of the district's linguistic, social, and cultural identity would not begin until after the end of the Empire.[132]

---

132 Research carried out with the support of the Canadian SSHRC/CRSH project "Les Kurdes de Syrie : Peuplement et occupation de l'espace à l'époque ottomane" (2017–21). The author is also grateful to Fexrî ʿEvdo, Muhannad Alkatee, and Şehnaz İyibaş for sharing document references and other insights and suggestions.

PART TWO

Kurds in Western and Urban Syria

4 Locating the Kurds in Ottoman Jordan and Palestine in the Sixteenth Century

ZAINAB HAJHASAN

The presence of Kurdish populations in Jordan and Palestine dates back to the Ayyubid period, when Salah al-Din al-Ayyubi employed Hakkari Kurdish troops in the coastal areas of Palestine as well as other groups settled in al-Salt. The Kurdish presence continued in the Mamluk period, when it was marked by the establishment of multiple Kurdish *waqf* (pious) foundations, and into the Ottoman period, which saw the community expand into various towns and *nahiyes* (districts) and become a significant factor in the region's socio-economic makeup. Archival documents from different branches of the Ottoman bureaucracy offer a detailed record of the community's demography, economic activities, and administrative role under Ottoman imperial rule. This chapter aims to provide a first overview of the historical Kurdish presence in Jordan and Palestine in the early Ottoman period on the basis mainly of sixteenth-century *Tahrir* (tax census) registers for Jerusalem, Safad, Gaza (Ghazza), Nablus, and 'Ajlun, as well as an *Awqaf* (pious foundations) register for the province of Damascus (Şam). These sources constitute a vital tool for imagining the Kurdish population and its economic activities and social dimension; most significantly, as will be shown, these materials help in understanding the continuing mobility of the Kurdish population in the region.

We have only a few studies on the historical Kurdish presence in Jordan and Palestine, chief among them the works of Muhammad al-Suwayriki and others which mainly describe the Kurdish community in the context of the important social and political transformations of the late Ottoman period.[1] The Kurds, however, also appear in works

---

1 Muhammad al-Suwayriki, *Al-Akrad al-Urdunniyun wa-Dawruhum fi Bina' al-Urdunn al-Hadith: Ma'a Lamhat 'an Akrad Suriya wa-Lubnan wa-Filistin* (Amman: n.p., 2004); Muhammad al-Suwayriki, *Al-Mawsu'a al-Kubra li-Mashahir al-Kurd 'abra al-Tarikh,*

focussing more specifically on the region's economy and social life under Ottoman rule, which highlight general demographic changes as well as the role played by Kurdish and other tribes in local society.[2] Except for one study by Amnon Cohen and Bernard Lewis using the Ottoman Tahrir Defters, these studies rely mainly on *shar'iyya* court registers.[3] However, Ottoman archival sources including the Tahrir Defters offer essential details that are not found in the *kadı* registers, and therefore serve to more accurately locate the Kurdish population in Ottoman Jordan and Palestine, understand the pattern of their distribution, and grasp information on their social and economic interactions, in a period that is often neglected in studies on the subject at hand.

The Kurds in Jordan/Palestine Tax Registers

The Tahrir tax registers encompass data on village or tribal population sizes, property holding, economic production, and tax liabilities in a given Ottoman province. As they provide a lot of incidental information on an area's topography, demography, agriculture, and administration, they are seen to constitute a key source for human geography and settlement patterns in the Ottoman period.[4] Amy Singer has pointed especially to the value of the marginal notes contained in the registers, which frequently refer to the previous tax conditions of specific areas, but also warned of the registers' limitations as a historical source, due to tax officials' limited knowledge of local society and inconsistent coverage.[5] Similarly, Heath Lowry has pointed to the problems of misreporting,

---

6 vols. (Beirut: Al-Dar al-'Arabiyya li'l-Mawsu'at, 2010); Muhammad al-Suwayriki, *Tarikh al-Kurd fi Bilad al-Sham wa-Misr* (Baghdad: Dar al-Thaqafa, 2007); Muhammad al-Suwayriki, *Tarikh al-Akrad fi Bilad al-Sham wa-Misr* (Amman: al-Kindi, 2010); 'Uthman 'Ali, *Al-Kurd fi'l-Arshif al-'Uthmani* (Erbil: N.p., 2010).

2 Hind Abu Sha'ar, *Tarikh Sharqiyy al-Urdunn* (Amman: Ministry of Culture, 2010); Ahmad Shuqayrat, *Tarikh al-Idara al-'Uthmaniyya fi Sharq al-Urdunn, 1864–1918* (Amman: Dar Khalid al-Lahyani, 2016); Ahmad Aybash, *Tarikh al-Sham fi Matla' al-'Ahd al-'Uthmani, 1520–1544* (Abu Dhabi: National Library, 2010), 27–33. See also David McDowall, *A Modern History of the Kurds* (London: I.B. Tauris, 2021); Muhammad Khuraysat, *Dirasat fi Tarikh Madinat al-Salt* (Jordan: Ministry of Culture, 1997), 36–7. Hirmis Aboona, *Assyrians, Kurds, and Ottomans: Intercommunal Relations on the Periphery of the Ottoman Empire* (Amherst, NY: Cambria Press, 2008).

3 Amnon Cohen and Bernard Lewis, *Population and Revenue in the Towns of Palestine in the Sixteenth Century* (Princeton: Princeton University Press, 1978).

4 Osman Gümüşçü, "The Ottoman Tahrir Defters as a Source for Historical Geography," *Belleten* 72, no. 265 (December 2008): 911–42, https://doi .org/10.37879/belleten.2008.911.

5 Amy Singer, "Tapu Tahrir Defterleri and Kadi Sicilleri: A Happy Marriage of Sources," *Tarih* 1 (1990): 96–107; see also Metin M. Coşgel, "Ottoman Tax Registers (*Tahrir Defterleri*)," *Historical Methods* 37, no. 2 (2004): 87–100, https://doi .org/10.3200/HMTS.37.2.87-102.

Locating the Kurds in Ottoman Jordan and Palestine   113

inaccuracy, and contradictions with other sources that are inherent to the Tahrir registers, and cautioned that many works using them suffer "from a complete absence of anything resembling a useful methodological approach."[6] Heeding these warnings, the following contribution will not take the Tahrirs as a final authority on the social and economic parameters of sixteenth-century Palestine and Jordan. Rather, in attempting to provide a general overview of the Kurdish presence in the region in the Ottoman period, the aim will simply be to draw on the sporadic references to Kurds in the Tahrir registers, where possible in combination with other sources, to locate villages, tribes, or neighbourhoods known to the Ottoman administration as associated either in the past or continuously with an identifiably Kurdish population.

In this study we have drawn on twenty-two Tahrir registers for the *sancak*s (provinces) of Jerusalem, Safad, Gaza, and 'Ajlun 1526 to 1597.[7] Kurds (*Ekrad*) appear in these registers in three ways: to designate a specific neighbourhood or quarter (*mahalle*); as a community or tribe (*cemaat/jama'a* or *taife/ta'ifa*) of a given village, *hass* (fiscal reserve), or *waqf*; or as individual families in non-Kurdish *mahalles*. The terms *cemaat* and *taife* usually refer to nomadic Kurds,[8] but they can also designate Kurdish groups residing in towns or villages.[9] These communities either existed in the area since before the Ottoman period or consisted of resettled nomadic families. It is worth noting that this terminology was also utilized for other social groups such as the Bedouins, Turkomans, and Moroccans, as well as for religious groups such as various Jewish and Christian communities (*Cemaat* and *taife* could also be the term for a shaykh's followers).[10] Specifically Kurdish quarters (*mahallat al-Akrad*) are mentioned in al-Salt, Safad, Hebron, and Gaza, while other cities did not have such neighbourhoods. Of course the existence of a Kurdish quarter in a given town does not necessarily mean that the Kurdish population was limited to that area, nor that only Kurds inhabited the quarter.

Some details absent from the census registers can be found in the Evkaf (*waqf*; pious foundations) registers. Our sole reference to the Kurdish population in Ramla, for example, occurs in the *waqf* register

---

6 Heath Lowry, "The Ottoman Tahrîr Defterleri as a Source for Social and Economic History: Pitfalls and Limitations," in *Studies in Defterology: Ottoman Society in the Fifteenth and Sixteenth Centuries* (Istanbul: Isis Press, 1992), 3–18.

7 T.C. Cumhurbaşkanlığı Devlet Arşivi (ex-Başbakanlık [BOA]), Istanbul: Tahrir Defteri [TD] 131, 258, 265, 266, 289, 300, 304, 312, 342, 346, 427, 522, 559, 602; BOA: Türkiye Kadastro Genel Müdürlüğü [TKGM] 2, 129, 130, 134, 148, 350, 161, 418.

8 See TD 300:70, 197–98; TD 427:31, 142; TKGM 161: 66, 69.

9 TD 300:71; TKGM 161:155; TKGM 148:117.

10 TD 265:69, 173; TD 289:110.

114   Zainab HajHasan

of Gaza in 1549.[11] The division of towns into specificquarters was often inherited from earlier times, that is, from the Seljuk (Ayyubid) and Mamluk periods.[12] However, studies drawing on the *shar'iyya* court records in the region have shown that, through regular social and economic interactions, some quarters originally inhabited by specific ethnic or religious communities underwent significant demographic changes and gradually grew less homogenous.[13] This is particularly important in places such as Acre and Nablus, which were not major cities in these periods.

Ottoman tax records can also point to the past and possibly continuing existence of a Kurdish population on the basis of pious foundations. The copy of a foundation deed (*waqfiyya*) dated 583/1187 contained in a Tahrir register for Gaza, Jerusalem, Safad, and 'Ajlun attests the establishment by Salah al-Din of a *waqf* for the benefit of the Hakkari shaykhs Ahmad ibn Abi Bakr and 'Ali ibn Ahmad and their descendants in Jerusalem. The *waqf* included the villages of Tur Sina and Abu Dis (in Palestine).[14] Another example is the *waqf* of the Ayyubid sultan al-Malik al-'Adil Abu-Bakr ibn Ayyub for the benefit of the chamberlain (*hajib*) 'Ali al-Hakkari, which included two farms (*mazra'a*) in Jerusalem, as well as the farm of Dayr Yazid and the farm of Dayr Hazem, for a total revenue of 2,750 *guruş*. The Ottoman document, which unfortunately does not provide the date of the original *waqfiyya*, is dated 970/1562.[15]

The Kurds of Jordan and Palestine also appear to have controlled other *waqfs* centred on Jerusalem, Hebron, and Nablus, most of them bequeathed by Hakkari Kurds in the Ayyubid and Mamluk period. These included a Kurdish *zawiya* (Sufi lodge) in Jerusalem or a benefice for a fighter (*murabit*) associated with Salah al-Din.[16] These foundations, around the properties of which Kurds often continued to reside, of course maintained their status in the Ottoman period.

---

11 TD 265:293.

12 Adar Arnon, "The Quarters of Jerusalem in the Ottoman Period," *Middle Eastern Studies* 28, no. 1 (1992): 1–3, https://doi.org/10.1080/00263209208700889.

13 Ibrahim Rabay'a, *Tarikh al-Quds Fi al-'Asr al-'Uthmani fi Daw' al-Watha'iq Khilala 1600–1700* (Nablus: Maktabat Kul Shay', 1991), 37; Amy Singer, *Palestinian Peasants and Ottoman Officials: Rural Administration Around Sixteenth-Century Jerusalem* (Cambridge: Cambridge University Press, 1994), 80–3; Dror Ze'evi, *An Ottoman Century: The District of Jerusalem in the 1600s* (New York: State University of New York, 1996), 23–4.

14 TD 522:19; TKGM 129:29.

15 TD 342:14; TD 522:28.

16 TD 602:458; TD 522:28.

Locating the Kurds in Ottoman Jordan and Palestine 115

The Ottoman Tahrir records do not yet offer evidence of Kurds exercising administrative roles in the region in the sixteenth century, as they are known from other sources to have done in later periods. Suwayriki, however, surmises that they began to obtain such roles in various parts of the Empire after the battle of Çaldıran, and indicates that the governor of 'Ajlun in 1555 was Kurdish.[17]

Kurdish Urban Neighbourhoods (*Mahalle*)

The history of the Kurdish neighbourhoods (sing. *mahalle*) of al-Salt and Jerusalem, also known locally as the *harat al-Akrad*, is thought to go back to the settlement by Salah al-Din of Hakkari and other Kurdish troops and their families during the campaign to reconquer Jerusalem in 1187 CE.[18] In Jordan, the Kurds settled in al-Salt seem to have remained in that area, with a possible expansion to Irbid.[19] The population fluctuated in the Ottoman period and occasionally Kurdish families also moved to Jerusalem and its surroundings, as attested by references there to the Hakkari Kurds (see below). In Palestine, the Kurds spread in Jerusalem, Hebron, Ramla, Safad, Acre, Nablus, and Gaza in the Ayyubid and Mamluk periods; the Mamluks, for example, are recorded to have employed "warlike Kurds" in the port cities to avert any naval attacks.[20] Suwayriki mentions a conflict that arose in Hebron between the Ayyubid Kurds and the Tamimi Arabs in the Mamluk period that ultimately contributed to the disbanding of the Ayyubid family in multiple cities.[21] While the growing Kurdish presence in Jerusalem was due in part to Kurdish ulama travelling to the city in that period, under the Ottomans, the *hajj* was the primary reason for Kurds to settle in Jerusalem, around the Zawiyat al-Azbakiyya.[22]

In the sixteenth century, and especially after the end of the Janbirdi al-Ghazali revolt in 1521, the administrative division of the Arab provinces became more tangible.[23] 'Ajlun, of which al-Salt was a *nahiye* (district), was made a *liva* (*sancak*) of the province (*eyalet*) of Damascus, along with Jerusalem (Quds), Gaza, Nablus, and Safad. Acre and Ramla

---

17 Suwayriki, *Tarikh al-Kurd*, 34.
18 Khuraysat, *Dirasat*, 65–7, 94.
19 Suwayriki, *Al-Kurd fi'l-Arshif al-'Uthmani*, 97–8, 109.
20 Cohen and Lewis, *Population and Revenue*, 34.
21 Suwayriki, *Tarikh al-Akrad*, 93.
22 Suwayriki, *Al-Kurd fi Bilad al-Sham wa-Misr*, 110–12.
23 Muhammad Adnan al-Bakhit, *The Ottoman Province of Damascus in the Sixteenth Century* (Beirut: Librairie du Liban, 1982).

116   Zainab HajHasan

became *nahiye*s of Safad and Gaza, respectively. The administrative status of Acre shifted towards the end of the sixteenth century, however, as it was joined to the *liva* of Sayda (Sidon), which itself became an independent *eyalet* (separated from Damascus) in the seventeenth century.[24] Within these areas, the Ottoman Tahrir registers detail the distribution of Kurdish tribes who frequently inhabited villages or quarters named after them.

Kurdish quarters existed in Safad and Gaza as well as in Hebron and al-Salt. Occasionally these *mahalle*s were named after a specific tribe rather than for Kurds in general. Names of tribes were also applied to villages and farms, such as the village of Kurdiyya in Ramla.[25] A general survey of the relevant Ottoman tax registers also enables us to locate the Kurdish population as follows. Al-Salt: one *mahalle*, two villages; Gaza: one *mahalle*, one tribe; Safad: one *mahalle*, four *cemaat*, and the village oddly named Kawkab al-Akrad ("Planet of the Kurds"); Jerusalem: one *mahalle*, two *cemaat*; Nablus: one *cemaat*.

In some cases, quarters identified generically as the Kurdish *mahalle* became identified with specific Kurdish tribes, or vice versa. In Hebron, the Kurdish quarter was designated the "Mahallat Akrad Qays" in 1566, suggesting its inhabitants were affiliated (for tax purposes) with the Arab Bani Qays tribe at the time, before being simply called the Mahallat al-Akrad again in 1597.[26] The neighbourhood known as the "Kurdish" Shuja'iyya quarter (Shuja'iyyat al-Akrad) of Gaza in 1549 and later called the Mahallat al-Akrad, in 1566, was known simply as the Mahallat al-Shuja'iyya in 1578.[27] In Safad, by contrast, the Kurdish quarter continued to be known as the Mahallat al-Akrad at the end of the sixteenth century.[28] On another level, the Arabic narrative literature corroborates the existence of a Kurdish quarter in Jerusalem. Khuraysat relates that the Kurds of Salt immigrated to Jerusalem, forming a community and a quarter called the "Harat al-Saltiyya" (block, neighbourhood of the Saltis).[29] On the other hand, Adar Arnon shows, on the basis of archival sources, that the Sharaf quarter was previously called the Kurdish quarter.[30] While the sixteenth-century Tahrir *defter*s

---

24   Muhammad M. al-Arna'ut, *Min al-Tarikh al-Hadari li-Bilad al-Sham fi'l-Qarn al-Awwal li'l-Hukm al-'Uthmani* (Amman: Al-An, 2018), 104–11.
25   TD 265:293.
26   TD 289:193–5; TKGM 129:72–3; TD 427:314; TKGM 130:85–6.
27   TD 265:18; TD 304:31; TD 427:165–6. This *mahalle*, unlike other Kurdish quarters, also encompassed a *suq* (market). TD 304:2–3 (*kanunname*); TD 312:98.
28   TKGM 161:13; TD 300:19; TD 427:1.
29   Khuraysat, *Dirasat*, 31–2.
30   Arnon, "Quarters of Jerusalem," 9.

do indicate a Kurdish quarter in Hebron, it is unclear what happened to the one in Jerusalem.[31] Whereas the records show "Ayyubid Kurds" to be residing in the quarter of Bab Hatta, they do not contain any references to a "Hayy al-Akrad" or a "Mahalle-i Ekrad" in the city itself.[32]

This could be explained by three reasons: first, that the Kurdish quarter was in fact only a smaller block (*hara*) of a larger quarter; second, that the interior conflicts that occurred prior to the Ottoman period and that scattered the Kurds throughout the region led to the disappearance of their quarters and the expansion of neighbouring quarters; and third, that a clear topographic division was not as evident in sixteenth-century Jordan and Palestine, and that the Kurdish population did not reside in one specific quarter or block. It is also worth noting that in other Palestinian and Jordanian towns, the Kurdish population occasionally appears as the *Jama'at al-Akrad* (the Kurdish community) under a specific village or *mahalle*.[33] This is similar to the case of the non-Muslim population or other social groups like the Turkomans, Indians, and Moroccans.[34]

Safad, Gaza, and early sixteenth-century al-Salt all hosted a large population of Kurds and other tribal groups. In the earliest record of Safad, the Kurdish quarter was home to around 196 families whose names (Hakkari, Canpolad, etc.) suggest they were overwhelmingly Kurds. This changes in later records, however, with the presence of names such as "al-Badawi," "Arab," and "Suri" (from Sur/Tyre in Lebanon).[35] The Kurdish *mahalle*s were frequently adjacent to those of the Turkomans, especially in Safad and Gaza. In the *nahiye* of Qaqun (*liva* of Nablus), the Kurdish *cemaat*s are recorded as being adjacent to the Arab (Bedouin) *cemaat*s.[36] This proximity resulted in much interaction between the two communities and an integration of certain Kurdish families into the Turkoman *cemaat*s, as in the case of Hasan al-Kurdi, who was recorded under the census of the Turkomans of Lahif in Safad.[37]

The Kurds also settled in villages. Gaza, Acre, Safad, Ramla, Nablus, and Hebron all had villages named after Kurdish families or farms (*mezraa*) affiliated with Kurdish tribes, especially the Xawalde tribe (*taife*). Such topographies appear to have developed under Ottoman rule,

---

31 TD 289:193; TKGM 129:72.
32 TKGM 129:12; TKGM 130:13.
33 TD 266:6; TD 427:9, 165; TKGM 161:21; TGKM 161:17.
34 TD 266:30, 47; TKGM 2:7.
35 TKGM 161:13–16; TD 300:19–21.
36 TD 258:241–3.
37 TD 247:90.

especially inasmuch as they do not yet appear in the earliest records.[38] Some of these villages were *waqfs* of Kurdish figures who bequeathed the land, or its harvest, to a specific beneficiary, as will be seen below.

The size of the Kurdish population in any given district could fluctuate significantly. The Kurdish quarter in al-Salt that was home to 130 Kurdish households at the beginning of the sixteenth century saw this number decrease to thirteen households at the end of the century.[39] Such decreases occurred in other districts and sub-districts such as Safad, Acre, and Tiberias, as well as in Gaza. The Kurdish population of Safad, and of Safad's Kurdish quarter in particular, underwent a marked decrease, from 196 households and forty-one bachelors in 1548 to 105 and twenty-six in 1556, only to increase again to 171 households in 1566.[40] Similarly, in Gaza the population decreased from 407 families to 380, then to ninety families in the two decades covered by these records.[41] In a different scenario in Ramla (province of Gaza), the aforementioned village of Kurdiyya, which had properties and *waqfs* indicating a Kurdish presence (see below), encompassed fourteen families as well as three bachelors in 1549, but no longer appears in later records.[42]

Sometimes, however, the decrease of the Kurdish population in one area was met with an increase in another. In Hebron, for instance, the Kurdish quarter saw an important increase from 237 households in 1553–4; to 304 households, twelve bachelors, and one blind person in 1563; before decreasing again to 180 households in 1597.[43] The records also indicate a pattern of interior and interregional migration. Kurdish families from regions such as Hakkari, the Hijaz, Rawand, and Fayyum settled in non-Kurdish *mahalles* in Palestine. Cohen and Lewis suggest that these "new arrivals" must have come because of economic or environmental reasons or, occasionally, conflicts and rebellions.[44]

The Tahrir registers generally do not state the religion of the Kurdish population. From the registers concerned, however, we see a Christian *cemaat* (group; community) residing in the Kurdish *mahalle* of al-Salt,

---

38 TD 300:77.

39 TD 266:36–8; TKGM 2:17.

40 TD 300:19–20; TD 427:1.

41 TD 265:18–24; TD 304:31–6; TD 427:165–6. In the second register for Gaza, dated 1557, the *mahalle*'s population includes fifteen sharifs; fifteen imams, *khatibs*, muezzins, and *muhassils* (tax collectors); and five handicapped and blind people.

42 TD 265:293.

43 TD 289:193–5; TKGM 129:72–3; TKGM 130:84–5.

44 Cohen and Lewis, *Population and Revenue*, 30; see also see Hind Abu Sha'ar, *Tarikh*, 47–50.

Locating the Kurds in Ottoman Jordan and Palestine   119

while in 1549 there was a Samaritan *cemaat* in the Kurdish quarter of Safad. Likewise, the records for Gaza for the same year show Jewish and Samaritan groups living in the Kurdish Shuja'iyya neighbourhood.[45]

In summary, Kurdish populations existed in many different districts and neighbourhoods of Jordan and Palestine in the early Ottoman period. Many of these, as indicated in the work of Boris James, had first been brought to the region by Saladin and the Ayyubids in the context of the Crusades, before coming increasingly under pressure in the period of Turkish and Circassian Mamluk rule.[46] By the time of the Ottoman conquest, the Hakkari soldiery and their families were still an important segment of the local population. In Ottoman tax censuses, this population was recorded at its highest level in the earlier period of Ottoman rule and started to fluctuate towards the end of the sixteenth century. While some districts saw the virtual disappearance of their Kurdish populations, Gaza and Safad, among other areas, maintained an evident Kurdish communal presence through the last records available. Many other Kurdish families, men, or women continued to reside in these districts and *mahalle*s as individuals too.

The Kurds as *Cemaat, Taife*, and Old Troops

As indicated earlier, a Kurdish population had been settled in Jordan and Palestine, particularly the latter, since the Ayyubid and Mamluk periods. This population included former military communities, which Ottoman records show were established mainly in urban areas (*mahalle*s). As these communities had essentially been recruited to protect the coastal cities and Jerusalem against the crusaders, records of such troops were not observed in al-Salt.

Remarkably, these former military communities continue to be identified as such in the Ottoman fiscal records of the sixteenth century, where they are listed under the title "Cündiyan" (Ottoman plural of Arabic *jundi*, 'soldier') or "Ecnad" (from Arabic *jund*, 'army'). These groups are often characterized as being established in the area "of old" (*kadimden mütemekkinler*) or, as in the 1566 Safad register, as "sipahis [cavalrymen] in olden times" (*kadim zamanda sipahileri*).[47] Many are noted to be resident in Kurdish quarters; others are mentioned as residents of Turkomans and other non-Kurdish quarters, including

---

45   TD 266:36–8; TKGM 2:17; TKGM 161:17.
46   Boris James, *Genèse du Kurdistan : Les Kurdes dans l'Orient mamlouk et mongol, 1250–1340* (Paris: Éditions de la Sorbonne, 2021).
47   TD 265:18, 26; TD 304:31, 36; TKGM 161:8, 17; TD 427:2.

Hikr al-Tuffah and Dar al-Khadr in Gaza and al-Wata and al-Jamiʿ al-Ahmar in Safad.[48] In Gaza, the Cündiyan also included "Jarakisah" (Circassians), referring either to the ethnicity of the original community or to later Mamluk military divisions.[49] A significant number of these communities, however, will have been remnants of the Kurdish groups settled there during the Crusades; the 1566 register for Jerusalem specifically identifies the "old troops" there as *"cemaat-ı Ayyubiyya"* (Ayyubid community) of the *"cündiyan-ı halka"* or soldiery of the provincial tribal militia (*halka*).[50]

While these old troops are usually encountered in urban settings, the Safad records also mention some in the villages of Iksal and Saruniyya (*nahiye* of Jira) in 1566 and 1574.[51] Other than the Cündiyan of the Turkoman quarter of Safad who are noted to have practised farming, we generally do not have information on these communities' economic activities.[52] Since they are clearly distinguished from other Kurdish *cemaat*s in the Ottoman Tahrir registers, it is likely that the Kurdish communities we see in Jordan and Palestine came about through pastoralism and migration rather than as remnants of old military divisions, and continued, irrespective of Selim I's sedentarization policies, to maintain a largely nomadic lifestyle. Such communities are generally identified clearly as *cemaat-ı Ekrad* in the registers, while the term *taife* is often used to label nomadic Kurds (temporarily) residing in villages (rather than towns). For Arab tribes, the term *taife* usually designates the larger confederation, of which the *cemaat* are individual branches, for example the *cemaat* of Shaykh Ahmad, Shaykh Salem, and Musa of the *taife* Bani Sakhr in Salt.[53] For the Kurds, on the other hand, the two are used interchangeably or together, as in *"Cemaat-ı ta'ife-i Kabaysha ve Xawalde ve Aşafere-i Ekrad"* or *"Xawalde ve Aşafere nam Ekrad taifesi."*[54] Since the term *cemaat* is used for both Arab and Kurdish tribes, it is not easy to differentiate between them when labels such as Akrad, ʿUrban, and ʿArab are not employed. The Kawabli tribe identified as Kurdish by Adnan al-Bakhit, for instance, is not in fact recorded as such in the available sixteenth century archival records.[55]

---

48 TKGM 161:13; TD 427:5–6.
49 TD 304:39–45; TD 265:27–36.
50 TD 289:25; TKGM 129:12.
51 TD 300:70; TD 559:142.
52 TD 304:45 TD 265:36.
53 TKGM 2:63–8; TD 265:24–6.
54 TD 427:32.
55 M. Adnan al-Bakhit, *Dirasat fi Bilad al-Sham: Filistin* (Amman: Greater Amman Municipality, 2005), 2:19. See also TD 559:295; TKGM 161:366.

Kurdish tribes were found in greatest number in villages of Safad, including in Tabgha and Saruniyya in the *nahiye* of Jira and Iksal in Tiberus, in addition to smaller communities in Lubiyya, Majdal, Hadtha, and Dallata in Tiberus and Safad. The earliest record of these clans is from 1549 and includes the Hasayki, Qaba'ili, Mahasne Kabayshe, 'Amre and Xawalde. The registers, however, suggest a discontinuous presence. For example, the Hasayki tribe settled in Tabgha village alongside the Qaba'ili tribe in 1549, appears in the village of Saruniyya in 1556, before disappearing entirely from later records.[56] While these tribes appear scattered across various villages as early as 1549, in later records they appear to have congregated. In 1556, for example, Saruniyya hosted three tribes (the Hasaykis, Kabayshes, and Mahasnes) and Iksal another three (the Kabayshes, 'Amres, and Xawaldes.)[57] By 1574, similarly, the Kabayshes, 'Assafs, and Xawaldes had settled in Iksal, replacing or displacing two of the previous tribes.[58] Unlike the other districts of Jordan and Palestine, Nablus was also home to one purely nomadic (*göçer ve konar*) Kurdish population, which lived alongside the local Turkoman tribes in the *nahiye* of Qaqun and shared in their agricultural and animal husbandry activities.[59]

Perhaps due to an increase in population or a tribal conflict, in 1566 the Kabayshes, Xawaldes, and Ashafres (a newly recorded tribe) are listed together as one *cemaat*.[60] Such a situation is evoked in 1549, where the register records an objection by the Mahasne and Qaba'ili tribes, apparently together, to their tax burden, which had not been reduced despite a decrease in their community's size. The tax assessment was subsequently modified to "fit their condition."[61]

Though these communities were nomadic and normally characterized by movement, some appear more settled and sedentarized than others. While the records lose track of some tribes that presumably ceased to exist in Safad, the presence of others including the Xawalde and Kabaysha is attested until the end of the century. Whereas the Hasayki only appear in one register, the Qaba'ili tribe is attested a second time in the village of Dallata (then in the *nahiye* of Safad) ten years

---

56 TKGM 161:67; TD 300:71.
57 TD 300:70–1, 197–8.
58 TD: 559:142–5.
59 TD 258 241–2.
60 TD 427:31–2.
61 TKGM 161:69. Interestingly, the entry refers to an earlier Safad register as "Defter-i atik" (old or previous register) that is however not available in the archives, while referring to the 1549 register of 1549 as the "defter-i cedid" (new register).

122   Zainab HajHasan

later.[62] The Xawalde, in contrast, who inhabited Safad as early as the Hasayki and Qaba'ili, appear to have been more settled and remained in the district at least until the end of the century. Similarly, while smaller tribes such as the Kabaysha maintained their existence in Safad towards the end of the century, the 'Amre disappeared.[63] One might speculate that these movements and discontinuities were the result of their farming and pastoral activities. The 1566 *defter* for Safad also suggests topographic and administrative changes such as the inclusion of a new *nahiye* of Sur (Tyre in South Lebanon); as well as a notable rise in the Arab Bedouin population in the *nahiye* of Jira, which had hosted several Kurdish tribes and which may have negatively impacted the Kurdish population.[64] On the other hand, the registers also bear witness to new villages with a Kurdish community, such as Iksal in Tiberias in 1566.[65] Unfortunately, we do not have any indication of the later location of Kurdish groups that ceased to exist in Safad by the end of the century.

The Tahrirs provide not only demographic information but also data on the economic practices of the Kurdish population in Jordan and Palestine and their interaction with other social groups. The Safad registers, for example, indicate that Kurdish *cemaats* were involved in tenant farming in Safad and its surrounding (*tevabinde*), whereby the clans worked the land and shared its yield with the landlord.[66] Similar information is found with regard to the nomadic Kurds of Nablus.[67] Other records highlight cooperation between Kurdish and Turkoman *cemaats*. A record from Safad, for instance, mentions Kurds farming a piece of land in Dallata village, together with Turkomans in 1566, in exchange for 1/8 of the harvest.[68] Another entry from the same Tahrir shows a Kurdish populace (*halk*) farming land in Kafr Buru'm in Jira alongside the people of the village.[69]

The agricultural activities of Turkoman clans sometimes involved tax exemptions or reductions in return for certain services. An entry from 1549 shows a Kurdish tribe protecting Turkoman farmers in Jira *nahiye* in Safad in exchange for a fiscal exemption (*bedel-i rusumat*).[70] Another

---

62   TD 427:31.
63   TKGM 161:147, 155; TD 300:198.
64   TD 559:154–60; TD 427:32.
65   TD 300:197.
66   TKGM 161:155; TD 300:197; TD 427:31; TD 559:143.
67   TKGM 148:117.
68   TD 427:31.
69   TD 427:39.
70   TKGM 161:67, 70.

Locating the Kurds in Ottoman Jordan and Palestine   123

document indicates the role of the Xawalde and Ashafare clans in farming and guarding lands from thieves in return for tax reductions:

> The aforementioned Xawalde and Ashafare Kurdish tribes farm some farmlands (*mezari*) belonging to Safad. After giving their revenues to the landlord (*sahib-ı arz*) ... and protecting the lands from thieves, they are not to be asked for more than 2,000 *akçe*.[71]

Just as much as the urban spaces, rural spaces in Jordan and Palestine encompassed an important Kurdish population in the sixteenth century. Kurdish tribes resided mostly in Safad, starting with the presence of only the three tribes Hasayki, Qaba'ili, and Xawalde. By the end of the century, however, Safad had been host to eight Kurdish tribes, with newcomers from the Kabayshe, Mahasne, Ashafre, 'Assaf, and 'Amre. These communities were involved in farming and forged working partnerships with Turkoman tribes and other communities, occasionally in return for tax exemptions when providing protection services on the land – no doubt similar in many ways as they had since the Ayyubid period.

Kurdish *Waqfs* between the Ayyubids and the Ottomans

Another critical type of information provided by the Tahrir registers are *waqf* records, including endowments made by or for Kurds. Many of the Kurdish *waqfs* in Jordan and Palestine date from the Ayyubid and Mamluk periods, maintaining their status under the Ottoman Empire. Some of these *waqfs*, which were found in Jerusalem, Hebron, Safad, Acre, and Ramla, were bequeathed by Ayyubid kings or Mamluk sultans.[72] Others were established by Qaymariyya emirs.[73] The Qaymaris (from Qaymur in eastern Anatolia, near Siirt) were of course one of the most famous Kurdish clans or tribes to have been established in the region by the Ayyubids, and they continued to form an important military body (*jund*) under the Mamluks.[74] According to the Ottoman-era chronicler al-'Ulaymi (d. 1552), the "Qaymariyya Dome" (Qubbat al-Qaymariyya) on the western outskirts of Jerusalem commemorated

---

71 TD 427:32.
72 TD 131:81; TD 289:49, 81; TD 342:5–6, 9–11; TD 522:26–7; TD 602:445, 453.
73 TD 131:106; TD 602:485.
74 Stephen Humphreys, *From Saladin to the Mongols: The Ayyubids of Damascus, 1193–1260* (Albany: SUNY, 1977), 252, 305–6, 341–2, 346, 352–3, 359–61; James, *Genèse du Kurdistan*, 202, 247, 257–8, 266–70, 285.

124 Zainab HajHasan

a group of Qaymari *mujahidin* (fighters) buried there. Later a Qaymari-yya mosque (Masjid al-Qaymariyya) was built right in the city of Jerusalem; the current building dates from Ottoman times.[75]

Kurds endowed *waqf*s with revenues from villages, lands, mills, and crops. These *waqf*s were not only local but could also be interregional. The beneficiaries of Kurdish endowments in Damascus, for instance, could be Palestinian Kurds, as with that established by al-Hajj Zayn al-Din al-'Amidi of Damascus for a *zawiya* (Sufi lodge) as well as some shops in Jerusalem.[76] Another *waqf* endowed by Kurds in Gaza benefited the sanctuary of Medina in Arabia.[77] The Hakkaris, meanwhile, bequeathed many properties in different villages of Jerusalem, including houses (*dar*) in Bayt Lifta and Bayt Lahya.[78] A certain Sayfeddin al-Kurdi, meanwhile, created an endowment for the benefit of his monastery (*ribat*) in Jerusalem.[79]

The most significant case is the endowment of shaykh Sa'id al-Kawkabani who had properties devoted to *waqf*s spread throughout Tiberias and Acre. These *waqf* incomes included villages, mills, and crops. The registers do not offer any clues on his identity other than his full name, Sa'id ibn Abi Bakr Abu'l-Hayja al-Kawkabani, and that he held the village of Kawkab al-Akrad (literally, "planet of the Kurds," but likely also a play on his name).[80] Another Kawkabani property owner in the area, 'Abdush ibn 'Umar al-Kawkabani (see below), for his part, is clearly identified in the records as being Kurdish. In any event, Shaykh Sa'id consecrated two villages, two farms, a piece of land, and a mill in the province of Safad, as well as a house in Lajjun, to his *waqf*, which appears to have remained under family control.[81]

Non-Kurdish communities established *waqf*s in Kurdish *mahalles* or villages. Some were for the benefit of religious or other public ('*amm*) institutions and others were purely familial. In 1550, Ahmad Fulayfil endowed a *dukkan* (small shop) in the market of the Shuja'iyya *mahalle* in Gaza for the benefit of the al-Tawsi *madrasa* in the same quarter.

---

75 Mujir al-Din al-'Ulaymi, *Al-Uns al-Jalil bi-Tarikh al-Quds wa'l-Khalil*, ed. Adnan Nabata (Amman: al-Dandis Library), 2:48, 77–8, 389; Ra'if Yusuf Najm, *Kunuz al-Quds* (Damascus: Wizarat al-Thaqafa, 2011), 318; Duaa Bdair, "Masjid al-Sitt Qamara," 14 September 2014, https://www.jerusalemaffairs-plo.ps/wp/?p=3188.
76 TD 602:429. The record of these waqfs goes back to 885/1451–2.
77 TD 427:168.
78 TD 131:89; TD 427:272–3; TD 552:25; TD 602:452, 455.
79 TD 602:458.
80 TD 427:127; TD 300:380.
81 TD 312:21; TKGM 418:198; TKGM 134:21; TD 559:74.

A Samiya al-Julqi, for her part, gave a piece of land in Shuja'iyya to finance a *hawd* (reservoir) and *sebil* (fountain) in Gaza city, while Samiya al-Tahmi bequeathed another piece of land in the "Kurdish quarter" (Shuja'iyya) to an unspecified local *waqf*.[82] Numerous non-Kurds of course possessed properties in Kurdish *mahalles*, like Hasan al-Masri of Hebron who owned a house in the city's Kurdish quarter, suggesting regular economic interactions and transactions between the communities.[83]

The Kurdish population in Jordan and Palestine not only endowed *waqf*s but also forged partnerships and purchased properties. Partnerships occurred as much between Kurdish and non-Kurdish individuals or families as between Kurds. A series of *vakıf* and *mülk* records stretching over five pages in the Safad *tahrir* of 1557–8 tells us about the shared ownership of a mill by the scribe (*katib*) Ahmad al-Halabi and his partners Muhammad ibn 'Aziz al-Din and al-Hajj al-Kurdi.[84] Another partnership is recorded in the same Tahrir between an Arab, Abu Harb 'Abd al-Qadir al-'Arabi (probably a Bedouin) and Muhammad ibn 'Ali al-Ghawri, known as "al-Hijazi al-Kurdi," in 1526. Their joint property consisted of three mills in the *nahiye* of Jira. Later, in 1573, their holdings expanded to also include olive groves (*ghiras al-zaytun*).[85] In another example, Abu Bakr 'Abd al-Qadir al-Kurdi joined forces with 'Usayli al-Kurdi in a partnership recorded in 1520.[86] Kurdish tribes also made partnerships with non-Kurdish communities. Some Qaba'ilis in Tiberias owned a mill in association with Shaykh 'Abd al-'Aziz ibn Ahmad al-'Urabi in 1583.[87]

Purchase and ownership of properties by Kurds did not occur only through partnerships. The Tahrirs frequently indicated ownership of land by identifiably Kurdish groups of earlier periods, especially in the Palestinian districts where Kurdish tribes had been brought to defend against the crusaders. One such land was named for Su'ad al-Qaymariyya, presumably a woman of the famous Qaymari tribe.[88] In al-Salt, a farm presumably owned by Kurds in the village of Sahur is recorded in 1579 as the "Qaryat al-Akrad" (village of the Kurds).[89]

---

82 TD 312:97–8.
83 TD 342:30.
84 TD 522:56.
85 TD 522:58, 60; TD 602:471.
86 TD 522:2, 58.
87 TD 602:472.
88 TD 289:206; TD 346:16.
89 TKGM 2:25.

126   Zainab HajHasan

Similarly, a Khadija bint 'Ala' al-Kurdi from Ramla owned (part of) a "garden grove" (*ghiras al-hakura*) belonging to the *khan* of the local al-Abyad (or Jarmadi) mosque.[90]

Many of these property titles date from the pre-Ottoman or early Ottoman period in the Arab provinces. In Tiberias, Sulayman al-Kadad al-Kurdi, Hasan ibn 'Abdu al-Kurdi, Faraj ibn Muhammad ibn Farajo al-Kurdi, and the above-mentioned 'Abdush ibn 'Umar al-Kawkabani al-Kurdi each owned a mill since earlier times.[91] And Ibrahim ibn al-Kurdi of Led village owned a vineyard in Ramla.[92]

Such landowning also occurred among the tribal Kurds of the villages of Safad. Three documents from as early as 1549, for example, record the ownership of two farms by the Xawalde in Tiberias.[93] Another document from 1556 shows a farm known as the Mazra'at Jund (farm of the "military unit") owned by the Qaba'ili clan,[94] while in 1579, a Ghannam ibn Nasir al-Hijazi of the Qaba'ili owned three mills in Safad.[95] Al-Hajj Thabit of the same tribe is shown as owner of a different mill in Safad in 1584.[96]

Overall, the Tahrirs give evidence of a large degree of economic interaction within the Kurdish population and with other groups. The registers include much information on their *waqf* activities, as well as commercial partnerships and property ownership. Endowments were passed on for the benefit of the Kurdish population established throughout Palestine. While many of these endowments were bequeathed by Kurdish men and women residing in the Palestinian districts, others were established for the benefit of poor local Kurds, Sufi lodges, or *madrasas* by rich, presumably Kurdish patrons in Damascus. It is safe to say the Tahrirs show the Kurdish community involved with other societal groups and well integrated into the social and economic fabric of the region in general in the Ottoman period.

Conclusion

Historically an identifiably Kurdish population existed in various towns and *nahiyes* of 'Ajlun, Jerusalem, Gaza, Nablus, and Safad. The

---

90 TD 602:474.
91 TD 522:58–61; TD 602:468.
92 TKGM 418:205; TD 522:57.
93 TD 300:200; TD 559:145.
94 TD 427:32.
95 TKGM 418:204.
96 TD 602:472.

Kurdish presence in the region began in the Ayyubid period and continued into the Ottoman era. It later expanded within Palestine and extended into Jordan. The hajj, trade, sheep herding, and farming all led to the immigration and settlement of Kurdish families from other districts to the region under Ottoman rule.

Kurdish families and tribes dwelled in quarters and villages and played an essential role in local agriculture. While some families resettled, others maintained their nomadic lifestyle. Tribal culture remained powerful in these areas as tribes, or their sub-branches, provided important stock-breeding, farming, or security services. The Kurds' economic role is more evident in Palestine than in Jordan since they were limited to one district in the latter. As Ottoman fiscal records show, the size of the Kurdish population fluctuated around the end of the sixteenth century. While some areas lost their Kurdish population, it often increased elsewhere. These shifts were likely due to the lack of security and economic opportunities in some districts and their enhanced availability in others.

Tribal mobility played a key role in the flux of the census count. The Kurds' nomadic lifestyle and their pastoral and agricultural activities required constant movement. Furthermore, many tribes or clans later settled in villages or farmsteads named after them. Tribes also played a role in protecting lands and farming benefices and cooperated with the Turkomans in animal breeding.

The Tahrir registers do not provide much information on the religious affiliations of the Kurdish families and tribes in the region under study. We do know that Kurdish families lived in both identifiably "Kurdish" and in ethnically and religiously mixed *mahalles* or neighbourhoods. Kurds owned *qit'as* (small land plots), mills, garden or olive groves, and houses. These properties, as well as the *waqfs* they occasionally established with their revenues, convey an image of intercommunal and interregional relationships. Some Kurds, members for instance of the Damascus elite, bequeathed properties to foundations in Jerusalem and Hebron; other *waqfs* stand as evidence of a Kurdish presence since the Ayyubid and Mamluk periods. The Ottoman Empire inherited these institutions and preserved their status.

Ottoman fiscal records demonstrate that the Kurdish population constituted an important demographic, social, economic, political, and administrative actor in Jordan and Palestine in the early modern period. Many more sources (local chronicles, *shar'iyya* court records, foreign consular reports, etc.) remain to be investigated to further flesh out our understanding of the history of the region's Kurds under Ottoman rule.

5 The Lebanese Junblats and the Canbolads: A Case of Mistaken Identity

ABDUL-RAHIM ABU-HUSAYN[†]

The Junblats (Jumblatts) have been unquestionably the leading Druze family in the Shuf region of Mount Lebanon since the early nineteenth century, if not much earlier. Yet their origin and rise to paramountcy among the Druze shaykhly class is still more in the realm of legend than historical fact. In this paper, an examination of the circumstances and the historical literature which gave rise to the commonly accepted account of the Junblat origin is undertaken and an alternative explanation is advanced on the basis of contemporary and more reliable evidence.

The earliest known record of the tradition alleging the descent of the Lebanese Junblats from the Kurdish ʿAli Canbolad (Janbulad) of Aleppo is to be found in Tannus al-Shidyaq's *Akhbar al-Aʿyan fi Jabal Lubnan*.[1] Shidyaq (c. 1794–1861), a Maronite scholar who provided clerical services to various families of Lebanese notables in his time, states that he derived his information on the subject of the Junblats, as on the origins of other Druze shaykhly families, from recorded genealogies, and also from oral accounts, naming one of his Druze employers, Shaykh Khattar Talhuq, as his principal informant.[2]

As is well known, the ʿAli Canbolad whom Shidyaq presents as the ancestor of the Druze Junblats of the Lebanon, was a nephew of Husayn Paşa Canbolad: a man who held appointment for some time as *beylerbeyi* of Aleppo. Following Husayn's downfall and execution, his nephew ʿAli assumed unofficial control of Aleppo and much of Syria between 1605 and 1607, during which time he rose in rebellion against the Ottoman state and, encouraged by some European powers

---

1 Tannus al-Shidyaq, *Akhbar al-Aʿyan fi Jabal Lubnan*, ed. Fuʾad Bustani (Beirut: Lebanese University, 1970), 136–42.
2 Tannus al-Shidyaq, *Akhbar al-Aʿyan fi Jabal Lubnan*, 6.

The Lebanese Junblats and the Canbolads   129

(mainly the Medici Grand Duke of Tuscany and Pope Paul V of Rome), attempted to establish for himself an independent kingdom in northern Syria.[3] The Druze emir Fakhr al-Din Ma'n, then *sancakbeyi* of Sidon-Beirut and Safad, in the *eyalet* of Damascus, was associated with the 'Ali Canbolad rebellion for some time. In 1607, however, the Ottomans sent against 'Ali "their most venerable (and feared) general, [the grand vizier] Kuyucu Murad Pasha."[4] Murad managed to defeat 'Ali, after which the man fled, was brought over to Istanbul, pardoned by Sultan Ahmet I, and appointed governor of Temeşvar, in present-day Romania. Ultimately, having become involved in some mischief, 'Ali Canbolad was arrested and imprisoned in the fortress of Belgrade, where he was put to death in 1610. And there his story ends. The known sources relate nothing about his progeny in Syria, although he was survived in Istanbul by one or more members of the family who, according to the sources, were his nephews.[5]

Shidyaq's account of the Canboladi origin of the Lebanese Junblats (the latter name being an Arabicized corruption of the first) runs as follows:

> In the year 1607, when Murad Pasha defeated 'Ali Pasha Janbulad of Aleppo, and when the latter fled to Malatya, as already mentioned, his relatives were dispersed, and some of his sons went into hiding in the regions of Aleppo and Kilis.
>
> In the year 1630, Janbulad ibn Sa'id came with his son Rabah from the region of Aleppo to Beirut, because of the friendly relations between [the Janbulads] and the Ma'ns. When the news of his arrival became known, the notables (*akabir*) of Mount Lebanon came [to Beirut] to greet him and invited him to stay in their region (*bilad*). Accepting the invitation, he took residence in Mazra'at al Shuf. Emir Fakhr al-Din respected him to the extent that he used to depend on him in important affairs. Shaykh Abu Nadir al-Khazin was the chief steward (*mudabbir*) of Emir Fakhr al-Din, and he became allied with Janbulad, a strong friendship developing between the two [of them].

---

3 On 'Ali Janbulad and his relations with the Medicis of Tuscany and Pope Paul V see Bulus Qara'li, *'Ali Basha Junblat* (Beirut: N.p., 1939). On the question of 'Ali Canbolad's sovereign pretensions, see William Griswold, *The Great Anatolian Rebellion 1000–1020/1591–1611* (Berlin: Klaus Schwarz, 1983), 110, 113–32.

4 Griswold, *Great Anatolian Rebellion*, 110.

5 The full story of the 'Ali Canbolad rebellion is told in a number of contemporary Syrian and Ottoman accounts. For a modem rendering of these accounts, see Griswold, *Great Anatolian Rebellion*, 110–208.

130   Abdul-Rahim Abu-Husayn

In the year 1631, Emir Fakhr al-Din sent Janbulad to the fortress of Shaqif Arnun with fifty men and put him in charge of this fortress to guard it against emir Turbay ibn 'Ali al-Harithi, the emir of Lajjun ... He stayed there for about one year.

In the year 1640, Janbulad died and was survived by [his son] Rabah who stayed on for some time in Mazra'at al-Shuf as a respected figure, after which he died, leaving three sons: 'Ali, Faris, and Sharaf al-Din. He was a man of good reputation and his [eldest?] son 'Ali married the daughter of Shaykh Qablan al-Qadi al-Tanukhi, the paramount shaykh of the Shuf ... Then ['Ali] moved [from Mazra'at al-Shuf] to Ba'daran where he built himself a residence (dar).

In the year 1712, when Qablan al-Qadi died without an heir, the notables (akabir) of the Shuf agreed that his son-in-law 'Ali succeed to his position as their chief (ra's). They requested Emir Haydar al-Shihabi to appoint him [in this position] and offered him 25,000 piasters [for the purpose]. Thereupon [Emir Haydar] appointed him to the muqata'at [fiscal districts] of the Shuf ... and he became the paramount shaykh (shaykh al-mashayikh) [of the region].[6]

At first sight, and taken by itself, this account of the origin of the Druze Junblats and their shaykhly ascendancy in the Shuf region of Mount Lebanon does not appear implausible, and the Junblats themselves, certainly since the publication of Shidyaq's work, have accepted it without question. In a book published posthumously, the late Druze leader Kamal Junblat (d. 1977) made a point of tracing the origins of his distinguished family back to the Kurdish Canbolads, the sancakbeyis of Kilis, in northern Syria, and the beylerbeyis of the eyalet of Aleppo throughout much of the sixteenth century and the first decade of the seventeenth.[7] And Kamal Junblat had good reason to do so, considering that no Lebanese or other historian since Shidyaq had in the least doubted what the latter had reported on the matter.

In the standard modern histories of Lebanon, the descent of the Junblats of the Shuf from the Kurdish Canbolads of northern Syria is taken for granted. Philip K. Hitti, for example, states:

Among the last was Ali Janbulad, Kurdish chief, who usurped the walayah of Aleppo. Fakhr al-Din had already entered into an alliance with the Aleppo

---

6   Shidyaq, Akhbar al-A'yan, 136–42.
7   Kamal Junblat, Hadhihi Wasiyyati (Mukhtara, Lebanon: Al-Markaz al-Watani, 1987), 46–8.

The Lebanese Junblats and the Canbolads   131

usurper, whose tribesmen migrated to Lebanon, where their descendants, known as Janbalats, still exercise leadership among the Druzes.[8]

Kamal Salibi, similarly, has the following to say on the subject:

Among the "great sheikhs" invested by Haydar Shihab [in 1711–12], the Janbalats enjoyed by far the highest prestige. An ancestor of this family, a Kurdish chieftain called 'Ali Janbulad (mispronounced Janbalat) had usurped the *vilayet* of Aleppo in the early seventeenth century, and rebelled against the Ottomans with the help of Fakhr al-Din II of Lebanon. The rebellion failed, 'Ali was defeated and executed, and his family were forced to seek refuge with Fakhr al-Din II, who allowed them to settle in the Shuf under his protection. Here the Janbalats soon rose to prominence and were accepted as Druzes, taking over the chieftainship of the region after the Ma'nid family became extinct in 1697.[9]

More recent scholarship on the subject has also taken the Canboladi descent of the Lebanese Junblats for granted. William Griswold, for example, states:

Many descendants of the original Canbulad still live in the Lebanon; ... on 25 Rabi'ulevel 1397/16 March 1977 Kamal Jumblat, the most famous descendant of Janbulad in modern times, was murdered near his home at Mukhtara in Lebanon.[10]

Other modern scholars, again relying on Shidyaq, have attempted to elaborate an allegedly more exact lineage. Thus, Pierre Rondot writes:

Djanbulat b. Said (d. 1050/1640), probably grandson of 'Ali, finally emigrated to the Lebanon in 1040/1630 with his sons Said and Rabah, settled in the Shuf, and from 1041/1631, joined the campaigns of the amir [Fakhr al-Din]. His son Rabah succeeded him, and 'Ali, his grandson (d. 1142/1712), outlived his brothers Faris and Sharaf al-Din, who were assassinated; he entered the service of the powerful Druze chieftain, Kablan al-Kadi al-Tanukhi, married his daughter, and inherited his fortune and influence which he increased by his generosity towards the

---

8 Philip Hitti, *Lebanon in History from the Earliest Times to the Present* (London: Macmillan, 1957), 375.
9 Kamal Salibi, *The Modern History of Lebanon* (London: Weidenfeld & Nicolson, 1965), 10.
10 Griswold, *Great Anatolian Rebellion*, 282.

132   Abdul-Rahim Abu-Husayn

common people. He helped the amir Haydar Shihab to carry the battle of 'Ayn Dara, 1123/1711, against the Yamani "party."[11]

A modern Lebanese Druze historian, Selim Hichi, introduces a parenthetical variation to Rondot's account, in an attempt to reconcile it with the fact that a person by the name of Junblat is known to have been politically active in the Shuf as early as the first decade of the seventeenth century.[12] Thus according to Hichi,

> It appears that the first [Junblat] emigrant to these [Shuf] parts was Junblat Junblat. The exact date of his arrival [there] remains unknown, but it is probable that it occurred shortly after his family was defeated, i.e. between 1607 and 1611.[13]

This parenthetical variation apart, Hichi agrees that the rise of the Junblats to social and political prominence in the Shuf occurred as a result of the marriage of a certain 'Ali Junblat to the daughter of Shaykh Qablan al-Qadi in the year 1712.[14] The late Kamal Junblat is in agreement with both Rondot and Hichi regarding the role that the marriage of the Junblats into the Qadi family played in raising the Junblati social and political status. On the other hand, he stated that the name of the member of the Junblati family who married Qablan al-Qadi's daughter was Rabah, which may indicate that the whole marriage story is dubious.[15]

One matter which is ignored by Griswold, Rondot, and Hichi is the presumed conversion of the Kurdish and Hanafi Sunni Muslim Canbolads to Druzism following their settlement in the Shuf. Speculating on the matter, Kamal Junblat reached the conclusion that no exact date may be fixed for this conversion. Moreover, as a Druze, Kamal Junblat correctly stated that it was not possible to admit converts to the Druze faith, since Druze doctrine explicitly rules against the acceptance of proselytes.[16] Accordingly, he advanced the suggestion

---

11   Pierre Rondot, article "Djanbulat," *Encyclopaedia of Islam 2* (Leiden: Brill, 1971), 2:443–4.

12   On this matter, see the relevant citation from Khalidi below.

13   Selim Hichi (Salim Hishi), *'Ali Basha Junblat* (N.p., 1986), 117–18; Selim Hichi, *Al-Murasalat al-Ijtima'iyya wa'l-Iqtisadiyya li-Zu'ama' Jabal Lubnan (1600–1900)* (Beirut: Salim Hishi, 1979–1980), 1:16–22.

14   Hichi, *Al-Murasalat,* 1:20.

15   Hichi, *Junblat,* 46.

16   Hichi, 47.

The Lebanese Junblats and the Canbolads   133

that the Kurdish Canbolads could have been originally Druzes – as some of the inhabitants of the Aleppo region in northern Syria were.

In summary, the consensus of scholarly and common opinion has it that the Druze Junblats are actually the descendants of the Kurdish Canbolads; that they arrived in the Shuf either immediately or some time after the defeat of the 'Ali Canbolad rebellion by the Ottomans in 1607; and that they only achieved shaykhly status among the Druzes of the Lebanon in the early eighteenth century, by the decision of a Shihab emir. This consensus regarding the Junblat origins derives, beyond doubt, from the real or alleged tradition related – and perhaps further elaborated – by Tannus al-Shidyaq: a Maronite historian writing in the 1850s, and more than two centuries removed from the period he fixes for his account of the arrival of the Kurdish Canbolads/Junblats in the Lebanon.

Turning, however, from Shidyaq to the seventeenth-century sources providing contemporary or near-contemporary accounts of the subject at hand, an entirely different story begins to emerge. Here, to begin with, is the negative evidence.

From the Aleppine historian al-'Urdi (d. 1660), one learns that the Kurdish Janbulads (so spelt) of the Aleppo region were staunch followers of the Sunni Muslim Hanafi rite and are applauded by him on this account. Hence, the assumption that they could have been Druzes of the Aleppo region may be dismissed. Furthermore, 'Urdi refers to members of the family by title as *amir* or *amir al-umara'* (Turkish *bey* and *beylerbeyi* respectively), the official appointments that members of the family actually held, and never as shaykh.[17] Had the Druze Junblats of the Shuf been of Kurdish Canboladi origin, they would have been historically known as emirs, and not as shaykhs.

The Damascene historian al-Burini (d. 1615) was directly involved in the Aleppine politics of the early seventeenth century, and left a detailed biography of 'Ali Junbulad (Canbolad). From his account, one learns that the followers of 'Ali Janbulad were killed to a man, following his defeat in 1607. Burini was aware of the anti-Ottoman collusion between Fakhr al-Din Ma'n of the Shuf and 'Ali Janbulad, and was actually a member of the Damascene delegation that went to Aleppo in 1607 to urge Murad Pasha to deal with Fakhr al-Din as he had dealt with 'Ali Janbulad. Yet he makes no mention of any member or members of the

---

17 Abu'l-Wafa' al-'Urdi, *Ma'adin al-Dhahab fi'l-Rijal al-Musharrafa bi-him Halab*, ed. Muhammad al-Tunji (Aleppo: Dar al-Malah, 1987), 306–13, 339–40.

134 Abdul-Rahim Abu-Husayn

Janbulad family taking refuge with the Ma'ns in the Shuf after their defeat by Murad Pasha.[18]

Another Damascene historian of the period, al-Ghazzi (d. 1651), speaks of Husayn Janbulad and the rebellion of his nephew 'Ali, and the role of Fakhr al-Din Ma'n in this rebellion. Like 'Urdi and Burini, however, he makes no mention of any Janbulads who arrived to take refuge in the Shuf at any time before or after the defeat of 'Ali Janbulad in 1607.[19]

A later Damascene historian, al-Muhibbi (d. 1699), left biographical accounts of both Husayn and 'Ali Janbuladh (so spelt), as well as a biographical account of Fakhr al-Din Ma'n; and referred to the affairs of both the Canbolad and the Ma'ns on numerous occasions but made no mention of any Kurdish Canbolad immigration to the Shuf at any time.[20]

More significantly, the Maronite patriarch and historian Istifan al-Duwayhi (d. 1704), who was a personal friend of Ahmad Ma'n and who resided in the Shuf for some time, makes no mention of the arrival of any Kurdish Canbolads in the Shuf in any period. Had any of them arrived, to become the political allies of the Maronite Khazins, as Shidyaq asserts, it is highly unlikely that Duwayhi, as Maronite patriarch, would have omitted any mention of the matter.[21]

Apart from this negative evidence, there is the following, illuminating evidence to consider. Ahmad al-Khalidi of Safad, a Sunni Muslim man of learning who served Fakhr al-Din Ma'n as an adviser, left a contemporary and highly informed account of the career of this emir in which he elaborated on the circumstances of the Canbolad rebellion in northern Syria and its ultimate failure. In the same book, Khalidi also speaks of a chieftain of the Shuf (presumably Druze) called Shaykh Junblat (also thus spelt), without the least indication of any connection between him and the Kurdish and Hanafi Sunnite 'Ali Janbulad of Aleppo. The two figures, in fact, are clearly distinguished from one another by appellation. While Khalidi consistently refers to 'Ali

---

18 Al-Hasan al-Burini, *Tarajim al-A'yan min Abna' al-Zaman*, ed. Salah al-Din al-Munajjid (Damascus: Al-Majma' al-'Ilmi al-'Arabi, 1959–63), 2:271–96.

19 Najm al-Din al-Ghazzi, *Lutf al-Samar wa-Qatf al-Thamar min Tarajim al-Tabaqat al-Ula min al-Qarn al-Hadi 'Ashar*, ed. Mahmud al-Shaykh (Damascus: Wizarat al-Thaqafa 1981–2), 1:107–8, 231–40, 415–16.

20 Muhammad Amin ibn Fadlallah al-Muhibbi, *Khulasat al-Athar fi A'yan al-Qarn al-Hadi 'Ashar* (Beirut: Dar Sadir, n.d.), 1:370–1; 2:84–7; 3:135–40, 266–8.

21 Istifan al-Duwayhi, *Tarikh al-Azmina, 1095–1699*, ed. Ferdinan Tawtal (Beirut: Catholic Press, 1951).

The Lebanese Junblats and the Canbolads   135

Janbulad by title as 'Ali Pasha, he just as consistently calls the Druze chieftain who was his namesake Shaykh Junblat.[22]

This Shaykh Junblat features in the Khalidi account as one of two leading Druze shaykhs of Fakhr al-Din's time, the other being his rival and enemy Shaykh Yazbak ibn 'Abd al-'Afif, who was Fakhr al-Din's father-in-law and faithful ally. In the year 1023/1614, says Khalidi, while Ahmad Pasha al-Hafiz, the Ottoman *beylerbeyi* of Damascus, was making war against the Ma'ns, Shaykh Junblat was imprisoned by Fakhr al-Din's brother Yunus in the fortress of Shaqif [Arnun], after an open quarrel had broken out between him and his rival Shaykh Yazbak. Khalidi also suggests that the enmity (possibly tribal-political) between the two antedated the quarrel.[23] In his account of the Junblat origins, Shidyaq, who cites Khalidi among the sources for his work, transformed the imprisonment of Shaykh Junblat in Shaqif Arnun by the Ma'ns in 1614 into a commission to defend that fortress on behalf of the Ma'ns, at the head of fifty men, in 1631.[24]

Khalidi further reports that following this Ottoman invasion of the Ma'nid territory, representatives of the Shuf Druzes who were partisans of Shaykh Junblat went to meet Ahmad Pasha al-Hafiz, in response to his summons, after which they returned to their respective villages with "striped robes of honour."[25] Clearly, Shaykh Junblat was imprisoned by Fakhr al-Din's brother in 1614 because he had seized the opportunity of the Ottoman invasion of that year to cause political embarrassment to the Ma'ns, whose chief Druze shaykhly supporter was his rival Shaykh Yazbak.

What needs to be pointed out here is that Khalidi, whose account of Fakhr al-Din's career covers the years 1612–23, and who also explains Fakhr al-Din's involvement in the Kurdish Canbolad rebellion of

---

22 Ahmad al-Khalidi, *Tarikh al-Amir Fakhr al-Din al-Ma'ni*, ed. Asad Rustum and Fu'ad al-Bustani (Beirut: Lebanese University, 1969), 5, 6, 33, 36, 75, 78, 82, 84, 93, 134.

23 Khalidi, *Tarikh al-Amir Fakhr al-Din*, 32.

24 Shidyaq, *Akhbar al-A'yan*, 6, 141. This Shaykh Junblat along with his rival Yazbak is also mentioned in the account of Shaykh Shayban al-Khazin. According to him, they quarrelled while both were in the service of Fakhr al-Din Ma'n and Junblat gave Yazbak a beating. Thereupon, Fakhr al-Din imprisoned Junblat in one of the fortresses under his control. He was released later by emir Yunus, Fakhr al-Din's brother. For this account, see Nasib al-Khazin and Bulus Mas'ad, *Al-Usul al-Tarikhiyya* (Beirut: Nasib Wahiba al-Khazin, 1956), 3:417. Haydar al-Shihabi also refers to the enmity between a certain Shaykh Junblat and Shaykh Yazbak ibn 'Abd al-'Afif and the imprisonment of the first by emir Fakhr al-Din Ma'n. Haydar al-Shihabi, *Tarikh al-Amir Haydar Ahmad al-Shihabi* (Cairo: Matba'at al-Salam, 1900), 636–7.

25 Khalidi, *Tarikh al-Amir Fakhr al-Din*, 36.

1607, nowhere refers to Kurdish Canbolads converging on the Maʻnid territory during this time. And it is highly unreasonable to suppose that the Shaykh Junblat, who opposed the Maʻns and was imprisoned by them in 1614, was a Kurdish Canbolad fugitive, rather than a Druze native of the Shuf region. Had he been a Kurdish fugitive seeking refuge with the Maʻns, he would have been their friend rather than their principal local opponent; and as an alien fugitive to one of the most esoteric sects and communities in Syria, he could not reasonably have gained acceptance and developed for himself a substantial following of Shuf Druzes within a period of seven years at the most.

Furthermore, the Khalidi account of Shaykh Junblat as the head of a substantial Druze faction indicates that the Junblats, as the family of this shaykh was or came to be called, were already established in a position of social and political prominence in the Shuf by the early decades of the seventeenth century, and did not owe their rise to prominence to the marriage (real or alleged) of one of their number to the daughter of Qablan al-Qadi about a hundred years later. Likewise, the Khalidi account makes it clear that the division among the Druzes between Junblati and Yazbaki factions was already a fact of Druze political life in the Shuf during the time of Fakhr al-Din Maʻn, long before the time of the Shihabs, in the mid-eighteenth century, when it is commonly believed to have developed.[26]

---

26 For more details on this Qaysi-Yamani factionalism, see Abdul-Rahim Abu-Husayn, *Provincial Leaderships in Syria, 1575–1650* (Beirut: American University of Beirut, 1985), 74–6.

6 Warlords and Landlords: The Kurdish Presence in Central Syria in the Eighteenth and Nineteenth Centuries

DICK DOUWES

The presence of Kurds may not have been that prominent in central Syria, that is, the districts of Hama and Homs. Kurdish tribes were not herding their flocks in the area seasonally and Kurds did not inhabit villages or towns in any substantial numbers until the early nineteenth century. But earlier Kurds participated in the politics, economics, and culture of inland Syria as soldiers, traders, and scholars and travelled as pilgrims along the Sultanic Road connecting the main cities of Aleppo with Damascus, and the steppes and areas beyond with the holy sites in the Hijaz. The core responsibility of the Ottoman authorities in inland Syria was to secure safe passage of the hajj pilgrims and to provision the towns and fortresses along that road. In this context, a number of Kurdish officers made a remarkable career in the late eighteenth and early nineteenth centuries and left their mark on the area. A few settled in the area and became part of the local landowning elite, moving from the military status of *agha* to the bourgeois one of *efendi* in the second half of the nineteenth century.

General Conditions in Inland Syria

In inland Syria, sedentary and nomadic modes of life coexisted and were mutually dependent. A range of semi-nomadic – or for that matter semi-sedentary – ways of earning a living offered opportunities to adapt to changing, often challenging circumstances varying from drought and plague to extortion by the military. Apart from traditional seasonal movements of people with or without livestock, both the eighteenth and nineteenth centuries witnessed prolonged states of insecurity due to political unrest caused by factional provincial infighting and pandemics, as well as by the arrival of new groups of nomads competing with other nomads and with sedentary communities.

138   Dick Douwes

Pandemics like the plague often followed upon a period of drought and food shortage. As a result, many smaller villages were abandoned, not always permanently, but staying in a larger village or town offered better conditions for having a livelihood in times of instability.[1] But inland towns also witnessed calamities such as pandemics, and in the eighteenth and early nineteenth centuries the central Syrian towns of Hama and Homs repeatedly came under the attack of nomads, be they Turkoman or Arab, in coalition at times with Kurdish officers. Unlike villages, however, town populations were in a better position to redress the challenges they faced, not only because of their size, but also because they performed key functions in the administration of inland Syria. Consequently, the Ottoman authorities invested heavily in retaining – or at times restoring – public order and recreating welfare in these towns. The districts of Hama and Homs were part of the province of Damascus for most of the eighteenth and nineteenth century but the governors of the adjacent provinces of Tripoli (later Sidon) and Aleppo also regularly intervened in their affairs.[2]

Situated on the Sultanic Road that connected the two large cities of inland Syria, Aleppo and Damascus, the Ottoman authorities had a keen interest to supply the towns along that road like Maʻarra al-Nuʻman, Hama, and Homs with enough food and guarantee an adequate level of security. The Sultanic Road was the main line of communication between Anatolia and the holy cities of the Hijaz, Mecca and Medina, and was key in the adequate provisioning and protection of traders, pilgrims, and other travellers. Along the road, fortress villages were manned by *muhafiz* soldiers (guardians), and efforts were made to keep control of some fortresses to the east of the road, such as that of Salamiyya located to the southeast of Hama (see map 1). The Ottoman authorities did not always succeed in providing these crucial services and some major incidents interrupted travel along the Sultanic Road in the eighteenth and the first half of the nineteenth centuries. For instance, in the eighteenth century Salamiyya was for decades the

---

1 For a description of the general conditions of the area, see Dick Douwes, *The Ottomans in Syria: A History of Justice and Oppression* (London: I.B. Tauris, 2000), 14–43, and James Reilly, *A Small Town in Syria: Ottoman Hama in the Eighteenth and Nineteenth Centuries* (Bern: Peter Lang, 2002), 13–24. Local histories include Ahmad al-Sabuni, *Tarikh Hama* (Damascus: Dar al-Qutayba, 1984); Munir ʻIsa al-Asʻad, *Tarikh Hims* (Homs: N.p., 1984); and Muhammad Salim al-Jundi, *Tarikh Maʻarrat al-Nuʻman* (Damascus: Wizarat al-Thaqafa, 1994). None of these sources contains much information concerning the Kurdish presence.

2 Douwes, *The Ottomans in Syria*, 85–103.

stronghold of the Mawali tribal chiefs who regularly challenged the provincial authorities and even attacked the two towns a few times.[3] However, even in times of fragile control by the provincial authorities, travel was not necessarily hazardous. The famous Swiss travel author John Lewis Burckhardt freely moved through districts to the north and west of Hama that were held by rebel Kurdish warlords in the 1820s.[4]

The population, both sedentary and nomadic, of the districts of Hama and Homs was by and large Arabic in language. The sedentary were referred to as *awlad al-'arab*, of Arab ancestry, *'arab* (Arab) being a general designation of semi-sedentary and nomadic tribes, including *badu*, bedouin tribes having a long range of transhumance deep into the Arabian Peninsula. Well into the second half of the nineteenth century, Arab tribes controlled large stretches of wasteland (*badiyya*) to the east of the Sultan's Road, in particular the Mawali and their associates and later the 'Anaza, arriving in the area in the closing decades of the eighteenth century.[5] Relations between villagers, townsmen, and Arabs were often close, occasionally defined by family bonds. More importantly, the sedentary depended on the products marketed by the nomads, such as sheep, as well as on their services, including herding flocks owned by urban investors or by villagers. The nomads depended on urban and village markets for a wide range of goods, from wheat to all sorts of utensils, including weaponry. The reciprocity in their relations implied that mechanisms of informing, negotiating, and regulating disputes functioned most of the time. In years that these mechanisms did not function properly, local order collapsed – as happened at various junctures in the second half of the eighteenth and in the early nineteenth centuries.

Being nomads by birth or migrants by force, local structures in inland Syria were tailored to the mobility of its population and that of adjacent regions, in particular Anatolia and the northern parts of the Arabian Peninsula. Khans – or caravanserais – had an important function in facilitating travel. Village elders often entertained passers-by, as did fortress villages and towns for particular groups of nomads as well as various military formations, such as the horse-mounted *deli* forces.

---

3 Ahmad Wasfi Zakariyya, *'Asha 'ir al-Sham* (Damascus: Dar al-Fikr, 1983).

4 John Lewis Burckhardt, *Travels in Syria and the Holy Land* (London: N.p., 1822), 125–38.

5 Astrid Meier, "Bedouins in the Ottoman Juridical Field: Select Cases from Syrian Court Records, Seventeenth to Nineteenth Centuries," *Eurasian Studies* 9, nos. 1–2 (2011): 187–211.

These forces were, at least partly, tribally based, many of them being Kurds and Turkomans.[6] They played a crucial role in provincial politics, both in the service of Ottoman governors and, at times, as rebel warlords. Kurdish officers and their cavalry were deeply involved in the politics of inland Syria at that time. Yet, in the Hama and Homs district many were only passing through, moving to other areas in which their trade was required; it is difficult to judge from existing sources how many settled in the two towns and became urban locals.[7] In the early decades of the nineteenth century Kurdish families settled in a few villages to the west of Hama, striking root in the area. The Kurdish presence in the seventeenth century comprised isolated communities to the west of Homs, in the area of Hisn al-Akrad, and specifically two Kurdish tribes, the Saçlo and the Kiliçlo. The latter two may have had a continued presence of some sort, but do not occur in the local sources of the eighteenth and nineteenth centuries.[8]

The most prominent non-Arab presence was that of the Turkomans. Gypsies perhaps also outnumbered the Kurds in this part of Syria, being locals in the sense that they regularly pitched their tents over prolonged periods of time in the area.[9] The Turkoman presence was partly the result of old-school Ottoman policies to resettle tribal groups, both to discipline them to orderly conduct after local revolts and to use them to strengthen Ottoman control in areas where it was contested, such as in border regions or along major roads. But the recurrent references to Turkoman attacks on villages and even the towns of Hama and Homs suggest that some Anatolian Turkoman tribal groups operated within a large geographical range.[10]

In the early eighteenth century Turkoman tribesmen were settled in villages to the south of Hama, along and to the west of the Sultanic Road as fortress villagers who, presumably, were to add security to

---

6 On provincial and local forces, see Abdul-Karim Rafeq, "Local Forces in Syria in the Seventeenth and Eighteenth Centuries," in *War, Technology, and Society in the Middle East,* ed. Vernon Parry and Malcolm Yapp (Oxford: Oxford University Press, 1975).

7 A post on the Facebook page for the city of Hama from 11 May 2019 lists the names of families of various ethnic backgrounds including Turks, Kurds, and Circassians: https://www.facebook.com/City.Of.Hama/posts/10156917577903153/.

8 Stefan Winter, "Les Kurdes de Syrie dans les archives ottomanes (XVIIIᵉ siècle)," *Études Kurdes* 10 (2009): 125–56.

9 For a description of the Gypsies in northern Syria, see M. Corances, *Itinéraire d'une partie peu connue de l'Asie Mineure* (Paris: P. Gueffier, 1816), 202–9.

10 Enver Çakar, "Les Turkmènes d'Alep à l'époque ottomane (1516–1700)," in *Aleppo and Its Hinterland in the Ottoman Period,* ed. Stefan Winter and Mafalda Ade (Leiden: Brill, 2019), 11, 17–19, 24–5.

Warlords and Landlords 141

local logistics, in particular along the roads connecting Hama and Homs to the coastal city of Tripoli, a most important centre of provincial administration and, importantly, the main outlet for the Hama and Homs region to the Mediterranean. According to al-Makki, a chronicler from Homs, it was the first scion of the al-'Azm family to make a career in provincial administration, Isma'il Agha, who was ordered to settle Turkomans in the area.[11] The Turkoman villages paid less taxes in compensation for their military services. The Turkomans expanded their settled presence to other villages, at times by force.

The Turkoman villages, referred to as *Turkman iskan*, gradually lost their fortress peasant function but continued to receive a favourable treatment by the fiscal authorities well into the nineteenth century. The Turkoman villages of the Hama district appear to have been well-integrated in the local administration, numbering about twenty in the early nineteenth century. Most nomadic Turkomans passing through the area were cattle traders that brought their sheep and goats to local markets, like Kurdish cattle traders did. In the second half of the nineteenth century refugees from the Caucasus were settled in deserted villages in the area to the east of Homs, well-armed by the state to resist bedouin encroachments on reconquered farmland. At the time the area was relatively well-watered, having rich pastures, a major attraction for the herding nomads.[12]

Who Is to Be Identified as a Kurd (or a Turkoman)?

The Kurdish presence in central Syria resembled that of the Turkomans, being mainly military in nature. Many Turkomans served in the provincial and local military units, be it janissary or mounted *deli* forces. They often cooperated – or competed – with Kurds when performing tasks ranging from keeping order to tax collection and rendering food supplies. It appears that with the rise to prominence of the al-'Azm family in the Syrian interior, not only did the presence of Turkomans increase in the Hama and Homs area with them settling in villages, but also that of Kurds, more as military than as settlers. However, a major issue in mapping the background of people living in the area, and even more that of the soldiery serving in garrison towns and fortress villages, is

---

11 Muhammad al-Makki, *Tarikh Hims* (Damascus: Institut Français d'Études Arabes de Damas, 1987), 371.

12 See on the expansion of sedentary agriculture, Norman Lewis, *Nomads and Settlers in Syria and Jordan, 1800–1980* (Cambridge: Cambridge University Press, 1987).

142   Dick Douwes

the difficulty of tracing their ethnic or regional background. Being local did not necessarily mean that one was of Arab ancestry, a clear example of which are the *yerli* forces, so-called "local" janissaries in Damascus who were frequently in competition with the *qabiqul* (*kapıkulu*), the "imperial" janissaries. *"Yerli,"* the Turkish term for "local," suggests that it in fact included non-Arab soldiery that had taken root in local society, constituting a domestic military class in Damascus.

Apart from a few career commanders in the provincial administration, only more general references are to be found in local sources to the ethnic or regional background of the various military formations. A late eighteenth-century overview of expenses for the fortresses along the Sultanic Road and adjacent areas, such as Khan Shaykhun, Tall Bisa, and Hasya, includes about 300 names of guardians (*muhafiz*) stationed at these fortresses, none of whom carried a family name or had any reference to a regional or ethnic background.[13] Yet, in the local histories several military formations in the province were known by their ethnic or regional origin, such as the *Maghariba* (from the Maghrib), the *Baghadida* (from Baghdad), *Arna'ut* (from Albania/the Balkans) and the *lawand al-Akrad*, mainly Kurdish mounted troops that were much feared by the population but also employed by the 'Azms.[14] Moreover, in local chronicles written by urban authors, Kurds as well as other migratory and rural groups are often treated with disdain.[15]

When tracing the background of local elites, family names may well give a clue to their origin and their career patterns serving in the provinces. Traditionally, family names were often lacking, except for those families having a career in religious learning in which the reproduction

---

13 Centre for Historical Documents, Damascus: Hama/Mahkama Shar'iyya [H/MS] 46:206, 1 Rajab 1209. In local Ottoman records, hardly any references are made to ethnic backgrounds of individuals and groups, the empire being a multi-ethnic entity in which religious differentiation, certainly in fiscal matters, mattered more than ethnic differences. In the rapidly increasing amount of data available in French and British consular and other reports, population estimates often follow religious identities with a keen eye to the variety of Christian communities and much less on the ethnic diversity among Muslims.

14 Mikha'il al-Dimashqi, *Tarikh Hawadith al-Sham wa-Lubnan*, ed. Ahmad Ghassan Sabanu (Beirut: Dar al-Qutayba, 1981), 148; Haydar Ahmad al-Shihab, *Lubnan fi 'Ahd al-Umara' al-Shihabiyyin*, 3 vols., ed. Asad Rustum and Fu'ad al-Bustani (Beirut: al-Jami'a al-Lubnaniyya, 1984), 1:117–18; Constantin-François Volney, *Voyage en Égypte et en Syrie*, 2 vols. (Paris, 1792), 2:375.

15 Bruce Masters, "The View from the Province: Syrian Chronicles of the Eighteenth Century," *Journal of the American Oriental Society* 114, no. 3 (July–September 1994): 353–62, https://doi.org/10.2307/605079.

of their knowledge and spirit was essential. The scholarly realm often involved specific family domains in which religious authority was reproduced and offices were handed from one generation to the next. Families of religious distinction, such as the Kaylanis and ʿAlwanis in Hama, had a virtual monopoly over religious institutions including the judgeship in *shar ʿiyya* courts and the administration of *awqaf* or pious foundations. Unlike Aleppo and Damascus, which had a tradition of having Kurdish quarters and religious scholars of Kurdish origin, the settled, permanent urban presence of Kurds in Hama and Homs was very small until the early nineteenth century.[16] Only then did a number of families, having arrived as military officers in the service of the governors of the province of Damascus, strike roots in the area, in particular in Hama and its western countryside. Some of them became landlords in the second half of the nineteenth century. In the course of the century a part of the al-Masharifa quarter – thus named after a prominent subsection of the Mawali Arabs – in Hama became known as the *harat al-Baraziyya*, referring to the by far most prominent Kurdish family of the late Ottoman period in the area. But it was also home to a number of lesser known Kurdish families who settled in the area in this period, including the al-Milli, a member of which would play a crucial role in the late eighteenth and early nineteenth century, Mulla Ismaʿil (see below). Members of the Kurdish Barazi tribe also lived in Damascus, in particular in the Rukn al-Din quarter. They were not known by the *laqab* (family name) al-Barazi, however, but rather as the Shamdin Agha family, a name which apparently refers to a subsection of the larger tribe.[17]

Adopting a family name may well have been a sign of being in the process of Arabization because prominent local Arab families were known by family name, such as the al-Kaylani in Hama and the al-Jundi in Maʿarra and Homs. The most prominent Kurdish families of central Syria in the nineteenth century are known by family names, the al-Barazi and Tayfur families, both of them relatively new arrivals, their

---

16 According to an internet source a Kurdish family called al-Murad, after Murad Agha, established a tradition of religious learning in Hama. See Hama Gharb al-Mashtal, "Al al-Barazi" wa-"Al al-Milli," family history and photo collection by National Geographic Hama, Facebook, 14 February 2020, https://www.facebook .com/hama.Almashtal/posts/2658290587559805/.

17 See Barazi Family Network, "Shajarat ʿaʾilat al-Barazi/Al-Barazi Family Tree," accessed 1 February 2024, https://www.barazifamily.net; Kurd Dimashq, Harat al-Baraziyya/Barazi Neighborhood (Hama), description and satellite image, 19 July 2016, https://www.facebook.com/damas.kurds/posts/907321289395257/.

144   Dick Douwes

presence dating from around 1800 or somewhat later.[18] In the case of some key players in provincial politics who are not known by a family name, their ethnic background is sometimes known from local sources. Several Kurdish commanders made a career in the service of the 'Azm governors who held provincial offices for much of the eighteenth and early nineteenth centuries, including Kunj Yusuf Pasha and Ibrahim Deli Pasha, both serving as governor of Damascus. Both started their career in the *deli* forces of the most influential warlord Mulla Ismail of the Kurdish Milli tribe and they may very well have been members of the same large tribe.[19]

Unfortunately, the background of some major players in the Hama and Homs region is less known, in particular that of Faraj Agha who dominated local politics during the 1820s and 1830s in central Syria. He may have been of Arab origin, namely of the small Turki tribe originating from the Najd, connected to the great 'Anaza confederation, and considered to be local at the time in the Hama and Homs area.[20] Local sources refer to him as the *hakim* (ruler) or *muhafiz* of Hama and blame him for the impoverishment and depopulation of villages, such as Murayj al-Durr, a Turkoman village to the south of Hama, in the second half of the nineteenth century, which was then repopulated by Circassians.[21] But he was employed by both the Ottomans and the Egyptians, ruling the area for over a decade.

Apart from the military, the Kurdish presence in Syria comprised trading and scholarly, mainly Sufi, networks that predated Ottoman rule but are likely to have expanded considerably in Ottoman times. Trade and travel within the empire brought together areas that had been separated administratively before, in particular Anatolia and the Bilad

---

18   According to a text published on Facebook the family name (*laqab*) of the al-Barazi was adopted in 1830 (see Kurd Dimashq's Facebook post in note 17).

19   On a Kurdish Facebook page Kunj Yusuf Pasha is referred to as Yusuf al-Milli. See Shakhsiyyat min al-Dhakira al-Kurdiyya, Isma'il al-Milli, family history and photo of Muhammad Salim al-Milli, Facebook, 31 August 2020, https://www.facebook .com/199678623718479/posts/1201806256839039/.

20   On Faraj Agha, see Douwes, *Ottomans*, 122–4; 178–83. According to an internet source he was a "Turki," that is, from the Arab Turki tribe. He married locally and the family was named after his son, 'Uthman Agha. See 'Abdallah al-Tawashi, National Geographic Hama, Mawsu'at Hama, Al-Tatawwur al-Sukkani wa-l-'Umrani fi Hama khilal al-Fatrat al-Hukm al-'Uthmani: Al-juz' al-Sadis, Facebook, 29 January 2019, https://www.facebook.com/Encyclopedia.of.Hama/photos /a.1407239766185310/2198780260364586/.

21   Douwes, *Ottomans*, 15–16.

al-Sham. Kurdish tribes moved into the eastern parts of the province of Aleppo and became fully absorbed in the provisioning of livestock, in particularly sheep, to towns and fortresses along the Sultanic Road that connected Aleppo to Damascus. Kurdish traders provided the inland towns and villages with sheep for slaughter, following the Sultanic Road south.[22] They herded the remainder of their flock in the Bekaa Valley and sold it to local salesmen who marketed the sheep in Mount Lebanon and neighbouring areas.[23] An example of the prominent Kurdish involvement in the livestock trade is the arrival of a Kurdish commander at the banks of the Orontes (Asi) river near Homs with "… God only knows how large an amount of cows, sheep, and goats" in 1802, an exercise likely connected to the supplying of Ottoman troops that had moved overland to Egypt and Palestine to battle the Napoleonic invaders.[24]

Villages and Tribes

The districts of Hama and Homs may have been frequented by Kurdish tribes other than sheep traders but there is hardly any record of Kurdish tribal transhumance. Burckhardt encountered in the 1820s some Kurdish families who had pitched their tents in the western part of the district, not far from the fortress town of Misyaf.[25] The most famed reminder of the history of the Kurdish presence in the area is Hisn al-Akrad, a large fortress situated to the west of Homs along the road to Tripoli. By the early nineteenth century, it was Kurdish in name only, referred to in European sources as the Crac de Chevaliers; but the area to the southwest of this huge castle was inhabited by Turkomans and some Kurds.[26] Around 1800 the district of Hisn al-Akrad was a melting pot in which a large variety of actors – differentiated socially, ethnically, and religiously – played an active role in local politics.[27]

The name of villages such as Qubbat al-Kurdi to the south of Hama and close to the Sultanic Road may indicate a past Kurdish presence; this particular village was deserted in the eighteenth century and repopulated in the second half of the nineteenth century by local *'arab*.

---

22 Reilly, *Small Town*, 91.
23 Burckhardt, *Travels*, 25–6.
24 Al-Makki, *Tarikh*, 163.
25 Burckhardt, *Travels*, 149.
26 Burckhardt, 161.
27 Stefan Winter, "Le District de Hisn al-Akrad (Syrie) sous les Ottomans," *Journal Asiatique* 307, no. 2 (2019): 232–3, https://doi.org/10.2143/JA.307.2.3287179.

146   Dick Douwes

Only two villages were evidently inhabited by Kurds, both situated on the western fringes of the districts of Hama and Homs. These villages, Akrad Ibrahim and Akrad al-Dayanisa, were most probably tribal settlements in origin; but unlike the Turkoman villages, they did not constitute a separate administrative unit and were classified as belonging to the largest fiscal category, the so-called villages of the granary (*hasil*). Akrad Ibrahim was the larger of the two, with a fifty-*faddan* surface of agricultural land, and hence belonging to the larger villages in the district of Hama. Akrad al-Dayanisa, having a mere twenty *faddan*, belonged to the smaller settlements.[28]

According to Wasfi Zakariyya, writing in the late 1920s and early 1930s, the settlement of Kurds in these places dated from the early nineteenth century, the Akrad al-Dayanisa belonging to the Milli tribe and being Yazidi. This seems probable because in the early nineteenth century the Kurdish *delibashi* Mulla Isma'il played a prominent role in central Syria, in particular in this area (see below). Zakariyya noted that only elderly people still spoke Kurdish. He also mentions the semi-nomadic Akrad 'Uthmanu who were making a livelihood in the southern part of the Ghab valley and in the process of settling in two or three villages, later moving to newly established villages to the east of Hama.[29] The German geographer Martin Hartmann who visited central Syria in the late nineteenth century reported that he met with tent-dwelling Kurdish farmers to the east of Hama.[30]

Provincial Careers

When highlighting the Kurdish presence in the districts of Hama and Homs in the eighteenth and nineteenth centuries, the careers of a number of Kurdish officers and governors come to the fore. The core responsibility of provincial authorities in the Syrian interior was to ensure safe passage along the major roads and provide nourishment to passers-by, including pilgrims heading for Mecca and Medina.

---

28 H/MS 49, 23 Rabi' al-Awwal 1245, 326–9. The largest village was Talldu (eighty-six *faddan*). The smallest hamlet was Kafr Yahud (four *faddan*, later often spelled as Kafr Hud, the rural Jewish inhabitants having migrated for larger places such as Aleppo). Note that a *faddan* is not a square measure, but translates the time needed to work the field with a pair of oxen, sometimes two pairs.

29 Zakariyya, *'Asha 'ir al-Sham*, 664–73. The two Kurdish villages only appear in the local records in the 1820s.

30 Martin Hartmann, "Beiträge zur Kentniss der Syrischen Steppe," *Zeitschrift des Deutschen Palästina-Vereins* 23 (1901): 75.

Hama and Homs were situated on that most important line of travel and communication, the Sultanic Road. A range of fortresses on and near this road constituted a vital asset in maintaining control. The organization of the yearly pilgrimage was the single most important task of the governor of Damascus, the city being a major assembly point for pilgrims who needed to be escorted by the governor's troops along the long road to the holy cities in the Hijaz. Damascus, being the point of departure for the pilgrimage, had strengthened its position as a centre of religious learning, attracting scholars from the wider region, including Kurds.

Sufi networks were spread all over the area and governed major parts of social and economic life in the cities, including Hama and Homs. Unlike Damascus, the local learned families that dominated religious offices in Hama and Homs appear to have been exclusively of Arab ancestry. The most prominent family was the Kaylanis of Hama, who belonged to one of the most widespread *ashraf* family networks of the Arab provinces of the empire, with family ties to Baghdad, Damascus, and Cairo. According to 'Abd al-Ghani al-Nabulusi, the family was held in high regard.[31] Members of the Kaylani family dominated religious offices such as the *mufti*ship and usually provided the *naqib al-ashraf*, the head of the descendants of Muhammad. A more locally oriented family of *ashraf* and religious learning, also held in highest esteem, was the 'Alwani family, descendants of the most venerated mystic of Hama, 'Alwan ibn 'Atiya (d. 1527), whose shrine constituted the most popular Sufi shrine in Hama.[32] Both the Kaylani and 'Alwani families predated Ottoman rule. Hama and Homs harboured numerous *madrasa*s, *tekke*s, and shrines. No doubt these also catered to travelling Kurdish Sufis and religious scholars, though it appears the latter tended to opt for residence in Aleppo and Damascus rather than in the smaller towns in between.

Thus, the Kurdish presence in the districts of Hama and Homs was neither religious in origin, nor pre-Ottoman, but obviously military and mainly established in the late eighteenth and early nineteenth centuries. With the coming to prominence of the 'Azm family in the eighteenth century, the Kurdish military gained a foothold in the administration of the Syrian provinces, including the large inland

---

31   'Abd al-Ghani al-Nabulusi, *Al-Haqiqa wa'l-Majaz fi Rihla ila Bilad al-Sham wa-Misr wa'l-Hijaz* (N.p.: Al-Hay'a al-Misriyya al-'Amma li'l-Kitab, 1986), 49–50.

32   Sabuni, *Tarikh*, 135–7. On the shrine, see Jean Gaulmier, "Pèlerinages populaires à Hama," *Bulletin d'études orientales* 1 (1931): 143–5.

148 Dick Douwes

province of Damascus, which comprised Hama and Homs for most of the eighteenth and nineteenth centuries.[33] Several high-ranking Kurdish officers were engaged in administrative functions, ranging from governors to commanders of military units that were intended to ensure orderly rule and public safety. However, they also contributed, at times, to widespread insecurity through infighting between various military factions as a result of the highly fragmented nature of policing the province.[34] Local elite families like the Kaylani family, being firmly rooted in the local administration, were quick to establish close ties with the newly arrived military, in particular the 'Azm family, and may have helped the latter's process of localization. Various branches of these two families owned great wealth and spread their network well beyond the two districts, in particular to Damascus, the core administrative and political centre.[35]

The speculation concerning the roots of this most powerful family of eighteenth-century inland Syria is well known, the 'Azms being perhaps of Kurdish, or possibly Turkoman or local Arab origin.[36] Given that Kurds were actively engaged in higher office by the 'Azms suggests that their roots – or at least their network – were situated in Anatolia. Apart from the engagement of Kurdish military, the settlement of Turkomans in over a dozen villages in the Hama and Homs regions during the early period of 'Azm dominance indicates that families and tribes from Anatolia acquired a clear and tangible presence in central Syria.[37] Some families of Arab ancestry also gained prominence under al-'Azm patronage, in particular the al-Jundi family from Ma'arrat al-Nu'man, a small town along the Sultanic Road less than a day's travel to the north of Hama in the southernmost district of the province of Aleppo, and key in the early career of the al-'Azm clan. Apart from dominating offices in Ma'arra, members of the al-Jundi family were appointed to offices in Homs where the family acquired a stronghold and were part of the local elite in the nineteenth century, possibly second to the al-Atassi family, also of Arab ancestry.[38] The 'Azms were not the only provincial governors recruiting Kurds for military services; the core of the military

---

33 Some temporary changes in the provincial division occurred, the districts being occasionally attached to Tripoli.

34 Douwes, *Ottomans*, 111–15.

35 Douwes, 72–5.

36 Abdul-Karim Rafeq, *The Province of Damascus 1723-1783* (Beirut: Khayats, 1966), 90–2.

37 Reilly, *Small Town*, 33, observes that the 'Azms are of non-Arab origin.

38 On the al-Jundi family and their connection to the 'Azm family, see al-Jundi, *Tarikh Ma'arrat al-Nu'man*, 2:334–9.

units of al-Jazzar Pasha, the family's most serious provincial competitor in the late eighteenth century, consisted of Kurds. According to a local chronicler, after his dismissal as governor of Damascus in 1795, his *Akrad* ruled the city for a while.[39]

The al-'Azm clan was successful in gaining office in the Syrian provinces during most of the eighteenth century and continued to do so in the nineteenth, though mainly lesser posts from the second half of the eighteenth century onwards. During their slow demise from power starting in that time, and in fierce and sometimes violent competition for local dominance against other factions based in Tripoli, Sidon, and Akka, in particular that of Jazzar Pasha and his associates, they gradually gave way to other contenders. Several Kurdish commanders made their career in this context, often starting in the service of the 'Azm family but also rendering services to their challengers. These commanders belonged mainly to cavalry units, serving various sultanic appointees, some running a business of their own of supplying troops to various provincial parties. Some officers who served the family actually replaced them, surpassing the authority of their former patrons with sultanic support, for example Ibrahim Deli Pasha and Kunj Yusuf Pasha. Others took a rebellious turn and acted as warlords to be hired by the various provincial powers, the most important being Mulla Isma'il, who operated mainly from the Hama area, also the rural stronghold of the 'Azms.

Two Kurdish tribal names figure prominently in the local history of the Hama and Homs area: that of the Millis and the Barazis. Local documentation and histories offer very little information on the relations between the two, except that members of both families or tribes arrived and made careers in the *deli* forces in the late eighteenth and early nineteenth centuries. Some stayed in the area, in particular in the town of Hama and a few villages, thus creating a Kurdish presence which was to leave its mark on local society.[40]

Kurdish Pashas

Because the 'Azms resided mainly in Hama, apart from Damascus, the Hama area became the scene of provincial contention between the

---

39 Muhammad Jamil Shatti, *Rawd al-Bashar fi A'yan Dimashq fi'l-Qarn al-Thalith 'Ashar* (Damascus: Dar al-Yaqza al-'Arabiyya, 1946), 40–3.

40 On the Millis and Barazis in northern Syria, see Muhammad Amin Zaki, *Khulasat Tarikh al-Kurd wa'l-Kurdistan* (Baghdad: N.p., 1961), 420–5, as well as the contribution of Muhsin Seyda to this volume.

150   Dick Douwes

coastal factions of Jazzar Pasha and the interior factions that included various high-ranking Kurdish officers. None of the factions constituted stable coalitions and several major players switched sides, sometimes more than once, offering their services to various local and provincial contenders for power or starting a business of their own as rebel officers.

The first Kurdish *delibashi* to become governor of Damascus, after having made his career in the al-'Azm household, was Ibrahim Deli Pasha.[41] Prior to his appointment to Damascus in 1788, he served briefly as governor of the province of Tripoli, before being removed from that post by Jazzar Pasha who dominated provincial politics at the time. In Damascus Ibrahim Deli Pasha soon faced a rebellion of the several military factions in the city. He retreated to Hama in order to collect troops. After receiving the backing of the Porte he retook Damascus and besieged the citadel of the rebellious janissaries. Following the mediation of one of the leading *deli*s, Mulla Isma'il, the janissaries surrendered. The fact that Ibrahim Deli Pasha was able to mobilize troops from Hama is indicative of his connection with the 'Azm household. However, locally the departure of troops to Damascus proved disastrous because the Mawali tribe took the opportunity to loot the Hama area. The counterattack by troops from Aleppo and Damascus visited further havoc on central Syria, as they brought the plague with them.[42]

One of the most serious incidents in the rivalry between coastal and interior factions was the brutal attack on Hama in 1803 led by 'Abdallah Agha al-Mahmud of the Dandashli clan. He was subordinate to Jazzar Pasha and then governor of the Homs district in the western part of which the Dandashli clan was rooted. Earlier, he had served as district governor of Hama when Jazzar Pasha was governor of Damascus. The 'Azms, led by the then governor of Damascus 'Abdallah Pasha al-'Azm and their allies, defeated the troops of 'Abdallah Agha al-Mahmud after heavy fighting, leaving many casualties.[43] Al-Jazzar Pasha died the next year, 1804. His death was celebrated in the inland cities and towns, many having had bad experiences with his harsh and at times cruel rule. With his death, the confrontations between coastal and interior factions came to an end. The interior factions took control of provincial affairs with the appointment of Kunj Yusuf Pasha as governor of Damascus.

---

41 Shatti, *A 'yan*, 25–6.
42 Muhammad Khalil al-Muradi, *Silk al-Durar fi A 'yan al-Qarn al-Thani 'Ashar*, 4 vols., (Bulaq: al-Matba'a al-Miriyya al-'Amira: 1301 H.), 3:11–20; Jundi, *Tarikh*, 2:336; Muhammad Kurd 'Ali, *Khitat al-Sham* (Damascus: al-Matba'a al-Haditha, 1983), 3:5–6.
43 Douwes, *Ottomans*, 98–9.

Like Ibrahim Deli Pasha he made his career in service of the ʿAzm household as *delibashi*, but this Kurdish officer had also been employed by Jazzar Pasha and turned against former associates of the ʿAzms in Damascus among the local military. Kunj Yusuf Pasha's period in office was troubled by the impact of the French invasion in Egypt and Palestine and the occupation of the holy cities in the Hijaz by the Saudi-Wahhabi coalition, thus posing a major menace to the reputation of the Ottoman sultan as guardian of the Holy Cities, and, subsequently, a threat to the position of his representative in Damascus. The pilgrimage to Mecca and Medina was interrupted and the Hawran, the area to the south of Damascus, was targeted by Saʿudi-Wahhabi raiders, causing Kunj Yusuf Pasha to take refuge in Hama in 1810, never to return to office.[44] Regionally, the province of Damascus lost imperial importance with the rise of Muhammad Ali Pasha of Egypt, whose armies were to regain the holy cities of the Hijaz for the Ottoman Sultanate.

The Fragmentation of Violence and Warlordism

In the post al-Jazzar, or for that matter the post al-ʿAzm period, inland Syria witnessed a continued rural crisis due to changing migration patterns of Bedouin tribes, who were moving into settled agricultural lands. The massive overland movement of Ottoman troops after the French invasion and the Saudi-Wahhabi takeover of the Hijaz had left many villages without assets to continue farming, the armies having taken nearly all livestock, food, and fodder. During the period of provincial factionalism between the coastal and interior factions, a degree of provincial order existed in which the households of al-Jazzar and that of the ʿAzms were able to organize coalitions that dominated provincial affairs for shorter or longer periods of time. After the demise of these factions, the military, already fragmented to a considerable degree, became tied to more local issues. Roaming soldiers were a considerable threat to local communities.[45] Following revolts in the inland towns and cities, several leading officers had been executed, but their troops were often given the opportunity to evacuate their positions. A number of experienced officers became warlords, marketing their services to various provincial players and creating independent rural territories of their own.

---

44 Douwes, 100–1.
45 Douwes, 112–14.

152   Dick Douwes

A key actor in the closing decades of the eighteenth and the first decade of the nineteenth century was Mulla Isma'il, a *delibashi* of the Kurdish Milli tribe. Little is known about his early career. In 1788 he pops up in local chronicles as a mediator between Ibrahim Deli Pasha and the rebellious janissaries of the citadel of Damascus, showing that he had a power base connected to the interior factions. Under the last 'Azm governor of Damascus, 'Abdallah Pasha al-'Azm, Mulla Isma'il took up residence in Hama, which served as a centre for negotiating in all sorts of provincial affairs, including those of Mount Lebanon. Hama also served as a place of refuge for Ottoman officials and even emirs from Lebanon when they were outlawed by the Porte or fleeing from local scenes of violence. Mulla Isma'il was not without competitors and he regularly changed sides, following his own strategy. He was also hired by Kunj Yusuf Pasha, who sought his mediation several times in local conflicts and called upon him for military assistance. When Mulla Isma'il sided with Sulayman Pasha, the former *mamluk* and heir of al-Jazzar Pasha, Kunj Yusuf decided to seek refuge in Egypt in 1810. Sulayman Pasha, who was appointed governor of Damascus, rewarded Mulla Isma'il by granting him the districts of both Hama and Homs.[46]

The alliance between Sulayman Pasha and Mulla Isma'il was not long-lasting. About a year after his appointment to Hama and Homs he was ousted from office. He first sought refuge with the Mawali and then established himself as a rebel chief in the Qal'at al-Mudiq, a fortress village situated at the entrance of the marshy valley of al-Ghab to the west of Hama, allying with other rebel Kurdish officers in the Jisr al-Shughur and 'Ariha districts of Aleppo province.[47] One of the last campaigns of Mulla Isma'il in the service of Kunj Yusuf was to restore the fortress of Misyaf to its Isma'ili inhabitants after it had been taken by the Alawi/Nusayri Rasalina clan.[48] From his rebel foothold in what was a relatively marginal region Mulla Isma'il continued to be involved in some larger conflicts in the Hama and Homs area, in particular involving recently arrived Bedouin tribes of the 'Anaza confederation. Their "sudden" arrival disturbed regional and local tribal relations and posed a severe threat to village life close to the Sultanic Road, as well as to the towns located on that road. Mulla Isma'il associated with the 'Anaza via the local al-Turki tribe, a connection that alarmed the local and provincial

---

46 Dimashqi, *Hawadith*, 45–6; Shihab, *Lubnan*, 556–9.
47 Burckhardt, *Travels*, 125–38. When Burckhardt travelled through the area he noted that "Milly Ismail" was eighty-five years old.
48 Douwes, *Ottomans*, 116.

authorities to the extent that they sought imperial support for moving against Mulla Isma'il. A large contingent of Arna'ut was dispatched to Hama. The conflict ended with the death of Mulla Isma'il, who was arrested and shot dead in a meeting with the district governor of Hama, Salim Bey al-'Azm, in 1818, thus concluding the long career of a provincial warlord.[49] This dramatic incident did not erode the old warlord's network, however, because two of his close associates were to dominate local policies for the next decades: Bakir Agha, a *delibashi*, later to be called Bakir Agha al-Barazi, and Faraj Agha, possibly of the al-Turki tribe and strongman of the area after Mulla Isma'il's death. Both the family of Mulla Isma'il and Bakir Agha with his family were ordered to leave the Hama area.[50] Faraj Agha did not leave; Bakir Agha was pardoned within a decade and both his following and that of the late Mulla Isma'il were allowed to return to Hama.[51]

Another remnant of the, albeit temporary, prominence of Mulla Isma'il in the Hama area, in particular in the western region of the Hama district, was the settlement of Kurds in the early decades of the nineteenth century in the villages of Akrad Ibrahim and Akrad al-Dayasina, as well as the presence of small groups of semi-nomadic Kurds. Most of these villagers and nomads were probably related to Mulla Isma'il, who recruited support from among his fellow tribesmen. It appears that Mulla Isma'il did not have direct heirs that were able to reproduce his military capacities, even though in the documents of the Hama court occasionally the name al-Milli, including the *agha's*, can be found in the 1840s and after. But another Kurdish household was to become the largest landowning family of the Hama and Homs area: the al-Barazi.

The Rise of a Landowning Class

The Ottoman reforms of the mid-nineteenth century – partly inspired by the episode of Egyptian rule over large chunks of the empire, including all of Syria – allowed the local elites, including the military, to turn their privileged position into a tool for acquiring rural properties. Former tax farmers of sultanic land were able to claim village land as their own property, often by way of making loans to villagers, but also by

---

49 Shihab, *Lubnan*, 636–8; H/MS 43 (27 Rajab 1233) 197–8 offers a list of belongings that his wife inherited.
50 H/MS 43:213 (dated early Sha'ban 1233).
51 H/MS 49:234 (dated 1242), H/MS 49/388 (dated 1245).

financing the repopulation of deserted villages to the east of the Sultanic Road. Because of the relative scarcity of local sources, it is difficult to fully apprehend the impact of the Egyptian occupation on inland Syria, but Egyptian authorities appear to have relied on existing networks, in particular on those of inland Syria, restoring Damascus as the main centre of administration at the expense of Sidon and 'Akka. They appointed Ahmad Bey, the adopted son of Kunj Yusuf Pasha, as *mutasallim* or deputy governor of Damascus and recruited officers from the Damascene military for regional positions, such as those in Hama and Homs. Some of these officers were recruited from the prominent al-Shamli family from the Maydan neighbourhood, members of which had served earlier in the Hama and Homs areas. Having been found guilty of exacting money from several villages, Rashid Agha al-Shamli was soon replaced by the local strongman Faraj Agha as deputy governor of Hama. In June 1833, he in turn was replaced by 'Abdallah Agha Tayfur, a local Kurdish *agha*. In 1834 Faraj Agha returned to office in Hama following revolts of the 'Anaza Bedouin who were protesting against the restrictions imposed by the authorities on their migratory patterns.[52] But 'Abdallah Agha Tayfur replaced Faraj Agha once more within a year, a pattern of quick rotation of offices that reflects suspicion towards local strongmen and is indicative of the failing of adequate central control. When conditions ran out of control, local strongmen were re-engaged, a model on which soldiers like Faraj Agha, and before him Mulla Isma'il, survived. When the Egyptians were forced to evacuate Syria, Faraj Agha was called upon once more following a petition of the notables of Hama.[53]

It is difficult to assess if and to what extent the elites of Hama and Homs suffered from the decade of Egyptian rule. Some may have, but when comparing the elite composition between the pre- and post-Egyptian period, local elite families were mostly able to regain their prominence, like the 'Azm and Kaylani families. But some new arrivals who had settled in the area a few decades before the Egyptian takeover gained local prominence, and these included principally Kurds who had started their career in the following of Mulla Isma'il of the Milli tribe. Several Kurdish families struck root in the area, some becoming landlords owning properties in several villages, some having huge latifundio-like estates by the final decades of Ottoman rule over Syria. Apart from land they also owned flocks of sheep and goats

---

52 Douwes, *Ottomans*, 198–200.

53 H/MS 277 (24 Dhu'l-Hijja 1256) and 297 (7 Muharram 1257).

tended by the local *'arab* tribes. The most prominent Kurdish landowning household was that of the al-Barazi. Hammu Agha, most likely a *delibashi*, was among the first Barazi military men to operate in the area in the early decades of the nineteenth century, in particular in the Misyaf district, part of the stronghold of Mulla Isma'il. His nephew Bakir Agha also started his career in the Misyaf district and became the dominant member of the family. Although he had been banned from the Hama area, he and his following were allowed to return, indicating that he could fall back on a local power base, regardless of his participation in an attack on Hama in 1819 in coalition with Faraj Agha and the 'Anaza Bedouin.[54] It appears that Hammu Agha first resisted the Egyptian armies led by Ibrahim Pasha, son of the rebellious governor of Egypt, Muhammad 'Ali Pasha, but later collaborated with his rule and left for Egypt when Muhammad 'Ali Pasha was forced to evacuate his troops.[55] Members of the Barazi family were soon considered to be of prominence, given the local support for Hammu Agha's nephew, Bakir Agha al-Barazi.

Other families that acquired a prominent position were the Turkoman Jijaklis and Turkumans and the Kurdish Tayfur, all of whom arrived, like the Barazis, in the area in the early nineteenth century, perhaps somewhat earlier. Data on their early careers is scattered and insufficient to trace their path to local prominence. 'Abdallah Agha Tayfur acted at least twice as deputy governor of Hama during the decade of Egyptian rule, whereas Khalil Agha al-Jijakli was appointed to the local council along with leading members of the 'Azm, Kaylani, and the highly respected 'Alwani families. The Egyptian regime stimulated – and at times forced – the local elite to invest in the rural economy, including in the repopulation of villages that had been deserted over the last decades or earlier. Most notables invested in villages to the west of the Sultanic Road, rather than in repopulating villages to the east. For instance, 'Abdallah Agha Tayfur made loans to relatively well-established but poor villages to the west of the road, including Kafr Buhum, Talldhahab, Talldu, and Halfaya, thus creating future prospects of ownership of village land.[56] Two *agha*s of the Jijakli family

---

54 H/MS 49/388 1245.
55 Barazi Family Network, "Muhammad Agha Bin Bakir Agha Al-Barazi," accessed 1 February 2024, https://barazifamily.net/index.php?page=display_node&nid=3; Bahzani, "Mujaz Ean Tarikh Alkurd fi Himah Wahims: Eali Shikhu Brazi," accessed 1 February 2024, https://www.bahzani.net/?p=81983.
56 H/MS 51/365 (dated 1257) and H/MS 51/439 (19 Jumada al-Akhira 1257).

156   Dick Douwes

invested a large amount in a village to the west of Hama in 1830.[57] The most important investors – apart from the state – in the repopulation of deserted villages to the east of the road were the Mawali chief Muhammad Khurfan Bey and the local strongman Faraj Agha, sometimes as partners.[58] With the retreat of the Egyptian regime in 1841 most of the repopulated villages were again abandoned. As a result of the nineteenth-century reforms, in particular after the Egyptian interlude, the organization of the state and provincial military changed significantly, with the fading of old-school structures that were often based on ethnic or tribal association and with it the prominence of Kurdish military figures such as the *delis*.

During the Egyptian episode, the ties between the urban elite, who earlier had acted as tax farmers and moneylenders, changed, forcing villagers into debts of magnitudes that could never be repaid. The later reforms allowed the elites of Hama and Homs to turn former state land (*miri* or *aradi sultaniyya*) into virtual property. After 1860 these families started to invest, at first reluctantly, in the expansion of cultivation to the east of the Sultanic Road, thus extending their rural possessions. By the close of the Ottoman era and into the French Mandate period, the Barazi households owned (most of) the land of over fifty villages and hamlets, nearly equal to the combined rural wealth of the more "notable" 'Azm and Kaylani families together. Like other renowned families, members of the Barazi family also acquired village properties in the adjacent districts of Idlib and Homs.[59] In the latter district, urban-based families of Arab ancestry owned extensive landed properties, including the Jundi, Atassi, Durubi, and Jandali families. Members of the latter acquired the village of Akrad al-Dayasina. Unlike the 'Azm and the Kaylani families, who enjoyed powerful family ties well beyond the Hama region, the Barazis' powerbase appears to have been primarily regional. Yet, the Barazi family became the largest urban-based land-owners in the wider region.

---

57 H/MS 49/388 (16 Dhu'l-Hijja 1245).
58 See for instance H/MS 51/33 (9 Rajab 1252) and H/MS 51/156 (28 Shawwal 1254) investments in Talldara and 'Izz al-Din, both of which were deserted after the Egyptian withdrawal and repopulated again in the second half of the nineteenth century.
59 Jean Gaulmier, "Notes sur la propriété foncière dans la Syrie centrale," *L'Asie Française* 33 (1933): 130–7. This short article gives an overview of landholding in the Hama district, the al-Barazi family being by far the largest, owning land in over fifty villages and often most of the village.

Conclusion

Apart from the settlement of Kurdish families in a few villages in the western part of the Hama region in the early decades of the nineteenth century, the rural Kurdish presence in this part of inland Syria was small. The presence of nomadic Kurds was marginal at best, except from livestock traders passing through with their flocks to be traded along the Sultanic Road connecting Aleppo to Damascus. The towns of Hama and Homs were situated on that vital connection from Anatolia and beyond to the holy cities of the Mecca and Medina. Their strategic location not only attracted pilgrims and traders, but also military migrants such as the mounted *deli* and *lawand* forces, which played a prominent role in local and provincial politics.

Despite its disputed origins, the ʿAzm household's exceptional career in the Syrian provinces triggered the increased involvement of Kurds in the administration. Kurds were engaged primarily in local and provincial military formations, most notably the *deli*. A few Kurdish *delibashi*s made a remarkable career, surpassing their earlier overlords of the ʿAzm family in authority, such as Ibrahim Deli Pasha and Kunj Yusuf Pasha, both becoming governors, including of the province of Damascus. But their careers in high offices were frustrated by the intense provincial factionalism of the last decades of the eighteenth century and the first of the nineteenth century; both faced low points in their career when they had to flee from Damascus, under differing circumstances.

In these hectic and violent times, which witnessed a rapid rotation of governorships in the Syrian provinces and outright military confrontations between competing factions, certain military commanders were well equipped to survive or even thrive in such conditions, their services being needed by various factions. The most prominent of such warlords was Mulla Ismaʿil, a Kurdish *delibashi* of the Milli tribe and a dominant player in provincial and local affairs for several decades around the turn of the nineteenth century. Hama served as his base, which indicates that the start of his career was connected to the ʿAzms. But Mulla Ismaʿil had an agenda of his own, like other warlords of the time. His prominence in the Hama area explains the settlement of Kurds in a few villages and the arrival of more Kurdish military in the early nineteenth century. The warlord's legacy consisted in the rise of a few Kurdish families to local prominence, in particular the al-Barazi household, but also some lesser-known Kurdish families including the Millis, who settled in the town of Hama. Not only Kurdish *agha*s made a career in this period, but also Turkomans, such as the Jijakli and

158   Dick Douwes

Turkuman households, who both settled in Hama in the early decades of the century too.

The decade of Egyptian rule witnessed what appears to be a consolidation of local power relations as they had evolved in the decade before the arrival of Muhammad 'Ali's troops. The Egyptian interlude is often seen as a turning point in the history of the Syrian provinces, but it was not so influential when it comes to the composition of the local elite in towns like Hama and Homs. Remarkably, families of *agha*s serving before, during, and after the interlude of Egyptian rule were able to strengthen their position by investing in rural estates, partly as a continuation of tax farming, but mainly through making partnerships and giving loans to villagers, as well as to semi-nomadic tribesmen. In the second half of the nineteenth century, these families profited from a variety of reforms, in particular concerning ownership of land, which turned them into a class of landowners – no longer *agha*s but *efendi*s or landowning bourgeois, spreading their networks into the fields of governance and culture. The Barazi family, in a sense heirs to Mulla Isma'il, *deli*s in origin, became the largest landowners of the Hama and Homs districts. By that time they had become Arabized, like other families including Kurdish villagers. A difficult question to answer is to what degree, and when, they were still seen by local society as being Kurdish, and to what extent they themselves expressed their Kurdishness.

PART THREE

Kurdish Tribalism and Tribal Control in the Jazira

7 *Waqf* versus *Miri* Nomads: Taxation, Endowment, and Settlement Practices in Northern Syria in the Eighteenth Century

KEIKO IWAMOTO

Introduction

In the history of the Kurdish people, the city of Raqqa has played a very significant role. A fairly small town situated near the Euphrates in northern Syria/Mesopotamia (and capital of the self-declared caliphate of the "Islamic State" from 2014 to 2017), in the late seventeenth and eighteenth centuries Raqqa was the principal location for the forced settlement of Turkish (Türkmen or Türkman; Turkoman, Turcoman) and Kurdish (Kürd or Kürt; Ekrad) nomads by the Ottoman government. This paper will focus on the reasons for this initiative and the differential treatments of these tribes by the Ottoman state.

Pastoral-nomadic tribes occupied vast spaces in the early modern Ottoman Empire, including large parts of modern-day Syria. However, the Ottoman government considered pastoral nomadism problematic and unwelcome, especially from the late seventeenth century. This led to the government-mandated resettlement of many nomadic tribes into the Raqqa area for various reasons, including as punishment for banditry (*eşkıyalık*), plundering, and tax evasion, among other legal offences.

Several researchers have investigated the settlement policies of the seventeenth- and eighteenth-century Ottoman government towards nomadic groups in northern Syria, especially the Raqqa area. Cengiz Orhonlu and other scholars have focussed mainly on imperial edicts (*ferman-ı ali-şan*; *emr-i şerif*) in studies on Ottoman settlement policy, including those recorded in the "Mühimme Defteri (Registers of Important Affairs; Bâb-ı Âsafî, Divan-ı Hümâyûn Sicilleri Mühimme Defterleri [MD])," as well as registers from the "Maliyeden Müdevver" collection [MAD] of the Ottoman Archives/T.C. Cumhurbaşkanlık

162   Keiko Iwamoto

Devlet Arşivleri Başkanlığı Osmanlı Arsivi [BOA].[1] Orhonlu analyzed Ottoman sedentarization practices from 1691 to 1699. He clarified that the policy aimed to develop deserted land for agriculture and to establish a buffer zone between the newly settled people and Bedouin raiders from the Syrian Desert and the Arabian Peninsula.[2] The Sublime Porte issued many edicts demanding that any fled settlers be returned immediately to their assigned settlements; the entire tribe could be punished collectively with resettlement to Raqqa if some of its members had taken to banditry. Orhonlu also reported that the government took several measures to entice nomad groups to settle in the Raqqa area, such as distributing arable land, providing irrigation systems, and exempting them from certain cultivation taxes.[3] Reşat Kasaba, in his studies on mobility in the Ottoman Empire, reviewed government settlement policies in the Raqqa district. He notes that these policies were indeed a punishment for bandit (şeki; eşkıya) tribes and indicates the last quarter of the seventeenth century and the first half of the eighteenth

---

1 For more on these administrative documents, see Bilgin Aydın, *XVI. Yüzyılda Divan-ı Hümayun ve Defteri Sistemi* (Ankara: Türk Tarih Kurumu, 2017), 27–49.

2 Cengiz Orhonlu, "Osmanlı İmparatorluğunda Aşiretlerin İskânı," *Türk Kültürü Araştırmaları* 15 (1976): 269–88; Cengiz Orhonlu, *Osmanlı İmparatorluğu' nda Aşiretlerin İskânı* (Istanbul: Eren, 1987). For other studies, see M. Çelikdemir, "Rakka Mukavelesi (19 Aralık 1692)," *Gaziantep Üniversitesi Sosyal Bilimler Dergisi* 5, no. 1 (2002): 245–58; M. Çelikdemir, "Osmanlı Devleti'nin Aşiretleri Rakka'ya İskân Etmek İstemesindeki Sebepler," *Türk Dünyası Araştırmaları* 143 (2003): 141–54; M. Çelikdemir, "Osmanlı Devletinin Rakka İskan Politikasında Önemli Bir Kaynak: Mühimme Defteri," in *Birinci Orta Doğu Semineri Bildirileri Elazığ 29–31 Mayıs 2003* (Elazığ: T.C. Fırat Üniversitesi Orta Doğu Araştırmaları Merkezi, 2004), 345–56; M. Çelikdemir, "Osmanlı Devletinin Aşiretleri Rakka'ya İskân Faaliyetleri," in *II. Kayseri ve Yöresi Kültür, Sanat ve Edebiyat Bilgi Şöleni (10–12 Nisan 2006) Bildiriler* (Kayseri: Erciyes Üniversitesi Matbaası, 2007), 279–89; Yusuf Halaçoğlu, *XVIII. Yüzyılda Osmanlı İmparatorluğu'nun İskân Siyaseti ve Aşiretlerin Yerleştirilmesi* (Ankara: Türk Tarih Kurumu, 1988); Faruk Söylemez, *Osmanlı Devletinde Aşiret Yönetimi: Rişvan Aşiret Örneği* (İstanbul: Kitabevi, 2007); Faruk Söylemez, "Bozok Sancağı'nda Rişvan Oymakları," in *I. Uluslararası Bozok Sempozyumu 05–07 Mayıs 2016 Bildiri I. Cilt: Yozgat ve Çevresindeki Arkeolojik Alanlar, Höyükler ve Kazılar, Yozgat'ın Siyasî, İçtimaî ve İktisadî Tarihi*, ed. Kadir Özköse (Yozgat: Bozok Üniversitesi, 2016), 140–9; Bruce Masters, *The Arabs of the Ottoman Empire, 1516–1918: A Social and Cultural History* (Cambridge: Cambridge University Press, 2013), 95–100; Sam White, *The Climate of Rebellion in the Early Modern Ottoman Empire* (Cambridge: Cambridge University Press, 2011), 229–48.

3 İsmail Kavırım points out that some tribes of *waqf* nomads settled in a few villages in Karaman province, central Anatolia, as *derbendci* or *derbentçi*, that is, as responsible for guarding important roads or mountain passes in exchange for tax exemptions. İsmail Kıvrım, "Haleb ve Rakka'dan Hotamış'a," in *Geçmişten Günümüze Göçler*, ed. Alaattin Aköz, Doğan Yörük, and Haşim Karpuz (Konya: Konya Ticaret Odası, 2019), 129–44.

Waqf versus *Miri* Nomads   163

century as the beginning and development of "the waves of sedentarization" for the Ottoman nomadic peoples.[4] The establishment of the "Sedentarization Bureau" (İskan Dairesi) also occurred during this time to settle many nomads systematically. Kasaba concludes that the settlement policy's enforcement is correlated with the Ottoman Empire's territorial loss and diplomatic changes with the neighbouring empires.[5]

This paper attempts to address the question of why some Kurdish and Turkish groups involved in the settlement process were categorized as state-owned (*miri*) nomads and others as *waqf*-owned nomads. In the so-called classical period, that is, the fifteenth and sixteenth centuries, the Ottoman government collected taxes under the *dirlik/timar* feudal taxation system, whereby it assigned or bestowed tax collection mandates to military officers, bureaucrats, or Islamic judges (*qadi* or *kadı*). This created a ruling class (*askeri*) that did not have to pay taxes, but was, in turn, obligated to serve the state as soldiers or other professional workers and rule their assigned tax-paying subjects (*reaya*). These taxation rights generally covered taxes on land, crops, markets, and livestock paid by settled and nomadic pastoralists, as well as *jizya* or *cizye* capitation tax paid by non-Muslims. Depending on the size or amount of the collected tax, the Ottomans divided *dirlik* into three categories: *timar, zeamet*, and *hass*, of which the latter, for amounts of 100,000 *akçe* or more, were allocated to the reigning Ottoman sultan (*padişah*) and the royal family, including the reigning sultan's mother, concubines, sons, and daughters, or to high bureaucrats and officials.[6] The reigning sultan's mother held the title of Valide Sultan and exerted significant power and influence over the harem court and beyond as the imperial harem's head.

Since the last decade of the sixteenth century, however, the Ottomans had begun replacing the increasingly outdated *dirlik* system with tax farming (*iltizam*), whereby the rights to a given tax source (*mukataa*

---

4 Reşat Kasaba, "Nomads and Tribes in the Ottoman Empire," in *The Ottoman World,* ed. Christine Woodhead (London: Routledge, 2012), 17–19, 21–2.

5 Reşat Kasaba, *A Moveable Empire: Ottoman Nomads, Migrants, and Refugees* (Seattle: University of Washington Press, 2009), 53–83; Reşat Kasaba, "Nomads and Tribes in the Ottoman Empire," 11–24.

6 *Akçe* was the official Ottoman silver coin minted by the coinage bureau. In the seventeenth and eighteenth centuries, however, non-Ottoman coins such as the *guruş* and *riyal* also circulated on the domestic market and were used for official transactions, taxes, and salary payments. See Şevket Pamuk, *Osmanlı İmparatorluğu'nda Paranın Tarihi* (İstanbul: Tarih Vakfı Yurt Yayınları, 1999); Ömerül Faruk Bölükbaşı, "Riyal," in *Türkiye Diyanet Vakfı İslam Ansiklopedisi* [DİA], supplement vol. (ek) 2 (Istanbul: Türkiye Diyanet Vakfı, 2016), 430–2.

164   Keiko Iwamoto

or *muqata'a*), such as a piece of land or other taxable production unit, would be auctioned off for a determined period or even for life (*malikane*). Those who obtained tax collection rights might subcontract the actual work of tax collection to their vassals, local dignitaries, or representatives of local communities (*ayan*). These people, who could even be non-state officials, were the face of Ottoman authority to the *reaya* and became indispensable actors of the Ottoman Empire in the seventeenth and eighteenth centuries.[7]

The Ottomans bestowed these tax collecting rights, which were *de jure* state-owned or *miri*, to particular individuals as private property (*mülk*). These persons, especially Ottoman family members, frequently converted their *mukataa*s into *waqf* (Turkish *vakıf*), an inalienable and charitable endowment established under Islamic law (*shari'a*). In Islamic law, *waqf* refers literally to the permanent cessation of the transfer of ownership of a specific piece of property, such as land or a building, belonging to the donor. The management of the property or goods is entrusted to a trustee or *mütevelli*. The *waqf* property, as well as products and revenues from the *waqf* property, are to be used for public, charitable, and religious purposes, such as operating educational and commercial institutions including mosques, *madrasa*s, hospitals, public soup kitchens, and caravansaries. Female members of the Ottoman family and their representatives operated many *waqf* institutions in various parts of the Ottoman Empire, including in many quarters of the imperial capital, Istanbul.

The Ottoman family's female members occasionally signed over the tax collection rights to their personal *waqf*s, which could be an important source of funds for political endeavours within the harem, the court, or the Ottoman central government.[8] One major *waqf* foundation that originated from the tax-collecting rights granted to the female members of the Ottoman royal family was the Atik Valide Sultan Mosque and

---

7   Halil İnalcık, "Military and Fiscal Transformation in the Ottoman Empire, 1600–1700," *Archivum Ottomanicum* 6 (1980): 283–338; Linda Darling, *Revenue-Raising and Legitimacy: Tax Collection and Finance Administration in the Ottoman Empire 1560–1660* (Leiden: E.J. Brill, 1996); Linda Darling, "Public Finances: The Role of the Ottoman Centre," in *The Cambridge History of Turkey*, ed. Suraiya Faroqhi (Cambridge: Cambridge University Press, 2006), 3:118–31; Baki Çakır, *Osmanlı Mukataa Sistemi (XVI–XVIII. Yüzyıl)* (Istanbul: Kitabevi, 2003).

8   John Robert Barnes, *An Introduction to Religious Foundations in the Ottoman Empire* (Leiden: E.J. Brill, 1986), 5–49; Leslie Peirce, *The Imperial Harem: Women and Sovereignty in the Ottoman Empire* (Oxford: Oxford University Press, 1993); Jane Hathaway, *The Chief Eunuch of the Ottoman Harem: From African Slave to Power-Broker* (Cambridge: Cambridge University Press, 2018).

mosque complex (*külliye*), located in the hills of Beylerbeyi above Üsküdar, an area on the Asian side of Istanbul.[9] The *waqf*-supported Atik Valide Sultan Mosque led the Ottomans to create the *hass* (privy reserve) *mukataa* of the Yeni-İl Türkmen and of the Aleppo (Haleb) Türkmen at the same time.[10] In other words, the *waqf* income allowed the Ottomans to form both the Yeni-İl Türkmen tribal confederation and the Aleppo Türkmen tribal confederation.[11] The members of the Yeni-İl and Aleppo Türkmen *waqf* reserve paid a fixed amount of money on pastoral products, which were recognized by the state as taxes, as did other pastoral-nomadic tribes, for the institution.

The following section gives an overview of the history of the Atik Valide Sultan Mosque *waqf* and the *hass mukataa* of the Yeni-İl and Aleppo Türkmen. The Yeni-İl *hass mukataa* was established in 1548, when the Ottomans bestowed the right to collect taxes from the pastoral products of nomadic Türkmen living in the Sivas region of central Anatolia to Mihrimah Sultan, the daughter of Süleyman I (r. 1520–66). After this, the term Yeni-İl came to mean the nomadic people paying

---

9 Pınar Kayaalp, "Vakfiye and Inscription: An Interpretation of the Written Records of the Atik Valide Mosque Complex," *International Journal of Islamic Architecture* 1, no. 2 (2012): 301–24, https://doi.org/10.1386/ijia.1.2.300_1; Pınar Kayaalp, *The Empress Nurbanu and Ottoman Politics in the 16th Century: Building the Atik Valide* (London: Routledge, 2018); Ramazan Pantık, "Atik Valide Sultan Külliyesinde İdari ve Mali Yapı (1590–1830)," in *Vakıf Kuran Kadınlar: Vakıflar Genel Müdürlüğü & Bezmiâlem Vakıf Üniversitesi Fatih Sultan Mehmet Vakıf Üniversitesi, 11 Mayıs 2018, İstanbul, Bildiriler*, ed. Fahameddin Başar (Ankara: Vakıflar Genel Müdürlüğü Yayınları, 2019), 265–83; Tijen Sabırlı, *Dindarlık, Ekonomi ve Sosyal Hayat: Nurbanu Atik Valide Sultan Vakfı Üzerine Bir İnceleme* (Istanbul: Libra, 2019). Ottoman female royal family members such as the queen mother, wives, and princesses of the reigning Ottoman sultan living in the harem were granted certain taxation rights under the name of "shoe money" (*paşmaklık* or *başmaklık*).
10 Yeni-İl meaning "new province." See also Ersin Gülsoy, "XVII. Yüzyılda Yeni-İl Türkmenleri," in *Oğuzlar: Dilleri, Tarihleri ve Kültürleri: 5. Uluslararası Türkiyat Araştırmaları Sempozyumu Bildirileri*, ed. Tufan Gündüz and Mikail Cengiz (Ankara: Hacettepe Üniversitesi Türkiyat Araştırmaları Enstitüsü Yayınları, 2015), 221–8.
11 For similar instances, see the cases of Yörük Voyvoda in the province of Hüdavendigar (Bursa). The *voyvoda* or voivode administered the *yörük* nomad group, who were the *reaya* of the *waqf* for the two Islamic holy cities, Mecca and Medina (Haremeyn-i Şerifeyn), and collected the *waqf*-income paid to the Haremeyn *waqf* institution. See Nilüfer Alkan Günay, "18. Yüzyıl Osmanlı Taşra Yönetim Düzeni Açısından Hudâvendigâr Sancağı'nda Yaşayan Vakıf Reayası Yörükler," *Uludağ Üniversitesi Fen-Edebiyat Fakültesi Sosyal Bilimler Dergisi* 18, no. 33 (2017): 317–38, https://doi.org/10.21550/sosbilder.311010; Nilüfer Alkan Günay, "18. Yüzyıl Osmanlı Taşra İdaresinde "Mültezim ve Reaya" İlişkisine Dair Bir Değerlendirme: Hudâvendigâr Sancağındaki Yörükân Voyvodaları ve Yörükler," in *Yörükler: Orta Asya'dan Anadolu'ya*, ed. İlhan Şahin (Istanbul: Bursa Osmangazi Belediyesi, 2019), 199–210.

166   Keiko Iwamoto

a fixed amount of money on their livestock production to Mihrimah Sultan's private treasury. After she died in 1578, the authorities changed the Yeni-İl *hass mukataa*'s financial status from her private property to *waqf* property, which was then utilized to maintain and administer a mosque complex dedicated to her in Üsküdar. In 1583, the Yeni-İl *hass mukataa* was given to Nurbanu Valide Sultan (d. 1583), mother of Murat III (r. 1574–95), as her *waqf*, to manage and finance her mosque and its complex with immunity privileges. This privilege strictly prohibited all officials and administrative powers from intervening in the tax-collecting right and its administration in any way (*mefruzül-kalem ve maktu'ül-kadem min külli'l-vücuh serbest*). Following this, the *waqf* institution annexed the Aleppo Türkmen *hass* to the *waqf* of Nurbanu's Atik Valide Sultan Mosque. It was customary to treat the two separate Yeni-İl Türkmen *hass* and Aleppo Türkmen *hass* as one single *waqf hass* in the financial and administrative records since the last quarter of the seventeenth century. At a later point, to better distinguish the Nurbanu Valide Sultan Mosque from the nearby mosque of Emetüllah Valide Sultan (d. 1715) built on the shores of Üsküdar, which was dedicated to the queen mother of Mustafa II (r. 1695–1703) and Ahmet III (r. 1703–30), the mosque began to be called the "old" (*atik* or *'atiq*) Valide Sultan Mosque.[12]

The Yeni-İl and Aleppo Türkmen *hass* constituted an essential part of the *waqf* income for the Atik Valide Sultan Mosque.[13] Consequently, the chief manager or *mütevelli*, and subcontracted tax collectors and managers, rather than state officials, had the right to collect the revenue for the foundation from the Yeni-İl and Aleppo Türkmen, as well as to have management control over the tribes. In this sense, the Aleppo and Yeni-İl Türkmen were not state *reaya*, but *waqf reaya*, paying a fixed amount of money or livestock to the foundation.

Therefore, in the seventeenth and eighteenth centuries of the Ottoman Empire, tax collecting rights and the management system of tax collection were inevitably complicated and multi-layered. This caused

---

12 Mehmet İpşirli, "Paşmaklık," in DİA (2007), 34:167–8; İlhan Şahin, "Nurbânû Sultan," in DİA (2007), 33:250–1; İlhan Şahin, "Üsküdar ve Türkmenler," in *Osmanlı İstanbulu: IV. Uluslararası Osmanlı İstanbulu Sempozyumu Bildirileri 20–22 Mayıs 2016 İstanbul*, ed. Feridun Emecen and Emrah Safa Gürkan (Istanbul: 29 Mayıs İstanbul Üniversitesi, 2016), 277–88; Betül İpşirli Argıt, "A Queen Mother and the Ottoman Imperial Harem: Rabia Gülnüş Emetullah Valide Sultan (1640–1715)," in *Concubines and Courtesans: Women and Slavery in Islamic History*, ed. Matthew Gordon and Kathryn Hains (Oxford University Press, 2017), 207–24.

13 The Yeni-İl *hass mukataa* constituted 70 per cent of all income of the Atik Valide Sultan Mosque *waqf*. See Sabırlı, *Dindarlık, Ekonomi ve Sosyal Hayat*, 108–10.

Waqf versus *Miri* Nomads   167

significant challenges in understanding the scope of tax collecting rights and the administration's authority over the *reaya*. Occasionally, state tax collectors and *waqf* revenue collectors insisted that subjects pay their dues as either state taxes or *waqf* income without confirming whether they were in fact state taxpayers or *waqf* subjects. The central government eventually received a significant number of complaints (*şikayet*) brought by the *reaya*, who suffered from the repeated demands of both state tax collectors and *waqf* income collectors.[14] The government introduced a financial and administrative document called "Book of Boundaries" (*hudud-name*) to solve this problem. The Book of Boundaries aimed to specify the sphere and limit of tax collection rights and their administration. Nevertheless, many disputes arose between state tax collectors and *waqf* income collectors in the seventeenth and eighteenth centuries because of the complexity of the revenue system.[15]

At the same time, from around 1691 onwards, the government forced settlement (*iskan*) policy for nomadic tribes was also being enforced on a large scale vis-à-vis various Turkoman and Kurdish tribes in eastern Anatolia, and who were directed to the area of Raqqa in northern Syria.[16] These included not only state-taxed (*miri*) Aleppo and Yeni-İl Türkmen tribes, but also, as Stefan Winter has shown in

---

14 For details, see Halil İnalcık, "Şikâyet Hakkı: 'Arż-i Ḥâl ve 'Arż-i Maḥżar'lar," *Osmanlı Araştırmaları* 7–8 (1988): 33–54; Murat Tuğluca, *XVII. Yüzyıl Sonu Şikâyet Defterlerine Göre Osmanlı Devlet-Toplum İlişkisinde Şikâyet Mekanizması ve İşleyiş Biçimi* (Ankara: Türk Tarih Kurum, 2016).

15 As mentioned before, it was widespread that the Ottoman state bestowed the tax collecting rights of the land belonging to the state to a person as their private property and that they subsequently transformed these rights into *waqf* property. Additionally, with the introduction of the lifetime tax collection contract system in the late seventeenth century, the number of disputes over the extent of the control of tax collecting rights among private, *waqf*, and state property rose significantly. The government therefore issued more boundary-defining documents and deeds to resolve or avoid such disputes. See Barnes, *An Introduction to Religious Foundations in the Ottoman Empire*, 20–49; Michael Niziri, "Defining Village Boundaries at the Time of the Introduction of the Malikane System: The Struggle of the Ottoman State for Reaffirming Ownership of the Land," *Journal of the Ottoman and Turkish Studies Association* 2, no. 1 (2015): 37–57, https://doi.org/10.2979/jottturstuass.2.1.37; Heather Ferguson, *The Proper Order of Things: Language, Power, and Law in Ottoman Administrative Discourses* (Stanford: Stanford University Press, 2018), 106–50.

16 Terms such as Kurd, Türkmen, and Arab refer to ethnic groups or nationalities in the present time. However, they also meant nomadic or tribal peoples generally in the period that this paper discusses; they did not directly refer to identity, ethnicity, or mother tongue. Even expressions such as "Türkman-ı Kürd," "Ekrad-ı Türkman," and "Arap Türkmanı" appear in several Ottoman documents. See for instance BOA: MD 140, no. 549.

168   Keiko Iwamoto

several articles, groups from the Reşwan and Kilis Kurd confederations.[17] These were not, however, as Winter suggested, *waqf* nomads, who (as we have shown elsewhere) were explicitly excluded from the *iskan* policy and prohibited from resettlement in Raqqa.[18] This can be demonstrated with the registry of Ottoman *waqf*-related orders contained in the archives of the Turkish Waqf Directorate/T.C. Vakıflar Genel Müdürlüğü Arşivi [VGMA] in Ankara. This collection contains many records on the Atik Valide Sultan Mosque foundation and its income, including from nomadic groups, a quantitative examination of which can demonstrate that the Ottomans implemented very different policies towards groups assigned as *waqf* income and nomads who paid regular state taxes. In doing so, this study will also shed light on the documents regarding Kurdish and other nomad groups in northern Syria, both *waqf* and state tax (*miri*) groups, and try to answer the question of what differences and divergences among the tribes caused the different assigned statuses of *waqf* and *miri* nomads.

Waqf and *Miri* Nomads in the VGMA Edict Registry

The VGMA edict registers of the State Treasury Secretary's Office (Bab-ı Defteri) concerning *waqf*-related matters include numerous records concerning the Yeni-İl Türkmen, the Aleppo Türkmen, and the Reşwan and Kilis Kurds.[19] These registers are listed in the VGMA archive catalogue under names such as "defter-i kuyudat-ı evamir-i

---

17   Stefan Winter, "Osmanische Sozialdisziplinierung am Beispiel der Nomadenstämme Nordsyriens im 17.–18. Jahrhundert," *Periplus: Jahrbuch für außereuropäische Geschichte* 13 (2003): 51–70; Stefan Winter, "The Province of Raqqa under Ottoman Rule, 1535–1800: A Preliminary Study," *Journal of Near Eastern Studies* 68, no. 4 (October 2009): 253–68, https://doi.org/10.1086/649610; Stefan Winter, "The Reşwan Kurds and Ottoman Tribal Settlement in Syria, 1683–1741," *Oriente Moderno* 97, no. 2 (October 2017): 256–69, https://doi.org/10.1163/22138617-12340151.

18   Keiko Iwamoto, "A Study on the Turning Point of the Ottoman Policy toward Nomads: The Settlement Policy of Turkish and Kurdish Nomads in the Seventeenth and Eighteenth Centuries," *Annals of the Japan Association for Middle East Studies* 32, no. 2 (2016): 69–95, https://doi.org/10.24498/ajames.32.2_69. This report and other articles written in Japanese led to this conclusion by all-out survey of the order records stored in VGMA archive. According to the over 1,200 orders, the Ottoman government usually ordered the officials to distinguish *waqf* nomads from state nomads and retain the former as nomadic pastoralists, not changing them to agricultural settling farmers, except for only five cases. See VGMA, Ahkâm Defterleri [AHK.d.] 328:46, 331; Evâmir Defterleri [EVM.d.] 323:244, 310–11, 318–19.

19   Kilis is a small city in southern Anatolia or northwestern Kurdistan, near the border of the present-day Syrian Arab Republic.

Waqf versus Miri Nomads 169

alişan, kalem-i muhasebe-i Haremü'ş-Şerifeyn [sic]," and others. Based on the VGMA catalogues, we located and surveyed a total of twenty-one registers.[20] The VGMA now classifies these in several fonds, including AHK.d., EVM.d., and Fermân Defterleri [FER.d.].[21] Among the registers, no. 316 is the earliest one recorded, dating from 1653 to 1666. No. 315 has records dating from 1692 to 1695, when large-scale forced settlement orders to Raqqa were first issued. No. 357 covers the period from 1768 to 1769 and is the latest VGMA *waqf*-related edict register. All the twenty-one volume registers contain edicts issued from the middle of the seventeenth century to the middle of the eighteenth century. Each register is forty-two to forty-four centimetres long and sixteen cm wide and is bound in leather, a typical style for Ottoman financial registers. Each register's cover indicates the range of record years and its name. The handwriting and style suggest these indications were added to the cover much later. The VGMA catalogue adopts the name written on the cover as a catalogue title without any critical analysis. On average, each volume encompasses 150 folio leaves or 300 pages, and each page contains two or three orders; some orders are written over two or more pages. A total of seven to eight hundred orders were issued over five or six years of each volume. In later times, archivists added page numbers at the top of each page in the register, but the orders themselves were not numbered as, for example, those in the Mühimme registers held at the BOA. In the following, we will reference the register and page number as well as the date, which is provided in the edict registry as in other registers prepared by the Treasury Secretary's Office.[22]

Of the twenty-one volumes consulted for this study, the total number of orders concerning the Yeni-İl and Aleppo Türkmen *waqf hass* was 1,227, or about 7–8 per cent of the total. Five hundred two orders relate to *waqf* income collection or to the appointment of *waqf* income collectors and *reaya* administrators. This represents approximately 40 per cent of the total.[23] The VGMA *waqf* edict registers include 243 orders to distinguish

---

20 Nos. 315, 316, 317, 319, 321, 322, 323, 324, 328, 329, 331, 332, 333, 335, 342, 344, 345, 351, 355, 357, and 362.

21 For details, see Mevlüt Cam, İbrahim Turhan, and Ridvan Enes Akçatepe, *Vakıflar Genel Müdürlüğü Arşiv Rehberi* (Ankara: T.C. Vakıflar Genel Müdürlüğü, 2020), 125–36.

22 This dating style contrasts with one of the order registers held by the Office of the Grand Vizier (Bab-ı Ali), which indicates only the beginning, middle, or ending decade of the month, not the exact day.

23 AHK.d. 317:7–8, 124, 159–60, 189, 197, 223, 232–3, 243, 273; AHK.d. 328:25, 41, 50–1, 69, 85–6, 90–1, 101–2, 114, 143, 179, 186, 191, 193–5, 197, 206–7, 211–12, 220, 222, 292,

170   Keiko Iwamoto

the *waqf* nomad tribes from others, to prepare a new *waqf* edict register, or to bring *waqf* nomads who had fled back to their original areas.[24] This number represents approximately 20 per cent of the total. One hundred sixty orders, accounting for approximately 10 per cent of the total, are commands to arrest, punish, and imprison bandit leaders of *waqf reaya*

302, 309, 316–17, 334, 337–8, 353, 365, 371, 386–7, 396, 398–9, 432, 434–5, 445–6, 451; AHK.d. 329:31, 35, 39, 41, 58, 63, 67–8, 73, 75–6, 79, 81, 85, 97, 99, 115, 122, 130, 134, 138, 144, 151–2, 195, 202, 208; AHK.d. 331:68, 74, 80, 97, 117, 123–4, 155, 159, 171–2, 178, 276, 298, 323; 342: 12, 24, 35, 41, 113, 119, 121, 125–6, 134, 140, 149, 175, 177, 196–7, 247, 253, 266; AHK.d. 345:19, 31, 33, 38, 44, 91, 95–7, 105, 112–15, 120, 141, 157, 172, 181, 184, 189, 195–6, 199, 208, 211, 229–30, 246–7, 271; EVM.d. 321: 17–18, 24, 35–6, 77, 84, 94 100, 119, 151, 160, 172, 175, 180, 184–5, 188, 190, 193, 196–7, 221, 234, 243, 248, 250, 253, 260, 267, 275, 277, 293, 297, 307, 310–11, 313, 318, 326, 341, 351–2, 360, 366; EVM.d. 323:42–3, 56, 58, 64, 69, 74, 83–4, 87, 89–90, 93–5, 106, 108–9, 127, 131–3, 135, 139, 143, 161, 166–7, 183, 193, 201, 211, 220, 238–9, 245, 253–4, 257–8, 279–80, 288, 290, 296, 308–10, 318, 320, 334, 345, 348, 356; EVM.d. 324:6–7, 20–1, 26, 60, 70, 76–7, 94, 155, 174, 179, 195, 211, 219–20, 228, 235–6, 246, 258, 291, 295–6, 341; EVM.d. 332:4, 10, 21, 26, 32–3, 40, 67–68, 74, 79, 84, 105, 117–18, 123, 135, 138, 141, 158–9, 162–3, 171, 176, 205, 221, 230–1; EVM.d. 333:39–40, 81, 163, 170, 183, 217, 251; EVM.d. 335:109–14, 116–17, 131, 155–6, 193–4, 255; EVM.d. 344:13, 24–5, 37, 50, 54, 91, 107, 110, 119, 128–9, 133 , 169, 171, 174–5, 185–6, 191, 199, 214, 250, 284–5; EVM.d. 351: 36, 88, 106, 108, 115, 121, 172, 177, 180, 202, 225, 229, 235, 275; EVM.d. 355: 16, 20, 58, 63, 67, 116, 167, 171, 176, 191, 215; EVM.d. 357:12, 27, 29–30, 32–3, 35–6, 38–9, 42–3, 48, 70–1, 108–10, 112, 138, 153–5, 159, 163, 166–8, 171–4, 178–9, 183, 186, 194, 198–9, 233, 250, 252–3, 257–61, 264–5; EVM.d. 362:14, 16–17, 28, 31, 33, 37, 40–1, 51–3, 57–8, 85; FER.d. 315:75, 81–2, 84, 100, 109, 114, 129, 139, 187, 200–1, 207, 210, 218, 231–2, 262–6, 278, 290–1, 294–5, 317–18, 325, 337, 363, 408, 415, 422–3, 431, 459, 489; FER.d. 316: 15, 25, 30–1, 61, 79, 89, 154, 158, 256, 297–8; FER.d. 319:10, 11, 211–12, 217, 220, 224, 249, 268, 270, 273, 285, 294, 333, 372. However, the number of pages does not necessarily correspond to the number of orders, as the record of one order may be written over several pages.

24 AHK.d. 317:18, 31, 39–42, 50, 53, 62–4, 72–3, 99, 123; 328: 24–5, 42, 46, 48, 77, 101, 126, 212, 220–1, 274, 340–1, 357, 385, 398, 428; AHK.d. 329:30, 39, 51, 86, 123, 128–9, 145, 147, 151, 193, 195, 201; AHK.d. 331:34, 53, 81, 86, 112, 153, 315; AHK.d. 342:7, 16, 31, 33, 45, 50, 57, 59, 62, 64, 71, 77, 87, 103, 106, 110, 113 , 116, 152, 168–9, 171, 179, 212, 223, 233, 243, 266; 345: 39, 61, 95, 111, 113–14, 158, 213, 238, 271; EVM.d. 321: 21, 28, 51, 53, 75, 85, 109, 136, 160 , 186, 228, 316, 330; EVM.d. 322:3–4, 18, 46, 75, 82, 87, 89, 134, 143, 212, 221, 260, 277, 279–80, 296–7, 321; EVM.d. 324:69–70, 76, 80, 83–4, 86, 88, 91, 96, 98–9, 111 , 159, 190, 228, 235, 242, 265, 295, 330; EVM.d. 332:6, 36, 67, 74, 163, 168, 171; EVM.d. 333:44–5, 94, 207–8, 235, 253; EVM.d. 335:26, 69, 82, 124–5, 269; EVM.d. 351:37, 100–1, 112–13, 117, 180, 229; EVM.d. 355:169, 173, 175, 192, 196, 198, 211, 216; EVM.d. 357:4–5, 16–17, 21, 63–4, 153, 157, 159, 162, 185, 242–5, 259; EVM.d. 362:35, 63–4; FER.d. 315: 56, 60, 62, 75, 82, 84, 100, 109, 118, 129, 139, 164, 187, 192, 200–1, 207, 210, 218, 231–2, 262–6, 278, 290–1, 294–5, 317–18, 325, 337, 363, 408, 415, 431; FER.d. 316:16, 20, 22, 28, 46, 92–4, 116, 120, 178, 182–3, 254–5, 274; FER.d. 319:59–60, 75–6, 207, 225, 306, 318, 333–4, 373.

origins.[25] Most records in the VGMA edict registers are memoranda (*tezkire*) issued by the Treasury Secretary as ordered by the Grand Vizier's Office, which had ultimate responsibility both for issuing imperial edicts and for defining the events, troubles, or contents of planned edicts.[26] Aside from these memoranda, the VGMA records also have a smaller number of copies of sharia court registers (*sicil*) or other financial registers.

The number of orders concerning the Kilis and Reşwan Kurds in the twenty-one VGMA edict registers is fifty-one.[27] Of these, twenty-one orders demand the collection of *waqf* income or appoint income collectors and administrators.[28] Thirteen orders concern the arrest, punishment, and imprisonment of bandit leaders, whether of *waqf* or state *reaya* origin.[29] Nine orders were issued to distinguish the *waqf* nomadic tribes from others, prepare a new *waqf* edict register, or bring nomads who had fled back to their original living places.[30] Only two edicts command nomads to settle in the province of Raqqa forcibly.[31]

As mentioned earlier, the complicated tax collection system appears to have caused many conflicts and disputes, as observable in the VGMA edict registers and others. This paper will analyze such disputes and classify them into various types in the following section.

The *waqf reaya* nomads make up the first category. They paid the equivalent of state taxes to *waqf* institutions, not the state. Four registers

---

25 AHK.d. 328:149, 198, 217, 224–5, 231, 253–4, 354, 377; AHK.d. 329:13, 30, 33, 38, 41, 43, 85, 101, 127–8, 153, 157, 175, 192, 194, 200, 203–4, 211, 217–19, 223, 232, 240–1, 246; AHK.d. 331:175, 179, 181, 184–7, 190, 193–4, 198; EVM.d. 321:147–8, 278, 306–7, 312; EVM.d. 323:3–4, 53, 58, 72, 82, 107 , 127, 136, 153–4, 239, 324; EVM.d. 332:2, 5, 12, 15–16, 19, 30, 36, 47, 49, 57, 85, 99, 102, 104, 230, 234; EVM.d. 333:236–7; EVM.d. 335:79, 99, 105, 107, 182, 215–16; EVM.d. 344:11–12, 24, 35–6, 40, 46–7, 71, 90, 97, 117, 172, 176, 185, 204; 351: 43, 47, 58–9, 67–8, 96–7, 121, 125, 135, 158, 171, 183, 191, 193, 196, 217, 223, 249; EVM.d. 357:73; EVM.d. 362:64–5; FER.d. 315:187, 192.

26 For more information on the characteristics of *tezkire* documents in the Ottoman administration, see Mübahat Kütükoğlu, *Osmanlı Belgelerinin Dili (Diplomatik)* (Ankara: Türk Tarih Kurumu, 1994); Yoichi Takamatsu, "Formation and Custody of the Ottoman Archives During the Pre-Tanzimat Period," *Memoirs of the Research Department of the Toyo Bunko* 64 (2007): 125–48.

27 The registers including orders related to the Kilis and Reşwan Kurds in the VGMA *waqf* order register are AHK.d. 328, 331, 342, 345, 355; EVM.d. 321, 323, 333, 351; FER.d. 315–16, 344. AHK.d. 331 alone contains over half of the total, that is, twenty-nine orders concerning the Kilis and Reşwan Kurds issued between 1742 and 1767.

28 AHK.d. 331:68, 74, 80, 97, 117, 124, 155, 159, 171–2, 178; AHK.d. 345:44, 229–30, 246; EVM.d 323:280; EVM.d 344: 50; EVM.d 351:88; 355:116; FER.d 316:79.

29 AHK.d. 331:175, 179, 181, 184–7, 190, 193–4, 198; EVM.d.323:136.

30 AHK.d. 331:53, 81, 112, 153; AHK.d. 342: 171; AHK.d. 345: 39, 61, 95, 111, 113–14, 158, 213, 238, 271; EVM.d. 321:51; EVM.d 333:44–5, 253; EVM.d. 344:171.

31 EVM.d. 321:288; FER.d. 315:318.

172   Keiko Iwamoto

describe the amount of *waqf* income paid by members of the Yeni-İl and Halep Türkmen to the Atik Valide Sultan institution. According to the registers, these nomads usually paid tithes (*öşür* or *'ushur*), sheep or goat tax (*adet-i ganem/ağnam* or *resm-i korı*), and a summer or winter pasture usage fee to the *waqf* income collectors.[32] These nomads frequently attempted to evade their payment levies or the management and control of the *waqf* administrators, giving rise to numerous orders by the Ottoman state for them to pay their dues quickly and according to the fixed regulations. Additionally, the government demanded that only qualified personnel be appointed to the foundation as income collectors and administrators, in order to prevent the abuse of administrative power.

A few typical cases may be discussed here in detail. The following is the summary of a record dated February 1756 and addressed to the governor of Sivas, the judge and the *voyvoda* of Yeni-İl, and the *waqf* income collectors for the Yeni-İl Türkmen *hass* tribes of the Atik Valide Sultan *waqf*.[33] Some background information: the Chief Black Eunuch of the imperial harem (Darüssaade Ağası), who since the late sixteenth century had taken over some important functions of the Chief White Eunuch (Babüssaade Ağası), was the supervisor (*nazır* or *nazir*) of the *waqf* foundation of the Two Holy Cities Mecca and Medina (Haremeyn-i Şerifeyn), which included that of the Atik Valide Sultan Mosque in Üsküdar. With his influence over the Ottoman harem section and by controlling the operations of the *waqf* properties of the queen mother and other princesses, he had gained immense power and wealth.[34] In late 1755 or early 1756, he had addressed an official

---

32 BOA: Tahrir Defteri [TD] 262; Maliyeden Müdevver [MAD] 6022; Tapu ve Kadastro Genel Müdürlüğü Defterleri [TKGM] 2180, VGMA: Mukâtaa Defterleri [MKT.d.] 905.

33 EVM.d 351:88. The term "*voyvoda*" is derived from a Slavic root that signifies a local governor or ruler in eastern Europe. However, in the Ottoman Empire, *voyvoda* also designated agents in charge of revenues from domains such as *hass* or *mukataa* fiefs granted to Ottoman family members, viziers, provincial governors, *waqf* institutions, and other dignitaries. See Erol Özvar, "Voyvoda," in DİA (2013) 43, 129–31.

34 Jane Hathaway, "The Role of the Kızlar Ağası in Seventeenth-Eighteenth Century Ottoman Egypt," *Studia Islamica* 75 (1992): 141–58, https://doi.org/10.2307/1595624; Jane Hathaway, *Beshir Agha: Chief Eunuch of the Ottoman Imperial Harem* (London: Oneworld Publications, 2005); Jane Hathaway, "Ḥabeşī Meḥmed Agha: The First Chief Harem Eunuch (Darüssaade Ağası) of the Ottoman Empire," in *The Islamic Scholarly Tradition: Studies in History, Law, and Thought in Honor of Professor Michael Allan Cook*, ed. Asad Ahmed, Michael Bonner, and Behnam Sadeghi (Leiden: Brill, 2011), 179–95; Jane Hathaway, "The Economic and Charitable Activities of the Ottoman Chief Harem Eunuch (Darüssaade Ağası) in the Ottoman Provinces," in

Waqf versus *Miri* Nomads   173

report (*arz*) to the Grand Vizier's office, stating that some Atik Valide Sultan *reaya* had recently abandoned the village Akçakale, whereupon members of the Kurdish Reşwan tribe had come there to graze their sheep. The Reşwan were state (*miri*) taxpayers, but the village was under the jurisdiction of the Atik Valide Sultan foundation, and it was strictly prohibited for nomadic pastoralists to move their flocks to unassigned areas without official permission.

To make matters worse, the Reşwan *voyvoda*, the chief administrator and tax collector of the Reşwan Kurds, as well as some tribe members, had then fanned out to other villages belonging to the foundation in the area and plundered them repeatedly. As the foundation supervisor, the Chief Eunuch complained that many *waqf reaya* were fleeing from the Reşwan Kurd invasion, which would cause a significant decrease in the foundation's revenues. The *waqf* income collectors and *reaya* also requested the Ottoman government to issue an imperial edict explicitly forbidding state taxpayer Reşwan Kurds to graze their livestock or squat in *waqf* villages, in order to protect the foundation's subjects and preserve its income.

Another VGMA edict tells of a dispute between non-Kurdish *waqf reaya* and Kurdish state *reaya*. The order is dated October 1750 and is addressed to the governor (*vali*) of Aleppo, the judge and *mukataa* administrators of Kilis, and the *mukataa* income collector or *voyvoda*.[35] The documents call the Kurdish tribes belonging to the Kilis *mukataa* "Kilis Kurds." According to regulations and previous edicts, the Kilis Kurds paid their "tax" to the Kilis *voyvoda*. The Kilis *mukataa* was one of the reigning sultan's state tax reserves (*hass-ı hümayun*), and this *voyvoda* had obtained the rights to the Kilis *mukataa* as a lifetime tax concession (*malikane*). It is important to note that the Kilis Kurds were state *reaya*, not *waqf*, and that the Kilis *voyvoda* was a state income collector, not a *waqf* income collector. The *voyvoda*, in turn, subcontracted Kilis Kurd tribal chiefs known by such titles as *boy beği*, *kethüda*, or *mir-i*

History from Below: A Tribute in Memory of Donald Quataert, ed. Selim Karahasanoğlu and Deniz Cenk Demir (Istanbul: Bilgi Üniversitesi Yayınları, 2016), 199–216; Ülkü Altındağ, "Dârüssaâde," DİA (1994), 9:1–3; A. Ezgi Dikici, "The Making of Ottoman Court Eunuchs: Origins, Recruitment Paths, Family Ties, and 'Domestic Production,'" *Archivum Ottomanicum* 30 (2013): 105–36; George Junne, *The Black Eunuchs of the Ottoman Empire: Networks of Power in the Court of the Sultan* (London: I.B. Tauris, 2016); Kayhan Orbay, "Account Books of the Imperial Waqfs (Charitable Endowments) in the Eastern Mediterranean (15th to 19th Centuries)," *The Accounting Historians Journal* 40, no. 1 (June 2013): 31–50, https://doi.org/10.2308/0148-4184.40.1.31.

35 EVM.d. 344:246.

174   Keiko Iwamoto

aşiret, as well as judges of the Kilis Kurds, for the purposes of tax collection and administration. Thus in 1750 or before, the governor and judge of Kilis and local tribal chiefs had sent a report to the central government, saying that some groups of the Kilis Kurd tribes had not paid their assigned taxes to the *voyvoda* or his subcontractors at the due date. After receiving this report, the government issued an imperial edict to reprimand the tax-evading tribes sharply and appoint "eminently suitable" personnel to the tribe chiefs to collect all the outstanding taxes without delay.[36]

The second category of VGMA edicts encompasses warrants for the arrest, punishment, or imprisonment of bandit leaders, whether of *waqf* or state *reaya* origin. An order dated July 1758 indicates that bandits from the Kilis Kurds were punished as follows: recently some nomads from the Qizil Qoyunlo (Kızıl Koyunlu) and Amîkî (Amık) tribes of the Kilis Kurds had plundered numerous villages in the ʿAyntab (Gaziantep) region. Several of these villages were of the Yeni-İl and Aleppo Türkmen *hass*, which belonged to the Atik Valide Sultan Mosque *waqf mukataa*. Tribal chiefs of the Amîkî Kurds were the bandit leaders. The Qizil Qoyunlo and Amîkî tribes were state taxpayers or state *reaya*. But because some of the plundered villages and people who had fled their homes were under the jurisdiction of the Atik Valide Sultan *waqf* and not the state, the provincial governors of Kilis and ʿAyntab could not solve the problem under their own authority, and instead requested orders from the Ottoman government. Only *waqf* administrators and overseers had the legal power to supervise, control, and direct *waqf* villages and their *reaya*.

The *waqf* administrators, however, were not authorized to issue imperial commands or orders; only state officials could do so. Therefore, the Chief Harem Eunuch, as overseer of the Haremeyn-i Şerifeyn *waqf*, including the Atik Valide Sultan foundation, needed to send the report to the central government in order to demand appropriate punishment for the Kurdish bandits, who were state *reaya*. The Sublime Porte finally issued an order to punish the bandits and force them to bring the stolen money, sheep, domestic animals, and produce back to the villagers to compensate them for the damage, entirely and immediately. In addition, the Ottomans ordered the *reaya* who had fled from *waqf* villages to return to their homes so that the *waqf* revenues could resume.[37]

---

36 *Imperial edict:* More precisely, this means the Treasury Secretary's Office had issued a memorandum. The memorandum required the Grand Vizier's Office to issue an imperial edict. For details, see Takamatsu, "Formation and Custody of the Ottoman Archives," 128–39.

37 AHK.d. 331:198.

The third category concerns orders about correctly classifying nomad groups, whether state or *waqf reaya*, and distinguishing them from other categories of nomads. The confusion between *waqf* tribes and non-*waqf*, namely state (*miri*) tribes, caused a great deal of trouble for *waqf* income and state tax collectors. Some tribal groups attempted to evade paying state tax or *waqf* income by claiming that they were not subject to the state or not under the jurisdiction of *waqf* administrators. It was difficult for collectors to discern whether a given group was state or *waqf reaya*. The Ottoman government took steps to combat this tax evasion by ordering the preparation of a register that would record the *waqf reaya* and firmly identify each nomad group and classify which tax unit they belonged to. For example, an order dated May 1720, addressed to the Kilis judge and the Kilis *voyvoda*, mentions that Kilis Kurd tribes had been registered as state (*miri*) *reaya* and paid state taxes (*mal-i miri*). When the Ottomans renewed the register of the Kilis Kurds, they found that some Kurdish nomads were claiming they were *waqf reaya* and thus did not have to pay state taxes. The central government checked the old records of Kilis Kurd registers and found their claims to be false and baseless. The government thus ordered the Kilis Kurds' claims to be rejected and imposed state taxes on them as before.[38]

An order dated March 1723 states that some of the Atik Valide Sultan *waqf reaya* belonging to the Yeni-İl and Aleppo Türkmen *hass* had settled in state-owned (*miri*) land in Ahsandere, near Maraş (today Kahramanmaraş), where they had cultivated fields in the summer and grazed their sheep and goats in the winter. They had paid both their assigned dues to the Atik Valide Sultan *waqf* and the Ottoman tithe, namely the state tax on their agricultural products, to state tax collectors. When the Ottoman government commanded state (*miri*) *reaya* Qilîçlo (Kılıçlu) and Tacîrlo (Tacirlü) Kurds to abandon their nomadic lifestyles and settle in Raqqa, some of these Kurds had disobeyed the order and escaped to Ahsandere. They had then plundered some villages in Ahsandere and mixed with the formerly settled *waqf reaya* of the Yeni-İl and Aleppo Türkmen *hass*. The provincial governors and the Atik Valide Sultan administrators thereupon sent a report (*ilam*) to the central government asking for the swift identification of the Kurdish state tribes hiding in Ahsandere among the *waqf reaya*. The officials and *waqf* administrators were able to locate the state Kurdish nomads and punish them through forcible resettlement to Raqqa. The central government accepted this report and attempted to issue a precise imperial edict.[39] A similar case appears in an

---

38 AHK.d. 342:16.
39 AHK.d. 342:171. The Ottomans issued similar orders several times throughout the seventeenth and eighteenth centuries. See FER.d. 315:318.

176 Keiko Iwamoto

order addressed to the governor of Aleppo and the Kilis judge in August 1705. According to this order, some Kilis Kurd *miri* (state) tribes, the Oqçî Izzedînlo (Okçu İzzedinlü), Şêxlo (Şeyhlü), and Amîkî, had disobeyed previous Raqqa settlement orders and plundered several villages and towns in the Kilis, Antep, and Maraş districts. The governor and judge of Raqqa had repeatedly sent petitions, and even the inhabitants of plundered towns and villages had sent a petition (*mahzar*) with joint seals to the central government, requesting that the Kurdish bandits be severely punished and resettled in Raqqa. The central government accepted these petitions and issued an imperial edict accordingly.[40]

By analyzing the Ottoman decrees on forced nomad settlement side-by-side, it is clear that the imperial government recognized seasonal migration and pastoral nomadism as enormously problematic in the late seventeenth and eighteenth centuries. Because of this, the Ottomans began forcing pastoral nomads to settle in villages in the province of Raqqa and engage in agriculture in the last decade of the seventeenth century.[41] On the other hand, it is also apparent that the Ottomans never forced *waqf* nomads to settle in Raqqa as farmers, but instead wanted them to continue their nomadic lifestyle and pay *waqf* dues to their *waqf* institution as before. The *waqf*'s inviolability and immutability as a perpetual endowment under Islamic law meant that the *waqf reaya* were not subject to state administration and taxation. Moreover, this enabled the *waqf* tribes of the Aleppo and Yeni-İl Türkmen *hass* to continue their nomadic lives without interference from state officials and policies – unlike the majority of Kurdish tribes in the region, who were state taxpayers or *miri reaya*.

Conclusion

The following section answers the question raised in the introduction: what divergence or disparity caused the different statuses of state nomads, *waqf* nomads, and Kurdish or Turkish nomadic groups? The Ottoman government strictly distinguished *waqf* nomads from state nomads, regarding tax and *waqf* income collection, because the *waqf* nomads were not included under state officials' control and administration. As a

---

40 EVM.d. 321:51.
41 MD 112, nos. 556–7; MD 115, no. 2955; MD 119, nos. 940, 1330; MD 139, nos. 1342–51. See also Rhoads Murphey, "Some Features of Nomadism in the Ottoman Empire: A Survey Based on Tribal Census and Judicial Appeal Documentation from Archives in Istanbul and Damascus," *Journal of Turkish Studies* 8 (1984): 189–98; Söylemez, *Osmanlı Devletinde Aşiret Yönetimi*, 157; Rhoads Murphey, "Bozok Sancağı'nda Rişvan Oymakları," 143–8; Iwamoto, "A Study on the Turning Point of the Ottoman Policy toward Nomads," 84–6.

Waqf versus Miri Nomads 177

result, the Ottoman central government strictly prohibited *waqf* nomads, including most of the Yeni-İl and Aleppo Türkmen, from following the state policy of large-scale nomadic tribe settlement in Raqqa. This did not apply to the Kurdish *miri* nomad tribes because they were under state jurisdiction. Another significant finding to emerge from this study is that most Kilis and Reşwan Kurds were state *reaya*.

In contrast to the *waqf reaya* Aleppo and Yeni-İl "Türkmen," state *reaya* Kilis and Reşwan "Kurds" were under the Ottoman state officials' direct rule and administration. A detailed investigation of the Atik Valide Sultan *waqf*-related edict registers confirms that there was a distinct class difference between state and *waqf reaya* living side-by-side in the seventeenth- and eighteenth-century Ottoman Empire. This difference determined whether or not these tribes would be forced to abandon their nomadic lifestyle and be relocated to Raqqa in northern Syria.

From the end of the sixteenth century, various factions and powers, such as bureaucrats, Ottoman royal family members, harem eunuchs, janissaries, other army groups, and ulama and sufis, that is, religious intellectuals competed with one another for primacy within the Ottoman state.[42] Through the historical documentation concerning state and *waqf reaya* and the Kurdish and Turkish nomad groups utilized in this paper, we find conflicts or alliances over interests and power between the Ottoman harem authority and the state bureaucrats.

The differences in taxation and administration between the state and the *waqf reaya* were dealt with strictly according to their financial and administrative status. The control systems resulted in state *reaya* Kilis and Reşwan Kurds and *waqf reaya* Yeni-İl and Aleppo Türkmen attempting to escape from the grip of either the state officials or the *waqf* administrators. In many instances, these tribes were well-equipped to do so due to their high mobility; they often ran away from their assigned living areas or mixed with other nomadic tribes under different taxation and administrative systems. *Waqf* nomads were outside the administration of state officials and never needed to pay any state taxes. Nevertheless, state officials demanded illegally that they pay state taxes and settle in Raqqa without permission from the state because of the parallel structure between the state tax collection and *waqf* income collection systems. This parallelism led to much confusion and numerous conflicts between state tax and *waqf* income collectors.

---

42 Baki Tezcan calls the post-classical Ottoman state in this situation "the second empire." See Baki Tezcan, *The Second Ottoman Empire: Political and Social Transformation in the Early Modern World* (Cambridge: Cambridge University Press, 2010).

The confusion caused by the parallel tax systems made it easy for nomadic peoples to "cross" the boundary between them, as a way to evade paying taxes altogether and escape the constraints of Ottoman government administration. Simultaneously, tax collectors and their subcontractors took advantage of the system's multiplicities and complacencies in order to protect and ensure their maximum interests.

The complexity also implies that the state or *miri reaya* Kurds could escape from the strict and direct Ottoman governmental control and forced settlement policies. Our study's findings suggest that Ottoman nomads, whether state or *waqf reaya*, and whether Turkish or Kurdish, had found a way to live freely and independently under seventeenth- and eighteenth-century Ottoman rule, which was otherwise directed against nomadic pastoralists by design and viewed seasonal migration unfavourably, and promoted settlement and commitment to agricultural life instead.

Our findings also contribute to understanding people's resilience and survival under extreme or hostile and oppressive conditions in pre-modern and modern times. However, the conclusion also provokes much larger questions. Which tribes were subject to *iskan* policy, and which were not? What are the criteria that separate the two? Did the Ottomans follow a conscious policy of "ethnic" differentiation between *waqf* "Türkmen" and *miri* "Kurds" for forced settling policy, or merely of a "class" difference?

An instructive comparison, albeit from a much later period, may be with the Hamidiye Light Cavalry Regiments, which were recruited from mainly Sunni and pro-Ottoman Kurdish and Arabic tribes by the autocratic sultan Abdülhamid II in the late nineteenth century. At first glance, the Hamidian system appears to have divided, classified, and ruled people by "ethnicity" (Kurds, Turks, Armenians, etc.). The central state, however, was above all concerned whether groups were loyal or not, using ethnic difference as an excuse to attack opponents, while some Kurdish tribal chiefs in the Hamidiye Regiments even claimed to be of Oğuz Turkish descent in order to acquire the sultan's favour and obtain permission to attack other Kurdish tribes who were also in the Regiments but who were their enemies.[43] More study is needed to account for these remaining questions. It is hoped this article's conclusions may have important implications for future research.[44]

---

43 See Bahattin Öztuncay and Özge Ertem, eds., *Ottoman Arcadia: The Hamidian Expedition to the Land of Tribal Roots* (Istanbul: Koç University Research Center for Anatolian Civilizations, 2018).

44 Acknowledgments: JSPS KAKENHI Grant Number 17K13547, 21K13121 and grants from the School of Global Humanities and Social Sciences/Graduate School of Global Humanities and Social Sciences [SGHS], Nagasaki University supported this work.

8 Bekir Bey and the Making of a Reşwan Nobility at Rumkale

MUHSIN SOYUDOĞAN

There was no end to the number of cut heads, and those doing the cutting did not even bother picking them up and bringing them to the illustrious vizier. As the Kurds were hit, their heads rolled down like stones to the feet of his excellency Baba's horse.

– Gazzizâde Abdullatif Efendi[1]

Taken from the biographical history of Pehlivan İbrahim Paşa (known as Baba Paşa; "Father Paşa"), this passage depicts an alleged scene from his siege of the fortress of Rumkale, on the Euphrates thirty kilometres north of Birecik, in 1814. Related archival documents suggest that an Ottoman military force was sent to Rumkale following the denunciation of a homicide suspect who had taken sanctuary there.[2] The lord of the fortress, the Kurdish notable Bekir (Ebubekir) Bey, and his tribal assembly of Reşwan Kurds had initially refused to hand him over, but after a siege of several months, gave in and expelled the suspect. However, this was not enough to avert the attack: On 20 July, tunnel diggers opened a breach in one of the wells, through which soldiers infiltrated the fortress. The resisters surrendered and their leader was executed.

Twenty-four years later, Prussian field marshal Helmuth von Moltke stopped by Rumkale and summarized the event as he heard it from local accounts: "A *derebey* [warlord] had taken over the castle, then a Kurdish notable had supplanted him. Then Baba Paşa drove the latter

---

1 Gazzizâde Abdullatif Efendi, *Vekayi'-i Baba Paşa fî't-Târîh* (Ankara: Türk Tarih Kurumu, 2013), 279.
2 T.C. Cumhurbaşkanlığı Devlet Arşivi (ex-Başbakanlık [BOA]), Istanbul: Mühimme Defteri [MD] 3:57 (no. 188); Cevdet Maliye [C.ML] 559/22954.

180   Muhsin Soyudoğan

out."[3] This of course suggests that the episode was not just a matter of punishing a criminal but marked a political transition in a small but strategically located Ottoman town; an event, in Braudelian terms, in both medium-term (*conjoncture*) and long-term (*longue durée*) changes in the region.[4] Collating different temporal and spatial relationalities in this regard will provide us with better insight into the event: To this end, this chapter considers both macro and micro factors that played a role in the process that brought about the execution of Bekir Bey.

Making a Local Dynasty

When Rumkale was brought under Ottoman sovereignty in 1516, a small garrison was installed in the fortress. Being far away from the Empire's frontiers, this military unit mainly ensured public order, kept the trade routes passing by Rumkale safe, and collected state revenues in the region. This lasted until 1697, when a sultanic decree was issued to disband the garrison on account of the soldiers' collusion with residents of Rumkale "who never avoided violence and malice"; their revenues (*timars*) were to be confiscated on the behalf of the state treasury.[5] At first glance, there seems to be nothing extraordinary in this decision since there was supposedly a situation of disorder which the state sought to remedy. However, the date of the decree gives us pause to think.

It was Yusuf Paşa, the governor of Raqqa province, who had sent the Sublime Porte a report of the problems in Rumkale, which was under his jurisdiction. However, more than just the governor of Raqqa, Yusuf Paşa was also the main figure charged with resettling tribes in Raqqa and northern Syria. From 1691 to 1696, thousands of tribal families were driven from central and eastern Anatolia to northern Syria.[6] The evident reason behind this policy was to create a buffer zone against Arab tribes such as the Aneze and Shammar who were moving northwards and invading Syria. More than that, however, the Ottoman Empire had undertaken a long (1683–99) and devastating war in Europe, and the revenues were failing to meet the war expenditure. To compensate the deficit, the state had resorted to a tripartite strategy of increased taxation, internal debt, and confiscation.

---

3 Helmuth von Moltke, *Türkiye Mektupları* (Istanbul: Remzi Kitabevi, 1969), 160.
4 Cheng-Chung Lai, "Braudel's Concepts and Methodology Reconsidered," *The European Legacy* 5, no. 1 (2000): 65–86, https://doi.org/10.1080/108487700115134.
5 BOA: Türkiye Kadastro Genel Müdürlüğü [TKGM] 236.
6 Cengiz Orhonlu, *Osmanlı İmparatorluğu'nda Aşiretlerin İskânı* (Istanbul: Eren, 1987), 107.

First, taxes that used to be levied in extraordinary circumstances, such as the *avarız* and *imdadiyye*, became regular. And new wartime taxes, as first seen in 1689, were levied on oxcarts (*araba-ı gav*), horses (*bargiran-ı mekari*), camels (*mehar-ı şütran-ı mekari, katar-ı şütran-ı miri*), or their equivalent in cash.[7]

Second, in the previous period state revenues (*mukataa*) were either collected by trustees (*emin*) or given out as three-year tax farming contracts (*iltizam*). In the first method, salaried state officials were charged with collecting taxes. However, the second method was more like a debt or a mortgage. Investors (*mültezim*) who won the auction had to pay some amount in advance and the rest at the end of the contract. The first instalment was a sort of debt since the *mültezim* had to pay an amount in cash before receiving anything of the revenues himself. In order to increase the amount of revenue this way, the state on the one hand implemented more confiscation; on the other hand, in 1695, it expanded fixed-term contracts into life-long (*malikâne*) contracts. In the short run, this new method proved quite profitable, as contractors had to pay a considerable sum of cash (*müaccele*) right at the beginning of the term. But over the long run, the state had to content itself with a sum far less than the actual revenues. As a result, a huge surplus accumulated in the hands of some local elites or tribal leaders in regions where tribal relations were strong and intact.

Lastly, tribes' communal lands, or, as in the case of Rumkale, revenue sources that had once been allocated for the salaries of fortress guards and cavalries, were systematically confiscated. This is why the resettlement of tribes in northern Syria cannot be seen solely as a matter of restraining Arab tribes, but also as a means of making up the fiscal deficit the state treasury was facing.

It is known from many cases that when tribes resisted their resettlement, they were almost always accused of partaking in banditry and violence. That is what the government called public disorder, which, in the case of Rumkale, very likely meant popular resistance against Yusuf Paşa's efforts to deport tribes. And it is reasonable to assume that the fortress guards who faced losing their revenues cooperated with these tribes. The government might succeed in confiscating the guards' revenues but it was much less easy to deal with tribes, especially with powerful ones. In many cases, those who were forced to resettle managed to escape from the assigned areas and return to their homelands.

---

7 BOA: Başmuhasebe Kalemi [D.BŞM] 606.

182 Muhsin Soyudoğan

The larger Reşwan confederation's dominance west of the Euphrates brought about an opportunity during the economic crisis of the last decades of the seventeenth century in that they were able to form powerful local or regional political dynasties. The Reşwanzades of Malatya and Maraş and the Köse-Paşazades of Sivas were the two most important Reşwan governor families of the eighteenth century.[8] Another such family was able to attain power in Rumkale.

According to a genealogical tree based on oral history, the founder of the Kuloğlu dynasty, with which Bekir Bey was affiliated, was a certain Muhammed (Mehmed).[9] The names and relationships given on this tree can generally be verified with archival documents, with the exception of the link between the first two members and the subsequent generation. Nevertheless, since the earliest member known from archival sources lived around the middle of the eighteenth century, the lineage's eponymous founder must have lived around the turn of the century. He was probably the person referred to in some documents as Kasapoğlu Muhammed Kethüda, whose existence in Rumkale can be traced to between 1703 and 1713.[10] The first reason for this assumption is the title *kethüda*, which in this context means the head of a community who mediated with the state authorities and was responsible for collecting state revenues. As will be seen, the family did indeed perform these two duties in the following period. Second, according to the family tree, the second person to exercise leadership of the family was Hüseyin, which was indeed the name of Muhammed *kethüda*'s son. What is less clear is the identity of the third family head. According to the genealogical tree, his name was Haccı İsmail, and archival documents do confirm the tie between him and his successors. However, his link with his predecessors remains murky since archival sources do not provide his father's name. In one document, his father is indicated as a *"kul"* (slave), which could mean anyone occupying an office in the state bureaucracy.[11]

---

8 See Faruk Söylemez, *Osmanlı Devletinde Aşiret Yönetimi: Rişvan Aşireti Örneği* (Istanbul: Kitabevi, 2011); Necdet Sakaoğlu, *Anadolu Derebeyi Ocaklarından Köse Paşa Hanedanı* (Istanbul: Tarih Vakfı Yurt Yayınları, 1998).

9 Kale Meydanı, "Soyağacı," accessed 26 June 2021, https://www.kalemeydani.com /soyagaci/.

10 Our knowledge about him is limited to two events: In 1702, his son Hasan accused a certain Kuloğlu Hüseyin of having robbed his house. Perhaps related to this, one year later Muhammed and his sons Hasan, Hüseyin, and Ali were themselves accused of violence. These events may have continued for years; in 1713 they were ordered to be exiled to Cyprus. It is not clear whether the orders were executed, as there is no more mention of him in the records. BOA: İbnülemin Dahiliye [İE.DH] 22/2029; MD 112:1359; MD 114:914, 988; MD 117:775; MD 121:203.

11 BOA: Ali Emiri Mustafa III [AE.SMST.III] 128/9921.

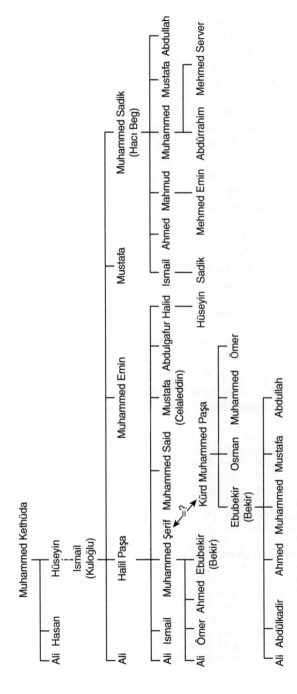

Figure 8.1. Kuloğlu family tree

184   Muhsin Soyudoğan

It is known that Bekir Bey had kinship ties with the family, but his exact filiation is not clear due to insufficient and contradictory references in the documents.[12] Bekir was known to be the son of Kürd Muhammed Paşa but information on the latter is very limited.[13] Since no document mentions anything about Bekir's grandfather and there was more than one person with the name Muhammed in the family, Bekir's position remains unclear. Nevertheless, there are many clues that lead us to think that Kürd Muhammed was the same as Muhammed Şerif, the son of Halil Paşa, son of İsmail. First, we do not know anything about the death of Kürd Muhammed Paşa. In one document he is claimed to have died in 1779,[14] but we know he did not die but moved to Kilis that year and lived there until 1782. No other document mentions his death before 1798, when Muhammed Şerif died. Shortly after the death of Muhammed Şerif, Bekir moved to Rumkale and lived in the house of Halil Paşa. Second, it is known that Muhammed Şerif had sons named Bekir and Ömer.[15] Third, neither Muhammed Şerif and Kürd Muhammed nor their sons of the name Bekir are recorded in the same documents or in the same period.

The Kuloğlu Revenue Farm

Though the family's sovereignty over Rumkale was built socially upon the dominance of the Reşwan tribe, economically it was ensured by the shares of state revenues (*mukataa*) that they held. In Rumkale state revenues were organized in two sections, the revenues from Rumkale (*mukataa-ı Rumkale*),[16] and the revenues of the "Reşi Kurds and their followers"

---

12 In BOA: Hatt-ı Hümayun [HAT] 632/31209 he is recorded as the brother of İsmail's son Muhammed Sadık. In HAT 446/22282:1 these two are described only as relatives. In C.ML 559/22954 Bekir is recorded as a shareholder in the tax farm together with his paternal cousins (*emmizade*). It is not clear who these cousins were, although we do know that Rumkale's revenues were traditionally under the administration of the Kuloğlu family.

13 In C.ML 577/23690 he is recorded as the son of Kul, while HAT 503/24778 indicates that the *bey*s of Rumkale including Bekir were known as sons of Kul. Therefore, Kul here probably refers to İsmail's father.

14 BOA: Maliyeden Müdevver [MAD] 9586:299.

15 However, a petition signed after the death of Bekir Bey by a certain Bekir (Mir Şerifzade), the son or grandson of Muhammed Şerif, may prove that Muhammed Şerif was not the same person as Kürd Muhammed. HAT 906/39718.

16 In the sixteenth century, this consisted of fees and taxes imposed on economic activities related to mills, dye houses, bazaars, transportation on the Euphrates, and agricultural production in some villages reserved for the state treasury. In later periods the capacity of this section was increased as confiscated and vacant *timar*s were added.

Bekir Bey and the Making of a Reşwan Nobility at Rumkale   185

(*mukataa-ı Ekrad-ı Reşi ve tevabiha*), which consisted of taxes and fees levied on the Reşi and Hevidi tribes. The Reşis had been the most populous tribe in the central district (*nahiye-i Merziman*) of Rumkale since the earliest days of Ottoman rule in the region.[17] The Hevidi tribe, on the other hand, represented a populous body around Behisni (Besni) and in the *nahiye-i Araban* of Rumkale.[18] The government organized some of the Hevidis of Behisni and the Reşis of Rumkale in the same fiscal unit (*mukataa*), perhaps because of their similar transhumance patterns.[19]

The revenues of Rumkale were under the management of Reşwan-zade Osman and Gergerizade Mehmed until their contract was annulled due to payment problems in the years 1718 and 1719.[20] By 1722, the *mukataa* was in the possession of a certain Abdi and İsmail Ağa. Around 1750, this İsmail made an agreement for his share with Battal Seyyid Mehmed Ağa,[21] according to which the latter would collect the taxes in return for a certain amount of profit. However, Battal did not engage in collection himself and charged one of his men instead, which lowered the profitability of the *mukataa* for everyone, including the state, and put the peasants under an increasing burden. Under these conditions, İsmail transferred his rights to his son, Halil, who became the overseer of the state revenues (*voyvoda*), the most important position in Rumkale, in 1758.[22] The profitability of the revenues from Rumkale improved under his administration throughout the 1760s; and his success led him to receive the support of the governor of Raqqa, Mehmed Paşa, so that he could procure tax farms for various tribes from the Ayntab district as well as some *mukataa* shares for his brothers.[23]

---

17 The hill country stretching west from Rumkale, referred to in Ottoman documents as the "Reşi Dağı" (Reşi Mountain, "Çîyayê Reşan" in Kurdish), was named for them. BOA: Gaziantep Şeriyye Sicilleri [GŞS] 56:49. In the 1580s, more than half the villages (56 per cent) located in Merziman are recorded as Reşi villages. The Reşi population was also dispersed among other groups. For example, in 11 per cent of the other villages there were at least four Reşi families in each. According to a document dated 1584, there were 1,000 Yezidi Reşi households around Rumkale. MD 55:49.

18 MD 115/387.

19 A.MKT.UM 514/66.

20 C.ML 384/15728; İE.ML 88/8349. According to Hüseyin Çınar, Gergerizade was from Ayntab. Hüseyin Çınar, "18. Yüzyılda Ayıntab'da Bir Yerel Gücün Yükselişi Ve Düşüşü: Battalzâdeler (Battaloğulları)," in *XIV. Türk Tarih Kongresi* (Ankara: Türk Tarih Kurumu, 2005), 438. However, his name connotes that he was from Gerger (Malatya), and probably had ties with the Reşwan.

21 Çınar, "18. Yüzyılda Ayıntab'da Bir Yerel Gücün Yükselişi."

22 BOA: Cezayir ve Rakka Ahkam Defterleri [CRAD] 24:138/3.

23 Serhat Kuzucu, "123 Numaralı Gaziantep Şer'iyye Sicili'nin Transkripsiyonu Ve Değerlendirmesi (H.1180–1181/M.1766–1767)" (master's thesis, Gaziantep Üniversitesi, 2006), 312–13.

186 Muhsin Soyudoğan

Halil's ability in managing state revenues landed him the title of *paşa* (*mirimiran*)[24] and the supervision (*mutasarrıf*) of the revenues of Kilis and A'zaz in 1770.[25] The following year he took on the administration of the revenues of Raqqa.[26] However, these gains also increased the burdens on him and dragged him into a fiercer competition with other state functionaries, which ultimately cost him his life. The *mukataa* of Raqqa was taken from him after just one year, in 1772. In 1774 he lost the *mukataa* of Kilis and A'zaz, which was awarded to the governor of Maraş under the pretext that Halil had not been able to pay the required instalments.[27] He was eventually executed in 1776. While several documents refer to his death, none gives the exact reason. He seems to have been killed because of his debts and was also accused of executing a man and seizing 300 *kile* (around 4,000 kg) of wheat, 800 *kile* (10,000 kg) of barley, and two horses from him, which can probably be attributed to an attempt to enforce payment. In the end, however, Halil was unable to pay his debts, and had all his wealth and assets confiscated after his death.[28]

Halil had made a major mistake right at the beginning. When he became a candidate for the *mukataa* of Kilis and A'zaz, the previous functionary had not completed his payments, so that there were outstanding debts on the *mukataa* from the previous year (1769). Halil was appointed overseer on the condition that he accept the liability for these arrears. He somehow believed he would be able to collect the amount from the taxpayers, but after occupying the post for six months, he could not transfer the money.[29] The main reason for this failure was the long-standing culture of resistance among residents of northern Aleppo to state taxation: the region of Kilis and A'zaz in particular was dominated by Kurdish clans who constantly challenged state authority in the area. In the early seventeenth century, these Kurds were organized under the Canpolad family, which was seeking to establish at least an autonomous polity, if not an independent state.[30] After the Canpolads

---

24 C.DH 233/11634. It is not clear if this title refers to his governorship of a province. However, a document dated after his death mentions him as the ex-governor (*beylerbeyi*) of Raqqa. C.ML 313/12845.

25 AE.SABH.I 133/8969; AE.SMST.III 198/15583; C.DH 297/14848.

26 C.ML 410/16776; C.ML 764/31132.

27 BOA: Ali Emiri Abdülhamid I [AE.SABH.I] 133/8969.

28 C.ML 735/30014.

29 C.ML 463/18831.

30 William Griswold, *The Great Anatolian Rebellion, 1000–1020/1591–1611* (Berlin: Klaus Schwarz, 1983).

Bekir Bey and the Making of a Reşwan Nobility at Rumkale   187

were defeated, the Kurdish clans of the region, especially the Oqçî Izzedînlu, often took part in preventive actions against tax collectors and resisted all demands for military recruitment.

Halil may still have been in trouble even if there had not been such a resistance, as arranging both the payment for the new year and the overdue taxes from the previous year at the same time would not have been easy. Not because of his lack of capability, but since the taxes were collected in kind, it would not have been possible for peasants to store cereals for a long period. Even if he could collect cereals and animals, it would not be an easy task to convert them into cash. Adding to the problem, his dismissal after only a short while from both the *mukataa* of Raqqa and that of Kilis-A'zaz made paying his debt nearly impossible.

Perhaps the experience of Halil was specific and personal, but he was only one case among many. Almost all the state or social elites we have come across in the documents for this research were either executed or faced the threat of execution at least once. Especially after the mid-eighteenth century, the region under consideration become a kind of elite farm where some people became powerful in a short period, then lost everything, including their lives, even quicker. This was the Ottoman mode of "the circulation of elites."[31]

The story of Halil Paşa would remain incomplete without mentioning the effects of the Russo-Ottoman War of 1768–74. It is known that the Ottoman treasury was in fairly good condition at the outbreak of war; it was this prosperity that emboldened the state to even undertake it.[32] However, the war quickly turned against the Ottomans and finally ended in a serious defeat. The heavy fiscal burden of the war forced the authorities to seek internal loans. In 1775 it was proposed to divide the revenues from *mukataa*s into multiple shares (*esham*) to sell to investors who would keep them for life, after paying a rate several times higher than the annual price. With this method, the state treasury would receive the revenues of several years in advance. In the short run this proved quite profitable, but things turned against the state so long as the shareholders were alive and kept their shares.[33] Maintaining this long-term deficit became increasingly difficult as the economy worsened. A solution therefore had to be found to the problem of shareholders who lived too long. A close look shows that the method of

---

31 "History is a graveyard of aristocracies." Vilfredo Pareto, *The Mind and Society*, ed. Arthur Livingston (London: Jonathan Cape, 1935), 3:1430.

32 Yavuz Cezar, *Osmanlı Maliyesinde Bunalım ve Değişim Dönemi: XVIII. Yüzyıldan Tanzimat'a Mali Tarih* (Istanbul: Alan Yayıncılık, 1986), 76–7.

33 Cezar, *Osmanlı Maliyesinde Bunalım* 79–80.

188 Muhsin Soyudoğan

esham division and of internal borrowing in general went hand in hand with a tendency to practice execution and confiscation. This does not necessarily mean that the state killed its elites arbitrarily to seize their properties. Rather, the relations and the competition that the practice of *esham* generated favoured a mechanism of eliminating shareholders, and so long as the state benefitted from it, other solutions tended to be neglected. As in Halil's case, the execution of shareholders provided the state with an opportunity to confiscate the whole family's assets and savings. If the deceased's assets would not cover his debts, the prospective new shareholder was normally required to pay them. And of course, since the share was resold after its possessor was eliminated, the state made extra gains almost every time.

Following Halil's execution, Kürd Muhammed became *voyvoda* of Rumkale in 1777.[34] Muhammed's career quite resembles that of Halil Paşa: like Halil, his competence in managing Rumkale's revenues earned him, in 1780, the post of tax-collector (*mütesellim*) of the *mukataa* of Kilis and A'zaz.[35] Here he had his work cut out for him, because the situation had considerably worsened in the region since Halil's death. The government was seeking new income sources due to the deepening economic crisis, which once again posed a threat to tribal life as well as to fief (*timar*) holders. Eventually, *timar* holders whose revenues were confiscated together with Kurdish tribes began to stand up against the appropriation of taxes through tax farming.[36] To repress them, Abdi Paşa was appointed governor of Aleppo in 1779.[37] He performed this task quickly, but the operation left the countryside around A'zaz devastated and empty.[38] This was the situation in which Kürd Muhammed tried to collect taxes. He did manage to collect some tax in cash as well as in livestock, which he sold through the intermediary of the tax collector (*muhassıl*) of Aleppo. However, he then suddenly fled to Rumkale for an unknown reason without delivering the revenues.[39]

---

34 RAD 24:267–8. In these documents he is presented as a notable (*ayan*) from Raqqa.
35 AE.SABH.I 254/17086; C.DH 29/1413.
36 AE.SABH.I 56/3964; AE.SABH.I 191/12789.
37 C.DH 187/9331.
38 C.DH 295/14730; AE.SABH.I 149/10105; AE.SABH.I 250/16795.
39 AE.SABH.I 254/17086. He might either have faced a problem trying to convert the livestock to cash or in fact been unable to collect the amount he had supposedly appropriated. Kilisli Kadri's interpretation is that Kürd Muhammed was incompetent and unable to handle the social problems which increased during his period in office. Being unsuccessful in maintaining control, he sought support from Abdi Paşa, who mistreated the people of Kilis. Since the people realized he was responsible for inviting Abdi Paşa, they sent the government a petition that led to his dismissal. He

Figure 8.2. Rumkale castle
Photo by Stefan Winter.

It nevertheless seems that he did eventually pay the collected amount to the shareholders, or was trusted to do so, as he was awarded the title of *paşa* (*mirimiran*) only a few months later.[40]

---

therefore stayed in that position for only five or six months. Kilisli Kadri, *Kilis Tarihi* (Istanbul: Burhaneddin Matbaası, 1932), 66. However, the duration of his appointment in Kilis was in reality much longer.

40 C.DH 29/1413.

190   Muhsin Soyudoğan

Kürd Muhammed was now the governor of Kilis-A'zaz as Halil Paşa had been. This promotion is attributed in the documents to his success in collecting taxes as well as to his efforts in retrieving goods that had been looted from a trade caravan by Kurds living in the Gâvurdağı (Amanos) mountains.[41] This event may have been related to Daltaban-zade Muhammed Ali, who first appears as an ex-fief holder and leader of rebellious clans in 1779. It was also more likely in the Kürd Dağı that Kürd Muhammed led the operation; both mountains were heavily populated by Kurdish tribes and Daltabanzade was from a village located in or near the latter.[42] Moreover, the final order addressed to Kürd Muhammed in 1782 asks him to resolve several problems related to Daltabanzade.[43] Shortly afterwards, Kürd Muhammed Paşa disappears from the record[44] and Daltabanzade became the new governor of Kilis.[45]

Rumkale in the Midst of Troubles

After Kürd Muhammed Paşa, Halil Paşa's brother Muhammed Sadık Bey was made *voyvoda* of Rumkale,[46] but he left the post to his nephew, Muhammed Şerif Bey, in order to perform the pilgrimage in 1783.[47] Şerif allegedly appropriated the taxpayers' (*reaya*) properties by force and imprisoned some of them in Rumkale during his reign. This was

---

41 BOA: Haleb Akham Defterleri [HAD] 4:21. The mountain range extends between Adana and Gaziantep. Gavurdağı in Turkish means "mountain of the infidels/ Christians"; among Kurds it is known as the "Çîyayâ Gewr" or "grey mountain." The "gavur" in the Turkish name is likely derived from "gewr."

42 Kürd Dağı: "Mountain of Kurds," the mountain range between Kilis and Hatay.

43 Kilisli Kadri, *Kilis Tarihi*; HAD 4:55.

44 The only reference to his death is in a document dated 1798, which says that since he died in 1779, he could not make his payments for that year. BOA: Maliyeden Müdevver [MAD] 9586:299. In fact, he did not die but was living in Kilis in that year and can be shown to have been still alive at least three years after that.

45 According to İsmail Kıvrım, Daltabanzade captured Kilis from Battal Seyyid Mehmed. İsmail Kıvrım, "Kilis ve A'zaz Voyvodası Daltaban-Zâde Mehmed Ali Paşa ve Muhallefâtı," *Osmanlı Tarihi Araştırma ve Uygulama Merkezi Dergisi (OTAM)* 24 (2008): 151. However, at that time Kürd Muhammed was the *voyvoda* of Kilis.

46 Muhammed Sadık had had a share of the revenues of Rumkale since 1761 and obtained a further one in 1778. C.ML 370/15229. It is not certain whether he became *voyvoda* in 1780, when Kürd Muhammed moved to Kilis, or in 1782, when the latter disappears from the record.

47 C.EV 476/24065. The reason behind this change may be related to the fact that Muhammed Şerif was the same person as Kürd Muhammed, to whom Muhammed Sadık left the post after returning to Rumkale.

Bekir Bey and the Making of a Reşwan Nobility at Rumkale 191

obviously related to the state's constant pressure on him to pay his father's debts. During the examination of Halil Paşa's inheritance it was revealed that some of his assets were in the hands of his son Şerif.[48] These assets were still being demanded from him ten years after his father's death. In a report dated 1786, Reşwanzade Ömer Paşa accused Şerif Bey of hiding state revenues that his father had once misappropriated, adding that when these had been demanded of him, he had taken refuge with Timur of the Kurdish Millî tribe.[49] It seems that Şerif had learned his lesson and would not die for the everlasting indebtedness that lifetime tax farming brought about.

Ironically, after Muhammed Sadık had fulfilled his pilgrimage, he and Muhammed Şerif were themselves accused of robbing a pilgrim caravan in a mountain pass of the Karadağ between Rumkale and Araban in 1789. Even more ironic, members of the family later received the title of "Mirü'l-hacc" or 'protector of the pilgrimage.' It seems the theft was well planned and targeted only certain people in the caravan: according to the report, the caravan consisted of more than one thousand pilgrims, but the thieves seized only seventeen animal loads, seven of them belonging to just one person, a well-known religious figure from Herat, whose goods were probably for trade rather than personal use.[50]

This robbery was very likely part of the of Millî Timur's rebellion that had broken out in 1789, which was sparked by the economic depression due to the ongoing war against Russia (1787–92), as well as the government's long-standing insistence on resettling tribes in Raqqa.[51] In a short period, the insurgency spread across a wide area.[52] The worst-case scenario for the state was if the rebellion were to spread among

---

48 BOA: Başmuhasebe Kalemi Muhallefat [D.BŞM.MHF] 59/72.

49 D.BŞM.MHF 78/5.

50 His stolen properties were estimated to be worth about 75 *kise* (4.5 million *akças*) of silver. The thieves also took his three slaves, four horses, and seven mules. C.DH 33/1639.

51 For example, from the province of Raqqa, the government requested 1,500 camels or 90,000 *guruş* in cash as its equivalent. MAD 8580:149. See also Tahir Öğüt, "XVIII. ve XIX. Yüzyılda Birecik Sancağında İktisadi ve Sosyal Yapı" (Istanbul: İstanbul Üniversitesi, 2008), 116–17.

52 Almost every effort, including poisoning Timur, splitting his forces by bribing someone close to him, or recruiting forces from neighbouring provinces ended in failure. The state was now confronting probably the most serious rebellion ever in Ottoman Kurdistan, which lasted for five years. Mehmet Rezan Ekinci, "Osmanlı Devleti Döneminde Milli Aşireti XVIII. – XIX. yy" (PhD diss., Fırat Üniversitesi, 2017), 134–43.

192 Muhsin Soyudoğan

the Reşwans: a Reşwan-Millî alliance would bring the most powerful Kurdish tribe from west of Euphrates together with that from the east. By taking precautions right from the beginning, the government was able to keep Reşwan participation to a minimum; the Reşwanzades were even mobilized against Timur.[53] Though there are no explicit references to the Reşwans of Rumkale being involved in this rebellion, as mentioned above, Muhammed Şerif had already joined Timur three years before to escape state oppression, and it is known that he was killed near Cizre in a skirmish between state and tribal forces approximately a month after the robbery.[54] It is therefore likely that the robbery had been conducted by a band, probably of Reşwan, under Şerif Bey's command. It would be wrong, however, to claim that his uncle Sadık Bey also participated. While Şerif had joined Timur, Sadık remained in Rumkale and cooperated with the government. Moreover, the robbery was not investigated subsequently, which suggests that those who had participated were no longer in Rumkale. Even if Rumkale did not suffer such a massive assault as happened to Birecik in 1792, the countryside was unluckily hit by a locust infestation in 1791 during the early days of the rebellion.[55] This obviously created a serious problem regarding Sadık's tax arrears. Worse yet was another conflict in nearby Ayntab.

Even though the Battalzades of Ayntab had significant economic power, they lacked a political patron until Battalzade Mehmed II's son Nuri Mehmed was made *paşa* and became governor of Ayntab in 1785. During his mandate, however, he became involved in a protracted dispute with the Janissary garrison of the citadel, who called in the help of the governor of Kilis-A'zaz, Daltabanzade Muhammed Ali and Kurdish contingents from the district to oust Nuri Mehmed in 1789. To improve his prospects for raising forces to take his revenge, Nuri Mehmed took to robbing traders and caravans and pillaging the

---

53 The strategy was to name a trusted and powerful Reşwan leader vizier and appoint him to the governorate of Malatya. The government thus hoped not only to prevent the Reşwans from rebelling but also to use them against Timur. In this intent, first Reşwanzade Ali was proposed, but this was not approved by the government. Then Reşwanzade Ömer II and Muhammed were named viziers. Ömer was also appointed governor of Malatya and in return took part in the military operation against Timur. On the other hand, Reşwan groups especially in Hısn-ı Mansur (Adıyaman) backed Timur against Ömer. AE.SABH.I 11/974; AE.SABH.I 362/25242; C.DH 264/13182.

54 MD 1:10–11 (nos. 33–4).

55 Rebels under the leadership of Ramazan Ağa of the Baziki tribe attacked Birecik in 1792, killing most of the state officials in town and looting their properties. HAT 260/15013; C.DH 315/15722.

Bekir Bey and the Making of a Reşwan Nobility at Rumkale   193

countryside of Rumkale. He was caught and imprisoned, but somehow regained his freedom and managed to reestablish the Battalzades' power in Ayntab after his supporters in town had killed Daltabanzade Muhammed Ali Paşa in 1791. But as the conflict with the janissaries flared anew, the governor of Raqqa, Mustafa Paşa (Köse), marshalled an army at Rumkale, besieged Ayntab, and executed him in 1791.[56] This briefly provided Sadık Bey of Rumkale with an opportunity to compensate his losses in these hard times, as Mustafa Paşa had gotten him appointed *voyvoda* of Ayntab in order to manage the revenues of Ayntab and Menbic.[57] Only shortly after, however, the governor of Maraş-Adana obtained the tax collectorship of Ayntab, and in 1793 Muhammed Sadık was reinstated in that post once more.

The fluctuation in Muhammed Sadık's position was not only related to the hostility between the governors of Raqqa and Maraş, but also to the ongoing friction between the Kuloğlus and Battalzades. When Battal Seyyid Mehmed had partnered with Kuloğlu İsmail to collect the state revenues at Rumkale, he was *voyvoda* of both Ayntab and Kilis-A'zaz. It is known that he derived much profit from these posts, to the point that it was rumoured he had found a great treasure at Kilis. After he died in 1765, his son Seyyid Mehmed II become *voyvoda* of Ayntab, then of Kilis, until the Kurds of Kilis attacked his house and ousted him from his position in 1769.[58] Thereupon Halil Paşa of Rumkale became *voyvoda* of Kilis-A'zaz, which would appear to explain the hostility of the Battalzades towards Halil's family.

Halil Paşa's execution five years later encouraged Battalzade Mehmed Sadık, who became *voyvoda* of Ayntab following the death of his brother Seyyid Mehmed II, to manifest his hostility. In 1776, when Muhammed Sadık of Rumkale and his two nephews, 'Ali and Halil, brought a load of barley and wheat to sell in Ayntab, Battalzade Sadık seized their grain by force and imprisoned the nephews. In the following years he continued mistreating traders and travellers from Rumkale by seizing their properties and throwing them in irons. When Sadık of Rumkale appealed the case in court nine years later, they were still being held.[59] Two questions need to be answered here: why did

---

56 C.DH 315/15722; Sakaoğlu, *Anadolu Derebeyi Ocaklarından Köse Paşa Hanedanı.*
57 C.ML 579/23778.
58 Çınar, "18. Yüzyılda Ayntab'da Bir Yerel Gücün Yükselişi Ve Düşüşü: Battalzâdeler (Battaloğulları)," 437, 445.
59 BOA: Maraş Ahkam Defterleri [MŞAD] 3:47/1; MŞAD 3:53/2. Sevde Nur Güldiken, "III Numaralı Maraş Ahkâm Defteri'ne Göre Ayıntab (H.1196–1229 / M.1782–1814)" (master's thesis, Gaziantep Üniversitesi, 2007).

194   Muhsin Soyudoğan

Battalzade resort to such violence; and why did Sadık of Rumkale wait so many years to appeal the case?

Like many other tax farmers, the Battalzades were also having difficulty in paying their debts.[60] This was the sort of vicious cycle that *malikane* and *esham* models brought about in the eighteenth century: once a shareholder was indebted, it was very difficult to repay without resorting to corrupt practices, which in return deepened the social and economic crises. Under these conditions, in order to survive or stand up against rival families, it became necessary to engage in clientelism. Families had two options: they either had to find a powerful patron such as a governor or raise a family member to become one. In that sense, Halil receiving the title of vizier (*paşa*) brought Kuloğlus an important advantage vis-à-vis their rivals. However, after Halil's death, the family lost this advantage, which is why they silently put up for years with Battalzade's abduction of their family members. When the government finally decided to investigate the allegations against the Battalzades, the inspector sent from Istanbul was none other than Halil Paşa's son Mustafa (Celaleddin). This Mustafa had probably been sent to the Porte back when Halil became a *paşa*, as a kind of insurance for obedience that the government often demanded of local ruling families. These security hostages could lobby for the family in the imperial capital or could be used by the government to curb the family's power.

Conflicting Interests

In the *esham* system anyone who had a certain amount of capital could acquire a share of state revenues. Those who did not have enough money borrowed from moneylenders (*sarraf*) or bought joint shares. The local people usually did not welcome alien tax collectors. For this reason, these had to transfer some of their shares to prominent local families, who had a certain degree of influence on taxpayers, to manage their revenue sources. Şevket Pamuk has called this interdependence in tax collection the "great coalition."[61] Such a conceptualization may mislead us to think of these relations as harmonious and constitutive of a kind of "class for itself."[62] In fact, these relations were based on a

---

60 BOA: Cevdet Askeriye [C.AS] 520/21706.

61 Şevket Pamuk, *Osmanlı-Türkiye Iktisadi Tarihi 1500–1914* (Istanbul: İletişim, 2005), 146–52.

62 In Marxist thought, this refers to the social classes that pursue their own common interest. For detailed discussion on this concept, see David Neilson, "In-Itself for-Itself: Towards Second-Generation Neo-Marxist Class Theory," *Capital and Class* 42, no. 2 (June 2017): 273–95, https://doi.org/10.1177/0309816817723299.

kind of dialectical division of labour and produced highly conflicting interests.

Celaleddin Mustafa, the son of Halil Paşa, occupied a post in the central bureaucracy in Istanbul and owned some shares in a division of the revenues of Rumkale, consisting of several villages around Nizib. In 1779, Celaleddin made an agreement with Kürd Muhammed to manage this share. However, as Muhammed reportedly died (or in fact moved to Kilis), Celaleddin did not receive his income. He therefore appealed to the court, which ruled that Kürd Muhammed's heir Bekir had to pay the debt. Though Bekir initially tried not to pay, he likely had no other option.[63] Thus did Bekir become another tax collector who began his career with a burden of debt.

Bekir Bey somehow paid his father's debt, but his payments over the next three years remained short of the expected amount. He expanded the family's holdings in 1784 with his brothers Osman and Muhammed getting some shares. Bekir regularly paid the instalments until the outbreak of Millî Timur's rebellion in 1789. Though he faced some difficulties paying in those hard times, he was able to increase his share towards the end of the rebellion by getting 25 per cent of the *timar* revenues of Rumkale, which had previously been managed by Muhammed Sadık. However, at the end of the tax collection contract's term the governor of Anadolu and Raqqa, Seyyid Ali (Alo) Paşa, tried to abrogate his rights under the pretext that he had been avoiding payment of his debts and had been involved in some untoward events.[64]

It is not clear in Seyyid Ali Paşa's report what sort of crimes Bekir was accused of. However, his debts were meticulously calculated in the same documents. The fiscal records show that he ran a serious deficit in 1789, when he was only able to pay 33 per cent of the revenues, and he did not pay anything at all the next four years. Thus, at the end of eighteen years his total debt had reached 42.5 per cent of the total expected revenues. His payment difficulties reflect to what extent the countryside of Birecik and Rumkale was affected by Timur's rebellion. The important question here is why the government did not just write off the debts, especially of small tax farmers like Bekir, when it was aware of the social and economic catastrophe in the region.

In point of fact, Seyyid Ali Paşa was not an ordinary state official. He was named governor of Anadolu and Raqqa in 1795 specifically to collect the unpaid revenues of Raqqa province.[65] To do so, he identified all

---

63 MAD 9586:299; C.ZB 25/1218.
64 C.ZB 25/1218; C.ML 581/23900.
65 HAT 198/9990.

debtor tax collectors in Urfa, Birecik, and Rumkale. His primary targets were Hamoyizade el-hacc Mehmed of Urfa, Deli Ömer Ağa of Birecik, and Muhammed Sadık of Rumkale.[66] This led Seyyid Ali to direct his forces against Urfa and besiege the city. After breaking the resistance, he marched on Birecik, but after two months of unsuccessful siege, he withdrew his forces to Ayntab. There he checked the fiscal records and seized almost all the revenues of Ayntab that had not been paid the last few years. When his stay at Ayntab got too extended, the citizens of the town petitioned the Porte, saying that their resources were nearly depleted; he was summoned to rush his troops to the Balkan front in 1796.[67]

Though Ali Paşa used force or threatened to use force against other debtors, his approach with Muhammed Sadık was smoother. Ali Paşa sent the Porte two reports, one regarding Muhammed Sadık and the other about Bekir. In the first, he asked the government to forgive Muhammed Sadık even if he had supported the "rebellious" Hamoyizade, the main reason being that he had after all played an important role in the efforts to bring order to Ayntab and its surroundings. He did have debts, but according to Ali Paşa, these could be tolerated because he had been unable to collect and send money due to the rebellions.[68] Conversely, in his other report Ali Paşa stated that Bekir Bey was a bandit who had intentionally never paid his debts and would not do so in the future.[69]

Though Muhammed Sadık and Bekir were equally accused of supporting rebels and not rendering their payments, Bekir was imposed harsher sanctions. Such a negative attitude towards Bekir cannot be explained without considering the relations of Sadık Bey with other governors in the region. The one of Malatya had once portrayed Sadık Bey as a lunatic who could not manage a tax farm.[70] As this was obviously not the case, it seems likely that intense rivalries, and the fact that he was now being seriously challenged by Bekir Bey, led Sadık to lobby effectively against him. The great imbalance in their treatment demonstrates their degree of competition for the governorship of Rumkale.

---

66 C.ML 20/939; C.DH 30/1459; C.DH 29/1416; C.ML 63/2855; Ayten Ertürk, "2 Numaralı Mühimme-i Mektume Defteri (H.1208–1211/M.1793–1796) Transkripsiyon ve Değerlendirilmesi (S. 31–60)" (master's thesis, Fırat Üniversitesi, 2018), 48.
67 HAT 206/10790.
68 HAT 187/8840.
69 C.ML 581/23900; C.ZB 25/1218.
70 D.BŞM.MHF 78/5.

After the incursion into Birecik in 1792, the town had been subdued by Bekir Bey. Later, a tax-farmer in Urfa, Çizmecizade Hasan Ağa, who was fleeing from punishment for not paying his instalments, found shelter in Birecik. There he convinced all but about fifty of the people of Birecik to not pay taxes to the government. In the dispute between these two groups, one of Hasan Ağa's opponents was killed, while others were expelled from the fortress.[71] One of these was probably Bekir Beg.

When Seyyid Ali Paşa came to Urfa, Bekir made contact with him and the Paşa welcomed his obedience and appointed him governor (*mütesellim*) of Birecik. Several months later, in 1796, he was appointed *voyvoda* of Rumkale.[72] This appointment was not welcomed by Sadık and his son Mustafa, who complained first to Ali Paşa and then to his successor Şeyhzade İbrahim Paşa. On the one hand those governors sent petitions, on the other hand Sadık went to Istanbul looking for a way to change the decision.[73] Eventually Bekir was dismissed and İbrahim Paşa was appointed in his stead in 1798. However, the efforts to obtain Bekir's expulsion from Rumkale backfired, as he somehow got himself appointed to the position again. In 1799, tension between the two rivals turned into open conflict, as Bekir attacked Sadık and expelled his family from Rumkale to Birecik.[74]

Though Sadık was supported by the governors of Raqqa, Bekir also needed help, otherwise he would not be able to impose himself on his rivals and the state authorities. Sadık, like the governors of Raqqa, saw Bekir as a bandit leader who oppressed people. However, in a report it was claimed that the people were supporting Bekir against Sadık.[75] It is certain that Bekir had the backing of the Reşwans. It should not have been a coincidence that Reşwan clans escaping from punishment in 1784 found refuge around Mizar village, where Bekir resided.[76] The

---

71 C.DH 33/1618; C.ML 268/10962.
72 C.ML 74/3381:2.
73 C.ZB 25/1218; C.ML 581/23900; C.ML 74/3381.
74 MAD 9586:301; C.DH 349/17436. In some documents it was mistakenly said that Bekir drove Sadık Bey and his nephew Şerif Bey out of Rumkale by force. See C.ML. 577/23690; Kadriye Demir, "3 Numaralı Mühimme-i Mektume Defterinin Özet ve Transkripsiyonu" (master's thesis, Sinop University, 2017), 416. However, as indicated before, Şerif Bey had already died during Timur's rebellion.
75 C.DH 349/17436.
76 Abdi Paşa, the governor of Aleppo, assaulted a group of Reşwan (Molikanlı) near Mizar on the pretence that they had looted a caravan. Muhammed Şerif Bey of Rumkale attempted to negotiate between them at first, but when that failed, he probably urged the governor of Raqqa and Millî Timur to save the Reşwans from

198   Muhsin Soyudoğan

second source of his power was the *voyvoda* of Ayntab, Hüseyin Ağa, who was the son of Nuri Mehmed Paşa of the Battalzade family.[77] This alliance makes sense when one thinks of Sadık's role in the death of his father. Finally, Bekir often received support from the governor of Maraş, Kalender Paşa, whose patronage was comprehensible given his rivalry with the governor of Raqqa, the former rebel and enemy of state Millî Timur Paşa.[78]

Due to the conflict between Bekir and Sadık, the state could not collect sufficient revenues from Rumkale and charged Kalender Paşa with their management; he then promptly made Bekir governor. But Rumkale was historically a part of Raqqa, sometimes of Aleppo, not of Maraş. Therefore, as had happened before, Rumkale once more became a disputed land between the governors of Raqqa and Maraş. The conflict between Timur and Kalender was however not limited to this appointment. According to Timur, Kalender had crossed the Euphrates (which served as the province's border), interfered with Birecik's affairs as well as agitated the Baziki and Reşwan tribes, and appointed Bekir Bey to Rumkale without the government's consent, allowing Bekir to pillage all kinds of commodities and animals and killing twelve of his men.[79]

In 1803, Timur Paşa went to Ayntab to break Kalender Paşa's hold over the town. During his presence there, he rearranged the government of Rumkale by dismissing Bekir Bey and appointing Sadık Bey as *voyvoda*. This once again provoked the aggression of Bekir, who stormed the houses of those who had sided with Sadık and killed Sadık's son Mustafa in 1804.[80] He was declared an outlaw and was ordered executed but managed to obtain the support of the new governor of Raqqa, Veli (Veliyüddin) Paşa, the son of Köse Mustafa Paşa,

---

the Paşa's anger. Söylemez, *Osmanlı Devletinde Aşiret Yönetimi*, 86–7. Sakaoğlu, *Anadolu Derebeyi*, 75. HAT 80/3322; MAD 9586:299; C.ML 559/22954. According to Tahir Öğüt, Mizar was located between the summer and winter pastures of Reşwan tribe. Tahir Öğüt, "XVIII. ve XIX. Yüzyılda Birecik Sancağında İktisadi ve Sosyal Yapı" (İstanbul Üniversitesi, 2008), 421, fn. 53.

77 C.DH 349/17436. See also marginal note in MAD 9586:301.

78 Timur remained governor of Raqqa from 1800 to 1803. C.DH 246/12289. On the career of Millî Timur, see Stefan Winter, "The Other *Nahdah*: The Bedirxans, the Millîs, and the Tribal Roots of Kurdish Nationalism in Syria," *Oriente Moderno* 86, no. 3 (August 2006): 461–74, https://doi.org/10.1163/22138617-08603003.

79 Serpil Acıoğlu, "137 Numaralı Ayntâb Şer'iyye Sicilinin (H. 1216–1220/M. 1801–6) Transkripsiyonu ve Değerlendirilmesi" (master's thesis, Gaziantep Üniversitesi, 2012), 113–14; C.ML 251/10391.

80 AE.SSLM.III 159/9538; RAD 25:93–8.

and was pardoned. However, Sadık Bey declared that he would not accept the pardon unless Bekir paid blood money, compensation for the properties looted and the tax instalments for 1802 and 1803, which he had not been able to submit because of Bekir. He also demanded he be awarded the *mukataa* from 1804 onwards.[81] Since this event did not turn into a blood feud, it can be assumed that Bekir agreed to at least some of the terms. It is also known, for instance, that one of Sadık's sons married a sister of Bekir.[82] It is likely that this marriage was part of the blood money, as women were often accepted as requital for blood money among tribes.[83]

When Bekir was declared an outlaw, it was Kalender Paşa who was ordered to punish him.[84] Instead, Kalender Paşa made him *vovyoda* of Rumkale in lieu of Sadık, Timur Paşa's candidate. Bekir kept his office for the next ten year and Sadık many times received orders and to pay his instalments properly.[85] At first glance, Bekir may appear as the victor in this battle, but every revenue overseer and shareholder in Rumkale began to lose from the disorder in management.[86]

Two Tribes, One Fate

Muro, the individual who ultimately brought about the death of Bekir Bey, was from the Hevidi tribe of Behisni (Besni), for whom Rumkale was not only a winter shelter but also a safe haven whenever they faced state oppression. In 1768, for example, the Hevidis were violently pursued by the governor of Malatya after they had gathered at the behest of the mufti of Behisni to protest against their excessive taxation, with many fleeing to Rumkale when they were ordered to be forcibly removed to Raqqa.[87] After passing considerable time in Rumkale in misery, they asked Halil Paşa to help them return to their homelands.

---

81 C.ZB 19/922; AE.SSLM.III 159/9538.
82 Kale Meydanı, "Soyağacı"; see also Cemil Cahit Güzelbey, *Gaziantep Şer'î Sicilleri (Cilt 142 İlâ 143)* (Gaziantep: Gaziantep Kültür Derneği, 1966), 3:70.
83 Şerefhan, *Şerefname: Kürt Tarihi* (Istanbul: Hasat Yayınları, 1990), 25.
84 Yusuf Sarıkaya, "5 Numaralı Mühimme-i Mektûme Defteri'nin Transkripsiyonu Ve Değerlendirilmesi" (master's thesis, Sinop University, 2019), 145–7, 183–4.
85 AE.SSLM.III 393/22713; AE.SSLM.III 270/15575.
86 AE.SSLM.III 270/15575; C.ML 206/8494; C.ML 519/21218; C.ML 547/22495; C.ML 733/29911; C.ML 370/15229.
87 AE.SMST.III 276/22051; MD 135:354, 1044, 1690. Faruk Söylemez and Muhammet Nuri Tunç, "18. Yüzyılda Behisni'de Camiler Ve Cami Görevlileri," *Kilis 7 Aralık Üniversitesi Sosyal Bilimler Dergisi* 7, no. 14 (2017): 77, https://doi.org/10.31834/kilissbd.352619; Söylemez, *Osmanlı Devletinde Aşiret Yönetimi*, 264.

200   Muhsin Soyudoğan

Halil's initiative on their behalf was finally granted by the government and they were able to return two year later, on condition that they pay their tax arrears.[88]

West of the Euphrates, it was the Kurds of Behisni who supported Timur's rebellion the most. After the rebellion, Seyyid Ali Paşa was assigned to collect taxes in Urfa while Reşwanzade Abdurrahman II was appointed *kaymakam* of Behisni to collect taxes that had not been paid the last several years.[89] The Hevidis once again objected to the demand and once again found support from the deputy mufti of Behisni.[90] Under the leadership of their *boybeği* (headman) Süleyman Derviş, the Hevidis not only refused to pay but also went out to villages to seize grains that were to be collected as the state's share, in addition to raiding Abdurrahman Paşa's house. When they saw it was no longer possible to stand against the army of the Paşa, they retreated once more to Rumkale in 1798 to take refuge behind Bekir Bey.[91]

In 1808, Abdurrahman Paşa was appointed to the province of Malatya, which had long been under his family's rule in the past and which he regarded as his rightful inheritance. Like his father and predecessor Reşwanzade Ömer, he quickly acquired a reputation for oppressing the local population but also of inciting Kurds and "bandits" around Malatya. This led the Porte to fear he might join forces with the Millî Timur in his renewed rebellion against the state, an alliance between the Millî and Reşwan Kurds in the mineral-rich mining region of Maden-Ergani being the worst scenario imaginable.[92] Abdurrahman was dismissed from office (and did in fact join Millî Timur), but was reinstated as governor of Behisni as a gesture of goodwill after Timur died in early 1811.[93] Many local clans including the Hevidis immediately protested the decision, but were again severely persecuted when Abdurrahman was permitted to re-enter the city with the active support of the governors of the neighbouring provinces.[94] The state

---

88 C.DH 259/12948; C.DH 297/14848.
89 Seydi Vakkas Toprak, "Osmanlı Devleti Hizmetinde Bir Aşiret ve Lideri Rişvanzâde Seyyid Abdurrahman Paşa," *İstanbul Üniversitesi Tarih Dergisi* 58 (2013): 65–85; C.DH 264/13182.
90 HAT 656/32061; Söylemez and Tunç, "18. Yüzyılda Behisni'de Camiler ve Cami Görevlileri," 77.
91 MD 3:57 (no. 188).
92 C.DRB 5/232; C.ZB 86/4263; HAT 1360/53516; TSMA E.1266/55.
93 TSMA E.299/20; TSMA E.682/39; HAT 503/24751; HAT 503/24749; TSMA E.721/9; HAT 502/24629; TSMA E.710/28; TSMA E.619/1.
94 TSMA E.4/89; TSMA E.619/1–4; TSMA E.478/5; TSMA E.619/11.

Bekir Bey and the Making of a Reşwan Nobility at Rumkale   201

imposed an unbearable fine of 250,000 *guruş* on the people of Behisni, which led many to disperse into the wider region.[95]

Nevertheless, the state did not give up punishing the fugitives. One such person was Muro.[96] When Abdurrahman Paşa attacked the rebels, Muro was headed towards Rumkale to take shelter with Bekir Bey. Soon after, in 1814, the forces of the governor of Sivas, Pehlivan İbrahim Paşa, appeared before Rumkale to arrest him. At first Bekir did not intend to hand him over, but when İbrahim's forces intensified their assault, a meeting was held with the Reşwan warriors, and it was decided to release him. Muro was immediately executed, but the siege was not lifted until the forces of İbrahim Paşa found a way into Rumkale through a stepped well. Bekir Bey thus had no choice but to surrender. He too was executed on the spot and Rumkale was totally devastated, not to be inhabited again.

Such an end makes us sceptical whether the real purpose of the operation was to punish Muro, to get rid of Bekir Bey, or to destroy the fortress of Rumkale. Indeed, it was one of the strategies of the Ottomans to destroy rather than conquer the fortresses that were hard to control or were in danger of falling into the enemy's hands. However, Rumkale does not fall into either category. It was supposedly an Ottoman fortress but was not even close to the Empire's borders. One may attribute such a result to Bekir's contumacy, but it had in fact been ten years since he had been pardoned and had not been involved in a serious crime needing capital punishment. Maybe it can be assumed that he was punished simply for protecting a fugitive and not obeying orders. However, Bekir Bey doubtless negotiated for the release of Muro and was given some assurances.[97] Otherwise, it would not have been logical to keep fighting after handing him over. We may never know if Bekir Bey's life was part of the bargain, but it is certain that he could have been spared. Here, the question is why İbrahim Paşa preferred to execute him.[98]

One of the reasons is of course related to the nature of such operations in the period. A governor was expected to maintain a standing

---

95 TSMA E.619/17; TSMA.E.620/30.

96 Muro is the Kurdish abbreviation of Murad or Murtaza. He was probably the same person as Murad the son of Mare, who was among the rebels that attacked Abdurrahman Paşa in 1798. See MD 3:57:188.

97 We know that İbrahim Paşa allowed his family to go to Birecik after they paid 6,500 *guruş*. C.ML 559/22954.

98 It is not certain whether Bekir Bey was executed immediately or only later once in İbrahim Paşa's custody. HAT 503/24778; HAT 503/24786; HAT 410/21305.

Figure 8.3. Stepped well in Rumkale
Photo by Muhsin Soyudoğan.

force to keep his post and defend his interests. The power of a governor depended on the number of his men, but more men meant a greater economic burden. Usually, the state revenues reserved for the men remained an acceptable amount. Especially during such operations, mercenaries expected something extra for the risks they took. That is why the governors usually passed on their expenditures to the targeted population. Such practices were forbidden on paper, but the government winked at them in reality and sometimes even encouraged them by declaring the whole community to be bandits or rebels.[99] This conflict was clearly present with İbrahim Paşa, who repeatedly mentioned in his reports how attentive he was not to harm the poor and the weak, while at the same time boasting how his forces had spoiled the abundant properties of the Kurds.[100]

---

99 In such cases the government would occasionally send orders specifiying "heads for us, belongings for you" (*başları bize, malleri size*), that is, giving permission to seize the victims' property.
100 HAT 807/37194; HAT 762/36026; HAT 503/24786; Gazzizâde Abdullatif Efendi, *Vekāyi'-ı Baba Paşa fī't-Târîh*, 276.

On the heels of the operation, an investigator was despatched to Rumkale to inventory Bekir Bey's wealth and assets to seize for the state treasury. The investigation revealed that one of İbrahim Paşa's officers had in fact taken all his money and possessions. The debt could not be assigned to the townsmen and clans who had assisted Bekir, because their wealth had also been seized. The investigator's second duty was to record the estates of those executed in Ayntab, but these had been seized by Kalender Paşa. So after spending two years in the region, the investigator left again without having located any significant sources of money, not even to compensate his own expenditures.[101]

Nevertheless, Bekir's death cannot be attributed merely to İbrahim Paşa's cupidity or his men's anticipation of remuneration for risking their lives. İbrahim Paşa's appointment to Sivas in 1813 was not an ordinary one. His principal task was to pursue and capture a whole list of troublesome governors in the region including Veli Paşa, son of Köse Mustafa Paşa, who attempted to recruit help among the Reşwan of Akçadağ in order to stand against the government forces.[102] In fact the scope of İbrahim's campaign went far beyond the list: he was also endowed with extraordinary powers to bring all the powerful Kurdish tribes and dynasties of the region under the Ottoman yoke.[103] Muro was thus not only accused of taking part in the murder of the son or grandson of the mufti who had led the tax protest in Behisni, but also of "replacing sharia laws with Kurdish traditions."[104] In other words, he was being accused of attempting to replace the Ottoman authority with a Kurdish one. This statement gives us a clue as to the real aim of the operation at Rumkale.

No doubt, the rebellions of Millî Timur epitomized the Kurdish question in eyes of the state. The primary solution was to curb Kurdish economic, political, and social power and to use these resources to build a modern army. The series of operations led by İbrahim Paşa that began at Sivas and extended eastwards as far as Çıldır can be regarded as a first step in that direction. While Kurdish notables were executed and their fortresses devastated one after another, many tribal assets

---

101 C.ML 559/22954; C.ML 307/12530.
102 Sakaoğlu, *Anadolu Derebeyi Ocaklarından Köse Paşa Hanedanı*, 179–80.
103 In his biography he states that he had to get rid of the tribes quickly "before Kurdistan stirred." Gazzizâde Abdullatif Efendi, *Vekāyi'-ı Baba Paşa*, 285. İbrahim Paşa is in a sense portrayed as the conqueror of Kurdistan. His depiction of Kurds as undefeatable warriors shows how much importance was attributed to the mission; Gazzizâde Abdullatif Efendi, *Vekāyi'-ı Baba Paşa*, 270–1, 276, 283.
104 Sakaoğlu, *Anadolu Derebeyi Ocaklarından Köse Paşa Hanedanı*, 201.

204 Muhsin Soyudoğan

were confiscated or stolen.[105] The operations were ended only after the people of Çıldır rose up against İbrahim Paşa's oppression. At the conclusion of these operations, Kurdish dominance, especially of the Reşwan tribes west of the Euphrates, was diminished by compelling them to resettle in Ankara and Konya.

Conclusion

Bekir Bey's life and death were the mirror, in the microcosm of a small town like Rumkale, of structural problems in the Ottoman Empire that had increased exponentially over the previous century. The economic crisis of the seventeenth century had gradually replaced self-sufficient *timar* landholding with tax farming that facilitated capital accumulation. As a result of this process, many individuals who possessed or were able to borrow money invested in tax farming concessions, often in partnership with influential provincial notables (*ayan*) or tribal leaders who founded local dynasties ruling over all kinds of administrative centres. Bekir's family was typical of such dynasties that emerged on the historical stage after the state had disbanded the garrison of Rumkale and converted the economic units reserved for their salaries (*timar*s) into tax farming.

This new fiscal system was a sort of internal indebtedness, and it functioned fairly well until the second half of the eighteenth century, when the imperial economy deteriorated drastically due to the long wars with Russia. To relieve the financial burden, the government sought to bring more investors into the system of tax farming, and therefore divided state revenues into ownable lifelong shares that could be sold even to small investors. In this way, people's savings were rapidly transferred to the state treasury, but the profitability of tax farming diminished with every additional party. There was a limit to how much shareholders could exploit the peasants before they fled the land, so that they frequently could not collect the required revenues and exposed themselves to reprobation and punishment. As a result, shareholders became involved in fierce competition with one another in order to preserve their positions. In such conflicts, small shareholders often sought the patronage of governors who were themselves in competition for more clients or to expand their area of governance. In such a situation, being on the wrong side could be deadly.

---

105 Before Rumkale İbrahim Paşa destroyed the neighbouring fortress of Altuntaş (Kelayê Zêrîn in Kurdish) on the Araban plain, which was under the control of the Hevidis. HAT 1264/48944.

In these circumstances, every tax farming shareholder had an innate criminal potential. And the state did not hesitate to execute them, if not for justice, then for financial gain. The government could expect a dual benefit from their execution. First, their death meant the confiscation of their wealth for the state treasury. The need for such revenue was so apparent that a sort of legacy hunting became widespread after 1789, whereby the government demanded from local agents that they report the death of every wealthy or heirless person and inventory all their assets to be confiscated.[106] Second, by killing them, the state could resell their shares or their posts for extra profit. This was a kind of venality of office that proved a subtle method of appropriating and transferring wealth to the state. In the end, the period constituted a massive graveyard of provincial notables, of which Bekir Bey was just one typical example.

On the macro level, the death of Bekir was a reflection of the state's centralization efforts in order to pull itself out of the systemic crisis that had lasted for more than a century. The year 1789 was a turning point for our case, as the rebellion of Millî Timur, during which Bekir first appeared as a political actor, erupted then. Timur may not have been driven by nationalist feelings sparked by the French Revolution of the same year, but it is certain that it had a significant effect on Ottoman politics. Selim III, who also ascended the throne that year, proceeded to undertake the first real reforms towards a modern central state. The 1814 military expedition of Pehlivan İbrahim Paşa against the Kuloğlu family at Rumkale that cost Bekir his life was surely part of that policy.

---

106 For some examples, see HAT 1381/54480; HAT 1411/57443; C.ML 187/7778.

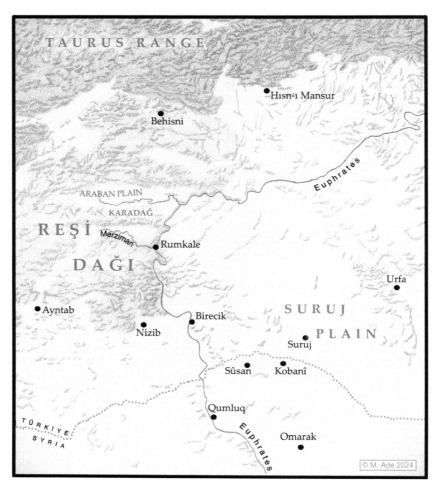

Map 3. The Reşi Dağı–Suruj region

9 The Berazi Tribe of Suruj and Their Rebellion in the Tanzimat Period

MUHSIN SEYDA

Introduction

In the fourth/tenth century, the Arab historian and geographer al-Mas'udi already spoke of the presence of Kurdish tribes in the Levant region. Among the tribes he describes living there are the famous and far-spread Dababala,[1] which then appear in the Ottoman Tahrir records of the sixteenth century alongside two other Kurdish tribes, the Berazis and the Izolis, inhabiting villages of the Suruj plain, as we will see shortly. The Kurds of "Syria," if we may be allowed the expression, have a clear presence in historical texts going back to different time periods. In addition to al-Mas'udi, both Yaqut al-Hamawi and Fadlallah al-'Umari highlighted this connection between Syria and the Kurds. This connection was uninterrupted from the tenth century until the emergence of the modern Syrian state, even if the Kurds did integrate into their Arab environment like other peoples who settled in the region.[2]

After the disintegration of the Ottoman Empire, new states were formed in the Middle East; Syria was one of these states that emerged from the legacy of the "sick man." With the demarcation of the boundary between the Republic of Turkey and Syria on the basis of the first Ankara agreement of 1921, the term "Kurds of Syria" was applied to the Kurdish populations living in the Kurd Dagh, Kobanî ('Ayn al-'Arab), and the Jazira regions, who found themselves inside the borders of Syria, and whose fate thus became linked with the state established according to the decisions of the first Syrian Congress held in 1919 to

---

1 Abu'l-Hasan ibn'Ali al-Mas'udi (d. 346/957), *Muruj al-Dhahab wa-Ma'adin al-Jawhar*, ed. Kamal Hasan Mar'i (Beirut: Al-Maktaba al-'Asriyya, 2005), 2:97.

2 Muhsin Sayda, "Lamha 'an tarikh al-Kurd fi Bilad al-Sham," *Medarat Kurd*, 16 June 2013, https://www.medaratkurd.com/2013/06/16/410/.

208 Muhsin Seyda

discuss the country's future. In the period just before the Congress, which would also host the international King-Crane Commission, most of the Kurdish areas that were later known as the Syrian Kurdish region still formed part of the Ottoman Empire and participated with Turkish forces in the Turkish War of Independence. In particular, branches of the Berazi tribe under the command of Buzan Shahin Bey (1890–1968) fought against the French and defeated a French division on the Plain of Suruj (south of Urfa) in 1920.[3]

This chapter examines a key moment in the history of the Berazis, and of the Syrian Kurds more generally, at the turn of the modern era: the tribal rebellion at Suruj around 1840–5. It argues that the rebellion, although a localized event, followed from new pressures exerted on the rural population in the region, through first the Egyptian and then the Tanzimat reforms, and therefore served to crystallize a Kurdish identity of anti-state resistance. Drawing on Ottoman administrative as well as local oral sources, it suggests, however, that the tribe was ultimately unable to parlay this resistance into a more effective movement or policy of demand.

Overview of the History of the Berazi Kurds of Suruj

Despite its great importance, the Battle of Chaldiran did not decisively end the Safavid presence in Kurdistan or the rest of the Kurdish lands in the Upper Jazira. The Kurdish diplomat and historian Idris al-Bidlisi made efforts in this regard by persuading the Kurdish princes to stand with the Ottomans in their struggle against the Safavids. In his *Tacü't-tevarih*, the Ottoman historian Hoca Sadeddin Efendi (d. 1599) cites the text of a message in which the people of Diyarbekir pledge their allegiance to the Ottoman sultan Selim I, disavow the Safavids, and ask for help and support to get rid of them.[4] In May 1516, the Ottoman forces confronted the Safavids under the command of Qara Khan Ustajlu at Koç Hisar southwest of Mardin near the Syrian town of al-Darbasiyya, the stronghold of the Kurdish Kîkî (Kîkan) tribe according to al-Mas'udi. This battle had many positive outcomes for the Ottomans, the most important of which was the entry of the fortress of Sinjar, Tell 'Afar, Ergani, Siverek, and Birecik under Ottoman sovereignty, so that "all of the lands of the Kurds were now Ottoman territories."[5] The

---

3 Jamil Bahri Kene, *Hikam wa-Amthal Kurdiyya wa-Maghaziha* (Aleppo: Al-Matba'a al-Sharqiyya, 1958), 37.

4 Fadil Bayat, *Al-Dawla al-'Uthmaniyya fi al-Majal al-'Arabi* (Beirut: Markaz Dirasat al-Wahda al-'Arabiyya, 2007), 249.

5 Bayat, *Al-Dawla al-'Uthmaniyya*, 250.

The Berazi Tribe of Suruj and Their Rebellion in the Tanzimat Period 209

Ottomans did not impose a specific type of rule on the Kurds or other peoples of the Empire, and one can deduce from the *Sharafnama* of Emir Sharafkhan al-Bidlisi the many different "means of power" and institutions through which the Ottomans ruled the Kurdish regions, and on whose shoulders the responsibility of maintaining security and collecting taxes fell.[6]

The motives behind the migrations of Kurdish tribes varied through the ages. Among the reasons were war, internal disputes, and conflict over pastures, in addition to the dryness and drought that periodically swept the country. It is difficult to determine exactly when the Berazis migrated to the Suruj Plain. The mystery of where they came from, what pushed them to migrate, and when they settled in Suruj has given rise to various accounts. One of the questions facing researchers who deal with the history of the Berazis is that of their union with other tribes under the banner of this confederation: was this union formed before their migration to Suruj or only after they settled there? Among the narratives circulating in the oral folklore of the Berazis is that they came a long time ago during a famine year from the region of Lake Van.[7] It would perhaps be worthwhile to compare the Kurdish dialects spoken around Lake Van to those of the Kurdish tribes of the Suruj Plain to ascertain the truth of this narrative. In any event, it does not agree with the claims of the Ottoman Kurdish historian Sharafkhan Bidlisi (1543–1603), who describes the Berazis as a branch of the Sulaymani tribe that was settled in and ruled the Qulp or Kulayb emirate near Diyarbekir. Bidlisi's account suggests there was an alliance between the religious power represented by the descendants of the Umayyad caliph Marwan II, who took refuge in Qulp, and the military power of the local Kurdish clans. Following their ascent to power and conquest of the Georgian and Armenian fortresses in the region, the latter eventually split into eight main groups, among them the Berazis.[8]

Regrettably, Sharafkhan Bidlisi did not devote much attention to the history of the Kurds in the Jazira (Mesopotamia), neglecting even so much as to mention the major tribes of his own era such as the Izolis

---

6 The "means of power" or the "medium of power" is an idea borrowed from the works of Wajih Kawtharani, who emphasizes the role of public institutions in the peripheries and their role as mediators between the people and the Ottoman state.

7 Mark Sykes, "The Kurdish Tribes of the Ottoman Empire," *Journal of the Royal Anthropological Institute of Great Britain and Ireland* 38 (July–December 1908): 475, https://doi.org/10.2307/2843309.

8 Sharafkhan Bidlisi, *Sharafnama*, trans. Muhammad ʿAli ʿAwni, ed. Yahya al-Khashshab (Damascus: Dar al-Zaman, 1985–2006), 1:226–7.

210   Muhsin Seyda

(Izuliyya) and others. Perhaps this was, as he himself described the aim of his *Sharafnama*, to preserve the reputation of the Kurdish families who had an important impact on the life of Kurdistan.[9] In this regard, the nineteenth-century Kurdish historian ʿAli Akbar Kurdestani relates that the great prince Tamerlane (1336–1405) deported two to three thousand Berazi families from the outskirts of Urfa to Iranian Kurdistan at the beginning of the fifteenth century.[10] Considering the fact that Kurdestani does not cite his sources, one may wonder if he got this narrative from a historical text or heard it directly from Berazis living in the emirate of Ardalan. If the story is true, we may conclude that the Berazis settled on the Suruj Plain in the late medieval period, and not in the context of the tribal sedentarization policies pursued later by the Ottoman Empire. The Suruj Plain also witnessed an exodus of some Berazi groups towards the Syrian interior and other regions. For example, Berazis settled nearly three hundred years ago in the valley that extends between the town of Tutak (Dûtax) in the Turkish province of Ağrı and Karayazı in Erzurum.[11] In the nineteenth century a number of Berazi families also migrated to central Syria and settled in the regions of Harem and Hama, from whence they came to play a prominent role in Syria's political history.[12]

Ottoman archival documents are of great importance for the study of the history of the Kurdish tribes of the Suruj Plain in general and of the Berazis in particular, from both a social and an economic standpoint. Among these documents are the (Tapu-) Tahrir records, which contain valuable and unique information about villages of the Suruj Plain that belonged to (*tabi-i*) the Berazis and other Kurds living in the region, including the Dunbuli, Izoli, and Rashidi tribes. To cite a few examples, the village of Tell Shaʿir, located three kilometres west of today's Kobanî, is mentioned in a Tahrir register dating from 1572 as belonging to the Rashidis and Dunbulis. Menas, now almost a suburb of Kobanî, was also affiliated with the Dunbuli tribe, as was Sûsan, situated eight km west of the city. Tell Raqaq was controlled by the Berazis and the Izolis.[13] However, the Izoli, Dunbuli and Rashidi tribes, whose presence

---

9   Bidlisi, *Sharafnama*, 1:51.
10   ʿAli Akbar Vaqayiʿ Nigar Kurdistani, *ʿAshaʾir va-Alat va-Tavaʾif Kurd*, ed. Muhammad Raʾuf Tawakkuli (Tehran: Kalban Jab Printing House, 2002), 39.
11   Information provided by Ahmad Aras (author of Serhildana Seyidan u Berazan), Izmir, June 2019.
12   Stefan Winter, "Les Kurdes de Syrie dans les archives ottomanes (XVIIIᵉ siècle)," *Études Kurdes* 10 (2009): 129, 155.
13   T.C. Cumhurbaşkanlığı Devlet Arşivi [BOA]: Tahrir Defteri [TD] 496:72, 82, 111, 155.

The Berazi Tribe of Suruj and Their Rebellion in the Tanzimat Period   211

is attested in these registers, are no longer mentioned in Ottoman documents of the nineteenth century. It is likely that they migrated from Suruj for unknown reasons, or merged into the more numerous and probably older Berazi tribe. Today, there are still families in the Kobanî region that claim descent from the Izolis.

In the seventeenth century, the Ottoman traveller Evliya Çelebi toured the region, writing down his observations and impressions in his famous *Seyahatname*. On his trip to Aleppo around 1648 he described the division of land and the inhabitants of the Suruj Plain, indicating that most were of the Dunyay (Dunay), Berazi, Kokh Bin (?), and Cum tribes. They were engaged in the cultivation of mulberries for silk production and paid the tithe tax on their revenues.[14]

By the early nineteenth century some documents begin using "Berazi" in reference to the entire Suruj Plain, thus adding a geographical meaning to the tribe name and juxtaposing the two. For example, in a document dated 1819 we read of the "al-Baraziyya District in Suruj," while another from 1858 mentions the "Suruj or al-Baraziyya District."[15] A report from the year 1898 speaks of "the dismissal of the director of the Baraziyya District in the *sancak* of Urfa."[16]

In the nineteenth century, the villages of the Berazis were administratively tied to the districts of Suruj, Birecik, and Harran. To cite a few examples, Koshkar, Göktepe, and Khrus east of today's Kobanî were part of the district (*nahiye*) of Harran, while Borazoğlu and Qumluq west of Kobanî were attached to the *kaza* of Birecik.[17] The *kaza* of Suruj, according to the Ottoman *Salname*s (provincial yearbooks), encompassed 175 villages including the town of Arab Pınar, whose name was Arabized to 'Ayn al-'Arab (from Kurdish Kaniya Araban, "spring of the Arabs") in 1937.

No major changes occurred in the administrative division of the Berazi villages in the Kobanî region under the French Mandate. The Mandate adopted the same basic divisions in effect under the Ottomans and passed them on to the republican period. When the region was partitioned between Turkey and Syria, catastrophic consequences resulted from the division of the Berazis' lands and the dispersion of the tribe itself on both sides of the border, depriving it of access to cities

---

14 Evliya Çelebi Mehmed Zılli ibn-i Derviş, *Evliya Çelebi Seyahetnamesi* (Istanbul: Darüssaadet, 1314/1898), 3:148.
15 BOA: Sadâret Mektubî Kalemi Meclis-i Vâlâ [A.MKT.MVL] 106/4683; A.MKT.MVL 99/90.
16 BOA: Sadaret Mektubi Kalemi Umum Vilayat [A.MKT.UM] 142/69.
17 Salname-i Vilayet-i Haleb (1285 h.), 194; Salname-i Vilayet-i Haleb (1284 h.), 153.

212   Muhsin Seyda

and commercial markets and leaving the Syrian Kurdish villages permanently occupying a non-urbanized space.

The Berazi Rebellion in the Tanzimat Era

The modern administrative reforms known as the Tanzimat had a direct impact on the rural communities of the Jazira region, including the Berazis. Among the institutions that had played a mediating role between the state authority and society in Suruj were the benefices (sing. *mukataa*) granted to the tribe in return for military and tax collecting services.[18] Ottoman documents from different periods inform us of the nature of the relationship between the Berazis and the Ottoman Empire; as with most tribes, this relationship did not fit a constant pattern but was often marked by changes of allegiance. Some documents report the participation of Berazi horsemen alongside regular Ottoman forces in the suppression of rebellions and the restoration of order in troubled areas. For example, a Mühimme decree from 1568 mentions that Berazi, Rashidi, Dunbuli, and Dedeli irregulars from Suruj joined in an Ottoman campaign against rebels in the swamplands of southern Iraq (the Jaza'ir/Cezair); the document in fact states that these troops were complaining of having been extorted by the ruler of Birecik.[19] Another order dated 1799 concerns the state's demand that the Berazi and Döger tribes of Raqqa province provide five hundred horsemen to send to Gaza, Ramla, and Egypt; due to its "very miserable" situation, however, the Berazis declared themselves incapable of equipping and sending the requested forces.[20]

The Suruj Plain and its surroundings began to witness a movement of tribal protests following the attempts of Sultan Mahmud II to abolish local entities and impose direct control over the provinces. An Ottoman order from 1831 reports that Ayyub Pasha al-Milli led a protest with the backing of "bandits" from the Berazi and Milli tribes, as well as the people of Urfa and Birecik, pushing the *mütesellim* (deputy governor) of Birecik, Lutfullah Ağa, to entrench himself in the castle. When news reached the *vali*s of Raqqa and Aleppo, they sent soldiers and artillery to relieve the *mütesellim*.[21] This uprising, according to the document, threatened the "Baghdad mission" that aimed to put an end to Mamluk

---

18 The different types or sizes of benefices given to urban and military leaders in Suruj (*zeamet; timar; hass*) are mentioned by Evliya Çelebi; see *Seyahetnamesi*, 3:148.

19 BOA: Mühimme Defteri [MD] 7:1359.

20 BOA: Cevdet Askeriye [C.AS] 312/12898.

21 BOA: Hatt-ı Hümayun [HAT] 20707/389.

rule over Iraq and restore it to Ottoman rule. The changes initiated by Sultan Mahmud II in the ruling structures of the Empire and his desire to extend direct control over the provinces progressively undermined the local order of Ottoman civil society. The Tanzimat beginning in 1839 confronted these communities with new laws and practices that stood in contradiction with their inherited traditions and the privileges granted to them in previous eras, while the concept of reform was reduced in the minds of many local actors to compulsory military service and taxes.[22]

The people of the region also bore the burden of the battle of Nizib between the Egyptian forces of Ibrahim Pasha and the Ottomans in 1839, which was fought near Berazi lands in Suruj and Birecik and which ended in defeat for the Ottomans. Ayyub Bey al-Milli, the *iskan başı* ("head of sedentarization") in Urfa, had originally welcomed the entry of the Egyptian forces to Aleppo, expressed his willingness to serve them, and attacked the region of Diyarbakir to subject it to Egyptian rule.[23] He rebelled against the Egyptians and helped the Ottomans regain control over the east of the Euphrates in 1834, but he died that same year and the Millis resumed their cooperation with the Egyptians under their new leader Timur (Timo) Milli, who was able to regain power over the tribe thanks to the Egyptians' victories in Syria. The information available on the Berazis in this period is insufficient to give a clear picture of their position regarding Egyptian rule over Urfa. It appears that they lacked a strong leader capable of uniting the whole tribe under his command, like the Milli chief Timo Pasha who built a veritable "tribal empire" in the northern Jazira, which threatened the provinces of Aleppo and Diyarbekir.[24] The power and hegemony of the Millis over the region ultimately made the Berazis subject to their influence. Some Ottoman documents refer to cooperation between the Berazis and the Millis, as in the previously mentioned rebellion in Birecik in 1831.

---

22 Odile Moreau, *L'Empire ottoman à l'âge des réformes : Les hommes et les idées du « Nouvel Ordre » militaire, 1826–1914* (Paris: Maisonneuve & Larose, 2007), 21–8.

23 'Imad 'Abd al-Salam Ra'uf, *Dirasat Watha'iqiyya fi Ta'rikh al-Kurd al-Hadith wa-Hadaritihim* (Damascus: Dar al-Zaman, 2012), 534. This book also contains the text of Muhamamd 'Ali 'Awni's "Taymuri treatise" that deals with the biography of the al-Taymuriyya family in Egypt and its descent from Milli Timur, leader of the Milli tribe.

24 Stephen Longrigg, *Four Centuries of Modern Iraq* (Oxford: Oxford University Press, 1925), 286; Stefan Winter, "The Other *Nahdah*: The Bedirxans, the Millis, and the Tribal Roots of Kurdish Nationalism in Syria," *Oriente Moderno* 86, no. 3 (August 2006): 469–70, https://doi.org/10.1163/22138617-08603003.

214   Muhsin Seyda

After the retreat of the Egyptian forces from Syria in 1840, the region witnessed a turbulent transitional phase. The influence of the Milli tribe declined in the Jazira, in addition to the mismanagement of the governors and the weakness of the Ottoman state in the periphery. In this turbulent atmosphere, the Berazi rebellion arose as a protest against the payment of taxes and forced conscription. The uprising was led by the brothers Hemê (Kurdish abbreviated familiar for Mihemed/Muhammad) and Kar'o, sons of Musko (for Musik; Musa), the *kethüda* of the Kitkan clan of the Berazis,[25] a position in which he was called upon to mediate between the tribe and the state in managing its affairs and collecting taxes. (The descendants of Kar'o still live in Omarak village, approximately forty km southeast of Kobanî). It is very difficult, in light of the available documents, to know the exact date of the Berazi rebellion. A petition sent by Mehmed Namık Paşa, the commander of the Arabistan expeditionary force, to the leadership of the imperial army in 1845 provides some details as to why the governor of Aleppo launched a military campaign against the Berazis and mentions the uprising of the Kar'o clan. According to the petition,

> [the tribe] has long failed to pay its financial dues and refuses to implement all noble orders in this regard, and it continues to this day to cut the roads for travellers and loot their money and belongings, just as they are used to killing souls and taking lives unjustly, in addition to the rogue bandits in the region who take refuge with him [the chief of tribe], who finds no shame in protecting them, and with the sword also hinders anyone who leans towards the state, as the members of his clan fear his tyranny, so that he uses them as he wishes. Therefore, the exalted authorities have sought to this day to seize and subdue him, and the regime of As'ad Paşa and Vecihi Paşa moved to collect costs and arrest him, thus As'ad Paşa himself led a force of regular and irregular soldiers equipped with sufficient numbers of cannons and ammunition, but without any result.[26]

With this information, it is possible to date the rebellion more precisely and to understand some of the reasons behind it. As'ad Paşa, who is mentioned in the report, took over the *eyalet* of Aleppo after the withdrawal of the Egyptian forces in 1840 and continued to rule it until 1842; he was succeeded by Vecihi (Wajihi) Paşa, who was dismissed in

---

25 Muhammad 'Ali Ahmad, "Al-Baraziyya fi Watha 'iq al-Arshif al-'Uthmani," *Medarat Kurd*, 13 May 2013, https://www.medaratkurd.com/2013/05/13/329/.

26 BOA: İrade Meclis-i Vala [İ.MVL] 66/1261.

The Berazi Tribe of Suruj and Their Rebellion in the Tanzimat Period   215

February 1845.[27] It is only in the reign of Osman Paşa, who took over in May 1845, that the Berazi rebellion ended.

Most of the Kurds of the Jazira under Ottoman rule lived, according to the expression of an older generation, in "their own Kurdish world" or "in pure Kurdishness," that is, without any direct interference of the state in their affairs.[28] However, Ottoman modernity undermined their "Kurdish world" with the two worst measures, compulsory military service and taxation. These were the measures that were at the root of almost every Kurdish revolt and rebellion in both the Ottoman and the republican eras.

In 1838 Sultan Mahmud II established the Ministry of Finance (*Maliye Nezareti*), which aimed to unify the process of tax collection in the provinces so as to increase the central state's hold over the periphery.[29] The petition submitted by Mehmed Namık Paşa to the leadership of the imperial army clearly stated the reason for the governor of Aleppo's campaign against the Berazis, namely to force them to acquit their financial dues. The Berazi tribe suffered under the bad administration of the governors, the oppression of its tribal chiefs, and the tax increases regularly imposed by the central government, and this situation worsened further in years of drought and epidemics because of the population's dependence on agriculture and livestock. The reforms that were supposed to protect the people from the oppression of officials and feudal leaders did not reach the eastern provinces and were barely registered by the local population.[30] In 1862, more than two decades after the declaration of the Tanzimat, the Russian traveller Takhtarov visited the Berazis' stronghold on the Suruj Plain and noted how the tribe was subject to extortion by state officials and tribal leaders, even though it paid all its dues and tithes from its grain production to the state.[31] If this was the situation during the Tanzimat, how must it have been before?

---

27 Na'um Bakhkhash, *Akhbar Halab kama Katabaha Na'um Bakhkhash fi Dafatir al-Jama'iyya: Al-Daftar al-Thani 1840-1846*, ed. Yusuf Qushaqji (Aleppo: Matba'at al-Ihsan, 1985), 153, 214, 288.

28 Interviews with local intellectuals Dr. Mustafa Mahmadu (b. 1950), French teacher Mustafa Bakr (b. 1951), and Dr. Khalil 'Abdi (b. 1940). The expressions "al-dunya al-Kurmanjiyya" or "al-kurmanjiyya al-nasi'a" refer especially to the transitional period between the end of the Ottomans and the early republican period when the local population lived free from any state authority.

29 Ekmeleddin Ihsanoğlu, *The Ottoman State: History and Civilization*, trans. Saleh Sa'dawi (Istanbul: IRCICA, 1999), 1:324.

30 Ankah Lahard [Édouard Engelhardt (d. 1916)], *Tarikh al-Islahat wa'l-Tanzimat fi al-Dawla al-'Uthmaniyya* [La Turquie et les Tanzimat, ou Histoire des réformes], Ottoman trans. Ali Raşid; Arabic trans. Mahmud 'Ali 'Amir (Damascus: Dar al-Zaman, 2008), 301.

31 B.M. Danzigh, *Al-Rahhala al-Rus fi al-Sharq al-Awsat*, trans. Mar'uf Khaznadar (Damascus: Dar al-Mada, 2008), 358.

216 Muhsin Seyda

The conditions under which the population was living made them ready to participate in any rebellion against the state. In 1839 the inhabitants of the region witnessed the defeat of the Ottomans at the hands of the Egyptians at Nizib, discrediting the Ottomans in their eyes and encouraging them to confront the state's armies. The state's constant portrayal of dissenters as "bandits" (*eşkıya*) was in line with its rhetoric of seeing any kind of uprising as sedition, of which there are numerous illustrations in Ottoman literature. The harsh economic situation did push members of Kurdish and Arab tribes to practice highway robbery in order to survive, and all rebellions in the Ottoman period were joined by bandits and other marginalized people. The author of the *Dawhat al-Wuzara* writes that the Milli chief Timur in 1791 "snapped the stick of obedience and started cutting roads and looting caravans."[32] Interestingly, Mehmed Namık Paşa's depiction of brigands joining the Berazi revolt and being shamefully protected by its leader whose brutality is feared by the tribe coincides in large measure with the story of the Kurdish historian and author Mela Mehmûdê Bazîdî about the brothers "Ahmi" and "Kalhi" (corresponding to the above-mentioned Hemê and Kar'o) and their fight against the Ottoman Empire. In other words, what Bazîdî wrote on the basis of popular local accounts is not very different from the official version, especially as regards the beginning of the rebellion and its development. After praising the two brothers' courage and honour, Bazîdî writes that "people came to take shelter with them and seek their protection from neighbouring areas, the number of families seeking refuge reaching nearly a hundred." The old *agha*s of the Berazi tribe began to harbour hatred for the two brothers and waited for an opportunity to attack them, but their attempts failed.[33]

Bazîdî tells the story of the two brothers as heroes defending the identity of the tribe, thus presenting a somewhat different picture than that given by the commander of the Arabistan army in his petition. Significantly, Bazîdî also praises the reforms of Sultan Abdülmecid, which in his words "put an end to the injustices of the Kurdish *agha*s against

---

32 Rasul al-Kirkukli (d. 1826/27), *Dawhat al-Wuzara' fi Ta'rikh Baghdad al-Zawra'*, trans. Musa Kazim Nawras (Beirut: Dar al-Katib al-'Arabi, 1963), 194.

33 Mela Mehmûdê Bazîdî, *Cami'eya Risaleyan û Hikayetan bi Zimanê Kurmancî*, ed. Zîya Avcı (Diyarbakır: Lîs, 2010), 87. Originally published by the Russian consul in Erzurum Alexandre Jaba, *Recueil de notices et récits kourdes, servant à la connaissance de la langue, de la littérature et des tribus du Kourdistan* (St. Petersburg: Académie Impériale des Sciences, 1860), 75–7, 87–9.

The Berazi Tribe of Suruj and Their Rebellion in the Tanzimat Period   217

the people and weakened their influence."[34] What is important to him is the social dimension of the rebellion: in his narrative the conflict is between the state, together with Arab and Kurdish tribes including the Berazis, against a protest movement of local residents who did not belong to a particular tribe. While Mehmed Namık's report focuses on the Berazis' insurrection against the authorities, it is understood that Kar'o "went to the leaders of the Berazi and Kitkanlo tribes to complain about the military conscription and abuse, saying they should stand united in the face of the imperial army and continuing to stir up the tribe daily."[35]

Popular stories from Kobanî speak of a Berazi tribal council that was held in a local village to discuss fighting the state army. What stands out in these narratives is that those who participated in the council were supposedly the warriors of the Berazi tribe and not its chiefs or *aghas*. Similarly, a Kurdish folk tale still celebrates the tribe members who attended the council as heroes of the rebellion.[36]

Aside from economic factors and state mismanagement, a principal cause of the Berazi rebellion was the compulsory conscription law that was promulgated by Sultan Abdülmecid in September 1843 and that gave rise to numerous protest movements in the region. According to the law, actual military service was limited to five years, with another nine years of duty in the reserves. Selection for service was determined by the drawing of lots (*kura*). The reforms also included new regulations dividing Ottoman territory into five military regions or armies, with a marshal (*müşir*) appointed to head each region.[37] The Suruj area, which was part of the district (*kaymakamiye*) of Urfa in the province of Aleppo, was included in the "Arabistan Army" that would ultimately be charged with suppressing the Berazi rebellion.

Another document regarding the rebellion is the response from the imperial army general Reza Paşa to a petition by the Field Marshal of the Arabistan Army requesting an award for a *kul ağası* (janissary corporal) who had been wounded fighting the Berazis and 'Anazas.

---

34 Mela Mehmûdê Bazîdî, *Adat û Rusumatnameyê Ekradiye*, trans. Jan Dost (Istanbul: Nûbihar, 2010), 99.
35 İ.MVL 66/1261.
36 "Delale Akitan," as popularized by Muhammad Mamed Kashu.
37 İhsanoğlu, *The Ottoman State*, 1:410; Erik Zürcher, "The Ottoman Conscription System in Theory and Practice, 1844–1918," in *The Young Turk Legacy and Nation Building: From the Ottoman Empire to Atatürk's Turkey*, ed. Erik J. Zürcher (London: I.B. Tauris, 2010), 156–60.

218 Muhsin Seyda

Although the order is primarily concerned with the award, it evokes the Berazis' refusal to submit to conscription:

> While carrying out measures to secure the required number of recruits from the Berazi tribe which lives in the *eyalet* of Urfa for the ... honourable Paşa and Marshal of the sultanic Arabistan Army, the tribe made excuses and violated the orders, which induced the army to launch a military campaign, take individuals by force, and seize the tribe's properties.

Resorting to military force, the state left a company of regular (*Nizamiye*) soldiers equipped with a cannon as well as a troop of irregular soldiers to "bring the Baraziyya back to the house of obedience." Accordingly, the tribe had to surrender before the might of the Arabistan Army and its chiefs sued for "safety and security and forgiveness for what they had committed."[38]

The leader of the revolt, Kar'o bin Musk, refused to surrender and urged the tribe not to either, but failed. He was forced to seek refuge together with about fifty families with the 'Anaza Arabs "who live on the other side of the Euphrates," but the 'Anazas "refused his request and turned him away, fearing military force would be directed against them if they received him." Kar'o and his brother Hemê therefore chose to confront the army rather than surrender. In the morning hours of 5 May 1845, an unequal battle took place between Kar'o and his partisans and the *kaymakam* of Urfa, which resulted in his capture and the killing of Hemê.[39]

Syria's first experience of forced conscription had occurred with the entry of the Egyptian forces under Ibrahim Paşa in 1831. Contemporary historians described at length the calamities and suffering faced by the population on account of these measures.[40] This and other reforms provoked the resentment of all groups, sects, and communities in the region, with most people wishing for a restoration of "Turkish" (Ottoman) rule instead of the Egyptians. Mikha'il Mishaqa, a leading historian of the period, asserted that the tradition of the people in the Levant was based on obedience to their immediate superiors and not to the government, linking their resistance to conscription and to the Egyptian reforms in general to their low state of awareness.[41]

---

38 HAT 1642/21.
39 İ.MVL 66/1261.
40 Anon., *Mudhakkarat Tarikhiyya 'an Hamlat Ibrahim Basha 'ala Suriya*, ed. Ahmad Ghassan Sabanu (Damascus: Dar Qutayba Publishing House, 2007), 73.
41 Mikha'il Mishaqa, *Mashhad al-'Iyan bi-Hawadith Suriya wa-Lubnan* (Cairo: N.p., 1908), 115, 131; Stefan Winter, "La révolte alaouite de 1834 contre l'occupation

The Ottoman Empire faced much the same difficulties as the Egyptians in trying to implement the conscription law in Syria, where modernizing reforms clashed with the social and economic structures of civil society. In rural areas in particular, force often had to be used to carry through recruitment.[42] Bazîdî mentions in this context how soldiers fled from the army lottery in Urfa and joined the rebellion. Moreover, among the Kurdish folk songs singing the praises of Karʿo and Hemê, there is one that illustrates the conflict between the Berazis and the state in the form of an imagined dialogue between an official seeking to integrate the periphery through the modernity represented by compulsory military service and tax collection, and the defenders of custom, tradition, and tribal values:

[State official:]
Come on, Hemê, draw your lottery slip
And pay what you're asked of the annual dues.
Follow one of the *agha*s
And don't go against the orders of the state; for violating the orders
    of the state is a heavy burden, like carrying salt or lead.
So give the state a few young men from the Kitkan and the Beraziyya.
[Hemê:]
I will not go back on my word
I will not let the Kitkan and Beraziyya go to the border
I won't let them carry spoons and go to pots [like enrolled soldiers]
As long as I'm alive, I will not have them wear tight military uniforms.
And I will not go to the lottery, I will not pay taxes, and I will not make
    myself a follower of the *agha*s
And I won't take the hands of Kitkan and Berazi boys to send them
    to the army.[43]

Hemê's rejection of tight military clothing recalls the position of the Arab Shammar tribe towards their sheikh Farhan Safuk, who encouraged them to take up farming on the banks of the Tigris River. Such work was contrary to the morals and nature of the Bedouin, which led half the tribe to separate from him. Irrespective of the differences between them and the Berazis, whom Tahrir records show to have been

---

égyptienne," *Oriente Moderno* 79, no. 3 (August 1999): 70, https://doi.org/10.1163/22138617-07903006.

42 Moreau, *L'empire ottoman*, [35].

43 Sefoyê Asê, "Hemê Mûsê (Hemê Gozê)," *Bîrnebûn* 15 (2002): 35.

220 Muhsin Seyda

engaged in agriculture and paying taxes on wheat and barley since the sixteenth century, both tribes rebelled against the fact of direct state control over their areas and defended an identity they saw threatened by the Tanzimat. Ottoman documents do not indicate that Kar'o and Hemê were fleeing from conscription or had been implicated in the army lottery. Their rebellion, as indicated in the documentation, seems indeed to have occurred prior to the conscription law of 1843.

After the death of Hemê and the arrest of Kar'o, the commander of the Arabistan Army wrote to the high command, urging it to apply the death penalty to Kar'o, as the penalty of hard labour or imprisonment in Istanbul would not deter him because he would be released after his sentence:

> It is certain that afterwards he will return as he began to tyranny and cor-
> ruption ... We embrace the position of the army leadership, knowing that
> nothing can be envisaged against this traitor except death and execution,
> and his execution under law depends on the will and order of the sultan.
> Seeing as this will be the end of the oppression and contumacy which this
> tribe has occasionally practiced, the people of this tribe will thereby enter
> into the realm of obedience just like all the other *kaza*s and *nahiye*s. It will
> thus become possible to implement at all times the sultanic order and will,
> from both the military and administrative standpoint, and to cleanse the
> people of this tribe from the machinations of the tyrants.

The Supreme Judicial Council (Meclis-i Vala) reviewed the Marshal's letter containing the charges against Kar'o over his leadership in the rebellion, and a copy was forwarded to the *fetvahane* (office of the mufti) to enquire about the legal requirements entailed by his actions. A *fetva* permitting his execution was delivered, and on 3 July 1845 the Supreme Judicial Council asked the sultan to issue a ferman to send him to the Army Command for execution.[44]

Conclusion

This contribution cannot claim to have covered all aspects of the Berazi rebellion, which falls under the framework of local history and which provides an illustration of the state's attempts to integrate the tribes of the periphery through modernizing reforms; what we have instead aspired to do is to situate this event in its historical context, far from current political considerations.

---

44 İ.MVL 66/1261.

The rebellion of the Berazi Kurds of the Suruj Plain in 1845 was a clear expression of Kurdish opposition to the policies of Ottoman state centralization. However, this revolt remained on the level of simple protest and did not transform into a movement of demand, as happened in other regions of the Empire. The Tanzimat period bore witness to several Kurdish revolutions led by emirs who had lost their hereditary principalities. The disappearance of the Kurdish emirates through modern state centralization was only a matter of time, as they quickly submitted to the Ottomans, but this did not mean the disappearance of the tribal system as such, which remained relatively coherent. The Hamidian regime would ultimately benefit from the fighting capacities of the local tribes. Despite the important differences between the revolts led by Kurdish princes and the tribal rebellions in the Tanzimat period, the two had in common the rejection of direct state control. One may therefore ask, in conclusion, two questions: if the state had proceeded to open schools and build public infrastructures, rather than impose conscription, as a first step towards instituting the reforms, would this have engendered opposition as well? And if we imagine, for the sake of argument, that the Kurdish leader Bedirxan Bey had imposed conscription on the tribes of his emirate, would they have obeyed his orders?[45]

Appendix

Text of folk song with imagined conversation between Hemê and the state official, from Sefoyê Asê, "Hemê Mûsê (Hemê Gozê)," *Bîrnebûn* 15 (2002): 35. Arabic translation by author.

Nifûsçî:
Hemo, were ser qurêo,
Bikşêne çîtikêo
Bide baş gumrikê salan û salêo
Xwe bike taba axa û axelerên di dinêo
Li xwe nerake fermaneke dewletêo,
Heçî barê hukumatê himlê risês e, barî xweo
Du xortikê Gêtîk û Berêz bide eskerîyêo

---

45 Translated from the Arabic by S.W. and Z.H. The author wishes to express his gratitude to Muhammad ʿAli Ahmad, Mustafa Mahmud, ʿAbdullah Dummar, and Ghiyath Husayn for answering his many questions about the Ottoman Turkish language and issues related to the Ottoman archives.

Hemê:
Ez çi bikim, mi xebera xwe gotîye
Ez nahêlim xortê Gêtîk û Berêz herne ser sînora
Rahêlne kevçîyê xwe, herne ser qerwana
Heta ez sax bim ez nahêlim destê xwe hilkêşînin di cilê nîzama teng e.

موظف الدولة :
هيّا يا حمي اسحب قصاصة القرعة
وادفع ما يترتب عليك من مستحقات سنوية
واتبع أحد الآغاوات
ولا تخالف أوامر الدولة، فمخالفة أوامر الدولة حمل ثقيل كحمل الملح والرصاص
فامنح الدولة بضع شبانٍ من شبان الكيتكان والبرازية.
حمي :
لن أتراجع عن كلامي
لن أدع شبان الكيتكان والبرازية يتوجهون إلى الحدود
لن أجعلهم يحملون المعالق ويذهبون إلى القدور
ما دمت حياً لن أجعلهم يرتدون اللباس العسكري الضيق.
ولن أذهب إلى القرعة ولن أدفع الضرائب ولن أجعل من نفسي تبعاً للأغوات
ولن أمسك بيد شبان الكيتكان والبرازية لإرسالهم إلى الجندية.

10 The Reşwan in Central Anatolia: Tribal Settlement and Sheep Trade in the Nineteenth Century

YONCA KÖKSAL

Tribes and the Ottoman state have a long history of coexistence, and they developed various forms of interaction over time. In the foundation period of the Ottoman Empire, tribes were both partners of the state for territorial expansion and an economic asset especially in terms of their livestock production. In time, they emerged as challengers to the state authority in the contested areas of taxation, security, and conscription. The complicated relations that developed through attempts of state control and tribal responses is well represented in the case of the Reşwan. Notable members of the Reşwan tribe became local governors and helped Ottomans to establish their authority in southern and eastern Anatolia in the seventeenth and eighteenth centuries. Through their animal trade, the Reşwans were also economically important for supplying meat to Istanbul. However, they became a source of tension when tribal groups threatened security through banditry and when they failed to pay their taxes especially in the nineteenth century. This chapter addresses the period of Reşwan settlement starting in the 1830s and analyses the effects of this settlement on the administration and economy of the tribe until the late nineteenth century. The Reşwan lived in a broad geographical area ranging from northern Syria to Ankara. Studies on the Reşwans mainly focus on tribal units in northern Syria and often overlook the history of their settlement in central Anatolia. This paper will therefore focus on the lesser-studied Reşwan settlement in central Anatolia, in particular in the provinces of Ankara, Konya, and Sivas.

Although the Reşwans were one of the most visible tribal confederations in archival documents, there are few studies on them. Their ethnic origins, social structures, and even the meaning of their name have been debated. While the majority agrees that the Reşwans were Kurdish,

224 Yonca Köksal

some studies argue that they were Turkomans.[1] The Reşwans were a confederation of different tribal groups and subunits (*cemaat*), and it is possible that in time there was an assimilation of various Turkoman and even Arabic groups to the Kurdish majority in the Reşwan confederation. Hence, scholars have argued for different meanings for their name, Reşwan meaning 'black' in Kurdish, or deriving from a family name of a probable founder of the tribe.[2]

The earliest records about the Reşwan show that they lived in the Urfa region in the sixteenth century and were possibly part of the Kara-Ulus (Black nation), a confederation of Kurdish tribes affiliated with the Akkoyunlu dynasty in eastern Anatolia. In the seventeenth and eighteenth centuries, they mostly lived around Urfa, Malatya, Hısnımansur, and Kahta (Adıyaman) in eastern Anatolia. The Reşwans were a seminomadic tribe, moving between winter and summer pastures. They were mobile in a large area from Aleppo and Raqqa in northern Syria to Konya, Ankara, and Yozgat in central Anatolia. They were part of the *hass* of the reigning Valide Sultan in the seventeenth century. The Reşwans seemed to have gradually moved from southeast to central Anatolia in the eighteenth and nineteenth centuries. Although there were still many archival documents regarding their presence in Adıyaman, Maraş, and Raqqa, they became visible in central Anatolia in archival documents of the nineteenth century. Smaller groups were also reported in broader regions such as Trabzon, Erzurum, and in the Balkans.[3] Since this paper focuses on the settlement of the Reşwans in the nineteenth century, it does not analyse the Reşwan units in southeastern Anatolia and northern Syria, which are well covered in the literature. The Reşwan in central Anatolia were confronted with more rigid sedentarization policies than the Reşwans in the southeast, and therefore they present an opportunity to analyse the processes and outcomes of sedentarization.

---

1 Faruk Söylemez argues that the Reşwan (Rişvan) were a Turkoman tribe that came from Khorassan to southeast Anatolia. See Faruk Söylemez, *Osmanlı Devletinde Aşiret Yönetimi: Rişvan Aşireti Örneği* (Istanbul: Kitabevi, 2007), 6.
2 Stefan Winter, "The Reşwan Kurds and Ottoman Tribal Settlement in Syria, 1683–1741," *Oriente Moderno* 97, no. 2 (October 2017): 256–69, https://doi.org/10.1163/22138617-12340151, and Söylemez, *Osmanlı Devletinde Aşiret Yönetimi*, 12, respectively.
3 Some Reşwan subunits (*cemaat*) such as Hamidli and Hacılar were reported to move to Edirne and Varna. See Söylemez, *Osmanlı Devletinde Aşiret*, 28–30. The Rumiyans, one of the Reşwan subunits, went as far as Erzurum. See Seyid Vakkas Toprak, *1835 Tarihli Nüfus Sayımına Göre XIX. Yüzyılın İlk Yarısında Hısnımansur (Adıyaman)* (Adıyaman Üniversitesi Yayınları, 2018), 156. See also Mark Sykes, "The Kurdish Tribes of the Ottoman Empire," *The Journal of the Royal Anthropological Institute of Great Britain and Ireland* 38 (July–December 1908): 477, https://doi.org/10.2307/2843309.

The Reşwan in Central Anatolia   225

This expansion towards the west can be linked to two reasons: an increase in the Reşwan population and the need to find pastures for their animals. With an increase in their population, the tribal members probably searched for new lands in an environment of scarce resources. There is only partial information about the population size of the Reşwan. Since they were mobile and were usually counted within their tribal subunits (*cemaat*), population figures only provide information on their presence in a certain locality at the time of counting in the sixteenth century censuses (*tahrir*). The figures were given for local *cemaat*s, not for the whole Reşwan tribe. Faruk Söylemez reports 15,400 Reşwans for the provinces of Ankara and Konya in 1880.[4] In 1540, the Kahta and Hısn-ı Mansur region, areas with the highest Reşwan concentration in southeastern Anatolia, had an estimated population of 6,773, while there is no information about the existence of Reşwan in central Anatolia at that time.[5] These numbers do not reflect the total population of the tribe, but they show the population increase and change in different geographical areas.

The Reşwan economy was dependant on animal husbandry, mostly sheep and some goats. They not only produced milk, meat, wool, and leather, but also traded live animals to local communities and long-distance merchants. In dry summer seasons, the Reşwan like many other nomadic pastoralists took their animals to fertile meadows of high altitude in central Anatolia. The expansive pastures of Uzunyayla, Çiçek Dağı, and Paşa Dağı became attractive destinations for the Reşwans increasingly in the nineteenth century (map 4). This annual visit in summer may have led to longer stays and eventually to a more permanent presence of the Reşwans in central Anatolia.

The next section will focus on the settlement process of the Reşwans in Ankara, Konya, and Sivas provinces in the Tanzimat era. It will discuss how and why the Ottoman state pursued a settlement policy, and the impact of this settlement on the Reşwan's administrative and social structures as well as its economy.

The Tanzimat Policy of Tribal Settlement

Although there were repeated attempts to settle tribes from the fifteenth to the seventeenth centuries, there was no permanent state policy of sedentarization until the nineteenth. These earlier attempts were made to

---

4 Söylemez, *Osmanlı Devletinde Aşiret*, 50.
5 Söylemez, *Osmanlı Devletinde Aşiret*, 37–45. Söylemez estimates that the Dalyanlı subunit of the Reşwan had a population of 10,000 in the Maraş, Antep, and Besni regions of of eastern Anatolia in the early nineteenth century (47).

226   Yonca Köksal

populate newly conquered territories, mainly in the Balkans, to prevent unrest, maintain security, and to enliven trade and economy. According to Cengiz Orhonlu, the first large-scale attempt at tribal settlement (*iskan*) was in 1690. Tribes that caused security problems in Anatolia were settled both in Anatolia and northern Syria. The Reşwan tribe was one of the tribes that were sent to Raqqa for settlement because some members of the tribe were reported to engage in robbery and banditry and disturbed locals. However, they deserted this settlement shortly and went back to the Maraş-Adıyaman region.[6] Throughout the eighteenth century, there was a series of reports sending Reşwan members who attacked and robbed caravans and stole animals and property to exile in northern Syria.[7] The Reşwan were not always considered disruptions to security, but sometimes also acted as providers of security. Leading members of the tribe received state appointments and became responsible for settling other tribes and providing security in the Maraş-Malatya-Adıyaman region. Members of the "Rişvanzade" (*zade* meaning 'son') family became district governors of Adana and provincial governor (*vali*) of Malatya in the seventeenth and eighteenth centuries.[8]

The Tanzimat sedentarization policy differed from these earlier settlement attempts in that it was a permanent policy. Rather than merely responding to local complaints and forcing tribal units causing problems for the state to settle, throughout the Tanzimat era there was a constant policy of settling semi-nomadic tribes whether they caused security concerns or not. Thus, settlement policy was applied in a wide region from Bosnia to Anatolia and to Transjordan.[9] The centralizing and reforming Tanzimat state needed tax revenue to finance its reform projects and conscript soldiers for the newly expanding army. When tribes settled and engaged in agricultural production, Ottoman statesmen hoped, they would pay more taxes and provide soldiers. In

---

6 Cengiz Orhonlu, *Osmanlı İmparatorluğunda Aşiret İskanı* (Istanbul: Eren Yayınları, 1987), 57–65.

7 In 1766, there were 12,000 Reşwan tents in the Aleppo region in winter. They went to Sivas in summer. See Yusuf Halaçoğlu, *18. Yüzyılda Osmanlı İmparatorluğunun İskan Siyaseti ve Aşiretlerin Yerleştirilmesi* (Ankara: Türk Tarih Kurumu), 112.

8 Jülide Akyüz, "Osmanlı Merkez-Taşra İlişkisinde Yerel Hanedanlara Bir Örnek: Rişvanzâdeler," *Kebikeç* 27 (2009): 79–97.

9 See Ahmed Cevdet Paşa, *Maruzat* (Istanbul: Çağrı Yayınları, 1980) for Bosnia; Martin Van Bruinessen, *Agha, Shaikh, and State* (London: Zed Books, 1992), 133–202 for patterns of state-tribe interaction before and during the Tanzimat in Kurdistan; and Eugene Rogan, *Frontiers of the State in the Late Ottoman Empire: Transjordan, 1850–1921* (New York: Cambridge University Press, 1999) for Transjordan.

The Reşwan in Central Anatolia   227

addition, eliminating robbery and banditry would increase security in the countryside and encourage trade and agriculture.

In addition to the advantages of tribal settlement for the Ottoman state, there were some disadvantages both for tribes and the authorities. Most of these tribes including the Reşwan were dependant on a form of pastoralism and bred livestock. Some of these tribes played an important role in providing the meat supply of the imperial capital, Istanbul. The Cihanbeyli confederation and seven smaller tribes under its aegis (*aşayir-i seba*) in the province of Ankara were major suppliers of meat in central Anatolia. When the meat supply of Rumelia shrank significantly in the nineteenth century as a result of territorial losses, Anatolian livestock became crucial for the meat supply of Istanbul. The Sultan provided a warrant (*berat*) and required the Cihanbeylis to send a certain number of sheep to Istanbul every year. The number of sheep the Cihanbeylis sent increased from 80,000 in 1819 to 120,000 in the 1840s.[10]

The Reşwans were not part of these seven tribes but lived in the same area as the Cihanbeyli confederation. While the Cihanbeylis were forced to provide a certain number of sheep every year and punished when they failed to do that, the Reşwan sheep merchants freely traded both within the province and with other cities and Istanbul. Throughout the nineteenth century, Reşwan merchants thus brought large flocks of sheep to Istanbul. Their sedentarization would have put pressure on this trade, since limiting their mobility between pastures could influence the number of sheep traded, especially in Istanbul. The decrease in animal supply from the central Anatolian tribes would have led to a considerable increase in meat prices of Istanbul where the market was vulnerable to climate change, famines, and epizootics. Thus, there was a need for some flexibility especially for movement between pastures, and for state subsidies for settlement. The settlement of the Reşwans reflects this tension between the two ends. On the one hand, the Ottoman state encouraged a permanent and large-scale policy of settlement because of financial and security concerns. On the other hand, economic activities such as livestock raising that were based on tribal mobility had to be tolerated and supported in order to provide meat for the region and the capital. The following pages will discuss the

---

10 Yonca Köksal and Mehmet Polatel, "A Tribe as an Economic Actor: The Cihanbeyli Tribe and the Meat Provisioning of İstanbul in the early Tanzimat Era," *New Perspectives on Turkey* 61 (November 2019): 97–123, https://doi.org/10.1017/npt.2019.19.

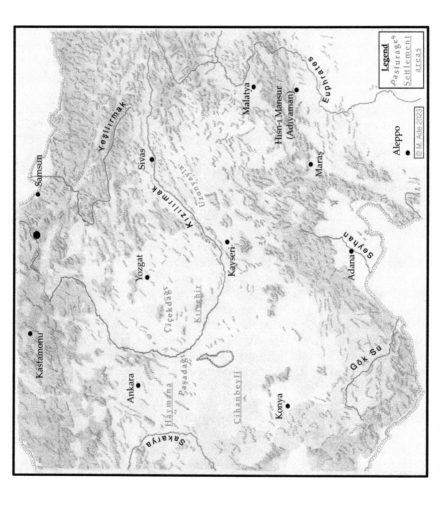

Map 4. Reşwan pasturages and settlement areas in central Anatolia

The Reşwan in Central Anatolia   229

Reşwan settlement by stressing how the Ottoman state struggled with these two conflicting concerns.

Settling the Reşwan

Even before the Gülhane Edict (1839) that started the Tanzimat era, there were discussions about settling the Reşwan tribe. Complaints about tribal members engaging in banditry and resulting clashes with military units in the Konya region led to considering the permanent settlement of the Reşwan. In 1830, the governor of Konya, Esad Muhlis Paşa, suggested settling Reşwan units in the provinces of Ankara and Konya. The Reşwan spent their summers on the Uzunyayla pasture in the east (near Sivas) and went to Paşa Dağı in the southwest (between Ankara and Kırşehir) in the winter (Map 4). The proposal was to capture the Reşwan immediately in their current locations and seize their sheep and properties. To entice tribe members to agricultural production, their cattle (black cattle) could be left to them, and land given for cultivation. The document also notes that this was a very difficult thing to do in the absence of a regular counting of Reşwan units and population. Thus, the settlement had to wait for the census, which was about to start. Meanwhile, the provincial governors should appoint tribal leaders (*beys*) who would be responsible for providing travel permits (*mürur tezkiresi*). Thus, the mobility of the tribe and banditry could be controlled.[11] Some Reşwan households were also to be settled in Sivas in their summer pastures, because seizing them and their animals would be easier during summer.[12] In 1842, the state ordered the settlement of several Kurdish and Turkoman tribes such as the Reşwan and Haremeyns in their winter pastures in Konya. The assignment of large military units, both cavalry and infantry, as well as cannon units, shows the coercive aspect and the state's determination for settlement.[13] As a result, 1,600 Reşwan households were settled around Esbkeşan in Konya. Diffuse Reşwan households were also settled in Haymana in Ankara province.[14]

---

11 Turkish Presidency State Archives of the Republic of Turkey – Department of Ottoman Archives [BOA], Hatt-ı Hümayun [HAT] 446/22289, 7.12.1830. Suat Dede also dates the start of Reşwan settlement to 1830. See Suat Dede, "From Nomadism to Sedentary Life in Central Anatolia: The Case of the Rişvan Tribe (1830–1932)" (master's thesis, Bilkent University, 2011), 47.

12 HAT 446/22289, 7.xii.1830.

13 A cavalry regiment, two infantry battalions, and four cannon corps were sent to the region. BOA: Cevdet Dahiliye [C.DH] 31/1548, 19.vii.1842.

14 Söylemez, *Osmanlı Devletinde Aşiret*, 170.

230 Yonca Köksal

Within a few years, the Reşwan seem to have deserted these settlements and engaged in banditry. They disturbed trade convoys especially when they travelled to their summer pastures. In 1848 and 1849, a second wave of settlement campaign targeted the Reşwan. The state's plan was to settle groups of a few Reşwan households in villages in the provinces of Ankara, Konya, and Sivas. The special target areas for settlement were Esbkeşan, Bozok, Haymana, and Kırşehir. Three thousand households were settled in Bozok, Ankara, and Sivas districts, and five hundred households were settled in Esbkeşan by military units.[15] Dividing tribes into several households and settling them in scattered villages over a wide region was a strategy especially for tribes that did not have well defined tribal chiefs, leaders, or headmen. When there was a well-defined hierarchy with a recognized chief and leaders in the tribe, the Ottomans preferred to negotiate with them and use them for settlement. When a strong tribal chief tended to resist state attempts at settlement, the policy was to strengthen the headmen of smaller units by giving them administrative responsibility, and thus to balance and contain tribal chiefs. This was the method for settling the Cihanbeyli and Yeni-İl tribes in the province of Ankara.[16]

When there was no generally recognized tribal chief, tribes were more likely to be settled through coercion. In the case of the Reşwan and Afşar tribes, the Ottoman state tried to create a centralized authority to negotiate settlement. With the Afşars, a tribal chief was imposed, and settlement negotiated with partial success in central Anatolia. The Reşwans were a geographically scattered confederation composed of various subunits (*cemaat*), located across a wide region ranging from Adıyaman and Raqqa to Ankara and Konya.[17] Ottoman archival documents frequently mention Reşwan notables and discuss giving more responsibility to *bey*s of smaller units, but there does not seem to have

---

15 BOA: Meclis-i Vala [MVL] 32/57 12.iv.1849; BOA: Mabeyn İrade [MB.İ] 2/76, 6.xii.1848.

16 Yonca Köksal, "Coercion and Mediation: Centralization and Sedentarization of Tribes in the Ottoman Empire," *Middle Eastern Studies* 42, no. 3 (May 2006): 469–91, https://doi.org/10.1080/00263200600601171.

17 Söylemez indicates fifteen subunits (*cemaat*) in the sixteenth century: Hacı Ömerlü, Hıdır Sorani, Kellelü, Çelikanlu, Mülukanlı, Mendubali (Mendollu), Zerukanlı, Bograsi, Rumiyan, Mansur, İzdeganlu, Mansurganlu, Karlu, Rişvan, and Çakallu. This number increased to thirty-five as the tribal population grew. Söylemez suggests the new subunits could have formed when previous subunits broke apart. See Faruk Söylemez, "Rişvan Aşireti'nin Cemaat, Şahıs ve Yer Adları Üzerine Bir Değerlendirme," *Sosyal Bilimler Enstitüsü Dergisi* 12 (2002): 39–52.

The Reşwan in Central Anatolia   231

been a single tribal chief. A Mustafa Bey was mentioned as the tribe's governor (*aşiret müdürü*) in a few documents in the 1860s, but there is no information whether he was a member of the tribe or an outsider, an official appointed by the state.[18] It is, however, possible that he was a member since he allied himself with tribal notables and petitioned the state against settlement.[19] In the absence of a permanent tribal chief with well-defined responsibilities, the Reşwan notables tried to mediate between Istanbul and the tribe, travelling to Istanbul to voice their complaints about sedentarization. They also tried to bribe local officials such as the Cihanbeyli chief Alişan Bey, Halim Bey, and the *agha* of Esbkeşan, İbrahim, to change their settlement destinations.[20] These demands were refused by the state: the Sublime Porte gave the order not to indulge the Reşwan notables but to send them back to their province.[21]

The Reşwan settlement combined several state strategies; there was limited use of negotiation with tribal notables especially in the earlier settlement attempts in the 1830s and 1840s. Starting with the second wave of settlement in 1848, there was frequent use of coercion. Military troops were employed; and a colonel from Istanbul, Mustafa Bey, was sent to complete the census (*tahrir*) of the tribe. There was discussion about sending troops from Istanbul, but using provincial troops from Ankara and Konya seemed to be an easier solution in winter conditions.[22] Tribal settlement and census were meant to go hand in hand: when they were settled, household numbers and their property, especially their animals, were counted. Since there were several allegations and also proven cases of robbery and banditry by some Reşwan members, the counted properties were seized to reimburse the plaintiffs. Some of these seized properties were also taken to cover the unpaid taxes of the tribe since the start of their settlement in 1830. A major purpose of the settlement was to increase taxation revenue and military conscription. Therefore, settlements were immediately followed with attempts to collect taxes and levy soldiers. In addition to these coercive and extractive aspects, there were also state incentives to encourage settlement and agricultural production. The Reşwans settled in Ankara were exempt from cereal taxes for the first year of their settlement. This could continue for another year if the yields were low. Additionally, the

---

18 For example, see MVL 699/82, 3.iv.1866.
19 MVL 671/76, 1864.
20 BOA: Sadâret Mektubî Kalemi Meclis-i Vâlâ [A.MKT.MVL] 23/55, 17.i.1850.
21 A.MKT.MVL 26/92, 24.iv.1850.
22 MVL 32/57, 12.iv.1849.

232 Yonca Köksal

distribution of sheep and lands to settled Reşwan households was also offered.[23]

The Reşwans responded to settlement in several different ways. One common reaction was to desert the settlement. Desertion was reported in almost every settlement project in Konya, Ankara, and Sivas. Limitation of their mobility between pastures was a big challenge to the tribal economy, and the Reşwans deserted their settlements for summer pastures in Uzunyayla.[24] Some deserted to escape military conscription and taxation; they went as far as Maraş and Aleppo.[25] Another destination for deserters was Haymana, which was located close (eighteen to twenty hours walking distance) to two popular winter pastures of the tribe, Paşa Dağı and Çiçek Dağı.[26]

The Ottoman state usually explained frequent desertion by the unruly nature of tribes. In the words of archival documents, the Reşwans were far from civilization (*medeniyet*), and their natural tendency was towards nomadism (*bedeviyet*).[27] Civilization was equated with urban living and sedentariness in this discourse, while the mobility of the tribe was linked to its unruly and nomadic nature. In the documents, there are also occasional acknowledgements of wrongdoing by state officials and other tribal chiefs, for instance by over-taxation, bribery, or other vexations, that are given as reasons for desertion.[28]

Aside from this discourse on civilization and maladministration, the desertion of the Reşwans was possibly linked to economic factors. The Reşwans fled to areas that were full of fertile meadows, where they had regular pastures for their flocks. In addition to being close to two important winter pastures, Haymana was home to a developed animal trade and a market for sheep. Availability of pastures and sheep trade must have played an important role for choosing desertion destinations, given that there were tensions between the Reşwans and locals over pastures in their new settlements. The Reşwans complained frequently about the lack of sufficient pastures, land, and irrigation in new settlement areas. There were complaints that the Reşwans had been

---

23 BOA: Sadaret Mektubi Kalemi Nezaret ve Deva'ir [A.MKT.NZD] 35/24, 26.v.1851. Both the Afşar and the Reşwan had this tax exemption. See MVL 240–35, 9.vi.1851.
24 MVL 301/58, 15.ix.1856.
25 BOA: Sadaret Mektubi Kalemi Umum Vilayat [A.MKT.UM] 330/50, 24.x.1858.
26 A.MKT.UM 409/49, 8.vi.1860.
27 "... aşayir-i merkume [Reşvan] dahi usul-i medeniyete refte refte alışmakta ise de malum-ı samileri buyrulduğu vechle bunların medeniyet canibine meyilleri kusri ve bedeviyete meyilleri tabii ve celi olmasıyla ..." MVL 592/49, 25 Kasım 1859.
28 For a case of bribery, see A.MKT.NZD 2/79, 17.i.1850.

The Reşwan in Central Anatolia   233

settled in ruined houses, were asked to pay high taxes, and did not have adequate pastures and lands in Bozok. They therefore requested resettlement to Haymana, which would be better for animal husbandry and agriculture.[29]

While commoners deserted the settlements, tribal leaders and notables tried to negotiate with state authorities. These negotiations sometimes took the extreme form of bribing officials who were responsible for settlement. At the other extreme, some Reşwan notables went to Istanbul to voice their demands. In 1850, three Reşwan *agha*s came to Istanbul and contacted a merchant named Petro who offered his help in their demand for changing the settlement region. The *agha*s had been settled in the province of Ankara, and they asked for approval for their return to Konya. Petro promised to help and took a bond from the notables in the amount of 40,000 guruş. He was to return the bond if he could not resolve the issue. Petro disappeared without providing the *agha*s any help; the bond was transferred to his son, Apostol, in the Bozok district. The *agha*s thereupon asked for and were granted the cancellation of the bond.[30] There were other reports of Reşwan notables (*rüesa*; chiefs) from Bozok and Ankara present in Istanbul. They requested either settlement in a different place or the grant of pastures and lands in their current settlement areas.[31] The Reşwan merchants sold their sheep on the Istanbul market, and therefore made regular trips to Istanbul. The frequent appeals of the Reşwan notables and their easy access to state authorities in Istanbul could be related to the use of these trade networks for the settlement problems. The fact that they bribed Petro, an important merchant (*bazergan*), also supports the possibility of activating trade networks for the Reşwans' demands about settlement.

The 1860s and After

Settlement attempts in the earlier decades were followed by taxation and conscription requests in this period. In 1860–1, the Ottoman state added the standard tribal sheep tax (*adet-i ağnam*) to the tax farming system in Bozok, Ankara, and Konya. Previously, the sheep tax had been collected from the tribe as a distinct unit. With the new regulation, the sheep tax on Reşwan households was included in districts where they were

---

29 MVL 101/66, 24.v.1851.
30 A.MKT.UM 41/60, 5.xii.1850.
31 For an example, see BOA: İrade Meclis-i Vala [İ.MVL] 228/7802, 2.i.1852.

234   Yonca Köksal

settled. The addition of the Reşwans' sheep tax to settlement districts would mean increased revenues for the state and a huge profit for tax farmers, who were mostly non-Muslims. The amount of taxes would have made tax farmers willing to obtain these tax farming rights. The Reşwan were reported for taxation purposes to have 108,000 sheep in Haymana, 100,000 in Çiçek Dağı, and 160,000 in Bozok.[32] In 1861, sheep taxes in the amount of 170,869 *guruş* in Esbkeşan and 550,000 *guruş* in Bozok, Kangırı, and Haymana were left unpaid by the Reşwan.[33] This attempt to integrate Reşwan units into the regular taxation system met with resistance, as seen from this huge amount of unpaid taxes.

Tax farmers were often unable to collect taxes from the tribe that encountered challenges with settlement. Only the Reşwans in Haymana were reported to pay their taxes. Others resisted fiercely. Bozok officials went to Reşwan households twice with the command of the provincial governor but could only collect 4,000 *guruş*. Their correspondence with Istanbul shows that they were tired of fruitless efforts to collect taxes and conscript soldiers from the tribe.[34] In another instance, the Reşwans fired guns at a tax farmer in Çiçek Dağı.[35] Tax collection was also a contentious topic among tax farmers. Since the Reşwan who had been settled in an area tended to desert and move to another locality, collecting their taxes could become a struggle among competing tax farmers. Tax farmers of Konya, Ankara, Bozok, and Sivas appealed to Istanbul and demanded a clear definition of who would collect taxes from the Reşwan units.[36] From 1848 to 1864, the Reşwans' unpaid taxes in the province of Konya amounted to the astronomic figure of 1,046,347 *guruş*.[37]

Security issues continued to bother state officials in this period too. Especially when the tribes moved to their summer pastures, they became a source of discontent for villagers. Groups of thirty to fifty vagabonds from several tribes, including the Reşwan, Afşars, Terkan, and Sarkıntılı, rambled around Niğde while migrating between their winter and summer pastures, stealing property and threatening locals.[38] The Reşwans in Mecidiye were required to send fifty-four conscripts to the Ottoman army, but refused to do so. Military units were sent to complete the conscription.[39]

---

32 A.MKT.MVL 126/7, 24.iii.1861 and A.MKT.UM 453/65, 6.ii.1861.
33 MVL 369/4, 15.v.1861.
34 A.MKT.UM 409/49, 8.vi.1860.
35 MVL 747/132, 1.v.1867.
36 BOA: Sadaret Mektubi Kalemi Mühimme [A.MKT.MHM] 387/28, 12.vii.1867.
37 MVL 705/92, 19.iv.1865.
38 MVL 571/30, 19.v.1858.
39 MVL 720/76, 20.i.866.

The Reşwan in Central Anatolia   235

Despite resistance to taxation and conscription, there was gradual settlement of tribes in the 1860s. The language of the archive documents is quite striking in reporting this process: There were around 2,000 households in the Haymana and Çiçek Dağı plains, and "while some of them have begun to settle and become civilized, most of them remain wild and are still camping in Haymana."[40] The analogy between settlement and civilization and between nomadism and savagery continued to be an important factor in Ottoman state policy towards the Reşwans.

In 1864, the administrative connection between the Reşwans in different regions and the district of Ankara came to an end, when Reşwan households were ordered to become parts of the districts and towns in which they were settled.[41] The Çelikanlı subunit of the Reşwans was settled in the newly established town of İslahiye through the Fırka-ı İslahiye campaign to the Kurd Dagh and Mount Kozan area in 1865.[42] In 1867, Reşwan households were integrated into local administrative units in Ankara, Konya, Yozgat, and Kırşehir.[43] A new residential area was created to complete the Reşwan settlement: Mecidiye was a new town created specifically for Reşwan settlement in Çiçek Dağı in 1849. There were new houses, a school, and a governor's mansion constructed in the town. The former Reşwan director (*müdür*), Mustafa Bey, played a role in the foundation of Mecidiye for the settling of Reşwan households. He was, however, accused of maladministration, bribery, and over-taxation in the town.[44]

According to another report, Mecidiye town was built for 4,000 Reşwan households that were settled in Bozok, but some of them had deserted the settlement and gone to Maraş and Aleppo. The members who stayed in Bozok engaged in banditry and conflict with Nogai groups that had recently come to the region from the northern Caucasus. The Reşwans in the region failed to pay taxes and resisted conscription. The author of the report, Hasan Ağa, a member of the Yozgat local council, blamed Reşwan notables for their unruly behaviour. He argued that it was crucial to reduce the control of notables over the tribe by appointing an outside governor.[45]

---

40   "İskan ve medeniyete bir mikdar yüz tutulmuşlar ise de el-halete haza vahşi ve ekserisi Haymana nişin bulunduklarından." See A.MKT.UM 409/49, 8.vi.1860.
41   MVL 696/42, 9.i.1865.
42   Söylemez, *Osmanlı Devletinde Aşiret*, 197. On the Firka-ı İslahiye, see also Andrew Gould, "Lords or Bandits? The Derebeys of Cilicia," *International Journal of Middle East Studies* 7, no. 4 (October 1976): 485–506, https://doi.org/10.1017/S0020743800024661.
43   MVL 1047/114, 14.xii.1867.
44   BOA: Dahiliye Nezareti Mektubi Kalemi [DH.MKT] 1328/102, 10.xii.1879.
45   DH.MKT 537/72, 3.ii.1866.

236 Yonca Köksal

The tribal chief of the area, *mir* Hüseyin, and headmen from the tribe presented a petition to the local council asking to open a secondary school (*rüşdiye*) in Mecidiye. Being aware of the state discourse, they argued that this school would help them transition from savagery (*bedeviyet*) to civilization (*medeniyet*). The Supreme Council responded stating that the town had been newly constructed, and that there was not even a primary school. Therefore, the construction of a secondary school did not have priority.[46] By 1879, most tribe members had deserted the town for cooler climates (possibly to Uzunyayla pasture) in the summer.[47] In addition to Mecidiye, another town named Turgutlu was established by joining twenty villages together for the Reşwans settled around Esbkeşan in Konya in 1865. Yet, the document notes that those Reşwan units settled in Konya were actually in the district of Yozgat (possibly in Çiçek Dağı pasture), and it was difficult to administer them from Konya.[48]

Local state officials as well as the tribe director capitalized on the Reşwans' resistance to settlement. To prevent their settlement in scattered areas, the tribe director Mustafa Bey tried to bribe two officials, Elhac Nasuh Ağa and Hafız Ağa, whom the provincial governor of Konya had sent to the region. Mustafa Bey took 56,000 *guruş* from the Reşwan notables who later collected this amount from all tribe members. Mustafa Bey claimed he had given this money to the two officials but had no solution to the settlement problems.[49]

When the problems with settlement did not end, the Council of State accepted a proposal in 1868 to form an autonomous district (*müstakil mutasarrıflık*) from Çiçekdağı to Nevşehir. This set the Kızılırmak river as a natural border to the movements of the tribe. The state plan was to have two bridges and gendarmerie to control the bridges in order to decrease the mobility of the tribe.[50] In 1880, 3,500 Reşwan households with an estimated population of 15,000 were reported in the provinces of Ankara, Sivas, and Konya. The sedentarization of the Reşwan appeared to be complete. The report notes that the Reşwan were sending conscripts to the army and obeying security forces, unlike other tribes in the region.[51] In later decades, the Reşwan settlement expanded towards the north. In 1899, some Reşwan households were reported to

---

46 MVL 598/67, 26.viii.1859.
47 DH.MKT 1328/102, 10.xii.1879.
48 İ.MVL 545/24486, 30.xii.1865.
49 MVL 728/46, 13.iii.1866.
50 BOA: Şura-ı Devlet [ŞD] 234/1, 13.vi.1868.
51 BOA: Yıldız Perakende Evrakı – Umum Vilayetler Tahrirâtı [Y.PRK.UM] 1/107, 30.ix.1880.

The Reşwan in Central Anatolia   237

be settled in Tosya in Kastamonu province.[52] After 1900, there are only a few documents about the Reşwan tribe in Kahta and Hısn-ı Mansur districts in southeastern Anatolia. The fact that there are no archival documents about the Reşwans in central Anatolia after this date can be seen as a proof of the completion of tribal settlement in the region by the turn of the twentieth century.

The Reşwan and the Sheep Trade

While there are some studies on the settlement of the Reşwan, the tribe's economic activities have not been studied much. The Reşwan earned their livelihood to a large extent with livestock. Sheep and goats were grazed for the subsistence of the tribe as well as for trade. To a lesser extent, camels were rented out for transportation, especially for carrying army supplies and materials from mines.[53] Raising livestock had been their most important economic activity since the sixteenth century. Based on the *tahrir* registers, Söylemez reports the amount of sheep tax as 69,440 *akçe* in 1519. This means that the Reşwan tribe in the Kahta district had around 69,440 sheep, since one *akçe* was taken per animal as tax.[54]

The Reşwan seem to have been an integral part of the sheep trade from central Anatolia to Istanbul in the nineteenth century. As early as 1794, Reşwan notables were reported to be supplying the Grand Vizier.[55] In 1802, the Reşwans were reported to have more than 150,000 sheep in Paşa Dağı close to Kırşehir. They failed to pay fleece wool tax to the official appointed by Cabbarzade Süleyman Bey, the famous notable of the region.[56] The tribe members not only bred and sold their own sheep, but Reşwan notables also bought sheep from other producers, possibly from local villagers and/or other tribe members, to trade.[57] In 1840, two Reşwan traders were accused of paying with false gold coins of lesser value when they bought sheep at Aksaray. They claimed to have gotten these coins from a Cihanbeyli trader who was the sheep director (*ağnam müdürü*) in Istanbul.[58] The traders regularly bought sheep from villagers in central Anatolia and sold them most probably in Istanbul.

---

52 DH.MKT 2252/78, 20.ix.1899.
53 Söylemez reports that there were one hundred camels in the Reşwan tribe in the Divriği Imperial Mine (Maadin-i Hümayun) region in 1827. Söylemez, *Osmanlı Devletinde Aşiret*, 87.
54 Söylemez, *Osmanlı Devletinde Aşiret*, 107, 113.
55 C.DH 340/16984, 17.ix.1794.
56 BOA: Cevdet Maliye [C.ML] 352/14463, 2.v.1802.
57 C.DH 4/180, 6.xii.1830.
58 BOA: Cevdet Darphane [C.DRB] 31/1509, 23.x.1840.

Figure 10.1. The Cihanbeyli *yayla* (pasturage), Ankara
Photo by Stefan Winter.

Reşwan traders were part of a wide commercial network that brought Anatolian sheep to the capital city. Before the nineteenth century, provisionism was a main economic policy of the Ottoman state.[59] Providing for the needs of Istanbul residents was a major concern. Having abundance of basic food supplies at affordable prices required directing animals from Rumelia and Anatolia to Istanbul. Increasingly, it was Anatolian sheep that arrived in Istanbul, in the late eighteenth and early nineteenth centuries, when wars and territorial losses reduced the Rumelian meat supply. Ankara, Konya, and Erzurum emerged as the provinces providing a considerable part of Istanbul's sheep supply.[60] As part of their obligation to provide a certain number of sheep to Istanbul, the tribal chief of the Cihanbeyli was given the title of "head trader" (*tacir başı*), and he had a representative who was to organize the arrival and trade of tribal sheep in the city.[61] The Reşwans were not part of the Cihanbeyli confederation and were not required

---

[59] For Ottoman economic policies, see Mehmet Genç, *Osmanlı İmparatorluğunda Devlet ve Ekonomi* (Istanbul: Ötüken Neşriyat, 2000), 43–67.

[60] Yonca Köksal and Can Nacar, "Marketing Sheep in the Ottoman Empire: Erzurum and Its Trade Networks (Circa 1780s–1910s)," *Archiv orientální* 91, no. 1 (2023): 41–67, https://doi.org/10.47979/aror.j.91.1.41-67.

[61] For more information on the Cihanbeyli's role in sheep trade and head trader position, see Yonca Köksal and Mehmet Polatel, "The Cihanbeyli and the Sheep Trade:

The Reşwan in Central Anatolia   239

to provide sheep to Istanbul. However, they lived in the same areas as the Cihanbeyli confederation and shared winter and summer pastures. They frequently traded with the Cihanbeylis and used Cihanbeyli connections in Istanbul to trade their sheep as in the above example.

These close connections with the Cihanbeyli traders sometimes created problems for the Reşwans. The Cihanbeyli chief, Alişan Bey, was in great debt to a Russian trader, David Savalan, in 1849. The debt was because of the credit that Savalan had provided to the Cihanbeyli confederation for animal trade to Istanbul. Hence, the debt was distributed among seven tribes in the Cihanbeyli confederation. The Reşwans were not part of this debt, but Savalan's servants attempted to seize their sheep in Istanbul and Bursa, claiming that these traders were part of the Cihanbeyli tribe, and that their sheep should therefore be counted towards the debt.[62] Savalan's men might have tried to seize as many sheep as possible when they identified Reşwan traders as part of the Cihanbeylis. Alternatively, some Cihanbeyli traders could have claimed to be from other tribes in order not to pay the debt. Both possibilities strongly suggest that the Reşwan and Cihanbeyli traders closely engaged with each other in the sheep trade.

Although we do not know the total number of Reşwan sheep sold in Istanbul, we have some information about individual traders. In 1849, one of the Reşwan sheep traders brought 345 sheep to Istanbul.[63] Another trader brought 820 sheep, but only 327 reached Istanbul.[64] It was difficult to walk sheep flocks from Central Anatolia to Istanbul; flocks were vulnerable to animal diseases, famines, and banditry. The high number of losses in the last example could be related to these factors.

In the mid-nineteenth century, the Reşwans' animal trade underwent some important transformations. There were major changes in the meat supply and animal trade of Istanbul, such as the elimination of price controls (*narh*) in 1862 and the establishment of the *ondalık* tax, which was collected on one out of ten sheep for the meat supply of Istanbul, came to an end in 1857. These changes meant a shift from provisionism to a free market economy for meat, in line with the general adoption of liberal

---

From Provisionism and Semi-Nomadism to Liberal Economy and Sedentarisation," in *Making a Living in Ottoman Anatolia*, ed. Kate Fleet and Ebru Boyar, (Leiden: Brill, 2021), 157–74.

62 BOA: Hariciye Nezareti Mektubi Kalemi [HR.MKT] 15/55, 29.xii.1846; MVL 19/28, 11.xi.1847; MVL 75/62, 5.vi.1849.

63 BOA: Bâb-ı Âlî Sadâret Evrâkı, Mektûbî Kalemi [A.MKT] 167/3, 1.i.1849.

64 MVL 75/62, 5.vi.1849.

240   Yonca Köksal

economic policies in the Ottoman Empire. The Ottoman state continued to provide meat for the needs of the palace and army but not for Istanbul residents. Thus, the sheep requirement from the Cihanbeylis came to an end, and meat prices began to be determined by market forces. However, the state continued to be concerned with keeping meat prices low and encouraged animal traders to bring their sheep to Istanbul.

From the 1830s to the 1860s, there were major attempts to settle the Reşwan tribe as discussed above. Settlement required the elimination of mobility between winter and summer pastures. Although tribes resisted and escaped to their pastures frequently, in the long run they became sedentary in scattered villages. Under the pressures of tribal settlement, it can be expected that the Reşwans' animal trade to Istanbul declined since feeding animals became more difficult in the absence of pastoral mobility. In fact, the earlier trade connections in Istanbul facilitated the Reşwan notables' visits to Istanbul, where they presented their objections to settlement to the state authorities. The complaints about the lack of lands and pastures that were discussed above should be understood in this context of animal breeding, which was not only necessary for the subsistence of the Reşwans but also for the sheep trade that was a source of income especially for the tribal notables. Reşwan notables' fierce objection to settlement could be related to their fear of a reduction in the sheep supply that would endanger their role in the animal trade.

Contrary to expectations of decline, however, the Reşwan's sheep trade to Istanbul continued to grow long after their settlement. As late as 1887, Reşwan traders were still active in Istanbul. One of the Reşwan merchants, Esseyid Mehmed Tevfik Efendi, and the deputy of meat merchants (*celeb*), Sheikh Hüseyin of the Cihanbeyli tribe, made an appeal to the Sublime Porte, complaining of over-taxation and of the mistreatment of the tax farmer of Uzunçayır, the pasture where Anatolian sheep were gathered before entering Istanbul.[65] The head trader position had been abolished a few years before. Taking advantage of this vacuum, the tax farmer of Uzunçayır, Ali Rıza Efendi, claimed to act as the head trader. The Cihanbeyli notables and traders had held the position of the head trader before its abolition. In alliance with the Reşwans, the Cihanbeylis complained about losing this position, which facilitated their sheep sales. In the absence of the head trader's mediation, these Kurdish traders who did not know the complexities of

---

65 Uzunçayır is close to Haydarpaşa and located between Kadıköy and Üsküdar on the Anatolian side of the Bosphorus.

The Reşwan in Central Anatolia   241

the Istanbul market were given low prices and lost money, and the tax farmer of Uzunçayır overtaxed them. In this document, it is reported that the Reşwans brought 10,000 sheep to Istanbul annually.[66] They seem to have increased their sheep supply to Istanbul after they were settled. Unfortunately, detailed information about how the Reşwans developed the sheep trade after settlement is not available. Their dispersion among various villages could have played a role in the continuation of breeding livestock. A similar trend was visible with the Cihanbeylis. Like the Reşwans, the Cihanbeyli animal trade to Istanbul grew after their settlement. They were sending 300,000 sheep to Istanbul at the end of the nineteenth century.[67]

After settlement, some tribe members became farmers, but the majority continued to seek its livelihood through activities linked to livestock. A further document shows the occupational distribution of the settled Reşwan members in 1851: Among 9,004 members who were settled in the districts of Bozok, Ankara, Amasya, Kangırı, Sivas, Yeni-İl, and Kayseri, there were 4,198 servants (*hizmetkar*), 3,479 farmers, 443 sharecroppers, 368 traders, and 289 non-working individuals because of old age or disability.[68] While a considerable number of them engaged in agricultural production, the majority of settlers became "servants," probably wage labourers. Their places of work are unknown, but we can assume that some of them worked in husbandry and as shepherds. The frequent complaints about inefficient land use, meadows, and irrigation mentioned above seem to have played a role in this large number of wage labourers, as well as in limiting the engagement of tribe members in agricultural production. The number of merchants was limited, and they were mostly in Ankara (247), Bozok (51), and Kayseri (43). Ankara and Kayseri were both important meat markets. Sheep and goats were sent from Ankara to Istanbul and other cities such as İzmid and Bursa. Kayseri was a city of *pastırma* (dried beef) production where cattle and sheep were traded in large numbers. There were also Reşwan notables who profited from the sheep trade and emerged as leading meat merchants in Istanbul. In 1893, three of the Reşwan traders were given a state medal for their continuous sheep supply and their hard work in reducing meat prices in Istanbul.[69]

---

66 ŞD 730/6, 28.i.1888.
67 Köksal and Polatel, "A Tribe as an Economic Actor," 115.
68 Söylemez, *Osmanlı Devletinde Aşiret*, 201–2. The original document is located in İ.MVL 219/7347, 13.viii.1851.
69 DH.MKT 145/85, 6.x.1893.

242   Yonca Köksal

Conclusion

Throughout the nineteenth century, the Reşwans underwent important transformations. During the Tanzimat era, their sedentarization was completed in central Anatolia. This was a contentious process. The Reşwans reacted to state settlement policies through both coercion and mediation: They deserted their settlements, tried to bribe local officials to change settlement destinations, went to Istanbul to negotiate with state authorities, engaged in banditry, and even fired weapons. When the Reşwans resisted settlement attempts persistently, the Ottomans used military troops to settle and disperse the tribes over a wide geographical area. The Reşwan units were ultimately settled in a region stretching from Bozok to Konya, and from Ankara to Kırşehir.

Economic transformations of the nineteenth century put additional pressure on their subsistence economy. The limitation of mobility between winter and summer pastures put pressure on sheep breeding and the animal trade. Yet, towards the end of the nineteenth century, some Reşwan members such as Mehmed Tevfik Efendi, were major sheep traders in Istanbul. The number of sheep they sold there reached a considerable number by the end of the century. The growth of this trade needs further explanation. We can only make some assumptions with the available data: The end of provisionist policies and the rise of meat prices might have made the sheep trade more profitable for Reşwan traders. More important, territorial losses in Europe meant a significant decline in the Rumelian meat supply. The increase in the need for Anatolian meat might have created more opportunities for the Reşwan. Despite these favourable conditions, there were also many challenges. There were two major famines in the Ankara-Konya region, in 1845 and 1874. In addition, cholera outbreaks and epizootics must have harmed a significant proportion of their animals. Although the rise of Reşwan notables in the animal trade can be traced in the Ottoman archives, there is unfortunately not much information about how these transformations and the difficult conditions of the time impacted ordinary tribe members as owners and herders of livestock.[70]

---

70 The author would like to thank Süleyman Ergüven for his assistance and the Scientific and Technological Council of Türkiye's (TÜBİTAK) 1001 Grant for funding.

11 Warfare and Alliances in Ra᾽s al-ʿAyn: Hamidiye Regiments, Bedouin Tribes, and Ottoman Governors, 1895–1905

ERDAL ÇİFTÇİ

Protecting the Ottoman Empire's integrity was one of the key anxieties of the state during its so-called "longest" (nineteenth) century. The Tanzimat and the Hamidian regimes confronted dangers to the empire from both the inside and the outside. Tribes were among the unwanted social types that the modernizing state sought to reform. The government focussed on them in order to control them and transform tribal outliers into sedate subjects. Whereas during the Tanzimat era (1839–76) the Ottoman state attempted to settle them, dispersing and limiting their power, during the Hamidian period the central government selectively empowered tribal chiefs, honouring and arming them. This shifting policy can be read as the traces of a transition from Ottomanism to Islamism, as the Hamidian regime preferred to negotiate with remote Sunni tribes in order to increase its control over its subjects. This created many obstacles to the institutional functioning of the state especially in less controlled regions. One of those tribal zones of the empire that witnessed such practices was Ra᾽s al-ʿAyn and its surroundings.

This study shows that under such circumstances, tribes found many arenas for their power struggles. Tribes competed against each other by fostering alliances and rivalries between themselves and with Ottoman governors and officers. This further weakened the functioning of the rule of law because the officials lost their neutral, bureaucratic role representing the state, which the Tanzimat government had tried to implement. As we will show, the Millî and Kîkî Kurdish tribes and the Shammar and Beggara Bedouins acted not only on their own behalf but also for governors or officers who shared common political or economic ground with them. Because the Millîs and Kîkîs were governed by the province of Diyarbekir, and the Shammar and Beggaras by the province of Zor, the Millî-Shammar rivalry also partly turned

244 Erdal Çiftçi

into a conflict between the two jurisdictions. As the Ottoman sources describe, relations between tribes and governors were ones of patronage (*sahabet*) and proxies. Although the existing literature shows that the Kurdish Hamidiye Light Cavalry disregarded the authority of the governors,[1] our case study suggests that governors and officers did not always stay above local politics but became involved in tribal disputes as allies, supporters, or opponents of various sides, leading to the further escalation of disorder in the region.

The involvement of officials in local disputes was partly the result of the expansion of the Hamidian and Bedouin tribes. Since the Kurdish Millî confederation extended its influence to Ra's al-'Ayn and further south to the Jabal 'Abd al-'Aziz, which was under the rule of the Zor government, the latter began to lose revenues as its officials were prevented from collecting taxes from area tribes.[2] While the Zor government supported enemies of the Millîs such as the Shammar Bedouin, the government of Diyarbekir supported the Millîs since they were aware of the power of Millî İbrahim Paşa, who was backed by both the sultan and the Fourth Army marshal.

Together with the conflicts between the Millîs and Shammars and their partnership with local government figures, other tribes in the region also had to ally with one side or another. This occurred via tribal warfare and/or tribal diplomacy. The Millîs' rivals such as the Karakeçi and other tribes in Siverek can serve as an example for this process. This chapter also suggests that collective identities of the tribal subjects and their boundaries were fragile, dynamic, and porous. The Millîs and Shammars continuously tried to absorb less powerful tribes in order to increase their power. Ra's al-'Ayn became a field for this conflict, as the region was a tribal borderland between the two tribes' headquarters, namely Viranşehir and the Desert of Zor. In order to better understand these developments, we will first discuss the disorders in the Ra's al-'Ayn region and demonstrate how the state rule over the area continued to weaken from 1890 to the end of Abdülhamid's reign in 1908. Then, an analysis of the tribal structure of the region and multifaceted representations of local politics in Ra's al-'Ayn and its surrounding regions will be provided. Lastly, the conflicts among the Millîs and

---

1 Janet Klein, *The Margins of Empire: Kurdish Militias in the Ottoman Tribal Zone* (Stanford: Stanford University Press, 2011); Bayram Kodaman, "Hamidiye Hafif Süvari Alayları: II. Abdülhamid ve Doğu Anadolu Aşiretleri," *İstanbul Üniversitesi Edebiyat Fakültesi Tarih Dergisi* 32 (1979): 460–1.

2 T.C. Cumhurbaşkanlığı Osmanlı Arşivleri [BOA]: DH.MKT 408/61 (Oct. 1899).

Warfare and Alliances in Ra's al-'Ayn   245

Shammar will be analyzed to see how the local administrations further sharpened the tribal disputes and supported their allied chiefs while antagonizing the other tribe.

Tribal Anarchy at Ra's al-'Ayn

Ottoman sources, British consular reports, and some travelogues all underline similar problems with tribes in Ra's al-'Ayn and the surrounding desert. Muslim immigrants from the Russian Caucasus who had settled in the area further contributed to the state of disorder. The *kaza* of Ra's al-'Ayn rarely had competent *kaimakams* able to quell tribal disputes and control the area, and as will be discussed below, officials appointed to Ra's al-'Ayn were often reluctant to stay. On account of Abdülhamid's policies, local authorities lacked the power to act effectively; and Hamidiye Regiment tribes, as well as the area Bedouin, had their own agendas. Ra's al-'Ayn became a haven for tribes as a region beyond state control in the Hamidian period.[3]

Complaints about tribal upheaval were regularly forwarded by the local government through the Ministry of the Interior or the War Ministry to the Fourth Army, but were generally ignored as Abdülhamid was intent on keeping the Hamidiye tribes on his side. In addition, the Bedouins of the region had always traditionally resisted state encroachment, the Syrian desert representing a free space similar to the interstate frontier zone between the Ottoman and the Iranian Empires. And finally the Abdülhamid regime consciously limited its own mediating and conflict resolving role in the highly politicized atmosphere of the late nineteenth century, paving the way for versatile local actors to conduct their own diplomacy and warfare.[4]

Located in the middle of this conflict area, Ra's al-'Ayn was a district (*kaza*) attached to the province of Zor, which was an autonomous *sancak* (*mustakil mutasarrıflık*) in the period under consideration. Northeastern Syria had little agricultural land and river basins provided the only suitable places for settlements and farming. Ra's al-'Ayn was a potentially well-to-do town on the northern edge of the Syrian desert, but was basically abandoned to the disorder of tribal conflict and contained only 5,000 houses in 1901. According to Mark Sykes, most of the inhabitants had left the town even after the government attempted to

---

3 Suavi Aydın and Erdal Çiftçi, *Fihristü'l Aşair* (İstanbul: İletişim, 2021), 215.
4 Mark Sykes, *The Caliphs' Last Heritage: A Short History of the Turkish Empire* (London: Macmillan, 1915), 331.

246   Erdal Çiftçi

rebuild and repopulate it with Muslim immigrants from the Caucasus.[5] The deserted lands and villages of Ra's al-'Ayn on the plains of the Khabur and Zerkan rivers were distributed to local tribe members for free (*meccanen*) in order to revive the region, settle the tribes, and "civilize" them.[6] The Chechens, who Ottoman sources indicate controlled the town centre, were also considered a sedentarized population. However, their presence only exacerbated the disorder already caused by Kurdish and Bedouin groups in the 1890s, and in which they participated as allies or proxies.

Since they were settled in Ra's al-'Ayn, the Chechen leader Mekki Bey usually aligned himself with the Zor government and its local allies such as the Shammar Bedouin – the sworn enemies of the Millîs, Kîkîs, and other Kurdish tribes.[7] Mekki Bey became deputy *kaimakam* of Ra's al-'Ayn with the support of the governor of Zor, Zühdü Bey.[8] Zühdü Bey in turn needed the Chechens as well as the Shammar in his struggle against the Hamidian-backed Millî and Kîkî Kurds, who were threatening his fiscal revenues by taking taxes from other tribes in the area.[9]

Numerous complaints were made against the Chechens as well. In 1890 the residents and villagers of Ra's al-'Ayn petitioned the government because their flocks were being seized by Chechen clans (*kabileleri*) when they brought them to pasture in the desert over the winter; they requested that Ra's al-'Ayn be governed from Mardin instead of Zor since the former was closer.[10] Complaints came from neighbouring provinces as well. In 1902, the Sherabin tribe of Diyarbekir complained that a Chechen named Muhammed and his supporters had stolen a

---

5 Sykes, *The Caliphs' Last Heritage*, 327. According to Sykes, the Circassians came to settle in the 1870s. However, a telegram sent by local Chechens suggests they had been in the Ra's al-'Ayn area since the Crimean War; DH.TMIK.S 45/35 (May 1903). Colonel Sir Mark Sykes (1879–1919) was a traveller, diplomat, and advisor to the British government. Between 1905 and 1906, he served as an attaché in the British Embassy in Istanbul. He published numerous firsthand accounts, based on his travels as well as on the reports of direct witnesses to events in the Ra's al-'Ayn region. He had a significant impact on British policy in the Middle East (and negotiated the Sykes-Picot Agreement) in World War I, before dying of the Spanish flu during the Paris Peace Conference.

6 DH.MKT 1947/17 (May 1892); ŞD 2597/14 (June 1892); İ.DH 1296/6 (Apr. 1894).

7 In the 1860s the Shammar had initially confronted the Chechens. See HR.SYS 1528/77 (Oct. 1867).

8 Nagehan Yılmaz and Halil Elemana, "İsmail Zühdü Bey," in *Kuruluşundan Cumhuriyet'e Sayıştay Tarihi, 1862–1923*, ed. Salih Kış (Ankara: T.C. Sayıştay Başkanlığı, 2012), 156–7.

9 DH.MKT 1890/91 (Nov. 1891).

10 ŞD 1464/26 (Mar. 1890).

flock of their sheep.[11] In Urfa, the Ceys (Qays) tribes and the Chechens were often at each others' throats around Harran.[12] Even in Mardin province, villagers sent telegrams saying they were under attack by Chechen tribes.[13] The Chechens frequently also collided with the Kurdish Kîkî tribe, whose lands lay between Kızıltepe and Viranşehir. The two groups repeatedly attacked each others' villages to drive away their flocks and steal their goods. We can surmise that these conflicts were mainly carried out with the aim of weakening the enemy economically: tribes in the region mostly targeted the assets of the enemy, rather than killing one another.[14] Most of the complaints appearing in Ottoman archival documents thus concern the seizure of animals and properties in the region.[15]

Because of the disorder brought about by the Chechen tribes, the central government several times considered their relocation. While some of them were resettled in northern provinces such as Muş, Maraş, and Sivas, others were divided between different villages in the hope that they would be assimilated as "peaceful" subjects. Some were employed as police forces in Baghdad.[16] Still others were forcibly removed to Daret 'Izze (Aleppo), but they subsequently petitioned the authorities to be allowed to return to Ra's al-'Ayn because the lands were too desolate and they were subject to Bedouin attacks at Daret 'Izze.[17] Despite these considerations, however, most Chechens were not relocated from Ra's al-'Ayn by the Hamidian government, and continued to sow conflict and chaos in the area.

Another important factor contributing to the disorder in the region was that Ra's al-'Ayn did not have powerful or able *kaimakam*s in the 1890s, with most remaining in office for only a year or two before requesting to be assigned elsewhere. This is what allowed Mekki Bey to serve as deputy *kaimakam* for so long. Between 1899 and 1901, there were five different nominations to the post of *kaimakam*. When Tevfik Bey was first named in July 1899, he was excused from accepting the appointment due to illness.[18] Another *kaimakam*, Osman Efendi,

---

11 DH.MKT 525/44 (June 1902).
12 DH.MKT 1654/10 (Sept. 1889); DH.MKT 1708/99 (Apr. 1890).
13 DH.MKT 1617/38 (Apr. 1889).
14 DH.MKT 1949/64 (May 1892). Sykes states that killing was not the main objective in these wars, even if the chiefs did also harbour clear desires for revenge against the other tribes. Sykes, *The Caliphs' Last Heritage*, 305.
15 A.MKT.MHM 637/38 (May 1892); DH.MKT 1608/116 (Mar. 1889).
16 DH.MKT 1952/120 (May 1892); ŞD 1465/33 (Dec. 1892); BEO 193/14467 (May 1893); DH.MKT 1651/130 (Aug. 1892).
17 DH.TMİK.S 45/35 (May 1903).
18 DH.MKT 2219/69 (July 1899).

248   Erdal Çiftçi

resigned from the post with the excuse of old age; he had been named with a specific mandate to solve the problems between the Millîs and the Chechens in the area.[19] The other appointees, Muhammed Edhem, İzzet, and Kadri, showed similar reactions. İzzet Bey did not even bother informing his superiors when he quit Ra's al-'Ayn in 1902; the central government later discovered that he had simply returned to his own village. Without anyone to collect taxes in the *kaza*, the appointment of an abler and younger *kaimakam* had to be requested yet again.[20] Although health concerns were usually cited as the main difficulty in finding *kaimakam*s, the authorities also admitted that "nobody requests" assignment to Ra's al-'Ayn since it was the "wandering areas of tribes" who were constantly at war with one another.[21]

Ra's al-'Ayn and neighbouring provinces had limited military might to stop intertribal wars (*ghazve*). Of course the central government sometimes protected specific groups, and the local tribes could not afford to confront the imperial army. Sykes asserts that the provincial governors could have established control over the region had they been permitted to do so by the state. The Hamidian regime, however, generally preferred to make concessions to certain tribes and otherwise ignore, if not actively encourage, the chaos and disorder.[22]

Under these circumstances, there was not even enough military power to subdue the tribes and collect the sheep tax. The *kaimakam* of Ra's al-'Ayn requested a squadron from Aleppo for this purpose in 1897, but his request was denied because the *vali* feared sending even a limited number of soldiers might lead to trouble back in Aleppo and surrounding areas.[23] Sometimes troops were called in from Aleppo, Urfa, and Diyarbekir to break up tribal disputes, but often this was not enough unless they were under orders from the Marshal of the imperial Fourth Army, Zeki Paşa, the only figure with sufficient authority against the Hamidiye tribes.[24] Occasionally not even Zeki Paşa could find the necessary forces in the field, as happened for example in July

---

19 BEO 1346/100934; DH.MKT 2219/69 (July 1899). Sykes also cites the criticism of a *kaimakam* from Mosul against the central authorities: "they send a young mektebli [graduate] who can neither ride nor rule, or a fond old man, on the brink of the grave." According to him, only experienced appointees would be successful in ruling this tribal zone. Sykes, *The Caliphs' Last Heritage*, 335.

20 DH.MKT 2586/99 (Feb. 1902); DH.MKT 660/68 (Nov. 1902).

21 DH.MKT 2507/121 (July 1891).

22 Sykes, *The Caliphs' Last Heritage*, 331.

23 BEO 927/69473 (Mar. 1897).

24 DH.TMIK.M 217/1; DH.TMIK.M 216/11 (Feb. 1906).

Warfare and Alliances in Raʾs al-ʿAyn 249

1901, when the Millîs were at war with some local tribes and a colonel from Diyarbekir by the name of Ishak neglected to follow the Marshal's orders to intervene. The desert heat, limited logistics, and a lack of money were cited as excuses. Instead, another officer, Kazım Bey, accepted the assignment and went to mediate between the Millîs, the Karakeçis, and other tribes in Siverek.[25]

The root cause of this disorder was of course the Hamidian regime's policy of ignoring the trespasses of powerful tribes it was integrating into the state apparatus, such as the Millîs, or of those who had traditionally been the patrons of the desert such as the Shammars. Before entering into the question of how these local disputes created alliances and rivalries including the local governments, an understanding of the tribal composition of the region is necessary.

Tribal Politics and Diplomacy in the Raʾs al-ʿAyn Region

Raʾs al-ʿAyn and northeastern Syria were largely under the control of Arab and Kurdish tribes during the Hamidian period. While the former mostly occupied the deep desert lands, the latter were in control of the northern spheres of Syria referred to in Ottoman sources as "the mouth of the desert" (çöl ağzı). Most of these groups were nomadic, which provided for a strong tribal identity. Fully settled tribes generally lost their collective identities, like the Tats of southern Mardin, and required the protection of another, nomadic, tribe.[26] All of northeastern Syria was subject to these rivalries and conflicts, increasingly in the 1890s. While large Bedouin confederations such as the Shammar and ʿAnaza drew their power from the desert and their masses of followers, others such as the Millî, Kîkî, and Berazi Kurds benefitted from the support of the Hamidian government.

Strong collective identities were an important factor in the power struggles between Bedouin and Kurdish tribes in the region. Modern anthropologists have posited that such identities were usually built around an existing noble family placing itself at the heart of an imagined community, rather than on actual blood ties.[27] In fact, Ziya Gökalp (1876–1924) already proposed this position at the beginning

---

25 National Archives, London: Foreign Office [FO] 404/202, Freeman to O'Conor, Mamuretulaziz, 22 August 1901.
26 Ziya Gökalp, *Kürt Aşiretleri Hakkında Sosyolojik Tetkikler* (Istanbul: Kaynak, 2011), 62.
27 Philip Khoury and Joseph Kostiner, eds., *Tribes and State Formation in the Middle East* (Berkeley: University of California Press, 1990).

250   Erdal Çiftçi

of the century on the basis of his field observations of the Millîs and the Shammars. For Gökalp, tribal identities were political rather than ethnic, and a tribe might house several different ethnic and religious identities. The Millî tribe, for example, included 'Adwan, Beggara, and Hadidi Arabs; the Kurdicized Turkish Terkans; Dinnan and Şarkiyan Yezidis; and other Sunni Kurdish clans.[28] The relationship between client tribes and their patrons was not constant because all tribes attempted to increase their own power by subduing others. The conflicts between the Shammar and 'Anaza Bedouin or between the Millîs and the Shammars were the result of such power struggles.

Beyond weakening the enemy economically, intertribal raiding also aimed to absorb sections of rival tribes into one's own domain. In order to preserve their prestige and power, chiefs had to be able to protect their subjects against other tribes, or risk losing them to the other tribes. We see many examples of sections of tribes joining other confederations. Thus while some Şeyhan Yezidis obeyed the rule of Millî İbrahim Paşa, others submitted to the Millîs' enemies in Siverek, the Karakeçis. In the south of Mardin, the sedentarized Tat tribe consisted of both Arab and Kurdish populations who had previously been members of other nomadic tribes in the region.[29] The Millîs, meanwhile, absorbed sections of vulnerable rival tribes as noted earlier. Even a section of the Shammars, the al-'Amr, joined the Millîs in 1903.[30] Although the Ottoman documentation mostly focusses on the short-term consequences of intertribal conflicts (raids, theft, killings, etc.), they were above all means for making the political power of tribal collectives on the ground.

The most successful tribes were able to incorporate large amounts of territory and human capital into their confederations, practicing *ghazwa/gazve* (tribal raids, although with overtones of "sacred war" in the Ottoman period),[31] and applying *khuwwa*, "brotherhood tax," on their followers and sedentary populations to affirm their tribal unity. Such formations were in fact characterized by Ziya Gökalp as "small nations," and by Richard Tapper as the "fourth world."[32] Expansion and inclusion were their defining features. Abdülhamid II's program of Islamist conservatism ultimately offered these tribes, through the

---

28 Gökalp, *Kürt Aşiretleri*, 18.
29 Gökalp, *Kürt Aşiretleri*, 58, 82.
30 DH.TMIK.M 149/14 (July 1903).
31 Ferit Devellioğlu, *Lugat* (Ankara: Aydın, 2000), 338.
32 Gökalp, *Kürt Aşiretleri*, 28; Richard Tapper, "Anthropologists, Historians, and Tribespeople on Tribe and State Formation in the Middle East," in *Tribes and State Formation in the Middle East*, ed. Philip Khoury and Joseph Kostiner (Berkeley: University of California Press, 1990), 48.

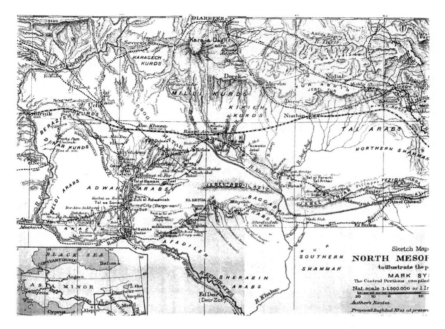

Figure 11.1. Extract from a map by Mark Sykes showing the tribal composition of northeastern Syria

Source: Mark Sykes, "Journeys in North Mesopotamia," *The Geographical Journal*, 30, no. 3 (September 1907): 237–54.

benefits of recruitment into the Hamidiye Light Cavalry, a means of continuing their mission. The most powerful figure to exploit this policy especially between 1895 and 1905 would be Millî İbrahim Paşa.

Relations among tribes were not limited to warfare. Already Mark Sykes drew attention to the other important aspect, namely tribal diplomacy. Millî İbrahim Paşa, according to Sykes, was "a politician, natural leader, a power of self-control, feudal baron, eastern despot, nomadic chief." Although this characterization may seem exaggerated, it calls attention to the fact that tribal leaders in northern Syria (and elsewhere) had to build delicate coalitions along shifting political lines; tribal conflicts did not erupt arbitrarily but were the result of precise planning.[33] Ottoman archival documents reveal little of this diplomacy but rather

---

33 Sykes, *The Caliphs' Last Heritage*, 302, 326. Sykes also romanticized tribal raiding as fun and sport, explaining it as a result not of inherent savagery but of nature's reawakening in the spring that pushed tribes to confrontation.

252   Erdal Çiftçi

refer to the prevalence of "tribal customs" (*âdât-ı aşâir*), a term often invoked when the state was unable to solve intertribal disputes through its own rule. The use of the term also suggests the Ottomans made a distinction between their state law and "illegitimate" tribal law. This is another reason why the Ottomans found it necessary to transform tribes into manageable subjects, their "customs" of raiding and plunder counting as nothing but banditry. As we will see below, the provincial governors on the spot also selectively used this vocabulary to delegitimize their rivals' military acts and diplomacy.

Referring to tribal relations simply as "customs" is of course reductionist and denotes the hegemony of the state archival record, as we have so few sources where the tribes speak for themselves. The term "*âdât*" reflects the fact that the state discourse was mainly produced in times of tribal war when the protagonists could be made to appear as robbers and killers, but conceals the complex relationships not only among tribes but between tribal leaders and other political actors in the region such as governors, military officials, and civilian notables. The characterization of Millî İbrahim by Sykes would have been equally true of Faris Paşa of the Shammar, Salt Paşa of the Cubur, or Halil Bey of the Karakeçis.

İbrahim Paşa of the Millî tribe

According to the literature, the Millîs were organized in two sections, one in Viranşehir and the other in Mardin. Although the Millîs of Mardin may have formed a tribal collective in previous centuries, in our period there was no real Millî tribal identity in Mardin beyond some residents of the city who went by the name of "Millî-zade" but who were urban notables rather than tribal chiefs.[34] The Milan Kurds of Van were not directly related to the Millîs. For the purposes of this chapter, we will focus only on the Millîs in Viranşehir and the Karacadağ region in northern Ra's al-'Ayn.

The leader of the Millîs at Viranşehir, İbrahim, was already one of the most successful tribal chiefs in the region and saw a further great increase of his power with the creation of the Hamidiye Light Cavalry Regiments by sultan Abdülhamid II in 1891. In addition to an imperial Mecidi decoration, third degree, he was awarded the rank of *mirülümera* and could henceforth carry the title of tribal "Paşa."[35]

---

34 See Gökalp, *Kürt Aşiretleri*, 59.
35 Mehmet Rezan Ekinci, "Osmanlı Devleti Döneminde Milli Aşireti (XVIII.–XIX. YY.)" (PhD diss., Elazığ University, 2017); Klein, *Margins of Empire*; Selçuk Günay, "II. Abdülhamid Devrinin Son Yıllarında Güneydoğu Anadolu ile

The Millîs' headquarters was the Karacadağ mountain between Siverek and Diyarbekir, from where they expanded towards Viranşehir as well as southwards. As a result, Millî İbrahim collided in the west with the Berazi Kurds at Suruj and the Qays Arabs at Harran, and with the Karakeçi and Bucak Kurds at Siverek. He also extended his power over villages belonging to the notables of Diyarbekir.[36] However, his greatest enemies were the Chechens and the Shammars in the south. He was ultimately able to crush them all, although he could not have competed with the Shammars without the military backing of the state. He was thus able to take control of the Ra's al-ʿAyn region where the Shammars had been.

Being awarded the command of a Hamidiye tribal regiment created uniquely powerful Kurdish tribal leaders such as Millî İbrahim, Mustafa Paşa of the Miran in Cizre, and Hüseyin Paşa of the Heyderan in Patnos. The Ottoman government had of course always been aware that there was no controlling the Syrian Bedouin without potent tribal intermediaries.[37] Without government support (and arms) Millî İbrahim Paşa would likely not have been able to confront the Shammar, before whom the Millîs had had to retreat into the Karacadağ and pay tribute to in the past.[38] Following his rise to power in 1891, British observers as well as later researchers stated that İbrahim Paşa presided over his own "little empire," "*imperium in imperio*" or "tribal emirate."[39] Such claims might be true regarding the Millîs' headquarters, but the fact is that neither Millî İbrahim nor his other Hamidiye counterparts could expand their spheres of control very far into neighbouring territories.

Kuzey Irakta Aşiret Mücadeleleri ve Milli Aşireti Reisi İbrahim Paşa," *Atatürk Üniversitesi Türkiyat Araştırmaları Enstitüsü Dergisi* 2 (1995): 103–32; Stefan Winter, "The Other *Nahdah*: The Bedirxans, the Millis and the Tribal Roots of Kurdish Nationalism in Syria," *Oriente Moderno* 86, no. 3 (August 2006): 467–70, https://doi.org/10.1163/22138617-08603003. The government, however, made a sharp distinction between Hamidiye tribal officers and officers of the imperial army; see BOA: Y.PRK.AZJ 19/53 (June 1891).

36 National Archives, London (Kew): Foreign Office [FO] 424/208, 5 August 1905; Oktay Bozan, "20. Yüzyılın Başında Eşraf-Aşiret Çatışması: Milli Aşireti ve Diyarbakır Eşrafı Örneği" *Atatürk Araştırma Merkezi Dergisi* 33, no. 96 (November 2017): 1–46.

37 The governor of Baghdad suggested placing three sections of the Shammars under a single shaykh to better control disobedient tribe members in the Ra's al-ʿAyn and Khabur regions; see DH.TMIK.M 158/18 (Nov. 1902).

38 Gökalp, *Kürt Aşiretleri*, 82; Mehmet Yaşar Ertaş, "Tanzimat Döneminde Mardin ve Çevresinde Devlet Aşiret İlişkileri," in *Makalelerle Mardin I: Tarih Coğrafya*, ed. İbrahim Özcoşar (Istanbul: Mardin Tarihi İhtisas Kütüphanesi, 2007), 497–528.

39 Klein, *The Margins of Empire*, 98; FO 424/202, O'Conor to Lansdowne, Constantinople, 29 May 1901.

254   Erdal Çiftçi

Figure 11.2. Mark Sykes's visit to Milli İbrahim Paşa's tent
Source: Mark Sykes, *The Caliphs' Last Heritage: A Short History of the Turkish Empire*
(London: Macmillan, 1915), 321.

This process occurred through both tribal warfare, which Mark Sykes characterized as "pastoral piracy,"[40] and tribal diplomacy. After 1891, the Millîs not only completely controlled Viranşehir but also dominated the tribes of neighbouring Siverek, Urfa, and Suruj, in addition to most of the villages of western Diyarbekir. In the south, they partly controlled Ra's al-ʿAyn through İbrahim Paşa's alliance with sections of the Chechens and the Shammars.[41] Although they would winter in the Jabal ʿAbd al-ʿAziz, the Millîs' hold on the region between the Jabal and Ra's al-ʿAyn was tenuous because the Shammars under Faris Paşa were powerful enough to defeat them if they did not receive help from the Ottoman imperial army.[42] Other Arab tribes, namely the Cubur, ʿUkaydat, Sherabin, and Beggara, also wintered in the region and did not

---

40 Sykes, *The Caliphs' Last Heritage*, 331.
41 Sykes, 324; FO 424/208, Maunsell to O'Conor, Constantinople, 12 June 1905; DH.TMIK.M 111/26 (Oct. 1901).
42 FO 424/208, O'Conor to Lansdowne, Therapia, 21 June 1905; FO 424/208, Anderson to O'Conor, Diyarbekir, 28 January 1902.

Warfare and Alliances in Ra's al-'Ayn   255

leave the Millîs sole control.[43] Considering the might of the Shammars and the 'Anazas throughout the Syrian desert, the Millîs still could not deal with these two players in an open war.[44] The notion that İbrahim Paşa had followers in Malatya as well as in the Saray area of Van seems unlikely since his power never reached that far.[45]

Like the Ottomans themselves, the Millî chief relied on divide-and-rule tactics to establish his authority over the periphery. According to Sykes,

> His first act was to make firm friends with the sturdy little colony of Circassians at Ras-el-Ain, and then to gather under his dominion the lesser Shaykhs of the surrounding tribes, and to part them from their own people, in this way securing parties of one hundred and two hundred tents at a time. So well did he manage his diplomacy, that before many years had passed the Millî Kurds began to present a far more powerful front than ever before.[46]

He used similar tactics with the Chechens and Karakeçi tribes, and even with a section of the Shammars, where he, "by wheedling, bribes, and oratory gained over the great shaykh Jurallah, who commanded 1,500 tents." Millî İbrahim apparently maintained a network of spies to keep abreast of developments in the surrounding cities and among other tribes, and was able to take over the Terkan clan, which had been under the authority of Karakeçi Halil Bey in Siverek, marry the sister of a Qays chief, and forge alliances with sections of the Kîkîs, 'Afadla, Beggara, and Sherabin tribes, all while retaining "a solid block of enemies" of the Tayy, Jabbur, 'Anaza, and Shammars.[47] Karakeçi Halil Bey, who was one of the local chiefs who had resisted against Millî İbrahim the longest, and who had sided with the Shammars against him, finally gave up and recognized his pre-eminence too.[48]

---

43 DH.MKT 2026/103 (Nov. 1902).

44 Sykes, *The Caliphs' Last Heritage*, 311, 454; FO 424/208, Anderson to O'Conor, Diyarbekir, 28 Jan. 1902.

45 While some clans in these areas declared their allegiance to İbrahim Paşa this was likely a reflection of their admiration for the Milli chief and not of his actual power in the field. Cf. Klein, *The Margins of Empire*, 100; Sykes, 424.

46 Sykes, 323.

47 Sykes, 323, 324. İbrahim Paşa had also been in conflict with the Karakeçi tribe since 1878; ŞD 1455/38 (June 1878).

48 FO 424/208, Maunsell to O'Conor, Constantinople, 12 June 1905; Klein, *The Margins of Empire*, 98, 100.

256 Erdal Çiftçi

Unlike most other Hamidiye tribal chiefs or the Bedouins, İbrahim Paşa also enjoyed a close rapport with the Armenians. He supported the Armenian merchants of his headquarters Viranşehir, invited others to come to the region, and built the city into a well-populated, well-connected commercial centre. Both the Armenians and local tribe members were free to trade in the area, where they were "perfectly safe once within the Millî limits, and treated with kindness and respect."[49] His relations were also good with the Armenians of Diyarbekir city, which provoked the anger of Diyarbekir's Muslim notables.[50] This in fact led the Fourth Army commander Zeki Paşa to suspect the notables were supporting the Shammars and accuse them of treason, hatred, disobedience, and incompetence when they complained about the Millîs.[51] For Mark Sykes, the sight of "government rifles" was a sign that he was approaching a Millî encampment. When the tribe came under threat they would be supported by military battalions called in from neighbouring provinces.[52] Needless to say, İbrahim Paşa would lose this power with the demise of the Abdülhamid regime and the end of the Hamidiye regiments in 1908.

Other Kurdish Tribes in Ra's al-'Ayn

Kurdish tribes were found mostly on the northern edges of the Syrian desert (çöl ağzı). Beyond the Millîs, there were the Kîkîs between Viranşehir and Kızıltepe; the Berazis in Suruj; and the Bucaks, Kırvars, and Karakeçis in Siverek. The Kîkî tribe was one of the most powerful and consisted of two main branches, the Xelecan and the Çerikan. While the former was situated on the western bank of the Zerkan River, the latter roamed on the eastern bank.[53] Because of the Shammars' attacks, some members of the Kîkî tribe abandoned their villages and returned to a nomadic life in the 1870s. Although they were driven up against the Karacadağ mountain by the Shammars, after the creation of the Hamidiye regiments, the Kîkîs were able to push the Shammars

---

49 Sykes, *The Caliphs' Last Heritage*, 313, 316–17.
50 Joost Jongerden, "Elite Encounters of a Violent Kind: Milli İbrahim Paşa, Ziya Gökalp, and Political Struggles in Diyarbekir at the Turn of the 20th Century," in *Social Relations in Ottoman Diyarbekir, 1870–1915*, ed. Joost Jongerden and Jelle Verheij (Leiden: Brill, 2012), 55–84; Bozan, "20. Yüzyılın Başında Eşraf-Aşiret Çatışması."
51 DH.TMIK.M 60/72–32 (Oct. 1898); DH.TMIK.M 67/59–47 (May 1899).
52 Sykes, *The Caliphs' Last Heritage*, 317.
53 Gökalp, *Kürt Aşiretleri*, 60.

Warfare and Alliances in Ra's al-'Ayn   257

back and take control of the region between Kızıltepe and Ra's al-'Ayn. The Kîkîs owed this success to their having Martini rifles.[54]

Most of the time the Kîkî chiefs aligned themselves with the Millîs. But when their interests collided, neither side hesitated to attack the other or the other's allies, as happened in 1899: When one section of the Harb tribe supported by Millî İbrahim attempted to settle and farm in the villages of the Zerkan River near Ra's al-'Ayn, the Kîkîs did not let them and prepared to fight them. The Akub al-Yusuf section of the Harb tribe had to flee their homes in face of the Kîkîs' attacks. İbrahim Paşa had tried to use the Harb to colonize a region closer to Kîkî territory but did not push the issue further, presumably because he did not want to enter into open conflict with the latter. However, another Harb section under the leadership of Halil bin Ubur el-Hindi settled in the same region. They were joined by some Kîkîs and allied with the Chechens of Ra's al-'Ayn, and were thus attacked by the main Kîkî tribe in its continuous battle with the Chechens.[55] The Chechens had previously raided the Tell Ermen area, which was usually under the control of the Kîkîs, while the latter had several times plundered the villages of Ra's al-'Ayn and various Chechen groups. According to the Fourth Army Marshall Zeki Paşa, the Kîkîs were allied with the Shammars against the Millîs, but had been prevented from attacking them by the Army.[56] This is one of the examples where the Kîkî and Shammar chiefs were brought together through "tribal diplomacy" – one of the Kîkî chiefs, Naif Ağa, going so far as to steal the mules of two imperial soldiers of Zor since that province was supporting the Chechens of Ra's al-'Ayn.[57]

In the Suruj region (south of Urfa), another powerful Kurdish tribe, the Berazis, were also integrated into the Hamidiye regiments, but nevertheless confronted aggressive attacks from the Millîs.[58] As indicated in a petition made to the government in 1896, they comprised one thousand families (*hane*) and paid 200,000 *kuruş* in tax annually.[59] Some Berazi members, who were probably sedentary, were also conscripted into the imperial army at Hama.[60] Like the Millîs, the Berazis were a confederation of several tribes including non-Kurds. According to Sykes,

---

54 Sykes, *The Caliphs' Last Heritage*, 328–31.
55 DH.TMIK.M 64/15 (Jan. 1899); DH.TMIK.M 74/33 (Aug. 1899).
56 DH.TMIK.M 67/59–63 (May 1899).
57 DH.TMIK.M 73/87 (June 1899).
58 Y.EE 139/47 (Sept. 1893). On the Berazis, see also the contributions of Dick Douwes and Muhsen Seyda to this volume.
59 BEO 884/66269 (Dec. 1896).
60 Y.MTV 180/157 (Aug. 1898).

258   Erdal Çiftçi

the Berazis controlled 360 villages in the Suruj region.[61] Their relations with the Millîs worsened when some Berazi horsemen switched to the Millîs in 1906. One of İbrahim Paşa's policies was in fact to raid Berazi villages in order to put pressure on them to accept his rule instead of that of the Berazi chiefs. In addition to the Berazis, several tribes of Harran such as Qays and Siyale were plundered because they did not submit to İbrahim Paşa.[62] İbrahim tried to justify his attacks on other tribes by accusing them of attacking his own domains; local officials tried to intervene but were powerless to stop him. During subsequent negotiations to return the stolen goods, the Millîs were once again supported by the Diyarbekir government.[63]

The tribes of Siverek were among the most powerful in the region and often clashed with one another and especially with the Millîs. While the Zaza Kurdish tribes of Bucak and Kırvar fought in the western and northern parts of Siverek, the Karakeçis and Millîs were at war in the southern and eastern parts.[64] According to the British vice-consul Anderson, these tribes had a "custom" of attacking each other's Christian villages – recalling how Ottoman documents refer to the same activities as "âdât." All the villages in the region were in fact under the protection and control of a tribal chief, a result of the war of expansion that began between Millî İbrahim and Karakeçi Halil Bey in 1901. Anderson suggests that the Millîs were initially less powerful than the Karakeçis and the neighbouring Kîkî and Dakori tribes, but he was ultimately able to expand his influence and overpower them.[65] With the exception of the Shammars, Karakeçi Halil Bey was thus the leader who stood most strongly against the Millîs until 1905.

The Karakeçis, one of the most populous tribes between Siverek and Ra's al-'Ayn, were also included in the Hamidiye Light Cavalry Regiments; their conflict with the Millîs thus ran counter to the Hamidian policy of incorporating and assimilating tribes into the state apparatus. When İbrahim Paşa's caravan was attacked by the Karakeçis, the Millîs attacked and pillaged their villages. The mutual attacks became

---

61 Sykes, *The Caliphs' Last Heritage*, 455; Gökalp, *Kürt Aşiretleri*, 56.
62 DH.ŞFR 359/164 (Feb. 1906); Sykes, *The Caliphs' Last Heritage*, 325–6, 454.
63 DH.TMIK.M 216/11 (Feb. 1906); Y.MTV 284/55 (Mar. 1906); Y.MTV 285/184 (Apr. 1906).
64 Gökalp, *Kürt Aşiretleri*, 58.
65 FO 424/203, O'Conor to Lansdowne, Constantinople, 28 January 1902. According to Anderson, the Bucak tribe could muster 10,000 gunmen, the Ashiti in Midyat 9,000, and the Karakeçis, Kîkî, and Dakoris (Dökeris) 1,500 each, while the main Millî divisions could only muster 500 in addition to those forced into their service.

Warfare and Alliances in Ra's al-'Ayn 259

increasingly violent in the spring of 1901 and men and family members fell victim on both sides, as did an army unit that was caught in between. A captain of fifteen soldiers was killed and others sent back to Urfa by the Millîs.[66] When the Shammars attacked the Millîs the same year, they allied with the Karakeçis, which led to a further escalation of the Millî-Karakeçi conflict.[67] While government soldiers sent from Urfa were meant to stop the Millîs, Millî İbrahim received help from Azimet Paşa, the top commander of the Ottoman imperial army in Diyarbekir.[68] The Millî and Karakeçi leaders, as well as the Shammar chiefs and others, were thus progressively becoming political actors and allies of local Ottoman officials in their own right, a process Talha Çiçek has described as the "provincialization" of nomad tribes in the region.[69] In the end, in 1903, it seems the two tribes made peace, since both were now accused of attacking other regions together *"bi'l-ittifak"* (in association). However, these relations remained unstable, and worsened again in 1904 after some Karakeçis went over to the Millîs.[70]

Just as the Zor government supported the Shammar leader Faris Paşa and Diyarbekir backed Millî İbrahim, Halil Bey of the Karakeçis was backed by the government of Urfa since this is where the tribe was attached administratively. The tribes, as Mehmet Rezan Ekinci has shown in his thesis, were not acting on behalf of their own interests alone. However, as Millî İbrahim enjoyed very close relations with the Fourth Army Marshal, the governor of Urfa could neither compete with him nor offer as much support to the Karakeçis as the Zor governor to Faris Paşa. When İbrahim Paşa fell from power in 1908, the Chechens of Ra's al-'Ayn, the Karakeçis, the Kîkîs, and other tribes did not hesitate to conquer the Millîs' territories.[71] This suggests that, in addition to his skill in warfare and diplomacy, İbrahim Paşa's dominance had above all been the result of the Abdülhamid regime's support.

---

66 Sykes, *The Caliphs' Last Heritage*, 324; FO 424/202, Jones to O'Conor, Diyarbekir, 22 January, 12, 19 March 1901.
67 FO 424/202, O'Conor to Lansdowne, Constantinople, 29 April 1901; DH.TMIK.M 108/67 (Oct. 1901); Ekinci, "Osmanlı Devleti Döneminde Milli Aşireti," 271. The Millîs had considered allying with the 'Anazas against the Shammars but ultimately refrained from doing so.
68 DH.TMIK.M. 87/34 (May 1901). Azimet Paşa was removed from his post in consequence.
69 M. Talha Çiçek, *Negotiating Empire in the Middle East: Ottomans and Arab Nomads in the Middle East* (Cambridge: Cambridge University Press, 2021), 187–92.
70 Sykes, *The Caliphs' Last Heritage*, 324; BEO 1899/142401 (Aug. 1902); Ekinci, "Osmanlı Devleti Döneminde Milli Aşireti," 289.
71 Ekinci, "Milli Aşireti," 300–2, 309.

260   Erdal Çiftçi

Alliances between Tribal Chiefs and Governors

Between 1895 and 1905, Ra's al-'Ayn and the surrounding region were hotly disputed between the Millî and Shammar tribes. In this period, the great majority of Ottoman documents dealing with Ra's al-'Ayn concern this conflict. While the former derived its power from the Marshal of the Ottoman Fourth Army and, indirectly, from the sultan, the latter was the most powerful tribe of the Syrian desert, if we discount the 'Anaza confederation, and enjoyed the support of the Zor provincial government. Thus the dispute was not merely one between two tribes but also involved various regional allies and proxies. For example the 'Adwan Arabs, who had previously been a sub-tribe of the 'Anaza, appear as allies of the Millîs and collided with their enemies around Ra's al-'Ayn several times at the end of the century.[72] The enmity between the Millîs and the Shammar also reflected a rivalry between the administrations to which they belonged: while the former were officially part of the province of Diyarbekir, the latter, led by Faris Paşa, belonged to the province of Zor, and both governments used the tribes to protect their taxation rights. Especially after the Millîs received additional rights and advantages from the Hamidian government, we will see that the governor of Zor turned to the Shammar to resist against the Millîs.

The most problematic question regarding the Millî-Shammar conflict was the violation of the Zor government's territories, of which Ra's al-'Ayn was part. The Millîs did not respect the integrity of the province, which lost many of its incomes when the Millîs prevented the collection of taxes from local tribes. The *mutasarrıf* of Zor, Zühdü Bey, therefore insisted that the border between Diyarbekir and Zor be demarcated (*tayin-i hudud, tefrik-i hudud*) as quickly as possible.[73] There are many examples of how governors and tribal chiefs competed to increase the number of their subjects for taxation. As early as 1892, or just after Millî İbrahim was recognized as a tribal "paşa," the *mutasarrıf* of Zor complained that the Millîs and 'Anazas were preventing his government from counting (*tadad*) the sheep of his province's tribes by hiding animals from the officers. Although they wandered in the territories of Zor, the Millîs refused sheep taxes to the officials there, claiming that they did not administratively belong to the Zor government.[74] The

---

72 DH.ŞFR 232/144; DH.TMIK.M 67/59; DH.ŞFR 245/117 (May 1896–Mar. 1900); Sykes, *The Caliphs' Last Heritage*, 315.

73 DH.MKT 2026/103 (Nov. 1892); DH.TMIK.M 74/6 (Apr. 1899).

74 DH.MKT 2026/103 (Oct. 1892).

authorities too sometimes tried increasing the size of their tax-paying population. In 1884, for example, the governor of Aleppo had accused the governor of Zor of encouraging sedentarized tribes who were living in the provincial borderlands (*hudud boyunda*) to migrate to his own territories.[75] The governor of Aleppo in fact requested the abolishment of the province of Zor, since according to him the region could not be ruled efficiently "because of the existence of another government in the middle of the desert."[76] What the Millîs and Shammars were doing was ultimately not so different from the conflicts between provincial governors who similarly tried to keep their territories prosperous by increasing their populations and collecting tributes.

Likewise, in 1892 the governor of Aleppo, Arif Bey, again accused Millî İbrahim of dominating his province's territory and its inhabitants, proposing to the central government that tribes of the region be registered into the Hamidiye Regiments separately from the Millîs to avoid losing control over them.[77] The *mutasarrıf* of Urfa made similar accusations that he could not collect animal taxes in his territories; if the Millîs were not stopped, the Urfa government could lose up to 70 per cent of its yearly animal tax income.[78] The Zor government, for its part, complained in 1898 that the Millîs had "dared to enter the territories of Ras al-'Ayn and 24,000 sheep were counted by them for taxation."[79] The following year, Zor's sheep tax official (*Zor ağnam tahkikat memuru*) reported that only 20 per cent of Ras al-'Ayn's sheep tax could be collected and that the government treasury had suffered great prejudice because of the ambiguity of the interprovincial border which the Hamidiye Regiments were violating. Tribes must remain within their own territories, he emphasized, otherwise taxes could not be collected properly.[80]

In addition to income losses, governors also stressed that they were unable to muster soldiers from the sedentarized tribes. In 1897, the Zor government wrote to the Ministry of the Interior that Millî İbrahim was recruiting Bedouin from the Beggara (Baqqara) and Sherabin into his own Hamidiye Regiments, along with some unregistered nomad tribes from Ra's al-'Ayn. Since the Zor government was levying soldiers among the settled members of these tribes as well, this was a threat

---

75 DH.ŞFR 120/86 (Feb. 1884).
76 ŞD 222/17 (Nov. 1889).
77 DH.ŞFR 153/59 (Feb. 1892).
78 DH.MKT 2284/71 (Dec. 1899).
79 DH.TMIK.M 50/61 (Mar. 1898).
80 DH.TMIK.M 74/6 (Apr. 1899).

262   Erdal Çiftçi

to the security and prosperity of the province.[81] The governor of Zor used this rhetoric to stop the expanding power of the Millîs. The Fourth Army marshal responded to the Ministry that any members of Bedouin tribes who were eligible for service in the imperial army would not be registered into the Regiments.[82] However, in 1900 Millî İbrahim himself petitioned saying that the Abadi clan of the Beggara was part of the Millî tribe, and since they were registered in the Hamidiye Regiments, they should not be counted for taxation (*tadad*).[83] Another document from the same dossier indicates that İbrahim Paşa even expelled tax officers sent from Ra's al-'Ayn in 1899.[84] According to İbrahim, the Beggara had always been part of the Millîs and were even the tribe of his own ancestors.[85] This meant an important loss of population, and taxes, for the administration of Ra's al-'Ayn and Zor.

As discussed above, the Millîs expanded their power as far as Jabal 'Abd al-'Aziz by allying with other tribes. They also pressed other tribes to recognize their power. İbrahim Paşa was able to obtain title deeds (*tapu*) for the region between Ra's al-'Ayn and Jabal 'Abd al-'Aziz that legitimized his being in control in the region.[86] This made the case more problematic since he thus had a legal right to roam in Zor territories. Inasmuch as he had the backing of military channels in the Ottoman central government, the local bureaucracy did not have any argument to expel the Millîs back to their headquarters in Viranşehir and Karacadağ.

Beyond the title deeds, İbrahim Paşa used some Bedouin tribes such as the 'Adwan as proxies to suppress or control other tribes. In 1899, the 'Adwan took over the region between Ra's al-'Ayn and the Khabur River, where clans of the Cubur and Ebu Salih tribes roamed as well.[87] Not only the 'Adwan but also some members of the Tayy and Kîkî tribes served as proxies in those years.[88] The shaykh of the Cubur, Musallat Paşa, resisted the Millîs and reported the case to the Zor government. According to the governor, even though Musallat Paşa was allied with him and fought against the Millîs, most of the Cuburs' sheep could not be counted for taxation (*tadad*).[89] During this

---

81 BEO 1046/78442 (Dec. 1897).
82 DH.MKT 2087/80 (Jan. 1898).
83 DH.TMIK.M 74/6–3 (Feb. 1900).
84 DH.TMIK.M 74/6–4 (Apr. 1899).
85 DH.TMIK.M 74/6–19 (Mar. 1899).
86 DH.TMIK.M 74/6–9 (Feb. 1900).
87 DH.TMIK.M 74/6–14 (Apr. 1899).
88 DH.ŞFR 232/144 (May 1896).
89 DH.TMIK.M 67/59–24 (Apr. 1899).

period, we rarely encounter Millî-'Anaza conflicts. On the contrary, it seems that Millî İbrahim maintained good relations with the 'Anaza since they shared their greatest enemy, the Shammar tribe. For example, when the 'Anaza attacked and captured 240 camels of the Harb tribe, İbrahim Paşa received these camels back from the 'Anaza and returned them to the owners.[90] These details show that the chiefs of the region had complex and multi-faceted political relations.

As İbrahim Paşa's tribal diplomacy empowered him in the region, he did not hesitate to use it against the Shammar tribe when different branches of the Shammars clashed. He for instance forged an alliance with Shaykh Jurallah of the Shammar since the latter's brother, Shaykh 'Isa, had the support of Faris Paşa in an intra-tribal conflict among the Shammars in Mosul.[91] İbrahim as a tribal "politician" could not miss this opportunity for his own interests: "To such a politician as Ibrahim this solid block of enemies was too dangerous to be left untouched. Profiting therefore by a long-standing feud between two parties of the Shammar, the Pasha by wheedling, bribes, and oratory gained over the great Shaykh Jurallah, who command 1,500 tents."[92] In addition, he led the al-'Amr clan of the Shammar to join his tribe in 1903 and later encouraged them to attack a Sherabin clan.[93] Such tactics were used by Millî İbrahim more than direct attacks against his enemies as a way of increasing his power.

İbrahim Paşa's dominance over the territories of Ra's al-'Ayn did not leave many choices to the Zor government. Since İbrahim had the support of the Fourth Army Marshal as well as the Commander in Chief (serasker), the governor of Zor, Zühdü Bey, attempted to use the Shammars' powerful leader Faris Paşa against him. Zühdü Bey sought closer relations with Faris Paşa, even punishing other local chiefs when dissatisfied with their service.[94] As reflected in their correspondence, this had previously already created tensions not only with Diyarbekir, but with the governor of Baghdad as well.[95] It can therefore be said that Zühdü Bey, more than Faris Paşa of the Shammar, became the Millîs' main enemy. With these entangling alliances, the provincial governors and local military figures themselves became involved in tribal disputes and lost their authority over parts of the tribal population.

---

90 DH.TMIK.M 39/21–13 (Nov. 1897).
91 DH.TMIK.M 132/34 (Sept. 1902).
92 Sykes, *The Caliphs' Last Heritage*, 324.
93 DH.TMIK.M 149/14 (July 1903). The Shaykh of al-Amr previously collected taxes from some Kurdish tribes. See Gökalp, *Kürt Aşiretleri*, 68.
94 ŞD 2237/1 (Nov. 1899).
95 DH.TMIK.M 51/22 (Mar. 1898).

Figure 11.3. Zühdü Bey, *mutasarrıf* of Zor
Source: *Tarih-i Osmani Encümeni Mecmuası* 2-14 (1328/1912): 862.

In 1896, the Millîs and Shammars were reconciled by the governor of Diyarbekir in Mardin. Faris Paşa signed a statement (*sened*) that he was going to return goods and animals previously seized from the Millîs. However, this treaty did not mark an end to their conflict. Faris Paşa did not in fact return the goods since he asserted that just after the peace, the Millîs had seized two hundred camels of the Shammar. And while the governor of Diyarbekir insisted that Zor fulfil the requirement, Zühdü Bey opposed the reimbursement of the goods, claiming that the ʿUkaydat (ʿAggedat) tribe of Zor had also been pillaged by the Millîs after the peace was made.[96] According to him, the Millîs had captured the camels and then forwarded them to the ʿAnaza tribe. Zühdü Bey also asserted that Diyarbekir's gendarmerie commander, Azimet Paşa, was under the influence of İbrahim's men and therefore had not

---

96 DH.TMIK.M 39/21 (Sept. 1897).

Figure 11.4. Shaykh Faris Paşa, chief of the Shammar
Source: Max Von Oppenheim, *Vom Mittelmeer zum Persischen Golf durch den Hauran, die Syrische Wüste und Mesopotamien* (Berlin: Dietrich Reimer, 1900), 2:42. Courtesy of Universitäts- und Landesbibliothek Sachsen-Anhalt.

266 Erdal Çiftçi

permitted the animals' return. Zühdü Bey opposed an investigation by the *vilayet* of Diyarbekir since both Azimet Paşa and the governor Halid Bey would only defend the Millîs.[97] He further asserted that if the Shammar had attacked the Millîs, the latter would be responsible since they had violated Zor's territories.[98] Zühdü Bey praised Faris Paşa for his service, describing him as considerate and reliable following the Millîs' attacks because Faris Paşa promised not to collect *khuwwa* (the Bedouin "brotherhood" tax) from the peasants in the region, instead raising his tribe's camel tax. Zühdü Bey requested a Mecidi decoration as well as the title of *mirülümera* for Faris Paşa, in addition to an annual pension as the shaykh of the Shammar in Zor.[99] In addition to his support for Faris, Zühdü Bey also backed Zor's ʿUkaydat tribe in their conflict against Baghdad's Dulaym tribe. In response, the governor of Baghdad accused Zühdü Bey of encouraging tribal warfare.[100] Zühdü Bey was eventually fired from his post over similar accusations.[101] In one example, he and his officers were accused of leading the Shammar under Faris Paşa's command to attack another tribe in the desert of northeastern Syria, sharing the booty among them in the centre of Zor in 1898.[102]

The governor of Diyarbekir, for his part, did in fact defend the Millî side. Just after the Mardin agreement, Halid Bey demanded the Zor government force Faris Paşa to pay for or return the stolen goods, arguing that otherwise the Millî-Shammar conflict would erupt again in the spring. According to his investigations, including testimony by the chiefs of the Harb and Sharabin tribes, the *müdir* of Viranşehir, the *mufti* of Raʾs al-ʿAyn, some Chechens, and others, the Shammars had not actually come near Viranşehir, and the two hundred camels were just an excuse for not reimbursing the Millîs; any further flare-ups would be solely the Zor governor's fault.[103] Halid Bey sent officers to retrieve the goods but they reported that Zühdü Bey did not recognize the Mardin agreement and insulted and threatened them, pushing his patronage of Faris Paşa so far as to falsely claim kinship and affirming "Faris Paşa is my tribe." According to Halid Bey, Zühdü Bey was

---

97 DH.TMIK.M 41/67 (Oct. 1897).
98 DH.TMIK.M 50/7 (Mar. 1898).
99 DH.TMIK.M 39/21 (Nov. 1897).
100 DH.TMIK.M 39/37; DH.TMIK.M 44/61; DH.TMIK.M 51/22 (Sept. 1897–Mar. 1898).
101 DH.MKT 1145/48 (Sept. 1899).
102 ŞD 2237/1–413 (Apr. 1902).
103 DH.TMIK.M 39/21; DH.TMIK.M 46/22; DH.TMIK.M 50/7 (Sept. 1897–Feb. 1898).

Warfare and Alliances in Ra's al-'Ayn 267

thereby acting against the sultan's order, protecting Shammar "bandits" who were "harmful to the public good and of no service or benefit to the state." Zühdü Bey was made to return some of the animals, but these were "injured and emaciated" and Millî İbrahim refused to accept them.[104] Halid Bey furthermore denied the Millîs had ever crossed into and attacked Zor territories, claiming they only roamed in their own areas.[105] In the end, the Ministry of the Interior sent the case to the sultan's aide-de-camp, Şakir Paşa, since "both provinces blamed each other for the root of the problem and for the deadlock."[106]

The rivalry between the two jurisdictions and allied tribes continued unabated. Later the same year, in September 1898, the government of Zor reported that a local clan, the Muhy al-Tala, had been attacked by proxies of the Millîs at Helobelo (Yukarı Taşyalak) near Ra's al-'Ayn, suffering many casualties and stolen livestock.[107] Zühdü Bey protested that one of the Millîs' foremost supporters, the Diyarbekir's gendarmerie commander Azimet Paşa, had been assigned to the investigation, noting that Diyarbekir officials were constantly providing Millî İbrahim with patronage (sahabetkarane) and taking his orders. Halid Bey again defended the Millîs, saying there was no proof they were responsible, as this region belonged to the tribes of Harran – the Qays, 'Anaza, Shammar, and Abu Khamis. The Millîs, on the other hand, never left the Viranşehir area. The Fourth Army Marshal Zeki Paşa also refuted the allegations, which he characterized as slander because İbrahim Paşa's eleven-year-old son Mahmud, who was accused of having orchestrated the crime, was not of an age to do so.[108]

The following spring, Zühdü Bey came to the aid of Mekki Bey, the deputy kaimakam of Ra's al-'Ayn and leader of the local Chechens, even though he was clearly the aggressor in a dispute with the Millîs. When the governor of Diyarbekir reported that Mekki Bey had attacked the Millîs, killing or capturing several men and stealing three herds of sheep along with seventy camels, Ra's al-'Ayn's administrative council unsurprisingly refused to acknowledge the crime, claiming no killings had occurred, accusing the Millîs of slander, and depicting Mekki Bey as an "oppressed innocent Muslim immigrant" and Millî İbrahim Paşa as a "tyrant." Halid Bey instead accused Mekki Bey of encouraging the

---

104 DH.TMIK.M 50/7; DH.ŞFR 223/38 (Feb.–Apr. 1898).
105 DH.TMIK.M 67/59 (May 1898).
106 DH.TMIK.M 46/22 (Jan. 1898).
107 DH.TMIK.M 60/72 (Sept. 1898).
108 DH.TMIK.M 60/72; DH.TMIK.M 64/15 (Oct. 1898–Feb. 1899).

268   Erdal Çiftçi

Shammar in their repeated attacks on the Millîs, demanding that he be punished in Siverek for his role. The Zor government made analogue charges, labelling İbrahim a "brigand leader" and the Millîs a "committee of bandits" (*eşkıya komitesi*); the Shammar, on the other hand, were in Jabal Sinjar and could therefore not be responsible. Mekki was apparently imprisoned in Siverek in May 1899 before being helped to escape by his men. He continued to enjoy the support of the Zor government, which also furthermore praised Faris Paşa and took the defence of the Shammar tribe as they returned to their places of origin (*meva-yı kadimleri*). The Shammars' peregrinations were portrayed as seasonal transhumance, the Millîs' as an illegitimate grab for power.[109]

Millî İbrahim continued to fight the Shammars between 1901 and 1905 while receiving military aid from Diyarbekir and neighbouring provinces. His relations deteriorated with the governor of Diyarbekir after 1901 but the latter was under orders from the central government not to harass the Millîs. Millî İbrahim, for his part, accused the Shammars of receiving support from the British government, which possibly heightened Istanbul's attention.[110] This close relationship came to an end when Abdülhamid II lost power in 1908. Zühdü Bey had already been dismissed from his post and sent into forced residence in Aleppo where he remained until 1908. Halid Bey, the governor of Diyarbekir, was not on good terms with the Unionists and supported Abdülhamid. His relations with the chiefs of the Hamidiye Regiments fluctuated,[111] but in the pursuit of his own interests, as we have seen, he generally remained pro-Millî.

Conclusion

Abdülhamid II's policy of Islamism, which was implemented in the Ottoman East through the creation of the Hamidiye Regiments among the area's Sunni tribes, paved the way for disorder in Ra's al-'Ayn and neighbouring territories. Together with the uncontrolled activities of Bedouin tribes in northeastern Syria, the arming of Kurdish cavalry units increased tension among various groups in the area. The chaotic

---

109 DH.TMIK.M 67/59 (Mar.–May 1899).

110 FO 404/202 (Apr.–May 1901).

111 Abdülhamid Kırmızı, "Kıbrıslı Halid Bey'in Diyarbekir Valiliği (1896–1902)," in *Osmanlı'dan Cumhuriyet'e Diyarbakır*, ed. Bahaeddin Yediyıldız and Kerstin Tomenendal (Ankara: Diyarbakır Valiliği ve Türk Kültürünü Araştırma Enstitüsü, 2008), 1:265–74.

atmosphere was further heightened by governors and local officials who became involved and took sides in tribal politics and often entered into alliances and partook in the tribal rivalries. Some of the tribes even came to represent the interests of local governors or high-ranking imperial military officers. The responsibility for the local disorder was therefore not the tribes' alone. These disputes occurred in a period when tribes were arguably being "provincialized." Alliances among the governors and their chiefs created a shared mission and local Ottoman officials lost their neutral stance in regard to intertribal and inter-provincial relations.

Tribes in Ra's al-'Ayn and adjoining areas carried out wars against one another in order to expand their territories and increase their power. The Kurdish Millîs emerged as the most powerful tribe in the region towards the end of the century. However, this success did not extend beyond the neighbouring regions, since many of their rival tribes were likewise supported by the Abdülhamid government at the same time. Tribal chiefs employed divide and rule tactics and engaged in what might be termed tribal diplomacy: Their enemy's enemy became their allies, and various allied tribes sometimes acted as proxies on behalf of leading tribal chiefs. Millî İbrahim Paşa epitomized this practice of tribal warfare and diplomacy, particularly while he was at the height of his power between 1895 and 1905. Overall, the examples we have cited show how tribal relations in the Middle East during this period were not marginal, isolated activities unique to tribes alone, but were rather at the heart of politics in rural northern Syria and southeastern Anatolia. These politics can only be understood if the multifaceted relations between government-supported Kurdish tribes, Bedouin Arab tribes, and local Ottoman officials are taken into consideration.

PART FOUR

Syrian Kurdish Elites of the Late Ottoman Period

12 Kurdish Naqshbandi-Khalidi Sheikhs of Damascus in the Nineteenth Century

METIN ATMACA

On a brisk, early morning of October 1820, Sheikh Khalid suddenly and secretly left the city of Sulaymaniyya for Baghdad. He took his family and left behind the school that produced hundreds of students of the Naqshbandi-Khalidi order and thousands of disciples all over Kurdistan and Iraq. James C. Rich, the British East India Company's resident in Baghdad and a guest of Mahmud Paşa, the ruler of the Baban emirate, witnessed the departure of the legendary Sufi sheikh and noted that the "cause of his flight is variously reported."[1] Some rumours had it that his prayers had failed to save the life of Mahmud Paşa's youngest son from smallpox, which was causing thousands of deaths in the city. Another claim was that he was involved in politics among the members of the Baban family to try to attain some influence over the region's governance. None of these claims is certain but there is one clear reason why he left the city: the newly established Naqshbandi-Khalidiyya order's sudden expansion over the region aroused the jealousy of the sheikhs of the Qadiri Sufi order, especially that of Sheikh Maʿruf Node (1752–1838). Rich allows that Sheikh Khalid was accused of many things that he did not commit, but that he was chased out of Sulaymaniyya because of Sheikh Maʿruf's unprecedented propaganda.

Khalid was not a stranger to Baghdad's scholars and notables. He had many followers in the city. First and foremost, Davud Paşa, governor of Baghdad, was a supporter of Khalid, who considered him a disciple.[2] In his earlier stay in Baghdad, Khalid came under the protection of a well-known Kurdish Haydari family. Through some of their family

---

1 James C. Rich, *Narrative of a Residence in Koordistan and on the Site of Ancient Nineveh*, vol 1. (London: 1836), 320–1.
2 Yusuf ʿIzz al-Din, *Dawud Basha wa-Nihayat al-Mamalik fi al-ʿIraq* (Baghdad: Matbaʿat al- Shaʿb, 1976), 49; Asʿad al-Sahib, *Bughyat al-Wajid fi Maktubat Mawlana Khalid* (Damascus: Matbaʿat al-Taraqqi, 1334/1915–16), 188–9.

274   Metin Atmaca

members, such as As'ad Sadr al-Din, the Hanafi *mufti* of Baghdad at the time, many scholars and dignitaries of the city were initiated into the order.[3] While in Baghdad, Khalid sent to Damascus two of his deputies, 'Abd al-Rahman al-'Aqri and Ahmad al-Khatib al-Irbili. Irbili initiated several dignitaries in Damascus into the order, including that city's Hanafi *mufti*, Husayn al-Muradi, and later advised Khalid to move there.[4] Leaving his family, disciples, and lands behind, Khalid travelled first to Istanbul and Jerusalem, finally arriving in Damascus in 1823. He remained there for the rest of his life and never returned.[5] Nevertheless, he kept his properties and continued to communicate with relatives and disciples in Kurdistan. Equally importantly, he referred to himself as "al-Kurdi" and "al-Shahrazuri" in letters written in Syria to followers in Jerusalem, Istanbul, Baghdad, and Dagestan.[6] Khalid's choice of titles implies his strong desire to retain his Kurdish identity even after he had left his homeland. As Sean Foley points out, "much like his ethnic background, Sheikh Khalid's titles balanced his need to simultaneously expand the Naqshbandiyya-Khalidiyya *tariqa* with his need to retain his Kurdish base."[7]

Sufism has long been a key part of Kurdish religiosity. Besides other initiatory traditions, the Naqshbandiyya order coloured the religious landscape in Kurdistan in the early modern period.[8] Despite the presence of Naqshbandi sheikhs throughout the seventeenth and eighteenth centuries, the Qadiriyya was more dominant among the Kurds, especially in southern Kurdistan.[9] Mawlana Khalid (Diya'

---

3 Butrus Abu-Manneh, "The Naqshbandiyya-Mujaddidiyya in the Ottoman Lands in the Early 19th Century," *Die Welt des Islams* 22, no. 1 (1982): 6, https://doi.org/10.2307/1569796.

4 Abu-Manneh, 8.

5 Sean Ezra Foley, "Shaykh Khalid and the Naqshbandiyya-Khalidiyya, 1776–2005" (Ph.D. diss., Georgetown University, 2005), 147–8.

6 Sahib, *Bughyat al-Wajid*, 173, 245.

7 Foley, "Shaykh Khalid," 302.

8 Dina Le Gall, *A Culture of Sufism: Naqshbandis in the Ottoman World, 1450–1700* (Albany: SUNY Press, 2005), 70–80, 83–5. The seventeenth-century Ottoman traveller Evliya Çelebi mentions numerous Naqshbandis in Kurdistan, to whom he refers interchangeably as "Nakşıbendi," "Hâcegân," and "Hâcegân-ı Nakşıbendi." Evliya Çelebi, *Evliya Çelebi Seyahatnamesi*, ed. S. Ali Kahraman and Yücel Dağlı (Istanbul: YKY, 2011), 1:23, 41, 44, 71, 73, 133, 261, 411, 413, 416.

9 C.J. Edmonds, *Kurds, Turks, Arabs: Politics, Travel, and Research in North-Eastern Iraq, 1919–1925* (London: Oxford University Press, 1957), 69–72; Muhammad Ra'uf Tawakkuli. *Tarikh-i Tasawwuf dar Kurdistan* (Tehran: Intisharat-i Ishraqi, 1378/1999), 133; Martin van Bruinessen, "The Qâdiriyya and the Lineages of Qâdirî Shaykhs among the Kurds," *Journal of the History of Sufism* (special issue on the Qâdiriyya order) 1–2 (2000): 131–49.

al-Din Khalid al-Shahrazuri, 1776–1827) undertook his short but intense education in the discipleship of Shah Ghulam ʿAli (d. 1824), a well-known Naqshbandi sheikh in Delhi.[10] Then he returned to Sulaymaniyya in 1811 and established his own branch of the order that would become known as the (Naqshbandiyya-) Khalidiyya. Over the course of his life, he appointed dozens of *khalifa*s who spread his message throughout various parts of the Ottoman Empire, especially among the Kurds. It is not surprising that it also became a key part of Kurdish identity in more marginal places like Syria, especially in cities such as Damascus. Because of the presence of his *khalifa*s and a Kurdish population to thrive among, Khalid likely felt welcome in Damascus.

Khalid had visited Damascus previously when he performed his pilgrimage to Mecca in 1805. He was therefore familiar with the city, its scholarly circles, and the milieu. Upon his second arrival in 1823 he was well received by scholars and notables in the city. One of the eminent families of the city, the Ghazzis, took him under their protection. Afterwards he bought a large mansion in the al-Qanawat quarter and used it both as a residence and a centre for the order.[11] Despite that, and the presence of numerous followers in the city, his first months were traumatic and difficult. He viewed the Damascenes as corrupt and their observance of Islamic practice as deviant, and thus longed to leave the city.[12] In a letter to ʿAbdullah al-Jali, his deputy in Koy Sanjaq (Koye; near Erbil), Khalid complained that "few people follow the exalted *sunna* here" in Damascus.[13] Besides, Sheikh Khalid was not immediately welcomed by the ulama, as he attacked Arabic and Islamic scholastic tradition during his stay in Baghdad. Thus, after Khalid's stay with the Ghazzis, a dozen established scholars met him to discuss religious matters, test his knowledge, and discern his real intention in moving to their city. Sheikh Khalid did so well and impressed the scholars that many of them subsequently joined his order or attended his classes.[14]

---

10 After nine or ten months of study, when Khalid attained the "greater intimacy with God" (*walayat-i kubra*), Shah Ghulam ʿAli gave him unconditional permission to guide disciples in the Naqshbandi, Qadiri, Chishti, Suhrawardi, and Kubrawi lineages. Arthur Buehler, "Mawlânâ Khâlid and Shâh Ghulâm ʿAlî," *Journal of the History of Sufism* 5 (2006): 66.

11 ʿAbd al-Majid al-Khani, *Al-Hadaʾiq al-Wardiyya fi Haqaʾiq Ajillaʾ al-Naqshbandiyya* (Cairo: Dar al-Tabaʿa al-ʿAmira, 1308/1890–1), 242–4.

12 Sahib, *Bughyat al-Wajid*, 229–31, 246–8.

13 Istanbul University Library AY 728, fol. 20b–21a, quoted in Abu-Manneh, "The Naqshbandiyya-Mujaddidiyya," 10.

14 Sahib, *Bughyat al-Wajid*, 88.

276   Metin Atmaca

Aside from these classes, Damascene scholars showed great interest in his personal library, which contained the city's best collection in both Arabic and Persian on diverse subjects in the Islamic sciences, linguistics, philosophy, and law.[15]

Damascus had a long tradition of accepting Kurdish scholars. Among those scholars Khalid found a number of Naqshbandi Sufis with intellectual links to India.[16] Many of these sheikhs found supporters among the Kurdish population, who mostly inhabited the Hayy al-Akrad (Kurdish quarter), a neighbourhood existing on the slopes of Mount Qasiyun since the twelfth century. Al-Akrad expanded mainly through Kurdish peasants and tribal groups from northern Syria escaping rural insecurity to seek shelter on the outskirts of Damascus. In the early nineteenth century, al-Akrad started to be recorded as a sub-quarter of al-Salihiyya, where the Kurds represented half the population. Some of these immigrants gained access to resources of the city and improved their economic status. Others continued to practice subsistence agriculture and stockbreeding.[17] Many Kurds also joined military and paramilitary groups to acquire wealth and political influence. This group later developed horizontal alliances with urban notables and occupied prominent positions in the military and bureaucracy of the city.[18] Some of these, who were referred to as *aghawat* (leaders of paramilitary forces), reached elite status and entered the mainstream of Damascus politics. Khalid found support among them as well as among the Arab population.

When Khalid arrived in Damascus, he left behind most of his family in Baghdad. Without a family in Damascus, he solidified his ties with 'Umar al-Ghazzi and Isma'il Efendi al-Ghazzi by marrying their sister 'A'isha. This marriage of convenience connected a leading Shafi'i sheikh with a prominent Hanafi family. Through the al-Ghazzis, Khalid also established contact with leading families from the Naqshbandi and Khalwati orders.[19] After securing his position, Khalid invited his wives,

---

15 Frederik de Jong and Jan Just Witkam, "The Library of al-Šayḫ Ḫālid al-Šahrazūrī al-Naqšbandī (d. 1242/1827): A Facsimile of the Inventory of His Library (Ms Damascus, Maktabat al-Asad, No. 259)," *Manuscripts of the Middle East* 2 (1987): 68–73.

16 Foley, "Shaykh Khalid," 150.

17 Philip Khoury, *Syria and the French Mandate: The Politics of Arab Nationalism 1920–1945* (Princeton: Princeton University Press, 1987), 291; Nelida Fuccaro, "Ethnicity and the City: The Kurdish Quarter of Damascus between Ottoman and French Rule, c. 1724–1946," *Urban History* 30, no. 2 (August 2003): 210–11, https://doi.org/10.1017/S0963926803001135.

18 Fuccaro, "Ethnicity and the City," 214.

19 Foley, "Shaykh Khalid," 159–60.

Khadija bint Yusuf/Umm Baha' al-Din and Fatima bint 'Abdullah/ Umm 'Abd al-Rahman al-Thabit, to come to Damascus. Khalid was especially looking forward to seeing his son Baha' al-Din, as well as his other son 'Abd al-Rahman, anticipating their support. However, both sons died of the plague in 1827.

Four different Ottoman governors were appointed to administer the province during the time Sheikh Khalid lived in Damascus between 1823 and 1827. Because of his importance and the high social status of many of his followers, one would have expected these governors to form a connection with him. Yet surprisingly, none of the hagiographies of the period mention any relations between Sheikh Khalid and Ottoman governors while he lived there. This despite the fact that he communicated with the governor of Acre, 'Abdullah Paşa, and counseled him on important political matters.[20] Khalid also corresponded with Gürcü Necib Paşa, Muhammad Ali Paşa's official agent in Istanbul. Both bureaucrats were loyal followers of the Khalidiyya and had close relations with Muhammad Ali. Such relations suggest the possibility that there were ties between Khalid and Muhammad Ali. The sheikh frequently expressed his loyalty to the Ottoman government and continued to maintain close relationships with administrators appointed by the central government.[21] His political connections angered certain scholars of Aleppo who sent letters in this regard to Sultan Mahmud II. Such complaints led the Ottoman sultan to assign agents to monitor Khalid in Damascus. The sultan also corresponded with one of his most ardent supporters, Davud Paşa of Baghdad. The reports from both the Ottoman agents and Davud Paşa were positive; the investigation of Khalid came out favourably for him and Mahmud II decided to reject the allegations against him. As a result, the Sheikh and his disciples from Baghdad and Kurdistan were allowed to remain in Damascus.[22]

During his period in Damascus Sheikh Khalid emphasized in his letters the necessity of supporting the sultan and the Ottoman government. Although he does not specify the factors that compelled him to support the Ottoman authorities publicly, it was probably related to 'Abd al-Wahhab al-Susi's expulsion from Istanbul in the mid-1820s. Al-Susi had been the head of the Khalidiyya in Istanbul before Khalid

---

20 Sahib, *Bughyat al-Wajid*, 85–7, 227–9, 244–5.

21 Sean Foley, "Temporal and Spiritual Power in Nineteenth-Century Ottoman Politics: Shaykh Khalid, Gürcü Necib Pasha, and the Naqshbandiyya-Khalidiyya," *Türkiyat Araştırmaları* 9 (2008): 230–1, 233.

22 'Abbas al-'Azzawi, "Mawlana Khalid al-Naqshbandi," *Majallat al-Majma' al-'Ilmi al-Kurdi* 1 (1973): 719–21.

278   Metin Atmaca

permanently barred him from the order when he acted too independently and attempted to found a suborder.[23] Thus, his official expulsion from Istanbul hints that Khalid had reached an agreement with Ottoman authorities at the time.

It seems that the Ottoman government needed sheikhs like Khalid in Damascus as the Empire and region went through an uncertain period. In 1810 the city was occupied by the governor of Acre, Sülayman Paşa, who was supported by Druze and Maronite levies. Damascenes, who considered their city one of the centres of Sunni Islam, felt humiliated by the challenge from local heterodox and non-Muslim groups.[24] In addition, the Greek Revolution in 1821 sent shock waves through the Ottoman Empire, especially in urban areas dominated by a Muslim population. In such a milieu, Sheikh Khalid, who sought to strengthen orthodox belief among the Muslims and keep them in high spirits, was welcomed in Damascus.[25] Despite his dissatisfaction with the outcome, he and his deputies succeeded in reviving interest in religion among the population. Because of the veneration shown to him by the Damascenes, Khalid was considered a renovator (*mujaddid*) by many poets and writers of the period. In spite of such admiration, he could not recruit any deputies from among the inhabitants of Damascus and perhaps not more than two *khalifa*s from all Syria, including Sheikh Muhammad al-Khani of Khan Shaykhun, who would stand at the head of the Damascus branch, and Sheikh Ahmad al-Arwadi of Tripoli, a supporter of the Khalidiyya. It is not clear how far the order spread in Syria but from his *khalifa*s and the activities of the order, it seems that the Khalidiyya was essentially confined to Damascus and Tripoli.[26]

In 1826 Khalid travelled on the hajj together with a large group of his followers. He cut short his journey and immediately returned to Damascus upon learning that the city had been struck by the plague, with the hope of saving the people. However, the Sheikh would die from the plague on 8 June 1827. Knowing that he would die, the Sheikh named Isma'il al-Anarani as his successor. Hagiographies also claim that a day after his death the plague ended, suggesting that he performed a miracle by sacrificing his life. In any case, he left an important

---

23 As'ad Rustum, *Al-Mahfuzat al-Malakiyya al-Misriyya* (Beirut: Al-Maktaba al-Bulisiyya, 1986–7), 1:100; Foley, "Shaykh Khalid," 182.

24 M. Ibn Abdin, *Radd al-Muhtar 'Ala al-Durr al-Mukhtar* (Cairo, 1271–2/1854–5), 3:253, 275 in Abu-Manneh, "The Naqshbandiyya-Mujaddidiyya," 9.

25 Abu-Manneh, "The Naqshbandiyya-Mujaddidiyya," 10.

26 Khani, *Al-Hada'iq al-Wardiyya*, 223, 243; Abu-Manneh, "The Naqshbandiyya-Mujaddidiyya," 10–11.

Kurdish Naqshbandi-Khalidi Sheikhs of Damascus 279

legacy in Damascus and the surrounding region as thousands attended his funeral.[27]

Khalid bequeathed most of his land and financial resources to several of his followers. He did not make any provisions for his wives or children, except for his wife Khadija, mother of his favourite son Baha' al-Din, who was to oversee his properties in Syria and manage his charitable resources.[28] Khadija lived a long life and played an important role in Sheikh Khalid's family and the rise of the Khalidiyya. This was only after a legal process that determined who would get what part of the Sheikh's inheritance. Each of Sheikh Khalid's daughters and wives received one eighth of Khalid's inheritance, while his only male heir, Najm al-Din, received a quarter. After the resolution of the case, almost all of Khalid's family left Damascus for Kurdistan.[29] Their departure first to Baghdad, then Sulaymaniyya was imposed on the family members as well as on the Khalidi sheikhs by the sultan, who felt threatened in his autocratic rule by the Khalidiyya's "activism" and the "orthodox revival" it sought to generate.[30] Following the destruction of the janissaries in 1826, Mahmud II outlawed the Bektaşi order, which had been dominating the elite infantry units for centuries. Although he handed over their properties in Istanbul to Naqshbandis in order to obtain their support against the Bektaşis and other rebellious agents, the sultan did not hesitate to turn against the Khalidiyya when he felt the reins of power were firmly in his hands.[31]

When Khalid's family was forced out of Damascus in 1828, it was the sheikh's younger brother Mahmud al-Sahib (1783-1866) in Sulaymaniyya who accommodated them. On that occasion Khalid's family informed Sahib that the deceased had bestowed on him his lands in Kurdistan. In fact, when Khalid had left for Damascus in 1823 he had appointed his brother as his deputy in the Sulaymaniyya lodge. However, Sahib did not actively lead the lodge there since he stayed with his brother in Damascus between 1823 and 1827. There he even married Daifa, the daughter of Hasan al-Muradi of the Muradi family. After his

---

27 Isma'il al-Ghazzi, *Husul al-Uns fi Intiqal Hadrat Mawlana ila Hazirat al-Quds*, ed. Muhammad Usama al-Tikriti (Damascus: N.p., 1970), 43–6, 51; Foley, "Shaykh Khalid," 183–5; Itzchak Weismann, *Taste of Modernity: Sufism, Salafiyya, and Arabism in Late Ottoman Damascus* (Leiden: Brill, 2001), 68.

28 Sahib, *Bughyat al-Wajid*, 259–64.

29 Foley, "Shaykh Khalid," 199.

30 Weismann, *Taste of Modernity*, 78–80.

31 John Kingsley Birge, *The Bektashi Order of Dervishes* (London: Luzac, 1937), 77–8; Abu-Manneh, "The Naqshbandiyya-Mujaddidiyya," 28–34.

280   Metin Atmaca

brother's death, Sahib returned to Kurdistan. When Sultan Mahmud II allowed the Khalidis in Iraq to return to Syria, Sahib came back to Damascus in early 1831 after an extended stay in Diyarbekir. He settled down in the city and began training novices and proclaiming ownership of his brother's estate, even though Khalid had not nominated him as his deputy. His claim to head the order was challenged by 'Abdullah al-Herati. Shortly thereafter, he decided to resettle in the Hijaz for the next seven years, because of the rising hostility with his rival, and also the city's occupation by Ibrahim Paşa of Egypt.[32] Once the Egyptian army withdrew from Syria in 1840, Sahib immediately returned.

After Sahib settled in Damascus again he resumed his teaching and sent deputies to other regions. His fame reached beyond Syria and Kurdistan to the capital of the Empire. Thus in 1843, Sultan Abdülmecid appointed him with an allowance as sheikh and teacher in the prestigious Sulaymaniyya lodge of Damascus. The sultan's patronage and generous support helped Mahmud al-Sahib advance his leadership position within the Naqshbandi-Khalidi order. His lodge remained as a rival branch to the order led by Muhammad ibn 'Abd Allah al-Khani in the Muradiyya mosque. Sahib maintained a correspondence with some of his deputies in Kurdistan. He also authorized a few deputies of his own in Syria. One of his most important *khalifa*s was Abu Bakr al-Kilali of Kurdistan, who had also had connections with Sheikh Khalid and Khani. Kilali was an erudite Sufi who taught many reformist ulama of the city. He dedicated himself to teaching not only the religious but also the rational sciences such as logic, philosophy, and the new natural sciences.[33]

Mahmud al-Sahib tried to enhance his position among the ulama of Damascus rather than focussing on the teachings of his brother. Anecdotes from his biography indicate that he kept his connections with many of Khalid's great disciples, who preserved their links with the Khalidi network while joining the local tendency of the day in the city, which was made up of ulama who remained loyal to the teaching of their master, abstaining from taking up administrative office and instead inheriting their posts from their fathers in mosques and colleges. These connections, however, were based on the respect given to Khalid rather than on any appreciation of Sahib's religious personality or the works he produced. On the other hand, Sahib focussed on

---

32 Weismann, *Taste of Modernity*, 93–4; Foley, "Shaykh Khalid," 159; As'ad al-Sahib, *Al-Fuyudat al-Khalidiyya wa'l-Manaqib al-Sahibiyya* (Cairo: Al-Matba'at al-'Ilmiyya, 1311/1893–4), 73–4.
33 Weismann, 95–6, 215; Sahib, 58–9, 63–5.

Kurdish Naqshbandi-Khalidi Sheikhs of Damascus   281

younger generations of madrasa students in Damascus who had no direct association with the legacy of his brother.[34]

More than a decade after Mahmud al-Sahib's death, his son As'ad al-Sahib (1855-1928) inherited his father's position in the Sulaymaniyya lodge in Damascus. According to him he had six masters, who were mostly Kurds. Among them were 'Ali al-Kharbuti of Kurdistan, Ahmad al-Zamalkani, and 'Isa al-Kurdi.[35] As'ad, with his conventional Khalidi principles of orthodoxy and service to the central Ottoman state, fit well with Sultan Abdülhamid II's Islamic policy. In return Abdülhamid showed As'ad his support by different means and gestures such as awarding him a letter of praise (*iltifatname*).[36] As'ad's attachment to the sultan's Islamic policy was contrary to the principles that Sheikh Khalid had emphasized of keeping distance from the rulers. As'ad's stance caused a further split that had already begun among the Khalidi leaders in Damascus in previous generations. Under Abdülhamid's regime As'ad edited and published primary sources of the Khalidi order in addition to his own writings. His writings contain many allusions to his struggle against Muhammad al-Khani and his son 'Abd al-Majid al-Khani. In his work As'ad demonstrated his position towards the sultan and state, and his views on the course of the Khalidiyya in the last decades of the Ottoman Empire. As'ad intensified his claim to the leadership of the Khalidi order in Damascus after 'Abd al-Majid published his biographical dictionary of Khalidi sheikhs, *Al-Hada'iq al-Wardiyya*, in which Mahmud al-Sahib was not mentioned. As'ad perceived this as a clear humiliation and severed his relations with the al-Khanis.[37]

As'ad, in order to establish his right to the leadership, reopened the old question of Sheikh Khalid's succession, thus refuting the claim of the Khanis. He asserted that his father, Mahmud al-Sahib, as brother of Khalid, most deserved to succeed him as his deputy. He added that his

---

34 Weismann, 96.

35 Sahib, *Bughyat al-Wajid*, 44–5; As'ad al-Sahib, *Nur al-Hidaya wa'l-'Irfan fi Sirr al-Rabita wa'l-Tawajjuh wa-Khatm al-Khwajagan* (Cairo: Al-Matba'a al-'Ilmiyya, 1311/1893–4), 25.

36 Cumhurbaşkanlığı Osmanlı Arşivi [BOA]: Y.PRK.UM. 29/88, 1.11.1311 (6 May 1894). As'ad was supported not only by sultan Abdülhamid, but also by succeeding Ottoman rulers. For instance, in 1911 he was given a piece of cloth from the Ka'ba to be used in Khalid's mausoleum (BOA: İ.MBH 6/29, 1.6.1329/ 30 May 1911), while in 1919 his travel expenses from Damascus to Istanbul were paid (BOA: MV 214/49, 29.4.1337/1 February 1919).

37 Jamal al-Din al-Qasimi, *Ta'thir al-Mahsam fi Ma'athir Dimashq al-Sham* (private collection, Qasimi library, Damascus, 1901, volume not specified), 57, in Weismann, *Taste of Modernity*, 111–12.

282 Metin Atmaca

father was the first and favourite deputy of Khalid and Sahib vigorously defended his brother against his Qadiri rivals in Sulaymaniyya when a conflict arose between the two orders.[38] After disputing the leadership of the other deputies like Isma'il al-Anarani, Isma'il al-Ghazzi, and 'Abdullah al-Herati, he argued that his father had nominated him as the successor three days before his death.[39] He thereby tried to establish a lineage of succession that would reach down to him.

As'ad dominated the Khalidi order in Damascus after 'Abd al-Majid al-Khani lost favour with the authorities during his visit to Istanbul in 1896. Two years after 'Abd al-Majid's return to Damascus, his father Muhammad al-Khani died. He was further devastated when he found out that his father's state allowance had been transferred to someone else. His father's death also led to fierce struggles among the members of the family over the succession, especially between him and his uncle Ahmad. To make matters worse, As'ad helped another brother of Muhammad al-Khani, 'Abdallah, to push his claim to replace his deceased brother. As'ad's interference in the struggle among the members of Khani family and his influence on the governor and his men proved decisive. He helped 'Abdallah to officially apply to become the head of the Khani branch and secured the approval of the *şeyhülislam* in Istanbul. As'ad even appointed 'Abdallah as his deputy, thus the Khani's lodge now became part of his network. As'ad al-Sahib's domination of the lodge in the Muradiyya mosque indicated the end of the Khani branch of the Khalidi order. 'Abd al-Majid departed for the last time to Istanbul to receive some compensation for his lost position and died there shortly after.[40] Meanwhile, As'ad had his brother Hafiz 'Uthman selected as head of the *waqf* of the Ahmad Paşa madrasa in 1891, while he himself was appointed head of the madrasa in the Sultan Selim mosque in 1902. As'ad allied himself to the Ottoman rulers during the administration of the Committee of Union and Progress as well. He won the patronage of Cemal Paşa, one of the top leaders of the CUP and governor of Syria during World War I, and had him sponsor the publication of an edited collection of Khalid's letters, *Bughyat al-Wajid fi Maktubat Mawlana Khalid*, in 1334/1915–16. As'ad

---

38 For the conflict between Mawlana Khalid and his adversary Ma'ruf Node, see Halkawt Hakim, "Le conflit Qâdiriyya – Naqshbandiyya dans le milieu kurde au début du XIXe siècle," *Journal of the History of Sufism* 1–2 (2000): 151–66.

39 Sahib, *Al-Fuyudat al-Khalidiyya*, 84; Sahib, *Nur al-Hidaya*, 25.

40 Qasimi, *Ta'thir al-Mahsam fi Ma'athir Dimashq al-Sham*, 52–4, in Weismann, *Taste of Modernity*, 121–2.

Kurdish Naqshbandi-Khalidi Sheikhs of Damascus   283

was shortly thereafter appointed chief judge of the Haramayn (Mecca and Medina), a prestigious judicial position.[41]

Besides As'ad and Hafiz 'Uthman, Mahmud al-Sahib also had a third son, 'Abd al-Fattah, on whom there is very little information. From the travel account of an Indian Muslim scholar, Shibli Nu'mani, who encountered 'Abd al-Fattah on his journey to Istanbul, we learn that the latter was well received by the Syrians in the capital because of his father's and brother's fame. It seems that 'Abd al-Fattah was very aware of the rising power of the non-Muslim population in the empire. On one occasion 'Abd al-Fattah shared with Nu'mani an annual report demonstrating that Christian students outnumbered Muslim students in the Mekteb-i Sultani (Lycée de Galatasaray).[42]

While Mahmud al-Sahib and later his sons, especially As'ad al-Sahib, dominated the Khalidi network in Damascus, sheikhs of Kurdish extraction continued to immigrate to Syria. Foremost among these sheikhs was 'Isa al-Kurdi, who As'ad greatly respected and even described as one of his principal masters.[43] Born in Tarham in the *sancak* of Siird, part of the province of Diyarbekir, in 1831, 'Isa came from a family related to the emirs of Bohtan and the Prophet Muhammad.[44] In 1851, on his way back from the *hajj*, he stopped at Damascus, where

---

41 Sahib, *Bughyat al-Wajid*, 311; Sean Foley, "Hagiography, Court Records, and Early Modern Sufi Brotherhoods: Shaykh Khālid and Social Movement Theory," in *Sufism and Society: Arrangements of the Mystical in the Muslim World, 1200–1800*, ed. John Curry and Erik Ohlander (London: Routledge, 2012), 61; Weismann, *Taste of Modernity*, 137–40. None of the sources, including Ottoman archival documents (see for instance a report prepared on him by Ottoman officials DH.KMS 44/57, 15 Şaban 1335/ 6 June 1917), clearly states that As'ad Sahib went to the Hijaz after he was appointed. Besides the judgeship (*kadılık*) of Istanbul, that of Mecca and Medina (*Haremeyn mevleviyeti*) was among the top judicial positions in the Empire below the *kazaskerlik* of Anadolu and Rumeli and the office of *şeyhülislam*. Starting in the nineteenth century, titles were given without appointment. Thus, most likely because of his close relationship with Cemal Paşa, As'ad received the title and position without actually performing the duty. For more on the *Haremeyn mevleviyeti* see the *İlmiyye Salnamesi* (Istanbul: Matbaa-ı Amire, 1334/1915), 649; İsmail Hakkı Uzunçarşılı, *Osmanlı Devletinin İlmiye Teşkilatı* (Ankara: Türk Tarih Kurumu, 1988), 99–100; Fatima Müge Göçek, "Mewlewiyyet," *EI2*; Fahri Unan, "Mevleviyet," *TDV İslam Ansiklopedisi*.

42 Shibli Numani, *Turkey, Egypt, and Syria: A Travelogue*, trans. Gregory Maxwell Bruce (Syracuse, NY: Syracuse University Press, 2020), 35, 67–8.

43 Itzchak Weismann, "The Forgotten Shaykh: 'Īsā al-Kurdī and the Transformation of the Naqshbandī-Khālidī Brotherhood in Twentieth-Century Syria," *Die Welt des Islams* 43 (2003), 377–8; Sahib, *Bughyat al-Wajid*, 43–4; Sahib, *Nur al-Hidaya*, 25.

44 On the last emirs of Bohtan see Metin Atmaca, "Resistance to Centralization in the Ottoman Periphery: The Kurdish Baban and Bohtan Emirates," *Middle Eastern*

284   Metin Atmaca

he paid homage at Sheikh Khalid's tomb and studied with Abu Bakr al-Kilali, who perhaps persuaded 'Isa to enter the Khalidi path. Upon his return to Kurdistan he studied under the tutelage of several scholars such as Hasan al-Nurani, 'Abdullah al-Baydari, and Qasim al-Hadi. He completed his religious studies with them and pursued the Sufi path, establishing his own circle of disciples while strengthening his Khalidi credentials. After the Russian-Ottoman war of 1877–8 caused further disorder in Ottoman Kurdistan, 'Isa immigrated to Damascus, where he settled in Salihiyya.[45]

'Isa directed much of his efforts towards the lower class rather than the urban elite who experienced Westernization and had a more reformist mind. Such a populist strategy shows the rupture between his methods and the traditional methods of the Khalidi network, which focussed mainly on the ulama, Sufi sheikhs, and state elites.[46] While in Damascus, 'Isa visited Mecca, Medina, Jerusalem, and Beirut. He also travelled twice to Istanbul, where he was a guest of Sultan Abdülhamid II. He maintained relations with other Khalidi sheikhs in Syria and dedicated himself to religious teachings and acquiring a large number of disciples until he died in 1912.[47] 'Isa al-Kurdi had many deputies, at least thirty-nine, from different parts of the Islamic world including Egypt, Bursa, Kazan, Bukhara, Albania, and Afghanistan. At least eleven deputies, including two of his sons, had a Kurdish background. Upon his death one of his close disciples, Amin al-Zamalkani, son of a Kurdish peasant from the Ghuta near Damascus, took over the post in the lodge next to Sheikh Khalid's shrine on Mount Qasiyun.[48]

Amin Kuftaru (1877–1938), whose family came from Karma near Hasaka in northern Syria to Damascus in 1878, was another influential Kurdish deputy of 'Isa al-Kurdi.[49] Like all other deputies of Kurdish

---

Studies 55 (2019), 522–6; Metin Atmaca, "Origins of the 'Kurdish Question': Yezdanşêr Revolt (1854–55)," in *Routledge Handbook of the Crimean War*, ed. Candan Badem (London: Routledge, 2022), 357–61.

45 Muhammad Abu al-Khayr al-Maydani, "Qabsa min anwar tarjamat mawlana 'Isa al-Kurdi," Leiden University library, Ms. 680A, 1–2, 57–8, in Weismann, " 'Īsā al-Kurdī," 377–8.

46 Abbas al-Azzawi, "Khulafa Mawlana Khalid," *Majallat al-Majma' al-'Ilmi al-Kurdi* 2 (1974): 182–222.

47 Weismann, " 'Īsā al-Kurdī," 378.

48 Muhammad Muti' al-Hafiz and Nizar Abaza, *Ta'rikh 'Ulama' Dimashq fi al-Qarn al-Rabi' 'Ashar al-Hijri* (Damascus: Dar al-Fikr, 1986–91), 1:425–6.

49 For biographical details of Amin Kuftaru see Muhammad al-Habash, *Al-Shaykh Amin Kuftaru fi Dhikra Khamsin 'Am 'ala Wafatihi* (Damascus: Dar al-Ma'rifa, 1989); Muhammad al-Habash, *Al-Shaykh Ahmad Kuftaru wa-Minhajuhu fi'l-Tajdid wa'l-Islah* (Damascus: Dar al-Nur, 1996).

Kurdish Naqshbandi-Khalidi Sheikhs of Damascus   285

extraction, he was a Shafi'i. Amin succeeded 'Isa as the leader of the Khalidi order after his master's death in 1912 and moved the centre of his order to the Abu al-Nur mosque at the foot of Mount Qasiyun. He had his own interpretation of Sufism, such that his movement was later distinguished as the "Kaftariyya" (Naqshbandiyya-Mujaddidi-yya-Khalidiyya-Kaftariyya) and spread beyond Syria. At Abu al-Nur he taught a wide range of Islamic studies while emphasizing the importance of Sufism. Kuftaru was known not only as an erudite scholar and Sufi but also as a political activist committed to resistance against the French mandate. His son Ahmad Kuftaru (1912–2004) continued his father's legacy and later held the position of the grand mufti of Syria from 1964 until his death in 2004.[50]

Damascus was long a centre of learning for Sufis from throughout the Ottoman Empire and the Islamic world. Among those who travelled to the city, Kurdish scholars made up an important proportion. There had already been Kurdish Sufis before Sheikh Khalid arrived in Damascus, though with little influence among the scholarly elites of the city.[51] After his arrival, Khalid built his influence by establishing close ties with powerful Arab families in the city. At the same time he brought his family members, deputies, and students to Syria. After his death his family members and non-local deputies were forced out of Damascus, but a decade later his brother, Mahmud al-Sahib, came back to the city, reclaimed Khalid's property and legacy, and dominated the scholarly scene even more than before. In fact the Kurdish sheikhs became so dominant and powerful in Damascus that Muhammad al-Khani, one of the leading Khalidi sheikhs of Arab extraction, felt it necessary to establish family connections with one of the Kurdish sheikhs, Ahmad al-Khatib al-Irbili, the first major deputy that Khalid had sent to the city. He thus married his son to the daughter of al-Irbili.[52] Khani was

---

50 For more on Ahmad Kuftaru see Annabelle Böttcher, *Syrische Religionspolitik unter Asad* (Freiburg: Arnold-Bergstrasser-Institut, 1998), 147–223, and Habash, *Al-Shaykh Ahmad Kuftaru*.

51 Before the nineteenth century, several Kurdish scholars and Sufi sheikhs chose to move to Damascus to study or teach. For instance, Hasan ibn Muhammad ibn Ibrahim al-Kurdi al-Suhrani and the Naqshbandi sheikh Mahmud ibn Abi Bakr al-Jazari settled in the city in the second half of the seventeenth century. Martin van Bruinessen, *Mullas, Sufis, and Heretics: The Role of Religion in Kurdish Society, Collected Articles* (Istanbul: Isis Press, 2000), 70–1, 106. On Kurdish scholars, including Molla Mahmud who settled in Damascus, in the Ottoman Empire in the seventeenth century see Khaled El-Rouayheb, *Islamic Intellectual History in the Seventeenth Century: Scholarly Currents in the Ottoman Empire and the Maghreb* (Cambridge: Cambridge University Press, 2015), 13–59.

52 Weismann, *Taste of Modernity*, 86.

286 Metin Atmaca

also patronized and protected by his followers like Haccı Musa Safveti Paşa, the governor of Damascus between 1846 and 1847. After his term ended in Damascus, Safveti Paşa went back to Istanbul, where he founded a Khalidi lodge at his private expense and nominated a deputy of Khani as its head. Safveti Paşa must have felt the power of Kurdish sheikhs in Damascus as he explicitly specified in the endowment charter that the head of the lodge must be a non-Kurdish Khalidi sheikh (*"shart an yakuna shaykhuha Naqshbandiyyan-Khalidiyyan wa-an la yakuna Kurdiyyan"*).[53]

Taking into consideration that the dominant school of law (*madhhab*) among the scholars and muftis of Syria was Hanafi, Kurdish Sufis of the Khalidiyya remained outsiders with their Shafi'i identity.[54] Despite this, many deputies of Sheikh Khalid and followers of his Kurdish *khalifa*s decided to change their *madhhab* to Shafi'ism. After a while it became very typical that Damascene Sufis and ulama were led by Kurds of the Shafi'i school.[55] Kurdish Sufis in Damascus adapted to their new home while they initiated many established scholars and novices into their network. They dominated the scholarly scene of Damascus from the time Sheikh Khalid arrived until the end of Ottoman rule in Syria. Kurdish Sufis not only established their place among the ulama in the city but also received political support throughout the Ottoman and post-imperial periods. What started as an exile for the Naqshbandi-Khalidi Sufis of Kurdistan turned out to be a great opportunity for them to spread their vision and belief beyond their homeland.

---

53 Khani, *Al-Hada'iq al-Wardiyya*, 272.
54 The majority of ulama followed the Shafi'i school before the Ottomans took over Damascus. During the eighteenth century many ulama switched to the Hanafi school, probably to strengthen ties with the Ottoman religious hierarchy and demonstrate their loyalty to the Ottoman Empire, whereas most ulama without official posts continued to adhere to the Shafi'i school into the nineteenth century. See Linda Schatkowski Schilcher, *Families in Politics: Damascene Factions and Estates of the 18th and 19th Centuries* (Stuttgart: Franz Steiner, 1985), 120; John Voll, "Old Ulama Families and Ottoman Influence in Eighteenth-Century Damascus," *American Journal of Arabic Studies* 3 (1975): 56–9.
55 Kenichiro Takao, "Sufi Genealogy of Shaykh Ahmad Kuftaru: Damascene Networking of the Naqshbandi Sufi Order in the 19–20th Centuries," *The World of Monotheistic Religions* 1 (2010): 115.

13 Alliances and Competition in Kurdish Networks in Late Ottoman Syria: The Example of the Bedirhani and Baban Families

BARBARA HENNING

In the following, the complex relationships and interactions between two Ottoman-Kurdish families, the Bedirhani and the Baban family, will be explored through the lens of a court case that took place in late Ottoman Syria. Hüseyin Bedirhan, who served as the local Ottoman governor (*kaymakam*) in the *kaza* of 'Akkar located in the *sancak* of Tripoli in the early 1890s, is the main protagonist of these proceedings: defending himself against accusations of malpractice, he petitioned against the conditions of his trial. One of his key arguments was that as long as Halid Baban, allegedly a sworn personal enemy of him and his entire family, was acting as Ottoman governor in Beirut, he could not hope for fair treatment of his case. But is there any evidence to support Hüseyin Bedirhan's claim, or was he playing on late-Ottoman stereotypes to secure advantages in the course of his trial? Contextualizing Hüseyin Bedirhan's argument, Ottoman-Kurdish networks, rivalries, and contested images of being Kurdish in late-Ottoman Syria and beyond come into focus.

Situating Hüseyin Kenan Bedirhan: Biographical Trajectory and Family Background

Hüseyin Kenan Bedirhan was born as one of the younger sons of Emir Bedirhan in 1855 or 1856 in the small town of Kandiye on the island of Crete.[1] At that time, his family had already been exiled from their homeland in the emirate of Bohtan in the surroundings of Cizre in

---

1   Biographical information on Hüseyin Bedirhan is taken from his *sicill* entry in BOA: DH.SAİD 1.00245; Malmîsanij, *Cızira Botanli Bedirhaniler ve Bedirhani Ailesi Derneği'nin Tutanakları* (Spånga: Apec, 1994), 138–50; Nazmi Sevgen, "Sosyal Tarih: Kürtler," *Belgelerle Türk Tarihi Dergisi* 17 (1969): 50–7; Nazmi Sevgen, "Sosyal Tarih:

288   Barbara Henning

eastern Anatolia for more than ten years. Hüseyin Bedirhan grew up within a large family and extensive household comprising more than one hundred individuals, including numerous brothers and sisters as well as a large retinue of dependents and servants. During their early years in exile, the Bedirhani family and their followers faced hardship and financial difficulties. They had been expropriated when they were expelled from their homeland, and payments of the income (*maaş*) they were assigned by the Ottoman state in compensation were often delayed or periodically discontinued altogether. When Hüseyin Kenan was still a young child, he set foot in Ottoman Syria for the first time: His entire family was permitted to move from Istanbul to Damascus, where his father Emir Bedirhan passed away in 1869, not long after the family's arrival. Following the death of Emir Bedirhan, the family petitioned for their state income to be continued. After some back and forth with the Ottoman authorities, their bid was ultimately successful, but Hüseyin Kenan, along with the other younger and still unmarried male descendants of Emir Bedirhan, was to receive only a modest share that amounted to a monthly stipend of 350 *kuruş*.[2]

As a teenager in Damascus, Hüseyin Bedirhan prepared for a career in the Ottoman military, enrolling at the local *askeri idadiye*. He left the school, however, without a degree. When he was fifteen years old, he entered the Ottoman Naval Ministry and began an apprenticeship in the field of accounting. Five years later, he was ready to take on his first appointment as a junior official in the provincial administration of Kozan in the province of Adana.[3] Soon, however, he left his desk job, opting for more practical military experience instead. Like two of his brothers at the same time, we find him leading units of Kurdish irregulars in the Ottoman-Russian war of 1877–8. His unit counted more than 3,000 individuals and was recruited from the surroundings of Adana to

---

Kürtler," *Belgelerle Türk Tarihi Dergisi* 18 (1969): 62–73 (two-part article published in two successive issues). A detailed but very positive sketch of his biography is also found in his obituary in "Bedirhanî Hüseyin Paşa," *Rojî Kurd* 3 (August 1329/1913 M). The text is unsigned but was probably authored by Hüseyin Bedirhan's nephew Mehmed Salih Bedirhan, the editor of *Rojî Kurd*. For a more detailed history of the Bedirhani family see Barbara Henning, *Narratives of the History of the Ottoman-Kurdish Bedirhani Family in Imperial and Post-Imperial Contexts* (Bamberg University Press, 2018), 86–151.

2 BOA: ŞD 370/34 (no date) for details on the payments allotted to each family member. See also Sevgen, "Sosyal Tarih: Kürtler" (part one of the two-part article cited in the previous note).

3 This trajectory can be reconstructed from his *sicill* entry in DH.SAİD 1.00245, where, however, no mention is made of his stint at the military school in Damascus.

Alliances and Competition in Kurdish Networks in Late Ottoman Syria 289

fight under the command of *müşir* Ahmed Şakir Paşa (1838–99) on the Balkan front.[4] But Hüseyin Bedirhan's mission failed badly: while many of the soldiers under his command perished, he himself fell severely ill at the front and returned to Istanbul having permanently lost his hearing. While his superiors spoke well of him and commended his abilities, nothing came of a promotion that had been promised.[5] After the war ended, Hüseyin Bedirhan drifted around, it seems, with no immediate prospects for employment in the military or the Ottoman administration. Unemployed and lacking an income of his own, he joined his older brother Osman Bedirhan, who was trying to make his way back to the family's former homeland in Cizre. Here, the family had once owned land and villages and it is likely that the two young men were hoping to assert financial claims. The Ottoman government was highly suspicious of the two brothers' activities, fearing that their presence would stir unrest among the local Kurdish tribes. After having spent two years in Cizre, Hüseyin was persuaded to return to Istanbul, where he was offered a promotion and a well-paying position as member of the city council (*şehremaneti*).[6] Back in the Ottoman capital, he also got married to Ayşe, a woman of Circassian origin who had been brought up in the Ottoman palace. By 1906, the couple had five children.[7]

In the meantime, however, Hüseyin Bedirhan had fallen out of favour with the Ottoman authorities.[8] In 1884, he was sent off to serve as district governor in the remote Hisnü'l-Ekrad (Crac de Chevaliers) in the foothills of the Syrian coastal range some thirty kilometres west of Homs. Other posts in the lower ranks of the Ottoman provincial administration followed: after his term in Hisnü'l-Ekrad, he served as *kaymakam* of ʿAkkar on the northern edge of Mount Lebanon from 1891 onwards – where we will encounter him in the episode to be discussed here. Having left ʿAkkar in 1895, Hüseyin Bedirhan moved on to the island of Lesbos as district governor of Molova.[9]

---

4 Sevgen, "Sosyal Tarih: Kürtler," 62 (part two of the two-part article).

5 Malmîsanij, *Cizira Botanli Bedirhaniler ve Bedirhani Ailesi Derneği'nin Tutanakları* (Spånga: Apec, 1994), 139.

6 Mehmed Uzun and Rewşen Bedir-Han, *Defter-i Â'malım* (Istanbul: Belge, 1998), and also his *sicill* entry in DH.SAİD 1.00245.

7 Two sons, Adnan and Ahmed, and three daughters, Mihriban, Hurşide, and Neyire are mentioned by Malmîsanij, *Cizira Botanli Bedirhaniler*, 144. All of them took the surname Çınar in Turkish Republican times.

8 Uzun and Bedir-Han, *Defter-i Â'malım*, 47–8. Along with a number of his brothers, who had fallen out with Abu'l-Huda as-Sayyadi, an intimate advisor of the sultan, Hüseyin Bedirhan was relocated to Syria.

9 According to his *sicill* entry in DH.SAİD 1.00245.

290 Barbara Henning

Then he went without employment for some time before he was appointed as *mutasarrıf* to Yozgat in central Anatolia in 1906. This was bad timing, as 1906 turned out to be a particularly difficult year for all members of the extended Bedirhani family: two of Hüseyin Bedirhan's close relatives, his older brother Ali Şamil Paşa and his nephew Abdürrezzak Bey, who both held high positions in the Ottoman capital, were implicated in the murder of the governor of Istanbul, Rıdvan Paşa. As a result, the entire Bedirhani family came under suspicion and many members and family relations were prosecuted.[10] In view of these developments, Hüseyin Bedirhan was dismissed from his post in Yozgat and found himself briefly exiled to Nablus, before the Ottoman authorities decided on more forceful measures and sent him off to Yemen, where he was imprisoned in Ta'if along with several other family members. Family legend has it that he occupied the very same cell that the reformer Midhat Paşa had once been interned in.[11]

Hüseyin Bedirhan was only able to return to Istanbul after an amnesty for political prisoners of the Hamidian era went into effect following the Constitutional Revolution of 1908. He appears to have spent some time in the surroundings of Cizre and was later able to find his footing with the Constitutional government in 1913, when he was offered a post as *mutasarrıf* in Kırşehir – which, however, he declined. Instead, he intensified his activities among the Kurdish tribes and planned to recruit and personally lead a unit of Kurdish fighters in the Balkan War. His plans did not come to fruition, however, as he unexpectedly fell ill and passed away while still recruiting in Midyat.[12] His biography depicts an Ottoman-imperial trajectory and career path, not untypical for members of the Bedirhani family in the late-Ottoman context, a time that finds many of them oscillating between imperial office and attempts to mobilize or influence Kurdish sections of the population.

Governing ʿAkkar, Making Enemies: Hüseyin Bedirhan in Ottoman Syria

In the context of the court case to be discussed in the following, we encounter Hüseyin Bedirhan in his mid-twenties in ʿAkkar. Still fairly early on in his career as an Ottoman provincial official, but already literally battle-scarred, deaf, and disillusioned, he was aware that the

---

10 See Henning, *Narratives of the History*, 259–95, for more detail on the events of 1906.
11 See the obituary in "Bedirhanî Hüseyin Paşa."
12 "Bedirhanî Hüseyin Paşa."

Ottoman state was not always a reliable partner or looking out for his best interests. Seen from an imperial standpoint, 'Akkar could be regarded as a place of internal exile, a mountainous periphery far away from the capital and also devoid of any contact to the Bedirhani family's former homeland in Cizre and its surroundings. At the same time, however, Ottoman Syria was by no means unfamiliar territory to Hüseyin Bedirhan, who had grown up in Damascus and some of whose close senior relatives were employed as Ottoman officials in the immediate surroundings and the wider region, thus providing a family network available to him. It is also debatable whether from Ottoman Syria, the Bedirhani family's Kurdish homeland was really as far off as the Ottoman authorities might have hoped. It is conceivable that in the 1880s, Hüseyin's brothers based in Damascus communicated with representatives in Cizre by means of letters smuggled by itinerant sheep traders who regularly crossed from the Kurdish regions of eastern Anatolia into Syria, supplying Damascus with meat.[13]

Hüseyin Bedirhan had transferred to the small town of 'Akkar from Hisnü'l-Ekrad, a neighbouring *kaza* that had a lot in common with his new post. The entire area was sparsely populated with the majority of its inhabitants Sunni Muslims, and also featured a long-standing Kurdish presence.[14] The town that was the seat of the Ottoman administration was home to barely 3,500 inhabitants. It was remote from the larger city centres of the province, and 'Akkar in particular was associated with disorder, backwardness, and tribal structures resilient against state modernization politics – an image that was perpetuated well into the twentieth century.[15] Literally not getting anywhere geographically or professionally with his new post, Hüseyin Bedirhan picked up on this gloomy atmosphere, feeling stalled in 'Akkar and under the impression that he had reached a dead end in his career as an Ottoman state servant.

Unfortunately for Hüseyin Bedirhan, the remoteness of 'Akkar did not mean that as local governor, he could relax at an easy and routine

---

13 National Archives, London: FO 106/64, "Notes on Kurdish tribes," report from Northern Mesopotamia by Francis R. Maunsell dated 2 February 1919.

14 Stefan Winter, "Die Kurden in Syriens im Spiegel osmanischer Archivquellen (18. Jh.)," *Archivum Ottomanicum* 27 (2010): 216–17.

15 Michael Gilsenan, *Lords of the Lebanese Marches: Violence and Narrative in an Arab Society* (Berkeley: University of California Press, 1996), 68–9. For this stereotype, see also Martin Hartmann, *Reisebriefe aus Syrien* (Berlin: Reimer, 1913), 51–2, who noted about 'Akkar specifically that a few old feudal lords in the mountains who for generations continued to exploit their subjects and harass travelers were not worth his time.

job. On the contrary, developments in the area were closely monitored and the local administration frequently came under pressure from both the Ottoman centre and European observers. Bordering the province of Mount Lebanon, which as a result of European interventions had been granted a special administrative status since 1861, 'Akkar did not escape the attention of European diplomats, businessmen, and investors in the region. Unlike Mount Lebanon, however, 'Akkar was inhabited by a Sunni Muslim majority and governed under conventional Ottoman provincial law. The local population also included Christian communities of different denominations and intercommunal tensions and arguments about special privileges carried over from neighbouring areas.[16] This was invariably closely monitored by European observers and an Ottoman administration anxious to demonstrate their claims of sovereignty over the area.

In addition, the plain of 'Akkar was fertile agricultural land, producing grain and livestock for the surrounding areas as well as for export to the wider Mediterranean. This was crucial, as in neighbouring Mount Lebanon itself, most agricultural lands were reserved for mulberry trees supplying the local export-oriented silk industry.[17] It thus fell to the surrounding areas, the plain of 'Akkar and the Syrian hinterland, to supply foodstuffs for local consumption. This arrangement was good business for large-scale absentee landowners based in Beirut, Homs, or Damascus and also attracted investors from Europe. The local peasant population, on the other hand, was often coerced into hard labour and continued to live in poverty. As head of the local Ottoman administration, Hüseyin Bedirhan was required to mediate between different groups, along with local as well as transregional interests.

Kurdish actors, notably military units and irregulars, also seem to have been part of the mix in 'Akkar and the wider area in the *sancak* of Tripoli, although it is not clear whether Hüseyin Bedirhan was in contact with them or enjoyed any particular authority among these groups. In the eighteenth century and again in the 1850s, the Ottoman government had repeatedly relied on Kurdish irregular units from Anatolia to keep a check on local resistance to state centralization efforts. Subsequently, Kurdish fighters had stayed in the region, and some had later

---

16 Bernard Heyberger, *Les Européens vus par les Libanais à l'époque ottomane* (Würzburg: Ergon, 2002), 47.

17 Vital Cuinet, *Syrie, Liban et Palestine : Géographie administrative, statistique, descriptive et raisonnée* (Paris: E. Leroux, 1896), 144; Fawwaz Traboulsi, *A History of Modern Lebanon* (London: Pluto Press, 2012), 46–7.

Alliances and Competition in Kurdish Networks in Late Ottoman Syria   293

settled down and were deployed to protect villages and trade routes against Bedouin attacks.[18]

On the one hand, governing 'Akkar was thus a challenge and an unrewarding task. Looked at from a different angle and notably from the perspective of the collective interests of the Bedirhani family, however, it made some sense for Hüseyin Bedirhan to be there. The town and its surroundings, as well as its wider transregional networks, were in many ways familiar territory to his relatives, the extended Bedirhani family. In the late nineteenth century, Hüseyin's older brother Bedri Paşa was the owner of considerable landholdings in the fertile Hawran region and the Bekaa Valley (Baalbek), and was involved in commercial agriculture producing, processing and exporting grain. In the late 1890s, Bedri Paşa himself served as *mutasarrıf* of the district capital Tripoli, thus continuing the family's influence over 'Akkar.[19] Tahir Bey, another relative, had invested in the large-scale cultivation of olives and pomegranates in the nearby region of 'Ajlun between Damascus and Jerusalem.[20] A presence in 'Akkar, close to the family's landholdings, was no doubt a useful and strategic addition to the Bedirhani portfolio. Accounts from within the Bedirhani family, notably the memoir of Mehmed Salih Bedirhan, who worked as a supervisor of the estate of Bedri Paşa Bedirhan in the Hawran and in Baalbek, illustrate that the family did indeed strategize and operate as a collective in the region, expecting compliance and loyalty from family members and, in particular, assistance from those employed in the Ottoman administration.[21] Even though in the case of the Bedirhanis, Ottoman Syria played a crucial role in terms of resources, especially landholdings for commercial agriculture, this dimension has not received wider attention. Instead, historical research focusses on family members' activities in the Kurdish regions of Anatolia or in exile in European cities. Looked at from the perspective of the family's late-Ottoman priorities and frameworks of interaction, Hüseyin Bedirhan's activities in 'Akkar are not exceptional, but form a coherent part of a broader continuum.

---

18 Alexander Schölch, *Palästina im Umbruch 1856–1882* (Wiesbaden: Franz Steiner, 1986), 168, 193–4, and Stefan Winter, "The Reşwan Kurds and Ottoman Tribal Settlement in Syria, 1683–1741," *Oriente Moderno* 97, no. 2 (October 2017): 264, https://doi.org/10.1163/22138617-12340151.

19 FO 195/2097 on Bedri Paşa's removal from his post in Tripoli in 1901, report dated 15 February 1901.

20 Martha Mundy and Richard Saumarez Smith, *Governing Property, Making the Modern State: Law, Administration, and Production in Ottoman Syria* (London: I.B. Tauris, 2007), 56.

21 Uzun and Bedir-Han, *Defter-i Â'malım*, 82.

294   Barbara Henning

His actions, including his conduct in the wake of the accusations and the court case he faced, also need to be read in this broader context of family interest and transregional concerns: his presence in 'Akkar ensured that his family's interests as landowners in the wider area were being looked after, at a time when both local actors and the Ottoman central government grew increasingly critical of their position.

Not least due to this difficult constellation, Hüseyin Bedirhan's term in office in 'Akkar did not go too well. Complaints were voiced against him by locals; the case built against him can be reconstructed from voluminous files in the archives in Istanbul. What was the matter? In a petition to the *Şura-yı Devlet* (state council), which he filed in hopes of speeding along the court proceedings that had already dragged on for a year and a half at this point and involved authorities on the local and provincial level as well as at the *Bab-ı Ali* in Istanbul, we hear Hüseyin Bedirhan's side of the story. A group of local *muhtars* (municipal leaders) from the village of Rejje in his district had ganged up on him, opposing him at every turn and throwing around accusations that he claims were completely baseless. But he did have a theory as to why these local officials took such a strong dislike to him: As local governor, Hüseyin Bedirhan had put pressure on them to repay a substantial sum of money that had somehow been misappropriated.[22]

This local conflict likely played out on the broader canvas of political and economic transformations in the region, in which *muhtars* were fairly recent arrivals on the political scene. While Hüseyin Bedirhan served as district governor in 'Akkar, a prolonged power struggle between new and old elites was underway across the Ottoman provinces. This struggle played out on multiple levels and prominently featured local elites opposing measures of increasing state centralization. The office of the *muhtar* was created in this context in 1871 and intended as a counterbalance against established local notable families and interests on the village level.[23] Members of the Bedirhani family came into conflict with *muhtars* in other locales as well: for instance, Bedri Paşa Bedirhan was accused by Faris Bey, the *muhtar* of al-Hara village, of unlawfully seizing land for himself.[24] In Hüseyin Bedirhan's case, the *muhtars* from Rejje got their way and he was – at first – replaced as

---

22 ŞD 2282/7, petition by Hüseyin Bedirhan to the *Şura-yı Devlet*, dated 18 Nisan 1310 M (30 April 1894). Mention is made of 32,000 *kuruş* in dispute.

23 *İdare-i Umumiye-i Vilayet Nizamnamesi* (Ottoman Law of Vilayet Administration) of January 1871, article 60.

24 BOA: BEO 190/14239 (1310 L 13).

district governor. When the *salname* (administrative almanac) of the province of Beirut was published for the first time in 1894, no mention was made of Hüseyin Bedirhan, but his position had not been filled; only a certain Ahmed Muhtar Efendi was listed as deputy governor (*kaymakam vekili*) of 'Akkar.[25]

Taking it to the Next Level: Hüseyin Bedirhan Argues His Case

The tensions, however, did not die down – not least due to Hüseyin Bedirhan himself remaining adamant and demanding a reopening and fair treatment of his case. His lengthy petition on the matter is dated April 1894. In particular, he was concerned that he stood no chance of being treated fairly in the provincial capital of Beirut, since the administration there was headed by governor Halid Bey, a member of the Ottoman-Kurdish Baban family.[26] The Babans and his own family, the Bedirhanis, Hüseyin argued in his petition, were age-old and sworn enemies, as was well known, and he could therefore only expect Halid Bey to be strongly prejudiced against him.[27] Thus, Hüseyin Bedirhan demanded his case be transferred elsewhere (*nakl-ı da'va*) and suggested another provincial centre in Syria, or, alternatively, Jerusalem or Adana as suitable places.

The broader argument for a mistrial and reopening of his case is interesting in itself. It revolves around a (relatively recent) ideal of a neutral and disinterested secular justice system. Claiming that the local *muhtars'* complaints against him were baseless from the start and that the proceedings had been drawn out over a lengthy period of time solely to wear him down, he built his case on his close reading of the Ottoman civil code (*mecelle-yi ahkam-ı 'adliye*) of 1877, explicitly referencing article 1703 of its statutes. He paraphrased the passage in question, which is found in the sixteenth and final volume of the *mecelle*, almost verbatim, stating that no one can at once be plaintiff and witness

---

25 *Beyrut Salnamesi* (1311–12 H, 1894 CE), 160.
26 Information on Halid Baban's term as *vali* in Beirut is sparse, but he was still in office until 1894. *Beyrut Salnamesi* (1311–12 H, 1894 CE), 126. In the same year, however, he was transferred to Kastamonu and served as *vali* there for the following two years, Ziya Demircioğlu, *Kastamonu Valileri 1881–1908* (Kastamonu: Doğrusöz Matbaası, 1973), 44–55.
27 ŞD 2282/7, petition by Hüseyin Bedirhan to the *Şura-yı Devlet*, 18 Nisan 1310 (30 April 1894), speaks of *aba'en 'an cedden ... vucudu herkese ma'lum olan husumet ve 'adavet.*

in any legal matter – *bir adamın hem mudda'i ve hem de şahid olamayacağı*.[28] We can imagine him with a copy of the *mecelle* nearby on his desk as he underscores his right to due process and demands to be tried not on the basis of personal bias and prejudice, but solely according to the letter of the law. This emphasis on justice and fair treatment also forms the basis for the second part of his argument: not only did the local *muhtars* have no right to accuse and simultaneously testify against him, but in addition, the deck was stacked against him in Beirut as well, with a personal enemy at the head of the provincial administration.

To successfully make this argument, however, Hüseyin Bedirhan needed to convince the authorities that, one, Halid Baban was indeed unduly prejudiced against him personally as well as his entire extended family; and that, two, there was a special quality to this rivalry, a long-standing feud between the two families, making Halid Baban a more biased interlocutor than the average Ottoman official who would also have competed with Hüseyin Bedirhan and his family members for prestigious and lucrative positions within the Ottoman administration. Members of both families did indeed wrangle for similar positions in the higher echelons of the Ottoman state administration. Hüseyin Bedirhan's nephew Abdürrezzak Bedirhan, for instance, had been considered for the position of second secretary at the Ottoman embassy in Tehran at the same time as Halid Baban was appointed Ottoman ambassador (*sefir-i kebir*) to Iran. Halid Baban's appointment was duly implemented, but Abdürrezzak was recalled to Istanbul on short notice before he had even arrived in Iran. It needs to be noted, however, that the job in Tehran was probably not too coveted by either of the two aspirants. At least in his later accounts of the events, Abdürrezzak Bedirhan does not make it sound as if he really wanted to go to Iran anyway, as he had hoped for a more prestigious position as an Ottoman diplomat in some European capital.[29] As to Halid Baban, the German ambassador in Tehran relates that the position in Iran was in fact a way of keeping him – as he was not allowed to leave his post to return home to the Ottoman lands for the entire six years of his time in office – a convenient distance away from Ottoman political circles. Sultan Abdülhamid II seems to have been wary of Halid Baban's personal

---

28 Hüseyin Bedirhan, ŞD 2282/7, 18 Nisan 1310 (30 April 1894). The article referenced in the *mecelle* is found in the subsection on the "fundamental conditions of giving testimony" and reads similarly: *Bir kimse hem mudda'i ve hem şahid olamaz.*

29 Abdurrezzak Bedirhan, *Otobiyografya*, trans. Hasan Cunî (Istanbul: Perî Yayınları, 2000), 15.

Alliances and Competition in Kurdish Networks in Late Ottoman Syria   297

connections to his own half-brother Mehmed Reşad, the later Sultan Mehmed V.[30]

Age-Old Enemies? Rivalries and Entanglements between the Bedirhani and Baban Families

Not all is as it seems at first glance here. In this section, we explore the relationship between the Baban and Bedirhani families further, interrogating and contextualizing Hüseyin Bedirhan's claim of age-old animosities and conflict. The two families had a lot in common, including their Kurdish background and eventful family histories. Their trajectories run almost parallel, taking them from a quasi-autonomous position as hereditary ruling families in the empire's east into exile, and from there into the circles of the imperial elite as high-ranking Ottoman bureaucrats.

While the Bedirhanis laid claim to the town of Cizre and its surroundings as their family's homeland, the Baban family traced its origins back to the Ottoman-Iranian borderlands where they made their first appearance in the sixteenth century, supporting the Ottoman struggle against Safavid incursions into Iraq. Kurdish tribes of the region, including the large Jaf confederation, paid tribute to the Baban family and formed a reservoir of Kurdish fighters to be mobilized under their leadership. The city of Süleymaniye in northern Iraq emerged as the family's stronghold in the late eighteenth century. Up until the first half of the nineteenth century, the Baban family made use of its position in the Ottoman-Iranian borderlands as a political resource, at times supporting the Ottoman side but also open to advances from Iranian interlocutors. The sources attest to local rivalries and conflicts with neighbouring tribes and families, among them notably the Kurdish emirate of Ardalan on the Iranian side of the border. From the 1820s onwards, Mir Muhammad of Rewanduz emerged as a serious competitor in the region, successfully invading part of the territory previously controlled by the Baban family.[31] Thus, in the mid-nineteenth century, prior to being exiled, the networks of the Baban family spanned

---

30 Malek Sharif, *Imperial Norms and Local Realities* (Würzburg: Ergon, 2014), 173–5. Halid Baban had been Mehmed Reşad's private tutor for Persian, see Demircioğlu, *Kastamonu Valileri*, 51.

31 See S.H. Longrigg, "Baban," *EI2*; David McDowall, *A Modern History of the Kurds* (London: I.B. Tauris, 1996), 32–6; Metin Atmaca, "Politics of Alliance and Rivalry on the Ottoman-Iranian Frontier: The Babans (1500–1851)" (PhD diss., Freiburg University, 2013), 28–35.

298   Barbara Henning

between Baghdad and Iran, and struggles for power and influence chiefly played out regionally. With their capital in Cizre, on the other hand, the Bedirhani family operated in different regional networks and does not seem to have mattered much as a rival, much less as an age-old enemy of the Baban family. The Bedirhanis expanded at the expense of their neighbours in the early 1840s, coming into conflict with the Soran rulers in the east and the emirate of Hakkari in the northeast of their domains.[32]

As the Ottoman central state sought to control the territories of northern Iraq more directly, the Baban family, headed by Ahmed Paşa Baban, was exiled from the area in 1850 and left without much resistance.[33] At that time, other Kurdish ruling families had already met with the same fate, including the Bedirhanis, who had been defeated by the Ottoman military and forced out of their homeland in 1846. Again like the Bedirhanis, the Baban family was expropriated, the Ottoman state taking over their vast landholdings in northern Iraq and promising to financially recompense the family.[34] Ahmed Paşa Baban was sent off to Istanbul, followed by some time in honorary exile as an Ottoman representative in Paris.[35] Then he was appointed to posts in the Ottoman provincial administration in Yemen, Van, and Erzurum. In 1875, he was appointed *vali* of Adana, and passed away in the same year.

Ahmed Baban was survived by two sons. The first, Mustafa İzzet Paşa Baban, made his career in the Ottoman military. The second, Halil Halid Baban, was *vali* in Beirut in the 1890s, when he was encountered by Hüseyin Bedirhan.[36] Towards the end of the nineteenth and into the early twentieth century, Baban and Bedirhani family members would

---

32   Michael Eppel, "The Demise of the Kurdish Emirates: The Impact of Ottoman Reforms and International Relations on Kurdistan During the First Half of the Nineteenth Century," *Middle Eastern Studies* 44, no. 2 (March 2008): 254, https://doi.org/10.1080/00263200701874883.

33   Martin van Bruinessen, *Agha, Sheikh, and State: The Social and Political Structures of Kurdistan* (London: Zed Books, 1992), 171–3. First published in 1978 as a doctoral dissertation.

34   Similar to the Bedirhanis, the Baban family advanced claims to have these landholdings returned in the post-war period. The *New York Times* reported on the matter under the headline "Kurdish Chief Claims $200,000 From Britain" on 25 November 1928.

35   The former Russian diplomat Aleksandr Chodzko was in contact with him during this time and commented on their working relationship in Aleksandr L. Chodzko, "Etudes philologiques sur la langue kurde (dialecte de Soléimanié)," *Journal Asiatique* 5, no. 11 (1857): 297–356.

36   The biography of Ahmed Paşa Baban is given by Mehmed Emin Zeki Bey, *Kürd ve Kürdistan Ünlüleri* (1945–7; repr., Spånga: Apec, 1998), 59–60.

Alliances and Competition in Kurdish Networks in Late Ottoman Syria   299

have run into each other in the same circles of late-Ottoman political elites and Ottoman-Kurdish intellectuals. Their relationship was complex, with encounters ranging from guarded cooperation to rivalry for leadership in the emerging Ottoman-Kurdish scene of publishing and political activism. Organizations like the *Kürd Te'avün ve Terakki Cemiyeti* (founded in 1908), the Kurdish student association *Hêvî*, and the *Kürdistan Te'ali Cemiyeti* (founded in 1918), for instance, counted members of both families among their leading representatives.[37] In 1901, Abdurrahman Bedirhan and Hikmet Baban crossed paths in exile in the city of Geneva in Switzerland, both of them active supporters of the Young Turk opposition. They seemed very comfortable around each other and quite close, judging from their exchange of frequent and amicable postcards. In one of these, Abdurrahman Bedirhan addressed Hikmet Baban affectionately as *akhi*, my brother.[38]

In many ways, these relations and shared networks also continued into the post-Ottoman period. Celadet Bedirhan, an influential figure in the Kurdish-nationalist movement of the early twentieth century, had been a junior staff member for Mevlanzade Rıfat Bey's journal *Serbesti* after the Constitutional Revolution of 1908 in Istanbul. He continued to collaborate with his friend and mentor in the Syrian Mandate territories throughout the 1920s and 1930s, when both were active members of the Kurdish association *Khoybun*.[39] The very same Mevlanzade Rıfat Bey had acted as confidant and private secretary to Halid Baban in the 1890s and accompanied him to his postings in Beirut and Kastamonu, later also following him into exile to Kayseri and eventually becoming the heir to Halid Baban's personal savings when the latter passed away there.[40]

In spite of their commonalities and regular encounters, the Baban and Bedirhani families never intermarried, and no clear hierarchical relationship with one family's legacy or claims for leadership conclusively

---

37 *Kürd Te'avün ve Terakki Cemiyeti*: Van Bruinessen, *Agha, Sheikh and State*, 275. *Hêvî*: Zinnar Silopi [Kadri Cemilpaşa], *Doza Kurdistan* (Ankara: Öz-Ge Yayınları, 1991), 28. *Kürdistan Te'ali Cemiyeti*: McDowall, *Modern History*, 93. Both Emin Ali Bedirhan and Hikmet Baban were prominently involved.

38 Malmîsanij, *İlk Kürt Gazetesi Kurdistan'ı Yayımlayan Abdurrahman Bedirhan (1868–1936)* (Istanbul: Vate Basın, 2009), 14–19, including reproductions of some of these postcards.

39 Hakan Özoğlu, *From Caliphate to Secular State: Power Struggle in the Early Turkish Republic* (Santa Barbara, CA: Praeger, 2011), 68, and Metin Martı, ed., *Mevlanzade Rıfat'ın Anıları* (Istanbul: Arma Yayınları, 1992), 5–6.

40 Demircioğlu, *Kastamonu Valileri*, 52–5.

300   Barbara Henning

outmatching the other can be established. As both adhered to the Shafi'i branch of Sunni Islam, there was also no reason for serious difference on religious grounds. But while they competed for prestige and influence in Ottoman and Ottoman Kurdish circles in Istanbul, the families were not in any direct competition for territory in the eastern parts of the empire. Any political rivalry between the leading Ottoman Kurdish families and infighting for positions and influence in the post-Ottoman order only really took off following the end of the First World War, when plans for autonomous Kurdish territories were on the table, prompting the question of who should become head of state or even monarch there. These rivalries, however, were much less pronounced in the context of the 1890s, when the large majority of Ottoman Kurdish actors still envisioned their future firmly within an Ottoman imperial setting. It is, in turn, this imperial setting and the competitions it encouraged that need to be looked at to understand more about the background of Hüseyin Bedirhan's grievances in 1894, along with his account of the relationship between the Bedirhani and the Baban families.

In regard to success within the Ottoman imperial system, it seems that the descendants of the Baban family of the second and third generation in exile outperformed their Bedirhani contemporaries. Numerous members of the Baban family held high-ranking positions as provincial governors, and two of Mustafa Zihni Paşa Baban's sons were graduates of the prestigious *Mülkiye* school for Ottoman bureaucrats in Istanbul.[41] By all accounts, Halid Baban himself had excelled at his post as Ottoman ambassador in Tehran, performing confidently and juggling delicate matters of protocol.[42] Sir Henry Drummond Wolff, the British ambassador to Tehran from 1888 to 1891, recalls Halid Baban in his memoirs as a polished and well-connected individual, "a Kurd by birth, with charming manners, who had been tutor and friend of Sultan Murad," and on top of all that an individual of formidable pedigree, as he was "said to be descended from Saladin."[43] The Russian czar was also strongly impressed by Halid Baban and awarded him a medal in 1894, which was matched in the same year by the Ottoman government with a promotion and pay raise.[44] Hüseyin Bedirhan – without much of a secondary education, with his hopes for a stellar military career

---

41 Ahmed Na'im graduated in 1894, and his brother Mehmed Asım followed suit in 1900. From among the Bedirhanis, only Abdurrahman attended the *Mülkiye*.

42 Anja Pistor-Hatam, *Iran und die Reformbewegung im osmanischen Reich* (Berlin: Klaus Schwarz, 1992), 154.

43 Henry Drummond Wolff, *Rambling Recollections* (London: Macmillan, 1908), 2:331.

44 Demircioğlu, *Kastamonu Valileri*, 47.

Alliances and Competition in Kurdish Networks in Late Ottoman Syria   301

crushed by his war injuries and lack of success he had incurred in 1877–8 and few additional credentials to show for himself – might have felt slighted, unjustly treated by, and just plain inferior to Halid Baban.

Contextualizing an Argument: Late Nineteenth-Century Transformations in Ottoman Syria

But there is more to this episode than just personal idiosyncrasies or inferiority complexes. It has been illustrated above that Ottoman Syria was an important political and economic base for members of the extended Bedirhani family throughout the late nineteenth century, a place where senior members like Bedri Paşa Bedirhan had been well-established for decades and, especially via the networks of Abu'l-Huda al-Sayyadi, with whom the Bedirhanis were intermarried, well-connected both regionally and in the Ottoman capital.[45] However, the administrative restructuring of Ottoman Syria, and in particular the establishment of the *vilayet* of Beirut in 1888, cut across existing lines of communication and patronage and dealt a blow to the well-oiled Bedirhani network. Resources were being redistributed; and newcomers to the region, like Halid Baban, emerged as serious competitors. Halid Baban had served as Ottoman ambassador in Tehran since 1885 and returned – accomplished and decorated with distinctions – to the Ottoman lands in the early 1890s.[46] Ottoman Syria seemed like a reasonable place for him to turn to: His father Ahmed Paşa had passed away in 1875, but had served as *vali* in Aleppo for an extended period of time between 1869 and 1873.[47] Halid Baban's uncle Abdullah Musib Paşa had chosen Beirut as his place of retirement after a successful career as an Ottoman provincial official in 1879.[48] He, too, had since passed away, but other family members likely survived him to welcome Halid Baban to the city.

---

45 Thomas Eich, *Abū l-Hudā aṣ-Ṣayyādī: Eine Studie zur Instrumentalisierung sufischer Netzwerke und genealogischer Kontroversen im spätosmanischen Reich* (Berlin: Klaus Schwarz, 2003), 273.

46 Pistor-Hatam, *Iran und die Reformbewegung*, 140.

47 Mehmed Süreyya, *Sicill-i Osmani* (Istanbul: Tarih Vakfı, 1996), 1:204 on Ahmed Paşa Baban.

48 Süreyya, *Sicill-i Osmani* 1:77 has Abdullah Musib's biography: He served as *vali* in Basra before coming to Beirut, where he died in 1881 and was survived by his son Rıza Bey. Halid Baban had several other paternal uncles who served as high-ranking Ottoman provincial officials: Mehmed Reşid Paşa (1822–96) was *vali* in Bitlis and Mehmed Paşa was appointed as *vali* in Basra as well. See Yılmaz Öztuna, *Devletler ve Hanedânlar* (Ankara: Kültür Bakanlığı Yayınları, 1990), 512–14.

302 Barbara Henning

Halid Baban's stay in Beirut was brief, however. He was recalled from his post around the time of Hüseyin Bedirhan's petition, in the second half of 1894, because of a matter completely unrelated to any disagreements with the Bedirhani family. Halid Baban's superiors in Istanbul had found his management of urban improvement projects in the city of Beirut wanting and recalled him from there. He was replaced as *vali* of Beirut by Abdülhalik Nasuhi Bey.[49] But even after his departure, the presence of the Baban family in Ottoman Syria was still making itself felt. Another branch of the extended family was established in Aleppo, where Mustafa Zihni Paşa Baban served as *vali* in 1895–6. It is perhaps indicative of the presence and connection of the Baban family to Beirut in particular that Musa Anter, a twentieth-century Kurdish activist and close friend of Mustafa Zihni Paşa's son Şükrü Baban, misremembered this fact and placed Mustafa Zihni Paşa not in Aleppo but in Beirut in his memoirs.[50] It might therefore be productive to look at the conflict between Hüseyin Bedirhan and Halid Baban in light of these developments and broader sociopolitical and economic transformations, rather than immediately buying into Hüseyin Bedirhan's own account of a long-standing family antagonism or reading the events in 1890s Ottoman Syria through the lens of constellations and rivalries which were only to emerge later, from the early twentieth century onwards.

Political and administrative changes in the province of Beirut were closely entangled with transformations in the regional economy, which also did not play out in favour of the established networks of the Bedirhani family centred on Damascus and its hinterland. Merchants and investors from Beirut sought influence over the agricultural lands in Ottoman Syria, and increasingly entered into competition with already established players in the region, seeking to redirect profits to Beirut instead.[51] Obviously, members of the Bedirhani family like Hüseyin and his older brother Bedri Paşa would not have enjoyed these prospects and were suspicious towards the new Ottoman administrators in Beirut enabling and promoting these changes. In addition to these

---

49 Toufoul Abou-Hodeib, *A Taste for Home: The Modern Middle Class in Beirut* (Stanford: Stanford University Press, 2017), 68–9.

50 Musa Anter, *Meine Memoiren* (Münster: N.p., 1999), 63. Among the sons of Mustafa Zihni Paşa was İsmail Hakkı Baban (1876–1913), probably the family member most well-known to posterity. He served as Ottoman parliamentary representative for Baghdad in 1908 and, briefly, as Ottoman Minister of Education in 1911, and was a prolific writer and politician.

51 Schölch, *Palästina im Umbruch*, 143.

economic motives, Halid Baban's commitment to his tasks as governor might have rubbed both locals and those serving under his administration like Hüseyin Bedirhan the wrong way.

While not much can be reconstructed of his day-to-day dealings in Beirut, Halid Baban's activities at his subsequent post are well documented and give an idea of his take on leadership and his general modus operandi. In the late summer of 1894, he was transferred from Beirut and took up office as *vali* of Kastamonu. Immediately upon his arrival there, he reached out to the local district governors under his command with orders to maintain close and constant correspondence with the provincial capital under all circumstances, taking note of and diligently forwarding any petitions and complaints from locals. That Halid Baban meant business is attested by subsequent notes in the historical record of his term in office that several members of the local administration saw their salaries severely cut back because they had neglected to keep him updated on events in their respective localities.[52] Halid Baban also personally supervised the selection of local officials such as *muhtars*, watchmen, and village security guards and followed their actions closely, taking swift disciplinary actions against those who had misappropriated funds. In terms of political priorities, infrastructure projects, improved water supply and fire protection, health policies, and education were high on his agenda. Judging from his term in Kastamonu, Halid Baban appears as a committed modernizer and reformer, micromanaging and multitasking with his subjects' alleged best interest in mind, but at times, he also seems patronizing, a perhaps overly-involved official who goes so far as to prescribe exactly what type of cart local peasants were allowed to use lest the roads be worn down too much.[53] If the impression he made in Kastamonu is any indication of his conduct in Syria as well, it is not difficult to imagine why Hüseyin Bedirhan found it challenging to work under him, closely monitored, while the local *muhtars* were already giving him a hard time.

Late Ottoman Perceptions of Kurdishness

Read against this backdrop, is the Bedirhani vs. Baban family feud a convenient legal fiction made up, or at least overemphasized, by Hüseyin Bedirhan? In the context of high-ranking career paths in the Ottoman administration, there is some evidence that family members did indeed

---

52 Demircioğlu, *Kastamonu Valileri 1881–1908*, 46.
53 Demircioğlu, 46–9.

304   Barbara Henning

compete, at times for similar posts, at times for economic resources and political opportunities. But again, this does not make the relationship between the two families qualitatively different from that of any other family of Ottoman imperial officials. For Hüseyin Bedirhan's argument to hold, the enmity needs to be of a different, more intense, almost primordial kind, going back to times immemorial – *aba'en 'an cedden*, to quote his own words from the petition of 1894. There seems to be less evidence for this. Even the otherwise very accommodating family historiography of the Bedirhanis themselves does not mention such a feud or even conflict between the two families,[54] and the historical record has little to add to this. Rather, whenever there is talk of the history of the Bedirhanis as former independent Kurdish emirs, ousted and exiled by the Ottoman central state in the mid-nineteenth century, the Babans are mentioned as fellow sufferers and victims of state violence.

Who might have been *primus inter pares* is a different question, and in some later accounts of their family history, the Bedirhanis do indeed claim preeminence among the former Kurdish emirs. But again, conflict over status does not necessarily make them primordial archenemies. In his study on the history of the Babans, Metin Atmaca points out that while the two families, and in particular their contributions to the Kurdish nationalist movement, are often compared and even pitted against each other in twentieth-century historiography, there are few indications of animosities between them reaching further back in time. One of the reasons for this is quite possibly that the history of the immediate Bedirhani family was a fairly recent one. The Babans had been established in northern Iraq for centuries already and are mentioned by the sixteenth-century chronicler Şerefhan Bitlisi in his *Şarafname* (1596). The tribe of the Azizan to which the Bedirhanis trace their descent had already been influential in the Bohtan area for centuries.[55] Emir Bedirhan, on the other hand, seems to have been more of a newcomer. His direct line of ancestors are not mentioned in these earlier sources, coming to power only in the early nineteenth century in the context of Ottoman centralization politics.[56]

---

54 Lütfi [Liceli Ahmed Ramiz], *Emir Bedirhan* (Cairo [?]: Matbaa-yı İctihad, n.d.).

55 Hakan Özoğlu, *Kurdish Notables and the Ottoman State: Evolving Identities, Competing Loyalties, and Shifting Boundaries* (Albany: SUNY, 2004), 47–59; Stefan Winter, "The Other *Nahdah*: The Bedirxans, the Millîs, and the Tribal Roots of Kurdish Nationalism in Syria," *Oriente Moderno* 25, no. 3 (August 2006): 462–3, https://doi.org/10.1163/22138617-08603003.

56 Atmaca, *Politics of Alliance*, 5–6.

Alliances and Competition in Kurdish Networks in Late Ottoman Syria 305

It seems to have been advantageous for Hüseyin Bedirhan to overemphasize this feud, in a way self-orientalizing himself and his nemesis Halid Baban and playing on the image of the vengeful Kurd known to hold a personal grudge against an opponent who would impact his ability to judge fairly. This is peculiar, to say the least, since both he and Halid Baban would have been perceived as educated and refined Ottoman bureaucrats with urban lifestyles and high rank, and both were known to entertain political ideas that would have been characterized as liberal and progressive at the time.[57]

That Hüseyin Paşa decided to play this card and chose to frame his complaint in these terms allows some insights into common late Ottoman stereotypes about Kurdishness and about the perception and image of his own family. The stereotype of a Kurdish *derebey* mentality, at odds with core values of Ottoman modernity, was widespread in late Ottoman times. Members of the Bedirhani family and their actions were frequently perceived through this lens, and even sympathetic family friends like Halide Edib relied on this image in her recollections of Bedirhani family members.[58] At least three elements come together in the stereotype of the vengeful Kurd deployed by Hüseyin Bedirhan. First, both in time and space, Kurds are seen as far removed from contemporary Ottoman modernity. In his *Kamus-ı Türki*, Şemseddin Sami places them at the margins of empire, in the Ottoman-Iranian borderlands and, in his entry on *derebey*, makes it clear that the despotic rule of petty chieftains was a thing of the past – "*vaktiyle*," once upon a time, they had wielded power.[59] Second, Kurds are thought of as actors in tribal contexts where personal loyalties and genealogical networks override individual obligations towards the state. And third, this leads to authoritarian and arbitrary ways of governing – incompatible with Ottoman modernity and ideas about justice and good governance.

This image of Kurdishness was familiar to Ottoman contemporaries. In 1894, the very same year Hüseyin Bedirhan penned his petition, a Kurdish-Arabic dictionary was published by the Ottoman official Yusuf Ziyaeddin Paşa, the district governor of Mutki in the province of Bitlis. The work was dedicated to Sultan Abdülhamid II and printed

---

57 For Hüseyin Bedirhan, see the obituary in *Rojî Kurd* 3 (August 1329 M), and for Halid Baban, see Demircioğlu, *Kastamonu Valileri*, 54–5, where his sympathies and tacit support for political exiles to Kastamonu are mentioned.
58 See her description of Ali Şamil Bedirhan in Halide Edib, *Mor Salkımlı Ev* (Istanbul: Atlas Kitabevi, 1979), 97–8.
59 Şemseddin Sami, *Kāmūs-ı Türkī* (Istanbul: İkdam Matbaʿası, 1899/1317), 1156 "كرد" and 608 "دره بكى".

306   Barbara Henning

with the title *el-Hediyetü'l-Hamidiye fi'l-Lugat el-Kurdiye*. In the preface, the author expresses his wish to bring his deplorable and backwards Kurdish compatriots into the folds of contemporary civilization, saving them from their current misery and ignorance.[60]

Framing his opponent Halid Baban in this way, Hüseyin Bedirhan thus plays on an ensemble of stereotypes and his depiction can be read as an attack on Halid Baban's integrity and suitability as an Ottoman official. But the accusation is even more complex, as Hüseyin Bedirhan himself was clearly identifiable as Kurdish and had likely been on the receiving end of stereotypes about Kurdishness frequently throughout his life and career. Bringing up this aspect in his petition is not only a way to vilify his opponent, but also a means to claim special treatment by the state administration by pointing to an additional, inner-Kurdish and personal dimension of a professional conflict with his superior. In doing so, Hüseyin hoped to unlock a different, more advantageous space of interaction and negotiation for his case. There is no telling whether this strategy could have worked, as he was outpaced by the events. While his petition was still pending, Halid Baban was recalled from his post in Beirut and transferred to Kastamonu for completely unrelated reasons. After two years in office in Kastamonu, Halid Baban was arrested on the orders of Abdülhamid II and permanently exiled to Kayseri, where he passed away before the Constitutional Revolution. The sultan had not feared him because he was too conservative or too biased by his Kurdish origins, as Hüseyin Bedirhan had tried to argue, but on the contrary because of his covert support for the Young Turk opposition and his having turned a blind eye to activities among political exiles in Kastamonu.[61]

Conclusions

Thus, taking Hüseyin Bedirhan's framing of his conflict with Halid Baban as part of an age-old and primordial family feud at face value does *not* contribute to a more nuanced understanding of Ottoman and Ottoman Kurdish network activities in Syria. However, contextualizing his account does. The emphasis on a simple dichotomy between

---

60   Yusuf Ziyaeddin, *El-Hediyet'ül-Hamidiye fi'l-Lugat el-Kurdiye* (Istanbul: Şirket-i Mürettibiye Matba'ası, 1310 [1894]), summary of the introduction in Mehmed Emin Bozarslan, ed., *Yusuf Ziyaeddin Paşa. Kürtçe-Türkçe Sözlük* (Istanbul: Çıra Yayınları, 1978), 13.

61   Demircioğlu, *Kastamonu Valileri*, 51, 54–5.

the two families obscures some of the connections and rivalries that might have gotten Hüseyin into trouble with the local administration in 'Akkar in the first place and, in turn, compelled him to request a trial in a different location.

There was no Kurdish family feud playing out in Ottoman Syria. What we find instead is a clash of opposing patronage networks, socio-economic interests, and incompatible takes on reform politics in the Ottoman provinces that crossed all kinds of lines. Hüseyin Bedirhan had pragmatic reasons to attempt to have his case moved away from Beirut and to Tripoli, Adana, or Jerusalem, to places where he himself or his relatives had accumulated no small amount of influence in previous years. And Halid Baban's priorities seem to have been reform and greater control of his local subordinates rather than getting back at an alleged personal enemy.

One final question remains to be addressed. How did the matter end for Hüseyin Bedirhan: was his petition successful? According to his personal record in the Ottoman archive, he was ultimately cleared of all suspicion and, in 1894, restored to his former post as *mutasarrıf* in 'Akkar, where he remained in office for another year before moving on to his subsequent post on the island of Lesbos.[62] For the extended Bedirhani family more broadly, however, the back-and-forth with locals and *muhtars* of 'Akkar did not come to an end with Hüseyin Bedirhan's departure. In 1900, Bedri Paşa Bedirhan was involved in the murder of two Muslim *beys* in 'Akkar and was caught trying to put the blame on a prominent local Christian, which fanned religious tension in the area. Bedri Paşa, who seems to have hoped to get rid of two factions of local opponents at once by pitting them against each other, ultimately lost his job as *mutasarrıf* in Tripoli over this affair.[63]

---

62 DH.SAİD 1.00245.
63 FO 195/2056, report from Beirut dated 13 October 1900.

14 Between Ottomanism and Kurdism: Mehmed Salih Bedirhan and ʿAbd al-Rahman Yusuf in Damascus

MARTIN STROHMEIER

Introduction

The presence of Kurds in Syria dates back to at least the eleventh century. This was a centre of gravity of the Ayyubid state with its Kurdish ruling class. Throughout Ottoman rule, Kurdish families were among local rulers who enjoyed relative independence. Until the middle of the nineteenth century, Kurds did not settle permanently in the *Jazira* ("island," referring to northwest Mesopotamia or northeast Syria), whereas they had been resident in northwest Syria in today's border area with Turkey for centuries. Damascus has had Kurdish inhabitants since the Middle Ages. Kurds were an important element and increasingly formed a power factor, especially in janissary regiments (*yerliyya*) and various paramilitary forces in which they served as policemen in the city, cavalrymen in the Bedouin and Druze regions, as well as guards of the pilgrimage caravan.[1] The opportunities to serve in these forces attracted Kurds from other parts of Syria. Over time, Kurds in the quarters of Damascus where they settled (Suq Saruja, Jabal Qasyun) developed a sense of belonging to a distinct group (especially those in the aforementioned military units), although this did not translate into an expressly ethnic identity until after the end of the Ottoman Empire. The leaders (*agha*) of these forces acquired administrative and economic functions as tax farmers (*mültezim*), grain traders, and governors in the countryside.

Kurdish families who rose to prominence in these functions included the ʿAbid, Ajalyaqin, Bozo (Buzu), Shamdin, and Yusuf families.

---

1 Moshe Maoz, "Muslim Ethnic Communities in Nineteenth-Century Syria and Palestine: Trends of Conflict and Integration," *Asian and African Studies* 19, no. 3 (1985): 283–307, esp. 293.

Especially the latter two succeeded in acquiring wealth, power, and posts; and by marriage with old-established Arab families, they rose to elite status. These connections resulted in an acculturation into the Arabic-speaking majority population.[2] Gradually they developed into influential players in urban politics and as such became detached from the Kurds who were part of the city's underclass, eking out a living in their traditional quarter of Hayy al-Akrad. There were a number of peculiarities among the Kurds of Damascus in terms of origin, language, customs, and traditions, that is, in their cultural identity, which differentiated them from Arabic-speaking townspeople, but these were not vehicles for a separate political identity until well into the twentieth century. Ethnicity, that is affiliation with an ethnic group, played hardly any role in their identity. What was more important in their relations with other members of their group (the Kurds) were social, religious, political, tribal, local, and kinship markers, as well as clientelist relationships.[3]

In the following I will portray two prominent personalities of the Kurdish community in Damascus, ʿAbd al-Rahman (al-) Yusuf (1873/4–1920) and Mehmed Salih Bedirhan (1873/4–1915). The kind and degree of their prominence, as well as their position in this community, were quite different. The nature of the sources for their respective biographies, as well as their life stories proper, make a comparison difficult. But by describing the differences in upbringing, lifestyle, worldview, offices, power, and wealth I hope to shed light on the wide range of Kurdish experiences and orientations. At the same time, the commitment of these two men to the Ottoman state will be illustrated.

Mehmed Salih Bedirhan: A "Passionate"[4] Ottoman and Advocate of a Kurdish Awakening (*İntibah*)

Family

Mehmed Salih was descended from the famous Bedirhan dynasty. His ancestors, the emirs of Botan in Upper Mesopotamia, could claim

---

2 Moshe Maoz, "Muslim Ethnic Communities," 296–7.

3 Jordi Tejel, *Syria's Kurds: History, Politics, and Society* (London: Routledge, 2009), 3–13. See also Nelida Fuccaro, "Ethnicity and the City: The Kurdish Quarter of Damascus between Ottoman and French Rule, c. 1724–1946," *Urban History* 30, no. 2 (August 2003): 206–24, https://doi.org/10.1017/S0963926803001135.

4 Mehmet Uzun and Rewşen Bedir-Han, eds., *Mehmet Salih Bedir-Han. Defter-i A'malım. Mehmet Salih Bedir-Han'ın Anıları* (Istanbul: Belge, 1998), 85: "rabitadar edecek marazi bir aşk."

310   Martin Strohmeier

an illustrious past, having ruled over large parts of Kurdistan for centuries. Wide-reaching changes to the balance of power in the region brought about their downfall and banishment (a privileged exile or rather résidence forcée) to Crete (1847). In 1863 they were allowed to leave the island and to settle in Constantinople with some members of the numerous and widely branched family entering the Ottoman bureaucracy. In 1867 or so, one year before his death in 1869, the last emir of Botan, Bedirhan, moved to Damascus, thus beginning the family's involvement with affairs in Greater Syria (*Bilad al-Sham*).[5] Having lost property and power base in their ancestral land due to their exile, it is remarkable how quickly they were able to rebuild influence and power. It was Bedri Bedirhan (1847/8–1914), one of the many sons of Bedirhan Bey, who was to play a pivotal role in Ottoman Syria for roughly a quarter of a century.[6]

Youth and Education

The nephew and future son-in-law of Bedri, Mehmed Salih Bedirhan, was born in Latakia in 1873 or 1874. His father Mahmud 'Izzet, a mid-level Ottoman official, was the nephew of the most powerful Kurd in the nineteenth century, Emir Bedirhan (d. 1870). Mahmud 'Izzet's father Salih was a brother of the Emir Bedirhan. Mehmed Salih's mother Leyla was a daughter of the Emir; she died in 1878 when he was four or five years old.[7] After her death, he grew up primarily with his maternal

---

5   Different dates are given; I follow Malmîsanij, *Cizira Botanlı Bedirhaniler ve Bedirhani Ailesi Derneği'nin Tutanakları* (Istanbul: Avesta, 2000), 65–6.

6   Malmîsanij, *Cizira*, 127–9. Bedri Bedirhan was banished to Rhodes, like his son-in-law Mehmed Salih. From the 1870s to 1900, he was appointed to the *Şura-yı Devlet* (Council of State) in Istanbul. Bedri had been a landowner and *mutasarrıf* of the Hawran district since 1885. He maintained close links with the sultan's advisor Abu l-Huda al-Sayyadi; see Thomas Eich, *Abū l-Hudā aṣ-Ṣayyādī. Eine Studie zur Instrumentalisierung sufischer Netzwerke und genealogischer Kontroversen im spätosmanischen Reich* (Berlin: Klaus Schwarz, 2003), 35–6, 183–4, 208–9. On the intricacies of Bedri Paşa's network of relationships see Barbara Henning, *Narratives of the History of the Ottoman-Kurdish Bedirhani Family in Imperial and Post-Imperial Contexts: Continuities and Changes* (Bamberg: University of Bamberg Press, 2018), 178–210, esp. 210. For the role which Bedri played in Mehmed Salih's life, see Barbara Henning, "Die Erinnerungen Meḥmed Sāliḥ Bedirḫāns: Osmanisch-kurdisches Selbstverständnis im spätosmanischen Syrien," in *Bamberger Orientstudien*, ed. Lale Behzadi (Bamberg: University of Bamberg Press, 2014), 381–413.

7   Uzun and Bedir-Han, *Mehmet Salih*, 30–1.

Between Ottomanism and Kurdism 311

grandmother Rewşen, one of Bedirhan's numerous wives. Stations of his childhood, often only briefly, were as follows: Damascus, Beirut, Jerusalem, Limnos, and Istanbul, where relatives of his grandmother lived.

In Damascus, the family lived in the quarter of Suq Saruja where Mehmed Salih was enrolled in school. Already at this early age he experienced the involvement of his family in Kurdish politics; his father and his uncle Bedri were arrested for allegedly participating in the Kurdish uprising that 'Osman and Huseyn Bedirhan had organized (1878–9).[8] During these frequent changes of place, he got to know other members of the Bedirhan family, including Khalil Rami, Nejib Paşa, and his son 'Abd al-Rezzaq. In the household of his aunt in Limnos he grew up with her daughters who were a few years younger than him. During his childhood, women (and not his father) were his constant caregivers and company; his aunt's husband became his *ersatz* father.[9] Salih and his grandmother spent one and a half to two years on the Aegean Island (around 1880–2), where he also attended elementary school. The next stop was Istanbul, where Salih was a pupil at a junior high school (*Rüşdiye*) for about a year.[10]

On his return to Damascus, Salih found that his father had remarried. He admitted hating his stepmother. His grandmother, father, and his new family, as well as other relatives now lived again in Suq Saruja. He was enrolled at the "Çakmakiye" school, corresponding to the *rüşdiye* level. Later he switched to the military branch of the *rüşdiye*. In 1886 he received his leaving certificate. He then registered at the military preparatory school (corresponding to a senior high school, *i'dadi 'askeri*). As he wrote in his memoirs, he knew nothing about mathematics, but he liked French and history; he had no talent for calligraphy and gymnastics. He had to repeat the school year and then only passed by the skin of his teeth. He got on well with his schoolmates, but not with the teachers whom he accused of "oppression." His performance in several subjects, especially natural sciences, deteriorated, and so did the relationship with his teachers. He dropped out of school but continued his education in Jerusalem for six months in 1890, living with his father's sister. He attended the famous Alliance school, but also

---

8 Uzun and Bedir-Han, *Mehmet Salih*, 31–2 and fn. 22; Günter Behrendt, *Nationalismus in Kurdistan: Vorgeschichte, Entstehungsbedingungen und erste Manifestationen bis 1925* (Hamburg: Deutsches Orient-Institut, 1993), 200–2.

9 Uzun and Bedir-Han, 35.

10 Uzun and Bedir-Han, 41–4.

312   Martin Strohmeier

hung around at a casino at Jaffa Gate and often had a little drink. In sum, the time at senior high school was depressing for Salih, but he was encouraged and comforted by his grandmother.[11] In retrospect, he describes his development as follows: "my self-respect gradually grew and with it my inclination and passion for righteousness, love of truth, and justice." He also had family responsibilities: after the death of an uncle, he was the only close male relative to take over the protection of his grandmother, aunt, and their four daughters. In this situation, his grandmother appealed to him: "Be diligent, do your best, become a real man. Feed us. You are our future and our life."[12]

Mehmed Salih's father (a mid-level official in southern Lebanon and later in Hawran) assigned him responsibility, entrusting him with the tax administration of several villages in the vicinity of Damascus.[13] His influence on his son was waning. Bedri imperiously declared himself to be his "real" father.[14] Mehmed Salih increasingly came under the thumb of his uncle, whose daughter Samiye he was expected to marry, but he resisted. In fact, he wanted to marry her from an early age, but he preferred to realize his professional ambitions first, probably in the endeavour to avoid Bedri's pressure. He had contemplated attending the *Mülkiye Mektebi*, the elite College of Administration in Istanbul, which was unrealistic considering his previous school achievements. Now he saw his future as rather bleak: "Tomorrow some of my friends will be officers, some civil servants and *kaymakam*. But not I." And again: "To face an unknown future, to be condemned to a life without a program ... and to remain a nothing." The embarrassing status of *iç güvey*, that is a son-in-law who lives with his in-laws, who is dependent and can be ordered around at will, made him shudder. He went into a deep crisis. He was sick for weeks when he swallowed medication with the intention of suicide. Seeing how worried his fiancée was about him increased his affection for her.[15] Salih married in 1891.[16] Although he was now a bit more relaxed about his future, his father-in-law would not "leave the young couple in peace" with his paternalism and "poisoned" their married life. In essence to punish his father-in-law for his

---

11 Uzun and Bedir-Han, 45–52.
12 Uzun and Bedir-Han, 52–3 Salih was not wealthy; a small amount of money flowed to him from the Bedirhan estate in Crete. He complained that he did not have enough money to buy tobacco.
13 Uzun and Bedir-Han, 68.
14 Uzun and Bedir-Han, 61.
15 Uzun and Bedir-Han, 64–7.
16 Uzun and Bedir-Han, 82: his first daughter Latife died at a very young age.

Figure 14.1. Mehmed Salih Bedirkhan in Damascus, January 1915
Source: © Archives Bedir Khan

tyranny, he had an affair with a woman named Taci. He suffered from hurting his wife through the affair and realized that this behaviour was not reconcilable with his moral concepts.[17]

There are a few remarks in Salih's memoirs that reflect his worldview. He mentions the husband (a judicial officer) of his grandmother's

---

17 Uzun and Bedir-Han, 71. See also Henning, "Erinnerungen," 396.

314   Martin Strohmeier

daughter in Limnos, a Kurd from Maraş, who was "Turkified" and "excessively religious," but also "uncorrupted" and "upright."[18] The fact that he emphasizes these characteristics probably meant that he made a distinction between different types of Kurds, namely those who (perhaps like himself) were Ottomanized, and those who had largely "forgotten" their "Kurdishness." Furthermore, the lines imply that he did not give religion a central place and that incorruptibility was a virtue to strive for, as he stressed in the context of his work for and his relationship with Bedri.[19]

Salih's political and cultural views emerge more clearly from his articles in the exile newspaper *Ümid* and in Kurdish journals published in Istanbul.

Exile and Editorship

Information about Salih's internal exile is scarce. The years 1893 to 1914 are not covered in his memoirs, making it difficult to precisely determine his whereabouts. Details gleaned from other sources are the stay in Cairo in (at least) 1900, his prosecution for "rebellious" activities in Aleppo in 1902 and the *résidence forcée* in Rhodes in 1906.[20] In 1907 he was imprisoned in Nablus. Salih's last station as internee was the Police Ministry (*Bab-i zabtiyye*) in Istanbul. In 1909, after Abdülhamid's dismissal, Salih returned to work as an official in the province of Kayseri.[21] From this timeline emerges that Salih did not hold a post for a period of roughly fifteen years and was at least temporarily separated from his family.

He may have spent some time in Istanbul in 1913 as his articles in *Rojê Kurd* bear the place name Kadıköy. At the time of his death at the end of March 1915 he was prison warden in Damascus.[22] The years 1894 to 1906 are a "black hole" in Salih's biography; this corresponds

---

18 Uzun and Bedir-Han, 34.
19 Salih condemns Bedri as corrupt. Bedri "bought" his office of *mutasarrif* for the amount of 800 lira. Uzun and Bedir-Han, *Mehmet Salih*, 79–80. See also Henning, "Erinnerungen," 396.
20 Malmîsanij, *Cizira*, 184. Uzun and Bedir-Han, *Mehmet Salih*, 99. In a telegram which Salih's father Mahmud Izzet sent to the *vali* of Beirut and to Beirut daily newspapers (July 1908), he states that his son was held in custody in Rhodes for ten years "for political matters" and was now being held at Akka prison. There is a photo with other exiles in Rhodes in Malmîsanij, *Cizira*, 24, appendix. Bedri was also exiled to Rhodes in 1906, probably having fallen out of favour. See also Henning, *Narratives*, 177.
21 Uzun and Bedir-Han, *Mehmet Salih*, 9–10; his daughter Rewşen was born there.
22 Uzun and Bedir-Han, 10.

to the fact that in this period (1896 to 1906) the regime's repression was most intense. Trying to put these details in context, we must rely on guesswork. Salih, after the failed putsch against Abdülhamid in 1896, might have been banished like other members of the Bedirhan clan who took up residence in Cairo, one of the centres of opposition to the Sultan. Here the first Kurdish newspaper, *Kurdistan*, was founded. Initially it appeared in Kurdish (to be precise, in the Kurmanji dialect of Botan); later, articles in Turkish were published as well. From July 1898 onwards the newspaper was transferred to Geneva and subsequently to London.

Two years later, in August 1900, Salih started to publish *Ümid* in Cairo. The only issue available to me does not - in contrast to *Kurdistan* - include any "Kurdish" theme. It was exclusively published in Turkish and had one thing in common with *Kurdistan*, namely an appeal to the Muslim identity of the projected readers by invoking Quran verses and *hadith*s. The newspaper appeared only briefly twice a month; two issues are confirmed.[23]

The journalistic orientation is expressed in the newspaper's masthead in three sentences and a symbol: "*Ümid gazetesi menafi'-i mülk ve millete khadim 'Arapça maqalati da qabul eder*" ("The paper *Ümid* serves the interests of the state and the nation, it also accepts articles in Arabic"); "*Enin-i milleti isma'a khadim siyasi gazetedir*" ("political newspaper serving to make heard the nation's groans"). The motto on top of the masthead is a hadith from the collection *Sunan*, by the ninth-century scholar al-Tirmidhi: "*Afdal al-jihad kalimatu haqqin 'inda sultanin ja'irin*," ("The best jihad is a word of truth before a tyrannical ruler").[24] Finally, the symbol of the Freemasons, the square and compass, is found on the masthead. The Freemasons had enjoyed the sympathies of Murad V, so they were persecuted when Abdülhamid came to power; there were close ties between the Young Ottomans, the Young Turks, and the Freemasons, regarding their resistance to the regime.[25]

The appearance of *Ümid* in August and September 1900 coincides with the anniversary of Abdülhamid's accession to the throne. In these

---

23 Nos. 1 and 2, August and September 1900, of which only No. 2 is presented by Seîd Veroj, "Mehmed Salih Bedirhan'ın 'UMMID' gazetesi," *Kovara Bîr*, archived 10 December 2023, at the Wayback Machine, https://web.archive.org /web/20231210162524/http://kovarabir.com /seid-veroj-mehmed-salih-bedirhanin-ummid-gazetesi/.

24 Al-Tirmidhi, *Riyad al-Salihin*, Book of Miscellany 194.

25 Dorothe Sommer, *Freemasonry in the Ottoman Empire: A History of the Fraternity and its Influence in Syria and the Levant* (London: I.B. Tauris, 2015).

316   Martin Strohmeier

articles, contrary to the usual congratulations and addresses of devotion, the Sultan is sharply attacked. The celebrations of the twenty-fifth throne jubilee are criticized from an Islamic-moral perspective: "disgraces which do not befit the honour of Islam nor humanity." All five articles are most likely written by Salih under the pseudonym Abu l-Baraka/ Ebu l-Bereket. The author denounces Abdülhamid for usurping the throne; like "a Genghis Khan," he was "the most brutal of creatures." His subjects had remained silent or had even collaborated for a long time. He calls Abu l-Huda, the influential Syrian adviser to the Sultan, a "scoundrel" (*rezil*), thereby attacking a sponsor and distant relative of his father-in-law Bedri.[26] The articles in this issue have no relation to Kurdish topics; they are solely dedicated to the oppressive rule of the sultan and his delegitimization employing religious arguments. Salih must have left Cairo by 1902 at the latest because he was reportedly involved in unspecified "seditious" activities in Aleppo that year.[27]

Mehmed Salih and the Kurdish Awakening

In her book about the Bedirhans and in two separate articles, Barbara Henning has dedicated several dozen pages to Salih.[28] They deal primarily with the content and character of his memoirs and the life path documented in them, but do not touch upon his journalism. She argues: "He is at home ideologically in the Ottoman nationalism of the early Young Turk movement. At no point does he make his Kurdish origins the basis for an ethnically grounded distinct identity."[29]

Reading Salih's memoirs and following his professional and political activities, and particularly his firm commitment to Ottomanism as well as his intention to go to war for his fatherland (on the Caucasus and Suez fronts), one can largely agree with this conclusion.

---

26   Eich, *Abū l-Hudā*, 208–9. Together with his grandmother, Salih had visited Abu l-Huda in the early 1880s: Uzun and Bedir-Han, *Mehmet Salih*, 36–7.

27   Malmîsanij, *Cizira*, 184.

28   Henning, *Narratives*, 231–49. Henning, "Die Erinnerungen," 381–413. Henning, "A Passionate Ottoman in Late Nineteenth-Century Damascus," in *Imperial Subjects: Autobiographische Praxis in den Vielvölkerreichen der Romanovs, Habsburger und Osmanen im 19. Und frühen 20. Jahrhundert*, ed. Martin Aust and F. Benjamin Schenk (Cologne: Böhlau, 2015), 233–54.

29   In German: "Ideologisch findet er damit im osmanischen Nationalismus der frühen jungtürkischen Bewegung eine Heimat. Seine kurdische Herkunft ist für ihn zu keinem Zeitpunkt Grundlage einer ethnisch begründeten separaten Identität." ("Die Erinnerungen," 409–10).

Between Ottomanism and Kurdism   317

In my opinion, however, things look different on the basis of Salih's articles in *Rojê Kurd*. Here, we find many references to the so-called awakening as propagated by intellectuals of many ethnic groups in the context of nation-building.[30] We observe an increase in ethnic awareness, a turning to Kurdish language and culture, the beginning of a preoccupation with Kurdish history and identity. This puts Salih in the same camp as more prominent Kurdish intellectuals such as 'Abdullah Cevdet (whose article Salih refers to) and İsma'il Haqqı Baban. Salih's statements are evidence of an emerging Kurdish identity, which could perhaps be described as complementary rather than as "distinct," existing parallel to his commitment to Ottomanism. Separatist views hardly existed among the Arabs and even less so among the Kurds in the Ottoman Empire, at least not until 1916. Even the most radical members of the Kurdish movement were not separatists at this point. Given the fact that Salih, in contrast to the young, independent, radical student members of *Hêvî* with whom he associated, was a descendant of the Kurdish aristocracy, a civil servant, and a family man, his commitment to the Kurdish cause is all the more remarkable. Salih was an avowed Ottoman, but in addition to his loyalty to the Ottoman Empire he also developed a Kurdish identity.[31]

After the dismissal of the Sultan, in lieu of the fight against the absolutist regime, there was an opportunity for a concentration on Kurdish issues, in the context of the greater freedoms for ethnic groups, if only for a short time. The small class of educated people who cared about Kurdism – which we can define very broadly here as a commitment to furthering Kurdish culture and concerns – was far removed from nationalist or separatist aspirations. As part of the Young Turkish opposition, their focus was on the struggle against autocracy, and on the relationship between Kurds and Armenians. Moreover, their efforts were aimed at showing Kurds the value of their culture, to enable them to be proud of themselves and to make their own leadership claims

---

30 I have defined the term "awakening" in "Das 'Erwachen' in kurdischen Zeitungen zu Beginn des 20. Jahrhunderts," in *Querelles privées et contestations publiques : Le rôle de la presse dans la formation de l'opinion publique au Proche Orient*, ed. Christoph Herzog, Raoul Motika, and Michael Ursinus (Istanbul: ISIS, 2002), 163–81; in a broader context in my *Crucial Images in the Presentation of a Kurdish National Identity: Heroes and Patriots, Traitors and Foes* (Leiden: Brill, 2003), 9–74.

31 Stefan Winter, "The Other *Nahḍah*: The Bedirxans, the Millîs, and the Tribal Roots of Kurdish Nationalism in Syria," *Oriente Moderno* 86 (2006): 461–74, esp. 467.

318 Martin Strohmeier

clear. In most of the Kurdish newspapers, members of the Bedirhan family were involved.

After his release from prison in 1908, Salih became a collaborator of the largely unknown newspaper *Kurdistan*, which appeared in the years 1908–9 under the aegis of the Bedirhans. It was closed after the counter-revolution of 31 March 1909.[32] The phase in which the Kurds and other ethnic groups could consolidate their following was brief. Before oppression of Kurdish associations set in, Kurdish students founded *Hêvî* in 1912. It became a sort of hotbed for Kurdish nationalists. The growth of Turkish nationalism aroused resentment in many "awakened" Kurds; the preoccupation of the Turks with their language and culture prompted the Kurds to take an interest in their own.[33]

Compared with previous Kurdish newspapers, *Rojê Kurd* demonstrated a more pronounced commitment to ethnic identity. The writings of Mehmed Salih constitute a significant contribution to a Kurdish awakening. He published the famous prologue (*dibacha*) of Ahmad-i Khani's epic poem *Mem u Zin*.[34] In "A Dream Comes True," Salih Bedirhan utilizes the rhetoric of victimization, a well-known element in nationalist discourse. The Kurdish youth had decided to proceed with progress and education in response to the ubiquitous insults directed against the Kurds. They had been neglected, exploited, and intrigued against, and now it was time for them to awaken. If the Kurds continued to sleep, they would lose their right to life (*haqq-i hayat*). The Kurdish youth, on the other hand, were in possession of the truth and were determined to awaken and thus save the Kurds from corruption. The author points out the importance of knowing and following model Kurds in the context of strengthening the initiative and feelings of the youth. He uses the well-established images of sleep as equal to death of the nation, the repression and deception of the Kurds by other nations.[35]

---

32 This was the second paper with this title, after the one established in 1898. The third appeared in 1919; its editor was Süreyya Bedirhan, one of Emin Ali's sons. Malmîsanij, *Cizira*, 100. See also Enver Yalçın, İlhan Kaya, and Gülşah Savaş Çakmakcı, *Osmanlı Dönemi Kürt Basın Tarihi* (Istanbul: UKAM, 2015).

33 Already in 1910 Celadet Bedirhan was shocked when he heard speeches by Yusuf Aqçura and İsma'il Gasprinskij, according to which only Turks lived in Turkey. Emir Celadet Ali, *Bir Kürt Aydınından Mustafa Kemal'e Mektup* (Istanbul: Doz, 1992), 21–2.

34 "Qasidat Hazret-i Sheykh Ahmad-i Khani" (Kurdish version "Berî Şîrê Qelem"), in Mehmed Salih Bedirhan, "Qılıçdan evvel qalem," *Rojê Kurd* no. 3, 11 Ramazan 1331/1 Ağustos 1329/14 August 1913. It had been previously published in *Kurdistan* 8, 5 Receb 1316/18 Teşrin-i sani 1314/20 November 1898.

35 "Khulyā ḥaḳīḳat oluyor," *Rojê Kurd* no. 2, 14 Şaban 1331/6 Temmuz 1329/19 July 1913.

Salih sincerely believed in Ottomanism (*'osmanlılıq*), the concept of a multi-ethnic state with several languages and religions in loyalty to the Ottoman dynasty. Yet, this belief seems to have suffered a blow which might have contributed to his Kurdism becoming more pronounced. In an article about an event in the First Balkan War in the *sancak* of Berat (Albania), two Kurdish soldiers of an Ottoman army unit were shot by "treacherous compatriots." In contrast, the Kurdish soldiers demonstrated "self sacrifice for their religion and their country."[36] As a result of this experience and other developments, namely the loss of the Balkan provinces and the aspirations of Christian Ottomans for a future outside the Empire, Salih appears to have lost confidence in the loyalty of Christian Ottomans and put his trust in an association of Kurds and Turks. This was by and large in line with 'Abdullah Cevdet, who advocated the unity of Kurds and Turks. Regarding the language question, however, Salih's opinion probably differed from Cevdet's: the latter proposed adopting "appropriate letters" by which he most probably meant the introduction of the Latin script for Kurdish. Salih, on the other hand, supported the proposal of the Kurdish "Society for the Spread of Education and Reform of Letters" (*Ta'mim-i ma'arif ve islah-i huruf cem'iyyeti*) for an addition of eight letters to the existing Kurdish alphabet.[37]

İsma'il Haqqı Baban had proposed a hierarchy of constitutive identities: first and foremost was Muslim identity, then Ottoman, and only in the third place Kurdish.[38] But this weighting was not shared by all educated Kurds. Writers for *Rojê Kurd*, *Hêvî's* mouthpiece, seem to have given the Kurdish part priority. Salih, on the other hand, stressed the primacy of Ottoman identity, subordinating the Kurdish aspect. At the time he was writing his articles for *Rojê Kurd*, his future son-in-law Celadet served in the Ottoman army on the Caucasus front. In 1913, together with his younger brother Kamuran, he penned an account of the Balkan Wars in which he dwelled upon the loss of Edirne. In the preface to their book, the authors (who after the Great War would become eminent leaders of Kurdish national aspirations), very much like Salih, expressed the wish: "May Ottomanism remain, may Islam be eternal!"[39]

---

36 Writing under the pseudonym Ebu Revşen: "Kürdlüğün menaqib-i hamasetinden iki sima-i besalet," *Rojê Kurd* 4, 10 Shawwal 1331/30 Ağustos 1329/12 September 1913.

37 "Hurufumuz ve Teshil-i qıra'at," *Rojê Kurd* 2, 14 Sha'ban 1331/6 Temmuz 1329/19 July 1913, under the pseudonym M.S. 'Azizi.

38 "Kürdler ve Kürdistan," *Kürd Te'avün ve Teraqqi Gazetesi*, no. 1, 11 Zulkade 1326/22 Tişrin-i sani 1324/5 December 1908, 3.

39 Kamuran and Celadet Bedirhan, *Edirne süqutunun iç yüzü* (Istanbul: Serbesti Matba'ası, 1329/1913–14), 8. However, the reference in that book to Ahmad-i Khani

320 Martin Strohmeier

Death and Legacy

Salih succumbed to typhoid fever at the end of March 1915. He was probably buried where other members of the family including his daughter
were laid to rest, that is, in the Shaykh Khalid Naqshabandi cemetery of
the Hayy al-Akrad neighbourhood.[40] For good reasons, what-if scenarios
are not part of the historian's trade. However, one cannot refrain from
thinking that, had he not died prematurely, Salih, especially after the end
of the Ottoman empire, would have further elaborated his commitment
to Kurdish culture, which was carried forwards by his descendants. It is
fitting that no less than Celadet Bedirhan, the eminent Kurdish author
and leader (for example, in the Xoybûn Committee), was to become Salih's son-in-law by marrying his daughter Rewşen in 1935. After Celadet's
death in 1951 she played a role in furthering Kurdish culture; her input
was indispensable in preserving and editing her father's memoirs.[41]
Rewşen's daughter Sīnemxan was born in Damascus in 1938. In 1960
she moved to Iraq, living in Kirkuk, Baghdad and from 2006 onwards
in Hewler/Erbil. She worked as a teacher and wrote about Kurdish language, literature, and history. In this way, three generations of Bedirhans
passed on the torch of the Kurdish cause.[42]

Abd al-Rahman al-Yusuf (1873/4–1920): A Staunchly Ottoman Notable and Politician of Kurdish Ancestry

ʿAbd al-Rahman Pasha al-Yusuf was descended from a family of
notables.[43] This family of Kurdish stock was, in comparison to long-
established dynasties such as the ʿAzms, a "relative newcomer"

---

reveals that Kurdish concerns were not absent. The authors had another theme
in common with Salih's "treacherous compatriots," namely the alleged treason of
Christian Ottomans when Bulgarian soldiers entered Edirne.

40 ʿIzz al-Din ʿAli Mulla, *Hayy al-Akrad fi Madinat Dimashq bayna ʿamay 1250–1979:
Dirasa Tarikhiyya, Ijtimaʿiyya, Iqtisadiyya* (Beirut: Dar Asu, 1998), 86; "Kürt aydın
Rewşen Bedirxan 28 yıl önce aramızdan ayrıldı," *Rûdaw*, 6 July 2020, https://www
.rudaw.net/turkish/culture/07062020.

41 Winter, "The Other *Nahḍah*," 463–6.

42 "Sinemhan Bedirhan," *biyografi.net*, ed. Mahmut Çetin, accessed 15 February 2022,
https://www.biyografi.net/kisiayrinti.asp?kisiid=6236. A family album of the
Bedirhans including Salih, Celadet, and his wife Rewşen can be found under the title
"The Kurdish Noble Family Bedir Khans: From Botan at late 1800 to 1960,"
accessed 30 November 2021, at https://www.saradistribution.com/bedirkhans.htm.

43 In the minutes of the Ottoman parliament, he is mostly called *bey*, and less frequently *efendi*. See Feroz Ahmad and Dankwart Rustow, "İkinci Meşrutiyet

Between Ottomanism and Kurdism   321

to Damascus.[44] In less than a century, the Yusufs rose from rather insignificant immigrants to members of the provincial elite. Most probably they came to the city at the end of the eighteenth century from Diyarbakır where they had worked in the livestock business.[45] The migration of the family perhaps had to do with the introduction of Kurdish troops in Bilad al-Sham to protect the pilgrimage routes to the Hijaz.[46] This is suggested by the fact that the post of commander of the caravan of pilgrims (*amir al-hajj*) became more or less a prerogative of the Yusufs in the second half of the nineteenth century. Furthermore, several members of the family gained positions in the provincial administration in Bilad al-Sham.[47] The rise of the Yusufs suffered only a temporary setback during the governorship of Midhat Paşa in the years 1878 to 1880.[48]

---

döneminde meclisler: 1908–1918," *Güneydoğu Avrupa Araştırmaları Dergisi* 4–5 (1976): 245–84. On account of his high standing he was given the honorary title of *paşa*. His family or ancestral name (*nasab*) is written with or without the definite article *al-*. This section is a shortened and modified version of my article "Abd al-Rahman Pasha al-Yusuf, a Notable in Damascus (1873/74–1920)," in Antonis Anastasopoulos, ed., *Provincial Elites in the Ottoman Empire* (Rethymno: Crete University Press, 2005), 349–67.

44 Butrus Abu-Manneh, "The Genesis of Midhat Pasha's Governorship in Syria 1878–1880," in *The Syrian Land: Processes of Integration and Fragmentation. Bilād al-Shām from the 18th to the 20th Century*, ed. Thomas Philipp and Birgit Schaebler (Stuttgart: Franz Steiner, 1998), 251–67, esp. 261.

45 The Bedirhans were newcomers to Damascus perhaps half a century later than the Yusufs who hailed from the same region, the difference between the two being that the former had been rulers in Upper Mesopotamia and now were exiles in Syria, whereas the latter were from humble origins and climbed the social ladder in approximately half a century. What helped both in their rise to influence was a policy of marriage alliances, though this was much less pronounced and successful in the case of the Bedirhans. See Henning, "Die Erinnerungen," 403–4. Philip S. Khoury, *Urban Notables and Arab Nationalism: The Politics of Damascus 1860–1920* (Cambridge: Cambridge University Press, 1983), 39. For another family with a Kurdish background, al-Muradi, see Linda Schatkowski Schilcher, *Families in Politics: Damascene Factions and Estates of the 18th and 19th Centuries* (Stuttgart: Franz Steiner, 1985), 19; ʿAbd al-Qadir Badran, *Al-Kawakib al-Durriya fi Tarikh ʿAbd al-Rahman Basha al-Yusuf* (Damascus: Matbaʿat al-Fayhaʾ, 1339/1920–1), 8.

46 Nelida Fuccaro, "Die Kurden Syriens: Anfänge der nationalen Mobilisierung unter französischer Herrschaft," in *Ethnizität, Nationalismus, Religion und Politik in Kurdistan*, ed. Carsten Borck, Eva Savelsberg, and Siamend Hajo (Münster: LIT, 1997), 301–26, esp. 303.

47 Badran, *Kawakib*, 8–10. Schatkowski Schilcher, *Families in Politics*, 151–3. Khoury, *Urban Notables*, 39–40.

48 Abu-Manneh, "Genesis," 253.

The Yusufs could not have acquired their extensive fortune and power if they had not allied themselves with another Kurdish clan, the Shamdin. Their eponym, Shamdin (d. 1860), succeeded in building a power base among the Kurds of the local janissary garrison (*yerliyye*) in Damascus. Sometime later Shamdin's son, Muhammad Sa'id (d. 1900), became commander of a newly formed garrison (*awniyye*), again consisting of Kurdish irregulars.[49] Sa'id's banishment to Mosul because his troops had participated in massacring Christians in Damascus (July 1860) did not result in a downturn of his career.[50] After his return he gained even higher offices. As district governor of the Hawran he took the place of Ahmad al-Yusuf and as *amir al-hajj* he replaced Muhammad Paşa al-Yusuf (his future or already son-in-law) in the late 1860s.[51]

The Yusufs' Landed Wealth

These offices laid the foundations for the fabulous wealth of the family, enabling Sa'id to buy large property, farms, and villages in the *Ghuta* (the green belt surrounding Damascus), the Hawran, and al-Qunaytira, as well as on the eastern shores of Lake Tiberias.[52] By the 1890s Sa'id was allegedly the biggest landowner in the whole province of Syria; in this position he was succeeded by his grandson 'Abd al-Rahman.[53] The incomes from dozens of villages that 'Abd al-Rahman owned in al-Batiha, the Ghuta, al-Marj, and the Golan, ranged from 7,000 to 10,000 Turkish gold liras.[54]

---

49 Khoury, *Urban Notables*, 40. Schatkowski Schilcher, *Families in Politics*, 147–9.
50 Leila Tarazi Fawaz, *An Occasion for War: Civil Conflict in Lebanon and Damascus in 1860* (Berkeley: University of California Press, 1994), 88.
51 Khalid al-'Azm, "'Zu'ama' al-Akrad': Mudhakkirat (Beirut: Al-Dar al-Muttahida li'l-Nashr, 1973), 1:12.
52 "Record on the Ottoman Senator Abdurrahman Pasha," German Foreign Ministry, Political Archive, AA 177, R 14039, A 40985, 10 September 1918, 6 (henceforth abbreviated as AA 177). The report illustrates the personal status of Abd al-Rahman, his relations with both foreign celebrities and prominent Young Turk politicians as well as the efforts of Austria and Germany to win him over to business transactions. Furthermore, the report lists 'Abd al-Rahman's properties and indicates his business ideas for the future.
53 Khoury, *Urban Notables*, 40. AA 177: 'Abd al-Rahman estimated the size of his properties at about 100,000 hectares. Cf. FO 882/24/128-34, 14 May 1919, "Who's Who in Damascus: The wealthiest landowner in Syria"; I am grateful to Jim Gelvin (UCLA) for making this and other Foreign Office materials available to me.
54 Hanna Batatu, *Syria's Peasantry, the Descendants of Its Lesser Rural Notables, and their Politics* (Princeton: Princeton University Press, 1999), 40–1.

Between Ottomanism and Kurdism 323

The Rise of the Yusufs through Marriage Alliances and Allegiance to Abdülhamid

The wealth and the landholdings of the family were enhanced by a marriage alliance between the Shamdins and Yusuf clans. In the 1860s Saʿid married his only daughter to Muhammad Pasha al-Yusuf. The couple had one son, ʿAbd al-Rahman, who inherited most of both families' fortunes, property, and offices.[55] The reasons and details for this alliance are not known to us, but it seems fair to guess that since both families competed for influence among the Kurds of Salihiyya (then a village to the northwest of Damascus, today a suburb), they decided to combine their wealth and power. Perhaps they realized that acting separately was less advantageous than joint action; one might also suspect a certain Kurdish solidarity. Finally, the above-mentioned loss of offices of the Yusufs to the Shamdins, happening at around the same time, might also have added to the impulse to merge power and fortune.

After the death of his father in 1896, ʿAbd al-Rahman became the head of the family and as such was responsible for the clans of the Shamdins and Yusufs. With the rise of the family to power, living in al-Salihiyya no longer befitted the rank of the Yusufs, although many distantly related Shamdins continued to live there. ʿAbd al-Rahman's father and grandfather had already moved to a more fashionable part of town, the extramural Suq Saruja, on account of its abundance of space and water, as well as its strategic location between the walled city and al-Salihiyya, probably in the 1870s. At the end of the nineteenth century the three wealthiest families in Damascus, the ʿAzms, ʿAbids, and Yusufs all lived in this quarter. The latter two had quarrelled over the *amir al-hajj* office before a marriage alliance offered more promising opportunities. These families became relatives by marriages that led

---

55 Khoury, *Urban Notables*, 39. According to Badran, *Kawakib*, 24, ʿAbd al-Rahman was born in 1873 or 1874. The German report (AA 177) states that he was fifty to fifty-three years old in 1918. FO 882/24/128-34, 14 May 1919, "Who's Who in Damascus" gives his age as forty-five. This latter number seems more likely; hence, the lifespan referred to in the heading of the chapter. According to Mulla, *Hayy al-Akrad*, 130, ʿAbd al-Rahman was born in 1871. Mulla has only scant information on the grandee. He credits him with having financed the al-Tiruzi Mosque in the quarter of Qabr ʿAtika, but this is incorrect because the mosque already existed in the 1850s when A. von Kremer visited it: A. von Kremer, "Topographie von Damascus," *Denkschriften der Kaiserlichen Akademie der Wissenschaften*, Philosophisch-Historische Klasse, 6 (1855): 1–36, esp. 22. In general, Mulla's book is full of gaps and suffers from a pro-Asad-regime bias.

324   Martin Strohmeier

to political alliances and resulted in shared economic interests.[56] They served as arbitrators and mediators in disputes. Suq Saruja came to be called 'Petit Istanbul' because of the wealth and refined lifestyle of its inhabitants miles apart from their humble origins (in the case of the Yusufs) and their Kurdish clientele.[57] The Yusufs established contacts not only with the imperial capital, but also with distinguished foreign personalities, such as the German Kaiser Wilhelm II and Kaiser Karl I of Austria-Hungary, thus acquiring a cosmopolitan outlook.[58]

'Abd al-Rahman hardly had any educational background beyond high school (*rüşdiyye*).[59] In contrast, his eldest son, after having attended the lycée (*sultani*) in Galatasaray (Istanbul), studied at the famous Theresianum in Vienna; the younger sons went to school in Beirut and the daughters were educated by a French governess.[60] British sources described 'Abd al-Rahman as "not intelligent, self-opiniated, but not fanatical."[61] On the other hand, his plans concerning the exploitation of his estates suggest that he was not lacking in ideas.[62] Furthermore, he is – somewhat contradictorily - described as a "strict" Muslim, although he did not fast during Ramadan. He employed many Christians in his service and took the duty of giving alms very seriously. During the famine in Lebanon in the First World War, 'Abd al-Rahman generously

---

56   'Abd al-Rahman took the daughter of Khalil Paşa al-'Azm as his wife. Hulu Paşa al-'Abid was also married to an 'Azm girl; two of his grandsons (the children of Ahmad 'Izzat Paşa, the influential scribe of Sultan Abdülhamid) married two sisters of 'Abd al-Rahman: Khoury, *Urban Notables*, 49. See also Caesar Farah, "Arab Supporters of Sultan Abdülhamid II: 'Izzet al-'Ābid," *Archivum Ottomanicum* 15 (1997): 189–219; Sami Moubayed, "Syria's Forgotten First President Mohammad Ali al-Abed," *British Journal of Middle Eastern Studies* 41, no. 4 (2014): 419–41, https://doi.org/10.1080/13530194.2014.942080. The Yusufs took an interest economically in the Hijaz Railway, the establishment of which was basically Ahmad 'Izzat al-'Abid's initiative, see Eich, *Abū l-Hudā aş-Şayyādī*, 184.
57   'Abd al-Razzaq Moaz, "The Urban Fabric of an Extramural Quarter in Nineteenth-Century Damascus," in *The Syrian Land*, ed. Thomas Philipp and Birgit Schaebler (Stuttgart: F. Steiner, 1998), 165–83, esp. 165–6.
58   About the fate of the Yusufs' palace see Samy Marwan Mobayed, "The Crumbling Palaces of Damascus," *Raseef*, 15 April 2021, https://raseef22.net/english/article/1082378-the-crumbling-palaces-of-damascus. According to Mobayed, 'Abd al-Rahman's children left their home in the early 1960s. During his visit in 1898, Kaiser Wilhelm II waited upon 'Abd al-Rahman in his palace.
59   He also had a private teacher. He spoke Turkish and Arabic very well, as well as some Kurdish, but knew only a few words of French. Badran, *Kawakib*, 25.
60   Badran, 100; AA 177, 1.
61   FO 882/24/128-134.
62   AA 177, 3, 6.

distributed grain to the poor. On the other hand, he paid considerably lower taxes than a Christian merchant.[63]

Abd al-Rahman Yusuf's Offices and Status

For roughly half a century the Yusuf and Shamdin families provided the *amir al-hajj*, the commander of the pilgrim caravan that went from Damascus to Mecca every year. However, this post was not obtained free of charge; 'Abd al-Rahman had to pay an extraordinary sum, two thousand gold pounds, to keep his office and to outmaneuver the 'Abids' claims by a marriage strategy.[64]

The post not only gave prestige to its incumbent, but also profit and influence; the *amir al-hajj* could allocate jobs and conduct business. The office brought 'Abd al-Rahman into contact with high-ranking personalities in the whole Muslim world, but it also caused conflict.[65] A case in point was his clash with the Sharif of Mecca, Husayn ibn 'Ali, over control of the caravan (1908–9) in which 'Abd al-Rahman came out the worst. His defeat increased the prestige of Sharif Husayn. Whereas the establishment of the Hijaz Railway had already reduced the significance of the *amir al-hajj*, Husayn's victory further contributed to the decline of that office.[66] 'Abd al-Rahman was suspended and the abolition of the office was considered by the Grand Vizier.[67] Moreover, if we are to believe 'Abdallah, Husayn's son (who, of course, as opponent, had an interest in portraying 'Abd al-Rahman in a bad light), the incident damaged 'Abd al-Rahman's standing. 'Abd al-Rahman's disparaging of Husayn was not well received by the public and led to death threats against him. 'Abdallah even seems to suggest a link between these threats and 'Abd al-Rahman's violent death several years later (August 1920).[68]

Damascene notables such as the 'Azms and Yusufs had not been on friendly terms with Husayn ibn 'Ali even before his appointment as

---

63 M. Talha Çiçek, *War and State Formation in Syria: Cemal Pasha's Governorate During World War I, 1914–1917* (Abingdon: Routledge, 2014), 241.
64 Khoury, *Urban Notables*, 48. Uzun and Bedir-Han, *Mehmet Salih*, 77.
65 AA 177, 6.
66 Given their involvement in the Hijaz Railway, it is open to discussion if the Yusufs had thought about this negative effect on the post that they had held for many years.
67 Hasan Kayalı, *Arabs and Young Turks: Ottomanism, Arabism, and Islamism in the Ottoman Empire, 1908–1918* (Berkeley: University of California Press, 1997), 151, 246.
68 Ernest Dawn, *From Ottomanism to Arabism: Essays on the Origins of Arab Nationalism* (Urbana: University of Illinois Press, 1973), 6–7. 'Abdallah ibn al-Husayn, *Mudhakkirati* (Amman: Al-Ahliyya li'l-Nashr wa'l-Tawzi', 1998), 42–5.

Figure 14.2. Abd al-Rahman Pasha al-Yusuf
Source: Courtesy of Sabah Kabbani.

amir of Mecca by the Young Turks in 1908. But the clash made 'Abd al-Rahman a fierce enemy of the Sharif.[69] Thus, when some years later the Arab movement gained momentum in Syria and received the encouragement of the Hashemites, 'Abd al-Rahman opposed the movement.

'Abd al-Rahman as Supporter of the Young Turks and Opponent of Arabism

We can assume that 'Abd al-Rahman had been a loyal follower of the Sultan, given his family's involvement with the post of *amir al-hajj*, especially in the context of the Pan-Islamic policies of Abdülhamid, the

---

69 Khoury, *Urban Notables*, 87.

"Father of the Kurds."[70] On the other hand, it is said that the Yusufs were on the Young Turks' side during their struggle against the absolutist regime,[71] even though it seems rather unlikely that a sympathizer of the oppositional Committee of Union and Progress (CUP) could have held such a significant post. In any case, we hear that 'Abd al-Rahman was a supporter of Young Turk activities in Damascus already in 1897, and that the government took measures against him and Muhammad Fawzi Paşa al-'Azm, then president of the municipality.[72] Later, 'Abd al-Rahman was in close contact with Talat Paşa and Enver.[73] In sum, the degree of allegiance to Sultan Abdülhamid and affiliation with the Young Turks, at least until the former's fall, are debatable. It is a fair guess that the political orientation of the Yusufs was not a matter of principle, but of strategic considerations, indicating their flexibility in adjusting to the vagaries of the political situation. The most succinct characterization of 'Abd al-Rahman's opportunism is contained in a statement by Hulusi Bey, governor of Syria in 1914–15, who noted that "whichever side was powerful, he would serve it" [*her ne taraf kavi ise derhal o cihetin amaline mütemayildir*].[74] After 1908 'Abd al-Rahman had excellent relations with the Young Turks. He was elected to parliament on the CUP ticket in 1908 and re-elected in 1912.[75]

'Abd al-Rahman proved to be a strong opponent of the nascent Arab movement. For example, he did not join the short-lived Arab Party (*al-Hizb al-'Arabi*), a group which included nearly all Arab deputies supporting Arab interests (such as the demand for Arabic as the language of instruction) in the Ottoman Empire. He nevertheless attended a group meeting in April 1911 where he opposed the foundation of an Arab party and voiced the opinion that the "Turks were the rightful

---

70 Martin van Bruinessen, *Agha, Shaikh and State: The Social and Political Structure of Kurdistan* (London: Zed Books, 1992), 268.
71 James Gelvin, *Divided Loyalties: Nationalism and Mass Politics in Syria at the Close of Empire* (Berkeley: University of California Press, 1998), 57.
72 Kayalı, *Arabs and Young Turks*, 123. Max Gross, *Ottoman Rule in the Province of Damascus, 1860–1909* (PhD diss., Georgetown University, 1979), 446, 466, quoted by Abd al-Aziz Duri, *The Historical Formation of the Arab Nation: A Study in Identity and Consciousness*, trans. Lawrence I. Conrad (London: Croom Helm, 1987), 262n20.
73 AA 177, 7.
74 M. Talha Çiçek, "Myth of the Unionist Triumvirate: The Formation of the CUP Factions and their Impact in Syria during the Great War," in M. Talha Çiçek, ed., *Syria in World War I: Politics, Economy, and Society* (Abingdon: Routledge, 2016), 9–36, esp. 22.
75 Rashid Khalidi, "Ottomanism and Arabism in Syria Before 1914: A Reassessment," in *The Origins of Arab Nationalism*, ed. Rashid Khalidi, Lisa Anderson, Muhammad Muslih, and Reeva S. Simon (New York: Columbia University Press, 1991), 50–69, esp. 59.

328   Martin Strohmeier

rulers of the empire and that their rule, under the CUP, was essentially enlightened and benevolent in nature."[76] These views suggest that 'Abd al-Rahman would also have had little sympathy for any manifestations of Kurdish self-awareness.

'Abd al-Rahman's influence at the national level is also indicated by his role as a deputy in the lower house (*meclis-i meb'usan*), and later as a senator (1914) in the upper house (*meclis-i a'yan*) of the Ottoman parliament. There is contradictory evidence concerning the details of his entering parliament as well as his party membership.[77] His recorded contributions were limited. There were several occasions when he took the floor; for example, to enquire about the state of locomotives of the Hijaz Railway.[78] Regarding another issue, he voiced the opinion that women should not be allowed to travel without being escorted by male members of their family.[79]

A person with such extensive power and wealth was bound to encounter opposition. When Cemal Paşa, the Commander of the Fourth Ottoman Army, Marine Minister, and Young Turk triumvir, set himself up as the unrestricted ruler over Syria during the First World War, he became suspicious of 'Abd al-Rahman on account of his extraordinary influence. But not even Cemal dared to take action against the Damascene notable, who was clever enough to demonstrate his loyalty to the "second Saladin" (*Salah al-Din-i sani*), as Cemal was referred to by his staff.[80] At Cemal's request he raised a Kurdish unit (which he equipped at his own expense), for the first of two disastrous expeditions against the Suez Canal.[81] Enver Paşa, always distrustful of Cemal, tried to sound out 'Abd al-Rahman about the General's activities in Syria. But he shrewdly told Enver that he did not know anything and that he did not want to get involved in politics. After Cemal left his post at the end

---

76 Samir Seikaly, "Shukri al-'Asali: A Case Study of a Political Activist," in *The Origins of Arab Nationalism*, ed. Rashid Khalidi, Lisa Anderson, Muhammad Muslih, and Reeva S. Simon (New York: Columbia University Press, 1991), 73–96, esp. 86.
77 He entered parliament as a successor of a certain Süleyman Efendi (perhaps in 1909) and as an independent (*müstaqil*); his profession and status were given as "toprak sahibi" (landowner) and "idareci" (state functionary, it is unclear to which function that would refer). See Ahmad-Rustow, "İkinci Meşrutiyet döneminde meclisler: 1908–1918," 280. Most studies have him as a "partisan" of the CUP; for example Khalidi, "Ottomanism and Arabism," 59. In 1912, he was in fact on the ticket of the CUP.
78 *Meclisi Mebusan Zabıt Ceridesi*, birinci dönem, içtima 95, celse 2, cilt 5, 10 Mayıs 1326/1910, 409–10.
79 *Meclisi Âyan Zabıt Ceridesi*, üçüncü dönem, içtima 32, celse 1, 9 Şubat 1332/1916 (sic, should be 1917), 511.
80 Ali Fuat Erden, *Birinci Dünya Harbinde Suriye Hatıraları* (Istanbul: Halk, 1954), 1:191.
81 Kayalı, *Arabs and Young Turks*, 189.

Between Ottomanism and Kurdism 329

of 1917, 'Abd al-Rahman was probably the most powerful civilian in Syria; he was often called on to arbitrate quarrels.[82]

'Abd al-Rahman and the New Regime

At the end of the war, however, 'Abd al-Rahman's prospects were not promising. The empire in which he and his family had risen to status and power had collapsed; the government and the party he had supported were gone. In Syrian politics the cards were reshuffled. The old guard, the notables, were ousted by their opponents, the victorious Arabists – officers of the Sharifian army and nationalists from modest backgrounds. There is no space here to describe in detail the shifting and peculiar alliances between leading families in Damascus. Once more the tried and tested instrument of marriage alliance helped the Yusufs to stay on top in post-Ottoman Syria, if only briefly. Thus, the anti-Hashemite Yusufs and the pro-Hashemite Bakris became allies, demonstrating that political affiliation and ideology were less important than the continued influence, welfare, and status of the families. This was also evident from 'Abd al-Rahman's admission (upon Faysal's recommendation) to the Arab Independence Party (*Hizb al-Istiqlal al-'Arabi*), which grew out of *al-Fatat*, the most important Arab nationalist group during the War.[83] The overwhelming number of delegates to the Syrian General Congress (May 1919), tasked with making plans for the "future" of Greater Syria, were members of the old guard with 'Abd al-Rahman as vice-president. This made the nationalists increasingly dissatisfied with Faysal's rule. Nevertheless, their continued influence did not prevent the notables from being deeply concerned about their future. Faysal, under pressure to find a balance between the nationalists and the notables, managed to persuade 'Abd al-Rahman and other like-minded grandees to found a new party, the Syrian Patriotic Party (*al-Hizb al-Watani al-Suri*).[84] When on 7 March 1920, the Congress voted for the independence of Greater Syria (that is, including Lebanon and

---

82 AA 177, 6–7.
83 Gelvin, *Divided Loyalties*, 57–60, points out that the commitment of the Bakris to "'Arab nationalism' was not firmly rooted in ideology." Khoury, *Urban Notables*, 87.
84 On the other hand, the notables were no less dissatisfied: "and would prefer Turks or French to Arabs," FO 882/24/128-134, 14 May 1919, "Who's Who in Damascus," quotation provided by Jim Gelvin. Archives Diplomatiques, Ministère des Affaires Étrangères Nantes, série Beyrouth, Mandat Syrie Liban, no. 2368, Damas, 25 March 1919, Cousse à Monsieur le Haut Commissaire de la République en Syrie et en Arménie. Khoury, *Urban Notables*, 90.

330   Martin Strohmeier

Palestine) with Faysal as monarch, the decision was presented to him by a delegation which included ʿAbd al-Rahman.[85]

At the conference of San Remo (April 1920), Syria was placed under French Mandate, leading to angry protests on the part of Syrian nationalists. Faysal could no longer evade the pressure of the nationalists and was driven even further into their arms. The increasing influence of the Arab nationalists made non-Arab minorities consider an insurrection with ʿAbd al-Rahman using the Kurdish community as a leverage.[86] This, in turn, would have served the French by putting Faysal and the nationalists (Haydar, Qadri, and others) in their place. However, the characterization of ʿAbd al-Rahman as an "ennemi irréductible" ["implacable enemy"] of Faysal is probably an exaggeration.[87] ʿAbd al-Rahman was opposed to Faysal primarily because he favoured the old guard's opponents. His threat of a Kurdish insurrection had nothing to do with a commitment to Kurdism, but rather with protecting his interests and keeping his privileges.

After the occupation of Damascus by French forces in July 1920, one of Faysal's last acts as "King of Syria" was to appoint a government to hand over authority to the French. It was headed by ʿAla' al-Din al-Durubi as Prime Minister, and one of its members was ʿAbd al-Rahman, who at the same time was 'President of the Consultative Council' (ra'is al-majlis al-shuri). One month later, in August 1920, Durubi and Yusuf (whom the French authorities had allowed to remain in office), travelled south by train as members of a delegation charged with solving a conflict with the population of the Hawran. At a station called Khirbat al-Ghazala, unidentified attackers shot both politicians. The circumstances of "the first state-level assassination of a Syrian notable by a peasant in modern times" were never cleared up.[88] The funeral procession for ʿAbd al-Rahman was attended by large numbers of the population, the leading

---

85 Gelvin, *Divided Loyalties*, 247–8.
86 "A Kurd and looked upon as Chief of that community in Damascus," FO 882/24/128–34, 14 May 1919, "Who's Who in Damascus," quotation provided by Jim Gelvin.
87 Archives Diplomatiques, Haut Commissariat ... en Syrie et Cilicie, no. 2346, dossier 1, 1920, s/d 15 [after 7 March 1920], "Forces à utiliser en zone est."
88 Linda Schilcher, "Railways in the Political Economy of Southern Syria 1890–1925," in *The Syrian Land*, ed. Thomas Philipp and Birgit Schaebler (Stuttgart: F. Steiner, 1998), 97–112, esp. 111. Badran, *Kawakib*, 112. Perhaps his murder had to do with the hostility that had developed between Druzes and Kurds due to "religious and economic rivalries"; see Maoz, "Muslim Ethnic Communities," 298. Philip Khoury, *Syria and the French Mandate: The Politics of Arab Nationalism, 1920–1945* (Princeton: Princeton University Press, 1987), 99. Najdat Fathi Safwat, ed., *Mudhakkirat Rustum Haydar* (Beirut: Al-Dar al-ʿArabiyya li'l-Mawsuʿat, 1988), 702 (22 August 1920).

Between Ottomanism and Kurdism 331

luminaries of Damascene society, and General Goybet.[89] ʿAbd al-Rahman was buried in the al-Dahdah cemetery.[90]

The Waning Power of the Yusufs

ʿAbd al-Rahman was the last powerful notable of the Yusuf clan. Eventually, the family also lost most of its assets, especially its landholdings. Muhammad Saʿid, the Austrian-educated eldest son of ʿAbd al-Rahman, ran up large debts to finance his lavish lifestyle. Moreover, the land rents sank enormously because of the depression, so that the use of land as security for borrowing money became nearly impossible.

To ease their economic woes, the Yusufs considered selling the large property of al-Batiha on the eastern shores of Lake Tiberias to the Jewish National Fund (1934). The outcry aroused by the imminent deal caused the French administration to promulgate a decree which "prohibited the sale to foreigners of lands on the frontiers of Syria-Lebanon with Palestine-Transjordan." In spite of this, the deal was pursued with Chaim Weizmann, the leader of the World Zionist Organization, visiting the residence of the Yusufs in Suq Saruja. Finally, under the aegis of the Syrian President al-ʿAbid (a brother-in-law of the late ʿAbd al-Rahman), a company was established with the aim of buying al-Batiha from the Yusufs, but nothing came of this scheme. Although Jewish organizations continued to try to buy the land, the Syrian government and the Mandate authorities stuck to their veto.[91]

Mehmed Salih's and ʿAbd al-Rahman's Collaboration in Raising a Kurdish Force for the Suez Canal Campaign

Mehmed Salih and ʿAbd al-Rahman must have been acquainted with each other before their short-term collaboration in late 1914. On the one hand, Salih, who was born in the same year as the grandee, looked up to him. On the other hand, given Salih's aversion to powerful people of Bedri's ilk, he would have had some reservations about the pasha. Certainly, ʿAbd al-Rahman was familiar with the Bedirhan clan, but since Salih did not live continuously in Damascus from approx. 1897 to

---

89 Badran, *Kawakib*, 114.
90 Mulla, *Hayy al-Akrad*, 130. The cemetery is located between Baghdad and Suq Saruja streets.
91 Khoury, *Syria and the French Mandate*, 446, 448–9. See also Moubayed, "Syria's Forgotten First President," 436–7.

332   Martin Strohmeier

1914, he was probably an unknown quantity. In any case, Salih reports one context in which they met repeatedly in December 1914, a month before the Sinai campaign started and roughly three months before Salih's death.

Cemal Paşa had requested the help of several Arab grandees like 'Abd al-Rahman (who was senator at the time) and As'ad Shuqayr to find auxiliary troops (Bedouins, Kurds, Druze) for the expedition against the Suez Canal.[92] In his memoirs Salih described his encounters with and impressions of 'Abd al-Rahman in a chapter entitled "On the Way to Egypt," referring to the attack on the Suez Canal. He wrote these lines on "11 Mart 1331" (24 March 1915), that is, several days before his untimely death; they concern his activities in December 1914 (he had organized the funeral of his father-in-law in İzmir and returned to Damascus on December 7, 1914). The heading, "On the Way to Egypt," probably refers to Salih's statement that he wanted to join the Kurdish volunteers.[93]

Assembling the auxiliary unit was a cumbersome affair. First, the number of 500 cavalrymen envisaged by Cemal turned out to be unrealistic. Eventually, only fifty to sixty volunteers were registered, and by no means all of them mounted. As depicted by Salih, 'Abd al-Rahman's efforts to muster a Kurdish unit ran into difficulties, in part because of rival Kurdish clans torpedoing 'Abd al-Rahman's efforts. Salih was highly critical about the lack of support for 'Abd al-Rahman's initiative. He complains about intrigues of members of the Bozo and Miro families who wanted to undermine 'Abd al-Rahman's initiative. This indicates that his influence on the community was not absolute. He singles out for his criticism Ahmad Ajaliyaqin, a distant relative. Having emigrated from his homeland as a "zero" and "nothing," he had now gained influence. That is, Salih believes that Ahmad should "give back" to the state to whom he owed his rise to power. Salih is concerned that the intrigues would diminish 'Abd al-Rahman's authority if in the end no Kurdish fighters could be organized. He wants the Kurds to participate in the war: "It is a duty to support this great Damascene Kurd whom I sincerely respect. Because the honour of my people there will

---

92 Behçet Cemal, ed., *Hatıralar. Bahriye Nazırı ve 4. Ordu Kumandanı Cemal Paşa* (Istanbul: Selek, 1959), 154. As'ad Shuqayr: also known as As'ad al-Shuqayri (1860–1940) of 'Akka, a deputy and close confidant of Cemal. See Ahmad al-Mar'ashli, ed., *Al-Mawsu'a al-Filastiniyya* (Damascus: Hay'at al-Mawsu'a al-Filastiniyya, 1984), 2:241–2.

93 Uzun and Bedir-Han, *Mehmet Salih*, 90: "... I felt rather happy to share the honour of participating in the cihad."

be elevated as well." On December 19, 1914, a month before the Suez Canal campaign began, the raising of the unit was celebrated after Friday prayers at the Sa'id Paşa Mosque with Cemal and 'Abd al-Rahman attending.[94]

Comparisons and Conclusions

Our aim was to portray two men of Damascus with Kurdish roots against the background of Abdülhamid's absolutist regime, Young Turk opposition, and the rise of Turkish and Arab nationalism, as well as the growing awareness and shaping of Kurdish identity. The comparison between Mehmed Salih Bedirhan and his contemporary, 'Abd al-Rahman Yusuf, reveals dramatic differences in their characters, outlooks, the circumstances of the context they were born into, and the courses of their lives. The dissimilarities, however, stem partially from the nature of the available sources from which our information has been gleaned. Whatever light is shed on the two figures emanates from almost completely different perspectives and foci. Nevertheless, the contours of two prominent lives in Damascus emerge.

Most of our knowledge about Salih comes from his memoirs, from his own pen (and his daughter's), while the narrative sources and archival documents regarding 'Abd al-Rahman are not by him, but about him. 'Abd al-Rahman was a dignitary, high-level politician, member of parliament, and entrepreneur, and the existing sources relate to his public, political and economic activities, and offices.

Our image of Salih is composed, to a large extent, of aspects of his private life and his output as an author. Although he descended from an old and noble family, he faced considerable hardship. He lost his mother early and was unable to realize his educational goals. We learn he lacked self-confidence, was plagued with doubt about his own abilities, and even contemplated suicide in his youth. However, because it is his self-presentation, Salih is able to highlight his positive traits, integrity and incorruptibility, which allow him to gain some self-respect. His little self-confidence rested on his general education, albeit not in the formal sense.[95]

---

94 Uzun and Bedir-Han, 92, 93. The palace of 'Abd al-Rahman al-Yusuf in Suq Saruja was destroyed in a fire on 16 July 2023.

95 Uzun and Bedir-Han, 65–6.

He accepted his position in the family network only reluctantly and was dependent on his family, particularly his father-in-law. Despite the family connections and his contacts with the highest circles of power, Salih never had any power of his own. He was able to attain merely a position as a mid-level civil servant. Apparently, he spent much of the period from the mid-1890s to 1908 as an exile or in prison due to his opposition to the Sultan. The "imperial career" he had envisaged never materialized.[96]

'Abd al-Rahman, in contrast, radiated an imperial aura. His connections, power, and wealth; his positions as deputy, senator, *amir al-hajj*, grandee, and big landowner; and his acquaintance with foreign dignitaries made him an imperial player. With his many hats and his links to Abdülhamid, he was a big mover and shaker in Syria; and he was the – perhaps not undisputed - leader of the Kurdish community in Damascus. After the Sultan's fall, the ever opportunistic 'Abd al-Rahman became a strong supporter of the Young Turks. At the apex of Damascene society, he was a powerful player not only in local politics, but also on the regional and international level.

Both men were steadfast Ottoman patriots. Salih, however, with a family history of intensive involvement in Kurdish politics, contributed to the development of the Kurdish awakening. It is fair to describe him as an actor in Kurdish affairs.

'Abd al-Rahman, as a leading notable with Kurdish roots, does not seem to have had any Kurdish agenda whatsoever.[97] He might have derived much of his power from the city's Kurdish community and supported it, but his influence had nothing to do with any sense of solidarity on ethnic grounds. He was beholden to the Kurdish community by ties of clientelism, although we know hardly anything about the means and mechanisms through which he exerted control. That he ran into difficulties when trying to recruit a Kurdish volunteer unit, points to limits of his authority.

We know that as an Arabicized Ottoman he was opposed to Arabism; it is unthinkable that he would have supported a separate Kurdish identity. It must have been embittering for Salih to witness the same-aged 'Abd al-Rahman's enormous wealth and power, as the latter utilized the very authoritarian methods that Salih had deplored in his father-in-law. Moreover, during the years when Salih was in exile or

---

96 Henning, *Narratives*, 231, 239, 245.
97 Therefore Khoury's characterization of 'Abd al-Rahman as "the leading Kurdish notable of Damascus" (*Syria and the French Mandate*, 309), is somewhat misleading.

imprisoned for his political stance, 'Abd al-Rahman continued to hold the reins as head of the family and member of "Union and Progress."

Despite the different orbits the two men moved in, they did come together on one project: the efforts to muster a Kurdish unit for the attack on the Suez Canal in the First World War. This was not unusual as the declaration of *jihad* motivated even Kurdish and Arab critics of the Young Turk Turkification policies to defend the empire. The mobilization of a Kurdish subidentity, stressed by Salih and largely ignored by 'Abd al-Rahman in the imperial interest, formed a link between them at a crucial moment. It is characteristic of times of crisis and change that a blending and confusion of identities take place. The lives of Mehmed Salih Bedirhan and 'Abd al-Rahman Yusuf show us the range and relationship of Kurdish and Ottoman identities, their thought, behaviour, and action; their place in late Ottoman society and administrative hierarchy; as well as their social status and economic power.

Afterword

Imperial Microhistory in Syria: An Agenda for Further Research

The purpose of this volume was to marshal a rather heterogeneous body of contemporary research on themes of direct relevance to the history of Kurds in Syria in the Ottoman period. As the field is still in its infancy, there remains a significant need for minute case studies on specific topics of the sort presented here before a more complete or synthetic approach can be envisaged. Needless to say, many topics or themes that are of vital importance to the subject, and that are sometimes indeed broached in other studies on Syrian, Ottoman, or Kurdish history, could not be addressed in the framework of the present volume and must be left for future investigation.

The studies in this collection do not generally partake in what it has become common in recent years to cast as global microhistory. The stories of individual pastoral communities, local tax agents or military figures, and Ottomanized notables and migrant families offered here remain essentially grounded in the provincial, rural milieu of northern Syria and adjoining areas, with only incidental connections to global currents of production, trade, or cultural exchange. They do, however, partake in what might be seen as imperial microhistory, in that they each take stock of intrinsic connections between, and movement across, purely local and wider Ottoman frames of reference: when Kurdish components of a tribal confederation labelled "Syrian" (Shamlu) play a fundamental role in the establishment of the rival Safavid Empire in Iran (Mustafa Dehqan & Vural Genç); when members of a Kurdish-dominated Sufi order in northern Iraq become key proponents of Islamic modernism in reform-period Damascus (Metin Atmaca); or when meat provisioning in the imperial capital is in the hands of fiscal collectives such as the Reşwan, who are based

338   Afterword

in the hinterland of Raqqa but with units historically assigned to palace interests and spread from central Syria to the vicinity of Konya (Yonca Köksal; Keiko Iwamoto), it is clear that the "local" history of the Kurds cannot be separated from, and in turn directly informs, the greater imperial context.

In lieu of a conclusion, it may therefore be useful to extrapolate from the contributions to this volume and attempt a brief overview of areas of Kurdish history or microhistory in Syria that need further exploration. For our purposes, these can broadly be divided into three sub-areas: local Kurdish communities present in continuity from previous periods; Kurdish pastoral nomads or semi-nomads, often defined by the state as tribes, who migrated periodically or settled more permanently in Syria under the strictures of Ottoman imperial government; and individual Kurdish notables (*ayan*), whether tribal, military, or scholarly, who first established themselves or came to recognition in Syria through their service to the Ottoman state.

Medieval Arab historians show Kurdish populations to have been established on Syrian territory since at least the eleventh century, although individual groups are also thought to have been migrating into the Mediterranean coastal mountain region since antiquity.[1] The contribution of Zainab HajHasan, and to a limited degree that of Stefan Winter, dealt with communities that were first settled in western Syria (Palestine; the Kurd Dagh) in the context of the Crusades or later under Mamluk rule. The echoes of this past subsisted in the names of urban neighbourhoods (*mahalle*) and agricultural villages in Ottoman records, in *waqf* foundations ascribed to Kurdish figures, and in the re-engagement of local tribal leaders as tax collectors and state intermediaries in the first decades after the Ottoman takeover. Many more such echoes are to be found across Syria. From the famous "Castle of the Kurds" (Hisn al-Akrad, today Qal'at al-Husn or "Crac des Chevaliers"), which was first manned by a Kurdish garrison in 1031, to numerous village names in the coastal mountains alluding to a Kurdish origin; a "Mosque of the Kurds" endowed in the port city of Jabala in the late Mamluk period; or the designation of the nearby highlands as the "Jabal al-Akrad" (mountain of the Kurds; not the same as Aleppo's Kurd Dagh), countless sites throughout coastal Syria continued to be

---

1 Ismet Chérif Vanly (d. 2011), "Le déplacement du pays kurde vers l'ouest (X^e–XVe s.) : Recherche historique et géographique," *Rivista degli Studi Orientali* 50 (1976): 353–63; Mehrdad Izady, *The Kurds: A Concise Handbook* (London: Routledge, 1992), 89–96.

Afterword   339

identified with Kurds in the Ottoman period or were known to still have Kurdish-speaking populations, in some cases until recently.[2]

A particularly high concentration of Kurdish clans, garrisons, or local dynasts appears to have subsisted – as per the cliché regarding Kurds and mountains – in the Lebanon range. The ʿAkkar district in the extreme north of Lebanon was dominated for much of the Ottoman period by the Marʿabi family of tax farmers, whose descendants and followers, although assimilated into their Arabic-speaking environment, continued to lay claim to Kurdish identity well into modern times.[3] If members of the Bedirxan family were transferred from Hisn al-Akrad and appointed *kaymakam* (governor) of ʿAkkar under difficult circumstances in the late nineteenth century (Barbara Henning), did this reflect an appreciation by the Ottoman authorities of the district's continuing Kurdish character? Several other "feudal" lords (in the sense of being recognized locally as notables, maintaining military retinues, and being invested with governmental tax collecting functions) in the region appear to have been of pre-Ottoman Kurdish extraction, including, if the contemporary Damascene chronicler al-Muhibbi (d. 1681) is to be believed, the famous Druze emir Fakhr al-Din Maʿn himself. After his execution in 1635, his daughter is said to have taken refuge with a Kurdish Sufi shaykh in Diyarbekir.[4]

Much remains to be done to illuminate the Kurdish presence in Ottoman Lebanon. Of particular note would be the Kurdish taxlord dynasty of al-Kura district near Tripoli, some of whose descendants go by the surname Ayyoubi today. Their history during the Ottoman period remains almost completely obscure, even though they were remarkably one of only very few families in Lebanon to have been officially recognized by the state under the title of "emir." As with numerous other feudal lordships in the region, it is almost certainly their military service to the preceding Ayyubid and Mamluk regimes

---

2 Stefan Winter, "Les Kurdes de Syrie dans les archives ottomanes (XVIII⁰ siècle)," in *Les Kurdes : Écrire l'histoire d'un peuple aux temps pré-modernes*, ed. Boris James (Paris: L'Harmattan, 2009), 129–34; Boris James, *Genèse du Kurdistan : Les Kurdes dans l'Orient mamlouk et mongol, 1250–1340* (Paris: Éditions de la Sorbonne, 2021), 104–6.

3 Faruq Hublus, *Tarikh ʿAkkar al-Idari waʾl-Ijtimaʿi waʾl-Iqtisadi, 1700–1914* (Beirut: Dar al-Daʾira, 1987); Michael Gilsenan, *Lords of the Lebanese Marches: Violence and Narrative in an Arab Society* (Berkeley: University of California Press, 1996), 12–13, 74.

4 Muhammad al-Amin al-Muhibbi, *Khulasat al-Athar fi Aʿyan al-Qarn al-Hadi ʿAshar* (Beirut: Dar Sadir, n.d.), 3:266–7; Martin van Bruinessen, "The Naqshbandî Order in 17th Century Kurdistan," in *Naqshbandis : Cheminements et situtation actuelle d'un ordre mystique musulman. Actes de la Table Ronde de Sèvres, 2–4 Mai 1985*, ed. Marc Gaborieau and Alexandre Popović (Istanbul: Isis, 1990), 345–6.

340   Afterword

that accounts for their continuing, hereditary status as emirs under the Ottoman sultanate, a *problématique* that could doubtless be verified and expanded through further research in contemporary archival sources.[5]

The most illustrious of these pre-Ottoman dynasties to have retained power in Lebanon is of course the Junblats. Professor Abu-Husayn's contribution demonstrates that the Druze shaykhs were not in fact descended from 'Ali Canpolad of Kilis but had been prominent in the Shuf since well before the latter's rebellion and putative migration in the seventeenth century. The Canpolad emirs' lack of any subsequent association with Lebanon appears to be corroborated by Alexander Hourani's research in the Ottoman Ruznamçe (government appointment) registers.[6] But then what of the Junblat shaykhs' actual origins, including their name, which nevertheless remains clearly of non-Arabic, Persian, or more likely Kurdish etymology ("heart of steel")? Were they of a separate family, and part of the larger phenomenon of pre-Ottoman Kurdish settlement in Syria, or can the reasons and means of their establishment in Lebanon yet be discovered in Ottoman sources?

The Canpolad emirs of Kilis were of course the most important representatives of a pre-Ottoman Kurdish "nobility" in Syria, and indeed the only ones cited as such in Şerefxan Bidlisi's *Şerefname* history of Kurdish families.[7] Their political career and especially their participation in the Celali rebellions have already been the subject of several documentary studies,[8] while new research by Charles Wilkins in the *shar'iyya*

---

5 See A.N. Poliak, *Feudalism in Egypt, Syria, Palestine, and the Lebanon, 1250–1900* (London: The Royal Asiatic Society, 1939).

6 Alexander Hourani, *New Documents on the History of Mount Lebanon and Arabistan in the 10th and 11th Centuries H.* (Beirut: N.p., 2010), 989–9.

7 Chèref-ou'ddine, *Chèref-Nâmeh, ou Fastes de la Nation Kourde*, translated and commented by François Bernard Charmoy (St. Petersburg: Académie impériale des sciences, 1873), 66–77. On the concept of nobility to describe leading Kurdish families of the modern period, see Nilay Özok-Gündoğan, *The Kurdish Nobility in the Ottoman Empire: Loyalty, Autonomy, and Privilege* (Edinburgh: Edinburgh University Press, 2023).

8 Şenol Çelik, "XVI. Yüzyılda Hanedan Kurucu Bir Osmanlı Sancakbeyi: Canbulad Bey," *Türk Kültürü İncelemeleri Dergisi* 7 (Fall 2002): 1–34; Metin Akis, "Kilis Sancağında Canbolatoğulları Ailesinin Yönetimi," in *Şehirlerin Sevdalısı İbrahim Hakkı Konyalı Armağanı*, ed. Hasan Bahar (Konya: Selçuk Üniversitesi Türkiyat Araştırmaları Enstitüsü, 2015), 391–404; Mustafa Dehqan and Vural Genç, "Kürdlükten Çıkmayub: Janfulad Husayn's Complaint against Sultan Mehmed III," *Journal Asiatique* 306 (2018): 167–71; Charles Wilkins, "Ottoman Elite Recruitment and the Case of Janbulad Bek b. Qasim," in *The Mamluk Ottoman Transition: Continuity and Change in Egypt and Bilad al-Sham in the Sixteenth Century*, ed. Stephan Conermann and Gül Şen (Göttingen: V&R Unipress/Bonn University Press, 2022), 2:155–80.

Afterword 341

court registers of Aleppo and other local sources is shedding light on the family's wealth, property holding, and participation in elite urban society in the Ottoman period.[9] Among the issues that remain to be explored are the Canpolads' dealings in the wider region, and perhaps most notably their tenure in the provincial governorships of Jabala (on the Mediterranean coast) and Balis (between Aleppo and Raqqa on the Middle Euphrates), both of which likely still had a Kurdish presence in the seventeenth century. How connected were they with local society here, and what do their continuing appointments, even after the execution of ʿAli Canpolad in Belgrade in 1610, say about the loyalty of the Kurdish nobility in Syria to the Ottoman state?

Finally in regard to pre-Ottoman Kurdish groups in Syria, special mention might be made of the Yezidis. With distant roots in a pre-Islamic "cult of angels," but originally equated with the ʿAdawi Sufi order of northern Iraq, members of this ethnically Kurdish religious community have been established in Syria, mostly in the Kurd Dagh and adjoining Jabal Samʿan district, since the fourteenth century. The contribution of Stefan Winter alluded to the fact that they, like other heterodox communities in Syria, were essentially left alone by the Ottoman state so long as they fulfilled their tax obligations and did not engage in brigandage and highway robbery (eşkıyalık). But it is also true that Yezidism became more severely proscribed in the sixteenth century than any other sectarian group in the Ottoman Empire, and that the history of Diyarbekir, Van, and the Jabal Sinjar was repeatedly punctuated by official campaigns of violence against Yezidis well into the nineteenth century.[10] What do we know of Syria? Much as with other groups treated as heretics by Muslim authorities (Kızılbaş, Twelver Shiis, Nusayris, Ismailis), the proscription of Yezidism was general and diffuse, and there is in fact only seldom reference to actual historical Yezidi figures named and

---

9 Charles Wilkins, "Mullahs, Merchants, and Mystics: Kurdish Townspeople in Early Ottoman Aleppo," paper presented at the Symposium in Honor of Jane Hathaway on the Occasion of Her Retirement, Ohio State University, Columbus, 20 May 2023.

10 Yavuz Aykan, "On the Legal Status of Yezidis: Law, Geography and Confession-Building in Early Modern Kurdistan (Sixteenth-Eighteenth Centuries)," in *Entangled Confessionalizations? Dialogic Perspectives on the Politics of Piety and Community Building in the Ottoman Empire, 15th–18th Centuries*, ed. Tijana Krstić and Derin Terzioğlu (Piscataway, NJ: Gorgias Press, 2022), 673–99; Amed Gökçen, *Osmanlı ve İngiliz Belgelerinde Yezidiler* (Istanbul: Bilgi Üniversitesi Yayınları, 2012). The systematic destruction of virtually every Yezidi site in the ʿAfrin district since 2018 can be understood in part as proceeding from the unequalled prejudice against Yezidism in the Ottoman legal tradition.

342 Afterword

identified as such in the Ottoman sources. The contribution of Muhsin Soyudoğan to this volume therefore also represents an important new point of departure in the study of Ottoman Yezidism, in that it treats a well-known local family (in Rumkale) which, though not identified as Yezidi in Ottoman documents, stemmed from or was closely linked to one of the most unmistakably Yezidi populations in the Empire, the Reşi tribe of the nearby eponymous Reşi plateau. The study is significant in this regard precisely because religion plays no role: beyond the predictable sectarian polemic of Ottoman religio-juridical discourse, we in fact need many more such studies of real-life Yezidi and other non-Sunni communities in Syria and elsewhere before concluding on the nature of Ottoman imperial "policy" towards heterodox minorities, confessionalization, and the like.

A second, complementary area that requires study is the Kurdish tribal formations that began to frequent, and in some cases settle in, Syrian territory following the Ottoman conquest. We already dispose of a large literature on Turkic or Turkoman groups, in particular the Yeni-İl confederation, that were established in administrative units called *ev* ("house") from the Amık and Reyhaniye plains northwest of Aleppo to Hama and Damascus in central Syria beginning in the sixteenth century.[11] More recently, historians of Anatolian Kurdistan have begun devoting monographic studies even to smaller individual Kurdish tribes, a critical addition to the imperial microhistory of the Ottoman world.[12] Book-length, in part very scholarly studies also exist for three of the most important central Anatolian Kurdish tribes that had branches settle in Syria in the Ottoman period, the Reşwan, the Lekwan, and the Izolis, yet none of these mention the tribes' Syrian past in any significant way.[13] The distant memory of settlement in Syria is at best kept alive today in the popular, oral-based accounts of the Kurds of "Interior Anatolia" (İç Anadolu; the Konya-Ankara region), essentially

---

11 İlhan Şahin, "XVI. Yüzyılda Halep ve Yeni-İl Türkmenleri," in *Anadolu'da ve Rumeli'de Yörükler ve Türkmenler Sempozyumu Bildirileri* (Istanbul: Yör-Türk Vakfı, 2000), 231–9; Enver Çakar, "Les Turkmènes d'Alep à l'époque ottomane (1516–1700)," in *Aleppo and its Hinterland in the Ottoman Period / Alep et sa province à l'époque ottomane*, ed. Stefan Winter and Mafalda Ade (Leiden: Brill, 2019), 1–27.

12 See for example Tuncay Şur and Yalçın Çakmak, eds., *Kürt Aşiretleri: Aktör, Müteffik, Şaki* (Istanbul: İletişim, 2022).

13 Faruk Söylemez, *Osmanlı Devletinde Aşiret Yönetimi: Rişvan Aşireti Örneği* (Istanbul: Kitabevi, 2007); Mustafa Akpınar and Ali Can Geliş, *Lek Kürtleri: Çukurova Lekvanikleri, Haymana Lek Şahbazanları, Bingöl Bermeki Lekleri* (Istanbul: Do Yayınları, 2016); M. Şahin Duman, *Tarihte İzoli: İzollular ve İzoli Aşireti* (Istanbul: Bilgeoğuz Yayınları, 2018).

the Reşwan and the Cihanbeylis.[14] The contributions of Keiko Iwamoto, Muhsin Soyudoğan, and Yonca Köksal to this volume each demonstrate how much more there is to learn about the Reşwan especially, quite possibly the best-documented of all Ottoman tribal confederations in the eighteenth century: the differential taxation statuses and seeming preference given to regional Turkoman tribes in Ottoman settlement projects; the indeterminate link between the Reşi Kurds (in the *sancak* of Ayntab) and the larger Reşwan confederation; the precipitation of the Reşvan-zade dynasty of governors in Maraş, Malatya, and Adana; and the rise of a Reşwan imperial merchant elite in the nineteenth century all have direct ramifications for the history of the Kurds in Syria proper.

Other Ottoman-era confederations with an important presence in Syria include the Berazi, who dominated the Suruj plain southwest of Urfa (see the contribution of Muhsin Seyda) but also had members serving as Ottoman military retainers settle in the Hama region, where they would eventually become one of the largest landowning families and wield political power down into republican times (Dick Douwes). Kurdish groups from further east which can be seen to have put down roots deep in central Syria in the Ottoman period include the Saçlo, Zirqî (Zirki), and Kîkî tribes, all of which await thorough study. The most famous of these was of course the Millî confederation, which has been the subject of numerous previous studies, and whose key role in intertribal politics, but also as Ottoman military and state figures in their own right, in northern Syria and Mesopotamia, is recalled in the contributions of Tom Sinclair, Dick Douwes, Muhsin Seyda, and especially Erdal Çiftçi. Many aspects of the Millîs' involvement in Syria, from the government's designation of their chiefs as *iskan başı* (head of tribal sedentarization) in Raqqa in the outgoing eighteenth century, to various Millî revolts in central Syria, to the famous Hamidiye regiment leader Millî Ibrahim Paşa's connection with Levantine and European consuls in Aleppo in the late nineteenth century, are extensively documented not just in Ottoman, Arabic, and foreign archival sources, but also in a rich local ethnographic and popular literature that has only rarely been incorporated and that awaits further investigation.[15]

---

14 Nuh Ateş, *İç Anadolu Kürtleri (Konya-Ankara-Kırşehir)* (Cologne: Komkar, 1992); Nuh Ateş, "Halikan ve Reşvanların Kökeni Üzerine Bazı İpuçları," *Bîrnebûn* 19 (2003): 56–61; Hacı Çevik, *Konya'da Kürt Var Mı? Orta Anadolu Kürleri ve Kürtlerin Siyasallaşması* (Istanbul: İletişim, 2021).

15 Ahmad Wasfi Zakariya, '*Asha'ir al-Sham* (Damascus: Dar al-Fikr, 1997), 664; Kamil al-Ghazzi, *Nahr al-Dhahab fi Ta'rikh Halab* (Aleppo: Dar al-'Ilm al-'Arabi, 1999), 373–6; Ahmad 'Uthman Abu Bakr, *Kurdistan fi 'Ahd al-Salam (ba'd al-Harb al-'Alamiyya al-Ula)* (Bonn: Kawa, 2002); 'Abd al-Hamid Muhammad al-Hamad, '*Asha'ir al-Raqqa wa'l-Jazira: Al-Ta'rikh wa'l-Mawruth* (Raqqa: N.p., 2003), 419–23;

344   Afterword

Beyond the question of mostly unknown rural and pastoral populations, which settled in large numbers in Syria and whose traces can be followed in the Ottoman archives, an important number of Kurdish state functionaries, military leaders, and religious notables also came to Syria under the particular conditions of Ottoman imperial rule, and in some cases had a lasting impact on Kurdish society and culture in Syria and beyond into modern times. The Bedirxan family, the traditional ruling aristocracy of Cizre (Jazirat Ibn 'Umar) on the Tigris, right by what is today the Turkish-Syrian border, and their profound contribution to the development of modern Kurmancî publishing, needs no introduction; the long-standing association of certain family members with Syria while in exile, as local Ottoman governors, or in rivalry with other leading Kurdish families, has been addressed in detail in the papers of Barbara Henning and Martin Strohmeier. The *agha*s or warlord-cum-landlords of the Berazi tribe discussed by Dick Douwes, whose progeny would ultimately go on to occupy the post of prime minister of republican Syria on two occasions, are another example, as are many more in lesser towns who have hardly been noted by historians. A leading local notable family of Hama at the turn of the seventeenth century, to judge by the city's *shar'iyya* court records for instance, was that named for a certain Hamo ibn Shaykh al-Akrad of nearby Salamiyya, raising the tantalizing and as-yet unanswered question to whom or what this apparently very local title owed its origin. Nor was the integration and assimilation of Kurds into Syrian urban society a purely elite phenomenon: the rise of popular Kurdish neighbourhoods in all the major cities of Syria, and their rapid growth in the late Ottoman period through land flight, industrialization, war, European occupation, and other displacements of modernity, also have yet to receive all the attention they deserve.[16]

Husayn Amin, *Durish 'Avdi wa-'Udul Milli: Riwaya min al-Turath al-Sha'bi al-Kurdi* (Beirut: Kawa, 2004); Azad Ahmad Ali, "Le rôle politique des tribus kurdes Milli et de la famille d'Ibrahim Pacha à l'ouest du Kurdistan et au nord du Bilad al-Cham (1878–1908)," in *Alep et ses territoires : Fabrique et politique d'une ville, 1868–2011*, ed. Jean-Claude David and Thierry Boissière (Beirut: Institut français du Proche-Orient, 2014).

16   See Bruce Masters, "Patterns of Migration to Ottoman Aleppo in the 17th and 18th Centuries," *International Journal of Turkish Studies* 4 (1987): 83–4; Ahmad Muhammad Ahmad, *Akrad Lubnan wa-Tanzimuhum al-Ijtima'i wa'l-Siyasi* (Beirut: Maktabat al-Faqih, 1995); 'Izz al-Din 'Ali Mulla, *Hayy al-Akrad fi Madinat Dimashq Bayna 'Amay 1250–1979 m: Dirasa Tarikhiyya, Ijtima'iyya, Iqtisadiyya* (Damascus: Dar Asu, 1998).

Finally, the lasting contribution of individual scions of Ottoman Kurdish families to the history not only of the Kurds but of Syria more generally, as exemplified *inter alia* in Metin Atmaca's study of the transposition of the reformist Khalidi-Naqshbandi Sufi order to Damascus in the nineteenth century, is beyond doubt. Two of the most interesting cases, which have not been addressed in the present volume, concern journalists and secular intellectuals who, while of immediate Kurdish ancestry, ultimately left their mark as pioneers of Syrian Arab nationalist thought: Khayr al-Din al-Zirikli, born in Beirut in 1893 to parents from the previously mentioned Zirqî community, who would go on to author the most important biographical encyclopedia of the Arab world, *Al-A'lam*, starting in 1926; and Muhammad Kurd 'Ali, born in Damascus to an Ottoman Kurdish civil servant from Sulaymaniyya, whose six-volume history *Khitat al-Sham* (1928) became the principal basis for the modern nationalist projection of a historical "Greater Syria" (Bilad al-Sham) as a foundation for Syrian identity. Long considered from the sole standpoint of the Arab national awakening, the investigation of these and other Syrian republican intellectuals and statesmen against their deeper Ottoman Kurdish social and cultural background is only just at its beginning.[17]

Acknowledgments

The editors are grateful first and foremost to all of our colleagues for agreeing to contribute to this in many ways unwieldy and unlikely collection, and for their patience and forbearance in submitting to multiple revisions before seeing it through to completion. The project was initiated in the early days of the pandemic, benefitted from very little institutional support on account of its subject matter, and met with important obstacles in the process of publication, but this end product of their generosity, we hope, will ultimately constitute a significant and lasting contribution to a field that is only just developing.

We are also very grateful to Mafalda Ade for drawing the original maps for this volume; to Layth Winter for image file editing; and to Fexrî Avdo for providing the cover photo of the Kurd Dagh. Special thanks are due to Stephen Shapiro, acquisitions editor at the University of Toronto Press, for all his care and efforts in guiding this

---

17 Muhammed Kürd Ali, *Bir Osmanlı-Arap Gazetecinin Anıları*, ed. İbrahim Tüfekçi (Istanbul: Klasik Yayınları, 2014).

work through publication and for setting up the new series in Middle East studies in which it appears as the first volume. Support towards publications costs was provided by the Canadian Social Science and Humanities Research Council (SSHRC/CRSH) project "Les Kurdes de Syrie : Peuplement et occupation de l'espace à l'époque ottomane" (UQÀM, 2017–22). Many thanks also to Melanie Magidow for her great care and expert advice in copy-editing, as well as to Mary Lui, associate managing editor, at UTP.

Montréal, 1 August 2023

Contributors

Abdul-Rahim Abu-Husayn (d. 2022) was professor of history at the American University of Beirut. The author of numerous works on Ottoman Syria and Lebanon, he was inducted into the Turkish Historical Society (Türk Tarih Kurumu) as an honorary member for his achievements.

Metin Atmaca is associate professor at the Social Sciences University of Ankara and associate member at the Centre d'études turques, ottomanes, balkaniques et centrasiatiques in Paris. He has published on Ottoman Arab historiography, microhistory in Ottoman studies, Ottoman-Iranian frontier societies, and the perception of the Kurds in Middle Eastern historiography.

Erdal Çiftçi is associate professor of history at Mardin Artuklu University. His research focuses on nomads in the Ottoman Empire, and his articles have appeared in *Middle Eastern Studies* and the *Journal of Balkan and Near Eastern Studies*. Together with various book chapters, he is also the coauthor of *The Last Tribal Census of the Empire: Fihristü'l Aşâir* (in Turkish).

Mustafa Dehqan holds a BA in history and an MA in historical linguistics from the University of Tehran. His research interests include Kurdish literature and religions, Kurdo-Syriac contact zones, and Garshuni manuscripts. He has published in numerous journals and is the author of an index to the *Sharafnama* by Sharaf al-Din Bitlisi (Nûbihar, 2014).

Dick Douwes is retired professor of global history at Erasmus University, Rotterdam. He has published on late Ottoman history in Syria, religious plurality in the Middle East, and Muslims in Western Europe.

348   Contributors

Vural Genç received his PhD in history from Istanbul University in 2014. His work focuses specifically on Ottoman–Safavid political relations and cultural contacts in the sixteenth century. He has published three books and numerous articles in the field.

Zainab HajHasan is a PhD candidate at Koç University. She previously studied at the University of Jordan in Amman and Istanbul Medeniyet University. Her work focuses on Arab coastal cities in the Ottoman period.

Barbara Henning is assistant professor at Johannes Gutenberg Universität in Mainz, where she teaches the history of the Eastern Mediterranean. She is an Ottomanist with an interest in imperial biographies, memory studies, and post-Ottoman transformations.

Keiko Iwamoto is associate professor at the Graduate School of Kyoto University. Her research, including a number of articles and her recent monograph *Nomads and the Early Modern Empire* (in Japanese; Kyoto University Press, 2019), focuses on the history of nomadic peoples in the Ottoman period.

Yonca Köksal is associate professor of history at Koç University. She completed her PhD at Columbia University in 2002. Her work focuses on the late Ottoman Empire, and she has published on the Tanzimat reforms in the provinces, tribes and livestock trade in Anatolia, and Muslim minorities in Bulgaria.

Muhsin Seyda is a native of ʿAyn al-ʿArab (Kobanî), Syria, and has a BA in history from Damascus University. His work revolves around the history of the Kurds in the Islamic period, and he is the editor of the online journal MedaratKurd.com.

Tom Sinclair was professor of Turkish history at the University of Cyprus. He writes mainly on economy and administration in Armenia during the late pre-Ottoman and early Ottoman periods. Among his recent publications is *Eastern Trade and the Mediterranean in the Middle Ages: Pegolotti's Ayas-Tabriz Itinerary and its Commercial Context* (2020).

Muhsin Soyudoğan is associate professor at Gaziantep University, Department of Sociology. His research focuses on gender, migration, and socio-economic history. He has previously published on tribes and the *timar* system in the Ottoman Empire, the Syrian civil war, and refugees.

Martin Strohmeier is retired professor of Turkish and Middle Eastern Studies at the University of Cyprus. His research focuses on the history of the Middle East during the modern era, and especially on education, the press, and nationalism. Presently he is writing a biography of Karl Neufeld, "the prisoner of the Khalifa."

Stefan Winter, from Sainte-Foy, Québec, studied in Toronto, Erlangen, Damascus, and Ankara before completing his PhD at the University of Chicago in 2002. He is professor of history at the Université du Québec à Montréal (UQÀM) and visiting professor at Koç University.

Index

Note: Page numbers in italics refer to maps.

Abadi clan, 262
Abbas I (shah), 66–68, 72–3
'Abbasid empire, 22, 54
'Abd Allah Khan (Uzbek), 72
Abdi Paşa (Aleppo), 188, 197
Abdühalik Nasuhi Bey (Beirut), 302
Abdülaziz (sultan), 105
Abdülhamid II/Hamidian, 11, 76,
    178, 221, 243–5, 250, 252, 256,
    259, 268–9, 281, 284, 296, 305–6,
    314–16, 324, 326–7, 333–4. *See also*
    Hamidiye Regiments
Abdülmecid (sultan), 216–17, 280
'Abdallah Agha al-Mahmud
    (Dandashli), 150
'Abdallah Agha Tayfur, 154–5
'Abdullah Cevdet, 317–18
'Abdullah al-Herati, 280, 282
'Abdullah Paşa (Acre), 277
Abdullah Musib Paşa (Baban), 301
'Abd al-Rahman al-'Aqri, 274
'Abid family, 308, 323, 324, 325
al-'Abid, Muhammad 'Ali (Syrian
    president), 331
Abu Dis (Palestine), 114
Abu'l-Huda al-Sayyadi, 289, 301,
    310, 316

Abu Khamis tribe, 267
Acre/'Akka, 114–18, 123–4, 149, 154,
    277–8, 314, 332
Adana, 2, 80, 96, 99–100, 102, 105,
    190, 193, 226, 228, 288, 295, 298,
    307, 343
'Adawi Sufi order, 98, 341
Adilcevaz, 62
Adıyaman. *See* Hısn-ı Mansur
'Adwan tribe, 250, 260, 262
'Afadla tribe, 255
Afghanistan, 22, 284
'Afrin, 2, 8, 75–6, 82–4, 85, 90, 92–3,
    96–9, 106, 107, 341
Afşar tribe, 64, 230, 232, 234
Ağa/agha (*aghawat*), 104–5, 137,
    153–5, 157–8, 216–17, 219, 231, 233,
    276, 308, 344
Ağrı province, 210
Ahl-i Haqq, 58
Ahlat, 34
Ahmad-i Khani, 318, 319
Ahmad Paşa al-Hafiz (Damascus),
    135, 152, 282, 283
Ahmed III (sultan), 166
Ahmed Cevdet Paşa, 104–5
Ahmed Muhtar Efendi ('Akkar), 295

352 Index

Ahmed Şakir Paşa, 289
Ahsandere, 175
Ajalyaqin family, 308; Ahmad, 332
'Ajlun, 111, 113–15, 126, 293
Akçadağ, 203
Akçakale, 31, 173
'Akkar district, 8, 11, 287, 289, 290–5, 307, 339
Akkoyunlu, 25, 224
al-Akrad. *See* Hayy al-Akrad
Akrad al-Dayanisa village, 146, 153, 156
Akrad Ibrahim village, 146, 153
Aksaray, 237
Alawi, 152. *See* also Nusayri
Albania/Albanians/Arna'ut, 142, 153, 284, 319
Aleppo, 2, 3, 6, 27, 29, 33–8, 43, 66, 76, 77, 81, *85*, 86, 87, 88–9, 93, 102, 104, 106, 137–8, 143, 145, 146, 147, 157, 226, *228*, 268, 277, 302, 314, 316, 341–3; court registers, 8, 75, 93, 96, 341; province, governor of, 75, 76–9, 82, 84, 86, 88, 93–6, 99–100, 102, 104, 105–7, 128–131, 133–4, 138, 145, 148, 150, 152, 173, 176, 186, 188, 197, 198, 208, 212–15, 217, 224, 226, 232, 235, 247–8, 261, 301, 338; Türkmen confederation (*see* Yeni İl)
Alevi, 60, 63
Alexandretta/İskenderun, 2, 38, *85*, 104
'Ali Bey (Janbulad?), 130
Ali Rıza Efendi (Uzunçayır), 240–1
Alikanlu tribe, 76
Alişan Bey (Cihanbeyli), 231, 239
Alqas Mirza, 59
Altuntaş fortress, 204
'Alwani family, 143, 147, 155; 'Alwan ibn 'Atiya 147
Amanos. *See* Gavur Dağı

Amasya, 241
Amid, 17, 22–3, 27, 34, 38–41, 43–4, 51. *See also* Diyarbekir
al-'Amidi, Zayn al-Din, 124
Amık/'Amq (lake/plain/district), 82–4, *85*, 91–6, 342
Amîkî Kurds, 83, 91–2, 96, 98, 101, 105, 174
al-'Amr clan, 250, 263
'Amre tribe, 121–3
Amuda, 46
'Ana, 33, 36, 54
al-Anarani, Isma'il, 278, 282
'Anaza/Aneze Bedouins, 139, 144, 152, 154–5, 180, 217–18, 249–50, 255, 259–60, 263–4, 267
Andkhud (Transoxiana), 73
Ankara, 34, 204, 207, 223, 224–5, 227, *228*, 229–36, 238, 241–2, 342; Ankara agreement, 106, 207; Vakıflar records, 9, 168
Anqele (Kurd Dagh), 93
Antioch/Antakya, 2, 8, 21, 38, 75, 83, *85*, 86, 89, 92, 96, 100–1, 103; court records of, 89–90
Arab tribes/Arabs, 35, 47, 49–51, 55, 87, 115, 120, 139, 143, 155, 180–1, 211, 216, 218, 250, 253–4, 260, 269, 317, 329. *See also* Bedouin
Arab Viran, 92
Araban plain, district, 185, 191, 204, *206*, 211
Arabgir/Arabkir, 65–6, 70
Arabgirlu tribe, 7–8, 65–6, 70–3
Arabia/Arabian Peninsula, 124, 139, 162
Arabic/Arabic sources, 3, 5, 6, 9, 10, 12, 13, 59, 77, 80, 82, 83, 116, 119, 129, 139, 221, 275–6, 305, 309, 315, 324, 327, 334, 339, 340, 343
Arabistan army, governorship, 76, 162, 214, 216–18, 220

Index 353

Aramaic. *See* Syriac
Ardalan tribe, emirate, 60, 210, 297
Arif Bey (Aleppo), 261
'Ariha, 152
Armenia/Armenians, 6, 17, 21, 29, 39, 41–3, 48–52, 55, 64, 68, 178, 209, 256, 317
As'ad Paşa, 214
As'ad Sadr al-Din (mufti), 274
Aşdi Kurds, 32
Ashafare tribe, 121, 123
'Assaf clan, 121, 123
Atassi family, 148, 156
Austria/Austrian, 322, 324, 331
'Ayn al-'Arab (Arab Pınar), 207, 211. *See also* Kobanî
'Ayn Dara, battle, 132
'Ayntab (Aintab/Gaziantep), 2, 33–4, 36, 76, 81, 93, 96, 106, 174, 185, 192–3, 196, 198, 203, *206*, 343
Ayyubids, 6, 8, 18, 82, 111, 114–15, 117, 119–20, 123, 127, 308
A'zaz/Azaz, 75, 78–84, *85*, 86, 88–9, 93, 95, 97, 102, 106, 186–8, 190, 192–3
al-Azbakiyya *zawiya*, 115
Azerbaijan, 66, 68
Azimet Paşa (Diyarbekir), 259, 264, 266, 267
Azizan tribe, 304
'Azm family, 141–2, 144, 147–52, 153–7, 320, 323–5, 327; 'Abdallah Pasha, 150, 152; Fawzi Paşa 324; Isma'il Ağa, 141; Khalil Paşa, 324; Kunj Yusuf Pasha, 144, 149, 150–2, 154, 157; Muhammad Fawzi Paşa, 327; Salim Bey, 153

Baalbek, 33, 37, 293
Baban emirate, family, 11, 273, 304; Abdullah Musib Paşa, 301; Halid, 287, 295–303, 305–7; Ahmed

Na'im, 300; Ahmed Paşa, 298, 301; Hikmet, 299; İsmail Hakki (Haqqı), 302, 317, 319; Mahmud Paşa, 273, 277; Mehmed Asım, 300; Muhammad Zihni Paşa, 300, 302; Şükrü, 302
Bab Hatta quarter, 117
Baghdad, 11, 17, 22, 29, 33, 35, 44, 47, 52–4, 63, 100, 142, 147, 212, 247, 253, 263, 266, 273–7, 279, 298, 302, 320
Baharlu tribe, 64
Bakir Agha al-Barazi, 153, 155
Bakri family, 329
Balikh river, 2, 45
Balis, 77, 341
Balkans/Balkan Wars, 101, 142, 196, 224, 226, 289, 290, 319
Baqqara/Beggara tribe, 4, 22, 331, 243, 250, 254, 255, 261–2
Barraziyya district, 211
Basra, 33, 47, 81, 301
al-Batiha (Tiberias), 322, 331
Battalzade family, 192–4, 198; Hüseyin Ağa, 198; Seyyid Mehmed Ağa, 185, 190, 193; Mehmed II, 192; Nuri Mehmed Paşa, 192, 198; (Mehmed) Sadık, 193–4
Bayburtlu tribe, 59
al-Baydari, 'Abdullah, 284
Bazîdî, Mela Mehmûdê, 216, 219
Bedirhan/Bedirxan emirate, family, 4, 11, 287–8, 293, 308, 309, 315, 321, 331, 339, 344; Abdurrahman, 299, 300; Abdürezzak, 290, 296, 311; Ali Şamil 305; (Emir) Bedirhan Bey, 49, 221, 287–8, 304, 310–11; Bedri (Paşa), 293, 301–2, 307, 310–12, 314, 316, 331; Celadet, 299, 319–20; Emin Ali, 299; Hüseyin (Kenan), 11, 287–307, 311;

354   Index

Bedirhan/Bedirxan emirate, family
(*continued*)
Kamuran, 319; Khalil Rami, 311;
Latife, 312; Mahmud `Izzet, 310,
314; (Mehmed) Salih, 11, 288, 293,
309–20, 331, 333, 335; Nejib Paşa,
311; Osman, 289, 311; Rewşen, 311,
320; Sinemxan, 320
Bedouin (`urban), 11, 32, 45, 87, 100,
113, 117, 122, 125, 139, 141, 151,
152, 154–5, 162, 219, 243–7, 249–50,
253, 256, 261–2, 266, 268–9, 293,
308, 332. *See also* Arabs
Behisni/Besni, 185, 199–201, 203, *206*
Behramlu Kurds, 67
Beirut, 11, 81, 129, 284, 287, 292,
295–6, 298–9, 301–3, 306–7, 311,
314, 324, 345
Bekaa valley, 145, 293
Bekir Bey (Kuloğlu), 10, 179–80,
182–4, 195–205
Bektaşi order, 60, 279
Bektaşlo Kurds, 96
Belgrade, 129, 341
Berat (Albania), 319
Berazi/Barazi tribe, 9, 10, 143, 149,
153, 155, 156, 157, 158, 207–221,
249, 253, 256, 257, 258, 243, 344
Berriye Ağzı (strait), 29, 35, 37
Berriyecik (Mardin), 35, 37
Bidlisi (Bitlisi), Idris, 62–3, 65, 208
Bidlisi, Şerefxan (Sharafkhan), 60, 62,
78, 209, 304, 340
Bingöl/Bingöl Dağı, 35, 60
Bitlis, 71, 301, 305
Birecik, 33, 45, 76, 78, 80, 179, 192,
195–8, 201, *206*, 208, 211–13
Bohtan/Botan, 49, 283, 287, 304,
309–10, 315. *See also* Cizre
Borazoğlu (Birecik), 211
Bosnia, 226
Bozo (Buzu) family, 308, 332

Bozok 230, 233–5, 241, 242
Boz Ulus confederation, 78, 81
British, 46, 50, 51, 103, 142, 245–6,
253, 258, 268, 273, 300, 324
Bucak Kurds, 253, 256, 258
Bukhara, 61, 284
Bursa, 34, 165, 239, 241, 284
Buzan Shahin Bey (Berazi), 208

Cabbarzade Süleyman Bey, 237
Cairo, 147, 314–16
Çaldıran/Chaldiran, battle, 69–71,
115, 208
Canberdi (Janbirdi) al-Ghazali
revolt, 76, 115
Canpolad/Janbulad family, 4, 9, 56,
75, 77–8, 81, 128–33, 135–6, 340–1;
`Ali, 75, 77, 101, 107, 117, 128–9;
132–3, 186–7, 340–1; Canpolad Bey
ibn Qasim, 77, 81, 95, 98; Faris,
130, 131; Husayn Pasha, 79, 128;
Ja`far, 81; Sharaf al-Din, 130, 131.
See also Ibn `Arabo; Junblat
Canpolad Kurds, 99
Caspian Sea, 33, 38
Catholic church (Church of Rome)/
Catholics, 19–21, 39–43, 49, 51–2,
54, 129. *See also* Armenians
Caucasus, 68, 141, 235, 245–6, 316, 319
Çavuşoğulları (Mûsa-Beylo) family,
92
Cebel-i Bereket, 103–4
Celali rebellions, 8, 77, 99, 101, 107, 340
Çelikanlı tribe, 235
Cemal Paşa, 282–3, 328, 332–3
Çerikan Kîkî branch, 256
Chaldaean church/Chaldaeans, 41,
52
Chamishgazak/Çemişkezeki (area/
tribe), 59, 65, 66–7, 69, 70
Chechen/Chechens, 246–8, 253–5,
257, 259, 266, 267

Chegeni tribe, 60
Christianity/Christians, 7, 18–20, 23, 26–9, 38, 51–2, 54–5, 101, 113, 118, 142, 190, 258, 283, 292, 307, 319–20, 322, 324–5. *See also* Armenians; Catholics; Chaldaeans; Protestants
Church of the East, 19–22, 26, 38–43, 48–9, 51–2, 54–5
Çiçek Dağı, 225, *228*, 232, 234–6
Cihanbeyli confederation, 10, 227, 230–1, 237–41, 343; pasturage, *228*, 238
Çıldır, 203–4
Cilicia, 21
Cindîres, 86
Circassians/Circassian Mamluks, 119, 120, 140, 144, 246, 255, 289
Çiyayê Kurmenc. *See* Kurd Dagh
Çizmecizade Hasan Ağa, 197
Cizre (Jazirat ibn ʿUmar/Gazarta), 2, 17, 20, 22, 35, 39, 41, 48, 49, 54, 94, 192, 253, 287, 289–91, 297–8, 344
Çobi Kurds, 76, 93
Çolak/Julaqan (Kurd Dagh), 105–6
Committee of Union and Progress (CUP), 268, 282, 327–8, 335
Crete, 287, 310, 312
Crusades, 6, 8, 119–20, 125, 338
Cubur tribe, 252, 254, 262
Cudi Dağı, 32
Çukurova, 103, 106
Cum/Juma district or tribe, 79, 82, 84–92, 95–6, 98, 100, 105–6, 107, 211
Cyprus, 3, 97, 182

Dababala tribe, 207
Dagar Su river, 66
Dagestan, 274
Dakori (Dökeri) tribe, 258
Dallata, 121–2
Daltabanzade Muhammed Ali, 190, 192–3

Damascus, 11, 37–8, 66, 76, 96, 111, 115–16, 124, 126, 127, 129, 133–5, 137, 138, 142–5, 147–52, 154, 157, 274, 277–86, 288, 291–2, 293, 302, 308–14, 320–34, 337, 339, 342, 345
Dandashli clan, 150
Dara, 17, 36–7
al-Darbasiyya, 208
Daret ʿIzze (Aleppo), 247
Darmık, *85*, 103
Davud Paşa, 273, 277
Dayasina. *See* Akrad al-Dayasina village
Dayr Hazem, 114
Dayr Yazid, 114
Dedeli tribe, 212
Deli Halil. *See* Hacci Ömer-oğlı
Deli Ömer Ağa, 196
Derbisak, 82, 84, *85*, 93–4, 95
Derne province, 63
Dersim, 66
Deyr al-Zor, 2, 11, 243–6, 257, 259–68
Dhuʾl-Qadr. *See* Zülkadir
Dinnan, Yezidis 250
Disimlu Kurds, 67
Diyarbekir/Diyarbakır, 2, 11, 17, 22, 23, 27, 31, 34, 41, 43, 47, 50, 78, 81, 208, 209, 213, 243–4, 246, 248–9, 253–6, 258–60, 264, 266–8, 280, 283, 321, 339, 341
Dohuk, 65
Druze, 9, 128–36, 278, 308, 330, 332, 339, 340
Dulkadir province. *See* Maraş
Dumancık, 92
Dunaysir, 23, 37
Dunyay/Dunay tribe, 211
Dunbuli tribe, 60, 210–12
Durubi family 156; ʿAla al-Din, 330
al-Duwayhi, Istfan, 134

356   Index

East India Company, 273
Ebu'l-Fazl Efendi (Bidlisi), 65
Ebu Salih tribe, 262
Edib, Halide, 305
Edirne, 88, 104, 224, 319–20
Egypt/Egyptian occupation, 18, 22, 37, 102–3, 108, 144, 145, 151, 152, 153–6, 158, 208, 212, 213–14, 216, 218–19, 280, 284, 332
Ekbez, *85*, 106
Elbistan, 95, 96
Enver Paşa, 106, 327, 328
Erbil (Hewler), 275, 320
Erciş, 34
Ergani, 23, 200, 208
Erzincan, 66
Erzurum, 34, 35, 43, 65, 210, 216, 224, 238, 298
Esad Muhlis Paşa (Konya), 229
Esbkeşan (Konya), 229–31, 234, 236
Euphrates river, 2, 10, 27, 33, 38, 45, 54, 65, 161, 179, 182, 184, 192, 198, 200, 204, *206*, 213, 218, 341
Evliya Çelebi, 23, 31–5, 48, 79, 211

Faraj Agha (Hama), 144, 153–6
Faraj ibn Muhammad al-Kurdi, 126
Farhan Safuk (Shammar), 219
Faris Bey (Janbulad), 130–1
Faris Paşa (Shammar), 46–7, 252, 254, 259–60, 263–6, 268
Fatima bint ʿAbdullah, 277
Fayyum, 118
Fırka-ı İslahiye, 103–5, 235
France/French, 6, 41, 75, 97, 106, 142, 151, 156, 205, 208, 211, 215, 285, 311, 324, 329–31

Gavur Dağı (Amanos), 84, *85*, 100, 103–4, 190
Gaza (Ghazza), 111, 113–14, 115–20, 124–5, 126, 212

Gazarta. *See* Cizre
Gemrik (Musabeyli), 92
Georgia/Georgians, 72, 73, 209
Gerger, 38, 80, 99, 185
Gergerizade Mehmed, 185
Germans/Germany, 3, 44, 48, 146, 296, 322–4
Ghab valley, 146, 152
Ghazzi family, 275–6; Ismaʿil Efendi, 276, 282; ʿUmar, 276
Ghazzi, Najm al-Din, 134
Ghuta (Damascus), 284, 322
Gökalp, Ziya, 249–50
Göktepe (Harran), 211
Golan, 322
Greek, 19; revolution, 278
Gregorian Church/Gregorians, 49, 51
Gürcü Necib Paşa, 277

Haccî Hannan Ağa, 106
Hacci Ismail-oğlu Osman Ağa, 105
Hacci/al-Hajj Ömer-oğlı (Oqçî-Izzeddinlo), 103–4; Deli Halil, 104–5; el-hacc Veli, 102
Hacci Şah-Kulu, 29, 35
Hacılar tribe, 224
al-Hadi, Qasim, 284
Hadidi tribe, 250
Hadtha, 121
hajj, 115, 127, 137, 147, 278, 283, 308; *amir al-hajj*, 321–323, 325–6, 334
Hajji Rustam Beg (Chamishgazak), 69–70
Hajji Shaykh Kurd revolt, 71
Hakkari tribe, emirate, 40, 52, 62, 111, 114–15, 117–18, 119, 124, 298
Halfaya, 155
Halil bin Ubur el-Hindi (Harb), 257
Halil-Beylu. *See* Alikanlu
Halil Bey (Karakeçi), 252, 255, 258–9

Index 357

Hama, 2, 9, 75, 80, 88, 89, 95, 99, 100, 102, 137–58, 210, 257, 342–3, 344
Hamidiye regiments, 11, 178, 244, 245, 248, 251–3, 256–8, 261–2, 268, 343
Hamidli tribe, 224
Hammu Agha (Barazi), 155
Hamo ibn Shaykh al-Akrad, 344
Hamoyizade el-hacc Mehmed, 196
Hanafi/Hanafism, 11, 132–4, 274, 276, 286
Hanano, Ibrahim, 106
Haqverdi Sultan Arabgirlu, 66, 73
al-Hara (Lebanon), 294
Harameyn. See Mecca; Medina; waqf
Harameyn tribe, 229
Harb tribe, 257, 263, 266
Harem, 210
Harran, 91, 211, 247, 253, 258, 267
Hasaka, 284
Hasayki tribe, 121–3
Hasirlu Kurds, 67
Hasya, 142
Hatay, 83, 190
Hawran, 151, 293, 310, 312, 322, 330
Haydari family, 273
Haydariyye/Haydarlar village, 92
Haymana (Ankara), 228, 229–30, 232–5, 254
Hayy al-Akrad (Damascus), 276, 309, 320
Hebron, 113–18, 123, 125, 127
Hekiçe (Kurd Dagh), 93
Helobelo (Ra's al-'Ayn), 267
Hemê (Katkan), 214, 216, 218–22
Hêvî association, 299, 317–18
Hevidi tribe, 185, 199–200, 204
Heyderan tribe, 253
Hijaz, 118, 137, 138, 147, 151, 280, 283, 321; railway 324–5, 328
al-Hijazi al-Kurdi. See Muhammad ibn 'Ali al-Ghawri

Hisn al-Akrad (Qal'at al-Husn), 100, 140, 145, 289, 291, 338, 339
Hisn Kayfa/Hasankeyf, 18, 30, 35, 39, 41
Hısn-ı Mansur (Adıyaman), 2, 80, 192, 206, 224–6, 228, 237, 354
Hit, 33, 36, 54
Hoca Sadeddin Efendi, 208
Homs, 88, 89, 137–41, 143–50, 152–4, 156–8, 289, 292
Hulusi Bey (Syria), 327
Humayun Shah (India), 71–2
Hurmas (Jaghjagh) river, 18, 23–4, 30, 32, 53
Husayn ibn 'Ali. See Sharif Husayn
Hüseyin Ağa ('Ayntab). See Battalzade
Hüseyin Paşa (Heyderan), 253

Ibn 'Arabo clan, 77. See also Canpolad
Ibn al-Hanbali, Muhammad, 77
İbrahim Ağa (Esbkeşan), 231
Ibrahim Deli Pasha (Damascus), 144, 149, 150–2, 157
Ibrahim Paşa (Egypt), 213, 218, 280
İbrahim Paşa Milli. See Millî
İçel/İç İl (Silifke), 95
Idlib, 156
Ikidam (Kurd Dagh), 92
Iksal (Tiberias), 120–2
India/Indians, 22, 23, 26, 33, 72, 117, 276, 283
Iran/Iranian, 3, 8, 17, 19, 22, 33–4, 37, 56, 57, 58–60, 62, 66–9, 70, 72–3, 210, 245, 296–8, 305, 337
Iraq, 6, 19, 22, 39, 41, 52, 69, 92, 212–13, 273, 280, 297–8, 304, 320, 337, 341
Irbid, 115
al-Irbili, Ahmad al-Khatib, 274, 285
'Isa al-Kurdi (shaykh), 281, 283–5
Isfandiyar Beg Arabgirlu, 73

358   Index

iskan (sedentarization), 87, 95–7, 99, 107, 120, 141, 162–3, 167–8, 178, 210, 213, 224–7, 231, 236, 242, 343
Iskandar Beg Munshi, 60, 66
İslahiye, *85*, 105, 235
Ismail (shah), 56, 58, 60, 62, 64, 66, 68–71
Ismail II (shah), 72
Ismailis, 152, 341
Ispir tribe, 65
Istanbul, 12, 96, 129, 197, 220, 233, 240, 242, 246, 274, 277–9, 281–4, 286, 288–90, 296, 298, 299–300, 311, 314, 324; as seat of government/administration, 5, 52, 75, 89, 194, 195, 234, 268, 294, 302, 310, 312; sheep trade, 10, 223, 227, 231, 233, 234, 237–42; *vakıf* foundations, 87–8, 164–5
Izla, Mt, 31, 51
İzmid, 241
İzmir, 332
Izoli Kurds/Izuliyya, 207, 209–11, 342
ʿIzz al-Din (Hama), 156
ʿIzz al-Din Bey/İzzeddin, 76–8, 82, 84, 90, 92–3, 98, 107; ʿIzzeddin Bey Kurds, 78–9, 81, 98
ʿIzz al-Din Shir Bey, 62
İzzeddin Efendi, 105
ʿIzzeddin (shaykh), 92
İzzet Bey (Raʾs al-ʿAyn), 248
İzziye district, 105–6, 108

Jabal ʿAbd al-ʿAziz, 244, 254, 262
Jabal al-Akrad, 338
Jabal ʿAmil, 8
Jabal Qasiyun, 276, 284–5, 308
Jabal Samʿan, 84, *85*, 92, 341
Jabal Sinjar, 35, 47, 49–50, 268, 341
Jabala, 77, 338, 341
Jabbur tribe, 255

Jacobites. *See* Syrian Orthodox
Jaf confederation, 297
Jaghjagh river. *See* Hurmas
al-Jali, ʿAbdullah, 275
Jamal al-Din Muhammad (Mosul), 26
Jandali family, 156
Jarjariyya tribe, 46–7
Jawanshir tribe, 68
Jazira. *See* Mesopotamia
al-Jazzar, Ahmad Pasha, 149–52
Jerusalem, 111, 113–17, 119–20, 123–4, 126–7, 274, 284, 293, 295, 307, 311
Jews/Jewish, 26, 28, 29, 50–1, 113, 119, 146, 331
Jijakli family, 155–6, 157; Khalil Agha, 155
Jira district, 120–2, 125
Jisr al-Shughur, 89, 152
Jordan/Transjordan, 3, 4, 8, 111–15, 117, 119–23, 125, 127, 226, 331
Junayd (Safavid), 62
Junblat/Joumblatt family, 9, 128–133, 136, 340; ʿAli, 132; Junblat (shaykh), 134–6; Kamal, 130, 132. *See also* Canpolad
al-Jundi family, 143, 148, 156
Jurallah (shaykh; Shammar), 255, 263

Kabaysha tribe, 121, 123
Kadıköy, 240, 314
Kafr Buhum, 155
Kafr Buruʿm, 122
Kafr Yahud, 146
Kaftariyya Sufi branch, 285
Kahta, 80, 224, 225, 237
Kalender Paşa (Maraş), 198–9, 203
Kalhur, 63
Kamal al-Din Ulugh Beg Arabgirlu, 71, 73
Kandiye (Crete), 287
Kangırı, 234, 241

Index 359

Karaca Ahmed Paşa, 76, 77
Karacadağ, 34, 252–3, 256, 262
Karadağ, 191, *206*
Karahöyük, *85*, 106
Karakeçi tribe, 244, 253, 255, 258–9
Karaman, 162
Karamort *khan*, 92, 96, 101
Karasu river, *85*
Kara-Ulus confederation, 224
Karayazı, 210
Karma (Hasaka), 284
Kar'o bin Musk (Kitkan), 214, 216–20
Kastamonu, *228*, 237, 295, 299, 303, 305–6
Kawabli tribe, 120
Kawkab al-Akrad, 116, 124
al-Kawkabani: Sa'id, 124; 'Abdush ibn 'Umar, 124, 126
Kaylani family, 143, 147–8, 154–6
Kayseri, *228*, 241, 299, 306, 314
Kazan, 284
Kendi-beli pass, 32
Kertuvan district, 30
Khabur river, 2, 38, 246, 253, 262
Khadija bint Yusuf, 277
Khalid al-Shahrazuri, 273–82, 284–6, 320; 'Abd al-Fattah, 283; As'ad ibn Mahmud al-Sahib, 281–3; Hafiz 'Uthman, 282–3; Khadija, 277; Khalidi family, 11; Mahmud al-Sahib, 279–283, 285;
Khalidi (-Naqshbandi) order/ Khalidiyya, 273–5, 277–86, 345
al-Khalidi, Ahmad, historian, 134–6
Khalwati Sufi order, 276
Khan Muhammad Ustajlu, 69
Khan Shaykhun, 142, 278
Khani. *See* Ahmad-i Khani
Khani family: Muhammad ibn 'Abdallah, 278, 280–2, 285–6; 'Abd al–Majid, 281–2
al-Kharbuti, 'Ali, 281

al-Khazin family, 134; Abu Nadir, 129; Shayban, 135
Khinis plain (Dohuk), 65
Khinislu tribe, 59, 65
Khirbat al-Ghazala (Hawran), 330
Khorasan, 66–7, 68
Khoy, 69
Khoybun/Xwebûn committee, 299, 320
Khrus (Harran), 211
khuwwa tax, 87, 250, 266
Kîkî/Kîkan tribe, 208, 243, 246–7, 249, 255, 256–9, 262, 343
al-Kilali, Abu Bakr, 280, 284
Kilis (city/province/tribal collective), 2, 9, 56–7, 75, 77–82, *85*, 86–92, 95–107, 129–30, 168, 171, 173–7, 184, 186–90, 192–3, 195, 340
Kirkuk, 320
Kırşehir, 229, 235, 237, 242, 290; settlement area, *228*, 230
Kırvar tribe, 256, 258
Kitkan/Kitkanlo clan, 214, 217, 219
Kızılbaş/Qizilbash, 7, 56–74, 97, 341
Kızılırmak river, *228*, 236
Kızıl Koyunlu tribe, 174
Kızıl Mağaralu Kurds, 67
Kızıltepe, 247, 256–7
Kobanî/'Ayn al-'Arab/Arab Pınar, 2, *206*, 207, 210–11, 214, 217
Koçhisar, 23, 37, 208
Kokh Bin tribe, 211
Konya, 204, 223–5, *228*, 229–36, 238, 242, 338, 342
Köse Bekir-oğlı Ahmed (Oqçî-Izzedînlo), 102–3
Köse Mustafa Paşa, 193, 198, 203
Köse-Paşazade family (Sivas), 182
Koshkar (Harran), 211
Kozan, 2, 106, 235, 288
Küçükalioğlu. *See* Mıstık Bey

360   Index

Kuftaru family: Ahmad, 11, 285;
    Amin, 284–5
Kuloğlu family, 10, 182–4, 193–4, 205;
    Bekir Bey, 10, 179–80, 182–4, 195–
    205; Halil Paşa, 183, 184–8, 190–1,
    193–5, 199–200, Hüseyin, 182–3;
    İsmail, 183–5, 193; (Kasapoğlu)
    Muhammed Kethüda, 182–3; Kürd
    Muhammed Paşa (Muhammed
    Şerif?), 184, 188, 190–2, 195, 197;
    (Muhammed) Sadık Bey, 183,
    184, 190–9; Mustafa, 183; 197–8;
    (Mustafa) Celaleddin, 183, 194–5;
    Ömer, 183–4; Osman, 195
al-Kura district, 8, 339
Kurd ʿAli, Muhammad, 345
Kurd Dagh/Kürd Dağı, 75, 82, 84,
    85, 91–5, 97, 100, 102–8, 190, 207,
    235, 338, 341
Kurdistan, 3–4, 8, 12, 17, 51, 65, 67,
    69, 168, 191, 203, 208, 210, 226,
    273–4, 277, 279–81, 284, 286, 310,
    342
Kurdistan newspaper, 315, 318
Kürdistan Teali Cemiyeti, 299
Kurmancî/Kurmanji, 5, 6, 10, 12–13,
    215, 315, 344

Lajjun, 124, 130
Lalesh valley, 92
Lar (Iran), 73
Latakia, 91
Lebanon, 3, 4, 8–9, 11, 3359, 117, 122,
    128–31, 133, 145, 152, 289, 292, 312,
    324, 329, 331, 339–40
Led (Tiberias), 126
Lek/Lekwan/Lekvanık tribe, 81,
    96, 342
Lesbos, 289, 307
Limnos, 311, 314
Liva-ı Ekrad, 75, 78–80

Lubiyya, 121
Lurs, 59
Lutfullah Ağa (Birecik), 212

Maʿarrat al-Nuʿman/Maʿarra, 138,
    143, 148
Maden-Ergani region, 200, 237
Madrasa/medrese, 25, 29, 53, 124, 126,
    147, 164, 281, 282
Mağaracık, 92
Mahasne tribe, 121, 123
Mahmud I (sultan), 88
Mahmud II, 212–13, 215, 277, 279–80
Majdal, 121
al-Makki, Muhammad, 141
Malatya, 38, 76, 80, 129, 182, 185, 192,
    196, 199, 200, 224, 226, 228, 255, 343
al-Malik al-ʿAdil al-Ayyubi, 114
Malik Jihangir revolt, 72
Mamluk empire, era, 6, 8, 18, 76–7,
    82, 90, 92–3, 98, 107, 111, 114–15,
    119–20, 123, 127, 338–9
Maʿn: Fakhr al-Din, 129–31, 133–5,
    136, 339; Yunus, 135
Marʿabi family, 339
Maraş, 2, 81, 95–100, 102, 106, 175–6,
    182, 186, 193, 198, 224–6, 228, 232,
    235, 247, 314, 343
Mardin, 2, 17, 23, 26–9, 32–41, 43–51,
    54, 208, 224, 246–7, 249–50, 252,
    264, 266
Marj Dabiq, 76
Maronites, 128, 133–4, 278
Maʿruf Node (shaykh), 273, 282
Marwan II (caliph), 209
Marwanid dynasty, 18
al-Masharifa quarter, 143
Matih tribe, 88
Matrakçı Nasuh, 59
Mawali/Mevali Bedouin, 32, 100,
    139, 143, 150, 152, 156

Mazandaran, 71
Mecca, 138, 146, 151, 157, 165, 172, 275, 283, 284, 325–6
Mecidiye (Çiçek Dağı), 234–6
Medici, house of, 129
Medina, 124, 138, 146, 151, 157, 165, 172, 283, 284
Mehmed IV (sultan), 87
Mehmed V (Reşad) (sultan), 297
Mehmed Paşa (Raqqa), 185
Mehmed Namık Paşa, 214–217
Mehmed Tevfik Efendi (Reşwan), 240, 242
Mekki Bey (Chechen), 246–7, 267–8
Menas (Kobanî), 210
Menbic/Manbij, 193
Mend dynasty, 77–8
Merwan (Kurd Dagh), 93–4
Merziman district, 185, 206
Mesopotamia/Jazira, 3, 10, 17–18, 20–1, 23, 33, 37, 40–1, 43, 45, 49, 54, 161, 208–9, 212–15, 308–9, 321, 343
Mevlanzade Rıfat Bey, 299
Midhat Paşa, 290, 321
Midyat, 258, 290
Mihemed Emîn Zekî Beg, 12
Mihrimah Sultan, 165–6
Millî tribe/family, 9, 11, 36–7, 45, 77, 79, 94, 98, 143–4, 146, 149, 152–3, 154, 157, 191–2, 200, 212–14, 243–4, 246, 248, 249–64, 266–9, 343; Ayyub Bey/Pasha, 212–13; İbrahim Paşa, 244, 250–63, 267–9, 343; Mahmud, 267; Mulla Isma'il, 143–4, 146, 149–50, 152–5, 157, 158; Timur Paşa, 191–2, 195, 198, 200, 203, 205, 216; Timur II (Timo), 213
Mir Muhammad (Rewanduz), 297
Miran tribe, 253
missionaries, 22, 41–3, 93, 97
Mıstık Bey Küçükalioğlu, 103

Misyaf, 145, 152, 155
Mizar village, 197–8
Molikanli tribe, 197
monastery, 20, 26, 40, 48, 51
Mongols, 7, 18, 22, 25–7, 92
Moroccans, 113, 117
Mosul, 17, 22–3, 24, 26, 27, 29, 33, 35, 36, 41, 43, 46–8, 50, 53, 248, 263, 322
Mudiq. See Qal'at al-Mudiq
Mughals, 72
Muhammad (Mehmed) 'Ali Pasha, 151, 158, 277
Muhammad al-Khani. See al-Khani
Muhammad Khurfan Bey (Mawali), 156
Muhammad Paşa al-Yusuf. See al-Yusuf
al-Muhibbi, Muhammad Amin, 134, 339
Mühimme registers, 6, 8, 75, 95, 101, 161, 169, 212
Muhy al-Tala clan, 267
Mulla Isma'il. See Millî
Muqaddam tribe, 68
Murad III (sultan), 87
Murad Pasha (Kuyucu), 129, 133–4
Muradi family, 274, 279, 280, 282; Hasan, 274, 279
Murat Su river, 65
Murayj al-Durr (Hama), 144
Muro/Murad (Hevidi), 199, 201, 203
Muş, 247
Mûsa-Beylo/Musabeyli tribe, 77, 79, 83, 86, 88, 92, 100, 101, 105; district, 92, 108
Musallat Paşa (Cubur), 262
Musko/Musa (Kitkan), 214
Mustafa II (sultan), 88, 166
Mustafa Bey (Reşwan), 235–6
Mustafa Paşa (Miran), 253

362 Index

Nablus, 111, 114–17, 121, 122, 126, 290, 314
al-Nabulusi, 'Abd al-Ghani, 147
Nadir Shah, 100
Naif Ağa (Kîkî), 257
Najd, 144
Naqshbandi/Naqshbandiyya, 11, 274, 276, 279, 280, 285, 286 245
Nevşehir, 236
Niğde, 234
Nizib, 185, 195, 206, battle of, 213, 216
Nogais, 235
Nu'mani, Shibli, 283
Nur Ali Khalifa, 69
al-Nurani, Hasan, 284
Nurbanu Valide Sultan, 166
Nusaybin/Nisibis, 2, 7, 17, 19, 23–36, 38, 40–55
Nusayri, 152, 341

Omarak, 206, 214
Ömer Paşa (Reşvanzade), 191, 192, 200
Ömer-oğlı el-hacc Velî (Oqçî-Izzeddînlo), 102–4. See also Deli Halil
Oqçî-Izzeddînlo tribe, 75, 81, 91, 95–6, 98–106, 108, 176, 187
Orontes (Asi) river, 2, 83, 85, 145
Osman Efendi (Ra's al-'Ayn), 247
Osman Paşa (Aleppo), 215
Otuz-iki tribe, 68

Palestine, Palestinian, 4, 8, 111–15, 117–27, 145, 151, 330, 331, 338
Paşa Dağı, 225, 228, 229, 232, 237
Patnos (Ağrı), 253
Payas, 38
Pazuki tribe, 60, 62–3
Pehlivan İbrahim Paşa, 179, 201–205
Persian, 58, 61–2, 276, 297, 340. See also Iranian

Persian Gulf, 33
Poche family, 86
Protestants, 97

Qaba'ili tribe, 121–3, 125–6
al-Qadi family/Qablan, 130, 132, 136; Rabah, 129–32
Qadiri Sufi order/Qadiriyya, 261, 273–5, 282
Qajar tribe, 64, 68
Qal'at al-Husn. See Hisn al-Akrad
Qal'at al-Mudiq, 101, 152
al-Qanawat quarter, 275
Qaqun district, 117, 121
Qarabagh, 68
Qarajadagh/Siyahkuh, 59
Qara Khan Ustajlu, 208
Qasyun. See Jabal Qasiyun
Qaymari/Qaymur; Qaymariyya tribe, 123–5
Qays/Keys Arabs, 32–3, 116, 136, 247, 253, 255, 258, 267
Qilîçlo/Kılıçlı tribe, 75, 77, 84, 87, 89–90, 93–8, 140, 175
Qizilbash. See Kızılbaş
Qubad Beg (Derne), 63
Qubbat al-Kurdi, 145
Qulp/Kulayb, 209
Qumluq (Birecik), 206, 211,
al-Qunaytira, 322
Qusayr district (Antakya), 89

Rabban Hormizd, 22, 39–42, 48
Rajo, 85, 106, 107
Ramla, 113, 115–16, 117–18, 123, 126, 212
Raqqa/Rakka, 2, 38, 45–6, 54, 89, 91, 92, 95–7, 99–100, 102, 161–2, 167–9, 171, 175–7, 180, 185–7, 188, 191, 193, 195, 197–8, 199, 212, 224, 226, 230, 338, 341, 343
Ra's al-'Ayn, 243–9, 251–63, 266–9

Rashid Agha al-Shamli, 154
Rashidi tribe, 210–11, 212
Raslan/Rasalina clan, 152
Ravendan castle/district, 82–3, *85*, 87, 92, 98
Rawand/Rawwadid tribe, 82, 118
Rejje (Lebanon), 294
Reş Ağa-zade Mehmed Ağa (Şêxlo), 105
Reşi Kurds, 10, 79, 99, 184–5, 342, 343; Reşi Dağı, 185, *206*, 342
Reşwan/Rişvan confederation, 9–10, 79, 81, 87, 89, 168, 171, 173, 177, 179, 182, 184–5, 192, 197–8, 200–1, 203–4, 223–42, 337–8, 342–3; Reşvan–zade dynasty, 96, 182, 192, 226, 343; Abdurrahman II, 200–1; Ali, 192; Ömer Paşa, 191, 200; Ömer II, 192; Osman, 185; Süleyman, 96, 100
Reyhânlo tribe, 96; Reyhaniye plain, 342
Reza Paşa, 217
Rhodes, 81, 310, 314
ribat, 26, 124
Rıdvan Paşa (Istanbul), 290
Rojava, 4
Rojê Kurd newspaper, 288, 314, 317–19
Rome/Roman. *See* Catholic church
Ruha. *See* Urfa
Rumelia, 217, 227, 238, 242, 283
Rumkale, 2, 10, 92, 179–82, 184–5, 187–205, *206*, 342
Rumlu tribe, 59, 64
Russians/Russo-Ottoman wars, 187, 191, 204, 215–16, 239, 245, 284, 288, 298, 300
Rustum Agha, Muhammad, 91
Ruzegi tribe, 60

Saçlo Kurds, 79, 92, 98, 99, 140, 343
Safad, 111, 113–26, 129, 134

Safavids, 8, 23, 32, 34, 56–74, 208, 297, 337
Safveti Paşa, Haccı Musa, 286
Şah Nasibi tribe, 31
Sa'id Paşa mosque, Damascus, 333
Şakir Paşa, 267
Saladin/Salah al-Din al-Ayyubi, 82, 111, 114–15, 119, 300, 328
Salamiyya, 2, 100, 138, 344
al-Salihiyya quarter, 276, 284, 323
Salmas, 20, 40, 41
al-Salt, 111, 113, 115–19, 120, 125
Salt Paşa (Cubur), 252
Samaritans, 119
Sami, Şemseddin, 305
Sarılı tribe, 30
Sarkıntılı tribe, 234
Şarkiyan Yezidis, 250
Saruniyya, 121
Sasanian, 19, 20, 54
Sasun, 51
Saudi clan, 151
Savalan, David, 239
Sayda/Sidon, 81, 116, 129, 138, 149, 154
Şekaki tribe, 33
Selim I (sultan), 70, 76, 120, 208
Selim III, 90, 205
Serbesti journal, 299
Sercihan, 36, 37
Serikanlo/Serektanlo tribe, 100
Şêxlo/Şeyhlü tribe, 89, 91, 95, 103, 105, 176; Şeyhli district, 108
Şeyh Avand Qizilbash, 59
Şeyh Ömerlu Kurds, 67
Şeyhan Yezidis, 250
şeyhülislam/shaykh al-Islam, 89, 282–3
Şeyhzade İbrahim Paşa, 197
Seyyid Ali (Alo) Paşa, 195–7, 200
Seyyid Mansur Kurds, 36
Shafi'i/Shafi'ism, 11, 276, 285, 286, 300
Shah Ghulam 'Ali, 275

364 Index

Shahrazuri. *See* Khalid
Shaltah (Kurd Dagh), 92
Shamdin family, 308, 322, 323, 325;
  (Muhammad) Saʿid, 322
Shamdin Agha family, 143
Shamlu confederation, 7, 64, 66, 337
Shammar Arabs, 11, 46, 180, 219,
  243–6, 249–50, 252–61, 263–8
Sharabin/Sherabin tribe, 246, 254–5,
  261, 263, 266
Sharaf quarter (Jerusalem), 116
Sharaf Khan I (Bidlis), 71
Sharafkhan. *See* Bidlisi
Sharif Husayn ibn ʿAli, 325;
  Sharifian army, 329
sharʿiyya court registers, 5, 8, 9, 45,
  75, 89–90, 93, 112, 114, 127, 143,
  153, 171, 341, 344
Shaqif Arnun, 130, 135
Shaykh al-Akrad, 344
Shaykh al-Hadid (Kurd Dagh), 84,
  93, 95, 99, 101
Shihabi emirs, 133, 136; Haydar,
  130–2
Shiis/Shiites, 8, 58–9, 61–3, 67–9, 341
Shirwan, 73
Shuf district, 9, 128–36, 340
Shujaʿiyya quarter, 116, 119, 124–5
Shuqayr, Asʿad, 332
Siird/Siirt, 39, 123, 283
Şikayet registers, 6, 8, 75, 101, 167
Silifke, 95
Sinara (Derbisak), 93
Sinjar/Jabal Sinjar, 2, 25, 32–5, 47,
  49–50, 52, 208, 268, 341; Sinjar Gate
  (Nusaybin), 24
Sivas, 34, 37–8, 81, 97, 165, 172, 182,
  201, 203, 223, 225, 226, 228, 229–30,
  232, 234, 236, 241, 247
Siverek, 2, 208, 244, 249, 250, 253–6,
  258, 268
Siyahkuh, 59, 62
Siyah Mansur tribe, 60

Siyale tribe, 258
Suez Canal, 316, 328, 331–3, 335
Sufi/Sufism, 11, 61, 64, 68, 114, 124,
  126, 144, 147, 177, 273–4, 276, 280,
  284–6, 337, 339, 341, 345. *See also*
  Khalidi; Naqshbandi; Qadiri
Sulaqa (patriarch), 39–42
Sulayman Paşa (Acre), 152, 278
Sulaymaniyya/Süleymaniye/
  Silêmanî, 11, 273, 275, 279–82, 297,
  345
Süleyman I (sultan), 29, 72, 165
Süleyman Derviş (Hevidi), 200
Süleymaniye tribe, 76
Sunni/Sunnism, 56, 62–3, 66, 69,
  97, 132–4, 178, 243, 250, 268, 278,
  291–2, 300, 342
Suq Saruja, 308, 311, 323–4, 331, 333
Sur. *See* Tyre
Suruj city, plain, 2, 10, *206*, 207–13,
  215, 217, 221, 253–4, 256–8, 343
Sûsan, *206*, 210
al-Susi, ʿAbd al-Wahhab, 277–8
Sykes, Mark, 245–8, 251–2, 254–7
Syriac (Aramaic), 19, 21, 53
Syrian Orthodox Church/Jacobites,
  21, 22–3, 48–49, 50

Tabgha, 121
Tabriz, 34
Tacirlo Kurds, 175
Tahmasb (shah), 60, 64, 71–2
Tahrir records, 5–6, 8, 53, 64, 75–6, 78,
  82–3, 91, 93, 95, 111–16, 118, 120,
  122–3, 125, 127, 207, 210, 219, 225,
  231, 237
Taʾif (Yemen), 290
Takkalu tribe, 64, 71
Talat Paşa, 327
Talish tribe/region, 59, 62
Tallaq (ʿAfrin), 92
Tall Bisa, 142
Talldara, 156

Talldhahab, 155
Talldu, 146, 155
Tamerlane, 210
Tamimi Arabs, 115
al-Tanukhi, Qablan al-Qadi, 130, 131
Tanzimat (reforms), 6, 8, 10, 50, 76,
86, 90, 97, 103–4, 108, 153, 156, 205,
207, 208, 211–16, 220, 221, 225–7,
229, 242, 244, 280, 284, 290, 298,
300, 301, 303, 307, 319, 338, 245
Tarham (Siird), 283
Tat tribe, 249
Tayfur family, 143–4, 155
Tayy Arabs, 32, 46, 50, 51, 52, 55, 255,
262
Tehran, 296, 300–1
Telbism district, 35
Tell ‘Afar, 208
Tell Ermen, 257
Tell Raqaq, 210
Tell Sha‘ir, 210
Temeşvar (Romania), 129
Terkan tribe, 234, 250, 255
Tevfik Bey (Ra‘s al-‘Ayn), 247
Tiberias, 118, 122, 124–6, 322, 331
Tigris river, 2, 17, 20, 22, 23, 30, 32–4,
35, 39, 47, 54, 219, 344
Tokat, 37–8, 43
Tosya (Kastamonu), 237
Tripoli, 89, 95, 100, 102, 138, 141, 145,
148–50, 278, 287, 292–3, 307, 339
Tur ‘Abdin, 21, 22
Turbay ibn ‘Ali al-Harithi, 130
Turgutlu, 236
Turhan Sultan, *valide sultan*, 87
al-Turki tribe, 144, 152–3
Turkoman (Türkmen)/Turkic, 6,
8–10, 56–61, 63, 69–70, 72, 76–8,
80–2, 84, 87–8, 95, 113, 117, 119–23,
127, 138, 140–1, 144–6, 148, 155,
157, 161, 165–9, 172, 174–8, 223–4,
229, 342, 343
Tur Sina (Palestine), 114

Tuscany, 129
Tutak/Dûtax (Ağrı), 210
Tyre, 117, 122

Üçpınar, 92
Ulama Sultan Takkalu, 71
‘Ukaydat/‘Aggedat tribe, 254, 264, 266
Ümid newspaper, 314–15
Urfa (Edessa/Ruha), 2, 17, 19, 23, 27,
29, 33–4, 36–8, 80, 94, 98, 196, 197,
200, *206*, 208, 210–13, 217–19, 224,
247, 248, 254, 257, 259, 261, 343
al-Urwadi, Ahmad, 278
Üsküdar, 87, 95, 165–6, 172, 240
Ustajlu tribe, 59, 64–5, 69, 208
‘Uthman Agha (Turki), 144
‘Uthmanu Kurds, 146
Uzbeks, 66, 72
Uzunçayır pasturage, 240–1
Uzunyayla, 225, *228*, 229, 232

Valide Sultan, 87–92, 95, 163–6, 168,
172–5, 177, 224
Van/Lake Van, 22, 34, 38, 62, 209,
252, 255, 298, 341
Varna, 224
Vecihi (Wajihi) Paşa, 214
Veli (Oqçî-Izzedînlo), 102
Veli (Veliyüddin) Paşa, 198, 203
Vienna, 9, 324
Vilayet-i Şark, 94
Viranşehir, 2, 35, 244, 247, 252–4, 256,
262, 266–7
voyvoda, 43–4, 47, 86, 88, 97, 99, 101–2,
165, 172–175, 185, 188, 190, 193, 197–8

al-Wahb tribe, 89
Wahhabi movement, 151
waqf/vakıf (evkaf), 6, 8, 9–10, 84, 86–7,
102, 111, 113–14, 118, 123–7, 143,
162–78, 282, 338
Warsaq tribe, 64
Weizmann, Chaim, 331

366 Index

Xawalde tribe, 117, 120–2, 123, 126
Xelecan Kîkî branch, 256
Xelîkanlo tribe, 76
Xoybûn/Khoybun committee, 299, 320

Yazbak ibn ʿAbd al-ʿAfif, 135, 136
Yazd, 33, 37
Yemen, 290, 298
Yeni-İl confederation, 9, 80, 165–9, 172, 174–7, 230, 241, 342
Yezidis, 10, 34, 47, 49, 50, 52, 75, 77–8, 81, 92–3, 98, 185, 250, 341–2
Yigirmi-dört tribe, 65, 67–8
Young Turks, 8, 11, 299, 306, 315–7, 322, 326–8, 333–5. *See also* Committee of Union and Progress
Yozgat, 224, *228*, 235–6, 290, 354
al-Yusuf family, 308, 320–5, 327, 329, 331; ʿAbd al-Rahman Paşa, 11, 309, 320–35

Yusuf Paşa (Raqqa), 180, 181
Yusuf Ziyaeddin Paşa (Mutki), 305

Zakho, 32
al-Zamalkani, Ahmad, 281
al-Zamalkani, Amin, 284
Zanganeh tribe, 60
zawiya/zaviye Sufi lodge, 25, 28, 37, 114, 115, 124, 126, 279–82, 284, 286
Zaza Kurds, 258
Zeki Paşa (Fourth Army), 248, 256, 257, 267
Zerkan river, 246, 256–7
Zervereklu Kurds, 67
al-Zirikli, Khayr al-Din, 345
Zirqî tribe, 343, 345
Zor. *See* Deyr al-Zor
Zühdü Bey (Zor), 246, 260, 263–4, 266–8
Zulkadir; Dhulqadr confederation, 64, 84

www.ingramcontent.com/pod-product-compliance
Ingram Content Group UK Ltd.
Pitfield, Milton Keynes, MK11 3LW, UK
UKHW041814300625
460150UK00016B/178/J